Fife Flyers On This Day

Fife Flyers shiny new home shortly after it was opened in 1938

Fife Flyers On This Day

John Ross

K&B

Kennedy & Boyd

Kennedy & Boyd
an imprint of
Zeticula Ltd,
Unit 13,
196 Rose Street,
Edinburgh,
EH2 4AT,
Scotland.

http://www.kennedyandboyd.co.uk
admin@kennedyandboyd.co.uk

First published 2022

All author's royalties will go to CHAS, https://www.chas.org.uk.

Hardback ISBN 978-1-84921-225-0
Paperback ISBN 978-1-84921-228-1

Acknowledgements

I am indebted to a number of people who have helped and encouraged me in the completion of this book.

To the directors of Fife Flyers for giving me this opportunity to satisfy an urge I've had for some time to put into print some of the clubs' rich history.

The *Fife Free Press* group, and in particular Allan Crow, for his assistance and permission for the use of material from the local newspaper archive. In particular the use of images taken by the following photographers who have worked over time with the newspaper:

Davie Ireland, Bill Dickman, Ian Alexander, Peter Jones, John Hutton, and Mike Drummond.

Also, the work of the many sports writers over the years who have diligently recorded the clubs' endeavours in the sports section.

Graeme Scott, Allan Crow, Gordon Holmes, Matthew Elder and those in much early days who wrote under the nom de plumes such as 'Canuck', 'Snow', 'Blue-Liners', 'Power play'. I hope I have done some justice to them in the retelling of their work.

Fact checking was a challenge, as I continue to build up my own records on the club, but the following people/sources provided assistance for which I'm truly thankful:

Iain Anderson, for allowing me access to his huge source of archive material and willingly answering the many questions I have posed over the years.

The custodians of ice hockey publications such as Stewart Roberts, (*Ice Hockey Annual*), and its predecessor the *Ice Hockey Herald* from Bernard Stocks. There were numerous times that I also had to dip into the archives of the *Ice Hockey News Review* and the *Ice Hockey World* all of which has, I hope, helped to make the following pages as accurate an account as possible.

In addition to images from the *Fife Free Press* I am grateful to the following photographers who kindly gave permission for the use of some of their material.

Derek Young, Gillian McFarlane, Mike Smith and Steve Gunn.

To the hugely talented Rebecca Thomson for providing the artwork for the cover of the book – you can follow her work here:

https://www.rebeccathomsonart.com/

Many thanks to Gordon Latto for taking time out to chat about his time in the game and giving me access to his memorabilia and of course for his time in providing the foreword to the book.

To the countless players over the years who have graced the ice, the coaches, club officials and volunteers and to all those who have poured in through the rinks iconic Art Deco entrance on winters nights to be warmed within its confines.

To anyone I have omitted, please accept my apologies; I hope I can make it up to you through your enjoyment of the pages to follow.

John Ross
January 2022

Contents

Season Reference Grid

Use the table below to identify particular seasons

Season	Dates
1938/39	Aug 20, Aug 25, Sep 30, Jan 10, Jan 19
1939/40	Dec 21, Jan 22, Feb 01, Apr 18, May 09, May 16, May 25
1943/44	May 14
1946/47	Aug 17, Sep 21, Oct 31, Mar 13, Mar 25, Apr 30, May 15
1947/48	Oct 07, Mar 11, Apr 27, May 06
1948/49	Aug 11, Sep 24, Nov 01, Dec 31, Feb 24, Mar 10, Apr 04
1949/50	Dec 08, Feb 20, Apr 11, Apr 22
1950/51	Oct 19, Oct 26, Nov 30, Dec 25, Apr 13, Apr 26
1951/52	Aug 04, Aug 18, Oct 24, Dec 05, Jan 14, Feb 21, Apr 17
1952/53	Sep 29, Dec 12, Jan 01, Jan 29, Mar 19
1953/54	Aug 12, Sep 09, Dec 11, Dec 24, Feb 10, Mar 04
1954/55	Aug 14, Aug 21, Nov 13, Nov 18, Dec 30, Feb 03, Apr 28, May 08, May 29
1962/63	Oct 14, Oct 28, Feb 17, Feb 23
1963/64	Nov 17, Nov 23, Feb 09, May 02
1964/65	Oct 18, Dec 06, Dec 20, Mar 21
1965/66	Oct 23, Nov 07, Dec 18, Jan 30, May 21
1966/67	Oct 09, Jan 07, Mar 05, Apr 02
1967/68	Dec 02, Jan 13, Jan 20, Apr 20
1968/69	Oct 06, Oct 13, Dec 07
1969/70	Feb 28
1970/71	Dec 19, Apr 10
1971/72	Sep 25, Nov 20, Feb 19, Mar 18
1972/73	Oct 21, Nov 11, Dec 09, Feb 16
1973/74	Mar 23, Apr 21, May 04
1974/75	Oct 12, Jan 05, Feb 22, May 11
1975/76	Oct 11, Feb 14, May 13, May 23
1976/77	Nov 06, Jan 16, Apr 09, May 01, May 22
1977/78	Oct 16, Nov 26, Apr 08
1978/79	Dec 16, Jan 28
1979/80	Oct 27, Apr 06
1980/81	Nov 08, Nov 29, Mar 31
1981/82	Sep 19, Jan 03, Mar 20

1982/83	Oct 02, Jan 08
1983/84	Nov 12, Mar 24
1984/85	Nov 21, Dec 01, Dec 22, Mar 09, Apr 14, May 05
1985/86	Sep 22, Dec 15, Mar 22, Apr 12, May 03
1986/87	Oct 25, Nov 15, Jan 04, Jan 17, Mar 28, Apr 25
1987/88	Nov 14, Jan 09, Jan 23, Mar 27, Apr 24
1988/89	Sep 04, Oct 08, Nov 05, Feb 05, Mar 12
1989/90	Sep 16, Apr 15
1990/91	Nov 24, Dec 23, Mar 02
1991/92	Aug 31, Dec 29, Apr 19
1992/93	Sep 05, Sep 26, Jan 24
1993/94	Jan 15, Feb 12, Feb 27, Apr 23
1994/95	Sep 03, Oct 29, Jan 02, Mar 26
1995/96	Sep 02, Nov 19, Dec 03, Feb 11
1996/97	Oct 05, Oct 20, Mar 08, Apr 29
1997/98	Sep 20, Jan 11, Mar 14, Mar 30
1998/99	Sep 06, Sep 12, Sep 27, Dec 26
1999/00	Dec 04, Dec 28, Jan 25, Apr 07
2000/01	Sep 28, Jan 06, Feb 13, Apr 03
2001/02	Sep 01, Nov 25, Nov 27, Mar 03
2002/03	Oct 15, Feb 02, Feb 25, Mar 16
2003/04	Sep 13, Nov 02, Nov 09, Feb 29
2004/05	Dec 27, Feb 06, Feb 15
2005/06	Sep 18, Dec 17, Feb 04, Apr 16, May 07
2006/07	Nov 04, Feb 26, Mar 29
2007/08	Nov 10, Jan 12, Jan 26
2008/09	Sep 14, Nov 22, Mar 15
2009/10	Oct 17, Nov 28, Mar 07
2010/11	Aug 28, Oct 03
2011/12	Sep 10, Sep 11, Sep 23, Oct 22
2012/13	Sep 15, Oct 30, Jan 27, Mar 17
2013/14	Sep 07, Nov 03, Dec 14, Apr 05
2014/15	Aug 30, Oct 10, Jan 18, Feb 07
2015/16	Aug 29, Oct 04, Dec 13, Jan 31
2016/17	Aug 27, Sep 17, Jan 21
2017/18	Aug 26, Dec 10, Feb 18, Apr 01
2018/19	Aug 23, Sep 08, Mar 01
2019/20	Aug 24, Nov 16, Feb 08, Mar 06

Gordon Latto sweeps the puck home against the Glasgow Dynamos 1977/78

Illustrations

Foreword

Gordon Latto

It's hard to believe that it's over 24 years since I skated out at Fife Ice Arena, or simply Kirkcaldy Ice Rink in my heyday, for the last time in a Flyers strip. At that time I was approaching the year that life begins and since then I've gone through a couple more big birthdays, it's hard to figure how that actually happened.

What will never escape me however is the length of time I have been associated with hockey in Kirkcaldy, and along with that comes the many fantastic memories, the occasional bad one and the countless friendships that I struck up along the way.

I suppose I was a rink rat; my brother Dougie and I used to walk to the rink and we used to chap the door at the rink at an ungodly hour on a Sunday morning to get the nightwatchman to let us in to skate before our training started with the Kirkcaldy Flyers.

Tommy Horne used to give us tickets to get in and I would stay there all day and I even cleaned out the café so they would feed me. I remember watching the team in the mid 1960s with Ian 'Eenie' Forbes, Sammy McDonald, Jimmy Spence and of course Harold 'Pep' Young, who really got the kids like myself in the area involved and laid much of the foundation for what came in the 1970s.

I'm sure I was once told that 'Pep' was derived from the fact that his brother was called 'Sal' and so they were Salt and Pepper? We started playing with borrowed equipment and I'm pretty sure I used one of Bert Smith's old chin guards, the style that was given a nickname by who knows who of the "rabbit hutch" — if you ever saw them you'd know — but I got rid of that when I moved to the half visor, although Dougie kept playing with his until he stopped.

Talking of equipment, I know people remark upon a particular style I had when I would "shoogle my shoulders" which was simply down to getting my shoulder harness into a comfortable position; maybe I should have gotten one that was a better fit but I think I did ok with what I had.

Hockey changed over the three decades that I played as you might expect, apart from me getting slower that is, but when I moved back into defence it was amazing how much more time I realised I had once I could see the whole game in front of me.

My short time in Sweden obviously opened my eyes to what was another world of hockey but I was happy to be at home and playing for the Flyers. The great home grown talents that were in the 1970s teams then gave way to the start of teams signing imports and there will be many people reading this who were first hooked on the Flyers of the mid-1980s, and what was a really proud moment in my playing career to lift the silverware at Wembley in 1985.

Not all of the imports who I've played with set the heather on fire but they were part of teams that left some sort of memory with people. You can't go through life only experiencing the highs and of course in my hockey days there were a number of lows too.

Former NHL goalie Ken Dryden once summed up just how huge a role an ice rink can play in a community. It is more than just a sports venue; it can be a community centre and a meeting point for old-timers like me, an *ad hoc crêche* for hundreds of kids who come to skate and play hockey, a place of competition and comradeship on match nights, a place where hopes and dreams are realised or dashed but certainly a place where memories are made. ;

It's important as our shifts become shorter that we preserve as many of these memories. The Flyers are the grandfather of hockey clubs in the UK and it's such a great sport, and it is with pleasure that I pen a few words for this book which I hope you all enjoy reading as much as I enjoyed playing.

Yours, Gogs

Introduction

I'm now well into my fourth decade of watching the Fife Flyers; some of you who are reading will pre-date that and I doth my cap to you. Others may only just be beginning to understand what it feels like to follow a team, investing heavily on time, money and most of all emotionally.

My first game was at the tail end of the 1976/77 season, not a bad season as it turns out to get hooked but it meant very little to me at the time. I was 11 years old. I hadn't even had a pair of skates on my feet, I played the round ball game and I already had a team, the "Best team in Methil" that I had followed since I was 5.

There was something about a Saturday night however that was oh so different from a Saturday afternoon. Even though the end result of both could be abject misery there was always the chance that both teams would win or at least one would compensate for the other. You can only imagine how some of my weekends have been spent as I've hared about all over the country at 4.45 pm on a Saturday to make the puck drop at the rink that evening. In more recent times that pressure has been relieved somewhat with more home games scheduled for a Sunday. Something I know I'm in the majority with, who feel this just aint right.

While I've spent a considerable time documenting and recording the history of my football club I was content to simply sit and watch the hockey. That was until a few years ago when I was fortunate to be able to make one of those big life choices and I then looked for projects to undertake in my early retirement.

The history of the Flyers was one such project, an obvious choice for me and one that I thought could be a valuable legacy for the club and its fans. Despite their longevity, and being the oldest professional hockey club in Britain, there appears to be a shortage of publications to record their achievements. The events of 2020 gave me that extra impetus and a great excuse to spend hours locked in my study in research of this book which does not claim to be anything like a full history of the club. The annals of history for the Fife Flyers is a whole other project which is already underway, please just don't tell the other half.

It's more of a historical diary which is aimed at providing glimpses into each and every one of the club's 69 seasons across its 83 years of existence, and hopefully provides a flavour of events that will rekindle or infuse memories or impart new information. What it is not is a collection of best bits; that's not how supporting a team works as even the sporting greats all have their bad days and there are plenty of such moments in the pages that follow.

It's random in its selection of games as hockey seasons spanned different months of the calendar and if you are looking forward to reading content from the traditional hockey months of June and July then I'll save you that disappointment now as you will find none.

The calendar used for this diary is a refined hockey version and as many of us already know there are really only two seasons in a year in any case, summer and hockey. So while some pages will reflect what some might call mere mundane moments there are other pages that recall great achievements with the winning of silverware, firsts and lasts, records to be impressed with and others to be kept locked away.

The truth however is that even with a book structure that often required simply a random selection of dates in history there appears to be, to the author at least, many more highs than lows in the Flyers history.

We will all have our favourite players, favourite moments and hockey like many sports appears to usually always have been better back in the day. Is that really the case though? The sport evolves, players come and go, systems and styles herald new outcomes in how the game is played and rule changes add in further nuances with the only constant being that the on-ice officials are always wrong even when they are right.

The atmosphere rink side changes too, cowbells, drums, sometimes more silence than noise. No more prodding players through the netting or indeed being on the receiving end of the butt of a stick. The more things change the more they stay the same, however. I'm guessing that if you are reading this you will have an enduring interest or passion for the Fife Flyers regardless of circumstance.

I hope that the pages that follow do some sort of justice to those that have managed the club, those that have pulled on a Flyers jersey and laced up for one or many games, the officials who enable games to be played and to the many thousands of people who have taken a seat or stood at the back and have been prepared to give their all from the stands.

I realise that I have many stones yet to un-turn but I hope that any mistakes that have been made are few and far between and my apologies in advance. Anyone with any addenda is encouraged to get in touch with me via the contact details below and I will ensure that any information is put to good use in any future publications.

On a final note the work I've undertaken is something of a labour of love and undertaken purely with the desire to share knowledge about this great club. One of the things that has made the Flyers such a big part of the community is the work undertaken off the ice over the years with local organisations and charities. Mark Morrison was instrumental in the link between the hockey club and Rachel House up in Kinross when it first opened in 1996 and the club has featured the CHAS logo on their jersey ever since as well hosting an annual charity fixture and having countless players visit the kids. It seemed wholly appropriate then that all money made by way of royalties on the sale of this book should be donated to CHAS so a huge thank you to all who have purchased a copy and who have previously supported such a deserving cause in the past.

A final, final plug is a personal one. To progress further with my research I'm hoping to reach out to people who may have historical items relating to the Flyers. Maybe you are of an age that you attended games and collected programmes or compiled scrap books, maybe a relative passed items on to you for safe keeping. Please see the details below and get in touch if you think you could help out.

You can contact me through the following:
Twitter, FifeFlyersHistorian @flyers_history
Facebook, FifeFlyers Historian
E-mail, FifeFlyersHistorian@btinternet.com

Abbreviations used

BIHA - British Ice Hockey Association
BNL - British National League
DEL 2 - Deutsche Eishockey Liga 2
EIHL - Elite ice Hockey League
ENL - English National League
ISL - Ice Hockey Superleague
NHL - National Hockey League
NIHA - Northern Ice Hockey Association
SIHA - Scottish Ice Hockey Association

Fife Flyers 1972-73 autographs

August

The advert from the local Fife Free Press heralding the new sport in town and the team called the Fife Flyers

2

Saturday August 4th 1951

Flyers fans were excited by the following headline in the *Fife Free Press*:

WEMBLEY STAR TO PLAY FOR FLYERS

After a week-end of intensive activity, Edwin McGregor, manager of Kirkcaldy Ice Rink, completed one the most sensational captures of the close season when he secured the services of Jack 'Stubby' Mason, Wembley Lions International and All-Star netminder, who put pen to paper to sign for Fife Flyers. 'Stubby', who still enjoyed the reputation of being the finest netminder in Britain, wasn't about to make his first visit to Scotland when he travelled north in September to join the Kirkcaldy club. In his first season with the Wembley Lions, which was four years previously, 'Stubby' had been a member of the Bobby Giddens' English Select combine that toured the country.

Mason would be replacing the hugely popular 'Pete' Belanger who had been Flyers custodian for the past two seasons before going south to play with the Harringay Racers. His resume however was impressive. 'Stubby' was selected for the English All Star 'B' teams twice. In 1948/49 when he was with the Wembley Monarchs and in the season, before he signed for Flyers, when he was with the Wembley Lions. The 27-year old was reputed to be slightly temperamental (Which goalie isn't? Right!) but was regarded as a real crowd pleaser who could be brilliant on his day. When the Lions visited Streatham in April 1951 the Programme Notes read as follows: "Welcome Lions – This evening we welcome Wembley Lions and Stubby (the people's choice) Mason."

He was afforded a slightly unusual, albeit prestigious, accolade early on in his time with the Flyers as the local paper reported.

ROYAL COMMAND FOR 'STUBBY' MASON

"One of the highest honours the world of sport can give has come to Jack Mason, Fife Flyers 27-year-old international netminder. Jack is to appear in the Parade of Sportsmen, part of the Royal Command Performance which is to be given before Her Majesty Queen Elizabeth and Her Highness Princess Margaret in Victoria Palace, London, on Monday. Asked how he felt about it, Jack said it was the greatest thing that ever happened to him. He hoped to be presented to the Queen. Jack was readily granted permission to miss practices by Kirkcaldy Ice Rink management and left for London yesterday."

Mason played for Fife in just the one season, 1951/52. He was an ever-present for the team and faced over 2000 shots, the most in the league, with a goals average of 7.51 and one shut out. His performances were enough over the season to earn him a unique place in the club's history as he was the inaugural winner of the Mirror of Merit Award, the popular feature that was in those days run in the *Kirkcaldy Times*. He was awarded five honourable mentions with runners up Floyd Snider and Mickey Linnell each receiving three apiece.

'Stubby' Mason in his days with the Wembley Monarchs

Tuesday August 11th 1948

SPECTATOR SUES ICE HOCKEY PLAYER: STRUCK BY
PUCK DURING BRAWL

The headline in local newspapers referred to a Kinghorn man who was pursuing a claim of £50 11s against Flyers defenceman Floyd Snider following an incident during the Flyers-Bruins game on April 11th, earlier that year. Mr McIlravie claimed he had paid admission to Kirkcaldy Ice Rink and obtained a seat in the fourth row from the front in Block M. During the game a dispute arose between the Flyers players and the referee. The referee suspended play and a noisy brawl arose between the referee and the players. During the stoppage Snider, apparently in order to emphasise his disapproval of the referee's decision and without any apparent cause, turned his back on the referee, skated a short distance away and struck the puck in the direction of the spectators where Mr McIlravie was sitting. The puck travelled in a straight line and struck McIlravie, going nowhere near the goal. As a result of this action Snider was penalised by the referee for misconduct and was disqualified from the game for 10 minutes. McIlravie stated that the puck struck him without warning on the bridge of the nose. His attention was not at the time directed to the game which had been suspended and he had no warning of Snider's action. Snider knew, or ought to have known, that it was dangerous to propel the puck in the direction of the spectators and in particular that there was danger of striking a spectator. Despite this knowledge, Snider recklessly and without any regard for the safety of the spectators struck the puck in the direction of McIlravie resulting in his injury.

McIlravie sustained cuts and bruises to his nose requiring medical attention. He was unable to follow his normal occupation for a number of days following, suffering from defective vision and severe headaches. In his defence, Snider denied he was in the employment of Kirkcaldy Ice Rink, and admitted that in the course of the game a dispute arose with the referee but explained that he took no part in this dispute. He claimed that he withdrew the puck from the goal-net and shot it for goal. Instead the puck hit the metal frame-work of the goal and went out of the rink. He admitted that as a result of this action he was disqualified from the game for 10 minutes. Snider explained that constantly throughout the game the puck is struck in the direction of the spectators sitting in galleries at the end of the rink behind the goal. There was a danger to the spectators in these galleries, and that McIlravie must have been aware of it, as he claimed he was a regular attender at hockey matches. Snider made it clear that in the entrance vestibule of the Ice Rink there is prominently displayed a notice stating "Skaters and spectators are only admitted to the building at their own risk and on the understanding that no claims can be entertained for any accidents which may occur from any cause". An identical notice is posted inside the Rink, one at each end. On the admission ticket issued to McIlravie there were printed the words: "This ticket is issued subject to the notice displayed in the box office."

It would take 15 months for the matter to be sorted with a ruling given on 15th December 1949 as follows:

FIFE ICE HOCKEY SPECTATOR WINS

Sheriff More has decided that 24-year-old Fife Flyers defenceman, Floyd Snider, must pay £50 11s, as sued for, to a spectator injured at an ice hockey match. The spectator made the claim in respect of injuries and loss of earnings. Sheriff More finds Snider at first took part, in a dispute over the referee's decision (award of a goal to the opposing team) and later, in a fit of bad temper gave the puck a smashing blow in McIlravie's direction. At the time it was struck, the puck was not in play. McIlravie's injuries were due to Snider's fault and negligence. Given consideration of the evidence there is little difficulty, said the Sheriff, in finding McIlravie has proved his averments. "It is significant that as a consequence of his reckless behaviour the referee suspended the defender for ten minutes and set him aside to cool like one of Kipling's 'brandered souls' ". The sheriff did not accept Snider's averment and evidence that when he struck the puck he intended having a shot at goal and that the puck struck the goalpost and glanced off it in McIlravie's direction.

Floyd Snider on the ice

Wednesday August 12th 1953

The *Leven Mail* carried the following headline:

FLYERS SIGN NEW PLAYER COACH

The Fife Flyers new player-coach for the season, it read, would be defenceman Ken Broughton. Announced by Ice Rink manager Alexander Bain who said that it was hoped to have more information regarding Broughton before the end of the week. So, who was Ken Broughton? Well, in truth, we are still none the wiser to this day because two weeks later the *Leven Mail* then advised Flyers fans of the following:

KENTNER SIGNS FOR FLYERS — BUT PLAYER-COACH CALLS OFF

Fred Kentner (as the *Leven Mail* was at pains to point out had been forecast exclusively last week) had signed for Flyers. That was in addition to a goalkeeper by the name of Ron Collins. However defenceman player-coach Ken Broughton would now not be taking up his duties. The club had received a cable from Canadian scout Gordon Gerrard in which no reason had been given for the change of heart on Broughton's part. At the same time Gerrard let it be known he was negotiating with another experienced player to take over the coaching chores. The season was a little less than a month from starting so it was with some relief the following week that the *Fife Free Press* picked up the story with the good news:

FLYERS SIGN COACH AND WINGER

Working under some pressure since the set-back involving the non-appearance of Ken Broughton, Gordon Gerrard beat the clock and a number of other Canadian clubs when he signed centre-ice Johnny Dobos who would also assume the player-coach duties. Dobos, a former Galt junior 'A' and 'B' player, who was familiarly referred to back home as 'Doughboy', hailed form Woodstock and according to reports was rated as one of the best playmakers in his league. Recently, Dobos had coached a representative team which included several of Flyers new recruits for the season ahead, goalie Collins and right-wingers Jack Lane and Lloyd Boomer. So that was surely that on the coaching front, well not quite with the *Leven Mail* first to break the news in the first week in November that:

FLYERS CHANGES ARE NOW ANNOUNCED

Appreciating that the renewed interest in ice hockey created by last season's team was being frittered away by the performances so far of the current Flyers squad, the directors at Kirkcaldy Ice Rink decided on a number of changes. First of these was the appointment of Henry Hayes as player-coach in place of Johnny Dobos. Hayes, who had played on the Continent and in the English league before taking over the running of Dunfermline Vikings last season was known as one of the better coaches in the country. He was a strict disciplinarian and his style was very reminiscent to that of a previous Flyers coach, Al Rogers, and he would not spare himself in his efforts to get the best out of a club. That was easily seen at Dunfermline last season and many people, including Hayes himself, would be greatly surprised if it did not soon become evident with Flyers too. Hayes' playing ability was not negligible either, even although he was in the veteran stages of his career at the age of 38.

He played smart positional hockey for Vikings last season and was always accurate in front of the net. Johnny Dobos, who was relieved as coach by Hayes, would continue to play for Flyers, although it was an arrangement that seemed untenable. Further alterations in the line-up were to be made in the coming weeks. Unsurprisingly, Dobos left three weeks later, but almost within days after that, there was a final twist in the coaching circus with the following headline

ILL LUCK STILL DOGS FLYERS AS HAYES BOUND BY SWISS CONTRACT

It was confirmed that Hayes was to be held to his contract with his former team in Switzerland and after only 4 weeks would return to the continent. He did however return the following season to coach the full season. Former fans favourite Floyd Snider was approached to return from Canada after two years away to coach the team and he duly arrived and stayed for the remainder of that season. Before his departure Wray Fallowfield took charge of coaching duties for two games including a 17-2 thumping in Paisley which still stands as the club's joint heaviest defeat on the road.

Footnote

Further research into Ken Broughton suggests that he may have played at that time for the Ontario Junior 'B' side the Newmarket Redmen and later became their coach in the 1960s.

One of the Club's Grand Slam seasons is commemorated with the raising of more banners at Fife Ice Arena

Saturday August 14th 1954

FLYERS TEAM BUILDING PROCEEDS APACE

Flyers coach Henry Hayes (yes, he was finally here), from his base in London had made a promising start towards fixing up a strong Flyers squad as they prepared to enter into the new British National League. Two players had already been signed. Goalie Walter Malahoff from Kamloops Senior 'B' and right winger Nickolas Jost who was a member of the Kanagan Valley Intermediate Championship team of last season.

None of last year's Canadian players were expected to return, with Hayes looking to make a clean sweep. Keen to make sure that for this season Flyers would have a strong and dependable defence, the coach had spent a considerable time concentrating on the makeup of the blueline. Along with an ex-team mate, who was well known to British and Continental ice hockey fans but who at this time would remain anonymous, he spent weeks pouring over various files on netminders and defencemen before starting to contact the players. 28-year-old Walter Malahoff was a very experienced player.

He started off as a junior for Trail B.C. and graduated to Trail All-Star Senior 'B' in season 1946-47, and while with them they won the Coy Cup. The following season he was with Spokane Spartans, a well-known Senior A outfit in the Kootenay League. He followed that by playing in 1948-49 for Vernon Canadians, and then had a three-season spell (1949-52) with Kamloops Elks. Last season he turned out for Kamloops Senior 'B'. Nickolas Jost had also had a successful career. Amongst other things he had been a member of the teams which won the B.C. Juvenile Championships and Junior Championships. A fast-breaking winger with a good shot.

The Kirkcaldy directorship were also vocal in support of the way in which Coach Hayes was getting on with the job. It was expected that in next season's British League there would be little room for a struggling team, so all efforts were being directed towards building up a team worthy of the occasion. Not only Scottish ice hockey, but British ice hockey, would be on trial in the coming season. If the opportunity was grasped, the game could be restored to its former prestige. This fact was thoroughly recognised and appreciated by all connected with the sport. The appearance of the three English teams — Wembley Lions, Nottingham Panthers and Harringay Racers — were expected to boost interest amongst local fans and at other Scottish rinks. The additional variety of fixtures afforded by the three newcomers would help to maintain interest, while the reappearance of Dunfermline Vikings was welcomed as there was no doubt the local rivalry added zest to the meetings between the Flyers and Vikings.

There was some difficulty in arranging the fixtures to suit all the clubs. With the travelling involved, both to and from England, a perfect solution was well-nigh impossible and a provisional list had already been circulated and rejected. From a financial perspective it was obviously better for a Scottish team to play as many games as possible during one visit to England and the same applied in reverse for the English clubs. Flyers fans were happy to hear that Thursday would still remain the regular home night with Tuesday as an occasional alternative. The Kirkcaldy Rink already had a new look with its updated interior decorative scheme. Next season meant a fresh start in more ways than one.

Milan Figala played the game with a smile but is in serious mood as he tries to shackle Tony Hand during the 1994-95 season

Saturday August 17th 1946

Flyers fans and indeed all ice hockey fans in Scotland were encouraged by the news that the game would soon return, following the shut down during the War years. The *Fife Free Press* sports section headline, along within many other newspapers, carried the following news:

ICE HOCKEY TO RESUME

Preparations for a new season were underway. The sport, which had been disturbed by the outbreak of war, had been gaining much momentum with the Scottish public. Hockey continued during the first year of the war but then had to give way to more urgent matters, although the Junior teams and occasional games played between Canadian service sides kept the game alive. It was good news to local enthusiasts to know that organised senior ice hockey was due to start up in October. There was little doubt that the game in Fife, despite having only been played for a couple of years before the outbreak of hostilities, had made a strong impression on sports lovers. Indeed, it was reckoned that it had been ready to experience a great boom all over Scotland when the War intervened.

Mr Fester Moffat, secretary of the Scottish Ice Hockey Association, had been unable to travel to Canada to arrange for a contingent of players to come over and join up with the Scottish clubs but this duty had been willingly undertaken by the Canadian Amateur Ice Hockey Association. They found a tremendous response with hundreds of Canucks willing to come to Scotland and take up the game here. A series of trial games had to be arranged to determine which of the aspirants would make the grade. The process resulted in 80 players being selected and they were due to make the trans-Atlantic trip early in September. On their arrival the players would proceed to the clubs to which they had been allocated. All of this selection process was done without the input from the individual clubs. Seven clubs were ready to take the ice. Paisley, Ayr, Falkirk, Dundee, Dunfermline, Perth and Fife.

This would make a decent line-up for the opening season with the prospect of an eighth team, a situation that could easily be resourced in view of the number of Canadians who were coming over. The fixtures list had been drawn up with two league competitions followed by a cup competition making in all a 30-week season. Since the last organised games in Scotland some of the local youngsters in the junior teams had made great strides in their development in the game. The facilities now afforded by ice rinks meant the Scots boys were able to get training comparable to that enjoyed by the youngsters in Canada. It was noted though that Scotland could not yet compete with the Canadian climate which ensured plenty of outdoor practice, a factor which accounted for the traditional expertness of Canadians at the game.

The Kirkcaldy Juniors had been fortunate in having former Fife Flyer Les Lovell (Senior) as their coach and as time passed it was expected that a number of the local lads would qualify for the senior game. Amongst other attractions in the offing for Flyers fans would be tours of the Scottish rinks by foreign teams and representative games between Scotland and England. Kirkcaldy ice hockey enthusiasts at first feared that the existence of a dance floor at the rink which reduced the ice surface to about two thirds might lead to difficulties in regard to the resumption of senior ice hockey. This had been resolved by replacement of the existing dance floor with a dancing surface which could be removed and replaced as the occasion demanded. Thus, the needs of both the dancing and ice hockey enthusiasts would not be sacrificed at the expense of the other.

ICE RINK
kirkcaldy
THE CENTRE OF ENTERTAINMENT

CLOSED FOR OVERHAUL

RE-OPENING FOR

SKATING & DANCING

SATURDAY, 31st AUGUST, 10 A.M.

ICE HOCKEY LEAGUE

COMMENCES

THURSDAY, 3rd OCTOBER, 1946

Advert in the Fife Free Press to herald the restart of organised hockey at the rink – the first for six years

Saturday August 18th 1951

SCOTTISH ICE HOCKEY ASSOCIATION CHANGES ITS MIND

What could the headline in the local paper relate to? The answer, the humble red line. For readers of a certain vintage this may mean absolutely nothing. However, the centre line in hockey had been a hot topic for a number of years. Last season the SIHA had been under some pressure to present a better and more entertaining product; now they had decided, amongst other things, that the day of the red line was to be consigned to history. It was a move that seemed to garner favour with the followers of the game but when the supporters' outcry was but a whisper from the past the Association had changed its mind and decided the red line would stay. This was a move that was not shared widely. Many thought that the centre line should be obliterated and that the playing surface be divided into three equal zones as it was before the war.

It was nearly eleven years ago that the Canadian Amateur Hockey Association, from whom the laws and practices of the game were applied pretty much world-wide, decided hockey needed something to speed it up. Some bright boy had thought up the red line idea and there had been nothing but complaint after complaint from all over North America ever since. The standard of play had deteriorated steadily and it was thought time somebody put a stop to the rapid decline. In a somewhat veiled dig at the general standard of professionals coming to these shores from Canada it was noted that to do without a red line would mean that there "would have to be considerable improvement in the stick-handling and general ability shown by the Canadians coming over here but isn't that to everybody's advantage?"

It was hoped the SIHA would think again on what was quite the hot topic back then; indeed the rule was still in place in the game in this country until 1998 when the I I H F scrapped it from their rule book and the NHL eventually abolished it for the 2005/06 season.

For those who have only followed the game since its abolishment the principle of the rule was very much like the offside rule at the blueline today but just applied to the red line. So essentially if the puck was being passed from the defensive zone side of the blue line you either needed to touch the puck before it crossed the red line or wait until it had crossed before skating over the red line and then touching the puck.

While the SIHA were being roundly slated for their red line decision they were being widely praised for another change they were to introduce. It would allow greater freedom to the individual clubs who were to be given permission to pay the players on their merits, as determined by the club's assessment.

Previously the Association kept a tight grip on the financial side of the game and they determined the value a player should be paid. This latter piece saw the further devolvement of player personnel responsibility to the clubs, rather than to the SIHA, who had been in the past also responsible for the "pooling" system where they allocated North American players to the clubs based on their own arbitrary, and of course wholly objective, decisions. One final change for the season ahead was the extension in size of the area of the goal crease from five to six feet, thus affording goalies greater protection; at the same time, it was hoped to avoid the ever-increasing number of disputed decisions in the goalmouth.

Mark Dutiaume, brother of player and coach Todd Dutiaume, in season 2001-02. The pair are one of what are thought to be 16 different sets of brothers who have played together for Flyers

Saturday August 21st 1954

FLYERS NOW HAVE EIGHT PLAYERS SIGNED

was the headline in the *Fife Free Press* as the report updated fans ahead of the team entering the British National League season. With the signing of Johnny Andrews from Fort William Ontario, and Don Cox, also from Ontario, coach Henry Hayes had now brought the total number of signings for Flyers up to eight.

Following on from the earlier article, that the Flyers had made a promising start in their recruitment of an entirely new squad for the season ahead with the signature of net minder Walter Malahoff and right-wing Nickolas Jost, there had subsequently also been four more additions to the team. They were Neil Matheson from Vancouver, Fred Hall from Medicine Hat in Alberta, John Popenuik from Regina, Saskatchewan and Walter Davison from Saskatoon, Saskatchewan.

Of the two latest signings, 21 year old Johnny Andrews had previously played for Fort William Canadians; last year following a tryout for Streatham he signed for Ayr Raiders. He proved to be a versatile and goal-getting winger, who notched 13 goals and 18 assists in 29 league outings. Don Cox, who would be the youngest member of the team at 20 years of age, turned out last season for the Fort William Hurricanes. He could play centre or left wing and came with a very good reputation. John Popenuik was expected to partner Fred Hall in defence. In the case of Neil Matheson and Walter Davison it was known that one played forward and the other defence but information as to which played which was not yet to hand. Matheson turned out to be the blueliner.

Coach Hayes was expected up in Kirkcaldy shortly when he would provide full information on all the players. However, based on the information gleaned so far there was a general optimism about the team that was being assembled. It was considered a pretty sound line-up and with Henry Hayes as player-coach and ready, if need be, to take the ice himself it had a blend of youth and experience that some thought had been missing in recent years. The new British National League was expected to be a stern test of team recruitment with great anticipation of the standard being set higher than previous years. It was also encouraging to note that many of the players came from Western Canada where, according to ex Flyers coach Al Rogers, a Saskatoon product himself, the most rugged ice hockey players were reared.

The new British League was attracting a good deal of attention and there were ongoing discussions, even at this later stage, to admit Brighton Tigers into the competition. Another English team and one that was so far south was not helping with the composition of the previously mentioned problematic fixture list. However, it was generally considered that the Brighton application should be accepted as four English teams (instead of the present three) and eight Scottish teams would give a more balanced series of fixtures. It was proposed that the season might have to be extended by three weeks to accommodate the Tigers inclusion but the view amongst most was "the more the merrier"! Brighton were indeed welcomed into the brave new world. The players arrived on 15th September and the official season start date was 27th September.

FIFE FLYERS AT WESTMINSTER

This photo was taken when Fife Flyers, fulfilling a London fixture, also took the opportunity of visiting the House of Commons, where Mr Tom Hubbard, M.P. for Kirkcaldy Burghs, acted as their host and guide. From left to right: Back row — Malahoff, Davison, Mr Victor Beattie (director, Kirkcaldy Ice Rink, Tom Elder (trainer, Mr Tom Hubbard, Andrews, Hayes (coach), Mitchell and Bruce. Front row — Sutherland, Matheson and Smith.

Paul Crowder who had the opening goal for the Flyers in their 80th season against the University of Manitoba Bisons.

Thursday August 23rd 2018

Fife Flyers 1 University of Manitoba Bisons 2

The Flyers hosted North American opposition for the first time in nearly three decades as they kicked of a pre-season programme that also featured the visit of two teams from Denmark and a couple from the German DEL 2.

The Manitoba Bisons, who hailed from Winnipeg, played their regular season games in the Canada West Universities Conference. Also known as the USports league. which had become more familiar with Elite Ice Hockey League fans in recent seasons as a number of former students of schools moved to the UK to take up their professional hockey careers after school. Indeed, Flyers coach Todd Dutiaume was a Bisons alumni, having played with them for two seasons from 1994-1996. Todd's coach at that time, Mike Sirant, was still in charge behind the bench for his 23rd season and he brought his youthful team to the UK for the second time, having visited the previous autumn.

The game would also see the emergence of local brothers Graham and Scott Rodger who, a few weeks later, became the first brothers to officiate in an EIHL level game in Scotland. The game saw Flyers ice a large bench with 21 skaters including several who were on trial. The coaching staff aimed to give them all ice time across the five exhibition games and fine tune their lines ahead of the EIHL season starting on September 8th.

It was one of the Flyers debutants, Paul Crowder, who had the honour of netting the first goal of Flyers 80th anniversary campaign, turning home the rebound off an Evan Stoflet slapshot to give Flyers an early lead. Bisons drew level through Jeremy Leipsic following a smart move where his line-mate split the defence to allow him to finish in front of Shane Owen.

Both sides carved out some good chances but it was fair to say Bisons were dominant in the second period — outshooting Fife a hefty 21-6 only to encounter a rock-solid Owen who made his art look effortless. It was no surprise he took the home Man of the Match award. The winning goal came with just 16 seconds to play and Owen could do nothing to prevent it when Carter Doerksen skated on to a great pass off the right boards before drilling the puck home.

For Head Coach Todd Dutiaume, the night was a first chance to see how his new-look team was shaping up. Post-game he commented: "We had only skated together three times as a group before the game; there is lots more to come from this team. We know we have an excellent group of players and they were keen to do well for the fans — I thought Owen was outstanding, particularly in the second period, and had a few chances gone in, then maybe things would have loosened up."

Others making their debuts for the Flyers were imports Scott Aarssen, Rick Pinkston, Joe Basaraba, Brett Bulmer, Mike Cazzola and British players Jordan Buesa, Bari McKenzie and Caly Robertson.

Saturday August 24th 2019

Fife Flyers 4 Herlev Eagles 3 (after overtime)

In the 2019-20 season opener the Flyers got their pre-season off to a positive start as they came from behind to secure an overtime win over the Herlev Eagles from Denmark.

New signing Kyle Just got the decisive goal at the end of a competitive fixture that also saw Chase Schaber grab a double on his return from injury. Mike Cazzola was also on target, netting an equaliser with just 13 seconds left of normal time as Flyers withdrew netminder Adam Morrison for a six-on-four power play.

The result was achieved with Flyers still waiting on the arrival of Danick Gauthier, Dylan Quaile and the Crowder brothers, Tim and Paul, from their respective Australian Hockey League teams. Emerging from a happy Flyers changing room coach Todd Dutiaume offered the following comments on the match to reporters. "It's nice to get a win under your belt early. It helps with confidence and camaraderie in the dressing room. For being together for just under three and a half practices and being short staffed we did a good job and the work ethic was there for sure. We were sloppy at times but that's the reason we have these games."

Flyers took the opportunity to give some ice time to a couple of younger players, Marty Simpson and Scott Jamieson, who were expected to be on two-way contracts with Kirkcaldy Kestrels during the season. The pair did their cause no harm, while Chad Smith, Jordan Buesa and Sam Jones all gave assured performances alongside the more experienced Bari McKenzie. Dutiaume added: "This was a great opportunity for the young guys to go out and get a regular shift. They put in a good shift, and while there were a few mistakes made out there, it was the same with the rest of the team. That's where they're going to learn, they need the experience so we rolled with them the entire game and we'll continue to do so tomorrow."

Flyers took the lead inside the third minute as Just pinched the puck to set up Chase Schaber who finished well from close quarters. The Danes, several weeks further into their preseason training, were dangerous throughout and goals from Acke Ringstrom and Christoffer Gath had them in front early in the third period. Schaber brought Fife level with his second of the night, a laser from the right wing on the power play on 47 minutes and Chase looked back to his old self after the previous season blighted by injury. Flyers were behind again however after a five-on-three power play goal from Johan Skinnars. That looked to be the decisive goal until a penalty called against Herlev in the final two minutes presented Fife with a power play and after calling a time-out, and withdrawing Morrison, a close-range finish from Cazzola took the game to overtime.

Herlev ran into more penalty trouble in the extra session and found themselves with two skaters in the box presenting Flyers with a five-on-three. They took advantage as Kyle Just fired home to seal the victory. Schaber was announced as Man of the Match and Dutiaume revealed why his ice time had been cut short following his summer surgery. "Chase is a natural athlete. He's had a significant period of time off, so we didn't really play him that much at the end. My natural instinct was to put him out on the ice but we were communicating on the bench and he felt he needed a rest and this is not the time to push him past a point where either of us feel uncomfortable. I thought he did a great job for us in his first competitive match free from injury since October." Todd was also pleased to score four goals given the firepower that was missing while the defence also coped well against the speed of the Danish attack. "We never question our offensive capabilities," he said. "We scored a couple of power play goals tonight so we're pleased with that and there were a lot of positive signs. Our big D back there looked pretty mobile and tidy and I know Jeff is happy with the performance all six guys put in which is a huge positive sign and affirms that we made some right decisions back there."

Bari McKenzie and Sam Jones celebrate as Kyle Just's overtime winner hits the net

Thursday August 25th 1938

ICE HOCKEY STAR FOR FIFE RINK

That was the headline in the *Dundee Courier* as the Flyers set about finalising their inaugural season roster with their first ever game just over four weeks away. The report read

"Mr J. C. Rolland, manager of Kirkcaldy Ice Rink, has secured a "scoop" with the signature of international ice hockey star Jimmy Chappell. For three seasons Chappell has been with the crack London team, Earls Court Rangers. Although only 23 years of age, he is regarded as one of the fastest players in the game. Born in Huddersfield, he went to Canada when 10 years of age, and learned his ice hockey in Oshawa, Ontario. He made his debut in organised hockey in 1931 with Oshawa Juniors, and three years later was in the college team which won the province championship. He was in the Whitby Intermediates the following year when they carried off the Ontario championship. Two years ago he joined the London club. Being British born, he was eligible to play for Great Britain in the Olympic Games in Germany and he played centre for the team which won the Olympic, World and European titles. He has played for Britain in the last two seasons, in London last year and in Prague in February of this year. On both occasions Britain won the European title. Chappell is 5 ft. 8 in. in height and weighs 11 st. 6 lb. He is a right-hand shot, and plays centre or right-wing, although he also played in defence for the Earls Court team."

In Flyers inaugural season Jimmy was one of three ever presents in the Flyers line up scoring 40 goals, second behind Norman McQuade's 49, in his 55 games. The following season he moved to the West side of Fife after Mr Rolland once again secured his signature, this time to play for the Dunfermline Vikings in their first season in the league. During his time in Dunfermline he married local girl Miss Marjorie Webster who was a figure skating instructor at the Kirkcaldy Rink.

As a member of the 1936 Olympic squad, Chappell scored two goals in six appearances and went on to add three more Olympic goals 12 years later when Switzerland hosted the Games. Including the two European Championships in 1937 & 1938, Jimmy totalled 16 appearances for Great Britain scoring seven goals and nine assists for a point a game record.

During the Second World War, Chappell saw active service including the D-Day landing in Normandy before returning in peacetime to playing hockey with the Brighton Tigers, winning league titles in 1947 and 1948. His post-war statistics saw him play 130 games, scoring 72 goals and 64 assists for 136 points with 121 penalty minutes. Upon retiring from playing Jimmy Chappell donned a referee shirt, for a spell with the whistle, before returning with his family to Canada. Described as a fine stick handler and a gentlemanly player Chappell also represented Canada at cricket and went on to develop an astute business career.

Jimmy Chappell in his Earls Court Rangers days.

Saturday August 26th 2017

Fife Flyers 4 EC Kassel Huskies 3 (after overtime)

Fife Flyers scored an overtime victory over German DEL 2 side EC Kassel Huskies in their opening match of the 2017-18 season. The game was a typical pre-season affair, competitive without being fully physical, as players shook off the rust from a long summer break.

The first period was evenly balanced and was heading towards a goalless conclusion when Huskies struck the opener with just five seconds left. It came on the power play as Danick Gauthier sat for hooking and they struck almost immediately through defenceman Mike Little to take a one-goal advantage into the room. Flyers fell further behind straight from the restart as John Rogl punished the space afforded to him by firing past netminder Andy Iles. That triggered a tough spell for Fife as they struggled with puck retention and were forced to work hard to stay in the game.

The team needed a goal to get going and Chase Schaber provided it on 38.23 with a sharp shot to finish off a three-on-one breakaway as the middle period ended without further scoring. The home side were again on the backfoot early in third as Gauthier caught an opponent in the face and sat out a double minor for accidental high sticks. The penalty kill however was solid with back up Jordan Marr in net and Flyers were rewarded with an equaliser on 47.11. With few options ahead of him, Shayne Stockton launched a hopeful shot from beyond the blue line that took a deflection on its way into the net via the post. After the bad luck with injuries suffered by him last term hopefully this was a good omen of better fortune in the season ahead for Stockton.

Flyers fell behind again five minutes from the end during a spell of four-on-four hockey when Adriano Carciola wasn't picked up and scored off his own rebound despite Marr's best efforts to keep him out. In a bid to avoid defeat Fife withdrew Marr for the closing two minutes to go for an extra skater and the move paid off when defenceman Ian Young fired a puck towards goal that found a way through traffic and into the net on 58.58.

The game went into an extra period of three-on-three overtime and Flyers struck the decisive blow after just 35 seconds. Following

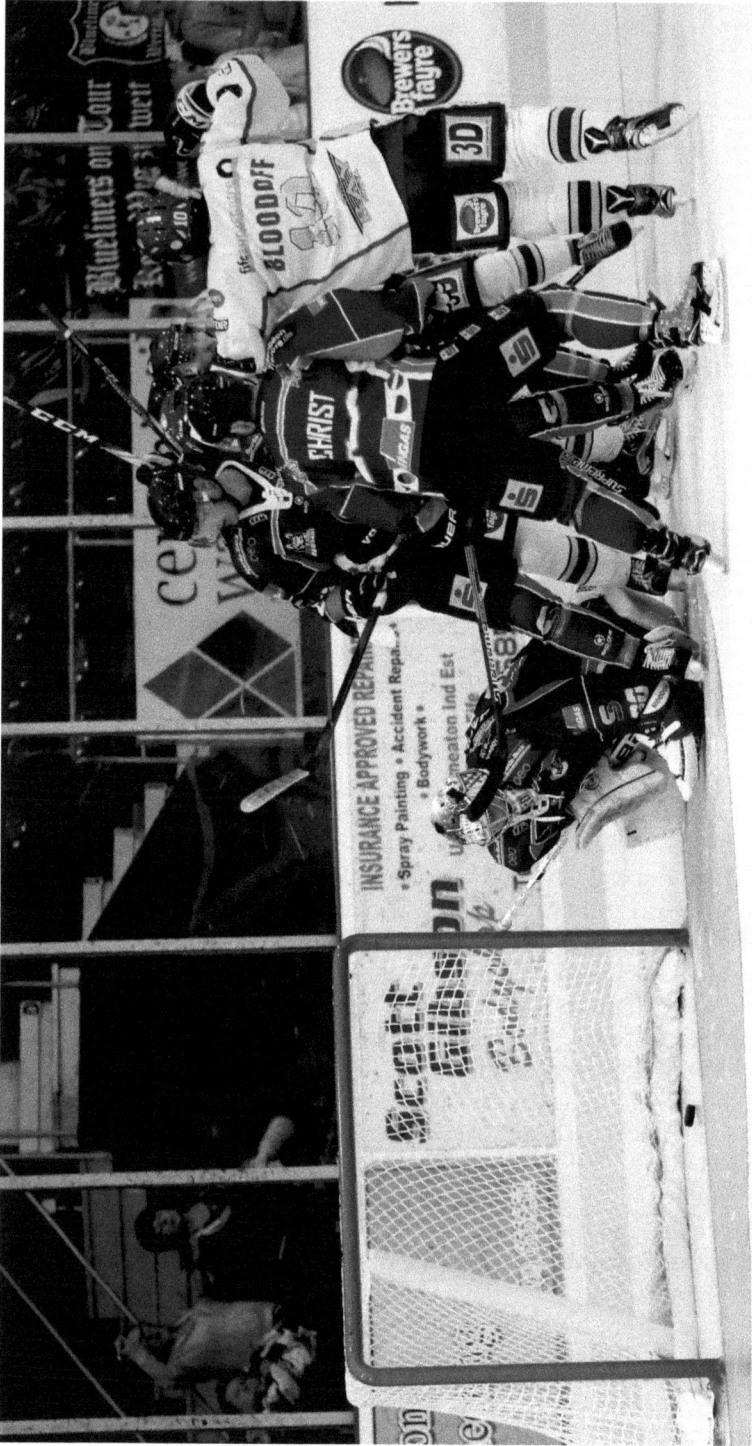

Shayne Stockton who was the first (re)signing for the 2017-18 season and wasted no time in getting off the mark with a goal against the Huskies

determined set-up work by Russ Moyer the puck fell to Peter LeBlanc who skated in from the wing and squeezed his shot past the visiting netminder at his near post.

While results in pre-season games tend at seasons end to not be at all important, it was encouraging to see Flyers claim victory against decent opposition and claw their way back from deficits during the game. It would suggest that after just a few days training there was already a good spirit about this group. The overall performance had its ups and downs, as you would expect at this early stage. The team lost its way in the second period, struggling to transition the puck and managing just three shots on goal, but there was a sprinkling of positives throughout the rest of the game.

Given they were familiar to the surroundings it was perhaps no surprise that Flyers stand-out men on the night were returning players. Schaber picked up a goal and the Man of the Match award, while Stockton also got on the scoreboard and showed glimpses of the skilful stick-handling centreman the team missed throughout his injury last season.

Of the new players it was hard not to be immediately impressed with the stature of forward Danick Gauthier. With his size and speed he was expected to ruffle feathers in the EIHL season ahead and as it transpired beyond. Also impressing was netminder Andy Iles with a number of good saves. Flyers used the match to ice every member of the bench which meant shifts for youngsters Chad Smith and Reece Cochrane, while back-up netminder Jordan Marr was given the third period to impress, which he did with some key saves, particularly during the Gauthier penalty kill. Head coach Todd Dutiaume was happy with the performance more so than simply the outcome.

Saturday August 27th 2016

Fife Flyers 5 EC Peiting 0

Fife Flyers made a solid start to the pre-season with a comprehensive victory over German third division side EC Peiting in front of 1500 fans at Fife Ice Arena. The main positives were the five goals, all from different scorers and a shut-out for debutant netminder Shane Owen, who looked composed throughout. As pre-season games go it was a good workout for the new-look side, which also saw first appearances for David Turon, James Isaacs, Matt Sisca, Russ Moyer, Brendan Brooks, Carlo Finucci, Chase Schaber and Sebastien Thinel. Flyers were also missing three imports with the arrival of Ric Jackman and Kyle Follmer, delayed due to paperwork (he would never eventually arrive in the country), while Phil Paquet missed out through injury. The injury to the returning D man was a significant concern and Head Coach Todd Dutiaume confirmed that Paquet would miss the start of the season and that he was currently looking to sign another import defenceman as cover.

"Any time you see a guy on crutches before the season starts, that's a huge concern. He picked it up in summer training and he let me know as soon as it happened. We brought him in and he was skating well but he was getting a bit of discomfort with it so we got a scan and it didn't come back with great news. It's a huge hole to fill but I'm working on that right now and hoping to get some cover in, either short term or long term. We do not want to be short benched, we've been down that road before."

While it was difficult to gauge the performance against a side some distance below EIHL standard there were encouraging moments of link-up play, particularly in the forward areas. Some late arrivals meant that Flyers preparations for their season opening match involved going over systems just 45 minutes before face-off. That was reflected in a rather scrappy start to proceedings which saw the visitors hold their own but the more Flyers settled into the match the more dominant they became. The opener arrived on 16.37 and it was one of the new boys, Brendan Brooks, who showed his skating prowess as he waltzed through the Peiting defence to slide the puck underneath netminder Florian Hechenrieder. Not many 37-year-olds were as quick across the ice as the former Braehead Clan forward. The goal gave the game more life and the Flyers second followed a minute later as Ryan Dingle picked up where he left off the previous season with a perfect back post pass for Sebastien Thinel who did not have to break stride as he guided the puck into the net. Flyers were getting into a groove. Carlo Finucci made an early impression with a stunning solo goal midway through period two, darting inside before sending a backhand effort inside the post. Chase Schaber seemed to be constantly making things happen and he got in on the act on 38.47 with a close-range finish making it 4-0 just seconds after a Flyers power play finished.

Flyers added a fifth early in the final period as Matt Sisca turned home Russ Moyer's pass at the back door, before the game petered out as both teams' legs clearly showed the effects of being so early in the season. Flyers also gave ice time to youngsters Marty Simpson and Chad Smith, two players who were to be under the wing of Jeff Hutchins this season in his player development role.

Dutiaume was pleased with his team's showing given the short preparation time and commented after the match:

> "For the first time together as a partial squad, it was good. We gave them information overload before the game but for the most part they executed okay. We saw some really positive signs and it was a good confidence boost all round."

Philippe Paquet was an early season injury worry for the Flyers

Flyers crash the net against their German visitors EC Peiting

Saturday August 28th 2010

NEWCASTLE TOURNAMENT

The Flyers had to settle for third place in the opening tournament of the new ice hockey season. The newly-revamped Northern League was given its official launch during a full weekend of hockey at the Metro Radio Arena in Newcastle. The League's eight member clubs competed over two days, initially in groups, and then in knock-out format, in a bid to reach Sunday's final. Flyers had been hot favourites to land the season's first silverware but travelled without several of last season's roster including netminder Blair Daly, brothers Steven and Derek King, defenceman Dan McIntyre and forwards Lewis Glasgow, Stephen Gunn and Iain Beattie. Regardless, Flyers travelled with a strong side including recent recruits Liam Greig, Daryl Venters, Chad Reekie and Chris Linton.

In their opening match of the weekend they met the Sheffield Spartans and got the tournament off to a positive start with a 5-3 victory.

MATCH 1 — SHEFFIELD SPARTANS 3, FIFE FLYERS 5
Spartans scoring: Humphries, Barron, Manning (1+0) Turner, Oliver, Millard (0+1).
Flyers scoring: Dutiaume, Greig (2+1) Venters (1+0) Wilson (0+3) Muir, Fowley, Scoon, McAlpine (0+1).
SOGs: Sheffield (Hartley) 18; Fife (Nicol) 17.
PIMs: 2-20

Next up came the host club Northern Stars, the Newcastle Vipers revamped ENL 2 winning side from the previous season, who proved too strong for the Flyers and they ran out 3-1 winners.

MATCH 2 — NORTHERN STARS 3, FIFE FLYERS 1
Stars scoring: Davies (1+1) Moutray, Telfer (1+0) Elder (0+2).
Flyers scoring: Lynch (1+0) Samuel, Linton (0+1).
SOGs: Northern (Lawson) 18; Fife (Nicol) 15.
PIMs: 8-4

In their final round robin game on the Saturday Flyers had little difficulty in disposing of the Bradford Bulldogs.

MATCH 3 — FIFE FLYERS 9, BRADFORD BULLDOGS 0
Flyers scoring: Linton (3+1) Greig (2+0) Venters, Wilson, Dutiaume, Wands (1+1) Fowley (0+4) Muir, Lynch, Reekie, Scoon (0+1).
SOGs: Fife (Nicol) 5; Bradford (Lawrence) 22, (Jackson) 15.
PIMs: 8-0

This set them up with a quarter final match up with the Flintshire Freeze who were also easily beaten 7-0 to conclude a satisfactory first day of the tournament.

Dutiaume was not overly concerned that his team failed to reach the final. For the record the Flyers fell 4-3 in an overtime game to the Solway Sharks in the first Sunday semi- final – Solway would lose in the final to Whitley Warriors as the Flyers picked up third place with a 4-3 win over Blackburn Hawks in the consolation game.

"We were missing a bunch of guys and we didn't use any special teams," he said. "It allowed me to see who came strong and prepared and who disappointed. From a coaching perspective, it was really educating. As far as the opposition was concerned I was pleasantly surprised with the level of the teams. Solway looked like they hadn't skipped a beat from last season and Whitley Bay always bring a good hard-working team. Those two deserved to be in the final. We've got a bit of work to do, and that's what we're using these two week-ends for."

Jamie Wilson, one of a number of returning players for season 2010-11

Saturday August 29th 2015

Fife Flyers 4 Belfast Giants 4

Ahead of the game it was revealed that Fife Flyers defenceman Nicholas Rioux would miss the clash with the highly-rated Belfast Giants. Flyers bosses had been hopeful that the defenceman would have been clear of the red-tape that was holding up his visa. Flyers Head Coach Todd Dutiaume hoped that the talented blueliner would eventually be able to arrive next week. The Flyers would open their pre-season following a hard week of training and Dutiaume said: "We pushed to get some Challenge games and we've got Belfast and Edinburgh at Murrayfield on Sunday. That's a good start for a new-look team but we're happy with the work put in so far and it's now time to test it out in games".

Fife Flyers new signings made a good first impression in a highly competitive curtain-raiser. Without Nicholas Rioux there were still 10 new imports who made their Flyers debut in front of an impressive 2236 crowd. An excellent attendance for a pre-season friendly and they were treated to an entertaining game. While such matches are primarily an exercise to shake off some rust and build match fitness, both sides appeared to treat the fixture as a dress rehearsal for the real thing. There was no holding back from either side as they played with a real intensity for most of the 60 minutes in a match that certainly whet the appetite for the new Elite League season.

Flyers fans had plenty to be encouraged with. The grit promised by coaches Todd Dutiaume and Danny Stewart was in evidence as Flyers stood up to a physical Giants side, often winning the 50-50 battles. There was also a noticeable change in style from last season with more emphasis on competing in the corners and less reliance on flashes of individual skill. Flyers made a stunning start, scoring the opener after just 57 seconds as Shayne Stockton raced onto TJ Caig's sublime back hand pass to nestle the puck past Giants' netminder Stephen Murphy. It was quickly 2-0 as the returning Kyle Haines zoomed up the left wing and squared for Caig to squeeze the puck past Murphy. A great start for a side that had only trained together for five days.

The returning Matt Nickerson was the subject of some pantomime booing from a section of home fans but the quality in the Belfast side became apparent as they turned a two-nil deficit into a 3-2 lead. Jonathan Boxill got the Giants on the scoreboard in the final minute of an adrenalin-packed first period with a simple back post finish. Derek Walser fired in the equaliser early in period two as Flyers started to dip. Giants took the lead through a Craig Peacock power play goal on 32.20, scoring at the third attempt after seeing two efforts blocked.

Flyers second period performance had been subdued compared to the first but the Kirkcaldy side picked up the pace again in period three to take back control of the game. Flyers drew level at 3-3 on 49.57 on the power play as a sublime flick from Ryan Dingle left Michael Dorr with a tap-in. A few minutes later it was 4-3 to the hosts with a goal born out of sheer determination. Jeff Lee, a menace to the Giants defence all night and a possible star in the making, simply wanted the puck more than his marker as he effectively bull-dozed a rebound over the line. Giants looked rattled but they grabbed a messy equaliser on 57.37 as Flyers new netminder David Brown appeared to lose his balance allowing Chris Higgins to fire home and claim a draw.

A scramble around the Flyers net results in the Giants beating netminder David Brown

Saturday August 30th 2014

Fife Flyers 4 Aalborg Pirates 2

The Flyers faced a baptism of fire when they squared up to Danish side Aalborg Pirates, coached by Paul Thompson, in what was a double header pre-season clash. Danny Stewart, associate player-coach, had a couple of objectives from the weekend. He was determined to see his men put on a good performance and also to record a winning start to the campaign. Flyers had invested in quality following their late-season charge last term which saw them qualify for the final four at Nottingham for the first time.

The opening game saw the rink buzz with the noise of a big crowd as the returning imports all picked up where they left off last season and new guys Chris Auger, Scott Fleming and Jamie Milam fitted in well. Jordan Fulton had the honour of scoring the first goal of the new season at 6.52 but the scoring honours went to Matt Reber who netted twice after Christian Nordentoft had levelled for Aalborg on the half hour mark. Reber was only denied a hat-trick as netminder Ervins Mustukovs (who would later play for Sheffield Steelers) pulled off a fine save after the forward had been left all alone in front of goal.

Tommy Grant cut the lead back to 3-2 in the third which allowed Thompson to pull his netminder for a six on five finish which saw Bobby Chaumont hit the empty net from deep within his own zone as the clock wound down. A good win and more importantly a solid workout against a good Danish outfit. Pirates came to Kirkcaldy with four games already under their belts and 24 hours later capitalised on some defensive mistakes to record an 8-3 win, giving the aggregate honours to Pirates.

The silverware may have been packed in the kit bags and shipped back to Denmark but Flyers still got what they wanted from this exhibition event, two good workouts. The matches against a good hard-working side were competitive and played with pace. The coach was also happy to look at the positives from the loss which saw Flyers give up four early goals before calling a time out to steady the ship and spike the momentum of a lively and very smart Danish squad.

"It was a kick up the back-side, and it worked because we got two short-handed goals. We tried some different things over the weekend and it was a good workout for us. That's what we wanted. I know we are feeling a bit down because it's the first time we've shipped eight goals in a while, but this will be a good learning curve for us and will help us get into game shape."

The results were kept firmly in perspective in the post-game analysis. Dutiaume was clear that he wanted his team to continue where they had left off last season but that they needed to show consistency. He reminded them that two seasons ago they started well and then fell away around Christmas and battled to make the play-offs. Last season they started slowly but came away in the second half of the season and made the semi-finals at Nottingham for the first time. In closing he said:

"We recognise that we need to work on our conditioning and that's what we've been doing this week. We've also been able to tighten up a few of our systems so we're pretty pleased with it. For our first time on the ice it was a heck of a performance over the weekend."

Fife Flyers 2014/15

The Flyers photo call for their fourth season in the Elite Ice Hockey League

Saturday August 31st 1991

Fife Flyers 11 Durham Wasps 5

The myth of three line hockey became a reality in this game when Fife Flyers crushed the Grand Slam Champions, Durham Wasps. The policy talked about by every coach at every rink was put into practice by Brain Kanewischer, and it worked to perfection. Flyers dictated the game and finished with a strength and style which was so glaringly absent last term. Seven minutes into the game and the coach had iced his entire bench and all three lines contributed to what could only be described as a demolition job of one of the most powerful teams in the country. They exhausted Durham's talented but limited personnel and crowned a memorable night with a quite unbelievable 6-1 final period. The goals came from no fewer than seven players with three others notching assists but the biggest plus factor in a superb all-round display was the rock-solid performance of stand-in netminder Colin Downie.

Flyers got off to a brisk start and called the shots with a series of slick line changes which gradually sapped the energy from Wasps established skaters. Kanewischer matched his third line with Durham's first and they came up with the opening goal after seven minutes of play. Craig Wilson and Chris Whitehill worked down the flank and Steven King fired the puck behind Frankie Killen. Wasps hardest working player, Mike O'Connor, made it 1-1 with a thundering power play strike at 11:05 and he then set up number two for Rick Brebant against Flyers third line. That, however, was the last time Durham were in front all evening. Downie defied Mike Blaisdell in the first of several head to head encounters and Flyers drew level just 70 seconds before the first buzzer. Frank Morris collected a loose puck in neutral ice and he beat Killen with a textbook finish.

Their confidence increased with every shift in a closely contested second period and the highly productive second unit claimed the go ahead goal at 23:13. Les Millie danced around Wilkinson and although Bobby Haig failed to find the net he managed to scramble the puck back to brother John who beat Killen from close range. O'Connor struck metal work with a vicious shot as Durham continued to rely heavily on their first line and Ian Cooper hauled them back to level pegging at 28:50. 24 seconds later and Flyers instant reply came from Frank Morris. Blaisdell finally beat

Downie on the half hour mark but his evening of misfortune continued when Morris calmly scooped the puck off the line. Damien Smith levelled at 4-4 with less than four minutes to play but Flyers struck again through Iain Robertson to take a 5-4 advantage into the second break. Les Millie made it 6-4 at 41:57 and Killen gifted John Haig number seven when he dropped the winger's angled shot just one minute later. A short-handed Blaisdell counter temporarily halted Flyers progress at 51:55, but it was swiftly cancelled out by Robertson's power play as Rick Brebant twiddled his thumbs in the sin bin.

With seven minutes left Cal Brown drifted into the Wasps zone and fired the puck off Killen's pads and netted his own rebound. It would be the big defenceman's last slice of action when, with the puck killed, Blaisdell took his frustrations out on Brown and cross-checked him into the boards. Flyers import was eventually stretchered into the dressing room and Blaisdell was dismissed on a game misconduct penalty. His departure opened up the ice to Laplante who boosted his own statistical returns with two late power plays.

Last season's Player of the Year, Iain Robertson, opens the Flyers account against Frank Killen in the Wasps net.

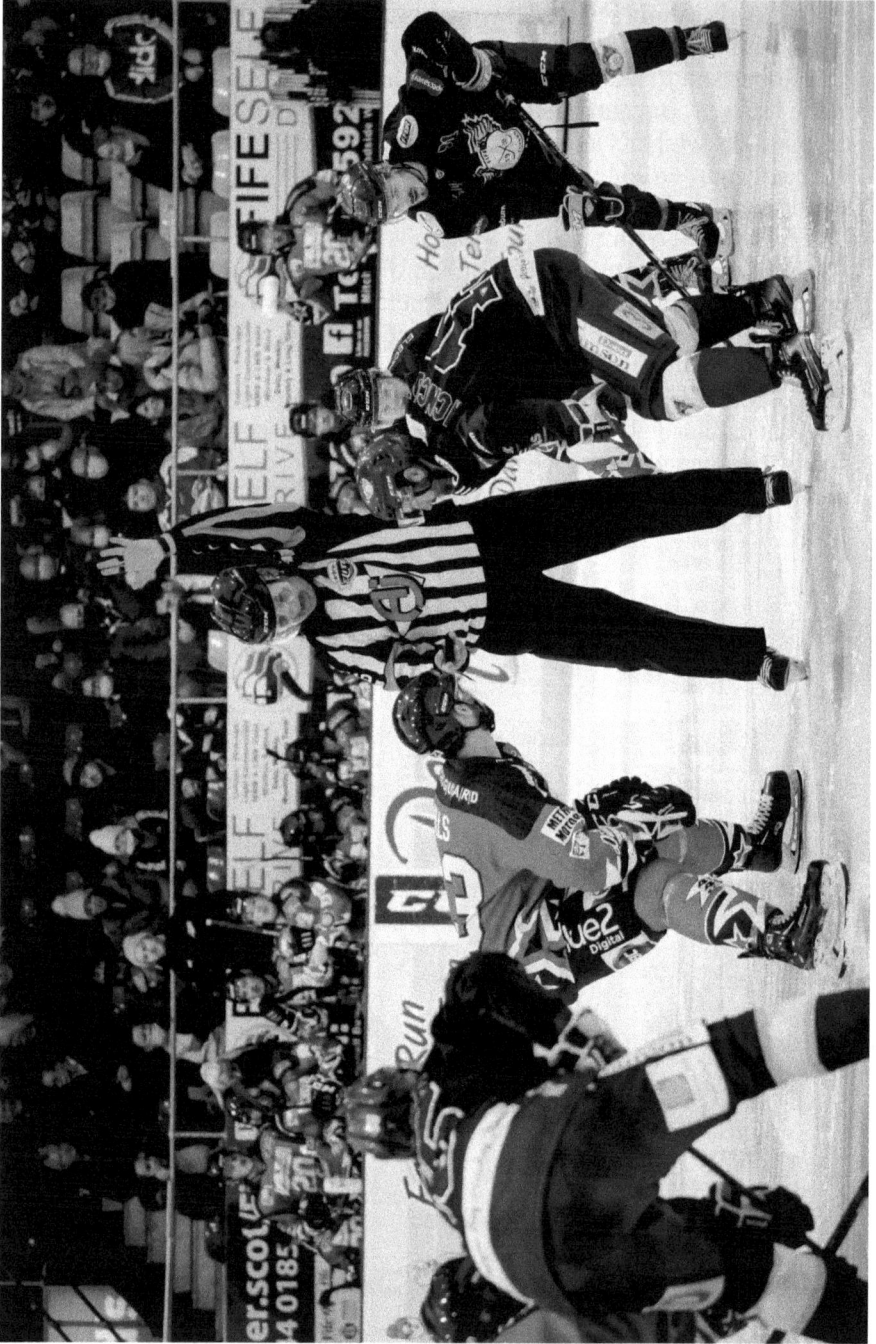

And the puck is about to be dropped on the post pandemic 2021-22 season as hockey returns to Kirkcaldy for the first time since February 2020

September

Frantisek Neckar who played for the Flyers during the 1998/99 season

Saturday September 1st 2001

Fife Flyers 3 Dundee Stars 2

The Flyers got the new season off to the best possible start with a closely fought 3-2 victory over the British National League new boys, the Dundee Stars. The Stars had brought top flight hockey back to the city of Dundee almost a decade after the Tigers dropped out into the Scottish National League. They also had a swanky brand new arena to play out of. Guided by Tony Hand, the visitors certainly had quality in their ranks, but not enough to outwit the more experienced Flyers.

The match was a classic end-to-end thriller for the greater part of the game, keeping the near 2500 crowd on the edge of their seats. Flyers new signings looked impressive with Karry Biette bringing a physical presence to the defence with some clean big hits while Mark Dutiaume showed why he was a 1995 draft pick for the NHL's Buffalo Sabres. In net Shawn Silver also caught the eye as he looked solid all night when tracking the puck.

The match started at a frantic pace as both sides went on the offensive. It was Flyers who broke the deadlock at 2:39, when Iain Robertson scored when he redirected a Frank Morris shot through the legs of last season's Flyers goalie, Stephen Murphy. Dundee almost levelled soon afterwards when Jan Mikel hit the post. Given the robust nature of play it was a surprise that the first penalty of the match wasn't called until 12:07 after a thunderous hit on the boards by Biette left Wayne Maxwell without a helmet and referee Moray Hanson called the Dundee player for a retaliation. Both sides had further chances in the opening period but neither could convert them.

The second period started slowly, with the game losing the tempo of the first but after the lull both sides were eventually back up to speed. Kyle Horne took the first Flyers penalty of the season at 28:13 for interference but the Stars were unable to make any inroads on the Flyers penalty kill and at 35:32 the Flyers struck again to go 2-0 up when Andy Samuel knocked the puck home from close range with Daryl Venters and Biette supplying the assists. Flyers were again short-handed as Robertson sat out a hooking call moments after Dundee had pinged a shot off the crossbar. Stars did eventually get on the board at 2:10 of the final period when

Martin Wiita was left unmarked in front of the crease and he coolly slotted the puck past Shawn Silver to break the shutout and get Dundee Stars first competitive goal. Shortly after that Karry Biette was penalised for tripping but after killing the penalty he endeared himself to the Fife faithful when he stretched the Flyers lead after he fired a one timer low past Murphy.

Dundee however were not done. When Teeder Wynne scored at 50:32 it was a goal that riled the home fans, who were incensed that referee Moray Hanson awarded the goal despite the goal judge not lighting the lamp. There probably is enough similar content to write another book on such instances from throughout the Flyers entire history. Stars almost snatched a point, when in the dying minutes, Silver once again had his pipes to thank. Despite the fact that the new kids on the block had outshot the home side 33-31 they came up short, but the formative signs of a new derby in Scottish ice hockey had however been on display.

It was an impressive debut by Shawn Silver against the Dundee Stars

Saturday September 2nd 1995

BENSON & HEDGES CUP

Fife Flyers 10 Blackburn Hawks 7

Flyers fans were thankful for one man in this one, Chris Palmer, as the Canadian goal ace almost single-handedly saved Fife from an embarrassing defeat by Division One upstarts Blackburn. He was involved in eight of the 10 home goals, banging home five and assisting on three. In what was the second weekend of the season Man of the Match Palmer also looked to be forming a useful partnership with last season's top scorer, Mark Morrison, who overcame his jetlag to net one goal and set up six helpers.

However, apart from that high-powered pairing the home side looked anything but impressive against a lively Hawks outfit inspired by import forward Oleg Sinkov. Morrison and Frank Morris were both added to the side which had comprehensively stuffed Murrayfield Royals the previous Saturday but coach Ron Plumb still wasn't behind the bench. Home fans missed the chance to see former favourite Ryan Kummu who was now in charge of the visitors as the all too common work permit delays at this time of the season denied him what would definitely have been a warm welcome back.

Blackburn had their plans disrupted even before the face off. After having travelled north with only their white home strips the Hawks were forced to change to a set of black Skate Attack All-Stars jerseys for the match. It didn't seem to put them off as they hassled and hustled from the opening seconds but it was Palmer who opened the scoring for Flyers on the power play at 5:41 when he let rip with a disguised shot which beat goalie Ian Young low on his glove side. Back came Hawks at 7:19 after somehow repelling a manic Fife attack they broke up ice and netminder 'Bernie' McCrone let a soft shot rebound off his body and Sinkov slid in to bury the puck. The Great Britain goalie, who went on to play excellently under severe pressure, continued his shaky start by giving away a tripping penalty. The visitors scored a second from the resultant power play when import Steve Chartrand flicked the puck past a screened McCrone after a nice drop pass by former Fife youngster John Haig. Palmer sent Morrison clear for an equaliser at 14:51, which relieved a long spell of Hawks domination, but a slashing call against Doug Marsden gave the visitors another goal scoring opportunity, which they duly took at 19:19

but not before Palmer and Morrison had combined for a brilliant short-handed strike at 18:09.

Indiscipline was to play a big part in Fife's second-period stutters, starting with Craig Wilson taking a silly roughing call just over two minutes in and Sinkov was left unmarked to convert yet another power play. A minute later Flyers hit back when Palmer was once more on target with a trademark spin and shot from bang in front of the nets and they looked to have finally wrestled control of the contest away from their English opponents when Steven King applied the killer touch to a smart passing move at 26:45. But once again Flyers were penalised — this time for too many men on the ice — and Hawks pounced on the opportunity to level matters when Haig made the score 5-5. Yet another daft penalty effectively handed the lead to the visitors before the end of the period when Morrison and Paul Hand were binned leaving Chartrand to plunder another on the 5 on 3 man advantage.

Flyers came out fired up for the final period and created the goal of the game at 44:24 when Alistair Reid resisted the temptation to have a slap shot and side-stepped his man to find Morris, who in turn slid a simple pass to team captain Iain Robertson for a tap-in. Just 26 seconds later Steven King put the Flyers 7-6 ahead with a super finish but Hawks hit back with yet another power play at 50:57 when Haig's weak shot trickled under McCrone. Fife then somehow shut the game down and finally moved up a gear with Palmer netting from a tight angle at 53:23 before turning provider for Steven King at 55:40. Palmer rounded off his stunning one-man display with the final goal of the match just 45 seconds from the final buzzer.

Flyers Chris Palmer
with a five goal performance

Saturday September 3rd 1994

Fife Flyers 10 Paisley Pirates 4

It was the opening night of the season with Flyers fans getting a look at their new star imports and Pirates supporters looking forward to seeing their team up against one the "Big Boys".

A constant in most sports is the 'critical assessment' of the men who are there to govern and administer the laws of the game. Officiating a hockey game is arguably one of the hardest jobs in sport but in a far from dirty or tempestuous Benson and Hedges Cup opener referee Drew Fraser handed out 119 minutes of penalties. These included punishment for such horrendous sins as holding the stick and some peculiar roughing calls when not a single punch was thrown in anger.

The big talking point, however, was the five-minute-plus-game penalty dished out to young Flyer Craig Wilson for spearing. If he was guilty of deliberately sticking his opponent with the blade of his stick then the B I H A rules are quite clear and any major penalty was now punishable with ejection from the match. But it looked soft and the youngster was clearly upset at having his copybook blotted after just over 13 minutes of the new season.

Forget the eccentric refereeing; the game was about two new stars in Kirkcaldy — Messrs Tony Szabo and Josh Boni. Both arrived in Scotland with little time to prepare for this game, yet looked a cut above anything Paisley had. Szabo was brought in with the unenviable task of filling Doug Smail's skates and he netted a hat-trick before the game was half over and finished with four goals. He looked fast, skilful and had a real sniffer's nose for goal. Boni was a different prospect altogether; he was big, bustling and hard-hitting and he completed his hat-trick with only six seconds left on the clock.

Flyers lined up with Szabo at centre on the first line and an extremely jet-lagged Mark Morrison on left wing and Steven King on the right. Ally Reid and a slimmed-down Milan Figala anchored the defence and Fife looked rock solid as they stormed to a 3-0 lead in the first seven minutes. Szabo was first to strike at 3:25 when he netted from point-blank range after good build-up on the power play and he was on target again at 5:50 when he received an inch perfect pass from Steven King to find a space past netminder David Roor high on his glove side. Flyers looked to be coasting when Boni opened his account with a fantastic snap shot from an angle on the left, which beat the goalie on his stick side, and he celebrated in style.

Paisley, with a huge squad on the bench, struck back through Canadian import Mike Bettens on the power play at 8:35. Young Lithuanian import Dino Bauba poked a bouncing puck into the empty Fife net at 13:10 as McCrone scrambled about his crease with the defence at sixes and sevens.

Wilson got his marching orders 30 seconds later but just as Fife began to look rattled up popped team captain Iain Robertson with a short-handed goal to savour as he buried the puck past Roor at 16:16. Pirates struck back again 34 seconds later when Downes fooled McCrone with a wrap-around and the West coasters tied things up in the second period when Bauba's wrist shot escaped from McCrone's grasp and found the net.

Yet another short-handed effort gave Flyers some much-needed breathing space when Roor blocked Morrison's one-on-one but was unable to stop Szabo's follow-up for his hat-trick. Fife coach Jim Lynch had been using his youngsters to good effect during the game and it was fitting that recent junior call-up Richard Dingwall should spark off Flyers third-period goal blitz which eventually sunk the Pirates. His quick shot at 50:05 probably should have been saved by the netminder but Dingwall certainly wasn't complaining. Another netminding error gave Szabo his fourth and within a minute at 52:11 Boni showed his heads-up style by collecting a fumbled shot before taking it around the back of the net and sneaking the puck in for a well-executed wrap-around goal. Youngster Andy Samuel also marked his recent signing with a goal on the 57th-minute mark and Boni completed his triple as the clock wound down when he made a great move on his marker to create space and pick his spot in the top corner for the goal of the game.

Flyers new import Tony Szabo got off to a fine start with four goals against the Pirates – he would top score for the Flyers in the Benson & Hedges Cup

Sunday September 4th 1988

Glasgow Eagles 4 Fife Flyers 11

It was game number two of the "Czech Experiment" as Flyers travelled West to meet a Glasgow Eagles side who were expected to provide very little resistance. This turned out not to be the case, as there were only two goals separating the sides after 42 minutes before Flyers finally put the home side to the sword. The First Division side had goals from Tim Horvat, with a double, Rob Coutts and Tony Redmond. For the visitors Jindrich Kokrment bagged four, with doubles for Ronnie Wood and Les Millie and singles from Vincent Lukac, Milan Figala and Jim Lynch.

Fife Flyers manager Jack Dryburgh, who enjoyed building up the club's high profile, had surpassed anything seen before in the UK game. Even his silver-tongued rhetoric was in danger of running out of superlatives for his three new Czech players after their first weekend in harness. But he still managed to accentuate the positive by saying; " . . . and they can do a lot better!"

As the summer was drawing to a close it had been a tense wait for everyone at Kirkcaldy, but the three European imports arrived safe and sound but astonishingly without a pair of skates between them. Jack said:

"That was the first surprise. I was astonished. Apparently in Czechoslovakia the skates belong to the club they play for and not the individual so when they were asked for their size they took the first pair that fitted them and that was that. Home players tend to be a bit fussy but not these lads. Irrespective of make all they wanted was a decent fit and not only that they just went to the rack and picked out a stick and they were off!"

Jack admitted that some of his Scots players were slack-mouthed watching the Czechs in their initial training session, but after 20 minutes or so they began to copy them and were not afraid to try what Jindrich, Vincent and Milan were doing. The night before, Vincent Lukac had helped himself to four goals in a noisy and emotional home debut against Tayside Tigers in front of 3500 fans, and on the following night, at Glasgow's Summit Center, his line mate repeated the feat. There was no doubt about it these guys were class players.

"I've heard the comments from other quarters about them being old men but that is sheer envy and they will please a lot of ice hockey fans this season" Jack, again.

But one area of key concern for the Fife boss was protection for his players. Said Jack:

"I'm not asking that they get preferential treatment but I hope they are allowed to play and are not brutalised. Fans pay good money to watch good players but naturally I don't expect any of our rivals to stand back and admire them."

A telling comment came from Scottish Ice Hockey Association president Frank Dempster after he had watched the three Czechs in the Sunday match at Glasgow when he said:

"I've had the advantage of seeing all three play before and watched them often on video films as well. In my humble opinion they are still playing in third gear."

Flyers spared no effort to ease their imports into the local scene. As well as local minister's wife Marie Ashcroft interpreting for them off the ice, they discovered Markinch restaurateur Peter Smith, who was born in Czechoslovakia. He volunteered to cook up as many National dishes as possible to please the players. With all clubs adjusting fixtures to suit their tastes over the Christmas and New Year period the Flyers management had also arranged for the three imports to holiday at home.

Milan Figala, Vincent Lukac and Jindrich Kokrment – the 'Czech Experiment'

Saturday September 5th 1992

BENSON & HEDGES CUP

Fife Flyers 13 Murrayfield Racers 10

With the Flyers returning to the big time after a season's jaunt around the British First Division this was a major scalp pinned to the Flyers dressing room wall. However, the victory over Murrayfield Racers was achieved at a cost — defenceman Cal Brown was stretchered to hospital following a frightening injury scare.

The game was balanced on a knife edge when he was stretchered out of the rink but Flyers rallied superbly to finally kill off their oldest rivals. A capacity crowd packed the arena for the opening Autumn Cup game and they witnessed a derby clash that overflowed with incident. Flyers ran out worthy winners but were made to fight for two precious qualifying points.

Inspired by an outstanding Frank Morris they built up an early lead only to lose their way in a difficult middle period. They certainly enjoyed a lucky break when referee Alex McWilliam halted Racers momentum, by stopping the second period two minutes early, to allow ice staff to carry out emergency repairs to a goal-net but the manner in which Jim Lynch's troops finished the job was impressive.

Flyers late goal blitz saw off international goalkeeper Martin McKay. By icing Rob Abel in a hugely effective man-marking role they also snuffed out the threat posed by Tony Hand. The fact that Tony lashed out seconds after the final buzzer underlined just how uncomfortable he felt at being monitored at such close quarters.

Flyers got off to the best possible start with two goals in as many minutes when Morris fired them ahead at 1:29 and Steven King cashed in on a delayed penalty call to make it 2-0 just 31 seconds later. They dominated every aspect of the early action and increased their lead at 12:00 when Morris seized on a loose puck in neutral ice and beat McKay with a clinical finish. Racers were awarded a disputed penalty shot at 12:55 after Moray Hanson lifted the nets off their moorings and player coach Newberry made no mistake. A power play goal from the classy Chris Palmer reduced the deficit at 13:25 but Flyers were in no mood to let their lead slip away. Their response was immediate as Morris supplied a superb pass and Abel netted while lying flat on the ice. The

The lesser spotted Ed Zawatsky who was released after just six games having recorded 11 goals and 6 assists

livewire Junior 'B' import then danced around Paul Pentland before striking metal-work with a great shot. Ed Zawatsky struck a beautiful fifth for Flyers 18:11 but the hosts seemed to lose their momentum after the break and as both sides enjoyed good spells of pressure the initiative was passed back and forth like a baton in a relay race.

Racers who benched Junior 'B' import Declan McNaughton for two thirds of the evening and went with Les Lovell in defence fought back to 5-4 at 24:59 thanks to a slapshot from Palmer and they squared the game just seven minutes later when Tony Hand netted at the near post. Palmer's hat-trick goal at 32:03 turned the game in their favour and a Hand power play capped the revival until the dodgy net sockets unravelled much of the good work.

When the players returned from the dressing-room Flyers immediately slashed the deficit through a Cal Brown slapshot and then drew level at 8-8 when Abel found Dean Edmiston in space and he netted a mere 29 seconds into the final period. The teams were deadlocked at 9-9 when Brown was struck in the face by the blade of Hilton Ruggles' stick and collapsed on the ice. The collision left the defenceman in distress and he had to be carried into the dressing room before being taken to hospital.

The Zamboni mopped up a pool of blood and Ruggles took a five-minute major penalty for accidental high sticks. Morris and Edmiston double-shifted along the blue line and Flyers cashed in on the extended power play to skate into an 11-9 lead. Zawatsky blasted number ten past McKay after Iain Robertson won a face-off on the right and Morris timed his hat-trick goal to perfection with the puck landing in the net just as Ruggles returned to the fray albeit in a subdued mood. With Tony Hand pushed out of the game by Abel Racers lost their composure and conceded further goals to Zawatsky and Paul Berrington.

TONIGHT'S GAME

CAPITALS

v

FIFE FLYERS

**Benson & Hedges Cup
Sunday 5th September 1998
at Murrayfield Ice Rink
Edinburgh**

The match programme, incorrectly dated, for the Edinburgh club's first win in a while against the Flyers

Sunday September 6th 1998

BENSON & HEDGES CUP

Edinburgh Capitals 4 Fife Flyers 2

Although the revamped Edinburgh Capitals made a winning start to their existence in their opening Benson & Hedges Cup fixture, they were undoubtedly helped by a lacklustre performance from Flyers, who were still clearly in the malaise that saw them drop a point at home to the Paisley Pirates in the season opener the night before in Kirkcaldy.

There was no doubt that Scott Neil had done a good job enticing some experienced and wily campaigners to Murrayfield. While they would certainly be a lot stronger and more competitive this season, their prospects were difficult to judge on this disappointing game. Whether the exertions of the previous night had taken its toll on Flyers, the plain truth was that Mark Morrison's side simply had too many passengers. The massive travelling support, which must have touched the thousand mark and caused the face-off to be delayed by ten minutes to allow everyone to get in, were left to taste defeat in Edinburgh for the first time in over three years and their first loss to a side from the Capital in 15 games.

It was altogether a rather low-key affair which only really burst into life in the opening period when antagonist-extraordinaire Dean Edmiston was up to his old tricks. However, when Deano didn't reappear for the second period, some of the edge went with him except for one moment when Doug Marsden found out that if you cheap shot Justin Bekkering you better watch your back!

What must have greatly concerned the fans however was the lack of a goal threat from Flyers who, despite out-shooting their opponents, failed to put any sustained pressure on John Finnie and as a result were reduced to firing hopeful long shots which the netminder dealt with easily. Of course it was early days yet; Mark Morrison was a shrewd enough coach to know that it would take some time to have the team firing on all cylinders. Even so, he would have expected more from some of his established stars.

Indeed, the one positive aspect was the display of the third line, who received quite a bit of ice time and displayed the desire and enthusiasm which was lacking in some of their more experienced colleagues. David Smith worked tirelessly and Andy Samuel put himself about. Bill Moody again showed the change in his game which convinced Flyers to bring him back. Ricky Grubb played the full game in goal and did very well but was unsighted as Roger Hunt scored Capitals first goal shorthanded at 10.15, When Marsden made it 2-0 at 13.37 Flyers were toiling. Morrison reduced the deficit on the power play at 31.24 but Marsden restored the two-goal advantage five minutes later and the visiting fans were left hoping for a final period like the one which salvaged a point against Paisley.

When Steven King fired home at 42.26 on the power play those hopes were raised but for all of the Flyers possession they couldn't create enough decent chances and a scrambled effort by Jeff Daniels at 52.49 enabled Capitals to see out the remaining minutes for a deserved win which was greeted with delight by their long-suffering and success-starved fans.

Saturday September 7th 2013

Fife Flyers 2 Cardiff Devils 5

As far as opening nights to a new season go the Fife Flyers have undoubtedly had better, much better. However the match would be remembered for a long time due to the impact made by a Flyer making his debut, a player of the type that the Fife fans had not seen in their line up in the modern era if indeed ever.

One look at Matt Nickerson's CV told you all you needed to know about the American defenceman's style. A hulking 6ft 4in and 234lbs with 56 career fights were the statistics of an ice hockey enforcer, This was not the type of player Flyers would normally recruit, but one which the current coaching staff viewed as essential in an increasingly physical Elite League.

Toughness was something Flyers could have done with the previous season particularly on the road; what they didn't need was their tough guy taking things too far. 18 minutes into his Flyers debut Nickerson crossed the line.

Flyers had made a bright start showing the difference that an extra week's practice could make and they led through Tim Hartung's well worked power play opener at 4.04. The game changed however in the 18th minute when Nickerson took exception to Andrew Lord and the big bearded American, who only stepped off a plane on the morning of the match, made a bee-line for the Cardiff forward after a flare-up behind the Flyers net. Nickerson menacingly circled his prey, resulting in Lord backing down. This display of posturing was enough to whip the crowd into a frenzy and leave some of the Cardiff players, none more so than the visibly spooked Lord shrinking into their shorts.

On the back of the energy generated by this moment alone the Flyers may well have gone on to record the win but what Nickerson did next however would define the entire hockey match and put a huge question mark against the 28-year-old's character. With the two staring each other out from the resultant face off and with Lord trying to skate away Nickerson swung a few punches that knocked him to the ground before cross-checking him in the back as he lay on the ice.

Nickerson was led away by the official and was assessed an unsurprising match penalty, ensuring he would play no further part while the cheers had turned to a stunned silence. It left Flyers to defend a five-minute penalty during which time Cardiff scored three times to take control of the match and Nickerson had sucked the energy out of the team as quickly as he had created it.

Cardiff went on to dominate the remainder of the match with netminder Kevin Regan collecting a deserved Man of the Match and Derek Roehl's debut goal nothing more than an overshadowed consolation. Nickerson had the potential to become a Flyers cult hero for all of the right reasons but first he would have to prove that he was not a liability. Following an automatic ban the following night at Edinburgh Nickerson was subsequently hit with another three game suspension by the Elite League's Department of Player Safety. Flyers player-coach Todd Dutiaume warned Nickerson over his future conduct saying

"The coaching staff let Matt know what to expect of him. A big part of his job is to be a presence out on the ice but he can't be a presence back in the dressing room. Something that people haven't seen from Matt yet is that he can play the game. He's not just a guy who goes looking for trouble. We need a bare minimum 20 minutes playing time from him every night so he's going to have to find a way to stay on the ice. We spoke to him and I believe we are on the same page".

The suspension left the roster even thinner following injuries to Jordan Fulton , Tommy Muir and the still recovering player-coach himself and the club were actively searching for some extra depth.

Another tussle with the Cardiff Devils and Matt Nickerson and Doug Clarkson get ready to engage

Saturday September 8th 2018

Elite Ice Hockey League Challenge Cup

Fife Flyers 5 Glasgow Clan 4 (after Shootout)

Flyers made their first competitive outing of the season against their West Coast rivals the Braehead Clan — no, wait a minute, Braehead was no longer the name on the badge and after a rebranding exercise it was the debut of the Glasgow Clan in Kirkcaldy.

There was however the same old rivalry in the stands though as the Flyers looked to extend their dominance over the team from Renfrewshire who had only beaten Fife once in their last nine outings. As games against the Clan had evolved in recent seasons this encounter was certainly not your average hockey game. It was thrills, spills and drama all the way at the packed barn.

Flyers started the game on the front foot and soon had their first power play opportunity when Clan forward Josh Gratton was penalised for a slash after just 19 seconds and it was soon a 5-on-3 advantage to the hosts when visiting goalie Joel Rumpel cleared the puck into the stands for a delay of the game minor. The opening goal soon followed as Evan Bloodoff was on hand to fire home from close range following a pinpoint pass from Evan Stoflet at 1:21. The home side doubled their advantage at 6.58 when Stoflet wristed into the top corner from Danick Gauthier's neat pass with the visitors visibly rattled even at this early stage. Flyers almost added a third goal short-handed when Bloodoff's excellent backhand pass was fired by Mike Cazzola at point-blank range but Rumpel got just enough on the puck to send it just wide of the net.

The middle stanza saw the visitors grow into the game and Zack Fitzgerald found himself one-on-one with Shane Owen but the returning netminder denied the Clan skipper with a smart pad save. Cazzola then broke clear short-handed but the former Edinburgh forward blasted wide of the target. Things began to heat up when Gauthier was given 2 minutes for hooking but was assessed a further 2 minutes for unsportsmanlike conduct and he was soon joined in the box by Stoflet after a roughing minor to give Clan a 5-on-3 opportunity.

Clan had their first spell of sustained pressure on the Flyers net during this power play with Matt Stanisz hitting the post after a stramash in the Flyers crease but Fife held out to retain their two goal advantage going

Evan Stoflet and Evan Bloodoff celebrate the Flyers opening goal against the Clan

into the final period. The third period saw both sides give possession away cheaply but the visitors got themselves off the mark when Josh Gratton's slapshot found the back of the net at 47.19. Astonishingly it was 2-2 less than a minute later when some indecision in the Flyers defence allowed Vaclav Stupka to snipe home the equaliser at 47.57. Clan then had Fife firmly camped in their own zone but a slashing call on Stanisz led to Fife regaining the lead on the power play when Bloodoff poked home his second of the game at 51.48.

The away side levelled again when Travis Ehrhardt's shot through traffic crept into Owen's net at 55.15. Incredibly Clan took the lead for the first time in the game as Connolly tucked his backhand shot into the corner of the Flyers net on 58.47 and with the clock running down Flyers pulled netminder Owen and the gamble paid off when Bloodoff got his hat-trick goal after another scramble in the crease to send the home support into a frenzy.

With sudden-death overtime unable to separate the sides the game went to penalty shots. Matt Beca, Mike Cazzola, Brendan Connolly and Chase Schaber all missed their opportunities while Paul Crowder and Scott Tanski both converted.

Into sudden-death and Cazzola and Ehrhardt failed to convert before Crowder scored his second penalty shot of the evening. Connolly had to score for Clan and his shot came back off the underside of the crossbar. The official immediately declared that his attempt hadn't crossed the line, leading to furious protests from the visitors. This resulted in the use of a goal line technology review, but the original call on the ice was upheld. Bloodoff was deservedly voted as Flyers Man of the Match for his hat-trick, in what was an excellent performance from the fan favourite.

Wednesday September 9th 1953

CHALLENGE MATCH

Falkirk Lions 6 Fife Flyers 3

Failing to make the most of their scoring chances, Fife Flyers suffered defeat when they opened their season with a challenge game at Falkirk.

The summer had provided yet another bump in the road for the stability of the sport when Mr Ian Stevenson announced that the final call had been made on the continuation of the Dunfermline Vikings. "Heavy costs" were the deciding factor.

While this was a regrettable outcome for the Flyers losing the 'derby' fixture it was hoped that some of the Vikings ice hockey enthusiasts would venture East to sustain their hockey needs. The Flyers had announced in August a new player coach in defenceman Ken Broughton. Broughton wouldn't appear and the saga is told earlier on in the book.

Flyers debutants included netminder Ron Collins, who played previously for Simcoe Gunners in the Toronto Intermediate league; Jack Lane, a right wing and 20 year old, 13 stone, left wing or center and Lloyd Boomer, both of whom had played Junior 'B' at Woodstock. The other newcomer was 23-year- old Acton, Ontario born Fred Kentner, who had turned professional at 19 with the Eastern United States League Washington D.C.

Scotty Dowle,who was one of the few bright spots from last term, returned and with Bert Smith being reinstated as a junior the Flyers had one space to fill. They offered Jim Fiddler from Falkirk Lions a trial, as well as free agent Dick Wolsherholme, but both were short lived.

On occasion, both teams enjoyed some measure of superiority but the Falkirk team made fewer errors when close to goal and thus deserved their victory. Considering it was the opening game of the season and there was nothing at stake, it was a hard fought contest and there was sufficient clever combined play to balance the phases when nothing much happened.

Both sides were under strength with the Lions using six Scots juniors, one of whom was a young Joe McIntosh, who would later feature prominently in the 60s and 70s with Flyers. Flyers iced four Scots which detracted from the value of the game as a guide to how either team would fare in the long season which lay ahead. Flyers looked as though they were going to be a fast team and if they learned to make the most their chances they would surely collect many goals. Lane was prominent with many speedy bursts down the right wing and finished Flyers best forward although Kentner made several grand openings for Smith and Dowle which were spurned.

Collins had a good game in goal and neither Wray Fallowfield nor Jimmy Mitchell made any serious blunders in defence. Strong saved Lions on numerous occasions and Hudson and Blair were always prominent in attack. An evenly contested first period ended with the score level at one each with Hudson opening in 10 minutes and Bert Smith replying for the visitors on 15 minutes. Flyers faded from then until midway through the last period when they faced a 5-1 deficit with Hudson getting his second and counters from Imrie, Paton and Flinn.

Sneddon and Fallowfield were both binned for a fight in the early stages of the third period and Lane threatened to spark a revival with a goal for Flyers with 10 minutes remaining but Blair put paid to that with another Lions goal. Boomer scored a consolation with a few minutes remaining as the home side outshot the visitors 30-28.

Lions – Strong, Sneddon, Carlyle, McIntosh, Morrison, Blair, Hudson, Paton, Flinn, Tyrell, Adams, Imrie.

Flyers – Collins, Fallowfield, Mitchell, Doig, Smith, Kentner, Dowle, Dobos, Lane, Boomer, Pearson.

Referee M. Beaton,   Linesman – S Cameron

Flyers in training ahead of the opening game at Falkirk 1953/54.
Left to right: Wray Fallowfield, Scotty Dowle, Jimmy Mitchell, Freddie Kentner, Johnny Dobos, Llyod Boomer, Ron Collins, kneeling on the right are Bert Smith and Jack Lane

Saturday September 10th 2011

Fife Flyers 0 Coventry Blaze 2

As difficult as this opening night was for Fife Flyers, the novelty of Elite League hockey ensured it was a night for the team and its supporters to cherish. After six frustrating years on the outside looking in, top flight hockey finally returned to Kirkcaldy and this sense of affiliation was more important than the score this Saturday.

Player-coach Todd Dutiaume had warned that the squad were on a steep learning curve and that it would take time for them to gel after playing in the Northern League for a number of years. It was a massive step up but one which was necessary to provide the club's emerging talent with a top-level platform to continue to develop their game.

Furthermore the fact that Glasgow-based Braehead Clan, Edinburgh Capitals and Dundee Stars were committed to the league was a huge incentive to take the plunge. Directors Tom Muir, Tom Muir senior and Jack Wishart took the historic decision in the summer to join the Elite League after much soul searching. It was a gamble for the Rosslyn Street club but one the trio felt was well worth taking. However, there had been a race against the clock from that moment to get a squad assembled in time for the puck drop that Autumn.

No one at the club failed to realise that it would take time before they could compete against the leading squads that included play-off and Challenge Cup champions Nottingham Panthers, Elite League champions Sheffield Steelers, Cardiff Devils — who were runners-up to Sheffield in the league and to Nottingham in the play-offs— Belfast Giants, who led the league for a lengthy spell last season and finished third, and former league champions Coventry Blaze.

As it turned out a 2-0 defeat against a top-class Coventry Blaze side that boasted four EIHL titles was better than most people expected. After all, in Elite League terms, Flyers were still in nappies. When the British National League broke apart Fife were a strong outfit with established Brits and long-serving imports who knew the British game inside-out. Contrast that with Saturday's team which was filled with local rookies and half a quota of imports that had just stepped off a plane and it was no surprise that the match was such a struggle. At times Fife were rabbits caught in the headlights. Coventry looked bigger, played faster, hit harder and their movement tied the home team in knots. But for an inspired performance by jet-lagged netminder Garrett Zemlak the home side could have been buried under an avalanche of goals.

That they kept the score to just 2-0 was an achievement in itself, as player-coach Todd Dutiaume acknowledged after the game.

"If I'm being honest, I don't think 2-0 reflected how the game went. We were more than a couple of steps behind and got out-classed in certain situations. But we identified that this was going to happen, and that we are going to go through growing pains. The score line, no matter how we got it, has to go down as a moral victory for us because I think those guys will be up there in contention for the league. I'm never pleased with a loss but I think it was a good opening night for us. It could have been a lot worse."

Flyers were behind within 98 seconds of their EIHL debut with Mike McLean capitalising on a rebound for Blaze's opener before a power play goal from Owen Fussey at 16.08 completed the scoring. The rest of the match was a damage limitation job as Flyers rarely broke forward and when rare chances to score did come along the forwards lacked the composure to make them count. It would clearly take time for Fife to get up to speed at this level but they hoped to do so before the novelty factor wore off.

FIFE FLYERS

History Tradition Success

Season 2011-12

Saturday September 10th

Elite League FIFE FLYERS v COVENTRY BLAZE

Progamme £2.00

The programme cover for Flyers first ever match in the EIHL

Jamie Wilson who was made the Flyers first Captain of the Elite Ice Hockey League era.

Sunday September 11th 2011

Coventry Blaze 9 Fife Flyers 0

The following night the Flyers were given a rude awakening to how difficult life on the road would be in the Elite League with a heavy defeat in Coventry. Despite playing with shape and refusing to quit they still found themselves on the end of a hammering. As hard as they tried the Flyers found it difficult to retain the puck or keep up to speed and as a result took a string of penalties with the first arriving as early as 44 seconds when Matt Siddall was called for a hooking minor.

Coventry needed just 13 seconds of their first power play to hit the opener but Fife's flirtation with the penalty box continued and after three more Fifers sat out two minute minors another power play goal finally put Blaze 2-0 up at 11:04.

When the home team's third goal hit the net before the end of the first period the game was already drifting beyond Flyers. Unlike the previous night in Kirkcaldy the EIHL newcomers were unable to prevent Coventry from inflicting further damage. The distance Flyers had to travel to get up to speed was underlined as Blaze cantered to a nine-goal victory with Robert Farmer hitting a hat-trick for the home side while the visitors only managed 14 shots on goal.

The final goal summed up Fife's night as netminder Garrett Zemlak went to collect the puck which bounced off the boards and dropped in front of Matic Krajl for the easiest of tap-ins. This result was clearly indicative of a team that had spent six years in the wilderness and it would take longer than one weekend for Fife to get old Scottish National League habits out their system.

Another small piece of unwanted history attached to the match was it was only the second time in history that a Flyers team had been shut out in back to back games. The previous time being in the 1998/99 season when they matched up in the knock out stages of the Benson & Hedges Cup against the Ice Hockey Superleague eventual runners up Cardiff Devils — but we'll cover that in a few pages time.

As has been mentioned it was to be a steep learning curve for all at the club but, for Garrett Zemlak — talk about being thrown in at the deep end! The new netminder only just completed a 22 hour journey from

Canada before being thrust into making his Elite League debut and over the course of the weekend he faced 89 shots in the two games against Blaze.

Despite the start made by his new team it did not phase the confident 22 year old as he later said he wouldn't have had it any other way.

> "Playing on a team like this can only make me a better player. Hirsch in the Coventry net wasn't busy at all he was just sitting around but I was busy and it felt good. Todd's already told me I'm going to be the go-to guy all year so if I can handle the workload and go every night; that's good for development of a goalie".

Zemlak had featured for four East Coast Hockey League teams the previous season and despite offers to stay, the Saskatoon-born goalie was tempted into a move to Fife after his agent was contacted by Dutiaume.

> "My agent knew Todd and there's nothing like going overseas to play hockey so I was excited when I got the offer. I had some offers again in the States but things weren't really as good as I thought I could get there. I'm young and wanted to try something new. This offer came up I took advantage of it and it's going to be a good experience, it already is".

Flyers smooth skating defenceman Matt Cohen

Saturday September 12th 1998

Benson & Hedges Cup

Fife Flyers 6 Telford Tigers 2

What a difference a week makes as Flyers netminder Frank Neckar probably reflected after this encouraging win over Telford. Seven days previous he had been pulled after two periods of his debut game and then sat out the action the next night in Edinburgh before having to then endure completely false reports in newspapers that he had been released. But any doubts about his credentials were surely laid to rest after Neckar served up 60 minutes of entertainment and action which thrilled another big Fife crowd.

The Czech goalie repelled all that Tigers could throw at him in the opening two periods and by the time he was finally beaten by a lucky deflection Flyers were six goals up and cruising to their first win. One save in the third period when he spread himself to deny Claude Dumas on a one-on-one was pure theatre and he celebrated with gusto on hearing that he had been credited with an assist on Flyers fourth goal.

Of course one game doesn't a netminder make, but surely he would now have the chance to settle into the team and his new surroundings. In what was definitely a game of three periods the opening 20 minutes was a tight defensive affair with neither side really coming close to making the breakthrough.

Flyers changed all that after the first break when Andy Samuel was set free by David Smith to beat Gavin Armstrong at 21.34 and the goal seemed to fire up Flyers. Steven King's brilliant backhand finish at 28.40 on the power play made it 2-0 and then came a burst of three goals in 88 seconds as Tigers were completely over-run. Gary Wishart knocked in number three at 30.10 after great play by Daryl Venters and Andy Finlay before King superbly finished a rink-length move started by Neckar 34 seconds later and Samuel beat the by now shaky Armstrong at 31.38 to leave the home side on easy street.

When King completed his hat-trick a minute into the third the game was over but Tigers finally found a way past Neckar through John Coyle on the power play and less than three minute later and with still 15 minutes to play Dumas netted. The visitors then decided to bare their claws as tempers became heated and Justin Bekkering showed remarkable composure as he was slashed and cross-checked in front of the visitor's net during a power play.

When he finally reacted, he was the victim of a vicious slash by Wayne Crawford which saw him thrown out on a 5+Game and Martin Smith and James Manson handed two minutes each along with the Flyer. The power plays came and went and the game rolled to its conclusion but even at the final buzzer referee Meier's work wasn't done as a confrontation between Wishart and David Fielder ended with both being handed 5+Game penalties for spearing.

Flyers scorers: Steven King 3+0, Andy Samuel 2+0, Gary Wishart 1+0, John Haig 0+2, David Smith 0+2, Frank Morris 0+2, Andy Finlay 0+1, Daryl Venters 0+1, Frank Neckar 0+1, Lee Cowmeadow 0+1, Bill Moody 0+1, Mark Morrison 0+1

Tigers scorers: Claude Dumas 1+1, John Coyle 1+0, Dwayne Newman 0+1, Ricky Plant 0+1, Mark Pallister 0+1

Shots on goal: Flyers (Neckar) 40; Tigers (Armstrong) 40

Penalty minutes: Flyers 33; Tigers 60

Referee: Glenn Meier Attendance: 2548

Justin Bekkering who was in 'the thick' of the action as always against Telford

Saturday September 13th 2003

FINDUS CHALLENGE CUP

Fife Flyers 4 Newcastle Vipers 6

The Flyers, unbeaten in their opening two matches, entertained the Newcastle Vipers, who arrived at the Fife Ice Arena knowing that they had to pick up something from the game to kick-start their faltering defence of the Findus Challenge Cup.

The game started well for Fife and after only two minutes Newcastle's Andrew Thornton picked up a hooking penalty. As the first power play of the game was coming to a close, Ian Fletcher managed to slide the puck to Dan Goneau and the big Canadian fired past Tommi Satosaari. That was it as far as scoring went in the first period but there were chances at both ends with Steve Briere having to look sharp to deny Jaruinen and former Flyer Jonathan Weaver and Satosaari doing well to stop Goneau and Karry Biette.

The second period started with some controversy as a Newcastle shot rose to hit Steve Briere in the mask which by rights should have ensured that the game was stopped; referee Cowan however allowed the game to continue and Vipers agitator-in-chief Rob Trumbley appeared in Briere's crease to stab home the rebound — much to the displeasure of the Fife players, not least Briere who lead the complaints.

Their protests were in vain however and the goal was allowed to stand. This seemed to unsettle the home team and it was Newcastle who next rang the red light at 24.30 when Jaruinen found Stephen Wallace in space for him to pick his spot. Flyers found themselves with a 5 on 3 power play after Simon Leach and Trumbley were binned within 30 seconds of each other and they took full advantage of their extra men as Karry Biette and Dan Goneau found Todd Dutiaume unmarked at the back post to give the latter the easiest of goals to tap in past an out of position Satosaari at 28.36.

The tie game was disappointingly short lived however as Newcastle went on the power play in the 35th minute when Steven King sat out a holding the stick minor. There was further controversy when Vipers goalie Satosaari appeared to trip Biette, who was clean through on goal, but referee Cowan wasn't interested. When play immediately returned up ice to the Flyers zone Marc West found Weaver unmarked at the point and the GB international scored by far the best goal of the evening — he unleashed one of his trademark rasping slapshots which snuck in the top corner via the underside of the crossbar and left Briere helpless.

Two minutes later and Newcastle extended their lead as Weaver and Jaruinen freed Paul Ferone, in the neutral zone, who skated in on Briere and found a gap on the goalie's glove side to poke the puck home to make it 4-2 to the visitors at the second interval.

The third period didn't start any better for the Flyers as Matt Beveridge scored only 1.39 after the restart. At that stage things were looking pretty bleak for Fife, but they started to mount a comeback at 45.48 as John Haig's pass found Goneau who shrugged off a challenge to find a hole in Satosaari and pull one back for the Flyers. At 52.27 it was game on again, as Todd Dutiaume scored straight from a Steven King face-off win. However the comeback was cut cruelly short at 53.31 when Beveridge found Weaver skulking just outside the crease and the former Flyer managed to tap the puck home from close range, much to the frustration and annoyance of Briere.

A disappointing result for the Flyers albeit against a team who were effectively battling to hang on to their trophy but according to captain John Haig speaking later in the week lessons had been learned.

> "It wasn't a great performance but I still think we could have got something out of the game and we know what we did wrong and we'll be working on that in training. We are a better team this year and we'll be able to bounce back."

Ian Fletcher and ex Flyer Jonathan Weaver battle for the puck

Sunday September 14th 2008

Fife Flyers 15 Dundee Tigers 1

If this rout proved only one thing it was that the Dundee Tigers were included in the Autumn Cup to make up the numbers. For the few hundred supporters dotted around Fife Ice Arena the Tigers participation at least meant they were treated to another Fife Flyers goal fest.

Those who had travelled the previous night up to Dundee saw almost an exact repeat of the score line — only tonight the Tigers at least got one on the board. It's when these types of lopsided score lines become the norm that any competition loses credibility and entertainment value. The truth was that over the last three seasons this was the Flyers 13th consecutive win against their opponents with a combined goals aggregate of 112 for and 13 conceded. Evidence enough that there was never much sport between the two in this fixture.

The nature of the game allowed Flyers to try out some new line combinations and new players with teenagers Aaron Greger, Dale Walker, Robbie Balfour and Craig Holland all being given ice time and 16-year-old Walker even managed to make a scoring debut when he notched a goal. The match also let Iain Bell show what he was capable of; he top scored with three goals and three assists, numbers not to be sniffed at regardless of the opposition. Flyers, in the main, managed to keep enough momentum going to make a very one-sided match watchable.

Just 74 seconds were on the clock when Steven Lynch opened the scoring but Flyers had to wait a further 10 minutes before beating John Robb again as Steven King forced the puck home.

Robb managed to make some credible saves but could do little to stop Lynch nonchalantly dumping the puck into the corner of the net in the 16th minute before Andy Samuel gave Flyers a 4-0 lead at the first break. A somewhat rare occurrence, a Tigers shot on goal — this was only one of 10 in the game — brought about a consolation goal a minute into the second period; 15-year-old netminder Robbie Balfour was deceived by Grant Reekie's shot from the point.

Flyers got back on track at 24:28 as Dutiaume drilled a slapshot across the ice while Robb stood tall expecting a higher trajectory. It was soon 6-1 as Bell deked past a Tigers defenceman on the blue line and crashed a shot home from the slot. The same player scored an identical strike at 35:17 to wrap up the second period scoring.

Clichéd perhaps, although Tigers had been brave up until now, the movement and fitness of Flyers finally saw tiredness kick in and the home side hit eight goals in the last 20 minutes. Started by Stephen Gunn 25 seconds in, defenceman Willie Nicolson couldn't hide his grin as he hit Flyers ninth before Bell followed up a rebound from the backboards to notch his hat-trick strike on 46:54.

It was now raining goals and great interplay between the line of Dutiaume, King and Samuel ended with the club captain firing home the 11th. Dutiaume tipped home King's pass on 49:04 for 12-1 before Samuel bagged an unassisted strike a minute later as Tigers weary troops ran out of steam. There was still time for two power play goals after all the other counters had been even-handed with the scorers Dale Walker at 54:33 and Lewis Glasgow with 55 seconds of the game remaining.

Tigers finished their Autumn games without a point and in the six games their goals total was 5 scored and 84 conceded. Flyers and Solway tied the group before meeting in the Final.

Flyers player coach Todd Dutiaume with two goals rushes the Tigers net

Fife Flyers 2008-09 line up

Saturday September 15th 2012

ELITE ICE HOCKEY LEAGUE & CHALLENGE CUP

Fife Flyers 5 Braehead Clan 1

Flyers kept up their encouraging start to their second season in the Elite League as they posted back-to-back home wins. It was the best yet on and off the ice. The rink buzzed with noise and the home side demolished Braehead in a manner which underlined why they just might have to be taken seriously this season.

It was game over in barely ten minutes as Flyers stormed to a 3-0 lead. Kris Hogg's first came in just nine seconds, fast but a full three seconds tardier than the all-time record for a Flyers goal scored almost 40 years ago to the month by Les Lovell. His second was on the power play at 4:03 and when Caisey Haines swept a third straight strike home from the right at 10:04 Clan's players could only look at each other in bewilderment.

Brock McPherson set up a toe-to-toe fight in the 13th minute to try to shake energy into his side when Tommy Muir stepped up for Fife and the duo produced a slug-fest which was one of the best seen at the rink for many a year. It brought the fans to their feet but it didn't change the game one iota, such was Fife's stranglehold. They hit hard and fast and broke with pace and determination and tormented Garrett Zemlak on his return.

He was given no time to settle. It showed to his credit that the young goalie came on to a solid game in the second and third periods when he even stopped a penalty shot from Hogg to deny him his hat-trick. Interestingly, Zemlak was beaten five times from attacks from the right wing with four on the power play but he undoubtedly saved at least another five or six goals possibly more as Fife produced some irresistible hockey.

Haines netted his second and number four at 44:58 but the fifth at 54:26 was a thing of beauty. Zach Carriveau sparked a passing move, very reminiscent of a Mark Morrison team at its most peerless, as the puck zipped from right to left with one touch per skater and back again before John Dolan converted from close range. Haines took the Man of the Match award but in truth there were numerous contenders. Bobby Chaumont was the Clan scorer in what was a mere consolation for the visitors.

Kyle Horne was outstanding and not just for shoving and skelping a yappy Robert Farmer around all night before the Clan man copped a

10+Game penalty for abusing the officials. The third line buzzed like atom bombs. Jamie Wilson put in some powerhouse shifts and the manner in which Todd Dutiaume smeared poor Steve Birnstill into the plexi was just vintage stuff.

The Flyers sparkling start to the new season had given a huge lift to the man who arguably needed it most. Player-coach Todd Dutiaume endured a torrid time last season as he shouldered the burden of a disastrous debut Elite League campaign. Dutiaume, along with assistant-coach Danny Stewart, were under considerable pressure to give the club's fans a team to be proud of again. Only four games into season two it was already looking like mission accomplished.

When asked what the team's flying start meant to him personally Dutiaume responded:

> "It's unbelievable. There were times last year when it was very difficult to come to the rink. There were troubles on and off the ice but this year it's just an absolute joy to come to the rink. You want to be here with these guys and play your hardest for them. It's a unit. We've got a tough season ahead of us but I think these guys are going to be make a few waves this year. For our second season in the Elite League the improvements that have been made already are vast and we want to keep building on that."

Player coach Todd Dutiaume finds the net against Clan in the earlier Autumn Cup Final match

Saturday September 16th 1989

Fife Flyers 4 Cleveland Bombers 6

Three games into the season and the Flyers bombed out of the Norwich Union Cup with a third consecutive defeat. Lingering hopes of a dramatic reversal in fortunes were blown away by Tim Cranston, who returned to haunt his former Kirkcaldy comrades. He shot a first period hat-trick and then, as Fife desperately sought a revival, he secured Cleveland's win with a last-minute strike.

The indictment read that Flyers had little to offer on a night when they needed a morale-boosting victory. Coach Rab Petrie could only contemplate the absence of Rick Fera and what might have been. The lack of a proven net-finder was emphasised in the final period when the home side failed to score, despite firing 17 shots on net in a total of 49 for the game.

Petrie could feel content with a captain's performance from Gordon Latto but his troubles outweighed the few positive aspects of Fife's current game. When it mattered most, Flyers seemed disinterested with their hockey and certainly never showed any of the fire which had been demanded by Petrie after the disastrous start to the cup campaign.

Fera's replacement was import Martin Boulaine, who made a cautious debut with a single assist, but he skated well enough and was one of the Flyers better players. The 24-year-old, who hailed from Quebec, had been a fifth round draft pick of the Washington Capitals in 1983; before that he had played Major Junior 'A' hockey for three seasons with Granby Bisons where he scored 319 points (132 goals, 187 assists) in 199 games.

The new Flyer, who also had 69 games for Team Canada, arrived at Kirkcaldy via Durham, having signed for Wasps in the summer and played in their early Norwich Union Cup games, before a financial dispute saw him leave the Premier League champions earlier that week.

Cleveland had a dream start with Cranston firing three goals, including two on the power play past Craig Dickson in the opening 11 minutes. Latto had pulled one back to make the score 2-1 in the eighth minute and seconds before the first period buzzer showed his determination with a second strike after Flyers besieged Terry Ward's goal on a power play and he converted the pressure, finding the net off a defender's heel.

The home side looked more assured in the second period but fell further behind when Bombers player-coach Andre Malo struck. The Flyers responded and Luc Beausoleil scored twice in the 24th and 29th minutes to tie the game with his first —a real cracker, when Neil Abel steamed down the left and crossed to Mike Rowe, who body-checked a Bomber and made the crucial assist for his fellow Canadian to fire home.

However, with the scores level, it was Bombers who took the initiative in the deciding final phase and two breakaway goals the first by Kevin Conway in the 50th minute and Cranston just before the end secured the points and a remarkable double victory. This put the Flyers out of the Norwich Union Cup knock out stages for the third consecutive season. Boulaine played a total of three games for the Flyers scoring 3 goals and notching 4 assists.

Martin Bouliane who made his debut against Bombers and after three games he was gone

Saturday September 17th 2016

Fife Flyers 3 Dundee Stars 6

It was to be a miserable weekend for the Flyers. Firstly they suffered their first home loss of the season on Saturday against the Stars. Then they then made the long bus journey to Wales on Sunday and returned empty-handed, following a 6-1 defeat to Cardiff Devils in the Elite League.

After previously winning three of their opening four games head coach Todd Dutiaume admitted that his team had been hit with a reality check.

"We may be guilty of believing our own hype, getting off to such a great start, and much was made of it. It was a blow losing to Dundee, especially at home. I've stamped it to our supporters that we won't be out-worked, but unfortunately that wasn't the case. We had a game plan but the guys didn't stick to it. Dundee were by far the better team. We've been running a bit short on the bench and pulling a few injuries right now, but that's no excuse. It's early days for us and we've only been together a few weeks, but I really need to find the right line combinations. With an older team this year we have to manage things a little different. These guys are maybe not accustomed to as much ice time as I put on my imports. But they'll find their feet and I'm sure we're going to be very pleased with this squad once we get them firing like they should be."

Another good crowd of just under 2300 was on hand at Fife Ice Arena to welcome the Stars with the majority expecting a home win, although games against their Tayside rivals throughout the Elite League era had always been incredibly tight. All the goals came at even strength with each side only picking up 6 penalty minutes in what was a fast open game.

The visitors opened the scoring midway through the first when Scott Brannon beat Shane Owen. Only three minutes later that advantage was doubled when Matt White converted. It was important the Flyers got the next goal and they did with 90 seconds on the clock before the first interval. Justin Fox was fed the puck by Shayne Stockton and he made no mistake. Flyers had a two man advantage to finish the period which carried over to start the second but were unable to convert.

A Chase Schaber unassisted goal tied things up though at 26:48 and it looked as though the Flyers would now go on and take control of proceedings. The ever dangerous Brett Switzer had other ideas as he once again gave the Stars the lead shortly afterwards. Justin Faryna then struck six minutes into the final period. Holding a two goal lead, it looked as though the Stars had killed off the Flyers chances of a comeback but when Shayne Stockton buried one past Joe Fallon just a minute later the home side were back in it.

It was a short-lived hope for the home fans, however, as Cale Tanaka regained the two goal advantage a further 60 seconds later before Joey Sides completed the scoring for the visitors, as the Flyers were outshot 38-25.

To demonstrate how competitive this fixture had been in the Elite League era, the overall results stood now at Fife 26 wins, Dundee 23 and goals of 162-157 in Flyers favour.

Chase Schaber beats Stars netminder Fallon to level the game

Sunday September 18th 2005

North Ayr Bruins 3 Fife Flyers 10

The Flyers headed to Ayrshire with a short bench and still won their sixth consecutive game to maintain their 100% record in their new lower tier surroundings. They eased past North Ayr with the bulk of the damage coming in the opening periods when they netted four apiece. The Bruins made more of a fight of it in the third narrowly losing the period 2-1.

Flyers were always in control, despite travelling minus the King brothers, defenceman Scott Plews, Marc McAndrew and Gavin Fleming. To add to their lack of depth they also lost Liam Greig in the opening period after he took a nasty looking hit from behind.

John Haig top scored with a goal and four helpers while a trio of players scored doubles: Chris Linton, Man of the Match Gordon Latto junior and Ian Simpson with Linton also adding an assist. Craig Mitchell had a goal and two assists while there were single goals for Stephen Gunn and Chris Wands and an assist for Paul Shevlin.

As if it wasn't already hard enough for the Flyers to find any opposition to match them with their dominance already looking ominous for the rest of their challengers they were still awaiting permission to sign the experienced duo of Dean Edmiston and Davie Smith. They were currently training with the team but the Scottish National League had still not given the go-ahead for them to begin playing. Even if clearance was granted Flyers coach Todd Dutiaume would have to change his line-up to accommodate them due to league rules regarding players over the age of 30.

"The league is a little concerned about us becoming too strong,We've got a limit on the number of over-age players a team can ice in one match. We're only allowed four per game. It's a rule that exists to give the young players in the league more of a chance."

Flyers were currently icing their full quota of over-age players in the form of John Haig, Steven King, Derek King and netminder Colin Downie. They had maintained their 100 per cent record in the Autumn Cup with a victory at home the night before over Edinburgh and although Flyers won the Forth derby 6-2 the match was a tougher test compared to earlier fixtures.

Dutiaume insisted that Flyers dominance so far was not just down to the influence of the experienced former British National League men in his roster but also the performances of the young former Kestrels players. "The talent base has always been here," Dutiaume said. "Instead of playing 14 times a season and training once a fortnight these guys are now playing and training twice a week".

Flyers remained unbeaten in the Autumn cup winning all 11 matches to take the first of many titles they would gather at this level of hockey over the next six seasons. The Scottish Ice Hockey Association ruled a few weeks later that they would deny the Flyers permission to ice both Edmiston and Smith in the Scottish National League and so they were both left to kick their heels for the season after preparing for a number of weeks to ice.

Gordon Latto (Junior) gathers the puck as Steven King circles behind the Bruins net in an encounter between the sides at Kirkcaldy

Saturday September 19th 1981

Fife Flyers 4 Glasgow Dynamos 5

A new player-coach was on board for season 1981/82 in the shape of Swede Ake Alm, who had coached in Edinburgh as well as for a couple of years in Liverpool. His player profile in the first programme of the season had an interesting comment: Miscellaneous Dislikes – "Poor standard of refereeing in Scotland and getting up in the morning!"

Young Andy Donald was in line to share netminding duties with veteran John Pullar and Willie Cottrell and the season would start with a home-based roster. The opening weekend saw a home loss to Glasgow Dynamos followed 24 hours later by a 10-2 demolition in Edinburgh from the Murrayfield Racers, in a game that saw the debut of some 14-year-old kid called Tony Hand?

Glasgow Dynamos certainly showed the benefit of summer ice training and the score line was an accurate reflection of play with the visitors marginally the better side on the night. Dynamos opened the scoring after only six minutes with a goal by Martin Shields and three minutes later John Hester again hit the Flyers net to give the West of Scotland side a two goal lead. Flyers big defenceman Kenny Horne pulled one back for the home team in 12 minutes and the score remained 2-1 for Dynamos at the end of the first period.

The Glasgow team took only two minutes and 40 seconds to regain their two goal advantage when Hester netted his second goal of the night. However Murray McLellan replied for Flyers just four minutes later and then a superb goal shot through goaltender John Tague's legs by Gordon Latto brought the scores level for the first time in the match at 3-3. Martin Shields edged Dynamos ahead again after 37 minutes to take the score at the second buzzer to 4-3.

Both teams notched a goal in the final period with Chic Cottrell netting for Flyers and Pat Travers for Dynamos and the visitors held on to their slender lead until full time. While this was a Northern League fixture the Autumn Cup was also at stake with the trophy being awarded to the team with the lead in the standings at the halfway stage of the Northern League fixtures.

Officials in the Flyers camp were not however disappointed with the result. Coach Ake Alm felt that his players still had a great deal of as yet untapped talent to offer.

"They are still trying out new techniques. You must remember that they are playing under a different system. It is very difficult to effectively simulate competition during practice sessions as both teams are making the same moves. The first few games will be very much a case of observing and taking notes,"

After just one week of training however the positional play of the team had improved although defence, which had never been a Flyers strength, was in need of some improvement. Flyers main problem following the opening weekends was in the position of goaltender. Andy Donald, who was to have replaced John Pullar between the posts, had received a serious cartilage injury playing rugby the previous Saturday, and specialists had not yet been able to say how long it would take to heal.

Flyers boss Sandy Nicol was also now trying to have lifted the suspension imposed on Pullar, based on the strength of a petition by 35 Murrayfield supporters regarding his conduct at the game on Sunday night. It was seen as if not a ludicrous but certainly dangerous precedent to be set and a situation that could very easily get out of hand he said. "I feel that a referee's report should be necessary before any player is reprimanded," he added.

The billboard poster for the Flyers opening match of the 1981/82 season

Saturday September 20th 1997

Fife Flyers 16 Murrayfield Royals 1

Chances of qualification in the Autumn Trophy had effectively been ended with back-to-back games against the Kingston Hawks the previous weekend in which the Flyers emerged without any points.

While those games were both close and nervy encounters for the Flyers fans it was the other side of the coin against the Royals as the home team put the poor Edinburgh outfit to the sword with a ruthless performance.

Flyers had opened the season by shutting out the Royals on their home ice. This game reminded everyone that there were too many similar score lines during previous encounters with the Capital club — who had switched their name from Racers to Royals a few seasons before — in which the Flyers won all of the so far ten match-ups.

It was hoped that the Edinburgh club were not discouraged by this reverse and would continue with their efforts to strengthen their squad, so that they would be able to put up more of a challenge in future games.

Missing the experienced duo of Scott Neil and Paul Pentland, the Royals were always going to be up against it but Flyers turned in a professional show to delight another sizeable crowd and scored some cracking goals in the process. Sharpshooter John Haig led the way with an amazing seven goal haul, just one short of the club record for a British player, held by Jimmy Spence. Yet again the line of Haig, David Smith and Steven King looked impressive which augured well for the much tougher clashes to come.

A clean contest with only 12 minutes in penalties actually produced two shorthanded goals for Haig while Colin Hamilton in net, who always seemed to perform well against Murrayfield, was beaten only once from 30 shots. Frank Morris set the tone for the evening by opening the scoring in just 49 seconds and Flyers had taken the tally to six by the end of the period with goals by Smith (3.14), Morrison (12.11), Haig (13.13 and 16:30 short-handed) and Morris again (19.55) hitting the net.

The pattern continued in the second period with scoring underway just 20 seconds after the restart and Haig and Morris both completed their hat-tricks. Royals replaced the over-worked Robert Jack with young Ryan Ford but this did little to stem the flow. Haig added a further two goals to take the score to 11-0 by the second break.

This had advanced to 14 through Morrison, Wayne Maxwell and Haig before Royals eventually found a way past Hamilton when Laurie Dunbar fired home at 49.30. Steven King answered almost immediately and when Haig grabbed his seventh and Flyers 16th at 52.54 a great number of the fans must have been thinking of reaching 20. However to their credit the Royals kept battling away and there was no further scoring as Flyers iced their entire bench.

Flyers scoring: John Haig 7+1, Frank Morris 3+2, Mark Morrison 2+4, David Smith 1+4, Steven King 1+2, Richard Dingwall 1+0, Wayne Maxwell 1+0, Gordon Latto 0+5, Mark Slater 0+2, Derek King 0+1, Bill Moody 0+1, Andy Samuel 0+1.
Royals scoring: Laurie Dunbar 1+0, Scott Carter 0+1, Neil Smith 0+1.
Shots on goal: Flyers (Hamilton) 30; Royals (Jack 29, Ford 26) 55.
Penalty minutes: Flyers 6, Royals 6. Referee: Graham Horner. Att: 2022.

John Haig in dominant form against the Royals as he came within a goal of tying a club record

Saturday September 21st 1947

FLYERS FIX A COACH

It was announced in the local newspapers that Al Rogers, formerly of the Dundee Tigers, had been appointed coach of the Flyers. The article went on to read

"A coach for the Fife Flyers has been fixed by Manager Wake at Kirkcaldy Ice Rink, yesterday. After being captain and coach of Dundee Tigers and Brighton Tigers Al Rogers should bring the new lads on a bit with his wide experience of the game. Manager Wake had other arrangements in view but is more than pleased in getting Rogers. He has high hopes that Rogers will prove himself to be the best coach throughout the whole Ice Hockey league. Rogers is in Liverpool but Mr Wake hopes he will be in Kirkcaldy at the beginning of the week. "

Al was of course a familiar name to all ice hockey enthusiasts. The 32-year-old Canadian came to this country with the first batch of pre-war Canadian ice hockey players and sported the colours of the Brighton Tigers for two years before he travelled North to Scotland to join the fledgling Dundee Tigers in 1938.

He had many a hard tussle at Kirkcaldy with George Horn and his Flyers colleagues and like most of the old hands he looked back on those old days with envy. Tigers had fared very well in their inaugural outing and were worthy of being thought of as the team of the season in 1938-39, after they won four trophies including the Airlie Trophy, Mitchell Cup, Bairns Trophy and the Canada Cup for finishing top of the Scottish National League Regular season; they only missed out by a couple of points from Falkirk of winning the Points League.

Rogers started his hockey career at the age of 16 and after he had gone through all the intermediate stages he played his first senior ice hockey with Saskatoon Quakers. In season 1933-34 his team won the Western Canadian Championship and Al on joining the Flyers was able to proudly show the silver watch presented to him by the citizens of the town which had the following engraved on the back: "To Al Rogers, from Saskatoon Citizens, Quaker Hockey Club, Western Canadian Champions, 1933-4."

During that season Al was one of the greatest young stars in Canada and he succeeded in gaining a life-long ambition when he was chosen for the right wing position of the international Canadian team, which represented his country at the Olympic Games in Milan, Italy. The following season he toured Japan as player coach with the Battleford Millers and then he returned to his old club in Canada. He stayed until he came to Britain for season 1936/37 with the Brighton Tigers, where he played on the top line with Bobby Lee and Gordie Poirier. In his two seasons for the Sussex team he scored 35 goals and 18 assists for 53 points.

He wasn't known for being on the wrong side of the officials, as his six penalty minutes testified, and so he moved to Dundee and the Tigers to become their player-coach and captain. He also played representative matches with Scotland that season along with the Flyers Len McCartney. The following season Roger's Tigers played second fiddle mostly to the Flyers and Panthers before war interrupted the sport.

Al would go on to coach the Flyers for six seasons where he helped them secure back-to-back league titles in 1948/49 and 1949/50.Other major trophies included the Autumn and Canada Cups, along with a host of minor trophies. In his first season he was voted the Coach of the Year — an accolade he picked up twice more, only matched in more modern times by Mark Morrison.

Al in his playing days
with Brighton

Sunday September 22nd 1985

Murrayfield Racers 6 Fife Flyers 6

It was the opening weekend of the 1985/86 season and the first Forth Derby saw another huge crowd squeeze themselves into the confines of Murrayfield Ice Rink.

The Flyers had won the previous night, when they demolished the Glasgow Dynamos 17-2 at Kirkcaldy. For the home side it was a chance for them to avenge their Wembley defeat by the Flyers in the final game of the previous season. The game would also provide the Flyers with a stiff measure of how their squad for this season would be expected to hold up against a Racers outfit many had as favourites for the honours before a puck had been dropped.

The Racers started the game very quickly and it took the Flyers the best part of the opening period to adjust to the speed and physicality of the game. However, as always with Ron Plumb's teams, he advocated patience and sticking to the game plan which is what they did. As Plumb said in his post-game comments

> "Until things started to sort themselves out we wanted to keep the game tight. If we could not win the game in the first and second periods then let's not let it slip completely away from us."

The team showed its continual determination in never quitting even at two goals down twice during the game. Praise was given in particular to the Flyers ability to support the top scoring line and generally keeping Murrayfield in check. Richard Black and Charlie Kinmond were alternated on left wing stints while naturally the offensive power came from imports Todd Bidner and Danny Brown. Craig Dickson, who had a fine game in nets for the Flyers, was expected to carry much more of the load, as Andy Donald was finding it ever more difficult to balance his hockey and university education commitments with exams on the horizon.

By the latter stages of the game the Flyers could argue they had regained the momentum but ultimately a share of the spoils on the road was seen as a positive result. Fife despite their slow start to the game opened the scoring in the eighth minute when Bidner despatched one behind Moray Hanson from a Brown pass. As was all too often the case, though, especially on Racers home ice, they would have difficulty in containing number 9, Tony Hand, and he struck twice from assists by Rick Fera in a space of only 16 seconds to give the Racers a 2-1 lead at the first break.

Midway through the game Brown popped in an equaliser with an assist from Plumb but the Racers repeated their trick of the first period when they notched two in an even shorter order with Hand and Fera netting just 11 seconds apart. Todd Bidner reduced arrears before the end of the second and then brought the teams level again less than two minutes into the final period. Incredibly the Racers caught the Flyers with another quick fire double when Tony Hand scored both to take his total to five with what was a relative lifetime between the two counters of 49 seconds!

It was important that the Flyers responded and within a couple of minutes Brown, from Plumb, brought the visitors to within a goal. The Flyers kept battling away and were rewarded, with less than four minutes on the clock, when Brown again converted a Plumb assist to send the right hand side of the rink into raptures. Shots on goal were 32-31 in favour of Flyers in a match that had only six minutes of penalties handed out to each side despite the intensity of the encounter.

Dougie Latto (left) with Flyers import trio of Bidner, Brown and Plumb – oh yes, and the Flyers mascot for season 1985/86- the 'Burrd'

Friday September 23rd 2011

ELITE ICE HOCKEY LEAGUE & CHALLENGE CUP

Belfast Giants 9 Fife Flyers 1

Yes, I know I'm a glutton for punishment, having already recalled the Flyers opening two games in the Elite League. By week three, faced with a triple header of games over the weekend, the enormity of their undertaking had not diminished as they suffered, in consecutive road games, another nine-goal hammering.

The visitors had bolstered their line up the previous weekend with the arrival of Mike Hamilton, who also had the honour of scoring the Flyers first Elite League goal, but they had no answer to a rampant Giants side who regained top spot in the league standings.

Giants established a commanding 4-0 lead going into the first intermission, before netting five further goals in the second period with doubles from Ryan Crane, Jeff Mason, Robert Dowd and Brock McBride. Danny Stewart grabbed Flyers consolation goal at 25.49 with the score at 5-0.

The only real positive for Fife was a third period shut-out for Blair Daly who stopped 18 shots after replacing Garrett Zemlak after half an hour. Similarly, Giants with the game won, replaced Stephen Murphy in nets for the third period with Andrew Dickson, who had no difficulty in dealing with only two shots giving Fife a miserly 13 shots on goal for the game.

Flyers player-coach Todd Dutiaume said:

> "That was embarrassing. It's a worry on my part that nobody showed up. Our guys have to realise that if you don't show up in this league you can get embarrassed quickly. For 50 minutes they gave us a lesson in hockey. It was men against boys. Maybe we've got an even bigger adjustment than we initially thought. We managed to come out with a 0-0 in the third period. I know that's not enough but it's a glimmer that we've got potential there. The guys are up against it when it comes to competing with these top five teams but you just never know on the night and we're hoping now that the game in Belfast was an anomaly. It was an awfully long day and the Belfast rink is on a different planet to what our guys are used to but we just stood back and watched them play hockey for most of the game."

Giants scoring: McBride (2+3) Dowd, Crane, Mason (2+0) Keefe (14) Doucet (0+4) Dignard (0+3) Garside, LeBlanc, Peacock (0+2) Kuiper, Lloyd (0+1).

Flyers scoring: Stewart (1+0) Samuel, Horne (0+1)

SOGs: Belfast (Murphy 11, Dickson 2); Fife (Zemlak 27, Daly 27) PIMs: 8-28. Att: 2194

The optimism from the coach was somewhat founded the next night as they returned to Kirkcaldy overnight to meet fellow strugglers Edinburgh Capitals who themselves had endured a 30-game losing streak to end the previous season. In game five the 'new boys' were on the board with their first ever Elite League win. Their next however would be almost two months and 15 games later in mid November! Sometimes you "hae tae hae a big hert" to follow your team, as some of the pages in this book no doubt testify.

Mike Hamilton who holds the honour of scoring the Flyers first ever Elite League goal

Friday September 24th 1948

Ayr Raider 2 Fife Flyers 5

The Flyers played their second of back to back Friendlies as the "pipe-openers" to the 1948/49 season. Ahead of the action commencing there was a "Go-Easy" plea as reported by 'Snow' in the local paper.

"Pressmen have been asked by the SIHA to refrain from making harsh comments on new players until they have had time to settle down. I think that this suggestion is rather superfluous as all journalists realise that it is impossible for a player to give of his best until he has become accustomed to his new surroundings. I don't propose at any time to rip the Flyers to pieces. Any comments or criticisms which I make will be in all fairness to the team and taking into account any background difficulties which may surround them. At present the local lads are hard at work putting Al Rogers' plans into action and taking in tips which his vast knowledge of the hockey world enables him to give them. It is for the coach himself to say how the team will line-up, but I venture to suggest that the forward lines will be Scrutton, Mann, Moreland and Scotty Reid, Joy, Smith. Al Rogers is making no rash promises at the moment and confines himself to saying 'the boys are banging away' line when I phoned him Friday afternoon. He's had injuries and hopes that the line-ups for the forwards will be as I have already mentioned."

After the disappointment of last season Rogers and his new charges looked to make it two wins from two before the start of the season. The Flyers initial victory was confirmed as no flash-in-the-pan effort when they travelled to the West Coast rink and battled themselves to a comfortable victory against the Raiders.

The first line were in scintillating form and four of the goals came from them. The second line were still a trifle shaky and apart from the two juniors, Jimmy Mitchell and Bert Smith, they were shot-shy. 'Pete' Belanger gave a steady game in nets, although there was a 15 minute spell in the second period where he had a really rough passage. Despite the fact that he was injured on one occasion he succeeded in keeping his charge intact.

The first-line forwards reproduced the previous night's form where they beat the Dundee Tigers 9-6 at Kirkcaldy. They had the beating of the home defence at every turn and each of them secured a goal. Floyd Snider was a forceful defenceman who could depend upon the stability of his partner Verne Greger alongside him to make plays up ice and consequently he greatly added to the driving strength of the forwards. The second-line were inclined to be erratic but there were plenty of signs that they would steady up as the season progressed. Junior Bert Smith was the real live-wire in attack and he capped a grand play by netting Flyers third counter while Jimmy Mitchell was also at his best and he set up a good partnership with Ken Joy. The centre, despite his lack of inches, was a nippy stick-handler and although he did not succeed in scoring he was always a source of danger for the opposition defence.

The game was keenly contested throughout, but Flyers always had the edge on their opponents. It was the visitors who did the bulk of the pressing in the opening period and went deservedly two goals ahead. Floyd Snider opened the scoring in the sixth minute when he collected a Chic Mann pass near the boards and cut in to net from close quarters. Two minutes later Hick Moreland collected the puck in his own zone and wormed his way through before he gave the net minder no chance with a terrific shot from just outside the goal crease.

In the opening minutes of the second session Al Bathe scored an unassisted goal to reduce the lee-way for Raiders. However Bert Smith regained the two-goal advantage for Flyers when he slapped home a Moreland assist from an oblique angle. Jack Heggie scored for Raiders before the session ended but Flyers were in command in the final period and 'Bud' Scrutton put them further ahead with a great solo goal. A few minutes later Chic Mann did likewise with his shot reaching the net via a post.

Things turned out fine for the Flyers as they went on to lift the Scottish National League trophy and the Coronation Cup. Back Row, left to right: Floyd Snider, Ken Joy, Chic Mann, Hick Moreland, 'Bud' Scrutton (Captain).
Front Row, left to right: Bob Reid, Verne Greger, Pete Belanger, Scotty Reid, Doug Smith

Saturday September 25th 1971

Fife Flyers 4 Dundee Rockets 9

The Northern League action started late September but a number of Scottish players had kept their hand in so to speak by competing in the Summer League in Aviemore.

Teams shared players on a number of occasions for the games that took place over June, July and August and Kirkcaldy finished third in the five-team league table. The top two Glasgow and hosts Aviemore met in the final at the beginning of September. With more than just a slight influence from Fife it was the home side who won 4-3, with the goals scored by guest Flyers Stuart Muir, John Taylor and Les Lovell.

Competitive action returned to Kirkcaldy when the Flyers took on the Dundee Rockets in the Autumn Cup competition. Three familiar faces were absent from the Flyers line-up as Roy Reid, Joe McIntosh and Joe Baird had all joined Ayr Bruins.

Rockets proved far too strong for Flyers, with most of the damage being done by Mike Mazur who scored a hat-trick and the veteran ex-Flyer Sam McDonald, who netted twice. Flyers trailed 3-1 at the end of the first period; within six minutes of the second period they had lost another two goals, and it was clear at that stage that it was not going to be their night. The home side pulled a couple of goals back but Rockets were able to raise their game and ran out easy winners.

Flyers goals were scored by Bill Dunbar, Kenny Horne, Norrie Boreham and John Taylor, with the other Rockets counters from Murray, George Reid, Joe Gullcher and another veteran ex-Flyer Jimmy Spence, now 36 years of age but still knew where the net was, as his 123 points in the season proved. So a defeat to start the season, not quite.

Perhaps both teams were still in Summer Cup thinking mode but afterwards the Northern Ice Hockey Association deemed that the game be void as both teams had fielded an unregistered player.

The game was rescheduled for the middle of November. While the Rockers were still in contention for the title the Flyers early season promise was already on the wane. The visitors won even more comfortably this time around with a 10-2 score line and it was the wily old Spence that grabbed the headlines as he netted five times and followed that up with four the following night as the teams met on Tayside in the same competition with Rockets again victors.

With Ian Forbes also a Dundee Rocket the "Perth Line" of the 1960s for Flyers were now inspirational across the Tay for the Rockets, who were starting to find heir feet in the game. The Flyers struggles were in large part due to a scoring drought for captain Les Lovell, although it did see Jimmy Hunter and John Taylor graft harder to pick up the weight off Les as they began to emerge as consistent scorers in their own right.

Chic Cottrell was nominated the best rookie of the year for season 1970-71 and was presented with the Montford Trophy ahead of the opening game of the season against Dundee Rockets by Tommy Horne.

Saturday September 26th 1992

BENSON & HEDGES CUP

Fife Flyers 5 Sheffield Steelers 5

Having lost their last three games in the competition, the Flyers fought hard to win back some respect after their disastrous exit from the Benson & Hedges Cup.

With angry words ringing in their ears, the squad took to the ice with a renewed sense of purpose against Sheffield Steelers. Coach Jim Lynch had threatened recriminations if his side failed to show character and commitment in their final Cup matches that weekend.

The reaction left Lynch with more questions than answers. Following a heroic struggle against Steelers on Saturday, the Flyers then suffered a humiliating reversal to their old rivals Murrayfield Racers in Edinburgh the following night. It was Steelers first-ever visit to the Rosslyn Street rink but the scoreline disguised the effort that Flyers put into the meeting.

They would probably have recorded their second win in the Cup had it not been for a major penalty collected by their most influential player, Cal Brown, who was drawn into a dust-up.

Flyers got off to an ideal start and scored twice within the opening two minutes. Only 20 seconds had ticked away on the rink clock. Former Flyer Andy Donald was left to pick the puck from the net when Cal Brown finished a three-man move by striking from the blue line and less than a minute later a superb cross-rink pass by Bobby Haig split the ice diagonally to find Frank Morris who picked his spot low past Donald.

Flyers import line were running riot and a third goal was added in the tenth minute on the power play as Brown jinked through Steelers defence to set up Ed Zawatsky. Before the celebrations died down, Paul Dixon checked the home side's surge at 10:16 with a goal, but Steelers were dealt another shock seconds later when Donald was struck on the head by the puck from a Morris close range effort.

His replacement, David Singleton, was tested by Dean Edmiston at 12:20 and lost his first goal in 15:52 when Morris and Iain Robertson set up Zawatsky for his second. Flyers failed to keep the pressure on the inexperienced netminder and it was the visitors who scored before the period buzzer though Steve MacSwain.

In a keenly-contested middle period Rob Abel rattled Singleton's upright but it was Dixon who got his second when he forced in MacSwain's assist during a goalmouth scramble at 22:40.

Bobby Haig celebrates a Flyers goal

Ex Flyer Ronnie Wood received a slashing penalty at 24:37 and just 14 seconds into the power play the home side restored their two-goal lead through Brown. The Flyers were still looking well in control of the match at this stage although their power play opportunities were not being converted. At 31:18 the incident occurred which changed the pattern of the match, when former Flyer Neil Abel elbowed Zawatsky in the face after catching the import behind the goals. This resulted in a fight with Brown and Plommer stepping in the help their team mates.

After calm was restored referee McWilliams issued a match penalty to Abel for fighting, a game misconduct penalty to Brown, and two-minute roughing penalties to Zawatsky and Tommy Plommer. Brown was Fife's most influential player in the opening half hour and his major penalty was a severe blow to Flyers in their bid to preserve their lead.

Certainly Steelers would have looked at his trade for Abel as a good bargain. Morris was pulled back into defence to cover but despite Steelers being shorthanded for five minutes after the melée, the second period ended without further score before two goals in 90 seconds wiped out Flyers lead in the third.

MacSwain scored his second of the night at 46:17 on a power play, before Craig Dickson allowed a speculative strike by Mark Mackie to slip between his pads. The Kirkcaldy crowd witnessed furious end-to-end hockey in the final 10 minutes. Steven King and Bobby Haig missed in front of goal while Rob Abel saw his shot well saved by Singleton, as the match seemed to be destined to end in a draw.

Sunday September 27th 1998

Fife Flyers 0 Cardiff Devils 9

In what was regarded as a crazy way to run a competition the Flyers, having finished second in their all BNL group, were "rewarded", as all BNL teams were, with a tie in the knock-out stages against Ice Hockey Super League opposition. They managed to restore a semblance of pride with an enthusiastic display in the second leg of the pointless Benson and Hedges Cup challenge round.

All the small crowd wanted was the goal the home side deserved but it was not to be. Flyers bowed out of the competition on the wrong end of a 22-0 aggregate scoreline. For the first time in their 60 year history they had been shut out in back to back games.

The result — combined with others over that weekend — did little for the credibility of the sport in this country or the sponsors of the event. At least Flyers gave a better account of themselves at home than they had been able to produce in Wales the night before and mustered 28 shots at goal which was a more reasonable number than the dozen they managed on Devils ice.

They created enough chances to score two or three goals but a combination of poor finishing and good netminding along with some downright bad luck meant that the Fife tally stayed blank. Flyers detractors were probably crowing over the weekend scores. While it did look like a humiliation, things had to be kept in perspective. It was fifteen imports against five; experienced pros against raw youngsters and genuinely a case of men against boys and it showed.

Flyers lacked nothing in effort but were always going to be struggling to contain a well-drilled machine like Cardiff who benefited from full-time training. Even small things like the ease by which they changed lines was superior to anything seen in the British National League. Devils did a very professional job and no malice could be directed towards them, except perhaps Kory Mullin, who found himself the target of the home fans light-hearted abuse after a series of incidents which made the big defenceman look rather foolish.

After being dumped by Mark Morrison on the boards Mullin tried to retract some revenge by charging the player-coach behind the goals but

Morrison was too quick for him and the Devil only succeeded in getting himself caught up with the netting! With a total of 14 minutes in the box Mullin probably wouldn't have been in a hurry to return to Kirkcaldy.

The outcome of the tie was obviously never in doubt after Saturday's game but Flyers tried their best only for Cardiff to more or less score when they wanted to. Martin Lindman (3.16), Ian McIntyre (11.48) and Vezio Sacratini (18.13) all found the net in the first period but Flyers enjoyed a fine spell in the middle stanza, counting 14 shots on Stevie Lyle's goal and only conceding one strike to former Fife favourite Steve Moria (28.37).

Unable to take advantage of a number of power play opportunities, the home side visibly wilted in the final 20 minutes and after Steve Thornton scored a fine solo short-handed goal at 44.47, Devils rubbed salt in the wounds with further strikes from Sacratini (45.07), Brent Pope (51.37), Moria (58.19) and Sacratini's hat-trick 18 seconds from the final buzzer.

Poor Frank Neckar must almost have been at his wits end having faced over 100 shots and conceding 16 goals over the weekend and the Czech must have wondered exactly what kind of hockey he had come to Britain to play. The fans gave both teams warm applause at the end but in reality it was a night to forget or one that should never have taken place at all.

Frank Neckar was under fire all weekend against the Devils

Thursday September 28th 2000

BENSON & HEDGES CUP

Fife Flyers 1 Newcastle Jesters 8

Three seasons on and the powers-that-be still hadn't figured out the relative futility of setting up the competition in this manner. As expected the Flyers found the challenge of facing the Jesters too much but at least they acquitted themselves well and finally scored their first goal against Superleague opposition in three attempts.

The Flyers had been winners of their British National League group — as had the Guildford Flames in their group — while the Jesters had finished fourth (bottom) in their ISL group, with only one win from six games. Bracknell were bottom in the other group.

So the theory being that the top placed BNL teams should be able to compete with the bottom placed teams from the Superleague was not evidenced again by this match; it took the Flyers until the final two minutes to get on the board, although their efforts deserved a better reward. The only saving grace this year was that it was a single game and not an aggregate over two legs!

Guildford Flames fared no better as they were hosed 9-1 on home ice by the Bees yet both they and Fife went on to be the dominant forces in the BNL that season with the Flames eventually edging to the title but it showed just how cavernous the gulf between the top two tiers of hockey in the UK was.

With Russell Monteith missing with flu Flyers had four imports against a Newcastle side featuring 18 and Jesters were quicker in everything they did. Their skating, passing and shooting was symptomatic of full-time professionals with plenty of practice time and fitness training which was exactly why no one was once again surprised at the outcome.

Jesters scored at regular intervals. With five minutes to go it was 8-0 with the game long over as a contest. With the home fans still cheering their team on, a long pass from Ted Russell found Mark Morrison high up the ice and the player-coach was able to use his speed to break free and finally shoot past Satosaari. The noise that greeted the goal wouldn't have been greater had it been the winning strike and both sides received warm applause at the end.

Speaking after the game and happy that the Flyers had come through the game unscathed player-coach Mark Morrison had been pleased with his side's performance despite the 8-1 score line and said; "We worked hard and that's all you can ask against Superleague opponents as the gulf is so great."

His side looked forward to unfurling the Championship banner 48 hours later when the Flames visited in the BNL opener, while the defeat also put the Flyers into the Benson & Hedges Plate competition where they were given a tough pairing with the Basingstoke Bison.

Flyers scoring: Mark Morrison 1+0, Ted Russell 0+1, Steven King 0+1.

Jesters scoring: Matt Oates 3+0, Jari Suorsa 2+1, Joel Poirier 2+0, Darren McAusland 1+1, Tero Arkiomaa 0+2, Daniel Lecroix 0+2, Rob Wilson 0+1, Craig Binns 0+1, Tommi Soya 0+1, Santeri Immonen 0+1

Shots on goal: Flyers (R Grubb) 44, Jesters (Satosaari) 25 Penalty minutes: Flyers 4, Jesters 8.

Referee: Moray Hanson. Att: 1108.

Ricky Grubb who had a busy night in Flyers net against the Jesters is helped out by Ted Russell

Monday September 29th 1952

Murrayfield Royals 2 Fife Flyers 2

After a wait of 13 years and a number of building alterations the Edinburgh Rink finally opened to the public in the first week of August 1952 as an Ice Arena.

The rink was built during 1938 and early 1939 at a cost of £60,000 and was due to be opened on 15th September 1939 by the Earl of Rosebery. However, because of the outbreak of the War on the 1st September and the government's ban on sport the planned opening was cancelled indefinitely with just a week's notice.

The final touches had been applied to the building and it was ready to stage exhibitions by famous skaters of the day Freddie Tomlins and Daphne Walker at the opening ceremony. The new rink management also had to cancel all contracts with ice hockey players and the Government requisitioned the premises as a Royal Army Service Corp Depot.

After the war, up to 1951, it remained under the control of the Government being used as a HM Stationery Office store. At long last, with a home to play in, the Edinburgh Royals took to the ice that September; this was the Flyers first ever trip across the Forth to commence an enduring rivalry.

Twice a goal behind, the Flyers fought back to gain a well deserved point in their third Scottish Cup game of the season, having won one and lost one. While the hockey itself was perhaps not of the highest standard, there was no lack of endeavour from both teams and there were many thrilling incidents.

Excitement mounted in the last period when Flyers piled on the pressure in an effort to force the equaliser and this arrived two minutes from time when left winger Moe Zubatiuk — he can legitimately lay claim to being the first Mo — finished off a move originated by Bobby Burns and Bud Stock.

Flyers owed a great deal to ex Detroit Red Wings goalkeeper Harry McQueston and Burns, who were inspiring when Royals had the better of the exchanges in the opening period. McQueston made his experience tell with his every move. Burns was never ruffled and always stuck to the methodical and determined style which had marked his play that season.

After a no scoring opening period how ironic that the first ever goal scored by an Edinburgh team against the Flyers came from someone called Fife, Moe Fife, who put Royals ahead after 11 minutes of the second.

The home side were next to threaten when a Nebby Thrasher shot was kicked out by McQueston. Gordie Blackman and Scotty Dowle were both guilty of shooting when passes would more likely have ended in the Flyers scoring before they equalised in the eighteenth minute. When Stock's pass found Zubatiuk completely unmarked in front of goal, the left winger's shot went into the net off Ray Gariepy's pad.

Flyers piled on the pressure after that but were caught napping when Fife broke away from the red line to give McQueston no chance for his second.

The visitors gained the initiative after that, but it took them 18 minutes of the third period to eventually break the home sides resistance. The Royals packed their goalmouth when Burns gained possession on their blue line, but the Flyers player-coach cleverly slipped the puck through to Stock who in turn transferred to Zubatiuk at the edge of the crease to score.

Flyers best were McQueston, Burns and Bert Smith although there were no weak links with the possible exception of Dowle who had been prone to forget his defensive duties and became over-eager to stick-handle his way through the Royals defence. Gariepy in the Royals net handled the puck cleanly and Nick Pyevach gave him excellent cover. Thrasher could not match Smith's speed and his play suffered in consequence. Cece Cowie, a fast hard-hitting left winger. was the Edinburgh team's best forward.

Royals – Ray Gariepy, Moose Sage, Nick Pyevach, Don Busch, Verne Greger, Nebby Thrasher, Moe Fife, Cece Cowie, Jim McGeorge, Roy Thompson, Cliff Baldwin

Flyers – Harry McQueston, Bobby Burns, Jimmy Mitchll, Gordie Blackman, Ron Biggar, Bert Smith, Nick Dubick, Marlowe McDonald, Bud Stock, Scotty Dowle, Moe Zubatiuk

Referee — R. Gemmell

MURRAYFIELD

ROYALS

OFFICIAL PROGRAMME 6^{D.}

Monday 29th Sept. 1952
SCOTTISH CUP
Royals
v
Fife Flyers
Face-off - 7.30 p.m.

Vol. I No. 3   MONDAY 29th SEPTEMBER 1952

The programme for the fist ever meeting between these two great Scottish ice hockey rivals

Friday September 30th 1938

CHALLENGE MATCH

Dundee Tigers 5 Fife Flyers 2

Interesting to note that the week before their first ever match the Flyers were making news in the area news sections of the *Fife Free Press*, this entry was under the Gallatown heading

HOCKEY PLAYER INJURED

"While the Fife Flyers were practising on Thursday forenoon one of the players was the victim of a mishap which was fortunately not of a serious nature. Three pucks were being used during the practice and two shots were sent in to 'Chic' Kerr, the goaltender, at the same time. One of them struck him on the head above the eye and he had to have the injury stitched."

Indeed the Flyers were to suffer a further training accident that led to Billy Fullerton sitting out the opening games. He injured his collar bone. So on to that first weekend of the Flyers existence. With both the Dundee and Kirkcaldy ice rinks opening over the same weekend, it made perfect sense that each would stage an ice hockey match and that the teams competing at both would be the Dundee Tigers and the Fife Flyers.

It was unsurprisingly a full house in Dundee, but even so the directors and management were taken by surprise by the extraordinary crowds which practically fought for admission to the gala opening. The rink held a capacity of 4000 people. At least 1000 more were turned away, as a queue stretched four deep along the Kingsway for 150 yards, causing the start of the match had to be delayed for a few minutes in order to allow spectators time to reach their seats.

Though this was merely a friendly encounter between the two newcomers to the Scottish game the crowd left in no doubt of their enthusiasm for a sport which was completely new to Dundee. The Tigers had the satisfaction of winning the match though they did not find their best form until the last period.

During the first two periods, which featured some slack play by both sides the Flyers were generally on top but the Tigers speed and combination play were too much for them in the closing session. Tigers were well served in goal by Scotty Milne who had been loaned for the evening by Perth Panthers. Chic Kerr in the Flyers net also got a great hand for his efforts especially when he resumed after a goalmouth spill with a large patch of plaster on his forehead.

The match was not without some periods of over exuberant play and the penalty-box had four occupants for brief spells. Al Rogers, the Tigers skipper, scored the rink's first goal in 10 minutes when he finished a solo run with a tight angled shot from the right which Kerr could only deflect into the net. Five minutes later Norman McQuade smacked in a smart shot which Milne parried and Len McCartney hit the return first-time to equalise for the visitors and the Flyers first ever 'road goal'.

The Flyers showed distinct improvement in the second period and Jimmy Chappell squeezed the puck home just behind the post but Tigers play was much faster in the last period and there was great excitement when Merrick Cranstoun levelled the scores from close in after a shot from Biff Smith had been saved. Tigers went all out and McNeil got through to score the best goal of the match. Now well on top, the Tigers added further goals through Jimmy Shannon, who streaked about 40 yards down the centre of the ice to net an unsavable shot, and a Jimmy Lightfoot hook shot from an almost incredibly acute angle.

Dundee Tigers: Scotty Milne (1) George McNeil (2) Biff Smith (3) Jimmy Shannon (9) Al Rogers (5) Merrick Cranstoun (6) Reserve defence; Doug Mitchell (4) Reserve attack; Jimmy Lightfoot (7) Fred Hill (8) Glen Braid (10)

Fife Flyers: Chic Kerr (1) Les Lovell (2) Jack Stover (3) Norman McQuade (7) Len McCartney (8) Tommy Durling (5) Reserve defence; Alex Fullerton (9) Reserve attack; Tommy McInroy (4) Jimmy Chappell (6)

Referee; J. B. McCabe Glasgow.

After the game full advantage was taken of the general skating with well over 500 skaters on the ice.

Action from the Tigers and Flyers match

Russ Parent, one of the Flyers three imports during the 1996/97 season

October

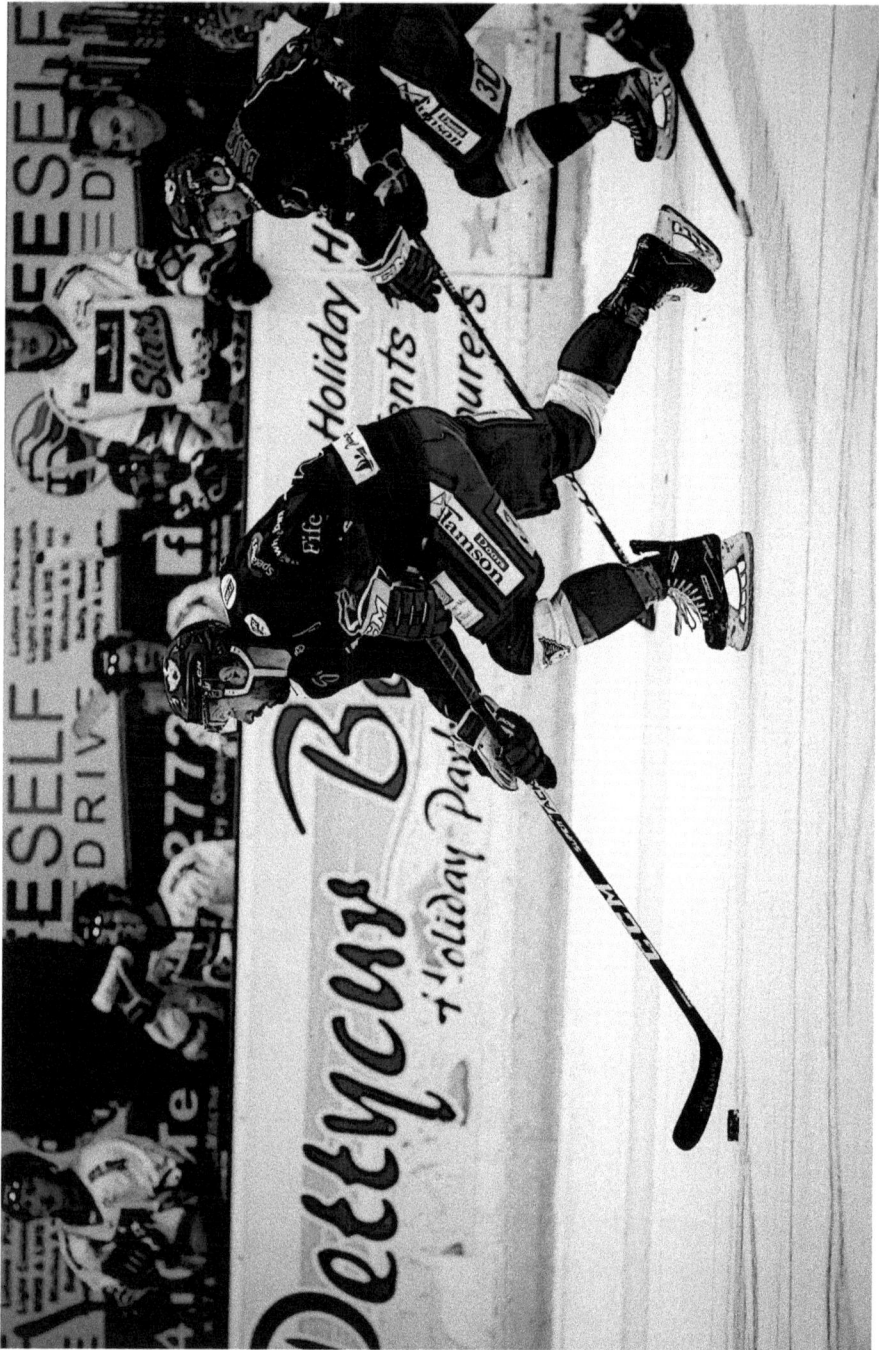

Bari McKenzie who celebrated playing his 600th game in the Elite Ice Hockey League on 7th November 2021

Saturday October 1st 1938

Fife Flyers 1 Dundee Tigers 4

The following evening, the Kirkcaldy public got its first taste of ice hockey when the Tigers deservedly defeated the Flyers in the return exhibition match following similar celebrations to open the new Gallatown rink.

Two miles of cars and thousands of people seeking admission reflected the enormous interest in the rink. Traffic to Gallatown was particularly heavy, and buses were packed. By the time the programme was due to commence at the rink, an audience of 4625 had assembled.

Billy Fullerton was due to compete in one of the speed skating events but was left a spectator as he had injured his collar bone in a training accident. The Flyers were then announced individually by Mr Graham, from Les Lovell, captain and coach down to "Wee Smith", the soon-to-become legendary Bert Smith, the team's mascot.

The visitors, although they lost the first goal, were always the more enterprising team, and it was not long before they were on even terms. The delightful manner in which the Dundee team combined was most effective, and it was on very few occasions that a pass went astray. On the other hand the Flyers were more or less dependent upon individual efforts, and although they succeeded on many occasions in penetrating the visitors defence their shooting was not on the same par as their opponents.

Perhaps the lack of combination play was due to the players not being together long enough as a team. Also that it was understood that the visitors were expected to have one the finest teams in Scotland that season. The Kirkcaldy team took all the honours in the first session, and if it had not been but for the brilliance of Mac Ross in the Dundee goal they might well have been on the lead. It was midway through this period that Norman McQuade, receiving a pass from Tommy Durling, went through on his own and gave the goal-tender no chance with a shot from well out. McQuade therefore had the honour of scoring Flyers first home goal. However, a few minutes later, Dundee were on even terms when Biff Smith netted following a brilliant individual effort.

In the second period Dundee did the bulk of the attacking, but although the Flyers defence was hard pressed they always succeeded in frustrating

Flyers line up on Kirkcaldy Ice for the very first time – without even standing room only available to the crowd.

the visiting efforts. They showed themselves to better advantage at the latter stages of this session, and on two occasions the Tigers were rather lucky to effect clearances from Durling and McQuade when all seemed lost from the visitors point of view.

The final session proved a thrilling affair. Right from the face-off Al Rogers worked his way down the left side and slammed in a terrific angular shot which Chic Kerr did well to stop. Les Lovell, who was showing a keen appreciation of openings, dispossessed Braid, and darted through on his own, but his parting shot went past. After four minutes' play the visitors took the lead, when Smith smacked home a pass from Merrick Cranstoun which gave Kerr no chance.

Following a melée in the home goal zone Rogers further increased the visitors' lead. Kerr, who was unsighted, made no effort to save. Nearing time Dundee got a fourth goal when Jimmy Shannon sent the puck into the net from the neutral zone following a face-off for a previous infringement.

The Flyers tried hard to reduce the leeway, but met with little success, as the visitors' defence was in tip-top form. McQuade, Durling and Len McCartney put in some wonderful stick-work but were inclined to be too selfish. Lovell was a strong resourceful defender and originated most of the attacks, while Kerr gave a grand display in goal. Outstanding for the visitors were George McNeil, Rogers and Jimmy Lightfoot.

Flyers — Kerr (1), Lovell (2), Stover (3), Chappell (6), Durling (5), McInroy (4), reserve attack—McQuade (9), McCartney (8), defence—A. Fullerton (9)

Tigers — Ross (1), Neil (2), Smith (3), Lightfoot (7), Rogers (5), Cranstoun (6), reserves — Mitchell (4), Shannon (9), Braid (10), Hill (8)

Referee—B. Bernie. Glasgow.

So, the Flyers were off and skating. Their first competitive fixture was just five days away with those inaugural hockey nights in Kirkcaldy being a Thursday evening, with a face-off time of 8pm.

Saturday October 2nd 1982

Fife Flyers 1 Dundee Rockets 16

After opening the season with a win against Glasgow Dynamos at home, the Flyers had only one point in their last three outings, so were keen to get things back on track as last season's all conquering Dundee Rockets made their first visit.

The Rockets signed off the Northern Ice Hockey Association era with a clean sweep of the trophies and were favourites for silverware in the inaugural season of the British Ice Hockey Association competition.

It was to be a weekend for lopsided scorelines. The Whitley Warriors travelled the short distance to Sunderland to whip the Crowtree Chiefs 16-5. The Rockets would not only humiliate the Flyers on this night but then returned home and put up the same score line against the visiting Ayr Bruins 24 hours later.

It was a disastrous night for the Flyers, who wrote another line in their history books with their most emphatic ever defeat (at the time of publishing) on home ice. Flyers were without the injured Jim Lynch and Rab Petrie. The game opened with both teams playing good constructive hockey, but after an evenly matched opening 10 minutes the floodgates opened on Flyers. Rockets went ahead through Chris Brinster and quickly added two further goals before Flyers stand-in Canadian Kelly Sproxton pulled one back while the home side were a man short. Gordon MacDougall then had a goal disallowed, but the Dundee side found the net four more times with a crippling three goals coming in the last minute of the period to lead 7-1 at the first buzzer.

A two-minute penalty for Flyers gave Rockets the chance to score their eighth five minutes into the second period and despite frequent attacks on the visitors goal the Kirkcaldy side failed to find the net. Frustration began to play its part and Rockets added three further goals before the second buzzer with Flyers once again short-handed.

Flyers substituted netminder Willie Cottrell with Andy Donald for the third period but he could not halt the deluge and at regular intervals the puck kept hitting the Fife net. The penalties against the now demoralised home side kept piling up and at one point the Flyers had three men in the penalty box but remarkably managed to kill those penalties without losing a goal! In the final 10 minutes the Rockets really rubbed it in with four further goals to bring their tally to 16.

This was the first experience of a "derby" game for imports Kelly Sproxton, Chris Reynolds and Gordon MacDougall and one they, and many Fife fans, would unfortunately not forget in a hurry.

For the record the Rockets scorers were — Roy Halpin (7), Allard Le Blanc (4), Ronnie Wood, Chris Brinster, Jimmy Pennycook, Joe Guilcher with one each and there was even one from Gordon Latto who spent the opening few weeks of the season on Tayside before returning to Fife.

Flyers 1982/3. Back, left to right: Stuart Drummond, Kenny Cruden, Brian Peat.
Middle, left to right: Chic Cottrell, Gordon MacDougall, Neil Abel, Allan Anderson, Kenny Horne, Jim Lynch.
Front, left to right: Dougie Latto, Murray McLellan, Andy Blair, Willie Cottrell, Steven Kirk, Chris Reynolds, Rab Petrie.

Sunday October 3rd 2010

Flintshire Freeze 0 Fife Flyers 12

The main story of the weekend had not been the Flyers comfortable victory over the Welsh side but for a game that did not take place.

Undoubtedly the credibility of ice hockey's Northern League suffered a blow as the Flyers match at Bradford Bulldogs on Saturday was cancelled because the home side could not raise a team. Bradford were one of five new English clubs to join the revamped Northern Ice Hockey League that season, but they had struggled to compete and sat bottom of the table, having lost all four games thus far.

The hosts only cancelled the match by email the day before the game, which was too late to allow several Flyers fans who had already booked accommodation in Bradford to change their plans. Supporters Club chairman Pam Clark explained: "There were a couple of fans that had rooms booked that they couldn't get money back on so they travelled on the Saturday anyway and stayed overnight in Bradford."

Fortunately for the team both the bus company and hotel agreed to waive cancellation charges. Flyers were awarded the double points on offer from the cancelled fixture but Bradford's Northern League future was now uncertain.

Player-coach Todd Dutiaume was less than impressed with the situation.

"It's not ideal because you have plans in place plus fans had booked a bus and you're left having to change things at the last minute," he said. "I'm more worried about the home game, because we're doing all this hard work with community groups and schools to get the rink filled. If a team was to then back out of the game at the last minute that would be a bad thing, not just for the new faces but all our regular fans as well who would be expecting to see a game. We'll just have to wait and see what happens with Bradford. I don't think it bodes well when you're pulling out of fixtures. Hopefully they don't drop out of the league and manage to fulfil the rest of their games."

So it was a frustrated if not rested Flyers who made the long round trip to Deeside on the English/Welsh border on the Sunday to take on

Flintshire Freeze. This was their only trip to that part of the country. As with Bradford and the Sheffield Spartans, the arrangement was that rather than meeting twice, home and away, to play just one game home and away with each game counting for double points.

The hosts were duly humbled despite the visitors missing Steven McAlpine, Josh Scoon, Liam Greig, Chad Reekie and Todd Dutiaume who again stayed behind the bench. Flyers were dominant from the start and rattled in four goals in the first period with Stephen Gunn completing a hat-trick inside nine minutes and Chris Linton also getting on the scoresheet.

The second period was more even as the hosts allowed Fife fewer scoring chances albeit a fine unassisted goal at 21.41 by Daryl Venters took the score to 5-0. A few power plays opportunities provided the hosts with a rare chance to trouble John Nicol's net but the stand-in Fife netminder held onto his shut-out.

A seven-goal salvo in the final period took Fife into double figures for the second time that season. Gunn notched his fourth while Steven Lynch matched his team-mates first period feat by hitting a 12-minute treble. Marc Fowley also bagged a brace while Linton scored his second. Young defenceman Aaron Greger picked up the Man of the Match award for Fife.

Dutiaume added: "Aaron didn't get ice time against Solway last week but he got 30 minutes on Sunday and we saw a lot of good things out of him."

*Stephen Gunn produced
a four goal performance
against the Freeze*

Sunday October 4th 2015

Dundee Stars 2 Fife Flyers 1

After losing their opening game in the Challenge Cup at home to the Braehead Clan, the Flyers had returned straight wins to occupy top spot in the table alongside the Belfast Giants.

Stars were a point behind and, with the Giants inactive in the Cup this weekend, a win for the Stars would see them take over top spot. The visitors' form had been decent so far this season and they had only suffered defeat once in their last five matches and had edged past Manchester Storm in a penalty shootout the night before.

Flyers were left to rue missed opportunities as they lost out in a close game when they failed to convert any of the seven power plays they had on the night — including a six-on-three man advantage in the closing minutes as they withdrew netminder David Brown in pursuit of an equaliser. Associate coach Danny Stewart admitted afterwards: "In a game like that your power play has to be the difference maker and it wasn't."

Flyers made a poor start and fell behind after just 32 seconds when Doug Clarkson caught the visitors sleeping with an unassisted goal. It remained 1-0 to the hosts until 5.21 into the second period when Justin Fox picked up the puck in neutral ice before driving forward and rifling a shot past Vlastimil Lakosil for the equaliser. Flyers had the momentum but the game became a tale of two netminders as both David Brown and Lakosil proved hard to beat as they kept the score line at 1-1.

The game was heading into overtime until a costly give away from Kyle Horne during a line change allowed Brett Switzer to pounce for Stars second and game-winning goal at 56.28. Flyers piled on the pressure and should have taken advantage of a six-on-three power play but came up short.

Stewart added

"It's easy to over dissect a game, but in the end we put ourselves in a position to win a game on the road and a bad line change gave away a goal with four minutes left which ultimately cost us a game." Shayne Stockton also added "We didn't have our best game. Give credit to Dundee they played a good game but we've got to be better on the road. There's no real excuses. We'll learn from it and have good training this week, watch what we did wrong, learn how we can improve and then go from there."

Stockton, who had three goals and five assists on the season, admitted that Flyers failure to take advantage of seven power plays ruined their chances of victory in Dundee.

"One of the big let downs for us was the power play for sure. We had a lot of opportunities and didn't capitalise and that was a big reason why we didn't score more than one goal. We're still getting there it's still a learning process" he said.

TJ Caig attempts to drive the Stars net

Saturday October 5th 1996

NORTHERN PREMIER LEAGUE

Dumfries Vikings 6 Fife Flyers 13

Vikings became the latest side to be ensnared by Flyers, but they must have fancied their chances against the Northern Premier League pacesetters, particularly after Dejan Kostic opened the scoring with the first shot of the match. For 20 minutes they more than matched Flyers and outshot them 12-10 while they created several good chances.

It was anyone's game at the halfway point but then Mark Morrison's side simply put its foot down and zoomed out of sight. The devastation caused by four goals in a little over two minutes was irreversible and a Frank Morris hat-trick was still to come! Vikings slithered out of sight in the final period and departed the ice a well-beaten side.

The game got off to an astonishing start when Kostic scored after 18 seconds. Steven King equalised in 34 seconds! The remainder of the period produced some excellent hockey from both sides and the hosts had a slight edge, thanks largely to the rapier pace of Kostic up front and the strength of fellow Swede Hastan Stromberg on the blue line. The defenceman fired them into a 10th minute lead before Martin McKay took a ten minute misconduct following a brief flare-up but then ex-Flyer Neil Smith lost possession on the red line to Morris who beat Moray Hanson for a short-handed equaliser at 13:52.

A couple of minutes into the second period, Vikings were penalised for having too many men on the ice, which looked rather harsh. The injured Gordon Whyte was holding up traffic as he hobbled through the bench door but with the man advantage Gordon Latto swept home a neat power play strike off Derek King's cross ice pass for 3-2. Flyers lost Frank Morris on a two minute hooking penalty and a ten minute misconduct, and were pulled back to level pegging when Ian Defty netted a screened shot.

And then came the blitz. A series of superb shifts paid off for the second line at 33:35 when Richard Dingwall knocked home from an Andy Samuel rebound. Number five came on the break-away at 34:14 with Steven King carrying the puck and setting up Morrison for a fine finish. Fast forward to 35:47 and Craig Wilson bagged his own rebound and only twelve seconds later a Morrison wraparound finished the swiftest of demolition jobs. Neil Smith had the final say to make it 7-4 before the break but Vikings still headed back to the dressing room looking shell-shocked.

Outshot 21-8 and outplayed, the home side simply had no answer to the relentless pressure which continued with three straight strikes early in the third period. Richard Dingwall made it 8-4 with a great finish at 45:31 and then Morris struck at full stretch after initially losing control of the puck. Smith countered with a goal against Flyers third line at 48:21 but the last ten minutes were dominated by Flyers who threatened to score with every attack. Morris netted twice and Wilson had the final word 48 seconds from time.

Vikings scoring: Neil Smith 2+2, Craig Johnston 1+2, Dejan Kostic 1+1, Ian Defty 1+0, Hakan Stromberg 1+0, Malcolm Bell 0+1, Richard Tasker 0+1, Martin Grubb 0+1, Paul Pentland 0+1.

Flyers scoring: Frank Morris 4+0, Mark Morrison 2+2, Craig Wilson 2+2, Richard Dingwall 2+2, Steven King 1+4, Andy Samuel 1+2. Gordon Latto 1+0, Derek King 0+1, Martin McKay 0+1.

Shots on goal: Vikings (Hanson) 51; Flyers (McKay) 35. Penalty minutes: Vikings 25 Flyers 44

Referee: Alex McWilliam. Crowd: 612.

John Reid bursts through against the Vikings at Kirkcaldy

Sunday October 6th 1968

Fife Flyers 8 Whitley Warriors 9

Flyers let a two-goal lead slip through their fingers to lose their opening match of the season.

They were ahead 7-5 with less than ten minutes left but just couldn't hold out against the Englishmen who turned the match around with four goals in as many minutes. Although the Flyers managed to pull another one back to make the score 9-8 with a minute remaining, they never really looked like snatching the equaliser.

One disappointed fan summed it all up so well when he commented "we could have done with Les Lovell out there" as the free scoring forward was even more noticeable in his absence than he usually was when he was out on the ice.

On the eve of the season the Flyers were shocked when it was confirmed that top scoring Lovell would be going to Murrayfield, stating that while he enjoyed his time at Fife the travelling was an issue for him. This however set alarm bells ringing around the league as such a signing could potentially make the Racers too big a powerhouse.

Youngster George Pearson was signed from Whitley Warriors as the man earmarked to take over Lovell's role, but it would be some time before it was appropriate to determine whether the newcomer was going to fit in. Certainly he took his goal well, but the scoring honours fell to a veteran on the team with Graeme Farrell enjoying a four-goal spree. Farrell was by far and away Flyers best forward. The Gallatown side would undoubtedly be depending upon his experience and skill to a greater degree this season, especially if they were to make a determined effort to compete with the Paisley Mohawks and Murrayfield Racers, who were the clear favourites for honours.

The biggest problems for the Flyers in the match were caused by brothers Terry and Kenny Matthews, who scored five goals between them. It was obvious right from the start that these two were going to trouble the Flyers defence as they were both involved in early raids which brought near misses. But the opening goal came at the other end when Joe Baird netted after help from Norrie Boreham and John Taylor. Flyers lost some of their early fluency after the goal and Warriors capitalised to the full. Terry Matthews levelled the scores and further goals by Tim

Owen and Kenny Matthews put them in front. The home side might have been lacking in the finer points of the game but were more than making up for it with their fighting spirit. Before the end of the first period, goals from Farrell and Baird had squared the game.

When Dave Medd was given a tripping penalty in the second period Warriors once again scored but Flyers were soon back on level terms through Farrell who netted a penalty shot. Back came Warriors and Ernie Clark scored his own second goal and his side's fifth; once again Flyers fought back with goals from Farrell and Pearson putting them ahead in the game. At the end of the period everyone agreed that although the standard of hockey left something to be desired the frantic pace and surfeit of goals made for a most entertaining game.

Into the final period and when Farrell added another goal to make the score 7-5 it really did look like the Flyers were going to go on and win. When many teams would have been content to let the game go the Warriors metaphorically rolled up their sleeves and tried twice as hard. They mounted a blitz on the home goal. Although Ian Nelson, who made his debut in net for the Flyers, played well throughout he couldn't stop shots by the Matthews brothers which levelled the scores.

Kenny Horne was given two minutes in the penalty box for slashing, leaving Flyers facing a hard task to hold on against the now cock-a-hoop visiting side and it was a task which proved to be beyond them. Terry Matthews put them ahead and Clark sealed the game. Home hopes were raised when Jimmy Hunter burst through to reduce the deficit to one but that was as close as the Flyers could get.

Jimmy Hunter who bagged a consolation goal against the Warriors

Tuesday October 7th 1947

Glasgow Bruins 5 Fife Flyers 4

Having won their opening two Autumn Cup matches the Flyers travelled West still without their netminder Babe Scholtz, who was recovering from breaking a bone in his hand; the 'pool reserve' Don Deacon continued to provide cover. Deacon would also play as cover for the Perth Panthers that season. Flyers had to swallow a bitter pill at the Paisley rink, when with just seconds to go the winning goal was scored by ex-Flyer and now Glasgow captain Jim McKenzie.

In the first period Deacon was tested very early by Chic Mann and with the visitors forwards not bringing the puck up ice with much success the Bruins did most of the attacking although their finishing was poor. Girard and Mundell were all over Deacon's net but Bob Londry was on hand to clear a shot and as the puck slid up ice to Ted Fowler he and Roy Hawkins had Belanger sprawling on the ice but could not convert.

Another goalmouth melée at Deacon's cage didn't bring the home team the desired result; when Floyd Snider poke checked the puck from Mann and skated up on his own, Belanger was equal to his effort. Deacon was settling down nicely and when he thwarted Jim McKenzie the play once again swung the other way; Les O'Rourke drew the defence and skated in on Belanger before flicking the puck over to the junior Bert Smith, who was making his first appearance of the season. He chose the right spot to give the Flyers the lead.

Into the second period and Flyers were the first to attack but it was Linter who tested Deacon at the other end with a shot. Hawkins and McKenzie both took two minute penalties for high sticks and then Wally Goodwin, Bruin's best defenceman, also received two minutes for tripping Cliff Ryan. On the power play Ryan skated for goal and lady luck smiled on Belanger, who somehow made the save before Mundell evened the score from a Chic Mann assist. The home side pressed for the go ahead goal and when Deacon lost sight of the puck Gecan flashed number two past him.

Gecan then took a trip to the cooler for charging Bob Londry and this gave the visitors the chance to level when Fowler sent a pass over to Jimmy Mitchell who steadied himself before slotting home. The

Bruins retaliated; Deacon's goal was under bombardment by Mann and company and it was no surprise when Goodwin whipped the puck over to Mann to put the Bruins ahead once more. They stretched their lead in the 15th minute when Mundell hit in a lovely shot at Deacon who failed to hold it and it somehow found the back of the net.

The home team were out to increase their lead at the start of the third, but it was the Flyers who scored next when Bill Bradbury with blood streaming from cut near his eye flicked the puck past the defence to Ryan who made no mistake. It was now the visitors turn to turn up the heat and Fowler and Hawkins both produced great stops from Belanger before Bob Londry and Goodwin accompanied each other to the penalty box for roughing; they were joined by Mundell, who was assessed two minutes for chopping, as it was described in the match report.

At the change-over Flyers were still lying one goal behind but they levelled when O'Rourke flew up the wing and his pass to Ryan was converted. Then came the heart-breaker for Flyers when McKenzie cracked the defence in a goal-or-nothing effort and he beat Deacon to the puck to slide it home. Right on time Snider had Flyers last effort.

Glasgow Bruins — Adrian Belanger, Wally Goodwin, Don Hibbs, Jim McKenzie, Chic Mann, Gary Hassim, Andre Girard, Ronald Lintner, Bill Mundell, Jack Gecan, Bob Lantz.

Fife Flyers — Don Deacon, Bob Londry, Floyd Snider, Bert Smith, Pat Good, Jimmy Mitchell, Les O'Rourke, Cliff Ryan, Bill Bradbury, Ted Fowler, Roy Hawkins

Flyers two goal man against Glasgow Bruins — Cliff Ryan

Saturday October 8th 1988

HEINEKEN PREMIER LEAGUE

Fife Flyers 15 Solihull Barons 2

Having failed by a single point to qualify for the next stages of the Norwich Union Cup the Flyers made a solid start on the opening night of their Premier League campaign. The two points were never really in any doubt against a poor Solihull Barons effort.

Since stepping up into the top league the Barons had enjoyed only one win in their ten meetings with the Flyers. With the home side already four up before the Barons opened their account it didn't look as though tonight would see an improvement in that record. Essentially the two goals scored against the home team were more isolated incidents than any concerted and serious pressure by the visitors who were simply outclassed. Flyers covered the rink far more efficiently and always with a man to receive or intercept a pass; with those two exceptions, when the visitors did go on the offensive the home team handled the attack coolly and quickly.

The Flyers were missing Blair Page, who had his original three game ban doubled to six for an incident in the Ayr game the previous weekend, but they went ahead when Dean Edmiston opened the scoring with a power play goal in the fifth minute before he hit a second less than a minute later when the visiting netminder was caught out of position. Gordon Goodsir and Ronnie Wood both reached the back of the net before Barons Tim Flannagan pushed in a power play goal in the 17th minute. Despite that lapse the first period ended with Flyers in control and Vincent Lukac scored the first of his trio in the 19th minute.

The second period saw no respite for the visitors with Jim Lynch putting in the first within two minutes of the restart after an almost static game of 'pig in the middle' which totally bemused the Solihull side. That opened up a goal bonanza for the Fifers with five more converted while the visitors seldom had a look-in despite trying valiantly. Lukac scored on another two power plays during the period which notched up the first hat-trick of the game with Ronnie Wood potting another and Jindrich Kokrment slipping in two more including a very impressive backward clip which took everyone by surprise.

Quick reactions from Milan Figala meant Flyers opened the third period with a short-handed goal in the fourth minute, when netminder

Ian Woodward sent the puck over the back of the net. Fielded almost instantly by Lukac, he flipped it to Figala's feet in time to slam it home before the goalie knew it was there. Five minutes later Goodsir scored his second of the match and, keeping up the almost constant attack, Wood completed his hat-trick just over a minute later.

After opening the scoring in the first period Edmiston closed the book for Flyers less than five minutes from the end to complete the home team's third hat-trick of the match. It was little consolation to Barons and of no consequence to the Flyers that Dominick Hardy finally scored their second and final goal 90 seconds from the buzzer.

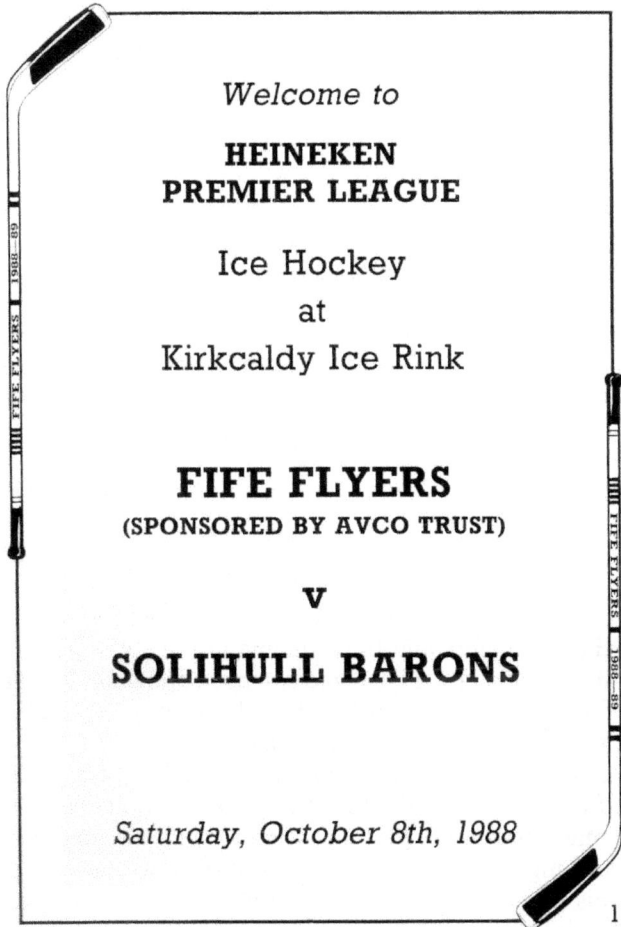

Welcome to

**HEINEKEN
PREMIER LEAGUE**

Ice Hockey
at
Kirkcaldy Ice Rink

FIFE FLYERS
(SPONSORED BY AVCO TRUST)

v

SOLIHULL BARONS

Saturday, October 8th, 1988

1

The match programme for the visit of the Solihull Barons as the Flyers got their Golden Jubilee season underway

Sunday October 9th 1966

Fife Flyers 7 Durham Hornets 1

A new season, a new league set up. The Northern League (initially known as the Scottish League) was launched. The League developed out of the far more limited Scottish League which had been established in 1962 and which by 1965 saw a regular but limited schedule played.

That summer the better British teams, mostly in Scotland, agreed to form a league to provide matches throughout the season. Initially, eight teams joined the Flyers with Paisley Mohawks, Murrayfield Racers, Glasgow Dynamos, Durham Wasps, Whitley Warriors, Ayr Bruins and Perth Blackhawks who, along with Paisley Vikings, played all of their games on the road for double points.

The Spring Cup served as the Northern League playoffs but would not be contested in the inaugural season. Flyers got the new season off to a promising start with a convincing win over Durham Hornets, who would later revert to being known as the Wasps. The team which took the ice wasn't last year's Flyers but, given time to apply some polish and — in the case of the younger members — experience, the new-look Flyers side, it was thought, could provide some real thrills and surprises in the coming months.

Although play at times was scrappy and many moves just didn't quite come off, there was excitement a-plenty for the fans and the game was by no means as one-sided as the score suggested. Hornets proved no easy meat for the new Fifers and the outcome of the game was never really certain until the very end. Flyers had two good attacking forwards in Bert Smith and Les Lovell but even they found difficulty in penetrating what looked at times to be an iron-hard Durham defence.

Flyers took an early lead, through Les Lovell, with a clever solo run through after only three minutes of play; five minutes later Bert Smith put the home side two up after a passing move between Jimmy Watson and 'Pep' Young had taken the puck well up into the visitors defence zone. At this stage Hornets began a forceful fight-back and it was ironic to note that just when it looked as though they were about to pull one back Flyers got their third goal when returnee 'Pep Young netted a swift Joe McIntosh pass.

The Durham side looked a lot more promising in the second period and in the 24th minute Pete Johnson flicked the puck past netminder Roy Reid after Frank O'Connor had taken it well up the ice. The Smith-Lovell combination again began to come into its own and in the 31st minute Les netted from Bert's pass. Shortly afterwards Durham defender Dougie Milner was given a two-minute penalty for interference but even with the extra man the Flyers found themselves faced with a difficult task in trying to find a chink in the visitors defence.

A chink however they did eventually find as they netted a further three times in the final period. Three minutes into the last stanza player-coach Bill Sneddon netted in grand fashion and three minutes later Bert Smith got his second and Flyer's sixth. Four minutes from the end youngster Danny Brown got goal number seven during a goalmouth skirmish. This had been a well-deserved win for a Flyers side which, although lacking in the punch and sparkle which was a feature of last season's side, had shown more than enough promise for the season ahead.

Flyers opening line up for 1966/67 season
Back Row ,left to right: Pep Young, Les Lovell, Danny Brown, Bill Sneddon,
Bert Smith, Jimmy Watson, John Taylor, Joe McIntosh
Front Row, left to right: Roy Reid, Kenny Horne, Dave Medd, Alistair
Crombie, Hugh Taylor

Friday October 10th 2014

ELITE ICE HOCKEY LEAGUE & CHALLENGE CUP

Braehead Clan 4 Fife Flyers 3

In a game played for both League and Challenge Cup points a capacity crowd of 3500 saw Braehead Clan edge past Fife in a cracking seven-goal game, to gain a measure of revenge for the Flyers earlier 4-0 win that season. It was the first of a gruelling three games in three nights for the visitors as they would also meet the Nottingham Panthers away and at home the next two nights.

First up, a derby match that had in the past produced many fireworks, but instead of the chirping and niggling the fierce rivals focussed on hockey and there was precious little to separate them. Clan had all the early pressure and the line led by Scott Pitt looked potent but once again they encountered netminder Kevin Regan in rock-solid form. When mistakes created openings for Clan he came to the rescue. The Flyers were often guilty of carelessly throwing the puck around and onto a Clan stick which put them under pressure at times during the game.

It was a night when the specialist teams came into their own with five of the seven goals coming on the power play and Clan's were courtesy of the highly predatory Scott Pitt and Neil Trimm partnership. Flyers got the go-ahead goal at 13:20 as Fitzgerald sat a roughing minor and Ned Lukacevic swept the puck home from the right. Clan replied at 16:28 with Matt Nickerson sitting for hooking Leigh Salters and Pitt followed Ned's move with a one-time shot home from the wing.

There was little between the teams throughout the second period, with great chances at either end but hot goal-tending and some solid defensive work along the blue lines kept the score tied. Clan went ahead at 26:35 when Ryan Kavanagh did well to block the puck on the point and keep it in the zone; when his shot came off Regan, Trimm was all alone at the back post to stuff it in. Two minutes later Fife were back on level terms as Jamie Milam's slapshot flew off a stick and the deflection deceived Jones. Lukacevic was called for boarding Derek Roehl at 36:30 and once again Clan's power play produced as Pitt swept the puck home from the right for 3-2.

Flyers had some golden chances to reply with Matt Reber setting up Scott Fleming at the back post but he couldn't finish. Reber found space in the defensive zone as he weaved around players, only to move one step too many before shooting and allowed Jones to stand strong. The home fans were back on their feet at 50:43 as Clan went 4-2 up. Kyle Haines pass out of defence was poor and went straight to a Braehead stick and Tristan Harper's finish was clinical.

Once again Flyers responded with a piece of Lukacevic magic which set up Fleming whose shot completely deceived Jones on the power play at 53:13. As the clock wound down Fife upped the pressure considerably and pulled Regan with 70 seconds to go and they played out the rest of the game in Clan's zone. Both sides called time outs in the dying seconds but Fife couldn't force the match into overtime.

Tommy Muir whose steady blueline performances had him sitting top of the Mirror of Merit Award

Saturday October 11th 1975

Fife Flyers 5 Murrayfield Racers 5

First leg deadlock but...

This was the first leg of the Spring Cup Final which had been held over from the previous 1974/75 season. It provided the crowd at the Gallatown rink with a cracker of a game which finished in deadlock with plenty of goals to remember. Flyers lined up minus Ally Brennan while Racers were without winger Willie Kerr.

It was the home team who got off to the best possible start with Law Lovell tucking the puck into the Racers net after only 27 seconds. The same player found himself in the penalty box before the first minute was over, giving Racers their first power play, but the Flyers survived before brother Les put the Flyers two up with five minutes of the first period left — only for Racers to cut the deficit right on the buzzer. Flyers netminder Johnny Pullar could only deflect a Gordon Inglis shot into his own net.

Racers started the second session as Flyers started the first and Inglis rifled in a long shot for the equaliser. A minute later with the Flyers on the penalty kill captain Les Lovell restored the lead as he bulged the net for a shorthanded goal. A cracker of a shot from Derek Reilly as he skated in on net gave Pullar no chance and once again the score was levelled. As the fans warmed to the cut-throat pace of this match Kenny Horne crowned his best performance for some time when he despatched a rebound off the keeper's pads into the back of the net. Only for Racers to come back once again, as 20 seconds later Freddie Wood put his side back on level terms. In the closing minutes of the second period Dougie Latto stuck one in the Racers net, and for the fourth time in the match Flyers were in front.

The crowd were back in their seats for the start of a pulsating final period, anxious to see if the Flyers could increase their slender lead but Willie Clark denied any addition in the goals tally with fine saves from the Lovell brothers. There was a sucker punch in the closing minutes, as Wood broke away to take an opportunist goal to level the scores yet again and leave the destination of the Cup seemingly finely poised.

Flyers put Racers on ice to lift the Spring Cup with some Murrayfield magic the following night as they really went to town in the second leg as they swamped Racers in a capital display. Flyers had Brennan back in the line-up as the sides resumed their battle. Les Lovell opened the scoring but instead of the Racers hitting back it was the Flyers who followed up with goals from big John Taylor, Lawrie Lovell and Dougie Latto.

A further four goals in the second stanza from the sticks of the Lovell brothers, Alex Churchill and Latto left the Racers sagging. Their only crumb of comfort came five minutes from the end of the period when they were awarded a penalty shot that Wood converted to rob Pullar of a well deserved shutout.

The final period proved to be academic with a further two goals in the first three minutes bringing up double figures and Lawrie Lovell got his hat-trick followed by a carbon-copy goal from Taylor. If this was the sort of performance the Flyers were going to turn in this season then the message was "Come back, hockey fans! The good old days have returned."

Law Lovell is up ended as he crashes the Racers net

Saturday October 12th 1974

Fife Flyers 9 Glasgow Dynamos 5

After a sequence of six defeats which stretched back to last season the Flyers finally broke their run. Glasgow Dynamos, who were in the habit in recent years of surrendering the points on Kirkcaldy ice, went down to their eighth consecutive defeat.

This was by far Flyers best performance of the season so far — a convincing victory over a much-improved Glasgow side, who had been very unlucky the previous weekend to lose to a very late goal at Murrayfield. Play moved from end to end in the opening stages. When Alex Churchill was sent to the penalty box, the visitors seized the opportunity to open their account through their Canadian forward Dino Befus. Flyers levelled the score when Lawrie Lovell found the net unassisted but a minute later Flyers found themselves behind again when a shot was deflected into the net. Things began to look bleak for the home lot in the 13th minute when Dynamos made it 3-1 while, incredibly, they were two men understrength and Martin Shields picked up the puck on the center line and went on to score a fine opportunist goal.

The loss of that goal seemed to put some bite into Flyers play and Ian Nelson in the visitors goal was by far the busier of the two keepers. With the period drawing to a close the Flyers made a vital breakthrough with Les Lovell shooting the puck through a ruck of bodies to make it 3-2.

Penalties were proving costly to Flyers and early in the second period Befus increased his side's lead to two goals when they were a man short. Flyers slowly regained their composure and once again were the team that was doing all of the pressing although they continued to scorn chances as they had done in the first period.

With 10 minutes on the clock Les Lovell eventually brought Flyers back into contention with a goal which heralded the start of a real purple patch for the home side. Firstly Joe McIntosh made it 4-4 with a rasping shot from the blue-line and then John Taylor put the Flyers ahead for the first time — not only in the match but after 153 minutes of ice hockey this season they were in the lead in a game!

The defence was now looking well in control of the Dynamos attack and helping set up the Flyers attacks with some great passes and from one of these Les Lovell was set free to score his hat-trick and give Flyers a 6-4 interval lead.

The third period saw the home team continue to dominate with Dynamos unable to be nearly as dangerous as they had been in the earlier parts of the match. Unsurprisingly, the next goal came from the Flyers, when Norrie Boreham increased the lead to three goals in the ninth minute. Somewhat unexpectedly, however, the visitors were given a little spark of encouragement when Alan Lavery beat netminder Pullar rather easily to make it 7-5.

However, this didn't alter the course of the match and a minute later Gus Cargill, with a rather nifty piece of play, dispatched the puck behind Nelson. It was enough to earn Gus the Mirror of Merit award for the week. After successfully captaining the Kestrels last season he had gradually worked his way into the Flyers team and his confidence was evidently growing, with a performance which showed good all-round positional play capped off with a well taken first-ever goal. It was then left to team captain Les Lovell to round off the scoring with his own fourth goal and Flyers ninth.

Flyers 1974-75
Back, left to right: Jack Latto, Jimmy Bell, John Taylor, Dougie Latto, Alex Churchill, Kenny Horne, Angus Cargill, Lawrie Lovell, Jimmy Jack, Joe McIntosh, Harry Cottrell
Front, left to right: Gordon Latto, Jimmy Hunter, Willie Cottrell, John Pullar, Norrie Boreham, Les Lovell, Chic Cottrell

Sunday October 13th 1968

Autumn Cup
Paisley Mohawks 8 Fife Flyers 4

The truth of it was that these were two teams at opposite ends of the hockey spectrum that season. Flyers crashed 8-4 to the Mohawks in their second Autumn Cup match.

The Mohawks had been the top team last season having retained their Northern League crown and were going to challenge once again for honours. While the Flyers had finished runners up in the league last term, they had an already wretched record against the West Coast side, having only one win in their last 10 games. This would be stretched by another seven games before Paisley would taste defeat against the men from Fife.

Unfortunately, that season Paisley weren't the only side the Flyers had difficulty beating! The home side were in command for most of the game and it was only by maximising their few opportunities that the Flyers put a better complexion on the score line. The Mohawks attacked strongly during the first period but they were held at bay by a determined Flyers defence in which netminder Ian Nelson was outstanding. The period ended goalless.

Nelson had signed from Glasgow in the summer, as replacement for Roy Reid as the senior goalie, and his performances that season could at best be described as inconsistent. He turned in some brilliant displays against the Canadian touring sides, as well as on the road at Paisley and Murrayfield, but there were times at home where fans would despair of him saving the simplest of shots. Perhaps not a fair reflection, because in truth the whole team that season struggled and never did come to terms with the loss of Les Lovell to Edinburgh on the eve of the season.

In the opening minutes of the second period, Norrie Boreham had a chance to put the Kirkcaldy side into the lead, but his shot was saved by the Paisley netminder Billy Laird. Finally the visitors resistance was broken as the home side went on to take a 3-0 lead in a two-minute burst with goals from Jackson McBride, Gordie Hughes and John Connor.

Flyers fought back hard and reduced the leeway with clever individual goals from wee George Pearson and Graeme Farrell but Alistair McCrae kept the Mohawks well in front when he scored their fourth goal. Pearson, who had moved to the area by taking up a job at Rosyth, was never going to fill the skates of Les Lovell but was the most effective of the newcomers. His bustling play soon won him the affection of the Fife fans along with another, George Wylie, an ex-Perth Panthers defenceman who played well enough but lacked speed and was unable to train regularly with the team.

The Mohawks maintained their pressure on the Fife defence in the third period and fully deserved the four goals they slammed home Although Sammy McDonald replied with two fine solo goals, which capped a great game for him, the visitors were unable to break through again.

A mid-December reshuffle saw the waygoing of the Perth trio of McDonald, Farrell and Wylie. They were replaced by some of the Fife Juniors, who brought a wave of fresh enthusiasm to the team. By the end of the season you could only feel sympathy for coach Joe McIntosh who, week after week, played his heart out in an attempt to lift the team by the boot straps. An effort that it was pleasing to see recognised in his selection for Scotland and a place in the All-Star 'A' team despite his charges finishing last in everything.

John 'Bernie' McCrone in GB action against France in 1992

Sunday October 14th 1962

Fife Flyers 5 Ayr Rangers 2

After dropping out of the British National League seven years ago the Flyers finally came back out of cold storage on the day that saw the commencement of the Cuban Missile Crisis.

It was a completely different hockey landscape in the country now from the fully professional game that had gone bang the previous decade as they faced off in the newly launched Scottish League, which was a fully amateur league founded by eight teams playing in two sections:

Section A: Ayr Rangers, Flyers and Murrayfield Royals would play each other twice home and away.

Section B: Paisley Mohawks, Durham Wasps, Glasgow Flyers, Perth Blackhawks and new addition Paisley Vikings, who were all without home ice and would travel twice to each of the Section A rinks and play for double points.

This was the first ice hockey league to be formed in either England or Scotland since the demise of the British National League in 1960. For the past two seasons only home tournaments had been played throughout Great Britain. It was modest in its outlook, but it gave the players a chance to lace up their skates and Kirkcaldy ice rink rocked to the cheers of 1600 excited spectators. The crowd was treated to a clean fast-moving brand of ice hockey as both teams were out to provide a thrilling opening to the new season.

The Flyers attacked the Ayr net in the opening minutes but their shots were too hurried and goaltender Billy Laird was able to deal with them without too much difficulty. As the home forwards slowly began to settle down they looked much more dangerous characters and there were a number of close calls, but over-eagerness prevented the Kirkcaldy team from opening the scoring.

Led by the two McCallum brothers, the West of Scotland team tested Johnny Pullar in the Kirkcaldy net with a few dangerous shots. When the Ayrshire line lost Hughes for two minutes for elbowing, it looked as if Flyers would break through, but the visitors put up a solid defence. Just after Gordie Hughes re-joined the line they opened the scoring through Walter Campbell in the 13th minute when Johnny Pullar left his net to smother a loose puck and it was flipped over his head to Campbell in front of the open goal. Reeling from the opener the Flyers lapsed again and Alex McCallum added to the Ayr total 30 seconds later.

The home side once again went on the power play when Archie McCallum received a two minute boarding penalty but Ayr stood firm. The second period was the slowest of the game but the Flyers, playing with more authority, cut the Ayr lead with a goal from 'Pep' Young who was assisted by Jerry Hudson in the 12th minute. Rangers had a chance to increase their lead when the Kirkcaldy line lost Dave Cook for two minutes on a tripping penalty but failed to breach the Flyers defence.

The pace increased again for the third period, the fastest and most exciting of the game, when the Flyers really came into their own and completely outplayed their opponents. Jerry Hudson equalised from Bert Smith in the fifth minute and Young put the Kirkcaldy side ahead with an unassisted goal five minutes later. Cook added another from an Andy Napier assist in the 16th minute before the visitors made a last-ditch effort to regain their lost lead. Archie McCallum led the rush and he pulled one back.

The Flyers turned up the power and Bert Smith picked up the puck behind his own blueline and carried over centre ice leading the Flyers rush in a single handed effort. With two Ayr defencemen back checking he crossed the Ayr blue line and unleashed a tremendous drive which ended in the top left hand corner of the net. A fitting goal to provide an exciting climax to a game which kept the spectators tense throughout.

After the game Pep Young was asked what he thought about how the game had gone in the early stages and whether the opposition might be too strong. He replied "There were still two periods left. The game was not over by any means". That was his attitude throughout and earned him the first Mirror of Merit Award for the week since 1955.

A quartet of the Flyers 1962/63 squad — Verne 'Bones' Greger, Harold 'Pep' Young, Andy Napier and Joe McIntosh

Tuesday October 15th 2002

CALEDONIAN CUP

Fife Flyers 3 Scottish Eagles 5

It was an eight-minute spell in the second period that proved costly for Flyers in their opening Caledonian Cup match. In that time the Ice Hockey Superleague Scottish Eagles bagged four goals which effectively sealed the win, although Flyers were never out-played.

Indeed, they matched their higher ranked opponents — who iced eight imports along with British players Jonathan Weaver and Paddy Ward and a bunch of kids from Paisley — all the way.

Over 40 minutes they would have won the game 1-0 had they avoided the middle session problems. The first period was played at a hectic pace and took only 24 minutes to complete with hardly any stoppages. Flyers created the better chances and Mark Morrison, John Haig and Jason Dailey were all denied one-on-one by netminder Eoin McInerney while Steve Briere had to look sharp at the other end to stop efforts from Dino Bauba and Mike Harding.

Neither Steve Roberts nor Frank Morris were able to continue after the break and this meant Flyers had to switch things around and that may have contributed to the sudden goal glut in the second period. Mike Harding opened the scoring from dose range at 22.01 but then picked up a roughing minor to go with Bauba's high sticks call and Flyers equalised with the two-man advantage at 27.16 with Davie Smith knocking in Morrison's pass. Eagles showed glimpses of their attacking style and one such quick break restored their lead at 31.27 when Jeff Williams converted Harding's pass.

However, almost immediately, youngster Alain Campbell picked up a tripping penalty and Flyers took just 12 seconds to level the game again with Morrison's attempted pass going in off the netminder at his near post. Luck turned against the home side when a speculative effort by Harding bounced into the air and rebounded into the net off Daryl Venters at 34.42 and just 13 seconds later Jonathan Weaver blasted a shot high past the glove of Briere.

When Williams netted his second and Eagles fifth 28 seconds from the interval it appeared to be game over and the final period saw the visitors content to sit on their lead. A superb finish by Karry Biette at 47.18 when he fired low past McInerney from the point produced the only goal of the final period but Flyers kept battling away and were unlucky not to reduce the gap on a number of occasions although Eagles also had their chances. Despite two late power play opportunities the Flyers couldn't add to their tally and it was the Eagles who made a winning start to the competition.

Flyers scoring: Morrison 1+2, Biette 1+1, Smith 1+0, Dutiaume 0+2, Haig 0+1.
Eagles scoring: Harding 2+2, Williams 2+1, Weaver 1+1, Marble 0+2, Swiatek 0+1, Quinnell 0+1. SOGs: Flyers (Briere) 43, Eagles (McInerney) 33. PIMs: Flyers 0. Eagles 10.
Ref: Neil Wilson. Attendance: 1070.

So, the very first game against the Scottish Eagles, but looking back through the history books now it's as though it never took place. The result was later expunged. The short but tumultuous existence of the Eagles came to an end a month later. Having made the move from Ayr to the Braehead Arena at the start of the season because the owners thought it would generate greater interest in the team, they also dropped the name Ayr but they managed to only complete six Superleague home games before folding. In what was the last season of the Superleague Manchester Storm would become the second team to go bust before it ended. Jonathan Weaver returned to Kirkcaldy when he signed for the Flyers in January after a short spell at Hull.

Flyers Karry Biette in action against Scottish Eagles Mike Harding

Sunday October 16th 1977

Murrayfield Racers 4 Fife Flyers 2

Flyers 100 per cent record on the season was ended at Murrayfield after they had started the season with 6 straight wins.

It was also the Racers' first success against their rivals in around 18 months and ended a sequence of 13 consecutive Flyers victories across all competitions. About 1000 fans were in attendance, which was reportedly the biggest crowd to see ice hockey in the Scottish capital since the commencement of the Northern Ice Hockey Association competitions.

Going a long way towards laying their bogey the home side had inspired performances by ex-Dundee man Jimmy Pennycook and ex-Flyers goaltender John Pullar.

Flyers, who were weakened in defence, started the game at quite a strong pace. Charlie Kinmond put them ahead with a well-executed score but Racers first power play of the night paid dividends when defenceman Bobby Hay playing at point rifled one home from the blue line. This brought the scoring to an end in what had been a very evenly contested first period.

In the second period Flyers almost regained the lead when a shot from Les Lovell smashed off the post with Pullar well beaten. Straight from the rebound, the Racers gained possession and moved swiftly towards Flyers goal where Jock Hay netted from close range. This gave the home team confidence and Flyers were kept pinned in defence for the rest of the period. The home side took control of the match when Willie Cottrell, who topped the goalie stats in the competition, made his only mistake of the night to let a blue-line shot from Ian McMillan slip through his glove and into the net.

Flyers had it all to do as they went into the last period behind by two goals but the travelling support were heartened when Chic Cottrell crashed home a shot to reduce the leeway. With just two minutes left for play they were nearly back on level terms when Gordon Latto missed an open net.

As the seconds ticked away the visitors were forced to kill a penalty but even then they went all out for an equaliser and Lawrie Lovell almost made it with 20 seconds left on the clock only to be denied once again by

Pullar, who made the save of the night from his close range shot. When the puck was cleared, it left Pennycook completely in the clear to race up ice and finally put the game beyond Flyers reach.

Flyers had a rest weekend seven days later. That allowed attention to focus on Kirkcaldy Kestrels. After two warm up matches, where they won one and lost one against the Glasgow Redwings, they would open their Second League programme with a home match against Whitley Braves

Just like buses the Racers had waited so long for their first win but their next win against Flyers came in the Flyers next game. The Racers won 7-5 at Kirkcaldy, and the destination of the Autumn Cup was settled, with the current holders relinquishing their defence to the Edinburgh side.

Flyers 1977-78
Back row, left to right: John Taylor, Jimmy Bell, Gordon Latto, Dougie Latto, Brian Peat, Kenny Horne, Dave Medd, Law Lovell, Jack Latto.
Front row, left to right: Joe McIntosh, Ally Brennan, Jimmy Jack, John Pullar, Les Lovell, Chic Cottrell, Rab Petrie, John Grant.

Saturday October 17th 2009

Fife Flyers 7 Charlestown Chiefs 0

Flyers finally turned on the style in front of their home crowd following some less than enthralling recent encounters for the visit to Kirkcaldy by the Chiefs.

The Charlestown Chiefs were not to be confused with those of the Hanson Brothers fame and were in fact the Latvian Hawks, who the Flyers had met several times over the last two seasons. The move had nothing to do with the movie *Slapshot* but simply the team who had previously been based in Dundalk would now be sponsored by Charlestown on Ice who ran the skating arena in Dublin which was now their new home.

The game was keenly contested and a much better advert of the hockey at this level as both teams played and hit hard. All three Flyers lines contributed to this win; Flyers strength in depth was a common feature of their seasons in the second tier league, while the high octane performances of the likes of Todd Dutiaume and Andy Samuel provided flashbacks of the glory years.

It was the Canadian player-coach who set the tone on 2.41 with an unassisted goal following a trademark dash towards the net. A second unassisted goal on the power play from Samuel was Flyers reward for a fired-up start. Chiefs were not prepared to be pushed around and the home players had to stand up and be counted in the physical battle. Steven McAlpine went toe-to-toe with the bullish Sergejs Selenkovs which saw both sit out 2+2+10 penalties.

Flyers made another power play count in the final minute of the period when Samuel fired home his second of the night. At 3-0 up, the norm so far that season was for Flyers to take a rest, and let the opposition find a way back into the match, but there was no letting up in this one. Flyers returned in the second period clearly eager for more goals.

They fired 19 shots at Deniss Kureless during the middle period which returned another two goals. Willie Nicolson skated half the length of the rink to set up Iain Bell from behind the net for a first-time finish on 22.08. Blair Daly made a stunning reflex save from a ferocious Jozef Hruska slapshot on 34 minutes when he tipped a howitzer onto the bar. Flyers all but wrapped up the game by the end of the second as Samuel latched onto Dutiaume's pass for his hat-trick on 39.45.

Flyers kept up the relentless pressure in the third stanza, with two clinical Stephen Gunn finishing off yet more good build-up work from Dutiaume. This was easily the best Flyers had played at home so far that season against a team that could have caused damage had it been allowed to. Steven Lynch Fife's assistant player/coach, said afterwards

"We wanted the win and we got it. We played well against the Chiefs and the performance was by far our best this season. I spoke to a few people after the game and they suggested that Chiefs didn't bring much to the table but that is taking away from the fact that we played really well. We controlled the game from start to finish and we now hope we've turned a corner."

The game marked a return to goal-scoring form for Andy Samuel. His hat-trick ensured that 'Sammy' had a big say in the Flyers win and a delighted Samuel said post match

"I thought we played well. It all came from during the week. We spoke about things we needed to improve on at training and everybody came in focused and knew what we had to do. Everybody came in with the attitude that we'd have to work a lot harder. We haven't really put in a good home performance this season so far but we went out and did that. We just need to keep it going now. Charlestown were a physical side but did not have the quality to break down Fife. They came out pretty hard but everybody in our team turned up we put the effort in and played as a team. It's always nice to score a few goals. Sometimes you can go a few weeks without scoring goals, even if you're playing well. I'm not one of the top goalscorers but when you're getting chances and scoring goals it gives you more confidence."

Iain Bell taking some punishment from the visiting Charlestown Chiefs

Sunday October 18th 1964

Brighton Tigers 11 Fife Flyers 2

Flyers received their biggest hammering since the return of hockey in 1962. Indeed, the only time the Flyers had conceded double figures during that time had been at the hands of the Brighton Tigers on their last visit to the South Coast last season.

The pattern continued after this latest shellacking. In their next three visits to the SS Brighton rink later that season they also conceded double figures twice more. These games were all in the Cobley Cup which was Brighton's home tournament, run along similar lines as the Flyers Skol Cup and the team with the best record against the Tigers would advance to the final. You will be unsurprised to hear it wasn't the Flyers; however, the Tigers mopped the floor with all comers and won all 11 of their matches while outscoring the opposition 107-47.

In what would, ultimately, be the last season for Tigers they were still able to draw sell-out 2500 crowds with fans clearly showing that they were not tiring of seeing so little competition in these matches. The smaller ice surface of the English rink had always unsettled the Kirkcaldy side where a decade ago they had lost in two of their three visits, having won the first ever meeting of the sides at the Tigers rink in season 1954-55.

It would have been easy to lay the blame squarely on the shoulders of netminder Roy Reid but his performance alone was no excuse considering the magnitude of their defeat. The Fife netminder saw action right from the start and the Tigers Scottish forward trio of Jackie Dryburgh, Les Lovell and Red Imrie gave him little respite. Tigers hit the target in the second minute of the match and were three goals up inside eleven minutes. Flyers countered through Lawrie Lovell with assists to Bert Smith and Graeme Farrell but Tigers added a fourth goal before the session ended.

The visitors were again outskated in the second session and retired seven goals down with little likelihood of getting back on level terms. In the final twenty minutes Flyers scored a second goal through Bert Smith following a set up by Lawrie Lovell which gave the veteran forward his first goal of the season but another three goals from Tigers saw them coast home easy winners. The Flyers normally potent first forward line of Ian Forbes, Jimmy Spence and Sammy McDonald failed to find the net and it was left to Flyers second line led by Smith and Lovell to make some semblance of a stand against the English side.

Seven of Tigers goals were scored by the Scots members of the team with hat-tricks for Kirkcaldy born Jackie Dryburgh — who was affectionately referred to by the Brighton fans as the "Wee McGregor" on account of his size and middle name — and Les Lovell, also got three when he won the battle of the brothers against younger sibling Lawrie. Falkirk born player-coach Thomas 'Red' Imrie who had started his career with Falkirk, Murrayfield and Paisley before moving south of the border scored once and to complete the rout there were doubles for Rupe Fresher and John Baxter. Flyers would have a chance to get revenge for this heavy defeat when the Tigers visited Kirkcaldy in the Skol Cup a few weeks later.

The optimistic words of the Brighton Tigers programme for the visit of Flyers who were humbled

152

Thursday October 19th 1950

Fife Flyers 2 Dunfermline Vikings 0

An Al Campone goal three minutes from time followed by an all-out Vikings power play brought the spectators to their feet for the closing minutes of play at Kirkcaldy Ice Rink. Flyers narrowly defeated Vikings to maintain their undefeated home record, following one of the most gruelling and exciting encounters to be staged at the Gallatown Stadium that season.

Hero of the match was 'Pete' Belanger. On the sounding of the final gong, he was absolutely mobbed by his grateful colleagues, after giving a most accomplished and entertaining display. Recording his first shut out of the season was a brilliant achievement considering the speed and intensity of the exchanges. Belanger, after an early attack of nerves, settled down to give one of his most spectacular and efficient performances on record. While he took most of the plaudits, Jimmy Burnett, who had been rather subdued since joining Flyers, was catapulted into the limelight by dishing out bodychecks that put the renowned Syme brothers into the shade. Leading the blue-line he appeared to revel in bouncing the diminutive but fiery Dunfermline forwards who, long before the end, were doing all in their power to give him a wide berth.

However, with astute Coach Al Rogers interchanging his defencemen with monotonous regularity, the Vikings forwards found to their dismay that if they were not laced by the hard-hitting Burnett they were opposed by the equally hard-checking Verne Greger or the genius of the stick-poking art Floyd Snider.

While most of the credit goes to the defence, the Flyers forwards were by no means unemployed; besides back-checking with amazing aptitude they were always a source of danger to a hard-checking but erratic Vikings defence. While Tuck and Tiny Syme tried to frighten them off their game both by word of mouth and action the forwards became more cheeky and composed as the game progressed. So harassed did the brothers become that at one stage to the amusement of the spectators they faced-up to each other and it was only through the timely intervention of referee Gemmell that peace was restored.

In attack Marsh Bentley and Bert Smith were tireless workers and they simply never allowed the Dunfermline defence a moment's respite.

Bentley's goal was a masterpiece of perseverance. He gained possession at the blue-line and was harassed all the way on his journey to goal by the two defencemen, but somehow he eluded their arms and sticks to whip home a beautiful shot which left don Anderson completely helpless.

Bert Smith in his new position in the second line was a dashing leader. Although he did not score he had many commendable efforts. While the remainder of the forwards were slightly off colour in attack, they made amends by back-checking accurately and promptly. Vikings were a clever robust team but the forwards were inclined to over-elaborate with their approach play, costing them numerous openings that might have ended in goals. Con Switzer was their most outstanding forward with Ross Atkins and Johnny Holland next in order.

In defence Don Anderson was an accomplished cage-minder with Tuck Syme and Ed McGibbon lending good support. The first period was goalless before Bentley struck in the second. In the final period the tempo increased as the game progressed and it was amazing the pace at which play swept from goal to goal. Switzer had a couple of sitting chances for Vikings when Flyers were short-handed, but on each occasion Belanger made brilliant clearances. With three minutes remaining Flyers added the decisive second when Campone guided a Bentley pass into the net to the relief of the home crowd.

Fife Flyers' Line-Up for 1950-51

Left to Right 'Pete' Belanger, Bert Smith, Jimmy Mitchell, Forrest Towns, Floyd Snider, Sherman Blair, 'Pep' Young, Jimmy Burnett, Marshall Bentley, Al Campone, Verne Greger

Sunday October 20th 1996

Fife Flyers 7 Castlereagh Knights 3

On paper this looked like Fife Flyers safest two points of the season as they went in search of their ninth consecutive win. It was the first ever visit of a team from Northern Ireland to Kirkcaldy. Bottom-of-the-table Castlereagh Knights had to endure a long journey from Belfast after playing a tough game the night before. They were up against a Fife side fresh after a rare Saturday off, and boosted by the appearance of Russ Parent in the line-up after he had received his work permit earlier in the week.

However, for two periods of this clash it was impossible to say which way the result was going to go as Flyers turned in their poorest performance on home ice to date. It was one of those nights when nothing went right and only the home side's strength and fresh legs pulled them through to another win.

As the shots on goal indicated the Flyers had plenty of opportunities to win handsomely. Chance after chance was missed and, with too many players off form, it was left to player-coach Mark Morrison to secure the points with a hat-trick, although on almost any other night he would probably have scored at least double that. Castlereagh deserved great credit for the way they went about their business. They played to a system which continually frustrated Fife and were hard and strong in defence without resorting to dirty or underhand tactics. In Dean Russell-Samways they had a netminder on top form as he performed miracles to turn away 51 of the shots fired in on him and this inspired his team-mates to give a performance that belied their lowly position.

Some fans even agreed that Knights were about the best team seen at the Rosslyn Street rink so far that season. Stevie Hamill gave the visitors a shock early lead and it took Flyers until 9.09 to draw level when Morrison pounced on a loose puck and rounded the netminder to score. Steven King put Fife in front before the first interval with a fine backhand finish.

Two goals in 20 seconds early in the second period by Garry McKeag and Vasili Vasilenko saw Knights regain the lead; the home crowd became a bit restless. Shots rained in on Russell-Samways but he stood firm until 33.41 when Morrison poked home after a scramble in front of the net and the game stood all square entering the final period.

In the end it was tiredness that seemed to catch up on the visitors. Russ Parent had fired Fife ahead with a fierce slapshot at 42.29 and Morrison notched his hat-trick goal soon after. The game was won. Castlereagh never gave up, however, and it took two late strikes to give Flyers a winning margin that frankly flattered them. Steven King scored short-handed at 57.06 with another neat finish and then Frank Morris wrapped things up in the final minute.

Before this however Richard Dingwall had somehow managed to get himself thrown out of the game on what looked a clean and fair contest, but he was adjudged third man in to a spot of pushing and shoving by referee McWilliam.

Castlereagh left the ice to generous applause from the Fife crowd who appreciated their efforts and Flyers also received a good reception although probably more out of relief than anything else.

Flyers scoring: Mark Morrison 3+0, Steven King 2+0, Frank Morris 1+2, Russ Parent 1+0, Martin McKay 0+1

Knights scoring: Stevie Hamill 1+0, Garry McKeag 1+0, Vasili Vasilenko 1+0, Dean Smith 0+2, Kevin Docherty 0+1, Jamie Brannigan 0+1, Igor Yurchenko 0+1

Shots on goal: Flyers (McKay) 31 Knights (Russell-Samways) 58

Penalty minutes: Flyers 24 Knights 18.

Referee: Alex McWilliam Crowd: 1900

Debutant Russ Parent, left, and Steven King in action against the Knights

Saturday October 21st 1972

Fife Flyers 15 Paisley Mohawks 1

At the start of the season Lawrie Lovell joined his brother in Kirkcaldy. This was the seminal moment in the rebirth of the Flyers as a top team not just in Scotland but in the UK.

Joe McIntosh tried his luck in Dundee and the Flyers had a 20-year-old Canadian, Bruce Libbos, a student studying in Edinburgh, from Ontario in their ranks. The Kirkcaldy Kestrels took a bow in their inaugural season in the Second League.

The Flyers made it three wins out of three to start the season and for the second game in a row Bruce Libbos stole the show. After scoring a hat-trick at Dundee the previous week he netted five times on his home debut in Flyers emphatic win. His skill and goalscoring flair quickly made him popular with the Gallatown supporters.

Tall and strong, the Canadian often appeared disinterested in this match, but when he burst into action the Mohawks defence could not handle him and his shots at goal looked as if they had been fired from a gun.

The game was not nearly as one-sided as the score might suggest. The Mohawks stuck grimly to their task until the final whistle, but Flyers gave a confident and competent performance which would put them in good heart for the future. Flyers had settled the game in the first period when they raced away to a 6-1 lead with three goals from Libbos and a goal apiece from Lawrie Lovell, Les Lovell and John Taylor.

Mohawks one moment of glory came when Billy Dempsey broke through the middle to fire in a shot which slipped through netminders Jim Taylor's catching glove and into the net. Five more goals in the middle period put Flyers on easy street with the scorers being Lawrie Lovell, George Taylor, Rab Petrie and two more from Libbos.

Into the third period and despite the big lead Flyers did not ease up and defenceman Dave Medd got a goal which he deserved while Jimmy Hunter and Alistair Crombie added two more. The final goal of the evening was a delight when Hunter wrong footed the visiting defence before drawing Ian Nelson out of his goal and then placing the puck into the corner of the net.

A guest at the match was Chic Mann, who starred for Flyers over two seasons between 1948 and 1950. Mann was a prolific scorer in the professional leagues dominated by players from North America. In his second season he had finished the top scorer in all Scottish competitions with 167 points and his 180 points the previous season had only been bettered by his team mate Bud Scrutton who notched four more points. 347 points in his 131 games played for Flyers! Later he married a local girl before he returned to Canada. He was back in Fife for the first time in many years for a holiday and was announced to the crowd before he performed the ceremonial puck drop before the match.

Chic Mann dropping the puck ahead of the Fife Flyers and Paisley Mohawks match, looking on is Ice Rink Manager, Mr Thomas Horne.

Saturday October 22nd 2011

ELITE ICE HOCKEY LEAGUE CHALLENGE CUP

Braehead Clan 7 Fife Flyers 4

The Flyers rookie season in the Elite League was already a full blown nightmare as they still had only one win to their name in their opening dozen games.

This was the first ever meeting between the Flyers and Clan and one small positive for the visitors was that it did at least produce their highest goals production in a game so far that season. Yet again the Flyers were a team who failed to skate for the full 60 minutes. In a league where they were late to the recruitment party, they still hadn't figured out that until they competed for the entire hockey game then all their hard work would deliver zero rewards.

There were some recurring bad habits. Yet again the first period was their main enemy when they coughed up three goals; in truth they could have lost twice as many, as they handed Clan control of the ice pad. Defensively the visitors were just awful as they looked disjointed and at times calamitous, with barely a check thrown in anger.

Up front there was almost zero creativity and Flyers looked like a side that had accepted defeat as a 'gimme' from the face-off. Three down after 11 minutes to goals from the sharp looking Jordan Krestanovich, Jim Jorgensen and Vince Connon, the writing was once again on the wall. Yet with just two seconds of the period remaining up popped Matt Siddall with the first decisive drive down the ice and suddenly it was 3-1.

As poor as they were in the first Flyers found their tempo in the second and worked incredibly hard. Albeit down 4-1 to Brock McPherson's early power play, which was one of four conceded on the night, they found their tempo and their self-belief. The away side were suddenly transformed and produced a strong, effective and hard-working period which brought them back to 4-3. They also started to hit with conviction and rattled Braehead enough to knock them off their stride. Siddall's second goal at 32:16 and Garrett Zemlak's huge back post stop to deny Drew Bannister were pivotal moments and paved the way for Mike Hamilton to make this a one-goal hockey game at 39:56.

Into the third and with new belief and optimism the Flyers killed the bulk of a minor penalty against Aigars Brencis at 42:29 raising hopes that little bit higher, but when Hamilton was called for high sticks Clan pounced with Krestanovich's back hand finding the roof of the net.

To their credit the Flyers rallied again. Danny Stewart netted at the back post for 5-4, but once again they were cut to three skaters with penalties to Kyle Horne and Siddall. Referee Neil Wilson made some strange calls during the game. Once again Clan punished them with Bayrack's top shelf finish for 6-4 effectively killing the game. Flyers pulled Garrett Zemlack with 1:20 remaining but coughed up an empty net goal to Krestanovich with 25 seconds remaining, leaving many feeling regrets that had they performed the way they did in the second period across the 60 minutes the result could have been oh-so different.

Clan scoring: Krestanovich (3+0), Bayrack (1+2) Jorgensen (1+1) McPherson, Connon (1+0) Galbraith (0+5) Bannister (0+2) Walker, Haywood (0+1).

Flyers scoring: Siddall (2+1) Hamilton (1+2) Stewart (1+1) Cohen (0+1)

PIMs: 10-14. SOGs: Clan (Suomalainen) 17 Fife (Zemlak) 39.

Following another defeat the next night against the Edinburgh Capitals player coach Todd Dutiaume said

"You can try to get by on a skeleton crew and hope that sometimes a team doesn't show up against you and you get points. But that's not what this team wants or this town needs. We need a team that's going to compete."

Within a couple of days the Flyers added former Newcastle Vipers forward Toms Hartmanis, who replaced fellow Latvian Aigars Brencis who left the club by mutual consent, with just a single assist to his name in nine games played.

Matt Siddall striking a pose many Flyers fans adopted in the first EIHL season

Saturday October 23rd 1965

Fife Flyers 8 Brighton Tigers 3

Despite the doors being closed on their SS Brighton rink the Tigers decided that they would try and struggle on with the assistance of some ice time at Wembley Arena. The receipts from a game next month against the Wembley Lions would pay for their equipment for the season.

The Lions themselves were only a couple of years away from extinction as there was now a huge hole in hockey resources in Southern England. The Tigers travelled North to meet the Flyers, and then the next night the Paisley Mohawks, in their opening games of the season and unsurprisingly were heavily defeated in both.

If things were not going well on the ice for Brighton it was equally bad for them off the ice. Flyers fans converged on the rink from all directions, with the indication that there would be a record crowd since the resumption of hockey in 1962, many supporters were in their seats unaware that there was no news about the Tigers arrival.

Word began to get around that they had not arrived and many fans hung around outside the rink just in case the game was going to be cancelled. It wasn't until the time of the scheduled face off that spectators were put in the picture with an official announcement that Brighton's plane had been diverted to Renfrew Airport because of fog and it was now anticipated that the game would begin around 9 pm.

The rink management staged an impromtu musical programme but many fans decided not to wait and they queued up to get their money back. It was nearer 10 pm before the English side eventually got to the rink and by the time the game ended well after midnight many of the supporters had simply gone home.

Right from the face off, there was fast exciting play by both sides but local fans received a shock after only two minutes when Kirkcaldy man Harry Pearson skated through Flyers defence and opened the scoring for the visitors after some hectic scrambling around the goalmouth.

The game continued at a terrific pace through the rest of the period and Tigers had several scoring opportunities but failed before, a couple of minutes from the end of the first period, Tommy Paton netted Flyers equaliser.

The pace slowed down in the second period but after only 90 seconds Bill Sneddon skated down the wing skipped past two defenders and flashed the puck into the back of the net with a tremendous shot. Law Lovell was prominent in this spell along with player-coach Jerry Hudson and it was from his pass that Andy Williams scored Flyers third goal. A couple of minutes later the coach hammered his way through Tigers defence to add another.

The final period proved to be the most exciting and in the first six minutes Flyers took their score to seven with goals from Bert Smith, Tommy Paton and Andy Williams. The first came three minutes in with the Flyers piling on the pressure and Smith grabbed a deserved goal. Less than 30 seconds later, Paton received a pass from Sneddon, bored through the defence and hammered home a beauty for his second. Andy Williams also got his second before Rupe Fresher flashed through the Kirkcaldy defence moments later to net Brighton's second. Not long after that, Pearson also got his second when he caught Flyers defence by surprise. Halfway through the period Gordie Hughes, who had been a constant thorn in the Tigers side, completed Flyers scoring. Hughes and Tigers defenceman Roy Yates almost came to blows but were sent to cool down for a couple of minutes as the game ended.

Flyers:- Roy Reid, Bill Sneddon, Joe McIntosh, Lawrie Spence, Gordie Hughes, Tommy Paton, Sammy McDonald, Jerry Hudson, Lawrie Lovell, Bert Smith, Andy Williams, Ian Shields

It was a frustrating week-end for Flyers fans. On the following night they rolled up at the rink expecting to see the Ayr Rangers but Murrayfield Royals provided the opposition instead. The West of Scotland side called off for their Skol Cup tie only a matter of hours before the face-off was due.

Bill Sneddon –
uncompromising player who would
also later coach the Flyers in a
similar manner

Wednesday October 24th 1951

Paisley Pirates 3 Fife Flyers 6

In a thrill-a-minute Autumn Cup game at Paisley the Flyers returned their best all-round performance of the season so far and deservedly won 6-3.

Pirates, for all their more cohesive movement, could not fight for possession as the visitors did and most of their plays broke down at Flyers blue line. Those that did get right through to 'Stubby' Mason were dealt with in grand style, as the goalie maintained his harshly judged reputation of being a star in most other rinks but Kirkcaldy. Mason was undoubtedly one of Flyers keys to success but it was more heartening that there were no real weakness in the Flyers team.

All four defencemen gave more than they got and the wingers skated back tirelessly. The man who deserved a special mention was junior Ian Granger who had the difficult job of shadowing Pirates high-scoring left winger Bob Kelly. Although the Pirate did net two of his side's three counters Granger was directly responsible for him not scoring any more.

Although Mickey Linnell showed the power of his terrific back hand shot to net twice, he didn't check the opposing winger as well as he might have done, and generally lacked the fighting power so essential in the scrambles. He had only been here two weeks however, and more skating time was hoped to help him a great deal.

Mason was still inclined to wander off the beaten path now and again. Bob Bergeron fell out of the game in the second period only to improve again in the third. Frank Facto was impressive throughout, if only by virtue of the fact that he never knew when he was beaten and that he notched two opportunist goals.

Pirates lost because their chief scoring threats, of Kelly and LeSarge, were bottled up and because their defence relied a great deal on the efforts of Bernie Hill. Ray Savard gave glimpses of the swerve which had made him such a menace in the past but his wingers were held at every turn and Flyers defence never gave enough scope for him to go through solo.

Despite this it was all Pirates in the opening minutes and it took Flyers just over ten minutes to get a direct shot on Orr. In this spell the whole

Paisley

SEASON
1951-52

ICE RINK

The Paisley Pirates

ICE HOCKEY

Programme - - - 3d.

The match programme for the Flyers visit to Paisley

team stood up to a beating before going on to prove that they could give one as well. In the 15th minute, two quick and direct passes from Williams and Facto left Linnell on his own on the right wing and he went in, to leave Orr helpless with a high back-hand shot into the top corner of the net. That was the turning of the tide for Flyers. Although they were often in trouble they never looked back. They should have added to their lead two minutes later but Verne Greger shot past from a Facto pass when a goal looked certain.

Flyers were denied what looked like a penalty shot when Empie pulled down Bergeron but that didn't upset their balance and soon into the second period Bergeron had his revenge when he netted from close range after Floyd Snider and Jimmy Mitchell had made the play. Hill got one back for Pirates when Williams deflected his shot past Mason but the visitors regained their two-goal lead when Facto stick-handled his way past the Paisley defence.

Linnell made a bad miss before the end of the period, when he passed across the goal instead of shooting into the big empty corner which was right in front him. He made amends at the start of the third which marked the beginning of a real goal rush for Flyers with three goals in a minute and twenty seconds. Linnell's was another backhand shot and then Facto netted only fifteen seconds later. If that wasn't good enough, Johnny Vanier notched Flyers sixth with a back-hander after Joe Millisin had barged through and a shot had been blocked. Kelly scored twice in goal-mouth scrambles before the end but Pirates never looked like fighting back to anything like level terms.

Pirates — Ian Orr, Hal Empie, Bernie Hill, Roy Hammond, Joe Brown, Scotty Logan, Rheal Savard, Maurice LaForge, Johnny LeSarge, Dave Hebenton, Hal Brown, Bob Kelly.
Flyers — Stubby Mason, Floyd Snider, Jimmy Mitchell, Verne Greger, Archie Williams, Bob Bergeron, Joe Millisin, Johnny Vanier, Frank Facto, Ian Granger, Mickey Linnell.
Referee — Gordon Gerrard

Saturday October 25th 1986

Fife Flyers 5 Solihull Barons 3

After completing their Norwich Union Cup group with a 100% record the Flyers welcomed Solihull Barons for their first ever competitive match on Kirkcaldy ice. The newly promoted Barons proved unexpectedly difficult opponents, as the home side made a rather hesitant start to their Heineken Premier League programme.

Having defeated the visitors 14-3 in a challenge match last month, the Flyers and their supporters must have anticipated a less demanding contest than that which developed. However, bolstered by the inclusion of Paul Hand and Paul Heavey from Murrayfield Racers, and backed by a large and vociferous travelling support Solihull were an entirely different proposition.

Perhaps simply by being too complacent Chic Cottrell's side made life extremely hard for themselves by not turning their superiority into goals, although they were faced by a netminder in inspired form. Flyers 59 shots produced just five goals and the home fans were unusually subdued as Solihull threatened to pull off a shock result.

There was no sign of what was to follow as Flyers established a 3-0 lead after 17 minutes. Neil Abel opened the scoring with a power play goal in the eighth minute, which was assisted by Mike Jeffrey and Dave Stoyanovich. Five minutes later Jeffrey himself added a second from a Jimmy Pennycook pass. Big 'Neily' again found the net with a slapshot from just inside the blue line but the home side were stunned as Barons hit back through imports Brad Schnurr and Jay Forslund before the buzzer.

Flyers dominated for long spells in the second period and struck the piping twice with shots by Stoyanovich and Gordon Latto while Barons always looked dangerous on the break. However the only goal of the period was well worth waiting for. Dave Stoyanovich showed determination and superb stick handling in beating three opponents before squeezing the puck into the net.

Two minutes into the final period and Solihull once again reduced the deficit when Forslund dragged the puck wide of Craig Dickson to score with a shot into the corner. As Flyers stepped up the pressure the visitors still threatened every time they broke out of their own end. Stoyanovich eased the tension when he netted the rebound after efforts by Jeffrey and Al Sims had been blocked.

The remainder of the game was played almost entirely in the Solihull end of the rink but, through a combination of slack finishing and fine goal-tending by Dave Graham, the Kirkcaldy side were unable to add to their score.

No one knew it at the time but this win was to be Flyers last win in seven games of which six were in the league and left the team at that point rooted to the foot of the Premier League table. It resulted in unprecedented action by the teams management, who decided to release top scoring import Mike Jeffrey in order to shake things up. His replacement was Steve Moria who will crop up at points in the book.

Flyers 1986/87
Back, left to right: Gordon Goodsir, Jimmy Pennycook, Dean Edmiston, Charlie Kinmond, Bobby Haig
Middle, left to right: Colin Braid, Stuart Drummond, Brian Peat, Andy Linton, Neil Abel, Allan Anderson, Jimmy Jack, Willie Cottrell, Jim McLean
Front, left to right : Andy Donald, Al Sims, Chic Cottrell, Gordon Latto, Robert Fernie, Dave Stoyanovich, Steve Moria, Craig Dickson

169

Thursday October 26th 1950

AUTUMN CUP

Fife Flyers 7 Perth Panthers 8

With the Flyers needing just a point in their final Autumn Cup match to win the title for the second time in three seasons, the Kirkcaldy faithful had little expectation other than to celebrate at the end of the night's action.

Panthers had already inflicted a defeat on the Flyers in an odd-goal-in-thirteen encounter in Perth. A third-placed Panthers win would however throw Ayr Raiders a life line as they were tied on points with the Flyers.

The home side were under the handicap of having played the night before and missing Sherman Blair, who now nursed a broken finger and was watching instead of playing. Within twelve minutes they also lost Al Campone with a re-occurrence of a knee injury. At the start of the third period Harold 'Pep' Young also retired with a cut leg.

Those personnel losses were a lot to absorb but Flyers biggest handicap on the night was their own surprising ineptitude in defence. Panthers, or rather the Forgie, Doig, Hamilton line, played well but it was the glaring blunders of Belanger, Snider and Greger which gave the Perth team the chance to win. Flyers even with their injuries would have won had the defence been anything like as tight as it had been all season.

A great example of that came at the opening of the third period when Flyers had just taken a 5-4 lead and the Panthers were under penalty. Instead of the home side piling on the agony as everybody hoped and expected, Bruce Hamilton got away twice in thirty seconds to put Panthers 6-5 up and rubbed it in making another goal barely a minute later.

That burst floored Flyers, even though they were enjoying spells of complete domination against the Perth lads, for whom it was only a case of playing out time. When Jock Harley pulled one back Hamilton promptly added another for the visitors. Jim Burnett's goal ten seconds from time was purely incidental. Flyers defence was wide open and Belanger never looked comfortable the entire night. Burnett had his best game yet but he and junior Jimmy Mitchell were the only defenders who could feel even a little satisfaction. Marsh Bentley and Bert Smith were the best attackers. Hamilton with four goals and three assists was Panthers star man with line mates Doig and Forgie close behind.

First Period: Flyers — Bentley (Snider) 2 min; Panthers — Hamilton (Doig) 5 min; Panthers -Forgie (Doig) 7 min; Flyers — Smith (Harley) 10 min; Panthers — Doig (Hamilton) 11 min

Penalties: Campone, Wilson, Hamilton.

Second Period: Panthers — Hamilton (Doig) 14 min; Flyers — Snider (Harley) 18 min

Penalty: Johnson

Third Period Flyers — Bentley (Thorne) 2 min; Flyers — Wardrope 4 min; Panthers — Hamilton (Perron) 8 min;Panthers Doig (Hamilton) 9 min; Panthers Johnson (Hamilton) 10 min; Flyers — Harley (Burnett) 14 min; Panthers – Hamilton 19 min; Flyers — Burnett 19 min

Penalties: Perron, Wilson

SHOTS ON GOAL Belanger 33; Siemon 40

Flyers: 'Pete' Belanger, Verne Greger, Floyd Snider, Jim Burnett, Jimmy Mitchell, Marshall Bentley, Lee Thorne, Al Campone, Bert Smith, Harold 'Pep' Young, Jock Harley, Alex Wardrope

Panthers: Jack Siemon, Ken Perron, Ed Wilson, "Mosh" Myhal, George Watt, Tommy Forgie, Ken Doig, Bruce Hamilton, Wayne Johnson, Jean Hotte, Paul Golden, Ian "Eenie" Forbes

Referees D. Cumming and R. Gemmell

Note – with the Flyers and Ayr Bruins ending equal on points it was decided that the season opening competition would be decided by a play-off which incredibly ended up taking place as some of the last games of the season in April. The Flyers lost the first leg 7-3 in Ayr but redeemed themselves spectacularly in the return in Kirkcaldy to win 11-4 in a game that doubled up for the Canada Cup to annex the trophy 14-11 on aggregate.

Pete Belanger clears his lines as Perth marksman Bruce Hamilton (left) strives to round Flyers Lee Thorne

Saturday October 27th 1979

Fife Flyers 5 Aviemore Blackhawks 4

Although the Blackhawks had visited Fife the previous season for a Skol Cup match this was their first match as a Northern Ice Hockey Association outfit.

The far-flung outpost of winter sports had decided to try out senior competition for the first time, having won the Spring playoffs of the Reserve League. They had no fewer than five signings from Canada including Scott Bodger who would later see service with Streatham, and ex-Glasgow goalie Pete Callaghan. The Hawks were coached by a man familiar to this parish, Les Lovell junior, and he got them off to a winning start with their 6-5 home win the previous weekend over Murrayfield Racers.

Flyers remained firmly entrenched at the top of the Scottish Section of the Autumn Cup and, with their two weekend victories, looked odds on to clinch a place in the playoffs. As predicted the match turned out to be a tightly fought contest but Flyers clinched victory over their Highland visitors by a single goal.

There were few good scoring chances created in the first period but it was obvious that the teams were well matched. Both goaltenders looked sound and Flyers new signing in net Fred Justason brought off a fine save in the closing minute of the period to keep the scoresheet blank. The 19-year-old Canadian Navyman provided cover in goals as starting netminder Willie Cottrell had broken his hand in a work place accident during the week. Justason had played junior hockey in New Brunswick and as luck would have it his ship was in dock at Rosyth at just the right time.

The following night 15-year-old Andy Donald would make his debut between the pipes for the Flyers. Seven minutes into the middle period Blackhawks broke the deadlock when Malcolm Wilkie skated in from the wing to beat Justason at the post with a fierce shot. The goal seemed to spur the home side into action and two minutes later Dougie Latto equalised.

Midway through the match Blackhawks captain and another well known face to Kirkcaldy fans, Robin Andrew, was ordered to take an early shower after he received a misconduct penalty following a heated exchange with one of the referees. Flyers took the lead shortly afterwards in the most unlikely fashion. Blackhawks were pressing forward with Flyers minus two players but they allowed Gordon Latto a free run at goal and he took full advantage.

Practically on the second period buzzer, Chic Cottrell first timed a Gordon Latto pass and flighted the puck past the Blackhawks tender to give Flyers a two goal cushion for the final period. Flyers appeared to be coasting to an easy win when Gordon Latto made the score 4-1 two minutes into the final period, but Blackhawks came storming back with Scott Bodger finding the net on two occasions.

Flyers came under pressure as the visitors pushed for an equaliser but Andy Blair relieved the tension when he powered the puck into the Highland team's net with only three minutes left. Blackhawks still found time to score again. Kenny McDonald beat Justason but time ran out on them and Flyers took the points in what had proved to be a hard game with the new boys to the senior ice hockey circuit. Unfortunately having won their opening four games the Flyers then went on to lose their remaining four games in the competition that stretched out into late December and therefore failed to qualify for the next round.

Gordon Latto notches one of his brace against the Blackhawks

Sunday October 28th 1962

Fife Flyers 3 Paisley Mohawks 3

This was the Flyers second game in the 'hockey restart' season and as was the case for much of the decade the amateur nature of the sport meant that teams were constantly shuffling players.

Jerry Hudson had left to take up a player/coaching position in Vienna. Canadian Dave Johnston, who hailed from Toronto, and who had played Junior 'B' for Lakeshore and Leeside, was to debut along with another new signing, ex-Falkirk Lion Johnny Bayne who would alternate with John Pullar in net.

It had also just been announced that the Flyers had made an application to join the British Ice Hockey league along with teams such as Southampton, Brighton, Durham, Ayr, Paisley and Murrayfield. In the meantime they were determined to show their worth over the season in the amateur league. Things didn't work out that way but from these humble beginnings the Flyers did indeed grow into a formidable team over the next few years.

The home fans didn't get the start they expected from their team though. Flyers were two goals down in the first three minutes of the game and trailed 3-0 early in the third period before they made a great recovery and managed to force a draw with the visiting Paisley Mohawks.

This game was similar to the opening game two weeks ago when the Flyers met Ayr Rangers as they were once more slow to settle down and their opponents were able to go ahead very early in the game giving the Flyers a big task to counter.

In the first minute of the opening session Jumbo Milne opened the account for the visitors and was followed by Billy Miller who added to the score a minute and 35 seconds later. Flyers were outplayed in the first period and the Paisley boys kept their lead through a skilled exhibition of hockey. In this early part of the game Dave Johnston was one of the very few Flyers who showed any promise. He followed the puck well and kept a watchful eye on his wing, while sticking close to his check and giving the Paisley man little chance to score. In fact over-eagerness cost him a two minute boarding penalty when he followed his man too closely.

The second period saw a little more life in the home ranks but Paisley still had the upper hand and player-coach Billy Brennan, a veteran of the

Scottish circuit, netted early in the session to give the West of Scotland team a commanding lead. Flyers defence line up received a boost shortly after Paisley's third goal when Pete Robertson took to the ice after he had been delayed on his way to the rink.

The referee handed out penalties one behind the other to two of the Paisley players, brothers Ally and Billy Brennan — forward Ally a holding call and defender Billy a tripping call. The Flyers were able to turn this to their advantage. With the superior manpower Flyers turned on the pressure and their power play paid rich dividends with goals coming from Verne Greger, who was assisted by Dave Cook, and within a minute of this opener a goal from Cook on an assist from 'Pep' Young.

The Flyers were now right back in the game and Paisley were unable to make their pressure pay off as they had done in the early stages of the match. Prominent in the Flyers defence, during this time when Paisley were making every effort to increase their lead, was Greger who ,besides scoring Flyers opening goal of the game, played well on defence giving Paisley little opportunity to score. The second period ended with the Kirkcaldy side slowly gaining the upper hand over the tiring Paisley team.

A Flyers power play continued into the third period where they equalised in the first minute, with the goal coming from 'Pep' Young assisted by Bert Smith. Pep was now the leading goal scorer with three goals to his credit and was closely followed by Dave Cook with two and Bert Smith, Verne Greger and the departed Jerry Hudson with one each.

The puck misses the Paisley net by inches following a goal-mouth scramble involving Jimmy Watson (center) goaltender J. Black and defenceman C. Forrest

Saturday October 29th 1994

HEINEKEN PREMIER LEAGUE

Fife Flyers 9 Milton Keynes Kings 6

Flyers made it four points out of four against the Milton Keynes Kings in the league so far that season with their second win on home ice against the visitors.

The team may not yet have been the finished article but they still won the points with ease. Four of their goals came on the power play and one was scored short-handed. Man of the Match Tony Szabo helped himself to another hat-trick, his eighth of a season in which he had already tallied 36 goals, having scored in all but two of the 16 games played so far.

Both sides also had a player thrown out by referee Alex McWilliam, whose handling of a late flashpoint left much to be desired; throughout, Flyers seemed to suffer the bulk of the minor penalties. Overall, it was a solid rather than spectacular performance but one which featured some worthy contributions. Szabo hustled non-stop. Mark Morrison put in a power of work. If the defence looked comfortable the penalty killing was first-class as was Josh Boni's exquisite stick-handling, which created some beautiful opportunities which must sooner or later light the red light.

The first line regained its cutting edge with three goals on the board by 3:30. Ryan Kummu, Morrison and Szabo all found ways past Scott O'Connor before the Kings kicked into shape. The English side, which relied far too heavily on blue-liner Doug McCarthy, came back to 3-2 at 11:43 without ever threatening to take control of the game away from the home side. Iain Robertson polished off a clever move to score a vital fourth for Flyers on the power play at 15:38 and 30 seconds later it was 5-2 via a devastatingly accurate blue line wrist-shot from Szabo.

The three-goal cushion was never really tested by Kings in the middle period and a McCarthy tip-in from a Paddy Scott shot at 27:23 was merely cancelled out by Szabo short-handed at 28:00. Forty-four seconds later Kummu floated a left-wing shot past O'Connor for 7-3 and the points were effectively sealed. With Lee Pow sitting out a triple minor for ingratiating himself in a dust-up between Boni and Simon Howard the Flyers moved further out of sight through a Steven King flick shot.

The hockey in the third period took second place to a procession of minor penalties and some curious calls from referee McWilliam. It also saw two players thrown out as tempers frayed. The antagonistic Pow departed at 51:15 for spearing Kummu, his second successive 'red card' at Kirkcaldy. The incident also saw Morrison collect his first penalty of the league campaign after claiming a piece of the Kings' enforcer.

Three minutes later, Craig Wilson reacted to a cheap shot from import Trent Kaese and drilled the forward with a flurry of punches. The duo were eventually separated but Kaese almost sparked a major mêlée as he dived in for round two, an action which should have been punished with an automatic game misconduct instead of a pitiful two minutes for roughing. Wilson clearly won the fight but was thrown out on a five plus game for high sticks but also had to be helped off the ice with a nasty leg injury.

Flyers: S. King 1+4, Szabo 3+1, Kummu 2+2, Morrison 2+0, Robertson 1+0.

Kings: McCarthy 4+1, Payne 1+1, Kaese 1+0, Perkins 0+1, Scott 0+1, Strachan 0+1

Steven Lynch behind the face cage battles in front of the Milton Keynes Kings net

Tuesday October 30th 2012

ELITE ICE HOCKEY LEAGUE & CHALLENGE CUP

Belfast Giants 5 Fife Flyers 1

Flyers wrapped up their Challenge Cup group section with a disappointing defeat in Belfast in a match which also doubled as an Elite League fixture. Inside the opening nine minutes Craig Peacock opened the scoring with a backhand shot. Robbie Sandrock doubled the score on an odd-man rush with the puck rebounding off the unfortunate Derek Keller on its way into the net. Fife silenced the home support five minutes into the second period when Casey Haines pounced on his own rebound to make the score 2-1.

However penalty trouble around the half hour mark proved Fife's undoing and Giants made a five-on-three power play count when Sandrock scored his second to restore his team's two-goal cushion while Kyle Horne and Jason Pitton sat in the sin bin. Another penalty near the end of period two this time a holding minor called against Steven McAlpine put Giants back on the power play and a Jeff Mason tap-in made it 4-1.

Giants were able to coast to victory in the third period and Dayman Rycroft wrapped up the scoring with a fifth goal less than four minutes from full-time. The result saw Giants leap-frog Flyers into second place in Challenge Cup Group A although Todd Dutiaume's men had already qualified for the quarter-final stage.

Afterwards the coach spoke and warned that his players were risking their place in the line-up by failing to perform on the road. The Kirkcaldy side were now currently on a six-game losing streak with five of the six defeats coming away from home and they had won just one road game from seven played and the coach was left wondering if he was in charge of two different Flyers teams.

"We play like two different teams at home and on the road. At home we're playing very well, showing a killer instinct and will to win, but that's been sorely lacking away from home. You need your best guys to lead and I don't think we've got the best out of our top line on the road. This is not a half-and-half league. You can't just show up at home. To compete you need to steal points on the road and that's something we haven't done. Behind the scenes we're trying lots of things but it's not transferring onto the ice right now."

Dutiaume admitted that a change of personnel may be required if results did not improve and he had shown he meant business by benching himself a couple of nights earlier in the defeat to the Nottingham Panthers.

"The puck wasn't my friend on Saturday night. My game has been pretty decent lately and I've been happy to be out there playing but I was garbage for parts of my shift out there. I said in the dressing room that if you're not performing you won't play, and it has to start from the top and go all the way down. I sit out, Scoony goes on and all of a sudden that line comes alive for a couple of shifts. It's another import down but these guys know if they don't show up on the road they'll be the ones sitting there hurting the team. Sometimes all it takes is for them to miss one shift to realise they are not in their comfort zone and they need to step it up a notch. Passengers will not play."

Dutiaume also considered a change of tactics in order to address his team's dismal away form. "We can look at a change of personnel but we could look at a few different systems," he said. "If guys are feeling they can't skate then we maybe go back to the trap we played last year —boring, bland, negative hockey. But when it comes to winning we'll do what it takes."

The Flyers went another six games with defeat on the road before they finally stemmed the bleeding when they won at Dundee in a shootout a few days before Christmas.

Zach Carriveau loses his helmet in a tussle with the Giants

Thursday October 31st 1946

SCOTTISH LEAGUE FLAG

Fife Flyers 8 Falkirk Lions 1

Completely out-skating and out-manoeuvring the Falkirk Lions, who had achieved fame the night before by beating the Flag League winning Dunfermline Vikings, the Flyers gave the Lions a severe drubbing at the Kirkcaldy Rink.

In doing so Flyers completed a nice double as they also beat the Lions 10-4 at Falkirk in their first game of the season. Jimmy Mitchell, the Kirkcaldy junior who deputised for Howard Duffield — unable to turn out owing to injury — scored a great success in his debut appearance with the senior line-up. Here was no raw product to be shoved on the ice for short spells and whipped off again when the going got tough; Mitchell took his full share in the game and his display on the right wing in conjunction with Bob Lantz and John Drummond was first-rate. His understanding with Lantz was particularly brilliant and to cap off a memorable night for the youngster he scored two goals in the first period. When he rattled in the first of his goals from an O'Connor assist he was nearly mobbed by the Canucks, who were obviously delighted that yet another local boy was making good.

Of the rest of the Flyers, Don Dougall performed heroics in the net while Bob Londry kept up the go-getting methods he showed in a recent game at Perth and Floyd Snider served up his usual whole-hearted display. Bud Scrutton, although not completely recovered from recent injuries, played a grand game and Harry O'Connor was tireless and dangerous as ever. Earl McCrone, who was Flyers most stylish skater, netted two goals but would have had more if luck had not been against him. Jim McKenzie, whether in defence or attack, was equally effective while Lantz and Drummond already mentioned stick-handled magnificently. A feature of the play was the quick passing and inter-changing movements of the Flyers as they had often been accused of over-doing the individualistic stuff but in this game they combined in splendid style and sold the opposing defencemen a few lovely dummies.

Scorers First Period: Flyers — Snider (Scrutton), McCrone (Scrutton), Mitchell (O'Connor), Mitchell (Lantz).

Second Period: Lions — Davis Flyers — Lantz (Drummond).

Third Period: Flyers — O'Conner (Snider), McCrone (Snider), Scrutton (Snider).

Flyers: Don Dougall, Bob Londry, Floyd Snider, Bud Scrutton, John Drummond, Earl McCrone, Jim Mitchell, Harry O'Connor, Bob Lantz, Jim McKenzie.

Lions: George Leonard, Rene Platt, Clair Morrison, Bun Glass, Johnny Savicky, Paul Pelow, Keith Tolton, Johnny. Carlyle, Frank Davis, Arnold Irwin.

Referees—G. Horn and E. Batson.

It was only the Flyers third win in the seasons opening dozen Flag matches as they finished bottom of the table with the Lions a place above them.

Before the game, Bob Page, secretary of the Supporters' Club said many supporters had been perturbed at the rumour that at the end of the present Flag series that all players were to be re-allocated. The reason why they were perturbed was that they wanted to keep the present Flyers line-up.

It turned out that there was to be no re-allocation of players and Flyers would retain their present line-up for the remainder of the season, a fact that Bob wished to be published and so put the supporters minds at rest. If this kind of support for a team which up to Thursday had only collected four out of a possible of twenty points did not encourage Flyers then nothing will. To put it plainly the supporters had faith in the present line-up and in the coaching of Al Rogers and after Thursday's display they must have felt their faith was justified.

Jimmy Mitchell marked his Flyers debut by scoring two goals

Moray Hanson and Gary Brine share a joke in the warm up, Brine had the last laugh as his Bracknell Bees shut out the Flyers 2-0 in October 1992

November

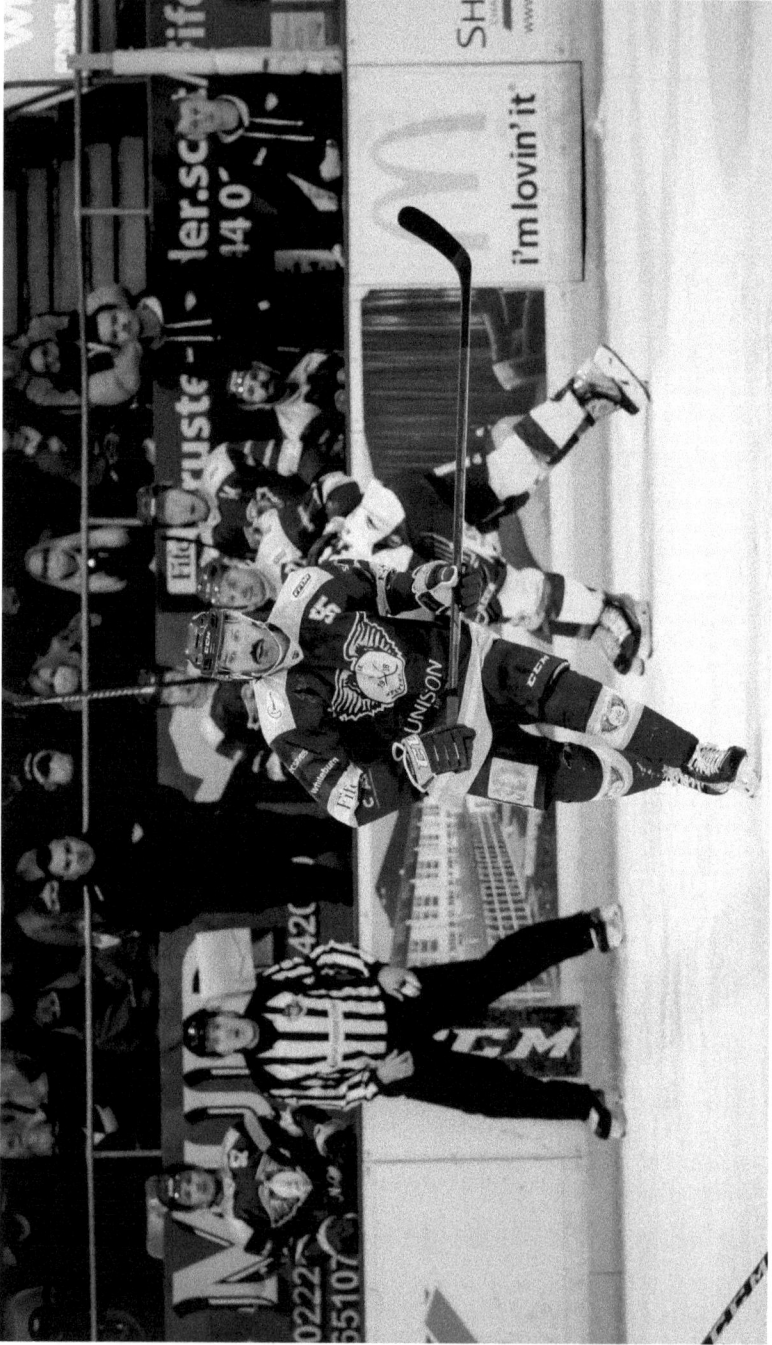

Matt Carter, who scored the club's 1500th goal in all Elite Ice Hockey League competitions in the game against Coventry Blaze on November 13th 2021

Monday November 1st 1948

Dundee Tigers 0 Fife Flyers 4

The Flyers with only one defeat in their opening dozen games were one victory away from clinching the Autumn Cup and their first significant piece of post war silverware.

The visitors played an outstanding game to make certain of the title and in the process Pete Belanger recorded his first shutout of the season. Harold 'Hick' Moreland almost scored in the opening minutes when he took the puck from a Dundee defender to send it skimming past the post. Johnny Evans tried hard for Tigers but Belanger held two shots from him. The home side pressed strongly and John Kennedy twisted his way into the goalmouth to unleash a stinger which Belanger cleared.

Back came Flyers via Chic Mann but he sent the puck wide of the net. Bobby Burns had another try for Tigers; Verne Greger stepped in to clear surrounded by a number of the home side. Floyd Snider worked his way into the goal-mouth from the right but his strong shot was saved in grand style by George Kovac. Seconds later the keeper was tested by Moreland who came in from the left wing and when Tigers retaliated Belanger was there to clear when they broke away.

At the other end Ken Joy slipped his marker but shot hastily as play continued to be of a fast end-to-end nature. Johnny Rozzini should have netted for Tigers but he shot past when well placed. Snider sent Scotty Reid away on the right and he too had hard luck to hit the post with a strong shot. A goalmouth scrimmage ensued round Kovac when Moreland, Bud Scrutton and Mann had shots saved.

Only twenty seconds of the second period had gone when Mann put Flyers ahead. Snider brought the puck down the middle; just as the defence thought he was about to shoot he flicked the puck to the unmarked Mann in the goal-mouth. Flyers were attacking strongly and Moreland sent a Scrutton pass narrowly past, to be followed by Bud having a shot saved by Kovac.

Eddie Michanik broke away but was tripped by Greger. He slid into the net along with the puck. To the displeasure of the home crowd the goal was disallowed as the whistle had already blown. With Greger in the cooler Tigers tried to equalise but a break away by Mann followed by a powerful shot brought Kovac into action. Back at full strength Flyers regained the upper hand and Kovac did well to save from Scotty Reid twice in succession. After a spell of pressure around Kovac's charge Russ Robertson broke away but Belanger saved his strong parting shot. Kovac left his charge to deny Mann but could not stop a shot from Moreland entering the net. This time the Flyers were denied as the counter was disallowed.

Evans working his way up on the right sent the puck to John Kennedy in the goal-mouth but Belanger stopped his point-blank shot. Flyers second was scored by Bert Smith, after Joy brought the puck up the right before parting to Smith in the centre who beat Kovac all hands down. Almost on the second period whistle Bud Scrutton netted from Moreland's rebound.

Two minutes had gone in the last session when Greger in the goalmouth sent home a pass from Scrutton to put Flyers four up. Two penalties in succession against Bob Reid and Greger saw Mann, Scrutton and Snider against five Tigers. Mann, however, was all set for a breakaway when he was tripped by Robertson to reduce the Dundee ranks. Tigers were trying desperately to score but were not allowed any scope by a sound defence and solid back checking. A pass back from Scrutton to Moreland saw the latter flick the puck over the cage then Mann hit the post. Archie Williams was through but Belanger saved his point-blank shot.

Flyers seemed content to lie back in defence in the last few minutes to help Belanger record a shutout. Consequently Tigers were attacking in waves but just could not break through the stout Fife defence. Belanger saved a shot from Bums and two from Bob Finlayson in successive raids. With forty seconds to go Kovac was withdrawn in an attempt to break down Belanger's shut out but to no avail.

Ex Glasgow Bruins and Harringay Racers Pete Belanger recorded his first shutout of the season

Sunday November 2nd 2003

Bracknell Bees 5 Fife Flyers 1

It had been a bit of an indifferent start to the season from the Flyers who, nonetheless, had managed to qualify for the semi-final of the Findus Challenge Cup by finishing second in their group.

They had won their last six matches, including their opening two in the British National League. It looked as though they were shaking off the early inconsistency as they met a Bees team a point below them in the league standings. The Bees, who were a Superleague team the previous season, had dropped out of joining the Elite Ice Hockey League to join the BNL. They had won both the earlier Findus Cup games in what were the first ever competitive meetings between the teams. On their previous visit to "The Hive" in Berkshire the Flyers were blanked 5-0.

The Flyers who travelled south, without Steven King and John Haig, faltered again as the Bees dominance over them continued. A Rempel double helped them move ahead of the Flyers after a delayed start to the game at Amen Corner. It was Bracknell's second league win of the weekend. They made light of the 45-minute delay to face off caused by the Flyers travel plans being disrupted by traffic.

Despite an 11-hour coach trip the visitors had the better of the opening exchanges before the home team started the scoring slightly against the run of play. Bees were also short-benched, after having just released Chris Crombie. With Flyers on their first penalty kill with Paul Spadafora in the box for hooking Greg Owen, Andrew Sande tipped in a Daryl Lavoie slapshot for the power play goal. Owen then turned provider for two further goals in the last three minutes of the period which all but sealed the Flyers fate. For the second goal Nathan Rempel found the net at 17.44 and this was added to shortly afterwards by Scott Allison at 18.28. The first period shots on goal were high with Bracknell outshooting Fife 19-13 and both goalies had to make big saves to keep the score down.

Flyers made it onto the scoreboard just past the half hour with a power play effort of their own when Todd Dutiaume fired past Stephen Murphy. Bracknell restored their three-goal lead with Daryl Lavoie netting his first of the season at 37.06. Less than 60 seconds later, Darren Hurley and Paul Spadafora clashed, with both men getting a 2+10 for roughing, and Hurley picking up an extra minor for cross checking. Bracknell made light of the penalty though as Nathan Rempel broke away and netted a short-handed tally for a 5-1 score at the second interval.

The third period was scoreless, but not without scoring chances. Stephen Murphy saved 15 shots in the session to maintain Bracknell's lead. Bracknell captain Dave Matsos spoke after the game and said: "Any time you can take four points from a weekend it's good. We played our systems well and got the results."

Meanwhile Flyers player coach Mark Morrison reflected in the defeat by saying

> "We've been on a great run, losing just once in seven games and I like the intensity we are playing to at the moment. I was happy with the home win against Guildford but we were missing a couple of players in Bracknell which was unfortunate. This is turning into a three line league and it gives you an advantage when you can have this on your bench. But the guys we have here believe in themselves which is great because confidence is everything in sport."

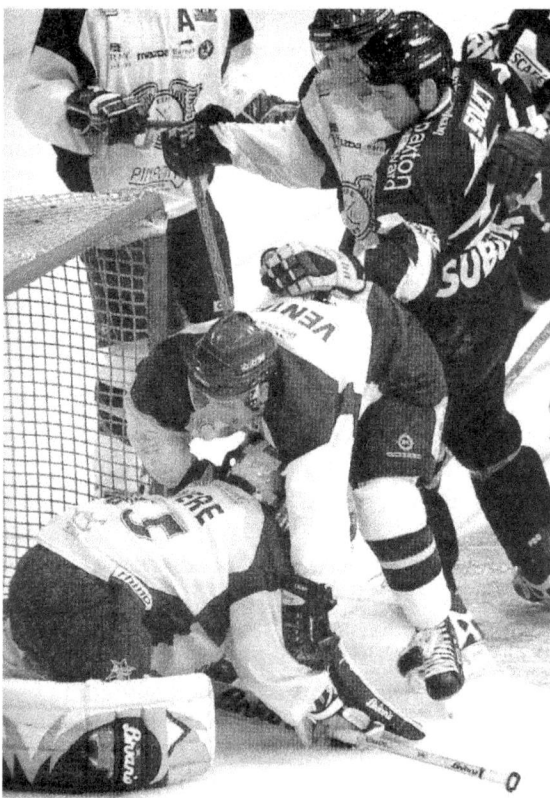

A net front melée as the Flyers try to shut down the Bees in their first ever game at Kirkcaldy

Sunday November 3rd 2013

ELITE ICE HOCKEY LEAGUE

Nottingham Panthers 7 Fife Flyers 1

A decade on. The Flyers travel plans were once again compromised as it took them over seven hours to get to Nottingham, which resulted in a delayed face off.

Less than nine minutes into the game, the reigning EIHL Champions Panthers had taken full advantage of the visitors' bus legs to move into an early 3-0 lead. Having already thrown away a three-goal lead at home to Dundee Stars just 48 hours earlier, there was little chance of the Panthers making the same mistake twice.

For Flyers it was already game over. They had been shut out at home by Sheffield the night before but had won their previous three games, all of which were on the road. From the moment American-born Chris Capraro opened the scoring with 95 seconds on the clock the writing was on the wall. Panthers doubled their lead with a power play strike from Bob Wren at 3.20 while Matt Nickerson sat out for an elbow before Brandon Benedict added a third on 8.30.

Flyers gave a better account of themselves in the second period when they almost matched the home side shot-for-shot but there was only one goal scored, from the stick of Nick Anderson to give Panthers a four-goal lead.

The home side cranked it up again in the third period with Benedict scoring twice to complete his hat-trick while Lee Salters also netted. At 7-0 down Flyers grabbed a late consolation, their first and only goal of the weekend when Euan Forsyth's effort deflected past Neil Conway.

After the previous weekend's memorable four-point haul this concluded a forgettable two days for Flyers. An entire weekend without a forward finding the net did not make for good reading and fans were losing patience. Flyers were now second bottom of the table and were the lowest scorers in the league, having scored a miserly two goals in their last three home matches.

Associate coach Danny Stewart admitted that patience was wearing thin and he commented:

> "We have the potential to be a good team but whether we have the right fit of guys who want to buy in, night in, night out, I'm

not so sure, that's yet to be seen. Leashes are getting shorter with some guys and although we've not jumped to make changes it's not because we're scared to. When the time is right if a guy is not getting the job done and someone else comes through that will improve the team then it's a no-brainer. We need more out of some guys – a lot more and it's got to come sooner rather than later. "

By the end of the month the Flyers added to their roster with the addition of defenceman Kyle Haines, who quickly became a fan favourite. With the return from injury of defenceman Justin DaCosta it left the Flyers with 12 imports signed but only able to ice 11 and later saw the release of Slovenian forward Rok Pajic.

One of the mis-firing Flyers forwards at that time, Jordan Fulton, who would go on to become the leading scorer that season

The Flyer

**Grand Slam Champions Fife Flyers
v Moray Tornadoes**

Scottish National League
Saturday 4th November 2006
Face-off 7.00pm

the
Fife Free Press

fifetoday.co.uk
because life is local.....

Price: £1.50

The Flyers match programme for the visit of the Moray Tornadoes

Saturday November 4th 2006

Fife Flyers 11 Moray Tornadoes 0

Hockey nights in Kirkcaldy thrive on atmosphere and excitement. In a fast physical competitive sport the crowd can be ignited by a great goal, a huge fight, a cheeky piece of opportunist play for a short short-handed goal, or simply a referee stinking the rink out giving the fans somewhere to vent their spleen. Come to think about it the referee doesn't always have to have made a mistake for some fans to be in state of apoplexy. But even the most ardent upbeat and positive supporter could not have made a case for this pointless match.

A foregone conclusion even before the Tornadoes team bus left Elgin, this monumental mismatch once again exposed the inherent weaknesses within the Scottish National League structure and questioned just exactly where Fife could go long-term to establish sustainable hockey. The harsh reality of the current situation was that Fife could most likely have iced their under-16 Flames team and still won this match.

Adding to the general apathy that was already creeping in just a few months into the season, the scheduling of this fixture for Bonfire Night meant that the already small attendance shrunk even further. There was hardly a bairn in the building and those that were in attendance must have had a real aversion to anything explosive happening on the night.

When the reported highlight of the night was the ice staff who put on an impromptu dance routine while the Zamboni cut the ice and at least raised a smile you know you've had better nights rink side. It was one-way low-grade sweat-free hockey. Fife declared at 11, they had clearly deployed the 'Mercy Rule' so often used in junior hockey because in truth they could have netted any number more than double that count.

The Moray lads won genuine applause for never giving up even although they knew it was a lost cause with their two lines working hard and their single goalie Craig Johnstone made four or five smashing saves to merit his Man of the Match award. It was 'shootie in' though as he faced a 66-shot barrage from a team which barely shifted out of first gear.

Not for the first time that season the Flyers were again left with a dilemma of playing at full tilt and possibly causing a meltdown of the scoreboard or sit back and take the pass rather than the shot and be accused perhaps of not trying. "Damned if they do, damned if they don't." The problem of being a big fish in a small pond was that ultimately they too end up going round in the same circles. They certainly treated their opponents with respect but still won at a canter with some smartly taken goals at regular intervals.

Young defenceman Lewis Christie was Flyers Man of the Match for a sparkling hat trick. He skated well all night and looked to have settled well into his new team. Player-coach Todd Dutiaume also weighed in with a six point haul with a 3+3. Richard Latto let rip for his counter and there were also singles from Steven King and Jamie Wilson while Stephen Gunn bagged a double. The big guns sat out as many shifts as they could without seizing up on a cold evening and became playmakers rather than goal takers.

The huge gulf in terms of shots on goal summed it up best of all. Netminders Daly and Marr shared an easy shut out as Tornadoes managed just seven shots in 60 minutes, arguably the lowest ever tally posted in a senior hockey game in Kirkcaldy in the last 30 years.

Some day I'll have a definitive answer on that.

Chris Linton, Gordon Latto (Jnr), Ian Simpson, Tommy Muir and Todd Dutiaume model the new look Fife Free Press sponsored 2006/07 jerseys

Saturday November 5th 1988

HEINEKEN PREMIER LEAGUE

Fife Flyers 8 Ayr Bruins 2

Surely on their way back to the West the Ayr Bruins had a whip round on the team bus for netminder John McCrone. It was the least they could have done after he single-handedly saved them from a hammering in this game at Kirkcaldy. He faced 53 shots and despite conceding eight goals he was responsible for preventing what looked like many more certainties and gave an overall impressive display of netminding all night.

'Bernie' rightly received the visitor's Man of the Match award for his part in a game which was completely controlled by a stronger and quicker Fife Flyers team. They were streets ahead of the West coast side which yet again tried to niggle their way into contention. With the emphasis on brawn rather than brain, which is usually a dubious tactic to play at Kirkcaldy, to say the least, the Bruins plans backfired when coach Rocky Saganuik collected a match penalty. He found himself in the dressing room barely halfway through the game, and with him went Ayr's hopes of creating anything resembling an upset.

Flyers won each of the three periods with ease and consistently outshot Bruins in a highly disciplined and encouraging team performance. Ayr had no answer to the electrifying speed of Vincet Lukac or the clever stickwork of Jindrich Kokrment, who was beginning to shine after shrugging off his shoulder injury. In attack they ran into a formidable defence marshalled by the towering Milan Figala and the impressive Gordon Latto. Flyers skipper enjoyed a tremendous tussle with his opposite number John Kidd. The Ayr stalwart tried every trick in the book to create mayhem in front of McKay's net but Latto was always one step ahead of him.

The hosts opened the scoring with six minutes on the clock when Kokrment launched an attack from deep within his own half and casually slotted the puck past McCrone. Lukac made it 2-0 in 9:50 but ex-Flyer Iain Robertson reduced the leeway before the buzzer. With Neil Abel off the ice after taking a heavy tumble, Les Millie fired home goal number three in 26:06 and the Czechs combined for a fourth which was scored by Kokrment just six minutes later. Flyers were cruising at this point and Lukac underlined their dominance with a power play fifth strike in 35:28.

Four minutes later Ayr's bump and grind brand of ice hockey brought about their own fall from Grace. Rocky Saganuik managed to tangle with three players as he drove his way to the Flyers net and when he used his stick on Figala even referee glen Reilly had no option but to point towards the dressing room. He went with a few grumbles and the bad feeling continued as several players jostled their way off the ice at the end of the period.

The final stanza was a foregone conclusion with Lukac and Kokrment teaming up for a sixth power play which was so quick Bruins' defence likely never saw the puck from start to finish. Kokrment did the spade work and Lukac obliged by firing past McCrone. With Ally Wood under penalty Ayr notched up their only power play of the day courtesy of Alistair Reid with an assist from import Frank Morris.

Flyers however kept the best until the end when Gordon Latto picked up the puck behind his own net and carved a firm path through the defence before firing past McCrone. With eight minutes left Les Millie followed suit with a sparkling move when Ayr's defence literally fell apart as the youngster surged forward for a superb unassisted goal.

This was Flyers 50th Anniversary season and the picture shows the Flyers first ever captain Les Lovell Senior welcoming the current Flyers captain Gordon Latto onto the ice.

Saturday November 6th 1976

Fife Flyers 12 Paisley Mohawks 0

With the home side on a run of 14 wins against their visitors in the last 14 games it was expected that the Flyers would maintain a 100 percent record after seven matches in the Autumn Cup.

This would maintain their lead at the top of the table ahead of hibernation for the winter before further matches in the competition were completed the following Spring. Unbeaten in all competitions so far the Flyers had disposed of the Mohawks the previous weekend when they won 14-3 in the West.

With such dominance it gave the Flyers management an opportunity to ice a young Kestrels line. George Ramsay, Stuart Winton and Jim Ross marked their debuts for the club with all three of them getting their names on the score sheet with a goal each. Mohawks came to Kirkcaldy with a larger squad than of late but any hope of a shock result was dashed with Flyers usual high-scoring opening burst. When the buzzer went for the end of the first period Flyers had lit the red light eight times without reply.

In comparison there was a significant lack of goals in the second period, mainly due to the Mohawks taking a more physical approach to the game, but in the final five minutes Flyers did manage to score once.

It was not until the final ten minutes of the last period that Flyers reached double figures when Brian Peat crashed one home. John Pullar was given a tough task to keep his shut-out when Mohawks were awarded a penalty shot but the Fife tender thwarted the effort. The scoring was rounded off by Chic Cottrell who netted his fourth goal of the evening with the other Flyers goals coming from Jimmy Jack and a Lawrie Lovell hat trick.

The Mirror of Merit award went to John Pullar who was always in control of the Mohawks efforts and after getting his first shut-out of the season he looked set to take his place in the Great Britain team once again that season. Flyers set up another Northern Ice Hockey Association record when they reached the 100 goal mark in only eight games, the fastest to reach that total in NIHA history.

John Pullar did indeed make the GB selection for the 1977 World Championships held in Denmark. The GB team finished bottom of Pool C on goal average along with Spain and Belgium who each had one win apiece.

Pullar was back up in all six matches to 30-year-old John Haney, who made his GB debut after spending his entire playing career abroad. He was now living in Denmark and played part-time for the Herning IK 'Blue Foxes' while, among other things, running a bookstore, doing freelance writing, acting and earning some extra money by working in a local slaughterhouse.

If that's something you didn't expect to find reading these pages then stay tuned. He later found fame, if not fortune, away from hockey. Along with his younger brother Chris, ex Colgate College friend Edward Werner and Scott Abbot the foursome went on to create the board game that would become a 1980s worldwide phenomenon. The four partners sold the rights to Hasbro for US$ 80 million and Trivial Pursuit was born.

Les Lovell and the 1976/77 Flyers receive the Dave Cross Memorial Trophy from senior N.I.H.A. referee Ian Black – it was presented to the least penalised team

Sunday November 7th 1965

Fife Flyers 13 Ayr Rangers 2

Although the home side were in top form to win this one the visitors seldom showed any real team co-ordination and it was always too easy for the skilful Flyers forwards to break through the weak Ayr defence with some classic manoeuvres.

It was a disappointing game for fans who had hoped to see a more competitive match but after a dull start it developed into an exciting match with tempers becoming increasingly frayed. Ayr went more and more to pieces as Flyers increased their lead. The match erupted in the middle of the second period when no fewer than five players, three Flyers and two Rangers, were sent off within seconds of each other. It seemed at this point that only strong handling by the referee would prevent the match developing into an all out battle.

With the majority of the play taking place round the Ayr net perhaps the most surprising fact of the game was that Flyers ended up scoring only 13 goals. At times it looked more like some shooting practice for Flyers rather than a two-sided tussle. Praise was undoubtedly due to the Rangers keeper Tommy Newell, who averted disaster for his side on innumerable occasions when his defenders left the way open for Flyers to attack. Bryce Penny, for the visitors, also showed promise and it was unfortunate that he was not backed up by his team-mates. He would guest for the Flyers later in the season.

The lack of someone to carry the puck over the blue line was the worst feature of the team, with their attacks mostly fizzling out before the puck was out of their own half. Once again Flyers first line of Bert Smith, Tommy Paton and Jerry Hudson were outstanding. Andy Napier, who played for the first time since the beginning of last season, also had a good game and fans hoped to see a lot more of him throughout the season.

Bill Laird, who took over from Roy Reid in net in the third period, was a bit unfortunate to lose an early goal with a deflection, but he stood no chance from the second goal scored by Penny. Paton had the first of his three goals only minutes after the start of the game after constant pressure by Flyers and this was followed shortly afterwards by a brilliant goal from Hudson, assisted by Bill Sneddon and Andy Williams. This was the best of Hudson's four goals for his side as he left the defenders standing, brought the keeper out, and skated right round him to flash the puck into the net with a fine display of stick-handling.

At the end of the first period the score stood at 3-0. It was after Hudson had further increased this lead in the second period that the game got out of hand. Flyers Sammy McDonald was sent off for tripping and he was followed almost immediately by team mates Paton and Sneddon and by Campbell and Penny of Rangers. After his two minutes off the ice McDonald went right back on to score two quick goals and Paton then completed his hat-trick to make the score 8-0 at the end of the second period. Hudson again scored in the opening seconds of the third period and then came Ayr's two quick strikes to make the score 9-2.

After this effort the visitors seemed to go to pieces and four additional goals by Flyers made the final score 13-2. Flyers scorers were: Paton (3) Hudson (4), McDonald (2), Smith. Napier (2), and Hughes:

Flyers — Roy Reid, Bill Sneddon, Joe McIntosh, Andy Williams, Gordie Hughes, Tommy Paton, Jerry Hudson, Bert Smith, Lawrie Lovell, Sam McDonald, Andy Napier, Ian Shields and Bill Laird.

Ice hockey was growing in popularity and the rink at Gallatown was acquiring quite a reputation for staging some of the most exciting matches. However, it was also acquiring a reputation it could well do without. Some of the language used by the players, being directed at the fans on occasions. was down-right objectionable and this was something which could do nothing other than harm to the game. During the Rangers game there was a certain amount of interchange between a player and a fan which built up into rather an unsavoury verbal assault by the player. Possibly the player felt he was being goaded by the fan but he would have done well to have remembered that there were many women within earshot and they should not have been subjected to such an incident. It was to be hoped this would not be repeated.

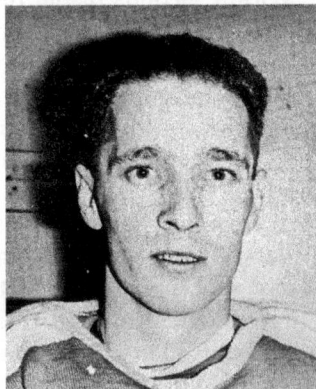

Roy Reid, who had a quiet night in net for the Flyers against the Rangers

Saturday November 8th 1980

Skol Cup

Fife Flyers 1 Murrayfield Racers 12

There were few highlights in November of 1980 and this match against the Racers certainly wasn't one.

Murrayfield brought their own special brand of hockey to Kirkcaldy and left Flyers stranded in their destructive wake. The Racers were the dominant force in the Northern League at that time and this game clocked up a fourth successive defeat for Flyers. To make matters worse three of these had been at the hands of their bitter rivals.

The Flyers would have to raise their standards, particularly on home ice, if they were to hold on to the large crowds that had been attracted by their success at the start of the season. Talking about home ice, there were a couple of improvements at this time with a new floor having been laid over the summer at the rink. A new £12,000 ice machine, the Zamboni, which would become infamously known later as Mabel, was about to make her debut. This was the end of the army of scrapers who went up and down the ice during the intermissions shovelling the ice smooth.

Home fans were given a foretaste of the humiliation to follow when in the opening 15 minutes Jimmy Pennycook had already netted a hat trick. Flyers were unable to stop the rout and further goals by Jock Hay and brothers Ally and Ronnie Wood left them six goals adrift at the end of the first period.

Within seconds of the restart Stevie Hunter widened the deepening chasm between the two teams with a goal whose build up was performed at breath-taking speed. Hay and Ally Wood also hit the net before the Flyers began to work their way back into the game, eventually putting some shots on the visitors net, albeit mostly of the long range variety. It was perhaps optimistic to say that it was essential at this stage that the Flyers did not concede another quick goal but it just wasn't to be their evening. Dampier smashed the puck across the goalmouth to Chris Kelland on the wing who trapped it skilfully before scoring from a well-placed shot that crept in by the post.

Flyers added to their troubles by taking five minor penalties by this point with Stuart Drummond and Jim Lynch both visiting the sin bin twice. Pennycook added to their misery by scoring in the final period and perhaps the sting of being 11-0 down galvanised the home team into action in an attempt to salvage some self respect.

Charlie Kinmond at last gave the home fans something to cheer about when he scored Flyers solitary goal of the match. Seven minutes later Pennycook ended a marvellous performance by hitting the net for the fifth time when Flyers had two men in the cooler. As the game slowly ebbed to its conclusion Kenny Horne and Hay had a pitched battle which ended with Horne getting his finger bitten and both players receiving five-minute penalties.

A week on and there were changes to the Flyers bench as firstly Law Lovell who had only returned to the club in September was replaced as coach by Bill Sneddon. He commented;

> "I am bitterly disappointed. It was only at the beginning of the season that Flyers asked me to come back as a coach. The deficiencies in the team are only too apparent to me but we just have to go with the stuff we have."

Then Canadian Tony Sgro went home before the arrival of fellow countrymen Neil McKay and Steve Crummey who both arrived in Fife having been playing in Aviemore for the Blackhawks.

Chic Cottrell is denied by the Racers netminder in a rare Flyers attack

Sunday November 9th 2003

Guildford Flames 4 Fife Flyers 3 (after overtime)

With Guildford having topped the Findus Challenge Cup table it was clear from this early stage in the season that the Flames would be a team the Flyers had to overcome if they were to be successful in their league endeavours.

Although the Flyers had already won their three meetings with the Flames so far that season, a trip to the Spectrum in Surrey wasn't one which the history books show was a particularly happy 'hunting ground'. Only three wins in 14 visits — the last of which was a few weeks ago in the Findus Cup — a huge result; as it transpired, the Flyers only victory on the road south of the border until early December.

So all wasn't lost although the point gained did in the end feel more like a point dropped as the Flames left it late to tie the match before Milos Melicherik netted the winner two minutes into the extra session. On a night when six of the seven goals were scored by special teams it was no surprise when Guildford netted the opener while killing the first penalty of the game. Jozef Kohut was sitting out a hooking minor when Ryan Vince skated away for the shorthanded marker. Marian Smerciak was binned for two minutes for roughing which led to Fife's power play equaliser from Daniel Goneau.

The visitors scored the only goal of the middle frame. It was at even strength when Greg Kuznik had the final touch past Stevie Lyle and the Flyers had a one-goal cushion to take into the last twenty minutes. All of the action in the last period was crammed into the final seven minutes. Firstly Guildford tied the game at 2-2 with a power play goal from Ryan Vince. Five minutes from time and Karry Biette gave the visitors the lead back and it looked as though both points were heading back North until Biette was penalised for tripping at 59.13 and Guildford gladly accepted the opportunity. Marian Smerciak netted with 26 seconds remaining to send the game into overtime.

In the extra session Biette was once again a guest of the penalty box — this time he was penalised for hooking at 61.14. Once again the Flames were clinical and at 62.51 the game was over as Milos Melicherik netted past Steve Briere for the game winning goal. An excited Stan Marple spoke after the game.

"It was an incredible finish. To score with under 30 seconds remaining, then to win in OT is a great accomplishment. This win was much needed."

Match Stats

Guildford: Vince 2+0, Smerciak and Melicherik 1 +0, Konder 0+3, Michnac, Plant, Dixon and Parlatore 0+1. Net: Lyle 26 shots, 23 saves.

Fife: Biette 1+1, Goneau and Kuznik 1+0, Dutiaume 0+3, Morrison and Spadafora 0+1. Net: Briere 34 shots. 30 saves.

PIM: 18-22 Power play conversions: Guildford 3 for 7, Fife 2 for 5

Attendance: 1322

Referee: Thompson. Linesmen: McPhee, Von Haselberg

Flyers Dan Goneau tangles with the Flames OT hero Milos Melicherik

Saturday November 10th 2007

Fife Flyers 6 Solway Sharks 0

The tie if not the game had already been decided even before the Sharks had loaded their kitbags on to the bus for the trip north from Dumfries.

Trailing 11-2 from their home first leg shellacking they had no option other than to go through the motions and fulfil a fixture in which they had as much hope of winning as there was of Wayne Gretzky serving chips in the café at Fife Ice Arena.

The Flyers won without any undue effort as they outshot an unsurprisingly disinterested looking Sharks team 40-25. They took their chances on the power play with four tallies and generally went about their business with one eye on the following night's game and tried to save as much energy as they could before their trip over the Tay.

As for the Sharks they had yet to deliver the level of performance which merited the talk earlier in the season of them being genuine and credible title challengers. The results between the two clubs didn't lie however. This was the fourth time that season that they had failed to lay a glove on the Flyers, who remained the bench mark team in the Scottish National League set up. Indeed the run of results endured by the Sharks against the Flyers since Fife dropped down into the lower tier of hockey was now just one win in 19 matches played.

Even with the addition of Anthony Payne, a blast from the past from the days when hockey included teams called Durham and Humberside, the Sharks looked little more than average; another throw-back to a different time in the sport— import Kevin Conway was utterly anonymous. As for Fife, well, it's hard to go full tilt when you are nine goals to the good even before the puck drops. By the end of the first period the gulf was 11 thanks to a Steven Lynch double with both goals coming on the power play.

The second period followed a similar pattern with Fife outshooting their guests 14-7 and having most of the play and occasionally getting in Payne's kitchen just for old time's sake. Someone remarked "if only his skates went as fast as his gums" A Chris Wands slapshot made it 3-0 at 22:04 before Todd Dutiaume drove the net for number four just four minutes later and when Tommy Muir added the fifth with a shot from the point at 35:23 thoughts were already drifting towards the next game.

The home side took two third period penalties and played them as if they had the man advantage and that pretty much summed up the night. Dan McIntyre declared the scoring over with number six at 46:32 to take Fife one step closer to their first silverware of the season. The challenge never did come from the Sharks, that season or next, as they would go another ten matches against the Flyers before eventually registering a win against them at the start of the 2008/09 season.

Todd Dutiaume stretches for the puck but his team were never stretched against the Sharks

Saturday November 11th 1972

Fife Flyers 8 Whitley Warriors 4

The clash between the two remaining unbeaten teams in the Autumn Cup drew a large crowd to Kirkcaldy Ice Rink. At the end of an absorbing match, it was Fife Flyers who came out on top, to retain their spot at the top of the table with 11 points from their opening six matches.

In a fast and exciting match, Flyers played some excellent ice hockey. They were quickly on top when Lawrie Lovell slipped in to open the scoring with Warriors playing a man short under penalty. In the ninth minute it was Flyers turn to kill a penalty when Kenny Horne sat it out in the sin bin. With the visitors pressing hard for the equaliser Lovell broke away to score his second goal. Before the end of the first period the home team had increased their lead to 4-0 with goals from Stuart Muir and Les Lovell.

Jim Pearson opened Warrior's account soon after the re-start to the second period. Lawrie Lovell maintained Flyers four-goal lead, when he completed his hat-trick with a goal just a couple of minutes later. Play raged from end to end with Terry Matthews pulling a goal back for the Warriors before Norrie Boreham scored Flyers sixth goal from a Bruce Libbos pass.

With what looked like a comfortable cushion for the home side there was to be no slackening off as the third period got underway. Canadian Libbos once again set Boreham up for a well taken goal and the Warriors responded when Matthews scored one at the other end. Les Lovell stepped in to score his second and Flyers eighth goal and with 10 minutes to go and with both sides still going at full speed Alfie Miller completed the scoring with what was merely a consolation goal for Warriors fourth of the night.

PENALTY!

The Flyers and Lawrie Lovell in particular would not want to hear any more about penalties for a while after this match as the Flyers had been awarded two penalty shots when Lovell was brought down twice in front of goal. He took both awards himself and after sending the first wide of the goal he saw the second brilliantly saved by the Warriors netminder, Bob Gilbert.

It seemed to be an unwanted bug that was catching with the Flyers as Jimmy Hunter had also missed a penalty shot the previous week.

Fife Flyers 1972-73. Back, left to right: Harold 'Pep' Young, Stuart Muir, Norrie Boreham, Alistair Crombie, Angus Cargill, George Taylor, Bruce Libbos, Brian Greenhorn, Iain Ritchie, Chic Cottrell, Harry Cottrell

Front, left to right: Les Lovell, Laurie Lovell, Rab Petrie, Jim Taylor, John Taylor, Jimmy Hunter

About this time Bill Sneddon, who had been a big favourite with Kirkcaldy fans when he played for the Flyers in the 1960s, was forced to retire after a long and successful career.

Sneddon, who was known as a 'robust' defender, played hockey both in the professional and amateur eras with his home town Falkirk Lions, and then with the Flyers and Murrayfield Racers, and had latterly joined Dundee Rockets. During his four seasons with the Flyers he also briefly had a stint as coach and he would do so again ten years from now. He had been troubled by a knee injury for some time but he was forced to "hang 'em up" after doctor's advice to quit playing.

Saturday November 12th 1983

Fife Flyers 2 Streatham Redskins 4

"Concentration lapse costs Flyers home record" was the *Fife Free Press* headline for this match.

Fife Flyers failed in their bid to become the first team to beat the Streatham Redskins that season and lost their own 100 per cent home league record in the process.

Without the suspended Steven Kirk, Flyers actually won both first and last periods 1-0, but a loss of concentration in the second session cost them the game. The match started with both teams playing cautiously and trying to gain the upper hand but both defences were in control. Shots were from long distance which posed no problems to the netminders. It became apparent that a defensive error might be the only way a goal would be scored and it was from such an error by a Streatham defender that Gordon MacDougall was able to intercept the puck and backhand it past the Redskins netminder to open the scoring after nine minutes. Shortly afterwards the Flyers found themselves a man short for five minutes but some fine defensive play and good goal-minding by Andy Donald kept the eager Streatham forwards at bay.

The second period continued in the same vein as the first with neither side quite able to take control until, with Flyers again skating a man short, Canadian Gary Stefan managed to force the puck home to tie the scores. Flyers seemed to lose concentration at this point. Within three minutes they found themselves two goals down, with both scores coming from Redskins Canadian centre Doug Merkosky. Flyers skated hard to try and get back into the game but once again they found themselves on the penalty kill and Merkosky scored to complete his hat-trick.

The last period started with Flyers knowing they had to get an early goal to try and pressurise the well drilled Streatham defence into making mistakes. However, as hard as they tried, Flyers were unable to disrupt the Streatham rear-guard which was well marshalled by ex-Flyer Robin Andrew. With barely five seconds of the match remaining the Flyers were eventually rewarded for their endeavours when, from a pass by Chris Orban, Gordon MacDougall scored his own and Flyers second. Flyers biggest failing was undoubtedly their inability to stay out of the penalty box. They picked up a host of unnecessary penalties and this allowed the Redskins to take full advantage of the situation. Special mention was reserved however for the roles played by Gordon Latto and young Gordon Goodsir, who both strove manfully to keep Flyers in the game when they were skating a man short.

Another positive factor to come out of the game was the welcome return to form of Andy Donald, who showed why he was so highly rated by opposing teams and deservedly took the Barr Printers Man of the Match award.

Shortly after the match Flyers coach Chris Reynolds decided that Jimmy Jack, Allan Anderson and Kenny Cruden would no longer figure in his plans for the rest of the season. Both Jack and Cruden joined Murrayfield Racers and both returned to Kirkcaldy a couple of years later when Jack played with the Flyers and Cruden the Kestrels. Anderson was back in the Flyers plans the following season and remained so for the following few years.

Neil Abel sweeps the puck home against the Redskins in a later visit that season to Kirkcaldy

Saturday November 13th 1954

Harringay Racers 8 Fife Flyers 2

After recording an encouraging 3-1 win in Nottingham against the Panthers, who were sitting second in the table just 24 hours earlier, the second bottom Flyers were no match for the fourth placed Racers in this Autumn Cup game.

Racers led 5-0 after the first session; although two quick goals by Bert Smith suggested a rally by Flyers the home lot were never in danger. It was the second success for the London side over the Flyers after they had won the earlier encounter 6-3 in Kirkcaldy. Racers goals came from Gene Miller and Fred Denny, each with a pair, Ray Maisoneuve, Les Lilley, Vic Kreklewetz and Art Hodgins.

Flyers team was Walter Malahoff, Roger Landry, John Petry, Jim Mitchell, Neil Matheson, Wayne Sutherland, Bert Smith, Johnny Andrews, Nebby Thrasher, Don Cox, Walter Davison, Ron Hemmerling

The programme notes for the visitors read as follows:

CAN FIFE FLYERS BEAT US? THEY ARE OUT TO FOLLOW EDINBURGH'S FOOTSTEPS.

Can Fife Flyers follow Edinburgh's example by beating Racers at Harringay? That is in the lap of the Gods but you can bet that coach Henry Hayes and his Merry Men will have a jolly good try. We recall earlier in the season that one very good authority on the game as it is played remarked "When Fife come down here you can bet they will give you a rattling good game. They never stop trying." Reports since then have confirmed this rating and Racers will have to be on their toes from start to finish. Motto of all Scottish Clubs coming down to Harringay is now "Anything Edinburgh can do we can do better" and there is no doubt the Royals victory here has given everyone else a boosted measure of confidence when they tread our ice. Although Flyers got beaten by (last placed) Dunfermline last weekend, we would hazard a guess that the main reason for their defeat was the fact that newcomers Petry and Landry had not settled down. This opinion is borne out by their 4-1 victory over Wembley on Tuesday! In our visitors line up this evening is red-headed forward

Nebby Thrasher, who answered the call to join Fife and arrived in Kirkcaldy this week. Thrasher played for Dunfermline in 1949-51 then joined Falkirk and wound up finally with Dundee. In his last four seasons Thrasher was never out of the top six league scorers in Scotland. In all he has netted 320 times which is not bad going in any language. One man only, Bruce Hamilton (Perth) could better this, according to records in the Ice Hockey World Annual. Looks like our defence will have to watch Mr Thrasher very carefully to-night. We understand he's as fiery as his hair!"

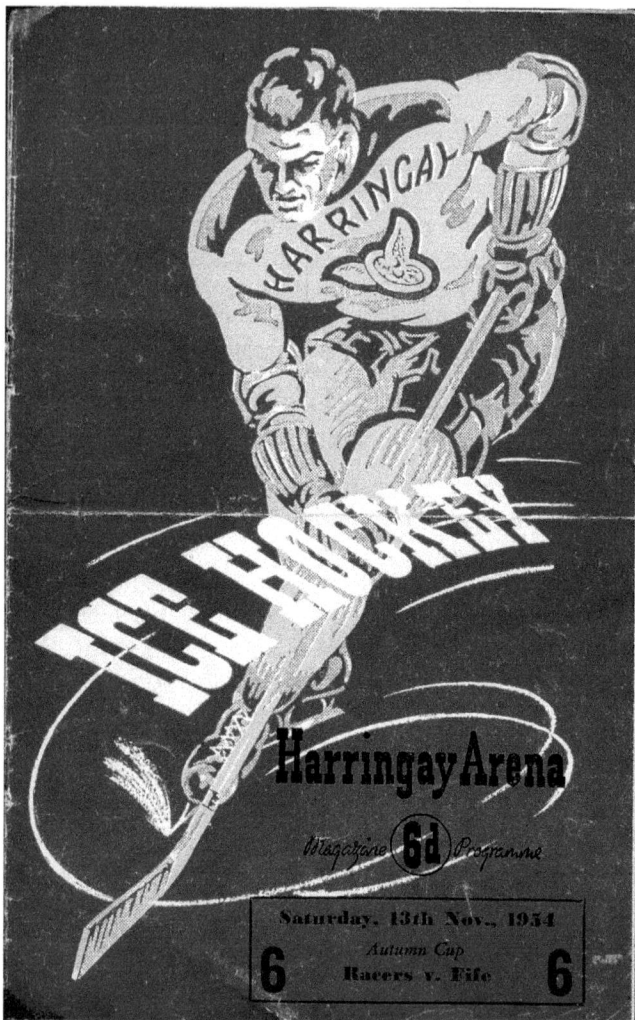

The match programme for the Flyers visit to the Harringay Arena to meet the Racers

Saturday November 14th 1987

HEINEKEN PREMIER LEAGUE

Fife Flyers 6 Solihull Barons 10

Solihull Barons, on the evidence of this visit to Fife, showed that they could be a force to be reckoned with that season.

A shock result this may have been but it was certainly no freak success against a strangely subdued Flyers outfit. The much-improved English side thoroughly deserved their triumph, in which netminder Martin McKay, who had been newly acquired from the Dundee Rockets, was in inspirational form.

Although Flyers out-shot the visitors 52-39 McKay continually broke the hearts of the Kirkcaldy offence with a series of magnificent stops. By contrast at the other end Craig Dickson in the Flyers net had a most unhappy evening and was beaten by a number of shots which he would perhaps have expected to save. Admittedly Flyers were without the play-making skills of injured Canadian Steve Moria as well as defenceman Neil Abel.

In Moria's absence Fred Perlini failed to make much of an impression and he scored just once. However, Jim Lynch, now reclassified as a non-import by the British Ice Hockey Association made his long-awaited return. The experienced Lynch proved that even at the age of 34 he would still be a valuable addition to the squad, as he claimed a pair of goals and assists to earn himself the Flyers Man of the Match award.

It was a skilful Barons team whose line-up included livewire Rick Fera and another former Murrayfield star, defenceman Paul Heavey, who punished Flyers ruthlessly by scoring on all four of their power play opportunities. Trailing 2-0 inside three minutes, to goals by Heavey and import Brian Mason, the Flyers levelled through Lynch and Al Sims before snatching a 3-2 lead with Lynch netting just 19 seconds from the end of the first period.

The match officials had incurred the wrath of the home support on more than one occasion and referee Glen Reilly was forced to call his two linesmen together; it was presumed to discuss the definition of 'icing'.

Flyers might have been expected to take control of the proceedings in the second period but they were in for a rude awakening as Barons scored three times without reply through Heavey, Jim Mayne and Mason to lead 5-3. Although skipper Gordon Latto pulled one back at the start of the final period Solihull always managed to keep their noses in front. Peter Smith made it 6-4 and although Perlini scored on a power play he foolishly gestured to Smith who had been under penalty and that earned the Canadian a two-minute penalty from which Fera immediately capitalised to restore Barons two-goal advantage.

A late goal by Ronnie Wood was a mere consolation for Flyers who lost further goals to Mayne, Fera and Smith to put Solihull into double figures. It was the Midland clubs first success against the Flyers since they joined the Premier League last season, having lost all four of these encounters. They would then have to wait another 12 games before being able to repeat their feat, when they once again won at Kirkcaldy in season 1989/90. Remarkably three of the only four wins against Flyers in their 24 game Premier league history were recorded in Kirkcaldy for the Barons.

Flyers Craig Dickson and Al Sims can do nothing to prevent Paul Heavey netting the Barons third goal

Saturday November 15th 1986

Fife Flyers 4 Nottingham Panthers 5 (after overtime)

There were raised eyebrows and not a little restlessness among the natives when Fife Flyers controversially decided to dispense with the services of popular player-coach Ron Plumb at the end of the previous season.

With Danny Brown and Todd Bidner also departing the scene, after a year bereft of silverware the Flyers had opted for a fresh set of imports. Well, not quite as when the Kirkcaldy club took the wraps off their trio of Canadians, just one name was enough to spark off an unprecedented stampede for season tickets.

The return of Dave Stoyanovich evoked memories of Flyers 1985 Wembley triumph, which capped a memorable season in which Stoyanovich smashed most of the British ice hockey scoring records. Predictably, Stoyanovich grabbed most of the headlines, but Flyers also brought back with them from Canada, the highly experienced defenceman Al Sims, a veteran of almost 400 games in the NHL, who had iced as a youngster with the legendary Bobby Orr, and 24-year-old forward Mike Jeffrey, who hailed from Nova Scotia.

With Chic Cottrell taking over as coach after hanging up his skates the Flyers fans began to think that perhaps the world was not such a bad place after all. And indeed a season keenly anticipated by the Fife faithful had so far shown no signs of letting them down. The initial target of reaching the Norwich Union Cup Final was achieved in some style despite a horrendous run of injuries which would have crippled lesser sides.

Having lost the 1984 final to Durham Wasps, largely through inexperience, Flyers were determined that there would be no repeat and after a slide of three straight losses in the league a victory in the final would hopefully provide a platform upon which they could get their season back on track.

Sadly that was not to be the case. In heart-breaking fashion not only did they lose out on the silverware but their season veered even more off track in the immediate aftermath. It was the first ever game staged at the

N.E.C. in Birmingham and a crowd of 5,600 were on hand along with an estimated 3,000,000 who watched the game live on BBC's Grandstand programme.

The game itself wasn't the prettiest to watch as neither side wanted to make a mistake but it could hardly have been any more exciting with never more than a goal between the sides. The Flyers opened the scoring through Jimmy Jack with less than three minutes on the clock but the Panthers were back on terms again five minutes later when Fred Perlini struck.

The game's only power play goal put the Flyers ahead again in the 13th minute when Gordon Latto beat Brian Cox. The Panthers levelled the scores again when Keyes pounced before the first period buzzer.

Nottingham went ahead for the first time in the 27th minute through the impressive Terry Kurtenbach and although outshout 21-9 in the middle frame a Stoyanovich 'dump' from behind the goal incredibly levelled the scores with a minute left.

The play was end-to-end in the third as the excitement level was somehow further increased. Panthers struck again early with Nigel Rhodes netting within three minutes. As the game progressed it looked ever likely that the Panthers would hang on for the win. With seven minutes remaining and the Flyers under penalty — with Peat sitting out a tripping call — Stoyanovich broke away to tally his competition-leading sixth short-handed goal of the campaign.

It was enough to take the contest beyond the regulation 60 minutes. The fans however wouldn't have long to wait for a decision. 24-year-old Layton Eratt gave Panthers their first major trophy since the 1955-56 season with less than two minutes on the clock. He beat the man principally responsible for the tie reaching this stage, Man of the Match Andy Donald, to spark wild scenes of celebration on one side of the rink and utter despair on the other.

To rub salt into the Flyers fans wounds they trudged back up the road for a Forth derby the following night at Murrayfield and were subjected to an utterly tortuous 14-2 demolition by the Racers. A weekend to forget so apologies to anyone reading who endured it. It was every bit as painful for me writing now as it was watching then!

Action from the NEC Final – Flyers Jimmy Jack (17) Dean Edmiston and Neil Abel (6) all try to protect Andy Donald from Panthers Randall Weber and Terry Kurtenbach

Saturday November 16th 2019

Fife Flyers 6 Glasgow Clan 4

The Flyers stuttering league form had seen them win only three of their last thirteen outings. The Clan rolled into Fife Ice Arena knowing that they had lost only two of their last ten in the East/West rivalry and had won all three so far that season. Flyers however answered some questions and exorcised a few demons along the way with a thrilling victory, made even more special as it was a night when they came from behind, something of a rare occurrence that season.

It was also a breakout night in front of goal when they scored six for the first time since mid-September — they needed these goals against a strong Clan side who came into the match as EIHL leaders. The performance was by no means perfect; even Todd Dutiaume admitted afterwards his team was sloppy at times, but there was character and heart in abundance.

It was a result that did not look on the cards early on as the visitors were two goals ahead inside 12 minutes and there was a sense of foreboding in the rink. The home side had enjoyed the better of the early back-and-forth exchanges but it was Clan who struck first on 6.38 through Jordan Heywood who found himself completely unmarked and finished well from a tight angle. The goal gave Clan a lift and they dominated for a spell which led to their second on 12.11 as Flyers netminder Adam Morrison left himself exposed at his near post and Nolan LaPorte fired past him.

Flyers rallied superbly led by the outstanding Danick Gauthier, Mike Cazzola and Tim Crowder line to turn a two-goal deficit into a 3-2 advantage in the space of three glorious minutes. Gauthier at 15.14 almost single-handedly turned the tide as he collected the puck deep in the neutral zone and set off towards the Clan zone at pace, leaving defencemen in his wake as he weaved this way and that. Patrick Killeen sprawled to prevent a stunning solo goal but Tim Crowder was rewarded for following in with a tap-in rebound. It was the boost Fife needed and two minutes later parity was restored as Cazzola's shot from the left was missed by Killeen as it nestled in the far corner. The turnaround was complete just 40 seconds later when Gauthier again drove the net hard to set up Tim Crowder for a back post finish, and the rink erupted.

The blistering pace continued in period two and Clan hit back on the power play at 28.47 as Rasmus Bjerrum finished off a quick passing move. Crucially Fife regained the lead inside two minutes with Cazzola converting from a tight angle after more good work from Tim Crowder and Gauthier. The momentum was now with the home side and newly announced club captain James Livingston capitalised on a clever reverse pass from Carlo Finucci to fire a first-time shot past Killeen for 5-3 at 34.47. Clan handed themselves a lifeline before the end of the period when a shot from Matt Pufahl took a deflection past Morrison to reduce the deficit to one.

Clan hadn't attained their lofty league position by being overwhelmed in games so far that season and they were never out of this one but crucially they never quite regained the momentum thanks to the hard work of the home team. As the game entered the final five minutes Clan were applying pressure in the Fife zone but a suicidal double penalty cost them dearly as Matt Stanisz was called for slashing and Mikael Lidhammer followed him to the sin bin after rather stupidly talking himself into a minor misconduct penalty. Criminal in any game but just daft in a one-goal game.

Fife, with the two-man advantage, killed the game at 55.51 as Scott Aarssen's slapshot nestled behind Killeen. Clan pulled their netminder for a late push but the home side battled hard to the final buzzer to ensure there would be no way back. Mike Cazzola's two big goals earned him Man of the Match but the inspiration behind this win was Danick Gauthier with three huge assists.

James Livingston and Kyle Just put pressure on Clan goalie Patrick Killeen

ICE HOCKEY

N⁰ 222

KIRKCALDY ICE RINK LTD.
FIFE FLYERS
v.
DURHAM BEES

SUNDAY, 17th NOVEMBER, 1963

Face off 7 p.m.

Programme   -   -   Sixpence

Flyers match night programme for the visit of the Durham Bees/Wasps. The Durham side used both monikers (Bees for away games and Wasps for home games) for a while before finally being known as the Wasps.

220

Sunday November 17th 1963

Fife Flyers 4 Durham Wasps 2

A fine hat-trick by Jimmy Spence was the highlight of the best game so far of the season at Kirkcaldy.

Flyers were always expecting a tough job on their hands to overcome the hard-skating Wasps, with the absence of Andy Williams. Bill Sneddon was ordered to the dressing-room in the first period, reducing their defence to just two men. That didn't make matters any easier. Bert Smith once again proved his versatility by taking turns on defence and Flyers held out to be narrow but deserving victors.

Wasps took advantage of some slack marking for Hep Tindale to slip home a Stark lateral pass but when Tindale and Greger were banished to the cooler only a great save by Metcalfe from Smith kept Wasps ahead.

Just after the half-way mark Sneddon high-sticked Adamson on the boards. When referee Beaton indicated that he would be penalised the Fife defender hurled his stick and gloves into the air before going to the box. Beaton had little option but to slam on a further 10 minutes and this incensed Sneddon who dashed out onto the ice. Joe McIntosh and two other Flyers fortunately restrained him before any further trouble developed but by that time Sneddon was automatically assessed a deserved match misconduct penalty.

Lammin only just failed to reach a Matthews rebound as play swung from end to end. Sammy McDonald was pulled down when almost in the clear. Jimmy Spence, of all people, missed an open goal but only ten seconds later he cracked in a terrific shot which left Metcalfe helpless. Thirty seconds from the buzzer Green slipped through the home defence to pick his spot after a neat Matthews pass to give the visitors the lead again.

Flyers squared the account early in the second when clever play by Smith put Spence in close for a neat finish. When McIntosh was sent off for using his elbow on Lammin, Weston hit the crossbar with a snapshot on the power play. Spence proved his worth at both ends of the ice when he came back to make a fine save on the goal-line after Reid had been drawn out. The pace and tension of the game came near to boiling point when Graeme Farrell cross-checked Metcalfe but somehow went un-penalised.

Spence scythed his way through with a mazy run but Tindale hooked him down in what looked like a penalty shot. With Smith dropping back on defence and the Spence, Forbes, McDonald line throwing the puck around in great style Wasps did well to hold out during the resulting penalty. Spence bided his time perfectly for Forbes to skate into position and then gave him the puck and he hit a great backhander past Metcalfe to give Flyers the lead for the first time. Reid stopped Stark at point-blank range and Metcalfe made a great catch from McDonald. Wasps put on the pressure and Reid was fully extended by Matthews and Lammin.

Flyers weathered the storm and Smith drew two men and slipped the puck across for the unmarked Spence to crash past Metcalfe. Wasps weren't finished though. Reid made an unbelievable save when Lammin shot for the empty net and he threw himself backwards to touch the puck past the post.

A bad offside decision when Lammin was straddling the line resulted in Matthews being given a 10 minute misconduct penalty and then Stark and Lammin received further 'twos' for "dissent" which meant Wasps were down to four men for the last couple of minutes but by this time the game had been won and lost. Spence and McDonald were the top stars for Flyers with Metcalfe and Dobson taking the honours for Wasps.

Flyers – Roy Reid, Bill Sneddon, Joe McIntosh, Verne Greger, Jimmy Spence, Ian Forbes, Sam McDonald, Graeme Farrell, Bert Smith, 'Pep' Young, Jimmy Watson

Wasps – Derek Metcalfe, Bill Hewitt, George Emmonds, Hep Tindale, Ian Dobson, Bobby Green, Terry Matthews, Dave Lammin, Pete Johnson, Johnny Weston, Ronnie Stark

Referees: M. Beaton and T. Watt

FIFE FLYERS

KIRKCALDY ICE RINK

OFFICIAL PROGRAMME 6d.

6805

Flyers match programme for the visit of the Dundee Tigers

Thursday November 18th 1954

BRITISH AUTUMN CUP

Fife Flyers 6 Dundee Tigers 4

Flyers recorded their third win in four games in the Autumn Cup but they had to fight much harder than had been anticipated and success was only made certain in the last few minutes.

It was far from being the clear-cut victory previous form had indicated and the Flyers could only scrape home against an off-form side which was further weakened with the absence of regular goalkeeper Don Grant and injury to star centre Bert Oig. Perhaps it was just as well for Flyers that the former Murrayfield Royals goalkeeper Ray Gariepy was substituting for Grant, as he made a nervous start and three of Flyers opening four goals were definitely of the saveable variety.

Given a boost like that, Flyers should have walked away with the game — but they didn't. It took Flyers 10 minutes to go ahead when a Ron Hemmerling pass left Walter Davison unmarked to cut in on goal, and the winger's shot found the net right between Gariepy's pads. A minute later Bert Smith took a pass from John Petry and outskated the Dundee defence before firing a shot from well out on the wing, which did not look particularly troublesome. Gariepy was late moving to it and it landed in the corner of the net.

Flyers then looked like piling up a big lead but they were brought back to earth with a bang when Jimmy Mitchell made a bad pass behind his own goal and before the error could be retrieved Marshall Key beat Walter Malahoff from the edge of the crease. Nebby Thrasher, who had frequently looked dangerous before this, scored with a brilliant solo goal in the 15th minute when he beat the labouring Oig at his own blue-line and raced past the defence to score with a fast shot right in the corner.

Two goals in a minute livened up the start of the second period when Jim McGeorge went through on his own for Tigers,then Smith took advantage of a good pass from Thrasher to restore Flyers two goal lead. Tigers were the better side for a long spell after this and it was definitely against the run of play when Wayne Sutherland scrambled the puck into the net for Flyers.

However, this was evened up when a Key shot was deflected past Malahoff and then a Red Kurz shot, into the crowded goalmouth, took

Tigers to within striking distance in the last period but the pressure on the home side was relieved when Verne Greger and George Marlin went to the cooler in rapid succession. Flyers didn't find the net on the power play, despite icing five forwards, but with only a couple of minutes to play Davison netted his second from a rebound to make the points safe.

The result was very satisfactory from Flyers point of view, but their method of gaining it would no doubt have caused some deep thought for Coach Hayes. The absence through illness of defenceman Roger Landry necessitated Hayes teaming up with Mitchell and this left Flyers with a weakness which could not be concealed. Hayes was astute when in possession but lacked pace and Mitchell made many mistakes. The other combination of Neil Matheson and John Petry was much more solid and they contributed to the success of the Thrasher-Andrews-Smith line in front of them by passing the puck up accurately and swiftly.

Nebby Thrasher and goalkeeper Malahoff were the top performers for the home side. While Malahoff inspired the Flyers defence it was Thrasher that kept the attack from falling to pieces. He was fast and tricky throughout; if he was reluctant now and then to pass the puck freely this contributed to the spectacle of the game. Both Bert Smith and Johnny Andrews worked hard and Ron Hemmerling made many nice moves for the other line attack, but neither Davison nor Sutherland quite hit it off despite Davison scoring twice. Marshall Key was the outstanding member of the Dundee side but he had little support from the temperamental Jim McGeorge and only occasional backing from Johnny Kent or Johnny Quales. Art Sullivan was kept well in check and Oig even before his injury never hit it off. The Dundee defence played well and former Flyer Verne Greger often caught the eye.

Sunday November 19th 1995

Newcastle Warriors 4 Fife Flyers 6

The Newcastle Warriors — who had been formed from the Whitley Warriors on the expectation of a shiny new arena in Newcastle, but who started the season playing at the Hillheads Rink in Whitley Bay — must already have been by now fed up with the sight of the Flyers.

They had already been beaten twice in the Benson & Hedges Cup qualifying campaign and again over the two-legged quarter-finals of the knock-out tournament. The Flyers were now in town again and this time ready to spoil the Warriors biggest night of all in their first game in their new 7000-seater arena in Newcastle. As house-warming parties go it wasn't spectacular. For a start the arena wasn't finished and this was very much a dress rehearsal for January's official launch. The match underlined that Warriors new coach Gary Douville also had a major rebuilding job to do on the ice.

Hopes of a first night victory to cheer the 4098 crowd — the biggest ever attendance at that time for a North-East ice hockey match — were thwarted within 20 minutes. Flyers 3-1 advantage killed the party mood and proved too much for a Newcastle side minus the drive of playmaker David Longstaff. Flyers played with a lot of guile and soaked up the pressure when required to do so and looked for their opportunities rather than charging gung-ho down the ice.

Execution of a classic road game strategy, but it might have been different. Kirkcaldy-born Dean Edmiston failed to convert at the back post from a peach of a pass from Simon Leach with just 40 seconds played but Ricky Grubb made the save and the Flyers gradually eased themselves into the game. A holding call against Martin King at 2:37 wasn't exploited by the visitors as the power play didn't even yield a shot on goal but it was a different story when Edmiston went for hooking Mark Morrison at 9:24 and Chris Palmer flicked the puck from the left and Mo netted the first ever goal at the new arena.

Steve Brown equalised within two minutes as Flyers defence dithered over a puck behind their own net but once again the Palmer/Morrison combination proved lethal when Mo's set-up was buried by Palmer with clinical accuracy at 13:42. Edmiston was binned for holding Morrison's stick at 17:48 and it proved a costly penalty as Palmer slotted home number three just 20 seconds into the power play. Flyers finished the period successfully killing a double penalty with brothers Derek and Steven King binned and then picked up where they left off in the second period with a killer fourth goal at 24:18.

Netminder Kevin Dean could only kick Ally Reid's shot into the path of Palmer who concluded his hat-trick with the rebound flick. A brief flurry of fisticuffs saw Les Millie and Martin King each collect double minors at 25:10 before Chris Norton grabbed Warriors second goal on the half hour mark. Hopes of a home revival were raised when Steven Brown scored at 41:54 but Warriors simply lacked the extra gear necessary to up the pace.

Morrison kept his side one step out of trouble with a right-wing slap-shot past Dean at 45:58 and he then won a face-off for Doug Marsden to seal the points with number six at 51:28. An interference call against Steven King gave Warriors a late power play but they needed almost the full two minutes before Edmiston netted off Leach's pass at 58:12 but it was a case of too little too late.

As it often had been throughout history, it was another tumultuous season for hockey in the North East as the Durham Wasps also found themselves in a different environment. Following the near end of their Riverside Rink they played out of the Crowtree Rink in Sunderland with talks of yet another rink backed by Sir John Hall being built in Newcastle.

History shows a very different outcome but it did start a chain reaction of Newcastle team names – following the Warriors there were the Cobras, then Riverkings, Jesters and finally the Vipers – I think I have that correct.

Flyers Frank Morris and Warriors Scotty Morrison tussle at Kirkcaldy earlier in the season

Saturday November 20th 1971

Fife Flyers 8 Murrayfield Racers 5

It was a night never to be repeated for defenceman Kenny Horne as he scored four goals and the Fife Flyers turned on a great display of ice hockey at Kirkcaldy to give Murrayfield Racers their first defeat of the season. It would also be the Flyers last victory over their rivals for almost 12 months.

Both sides made a late change through injury with the Flyers having John Pullar in goal in place of the injured Jim Taylor and Racers being without their captain Eric Grieve. The first period produced no scoring and no penalties but plenty of exciting hockey with the visitors just having the edge territorially. Stuart Muir shot Flyers into the lead early in the second frame. It took Racers less than two minutes to equalise through Lawrie Lovell only to see Kenny Horne put Flyers in front again with a long drive. Halfway through the period Norrie Boreham scored to increase the Flyers lead; this seemed a signal for the home side to turn on the heat. Although both forward lines were looking dangerous it was defenceman Horne who applied the killer touch with two goals.

In the third period Flyers resumed where they left off and buzzed about the Racers net which led to further goals by Boreham and Les Lovell to give the Flyers a 7-1 advantage with only five minutes remaining. A free-for-all following a clash between Rab Petrie and the visiting netminder Willie Clark resulted in both teams being depleted through the subsequent penalties and Racers used their greater experience to make the score more respectable with a trio of goals from Lovell, Gordon Inglis and Derek Reilly.

Flyers were still not finished however and as both teams returned to full strength Kenny Horne added to an already great night's work with his fourth goal. Right on the final bell Reilly netted a fifth for Racers making the score 8-5. The Flyers had been more than a match for Racers and, behind a well drilled defence, netminder Pullar who was playing only his second game in four years dealt competently with all that Murrayfield could throw at him.

This was an excellent win for Flyers after being beaten twice by Dundee Rockets the previous week although the happiest team would have been the Whitley Warriors who were heading the Autumn Cup table in what was a straight three-way battle with the Racers and Rockets as Flyers lay 5th behind the Ayr Bruins. The Warriors would go on to lift the trophy by a single point over the Racers.

It was a career night for Kenny Horne with his four goals against the "auld enemy"

Wednesday November 21st 1984

Dundee Rockets 6 Fife Flyers 11

This match was originally due to be played on October 28th but was rescheduled due to the Kingsway Rink hosting a curling bonspiel.

It was the last of the Bluecol Cup qualifying matches and with the Flyers having already qualified for the Final in Streatham in December by virtue of beating Murrayfield Racers at Kirkcaldy on the night before the original scheduled date this contest was for pride only.

Flyers ensured they would finish the qualifying group with a 100 percent record while at the same time they notched up their third win that season over the Rockets. That said, this was the first time the Rockets had tasted defeat in a home fixture against the Flyers in 11 matches (albeit two of these were also played at Kirkcaldy when they had some ice issues a few seasons back.)

The match was closely contested until Rockets Charlie Kinmond picked up a seven minute penalty early in the third period during which Flyers scored four times. Flyers led twice in the first period through Dave Stoyanovich and Jimmy Pennycook but a double by Rockets Canadian Roch Bois made it 2-2 at the buzzer.

Stoyanovich scored a short-handed goal early in the second period but Roy Halpin and Ronnie Wood put the Rockets ahead for the only time in the match. The visitors however fought back to lead 5-3 at the second interval with goals by Danny Brown and Pennycook.

Brown and Bois were on target in the final period before Kinmond's penalty turned the match. Stoyanovich and Brown netted two apiece to stretch Flyers lead to 10-5 with Brown's first the best goal of the evening when he finished in style following a patented solo rush. Although Halpin pulled one back for Rockets Dave Stoyanovich completed the scoring to bring up his personal nap hand.

The Flyers by this time knew who their opponents in the Final in London would be in just 10 days time. They would face the Durham Wasps, who at that point were the only team to have beaten the Flyers over their 15 games played that season. They also completed their qualifying group without dropping a point, before beating the Solihull Barons in a two-legged play off between the English North and South group winners.

Stoyanovich ended as top scorer with 48 points in the Scottish qualifying section with 31 goals and 17 assists. Rockets, who finished runners up in the table, had the next two top scorers on the list with Roy Halpin notching a 24+18 for 42 points and Roch Bois with 38 points while Danny Brown was fourth with a 20+12 for 32 points.

Durham's Jamie Crapper and Paul Tilley were way out on top from the English qualifying sections with a 33+28 and a 33+24 respectively and would naturally be considered the main threat in the final. How true that was!

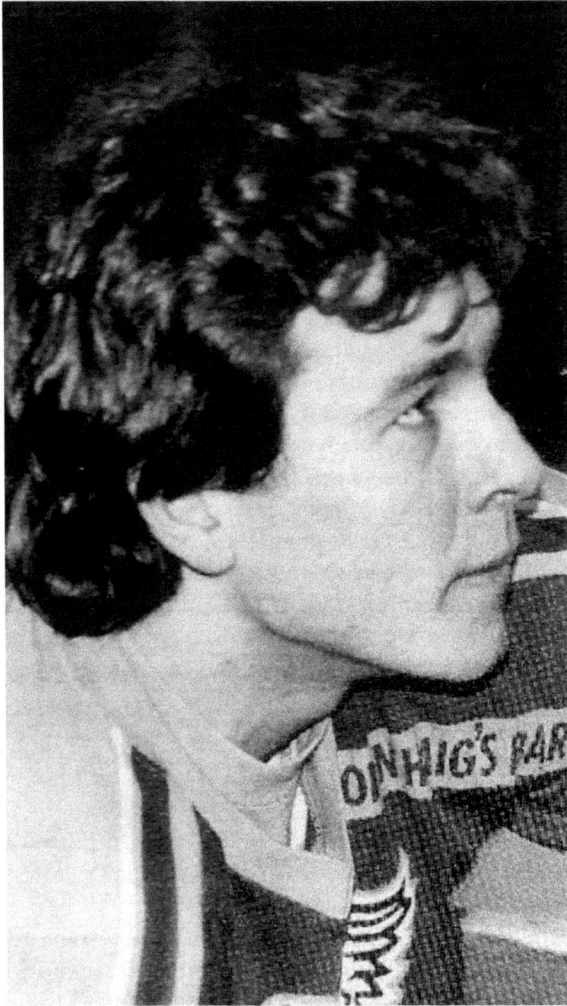

Flyers Danny Brown helped himself to a double against the Rockets

Saturday November 22nd 2008

Dundalk Latvian Hawks 5 Fife Flyers 3

The Flyers players faced a daunting early rise as they strove to keep their Celtic Cup title bid on track in Ireland.

The Kirkcaldy squad boarded a coach at 5.30 am on Saturday morning at the rink for the long road trip to Stranraer before boarding a ferry for the crucial double-header against both Dundalk teams. Flyers coach Todd Dutiaume admitted that the travel could give his side problems but with injured stars Steven Lynch and Jamie Wilson set for a return his aim was to return with maximum points.

"If we can come out of this weekend with full points I'll be really pleased with where we're sitting in the Celtic League. It's a big ask but we've got close to our full line-up back. It's been a hard month on the guys because we've been playing with a limited staff and we've been asking a lot especially from our centre men and d-men and our goaltenders have been a lot busier than normal. Hopefully we've pulled through this spate of injuries we've had.

It's been great having a level-head [assistant coach Steven Lynch] on the bench but the main reason we brought him here was for his ability on the ice. Whether we get one or 20 shifts out of him in Ireland it's a real positive for our team to have him back."

This would be Flyers first trip across the Irish Sea since Mark Morrison took his side to Belfast in a BNL /Elite League crossover match four years ago. "It's exciting and promises to be a lot of fun and so it should be, that's what hockey is all about" Dutiaume said. Flyers would hop off the ferry and make the one hour drive down across the border to the Dundalk Ice Bowl for a match against the Latvian Hawks on Saturday evening before facing Dundalk Bulls in the same rink on Sunday afternoon.

Dutiaume expected to face a stronger Latvian side than the one that was comfortably beaten in Fife last Saturday. "They were missing three or four of their better players which was a little disappointing from our perspective" he said. "They will likely be at full strength this weekend so we know it will be a lot tougher. Our guys have never played in this rink before either so we won't know what to expect. If we come out and play there's no reason why we shouldn't win these games but we've been a little inconsistent lately. I put that down to injury and tiredness."

Flyers were finding victories a lot tougher to come by that season but Dutiaume was also relishing the genuine challenge his team faced in winning silverware.

"Three years ago the league was a foregone conclusion by now but we're sitting in second or third place and that's despite hardly dropping any points. It must be interesting for the fans to not always see Flyers name at the top of the league and know we'll have to battle to March to win this thing."

He was certainly getting his 'wishes' as Flyers led the Latvian Hawks 2-1 at the end of the first period thanks to goals from Andy Samuel and comeback forward Steven Lynch. However, it all went wrong for the visitors in a four-minute burst during the middle stanza as Hawks scored three times to lead 4-2. Flyers pushed hard in the third period but it wasn't until they pulled netminder Blair Daly that Todd Dutiaume reduced the deficit. However, with Daly still off the ice Hawks grabbed a last gasp empty netter to finish them off.

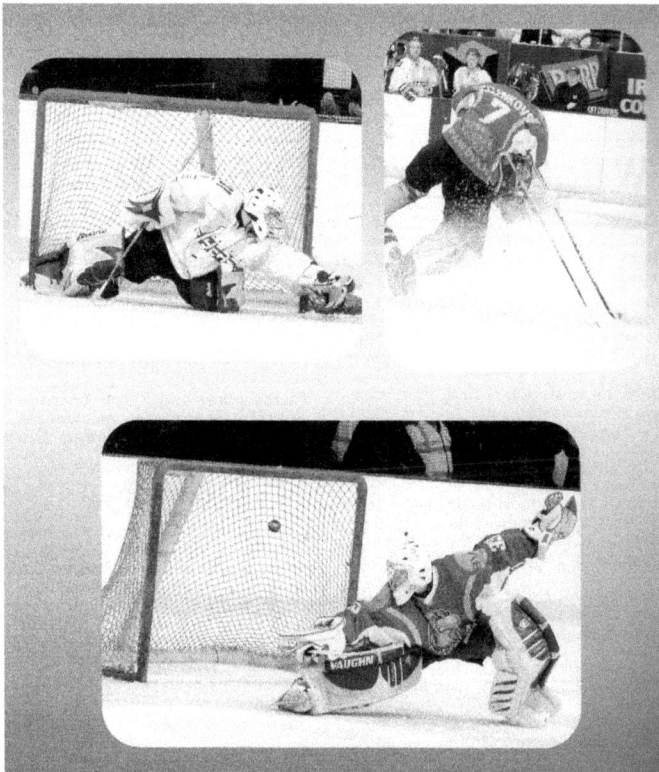

Action shots from the Latvian Hawks visit to Kirkcaldy a week earlier

WEMBLEY

EMPIRE POOL AND SPORTS ARENA

THE HOME OF THE LIONS!

OFFICIAL PROGRAMME—SIXPENCE

Saturday, November 23rd, 1963

WELCOME TO THE FLYERS!

GOOD evening everybody and a hearty welcome to the Empire Pool. Tonight we have much pleasure in welcoming that ace Scottish squad, Kirkcaldy Flyers, to Wembley and we know that sixty minutes of thrills and spills are on the way.

These Flyers from Fifeshire are acknowledged as Scotland's best and a glance at recent results indicate why, having licked Paisley 5-0, Ayr Rangers 10-1 and Glasgow Flyers 16-1. Tot up that little lot and you'll find that they possess the imposing goal record of 31 goals scored with only two against!

So Lions will have to pull out all the stops tonight if they are to clip the wings of the Flyers.

Our boys are in good heart and shape which isn't surprising following that remarkable drubbing of the Canadian Navy squad here on Thursday of last week.

This very one-sided game produced an avalanche of Lions' goals—five in the first period, eight in the second and six in the last.

Unluckiest guy of all was United States Air Force Lieutenant Walt Bohland, who took over the netminding job following injury to the regular Canadian Navy custodian at Brighton the previous Tuesday.

Bohland felt the full weight of the Lions' attack and, for most of the time, was hopping around like a scalded cat. Just the same, give him full marks for his gameness and pluck.

At the other end, Glyn Thomas had a trouble-free night, no wonder he chalked up his first-ever Empire Pool " shut-out."

Last 1963 Game

Next Saturday the curtain is lowered on Wembley ice hockey for 1963 with a visit from another hot Scottish squad, Paisley Mohawks. Coached by Bill Brennan and skippered by Bill Crawford these Paisley lads are quite a handful, so come along and see how the Lions handle them.

Ice hockey will return to Wembley when the ice show " Around the World in 80 Days " finishes its run on March 10th.

See you all next week.

The programme for the Flyers first visit to Wembley Arena since April 1955

234

Saturday November 23rd 1963

Wembley Lions 8 Fife Flyers 4

This was a match all Lions fans had been awaiting eagerly for and perhaps it was the mystique of a Flyers team — who were going great guns up in Scotland — that piqued their interest but in truth the result turned out to be much easier for their favourites than the most optimistic would have predicted.

Lions played by far their best hockey of the season. After a thrilling first period, in which they more than held their own, the Flyers fell to pieces in the later stages and rarely looked like forcing their way back into the game.

George Beach put the legendary Johnny Murray through to beat Roy Reid to the near corner after only two minutes. Lions almost added another when shots from narrow angles by both Board and Whitehead went right along the goal-line. A move which had resulted in so many goals for Flyers (and Altrincham Aces) in the past couple of seasons paid off yet again when Jimmy Spence won a face-off in Lions end and slid the puck back for Ian Forbes to blast home.

Both sides were playing canny hockey and waiting for their opponents to make a mistake. There was still plenty of excitement but ominously that was mainly round Flyers net. However a neat pass by Bert Smith put 'Pep' Young away and Graeme Farrell scrambled home his cross at the second attempt.

Lions paid the penalty of not backchecking when Spence broke away with Forbes and Sammy McDonald in close attendance. As the Lions defence covered the Flyers wingers waiting to intercept a pass Jimmy just kept going and picked his spot to give Flyers a 3-1 lead. The first real sign of weakness in Flyers defence left Zamick with only Reid to beat but, having drawn the goalie, he pushed the puck wide of the open net. That lesson failed to be learned and seconds later a fine pass by Bremner gave Lions Captain Beach a similar opportunity and he took full advantage.

A fine move started by Beach in his own zone culminated in Bremner flicking the puck cleverly past Reid from close range early in the second to tie it up. Zamick hit a beauty over Reid's right shoulder from just inside the blue-line and a minute later along range shot from Hodgins found a way past the unsighted netminder. These reverses took the sting out of Flyers for a while but just before the end of the-period a well judged lateral pass from McDonald put Spence through and he shifted round the defence. Although Thomas made a great stop the Flyers centreman backhanded home the rebound.

Spike Bremner — who had been skating well all night, before he had to be been carried off after an attempted check by Verne Greger midway through the second — returned for the last twenty minutes, thankfully showing no ill effects. A peach of a through pass by Hodgins put Whitehead in the clear to beat Reid in style. A well executed three-way play with Beach and Murray saw Bremner steam in unmarked to crash the puck past Reid and give Lions an almost unassailable lead. Five minutes from the end Beach slipped a perfectly judged pass between Bill Sneddon and Joe McIntosh and Bremner, who was the only Scot in the Lions line-up, cut in from the wing to beat Reid all-ends up and complete a well deserved hat-trick.

Hodgins, Beach and Bremner were outstanding in a great all-round performance by Lions but for Flyers only the Spence-Forbes-McDonald line enhanced their reputations. This was definitely an off-night for the Flyers defence and their second forward line apart from the never-give-up Bert Smith were too slow to make any impression on Lions strong defensive quartet.

Lions – Glyn Thomas, Red Devereaux, Vic Fildes, Pete Murray, Art Hodgins, George Beach, Spike Bremner, Johnny Murray, Tony Whitehead, Chick Zamick, Reg Board

Flyers — Roy Reid, Joe McIntosh, Bill Sneddon, Verne Greger, Jimmy Spence, Ian Forbes, Sam McDonald, Bert Smith, Pep Young, Graeme Farrell, Jimmy Watson.

Saturday November 24th 1990

HEINEKEN PREMIER LEAGUE

Fife Flyers 3 Cleveland Bombers 3

In what had become a fractious season a new chapter was written as a section of Flyers disgruntled fans had already jeered the club's imports *on* to the ice. They had drowned out individual Man of the Match awards and even often barracked them while sitting in the penalty box.

After watching an apparently solid 3-1 lead against the visiting Bombers evaporate they went for the jugular. Every first line shift started and finished amid choruses of abuse with the three Canadians taking the flak.

While every pass from Neil Abel was warmly applauded any moves involving Tim Coghlin, Rick Fera or Steve Gatzos were derided. To ram home the point, the fans heaped praise upon the all-British second line. The right to criticize had often been exercised more stridently in Kirkcaldy than any other rink in the country but it was rapidly reaching new heights of absurdity.

There was little to choose between the two teams from start to finish and Flyers even outshot Bombers with something to spare while they sat in the driving seat for the opening 30 minutes. Ultimately they paid the penalty for missing so many chances and a 3-1 second period reversal turned this game upside down and the result clearly pleased Bombers boss Noel Wallace more than it did Mike Fedorko.

The tone was set in the opening minutes when Gatzos fired an angled drive off Foster's pads and Iain Robertson's darting run between two defenceman carved out a half-chance for linemate Bobby Haig. Flyers drew first blood after 13 minutes when skipper Gordon Latto's excellent pass laid the foundations for Haig to drift across the blue line before thumping a cracking drive into the corner of the net.

Flyers struck again within 60 seconds as Les Millie and Mike Rafferty served roughing penalties and Fera worked his way along the blue line before a quick change of direction created the opening for Coghlin to score. An interference call on Clive Oakley gave Flyers a five on three power play but they failed to capitalise on the extra bodies which in hindsight was a costly slip.

The goal of the evening came just 41 seconds into the second period when Fera gazumped Foster with a deft back hand flick but crucially only ten seconds later Bombers were back in business courtesy of Kevin Conway's close range shot.

The hosts at this point however still looked cool under pressure. When Abel took an interference penalty at 25:35 they almost snatched a short-handed strike when Gatzos and Coghlin worked a neat move down the ice. The game finally burst into life around the half hour mark as Flyers second line started to click and Bombers responded with some sharp attacks. Tim Cranston ignited the visitors at 35:55 with a long range grounder which flew past Dickson to make it 3-2 and the former Flyer struck again at 36:46 to tie the game.

The third period was played out to the soundtrack of jeers and catcalls as the first line tried and failed to prise open Bombers goal. It was just not their night as Foster caught everything which came his way. With time and the fans' patience running out, Dickson denied Rafferty on a solo jaunt but was beaten by Conway's last-gasp flick which flew in and out of the net. This time the goal judge came to Flyers rescue with a controversial 'no goal' ruling and Cleveland's protests were long, loud and entirely justified.

The Flyers languished in the bottom three of the league with Whitley and Solihull.

One of the Flyers shining lights 'Robbo' getting round Bombers Mark Pallister

Sunday November 25th 2001

Fife Flyers 6 Coventry Blaze 3

Flyers lifted the Findus Challenge Cup with a superb display of controlled hockey which mixed their natural flair and skill with strong forechecking and commendable teamwork.

They blunted the threat of the bigger and stronger Coventry side by closing them down quickly and prevented them from finding any sort of rhythm, mindful of the fact that the Blaze had been taken to penalties the day before. There certainly seemed to be a lethargy about many of the Coventry side —that had also been evident the day before in the semi as well — and on this occasion there was no doubt the better team won.

It was always going to be important for Flyers to get in front and make Blaze chase. After killing off a cross-checking penalty on Karry Biette inside the first minute they took advantage when Steve Carpenter was binned for hooking. Russell Monteith showed his usual tenacity in front of goal to shoot home despite being flattened at 5.21.

Flyers survived a short spell of 5 on 3 and at 14.23 extended their lead with a goal worthy of any final in the world. Biette collected Derek King's pass inside his own zone and picked up steam as he went straight down the middle going between two defencemen; skipping over their sticks he reached the puck before netminder Ian Burt to round him and knock it into the empty net.

It was a sensational moment but Flyers were soon reminded they were still in a game when at 16.25 Hilton Ruggles set up Claude Dumas to score from close range and keep it tight at the first break. Flyers failed to make use of a brief 5-on-3 of their own at the start of the second period but restored the two-goal cushion at 26.41 when Biette picked up a loose puck and from a tight angle found the net.

This was the period which won the cup. Flyers prevented Blaze from creating any good chances and at 34.26 Mark Dutiaume broke clear and finished superbly for number four. The same player looked to have scored again soon after but the referee ruled the puck had hit the bar and had not entered the roof of the net and bounced back out.

Tensions grew as Flyers tried to kill the game off in the final period and Mark Morrison and Ruggles sat out high sticking minors, before a tripping call on Steve Chartrand proved crucial. Flyers worked the power play well and when it came to Biette, the man of the moment blasted his hat-trick strike high past Burt seemingly to seal the win. However Blaze had other ideas and when Dumas showed good skill to skate in and beat Shawn Silver just 16 seconds later there remained a glimmer of hope.

Needlessly Dumas then talked his way out of the game with a 10 minute misconduct for arguing over an offside decision. However, a lucky strike by Steve Roberts with the puck deflecting into the net off Silver's skate at 55.48 suddenly had the Fife fans anxiously looking at the clock. They needn't have worried as Flyers responded in the best possible way 23 seconds later when Monteith set up Mark Morrison to squeeze the puck home and finally kill off any Coventry revival and the party was started.

Fife Flyers: your 2001 Findus Challenge Cup Winners

Saturday November 26th 1977

Scotland 'A' 7 Scotland 'B' 8

The Flyers have over the years have provided many players for International teams. That was particularly the case during the 1970s when they were enjoying their period of almost complete domination of the game North and South of the border. The rink has also hosted many International matches and tournaments. Too numerous to go into at this time as I write, a seed has already been planted for a possible future book.

On the same day a trial was held for the England Senior squad at Billingham when the North East combine comprehensively overwhelmed their Southern counterparts 16-2. These trials coincided with a British Ice Hockey Association announcement. The GB National team, who had been invited to compete in the Pondus Cup in Denmark — a tournament that they had competed in over the last couple of years as a warm up to the World Championship tournaments — had now been uninvited.

Despite a verbal agreement with the Danish Federation at last year's tournament, there was no explanation given as to why they would not be participating next month. It was hoped that they would participate again in the future. GB had finished bottom of Pool C earlier in the year and despite the I I H F being provisionally willing to have them compete again in March 1978 the spot was taken by China, who had last competed in 1974. So this left the International calendar somewhat bereft of fixtures and the Home International double header between the Auld Enemies took on even greater significance.

Scotland team selectors Frank Dempster and Willie Clark did not have easy choices to make as the more fancied 'A' team went down by the odd goal in 15. Flyers player-coach Lawrie Lovell missed the game due to bruised ribs he sustained during a recent Edinburgh match. Most of the players on show had their purple patches and a number of the 'B' team members would be in with a good chance of making the national side.

A victory for the 'A' team looked an odds-on certainty during the early play and that would have been the outcome had the game been stopped at the end of the second period. But the favourites were dumped in a goal blitz in the last 20 minutes.

Goals from Jimmy Jack, Alastair Brennan and Steve Hunter against one from Dougie Latto gave the 'A' team a 3-1 lead after the first period.

Scoring was tight in the second stanza with one goal for each side scored by John Hay and John Hester. Then came the turnabout in the final period.

Charlie Kinmond pulled one back but John Hay restored the 'A' side's two goal lead before Dougie Latto scored his second of the night only to see it cancelled out 10 seconds later by Jimmy Pennycook. John Taylor and John Gibson netted a brace each in just over three minutes to move the 'B' team into the lead for the first time in the game. Although Les Lovell managed to pull one back in the dying seconds any hopes of a fight-back were too late.

On 17th December in the first of the two game series the Scots overwhelmed the English 15-4 at Kirkcaldy, although a little over a month later the English got revenge with an 8-6 win in the return at Billingham. In the first game there were Scotland debuts for Flyers Jimmy Jack and the Cottrell brothers Willie and Chic, with the other Flyers representatives contributing over 50% of the goals with Law Lovell netting five, Les a double and a single from Gordon Latto.

For the return the Scots were without coach Johnny Murray and six Murrayfield Racers; the Murrayfield side — with a Northern League game the following night — refused to release them. Joe McIntosh took charge of what was essentially a Flyers select with the brothers Cottrell, Lovell and Latto all icing along with Dave Medd, Charlie Kinmond, John Taylor, Jimmy Jack and Ally Brennan. All six goals came from the Flyers contingent of John Taylor with a hat trick and Law Lovell, Kinmond and Jack. Kenny McLennan, John Hester and Martin Shields of Glasgow were the non-Flyers. Hendrie, Wells and Gibson of Ayr should also have played but missed the match due to their car breaking down en route.

Gordon Latto sweeps the puck home in a match against the Glasgow Dynamos in season 1977/78

Tuesday November 27th 2001

Fife Flyers 2 Romania 6

It was the first visit of a national side to Kirkcaldy since December 1965 when the Flyers went down 5-3 to the Polish National touring team.

Over the years and in particular in the late 1940s and early 1950s, the rink had hosted a number of 'National' teams who were usually represented by a club side who had taken part in the World/European Championships and were finishing off with a tour of the UK.

Certainly there have been Canadian and USA sides who have visited in that guise although Czechoslovakia were famously beaten 6-1 by the Flyers in March 1948. This Romanian side had two days earlier played Team GB at Nottingham in what was called a "Friendship Game" which was part of the Findus Challenge Cup Final festivities.

The newly crowned Findus Challenge Cup winners appeared to be still suffering from the effects of their success although they also took the opportunity to blood a number of junior players on the night. Romania, who were beaten 6-1 by Great Britain at Nottingham before the final on Sunday, looked far sharper and talented on this occasion and always had the upper hand. The Fife team used the game more as a training exercise with Mark Morrison opting not to play the last two periods and instead watched from the bench.

The Challenge Cup was paraded beforehand and the Romanians were given a warm welcome on to the ice but they then proceeded to spoil the party by racing into a three-goal lead. Attila Gergely (5.17), Viorel Nicolescu (6.06) and Levente Hozo (10.35) all found a way past Colin Grubb as Flyers struggled to find their feet after the exertions of the weekend.

The second period saw juniors Chad Reekie, Euan Forsyth, Adam Walker and Scott McAndrew log plenty of ice time and referee Moray Hanson dish out a string of minor penalties as international relations became strained especially between Karry Biette and most of the Romanians.

Gary Wishart finally put Flyers on the board at 30.45 from Andy Samuel's pass but Catalin Geru finished well at 35.40 to leave the visitors in control at the second break.

Silly penalties again interrupted the somewhat lacklustre third period proceedings and there were no more goals until the closing stages when Gergely (55.17) scored his second before Russell Monteith pulled one back 13 seconds later and Gem also claimed a brace with 46 seconds of the game remaining.

Flyers scoring: Wishart 1+0, Monteith 1+0, Venters 0+1, Samuel 0+1, M. Dutiaume 0+1.

Romania scoring: Gergely 2+1, Gem 2+0, Nicolescu 1+0, Hozo 1+0, Sabolch 0+1, Cazacu 0+1, Kosa 0+1, Dimache 0+1, Andrei 0+1, Corduban 0+1.

Shots on goal: Flyers (Grubb) 34; Romania (Radii) 32.

Penalty minutes: Flyers 18, Romania 16. Referee: Hanson

Attendance 1004

Gary Wishart with one of the goals against Team Romania

Saturday November 28th 2009

Paisley Pirates 0 Fife Flyers 6

Flyers expected no slip-ups despite, being understrength, as they travelled West to Braehead Arena to meet the Pirates before entertaining them at Kirkcaldy the following night.

In the absence of Todd Dutiaume, who was attending to some family matters, assistant coach Steven Lynch took the reins.

> "Pirates have improved since the last time we played them. I think Dino Bauba is back playing for them and he can make a big difference, They also beat Whitley a couple of weeks ago. We'll be expecting to take four points but we know it's not going to be a walk in the park. There are no bankers where you are guaranteed two points any more."

Flyers had Dan McIntyre back in the squad, but Iain Beattie, who had been missing for the past month with a shoulder injury, was not quite ready yet to return to the fray. Despite the cautious 'coach speak' the visitors on Saturday night had little difficulty. In securing the two points against the Pirates they also posted a third consecutive shutout, which still stands at the time of writing as a club record. Having already disposed of Dundee Tigers in the Scottish Cup 11-0 and Whitley Warriors in the Northern League 6-0 the previous weekend — both of these also road games — the Pirates were similarly vanquished with a Stephen Gunn hat trick a double from Andy Samuel and single from Chris Wands.

Blair Daly, as he had done the two previous games, took the honours between the pipes in what may well be a record that endures forever for a Flyers netminder. That season the Flyers recorded eight shutouts. Daly was in net for them all, although two were shared with John Nicol. That number of clean sheets was also a club record for a season — one that had already been set in season 2006/07 and repeated in season 2008/09, such was the dominance of the Flyers in the lower tier of hockey.

Blair Daly recorded six of the 2006/07 shutouts, sharing two with Michael Haston and Jordan Marr, who was in net for the other two. Similarly, in 2008/09 Daly had six of the eight, with two shared with Holland, who had the other two. Remarkably for Daly, in two of the above seasons, 06/07 and 08/09 he also managed 10 assists in both which also stands as record points totals for a Flyers goalie in a season.

Blair Daly taking care of business in the traditional way for a goalkeeper whilst setting records at both ends in recent seasons.

Saturday November 29th 1980

Fife Flyers 6 Glasgow Dynamos 4

Tony Sgro was on his way back home to Canada after a short stay in Fife. The reinforcements from Aviemore of Neil McKay and Steve Crummey were still a week away, but the Flyers did manage to regain some of their recently battered pride with a competent if unconvincing victory against a never-say-die Glasgow outfit.

The visitors fought back from a two goal deficit on two occasions but in the end a brace by Chic Cottrell within the space of 60 seconds in the final period proved to be the last straw that broke the Dynamos back. Play was reasonably fluid despite there being a constant stream of players from both sides who made their way to the sin bin during the course of the game.

It looked as though the visitors were going to be on a hiding to nothing with the game just two minutes old, as Jim Lynch and Chic Cottrell netted without reply. But the goal avalanche that might have been expected never materialised as Dynamos managed to contain if not exactly threaten the home side.

Although Flyers kept buzzing around their opponents goal area they were restricted to firing in a number of long range shots as their principle offensive play.

Just as Flyers had started the first period, the Glasgow side stormed back in similar fashion in the second. Goals by Tony Daly and Peter Murphy in the first four minutes pegged back the home side's lead. Flyers were quick to reply through Gordon Latto, who netted his side's third before Jim Lynch scored the best goal of the game on the half-hour mark with a scorching shot which whipped past the goaltender before he could move. On the interval buzzer, however, Neil McLennan pulled one back for the Dynamos.

The final period was just 43 seconds old when Colin Wilson levelled the scores again as the game burst into life with thrust and counter-thrust. It was Chic Cottrell, however, who put paid to the visitors' challenge with two well-taken goals in the space of a minute, his second arising from a bad mistake by the goaltender. The Flyers held out for their second win against the Glasgow side that season after they had beaten the Dynamos the previous month to win the Skol Cup Final at Kirkcaldy. There was an added attraction for Kirkcaldy fans with the appearance of Olympic sprinter Allan Wells who performed the ceremonial puck drop and was presented to the players.

Olympic medal winner Alan Wells dropping the ceremonial puck in the match against Glasgow Dynamos

Thursday November 30th 1950

Fife Flyers 7 Falkirk Lions 2

This was the third meeting of these two teams in a 10 day span after the Flyers had emerged victorious in the Scottish Cup on a 12-8 aggregate over two games. Despite the heavy score against them the Falkirk Lions had provided the biggest advertisement yet for the inclusion of home-bred hockey players when they visited Kirkcaldy.

Ahead of the game Lions coach George McNeil had released all but five of his professional Canadian players and had decided to ice juniors in their places since he reckoned the Lions would be better served by "Scotsmen who never stopped trying, rather than by Canadians who had the ability but wouldn't use it."

And this game proved his theory was correct to a point. Although his five Falkirk Juniors never matched Flyers in science or guile they gained the admiration of the crowd for their enthusiasm for the game. They skated hard both ways and how successful they were showed in the 2-1 score at the end of the second period.

Even after being penalised in the last session, they managed to equalise before Flyers came away with one of their scoring bursts which were now an almost familiar trait. It really was only because their opponents were tiring that the home side got so much of its own way late on. Until then the teams had been well matched.

Flyers had the edge, but brilliant goalkeeping by Finch and poor finishing by the forwards kept them forging ahead, while the Lions always looked dangerous on their fast break outs. In the last ten minutes, however, the Falkirk team clearly wilted and Flyers scored with almost every shot. This was hardly in keeping with the previous run of the game, where in the early stages the play was so much towards Flyers goal that it was five minutes before Finch stopped his first shot.

Having lost their opening game in the National league the previous night, the Flyers got big performances from Marsh Bentley, who looked like hitting up a partnership with Al Campone, while Archie Williams had his best home game to date for Flyers.

Floyd Snider would have been included in honourable mentions but for the many loose passes he slung out of defence which far too often ended up on the end of a Lion's stick. Finch, Sneddon, Ormond and Nicholson were Lions best players.

Match Statistics:

First Period

Goals: Lions — Sneddon, Flyers- Bentley (Reid & Campone)

Penalties: Flyers — Reid, Sneddon

Second Period

Goals: Flyers — Thorne (Blair & Williams)

Penalties: Lions Gallacher, Penner and Green (2)

Third Period

Goals: Lions — Penner, Flyers — Thorne (Williams), Campone (Bentley), Bentley (Campone), Burnett, Snider (Williams)

Penalties: Flyers — Campone, Reid, Lions — Nicholson, Reid

Shots on Goal; Belanger 22 Finch 35

Flyers — 'Pete' Belanger, Verne Greger, Floyd Snider, Jimmy Mitchell, Jimmy Burnett, Marshall Bentley, Scotty Reid, Al Campone, Bert Smith, Archie Williams, Sherman Blair, Lee Thorne

Lions, Hap Finch, Lloyd Penner, Bill Sneddon, Bill Gallagher, Ken Nicholson, Johnny Sherban, Ken Green, Alex Ormond, Tommy Paton, Jack Smith.

Referees D. Cumming and D. Cross.

Al Campone (number 4) was a star against the Lions – seen here in action in an earlier game against the Ayr Raiders

December

Action from the Bluecol Cup Final:
above, Jimmy Pennycook is outnumbered around the Wasps net;
below, Steve Kirk awaits his chance.

Saturday December 1st 1984

Autumn (Bluecol) Cup Final

Streatham Ice Rink

Durham Wasps 6 Fife Flyers 4

The Flyers first major final for six years turned out to be a huge anti-climax as they failed to live up to the high-standard they had set for themselves that season. The Wasps deserved the victory but it was a bitter disappointment for the hundreds of Fifers who travelled to London, fully confident that they would see Gordon Latto lifting the first silverware of the ice hockey year. Yet the biggest disappointment of all was felt by the players themselves who knew they did not do themselves justice, coming off second best on the day despite winning the first and third periods.

The trophy was won and lost in the second period when Durham overturned a one goal deficit to score four times without reply and leave Flyers an uphill battle which proved just too much.

Although the Flyers outshot their opponents 36-34 and Durham netminder Neil Campbell was voted Man of the Match it was Durham who made better use of their scoring opportunities.

Wasps Canadians Paul Tilley and Jamie Crapper scored five goals between them while Danny Brown and Dave Stoyanovich were unable to make much of an impression in the tight confines of the Streatham rink.

Nevertheless, Brown came close to pulling the game out of the fire for Flyers, scoring twice as the Kirkcaldy side mounted a thrilling fightback.

Alas! It all came too late. A couple of penalties in the last six minutes ensured that Durham collected their first ever major trophy.

Player-coach Ron Plumb had emphasised the importance of making a good start to the match, but it was Wasps who drew first blood after just 67 seconds when Tilley beat Andy Donald from close range.

The first five minutes were played almost entirely in the Flyers half of the ice but gradually they came back into the match and after eight minutes Dougie Latto found the corner of the net with a low shot from wide on the blue line.

Both sides had chances to go in front but with just 11 seconds from the buzzer it was Ron Plumb who fired Flyers ahead with Durham short-handed.

The vociferous Fife fans expected their team to consolidate their lead in the second period but it took Wasps only 42 seconds to get back on level terms when Crapper accepted a simple chance set up by Tilley.

Three minutes later, Durham went 3-2 ahead when Crapper fired a superb shot out of Donald's reach.

Dave Stoyanovich had a chance to tie the scores when he skated clear following a mistake by Cooper, but he was unable to force the puck home. Just two minutes later Durham scored their own shorthanded goal through a swift break by Tilley. With less than a minute of the period remaining Ivor Bennett really put Durham in the driving seat with a tremendous goal to make it 5-2.

Flyers badly needed an early goal in the third period but once again it was the Wasps who scored within seconds, when Crapper picked up the rebound of his own shot to beat Donald.

The Kirkcaldy men needed something special now. Danny Brown gave them hope when he diverted a Stoyanovich shot into the net seven minutes into the period. Five minutes later Brown tucked away the rebound of another Stoyanovich effort to set the scene for a rousing climax.

Gordon Goodsir had desperate luck, striking the post with seven minutes remaining but immediately took a penalty to ease the pressure on Durham. And when Dougie Latto also picked up a penalty three minutes later Wasps were content to simply play out the remainder of the match.

The final buzzer signalled tremendous scenes of celebration among the Durham players and fans with the Flyers sportingly congratulating the victors before receiving their runners-up trophies.

As Wasps displayed the trophy to their jubilant supporters, Flyers applauded their own fans for their backing, reflecting on what might have been, and perhaps daring to dream about Wembley in May.

Saturday December 2nd 1967

Glasgow Dynamos 6 Fife Flyers 7

Fife Flyers must have taken their cue from their football equivalents at Stark's Park as, at Crossmyloof on Saturday night, they fought back after being two goals down with only eighteen minutes left.

There was a difference in their fight-back; earlier that afternoon Raith could only manage to draw, while the Flyers went one better and recorded a win!

It was the Flyers penultimate Autumn Cup game. The result exacted some measure of revenge over the Dynamos, who had earlier won in Kirkcaldy. In truth, though, for either side there was little to play for, as the Paisley Mohawks, with a 100% record, had long since clinched the title.

Flyers showed greater determination, speed and penetration in their late rally than had been shown for most of the season. They were forced to, though, by making things difficult for themselves after leading 2-1 they then lost the place in the second period and went behind 4-2.

In the third period they found themselves 6-4 down before the dramatic closing rally. Up front Les Lovell was at last showing his full potential. His four goals marked back-to-back games where he had enjoyed such a goal spree. It brought his total to 16 goals in the competition —10 ahead of Joe Baird. Norrie Boreham and Sam McDonald skated hard but Bert Smith had one of those games no doubt he would want to forget.

Flyers opened on the offensive but in the third minute it was the Dynamos who took the lead. Bob Stevenson sent Robert Ormond through; he outpaced the Flyers defence to score from close range. Within a minute, however, Flyers equalised through Les Lovell, with Norrie Boreham providing the assist.

In the seventh minute Ian Forbes found Graeme Farrell all on his own on the blue line with a long pass and the Perth man put the Flyers back in the lead with a fine shot. Dynamos increased the pace at the start of the second period. Within two minutes they had equalised through Rudy Carroll from a Bob Stevenson pass.

Worse was to come for the Flyers when in the ninth minute, with Kenny Horne in the cooler, the Glasgow side went into the lead through Alan Lavety with a hard shot from the blue line after intense pressure around the Fife goal.

A minute later and Flyers were again a man short when Ian Forbes was penalised. Bob Stevenson took advantage to make the score 4-2 for the home side with a fine solo goal. Flyers fought back and with four minutes remaining in the period 'Pinky' Farrell scored from a Joe McIntosh pass to reduce the leeway. A minute later Lovell equalised for the Fifers from another Norrie Boreham assist.

It was once again a bad start for the Flyers when, within two minutes of the start of the final period, Bob Stevenson sent Danny Ballantyne through and he beat Roy Reid with a rather soft looking shot. The Fife side fought back, but could not score. In the ninth minute, things looked really bleak, when that man Stevenson struck again to make the score 6-4 in favour of the Dynamos. Flyers then piled on the pressure and, after a terrific melée in front of the Glasgow goal, Forbes got one back for the Fifers with seven minutes to go.

Lovell twice came close before Bob Stevenson was penalised with five minutes to go. Les was on hand to net the equaliser on the power play from close range. Immediately afterwards Horne was penalised but a fantastic penalty-kill denied the home side taking the lead once more. With under three minutes remaining Les Lovell scored the winner, with a backhand shot high into the corner of the net after he had made a fine dash up ice.

Glasgow Dynamos — I Nelson, D Ballantyne, G Hysert, J Purcell, A Lavety, F Soulis, R Stevenson, B Stevenson, D Sinclair, F Burns, R Ormond, R Carroll

Fife Flyers — R Reid, J McIntosh, I Forbes, K Horne, B Brown, G Farrell, B Smith, S McDonald, J Baird, L Lovell, N Boreham, D Medd, P Reilly, J Taylor, I Shields

Fife Flyers 1967-68. Back, left to right: Tommy Horne (Manager), Joe McIntosh (Coach), Danny Brown, John Taylor, Norrie Boreham, Ian Forbes, Joe Baird, Bill Brown, Kenny Horne. Front, left to right: Ian Shields, Jim Taylor, Bert Smith, Sammy McDonald (Captain), Roy Reid, Dave Medd

Sunday December 3rd 1995

HEINEKEN PREMIER LEAGUE

Fife Flyers 7 Nottingham Panthers 7

As we were winding our way to the festive season both teams served up a cameo of a classic Christmas movie, The Great Escape, which for one night only was playing at the Ice Rink in Rosslyn Street.

That said, most of the game had been played out in a fairly low-key manner with little to suggest the drama that lay ahead. The Flyers found themselves, with just over a minute left in the game, trailing the beaten Benson & Hedges Cup finalists by a goal. Player-coach Mark Morrison took the ultimate gamble, pulling netminder Bernie McCrone to add a sixth skater.

Frantic was the only word to describe the action that ensued, amidst a frenzied atmosphere from the stands. Flyers battled to pin Panthers in their own zone. The new roof was almost blown off the old arena when Morrison fought like a tiger in the left corner and centered for Frank Morris to score the equaliser with just 19 seconds remaining.

The moment of glory was only slightly spoiled by Nottingham import Garth Premak starting some aggro, which he wanted to carry on even when the teams were shaking hands. There had been plenty of aggression shown in the previous 60 minutes, most of it directed at referee Paul Branch, who had bumbled his way from stoppage to stoppage without appearing to take any real grip on proceedings.

Panthers opened the scoring on a 5 on 3 power play with Steven King off for holding. Fife had also been handed a bench penalty after a water bottle had been tossed onto the ice. Morrison, who was also in the sin bin, remonstrated with the official that he had asked for the water to be thrown to him across the ice.

The Panthers gratefully accepted the opportunity. When a Mike Blaisdell shot came back off the boards Simon Hunt buried the rebound. Flyers equalised on a power play at 8:47 with Morrison tipping Derek King's slap shot past goalie Scott O'Connor. The visitors then streaked to a 3-1 lead through Randall Weber and, straight out of the penalty box, Ashley Tait. Morris pulled Fife back into the game at 16:40 and with 11 seconds remaining on the period a Doug Marsden interception presented Morrison with his second to tie the game up. Nottingham edged ahead again just over half-way into the second period, when dual national Neil Morgan was on hand to knock the puck past McCrone after a shot came off the back netting. The visitors once again stretched their lead when Paul Adey was allowed to waltz in unchallenged from the right corner to give Panthers a 5-3 lead.

Patience on a 5 on 3 power play dragged Flyers back into contention as the five-man unit resisted the crowd's cries to just blast away at goal. They moved the puck around perfectly until Doug Marsden was presented with the opening for Fife's fourth. Flyers tied the game up once more early in the third period, Morrison calmly netting after a great pass from Les Millie.

The lead however lasted a mere 19 seconds. Adey restored the visitors' advantage. With about 10 minutes to go, the Panthers had another two-goal lead. Adey completed his straight hat-trick to put Panthers 7-5 up. A wonderful crisp cross-ice pass from Millie, which was tipped home by Marsden, reduced the deficit to just one goal at 56:50.

The scene was set for the last-gasp equaliser which finally brought almost all of the subdued 1203 crowd to life.

Shots on Goal — Flyers 33 Panthers 35

Flyers: Morrison 3+3, Marsden 2+1, Palmer 0+3, Morris 2+0, Millie 0+2, Derek King 0+1, Steven King 0+1, Robertson 0+1.

Panthers: Adey 3+0, Hunt 1+1, Morgan 1+0, Tait 1+0, Weber 1+0, Blaisdell 0+1, Durdle 0+1, Kelham 0+1, Tricket 0+1.

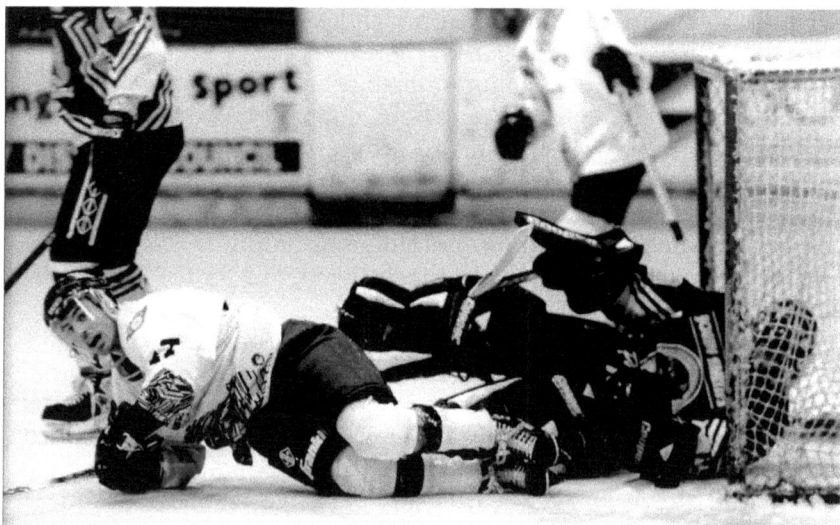

Frank Morris thinks he has scored but Panthers netminder O'Connor is about to glove the puck

Saturday December 4th 1999

Peterborough Pirates 2 Fife Flyers 3

A crowd of nearly 1000 witnessed this game, which more than lived up to expectations.

Flyers travelled south, knowing that they needed a win to level the season series, as the Pirates had plundered a 3-2 win at Kirkcaldy the previous month. Indeed, a strong rivalry between these two sides was already at boiling point. The Pirates had knocked the Flyers out of the Benson & Hedges Challenge Cup with a couple of single goal victories in September.

Pirates were on a nine-game unbeaten run but it was clear that Fife didn't have to worry about shaking off their bus legs as they quickly set the pace in this one. The first power play went to Fife and the teams ended up playing four on four as the intensity was increased.

Fife surrendered the opening goal to the veteran Doug McEwan at 17:58 but, importantly, were back on level terms seconds before the break. David Smith had the initial shot and the rebound from keeper Lindsay fell for Mark Morrison to net. Craig Lindsay and Stephen Murphy were in fine form in the nets and for most of the second period perfectly showcased their talents.

The Flyers went on a 5 on 3 power play midway through the period, a huge moment in the game. However Pirates penalty killing was strong as they emerged at even strength with the score still tied. The Pirates were soon back on the kill, however as Andrew Milne was ejected on a five-minute major penalty for boarding Kyle Horne, who was left with a face cut from the incident. Lindsay again was stellar in net and the power play was negated with Fife taking a minor tripping penalty.

Into the third period with both sides looking for the all-important go-ahead goal, Todd Dutiaume almost sneaked one short-handed. Home coach Randy Smith had the puck in the net but the whistle had already blown. Smith was not to be denied however as he beat Stephen Murphy at 51:30 with a shot to the youngster's near post.

Fife were not done, however. When Neil Liddiard and David Clarke were penalised within 20 seconds of each other, the Flyers this time made no mistake with the two-man advantage. Russell Monteith needed only 5 seconds to bundle home the equaliser.

Monty, the man they also called 'Cunndies', was to top off the heroics with just 13 ticks left on the clock as he struck the winner to leave the home side crestfallen. The Flyers had secured the sort of win that often defines title winners.

They had enjoyed only one win in the Fenlands rink in their last eight visits, so without doubt this was a massive two points to take. There was obviously still a long way to go in the season, but the Pirates capitulated the following night at Solihull. They probably looked back at that weekend as the point where their league aspirations took an almost unrecoverable blow.

Match winner as he was on a number of nights, Russell Monteith

Wednesday December 5th 1951

Falkirk Lions 4 Fife Flyers 0

The Flyers were embarking upon the start of their National League campaign after mid-table finishes in the opening two competitions of the season, the Autumn and Canada Cups.

The Lions had the upper hand in the games played between the two sides so far this season, winning both of the meetings played on their home ice.

Behind in the game by a couple of goals with fourteen minutes still to play, the Flyers seemed to have been thrown a life-line. Lions new Canadian goalie Murray Dodd was injured and replaced by junior George Brown. This would surely be their time to get pucks on the net and pressurise the young net minder. They failed to take advantage and they even failed to get a shot on goal!

This had been a typical Flyers performance so far this season; they always managed to flop just when they seemed to be on the point of doing something great and fully deserved to be shut-out for the first time on the season.

Outplayed for long spells, the visitors nevertheless had many opportunities to take the lead, long before Lions did in the second period. Mickey Linnell, Joe Millisin, Johnny Vanier, in fact almost every forward, missed when well-placed and their errors proved costly in the long run.

Lions, always the aggressors, never looked like losing after they took the lead. Their hefty defence was much too hard-hitting and powerful for the Kirkcaldy forwards. Both the speed of the nippy Thrasher and clever plays by Sinfield always looked like creating goals up front. Neither actually hit the mark, but it was they who softened up the Kirkcaldy defence.

Jack Mason and Floyd Snider were Flyers best. Fife were mainly on the receiving end in the first period. Lions definitely held the initiative and would have taken the lead but for some brilliant saves by Mason. New defenceman Jim Szabo showed clever enough touches on occasion, yet made one or two blunders which could, and should, have proved fatal. The ex-Brighton Tigers man would remain with the Flyers for a fortnight before moving on to join the Perth Panthers.

Up front for Flyers the Kewley, Millisin, Vanier line played neat hockey in bursts but Millisin was guilty of an atrocious miss in front of goal.

There was more life in the game in the second period with Lions putting more fire into their efforts. They fully deserved to take the lead when Henry netted. Mason did well to prevent the deficit growing rapidly in several goalmouth scrimmages, but he was beaten again before the interval by Sherban.

The last period was when Flyers really beat themselves. Following Dodd's injury they never looked like scoring. The Falkirk defence closed up and stopped them at every turn, often before they had really got an attack on the move. The Lions added further goals through Sherban and Ormond as they comprehensively outshot the visitors 42-17.

Lions, Murray Dodd, Bobby Burns, Bill Sneddon, Stu Cruickshanks, Jim Fiddler, Nebby Thrasher, Moe Fife, George Sinfield, Johnny Sherban, Jim Yeaman, Alex Ormond

Flyers, Jack Mason, Floyd Snider, Jimmy Mitchell, Verne Greger, Jim Szabo, Hal Kewley, Joe Millisin, Johnny Vanier, Archie Williams, Frank Facto, Mickey Linnell

Referee, Dave Cross

Two Fife Flyers, converging the Falkirk Lions' goal, beca entangled with cageminder Fi during the ice-hockey match Kirkcaldy last night.

Action from an earlier season encounter with the Falkirk Lions at Kirkcaldy

Sunday December 6th 1964

SCOTTISH LEAGUE

Fife Flyers 18 Glasgow Flyers 5

SPENCE LEADS GOAL AVALANCHE

Top scoring centre-ice Jimmy Spence bagged eight goals. This put Flyers well on the way to their second biggest win of the season, and brought Spence's personal goal tally to over the 40 mark.

Despite the huge margin which separated the two teams, Flyers Canadian netminder Bill McNab was still called into action regularly and went a long way to redeeming himself after a somewhat shaky debut the previous week. McNab was a 20-year old who had signed a few weeks ago, having previously played with Junior 'A' side the Toronto Marlboroughs.

Although the Flyers led 6-0 at the end of the first period, their lead had been cut by two goals when the teams skated off at the end of the second session with the score standing at 8-4.

A magnificent six-goal burst by the home side in the first five minutes of the final session sealed the West of Scotland side's fate. The Flyers slammed four of these goals home inside two minutes. Sammy McDonald opened the scoring in the fourth minute of the game and then Spence scored three times in quick succession.

Additional goals from Bert Smith and Spence put the Flyers six goals ahead at the end of the first twenty. Glasgow Flyers countered with a surprise goal by Don Brown against the run of play five minutes into the second period. A minute later, future Fife Flyer Joe Baird added a second goal.

Spence increased the home tally at the midway point but Bryan Bott, who also played a few games for the Flyers that season, pulled another one back for the Glasgow side. Brown added a fourth in the 14th minute. 50 seconds later he was benched for interference, with an additional 10 minute misconducted tagged on for arguing with the referee.

Team captain Baird incurred the referee's displeasure when he inquired about Brown's penalties and he too sat out for 10 minutes. Spence had brought the Flyers total up to eight before they lost Canadian Garry Holden, who was carried off in agony after being speared in the mid-rift by Gordie Hughes.

The Glasgow player was immediately benched for five minutes. A situation that the Flyers took full advantage of as they turned on the pressure at the start of the final period. Hughes had four minutes left to serve in his penalty at the start of the third session and the Glasgow side were also missing the services of Baird and Brown who still had five minutes of their respective misconduct penalties to serve.

Flyers turned this advantage into goals and brought their total to 13 through a double strike from Graeme Farrell and singles from Joe McIntosh, Law Lovell and Bill Sneddon before Hughes returned to bring the West of Scotland side back to full-strength. Shortly after, however, Spence soloed through to net the home side's 14th goal and a minute later Ian Shields was on hand to slam home another. Smith made it 16 before Glasgow scored another consolation goal, through John Hogg, but goals from Spence and McDonald hammered the final nails into the Glasgow side's coffin before the end.

Eight goals in a single game from a British player is still a club record held by Jimmy Spence; this wasn't him setting the record, though, but *repeating* it. It was almost 12 months to the day that he set the original record against the same opposition in a 19-1 win at Kirkcaldy.

The prolific Jimmy Spence

Saturday December 7th 1968

Fife Flyers 10 Durham Wasps 8

A GAME TO BE FORGOTTEN was the headline in the local paper. Hardly surprising perhaps given the position of both teams.

Flyers were bottom of the Autumn Cup table with two points to their name from a couple of draws. "A win is a win" is what they say – well, this was the Flyers first of the season, as they gained both points in the meeting with the team who sat just a place above them.

Despite the relief of a long-awaited victory, the Flyers remained bottom. It did little to enthuse the now long-suffering home fans in a game that most would have forgotten before they had stepped foot into the night onto Rosslyn Street.

It was a scrappy match between two teams who looked more as if they were out for a practice knockabout than for a real contest. As one spectator was heard to comment "Some pantomime – it's like Cinderella on ice". But if a pantomime it was, it was not one which was suitable for a younger audience, as tempers began to fray and the language of some of the players left much to be desired.

The attendance at Flyers matches was still extremely poor, despite the many appeals for fans to turn out and give their support to their team. A few weeks before, Ice Rink manager Tommy Horne had warned that unless the position improved there was a distinct possibility that all ice hockey at Kirkcaldy could be discontinued.

This would undoubtedly have been a huge disappointment both for the ice rink and for the town, where there was still a small band of staunch supporters who regularly turned out to cheer Flyers on. It is however a sad fact of life that when a team is consistently losing then interest quickly fades. It was felt that unless Flyers pulled up their socks and injected some new life into their team it may well be that the end was near.

Durham were quickly off the mark in the first period and had two goals to their credit before Flyers replied. The visitors notched up two more to a reply of one by the home side to make the score 4-2 at the end of the first period in favour of the visitors. Flyers pulled one back in the second session and then levelled the score before taking the lead.

Durham equalised before the Flyers once again got their noses in front only to allow the visitors to tie things up again at 6-6.

Into the third period and the Flyers eventually put some daylight between themselves and the Wasps. They scored a couple of goals but the see-saw battle continued. Wasps hit back with two of their own, to once again level matters. Graeme Farrell and Jimmy Hunter, who completed his hat trick, made sure of a win by notching the final two goals of the game without further reply.

George Pearson notched a double for Flyers with single goals coming from Bill Brown, George Wylie, Joe Baird and Ian Shields. For Wasps they had a hat trick from Peter Johnston, doubles for Denny Brown and Frank O'Connor and a single from Hep Tindale.

Flyers, Ian Nelson, Bill Brown, Joe McIntosh, Dave Medd, George Wylie, Peter Reilly, Jimmy Hunter, Graeme Farrell, Norrie Boreham, Ian Shields, John Taylor, George Pearson, Doug Wilson, Rab Petrie.

Wasps, Derek Metcalfe, Dougie Milner, Philip McDonough, Hep Tindale, Eddy George, Bert Greenwell, Frank O'Connor, Pete Johnston, Denny Brown, Wilson, Dave Raine.

Joe Baird seen with a couple of aspiring young hockey players by the name of Dougie and Gordon Latto

Thursday December 8th 1949

Fife Flyers 3 Dunfermline Vikings 1

The Flyers were becoming a dominant force on the Scottish circuit following their successes the previous season.

They had lost only four of their opening 21 matches and had just narrowly been pipped by Dundee Tigers in their effort to retain the Autumn Cup. They lead the Canada Cup table and knew that a win in this game against second-placed Dunfermline would secure them the title with a couple of games still remaining.

A Marsh Bentley inspired Flyers came out in top but it was a less than convincing performance by recent standards. It was felt that they couldn't be feeling too pleased with their performance. That certainly appeared to be the undoubted feelings from the report by the local hockey correspondent.

All round the Vikings were a smoother moving combination and only the hard work of Flyers second line and the steady blocking of Ray Dinardo, Floyd Snider and Co. on the blue line prevented them from recording an easy victory. Flyers first line had no answer to the plays of the Rowett, Watson, Gaudette line and the bulk of the work was thrown on the defence, which, with Dame Fortune lending a hand now and again, was just able to cope.

Snider had an unfortunate moment when he slapped the puck through 'Pete' Belanger's legs for what turned out to be Vikings only counter but he recovered well and played one of his best games this season. On their showings over the past few weeks Flyers first line just wasn't living up to expectations.

Chic Mann's trickiness would start to pay greater dividends when he had some decent support but that wasn't expected while pivoting Johnny Vanier and Bert Smith. It was to be expected of Smith, who was playing both senior and junior games, that at times he would be somewhat lethargic but there was no such benefit of the doubt given to Vanier's efforts which were described in black and white as "pathetic" these past few weeks.

There was only a week until the start of the 24-game National League and Al Rogers wasn't without his worries. It was doubtful if the few Flyers who were really pulling their weight could continue to carry the team and a new right-winger for the first line seemed to be the best solution.

Returning to the game, Bentley was once again the man who really counted for Flyers. He netted two goals and was entitled to a two-way assist on the third in addition to doing his share of the back-checking. He was always a menace and with Earl McCrone and Scotty Reid backing him up the Flyers second line once again took all the honours.

In defence, Belanger and Snider caught the eye more than the others but Dinardo, in his cool collected way and Greger, with his aggressive checks, were every bit as good. Nebby Thrasher, Ted Watson and Jerry Hudson, the Vikings sharpshooters, could make little of them, which was a direct testament to the Flyers defensive play.

The visitors looked to have their own worries but their fast swinging plays which had brought results in the past were expected to do so again in the future. Tonight was just not their night, but they played well with Thrasher, Watson and Ed Rowett in attack and Tuck Syme and Bill Melville in defence showing up best. Flyers were first to flash the red light when Marsh Bentley raced up the middle in a brilliant solo effort before he crashed the disc past a bewildered George Leonard.

The home lead was short lived however when Watson 'scored' for Vikings when he flicked the puck into the middle and Snider, attempting to clear, sent the rubber into his own net. Flyers again went ahead in the second session when Reid collected the puck and smashed it into the net. Although Vikings rallied and Belanger was kept busy, the score remained at 2-1 going into the final period. Vikings tried vainly to pierce the solid Fife defence in the last period but it was Flyers who scored again. Bentley raced through and made it 3-1 with a neat low shot.

The 1949-50 Flyers team. Back Row, left to right: Chic Mann, Ames Brown, 'Pete' Belanger, Earl McCrone, Verne Greger. Front Row, left to right: Floyd Snider, Ray Bouchard, Marshall Bentley, Johnny Vanier

Saturday December 9th 1972

Fife Flyers 9 Murrayfield Racers 4

THAT CUP-WINNING FEELING

Flyers clinch trophy

It was certainly going to be a Merry Christmas for Fife Flyers and their supporters, with every indication that they would go on to enjoy an even happier New Year.

Against their bitter rivals they annexed the Autumn Cup, their first-ever success in the Northern Ice Hockey League. Requiring only two points from their last three matches Flyers needed only one bite at the cherry to clinch the trophy with this fine victory against a Racers team, against whom they had not recorded a win in their last six outings.

Let alone such a handsome win! With a seven-point lead, Flyers couldn't be caught by any of their rivals. It was thought that, if they were able to maintain the form that had seen them drop only one point since the start of the season, there should be more silverware to keep the Autumn Cup company in the Kirkcaldy boardroom.

There really could not have been a better start for the home side. A fantastic goal by captain Les Lovell after only *six seconds* put Flyers on the road to victory. It was a goal that was claimed to be the fastest-ever scored in Northern League history and definitely set a club record, that stands at the time of publication, as the fastest-ever in a Flyers match.

Lawrie Lovell won the draw at the opening face-off and fed Chic Cottrell on the left. The young winger zipped over the blue-line and passed to his captain who blasted the puck first-time into the net. Then before Racers could get going Law added a second goal and brother Les, assisted again by Cottrell, made the score 3-0.

Racers showed they could be dangerous however scoring through Freddie Wood and Willie Archibald before the end of the period. A reminder to Flyers that it was not going to be as easy as the early play had indicated.

The second period opened with another quick goal for the Flyers, this time by Lawrie Lovell and although Derek Reilly pulled one back for the visitors Flyers played with great confidence. Even when penalties gave Racers a man-power advantage, home-netminder John Pullar was seldom troubled.

On one occasion, when the Flyers were two men short, Lawrie Lovell delighted the crowd with an amazing exhibition of stick-handling. Retaining possession of the puck for the best part of a minute Lawrie certainly put his former team-mates through the mill. He then set Ally Brennan up for a well taken goal. In the last 40 seconds of the middle frame he laid on an easy chance for brother Les and then scored the seventh himself.

Excitement mounted as the final minutes of the third period ticked away. Just before the halfway stage Willie Kerr had raised Racers hopes with a goal from close in, but Flyers were too near to success to be denied. Further goals by Lawrie Lovell and Cottrell boosted the home tally to nine.

CANADIAN STAR BREAKS ANKLE

Prior to the game there was a presentation by Mr James Fyfe, honorary treasurer of Flyers Development Club, for an injured Flyer. Canadian Bruce Libbos, who broke an ankle playing against Glasgow Dynamos two weeks ago, was presented with a cheque in appreciation of his good work for Fife Flyers that season.

THAT CUP-WINNING FEELING – a jubilant Flyers dressing room after their Autumn Cup clinching win

Saturday December 10th 2017

ELITE ICE HOCKEY LEAGUE

Fife Flyers 5 Milton Keynes Lightning 2

A second period goal blitz was eventually all that was required for the Flyers to unlock this game.

Three strikes inside six minutes saw the Lightning wilt and there was no way back for the English visitors. The result was no more than Flyers deserved.

They worked hard, had clicked early on when the game was finely balanced and indeed should have gone into the first period break a goal up, thanks to Chase Schaber's sixth minute strike. The forward skated on to a neat pass which found a gap in behind the Lightning defence, and he beat netminder Miika Wiikman with a good finish.

Just seconds were left on the clock when Lightning struck with an equaliser that was entirely down to a momentary lapse in concentration. Andy Isles blocked a shot and defenceman Jim Jorgensen didn't deal with the rebound which allowed the quick-thinking Guilliaume Ducet to pounce.

Fife's response in the second period was emphatic. They grabbed the lead at 22:28 on the power play as the puck was dug out of the right-hand corner and thrown across to Ricards Birzins who simply roofed it. Then came a (no pun intended) lightning-quick double which effectively saw Milton Keynes appetite for this game diminish.

Evan Bloodoff drove the net where he set up Liam Heelis to shoot and his re-bound was swept home by trailing man Peter LeBlanc for 3-1 at 26:40. Within 40 seconds it was 4-1 as James Isaacs got a glorious tip on Russ Moyer's rocket of a shot from wide.

Lightning coach Peter Russell was clearly furious on the bench. He had no choice but to call a timeout to steady the ship before it sank without trace. But his team looked rattled and slightly narked, a mood not helped when LeBlanc turned home an Ian Young pass for 5-1 on the power play at 33:12.

Lightning threw some tasty hits to raise the temperature among the crowd, no bad thing on a bitterly cold Sunday night. Former Fife fan favourite, Matt Nickerson, incurred the wrath of the crowd as he hit Liam Heelis with three cross checks behind the net. Nickerson had already headed down the tunnel presumably anticipating a game misconduct, only for referee Alan Craig to summon him back to sit a double minor.

Fife started the third period in control, and never looked in any great danger. Denny Kearney's power play counter at 49:05 did cut the deficit to three but as the shifts rolled over, the gap between the teams both on the ice and on the scoreboard was never in any real danger of being breached.

The Flyers were on a decent run of form, having lost only two of their last nine matches and were in a mid-table position. With three games in hand over the teams immediately above them they were in position to strike for a top three position.

A Peter LeBlanc double helped secure the points against the visiting Lightning

Liam Heelis sets up another Flyers attack as he evades his Lightning marker

Friday December 11th 1953

Paisley Pirates 17 Fife Flyers 2

It is fair to say that the season so far had not been a spectacular success for the Flyers. In the Autumn Cup they recorded a couple of wins from their dozen games to finish bottom of the table on goal difference to an equally hapless Dundee Tigers. Next up was the Canada Cup and it was a repeat story for those two, although this time the Tigers at least managed to put four wins on the board against the solitary victory by the Flyers. Both competitions had seen the Paisley Pirates win the titles, and in the process drop only three games across both competitions.

There was some hope for the Flyers, who naturally had lost on both their previous visits to the West this season, and that was the 10-2 shellacking that the Lions had handed the Pirates just a couple of nights before in the Scottish Cup.

Such optimism was quickly dispelled however as the Flyers really ran up against it and sustained their biggest-ever defeat at that time. In fact this game still stains the Flyers record books as their worst ever road reverse in history – a shared 'honour' with the exact score line being replicated amazingly twice in a calendar year in 1989 when in March at Whitley and then in December in Cardiff the Flyers were sent home with their tails firmly between their legs.

Returning to the 'present', Flyers had been somewhat in disarray with their coaching appointments from the close season, detailed elsewhere in the book. At this point Wray Fallowfield was in temporary charge before the return of fan favourite Floyd Snider.

For Flyers to lose 17 goals in their second National League game was indeed something of a crowning blow following their long spell in the doldrums so far this season. Playing two games in successive nights — Fallowfield had also presided over the 6-6 draw the previous night in Dundee —was tough for the Flyers, who had a depleted side.

To make matters worse tonight Jimmy Mitchell had to call off due to a leg injury. With Jim Smith still side-lined the Flyers had only eight players available. Taking this into consideration the apparent débacle was not quite so surprising.

Few teams would have fared any better against the mighty Pirates under similar circumstances. Until Flyers were able to get replacements into their line up, anything could happen for a team clearly low on confidence as well as bodies.

Two players who deserved the highest praise for a tremendous, whole-hearted display were defencemen Wray Fallowfield and Bob Reid who simply refused to give up the fight. Fallowfield was in fact quite the hero of the match.

Hal Schooley was the outstanding marksman in the Paisley side and he bagged seven goals to his credit. Other scorers were Harry Bentley, Tuck Syme and Cece Slack who each scored a brace. There were singles from Dave Ferguson, Bill Crawford, Johnny Trandle.

Murray Banks would also score his final goal for the Pirates before signing for the visitors, making a scoring debut just four days later at Falkirk. He went on to be the Flyers top scorer in the National League that season. Flyers consolations in the rout came from Scotty Reid and Bert Smith, who got the biggest ovation of the night as he stick handled his way past the Pirates defence with the Flyers short handed to score with five minutes remaining.

Flyers early season line up. Back, left to right: Scotty Dowle, Wray Fallowfield, Jim Fiddler (made only two appearances), Bert Doig, Fred Kentner
Front, left to right: John Dobos (player-coach), Lloyd Boomer, Craig Cooper (made only one appearance), Jack Lane, Ron Collins
Bert Doig was a Fife junior player who was reputed to be the only bearded player in the league at that time.

Friday December 12th 1952

Paisley Pirates 5 Fife Flyers 0

Flyers travelled West to the Paisley Ice Rink in what was their last game in the initial schedule of the Canada Cup series before it returned for the final four games at the end of the season. Fife had already tasted success on Pirates home ice in a Scottish Cup win as well as following that up with a similar result at Kirkcaldy.

The Pirates however had won the corresponding Canada Cup game at Kirkcaldy earlier in the season; with only one win in their last eight outings the Flyers were looking for a much-needed confidence boost ahead of the National League starting.

It was not to be. More target practice was clearly going to be necessary if Flyers were to rise from the bottom of the Canada Cup standings. Based on the evidence offered up by the team in this game there would be many struggles ahead in the National League.

Pirates scored two goals in the first period and two in the second but the ex-Detroit Red Wing, Harry McQueston, in Flyers net barred the door on many other occasions when all seemed lost.

Flyers missed the injured Bob Burns. The ex-Dundee Tigers and Falkirk Lions defenceman had been recruited that summer as player coach to replace Al Rogers and was also team captain.

Bud Stock and Marshall Bentley, while always prominent, failed to make anything happen around the Paisley net. They, however, were not alone in that regard.

The Paisley forwards were alive to every chance which was in stark contrast to the visitors. It was an easily earned shutout for Ed Lockhead, although he did have to show some greater attention to the game in the final period as Flyers eventually found some glimpses of his net.

Pirates goals came from Bob Kelly, Whit Mousseau with a double, George Sarkisian and Jerry Goodwin.

It left the table looking like this:

	P	W	D	L	F	A	Pts
Lions	10	9	0	1	32	23	18
Pirates	9	6	2	1	43	26	14
Raiders	9	5	0	4	31	23	10
Royals	10	4	1	5	36	35	9
Panthers	9	3	2	4	41	43	8
Tigers	10	2	2	6	31	46	6
Vikings	9	2	2	5	18	21	6
Flyers	10	2	1	7	23	40	5

In more positive news it was announced that two Flyers had been selected to represent Scotland. Two teams to represent Scotland in games with English teams were chosen at a meeting in Falkirk, somewhat curiously by the Scottish Ice Hockey Association Referees Committee.

For the game against Streatham at Murrayfield on the afternoon of Saturday December 27, which was televised, player coach Bob Burns and net minder Harry McQueston were included in the line-up. For the game at Earls Court London, on January 11th, Bob Burns would be Flyers only representative.

The teams were: Edinburgh – McQueston (Flyers), Greger (Royals), Hill (Pirates), Kewley (Raiders), Burns (Flyers), Sarkisian (Pirates), Mousseau (Pirates), Domenico (Raiders), Fife (Royals), Crowder (Royals), Baldwin (Royals), Cowie (Royals). Coach — Sandy Archer (Murrayfield)

London — Melnechuk (Lions), Burns (Flyers), Hill (Pirates), Baker (Lions), Cruickshanks (Lions). Mousseau (Pirates), Hudson (Vikings), Arnold (Lions), Doig (Panthers), Thrasher (Vikings), Hamilton (Panthers), Domenico (Raiders), Coach — George McNeill (Lions).

The Scottish Select side gained a 3-3 draw against Streatham and went down 3-2 to the Rangers at Earls Court.

Match programme for Flyers visit to play the Paisley Pirates

Sunday December 13th 2015

Elite Ice Hockey League

Fife Flyers 5 Nottingham Panthers 2

There are nights when Fife Flyers have given their fans a glimpse into their true potential and they go on and deliver the sort of win that is needed to underpin their entire season. There have been nights, of course, where the opposite is sadly all too common.

On a bitterly cold night against the Panthers they pulled out a performance defined by the former and thoroughly deserved their victory.

The Flyers so far that season had been a team in search of consistency, which made this win huge. It was gutsy and hard-earned. The hope was that they would draw confidence from it, which would surely allow them then to join the dots between games and finally put an end to their somewhat erratic performances and results to date.

A crowd of 1753 turned up. This wasn't bad for a Sunday night, even better considering that it had been a home double-header weekend so close to Christmas.

Those that strayed from the warmth of their homes were rewarded with a great finale. Flyers took an early lead in a closely fought opening period and were then hanging on a bit at 2-2 after two. They broke out in the third as Panthers punishing schedule of three games in three nights took its toll. To put the win down to Nottingham's fatigue, though they clearly didn't have as much in the tank, would be unfair to Flyers work ethic and determination to dig in.

They got big performances out of a number of players and when they had the momentum they certainly made the most of it. They had already scorned a couple of decent chances before grabbing the opener at 18:06. It came via the unlikely source of defenceman Tommy Muir, who left Dave Ling on his backside and took off on a mazy run down the ice pad. He chased the puck, got it back and his shot delivered the perfect rebound for Jeff Lee to bury.

Panthers upped their game in the second period and were level at 23:09 when Stephen Lee ripped a shot from the blue line through traffic on the power play. Back came Flyers and Phil Paquet scored a soft looking goal at 26:44 when his flicked puck rolled under the netminder and trickled over the line. Panthers responded and Logan MacMillan bagged a rebound from a spilled shot to make it 2-2 going into the second break.

It was clear the next goal would be significant. It was Fife who got it on the power play as referee Alan Craig binned MacMillan for a slash off the puck. Nicholas Rioux's shot was blocked and it fell neatly for Justin Fox to bury at 47:59.

Within four minutes it was 4-2 as TJ Caig faked the shot, as a player dived in to block. With the defenceman committed he hammered it home. Panthers stepped up the pressure in the closing five minutes but Fife didn't flinch. As the clock ran down Nottingham pulled netminder Miika Wiikaman only to see Michael Dorr slide the puck home from wide on the right for 5-2.

Second-placed Panthers missed the chance to close the gap on leaders Cardiff Devils and it was Flyers only win in league meetings with Nottingham that term.

Matt Delahey gets his shot off against the Panthers

Saturday December 14th 2013

ELITE ICE HOCKEY LEAGUE

Fife Flyers 7 Braehead Clan 6 (after overtime)

This was a different Fife Flyers team to the one that had been shut out 4-0 by the Clan at home just three weeks ago. Bobby Chaumont returned to form with a second hat-trick in three games.

It was far from a perfect performance but there was heart and passion on display that suggested the individuals were finally becoming a team. With the TV cameras in town and new signing Ned Lukacevic in the line-up Flyers made a storming start. It didn't take long for Andy Contois' replacement to match the goal tally his predecessor managed in 21 games when on the power play at 3.19 Lukacevic opened his account.

Braehead, considered an outside title challenger, hit back with goals from Joe Cullen (13.53) on the power play and Ash Goldie (15.52). Flyers were quickly level through Derek Roehl on 16.24 but Kenton Smith's slapshot gave Clan a 3-2 lead at the end of an engrossing first period.

Clan flexed their muscles at the start of period two with Matt Haywood making it 4-2 after 23 minutes. Almost instantly Flyers pulled it back to 4-3 with their second power play goal as Chaumont finished off a clever move. Flyers lost Matt Nickerson to a match penalty for excessive roughness after 28.08 when he dragged Chris Frank to the ice and administered a beating. Ed McGrane put Clan 5-3 up after a minute of the third but Flyers again hit back quickly via Chaumont.

Joel Champagne restored Clan's two-goal lead for a third time with five minutes left and the game was starting to look like a lost cause. For the fourth time in the match Flyers scored within a minute of Clan to pull it back to 6-5 thanks to Jordan Fulton's power play goal at 55.19. Flyers threw everything at the Clan defence and as the visitors continued to take penalties Flyers removed Kevin Regan from nets to go on a six-on-four power play for the final minute.

When Chaumont shot through a crowd of bodies to tie the game at 6-6 with 34 seconds left the rink exploded. Into overtime and the outstanding Danny Stewart (who gave a non-stop display) popped up in the right place at the right time to slot home the sudden death winner.

The aftermath of the Nickerson/Frank incident saw the Flyers defenceman handed a hefty ban. After reviewing the incident, the Elite

League head of discipline, Moray Hanson, hit Nickerson with a 12-game suspension accusing the Fife player of attempting to "choke" the Clan defenceman.

The EIHL chief also suggested that Nickerson ignored instructions from officials to stop and that Frank suffered a facial injury and was in "clear distress" at the time of the incident. It was Nickerson's fourth match penalty since joining Fife in September and Hanson described him as a "multiple repeat offender"; the 28-year-old American now faced over a month on the sidelines.

Flyers coach Todd Dutiaume questioned whether the punishment fitted the crime and if Matt Nickerson's reputation was counting against him. He also criticised Braehead's PR war of words and the conduct of Chris Frank and insisted talk of a grudge between the teams was misguided.

Dutiaume said:

> "I don't think 12 games reflects the crime because in every one of Matt's suspensions there has never been a resulting injury. The rules state that you don't have to injure a player to get a match penalty but we've had players hurt for several weeks and the opposing player was back in half, or a third of the time."

The 12-game suspension was subsequently reduced to 9.

The Matt Nickerson and Chris Frank incident that resulted in the Flyers defenceman receiving a substantial suspension

Sunday December 15th 1985

Durham Wasps 8 Fife Flyers 5

Murrayfield Racers and Durham Wasps continued to set the pace at the top of the league but there was very little between the Dundee Rockets, Ayr Bruins and Flyers who were all in hot pursuit, just a few points behind.

Visiting Durham Ice Rink during the British Hockey League years of the '80s and '90s was never usually an 'enjoyable' experience for the Flyers or, dare I say, the fans. The Flyers, coming into this game, had yet to win on Durham ice in five attempts over the previous three seasons.

Their only losses in the Premier league so far that season had come on the road at Streatham and Murrayfield, but they knew that to make an impact in the league that they would have to take points from teams like Durham and Murrayfield at every opportunity.

Minus Gordon Latto and Jimmy Pennycook, whatever plans they drew up on the bus heading to the North East were most likely ripped up inside the opening five minutes when John Ciotti and Paul Smith had the home side a couple of goals ahead.

Danny Brown, with an unassisted goal, a minute later steadied the ship. However, it was to be a Wild-West shoot out in the first period and Anthony Johnson regained the home side's two-goal advantage a further 60 seconds later. Not to be outdone, Brown pounced again to net unassisted with just a further 30 seconds on the clock. Smith, once again for Durham, kept the scorekeepers busy before Ron Plumb got Fife to within a goal from a Todd Bidner pass. The Wasps however pretty much put the game to bed before the first buzzer when they struck twice through Ian Cooper and Ciotti.

Any thoughts of another Flyers fightback were killed within 66 seconds of the restart when Paul Smith completed his hat trick; it looked as though the Flyers might be routed when, a couple of minutes later, the home sides power play cashed in with Wasps leading goal scorer John Ciotti also grabbing a triple.

A goal from Bidner less than a minute later made the score 8-4 but with over half of the game remaining it was still a long way back.

Remarkably after that it was all about the goalies with Frankie Killen facing 37 shots to Craig Dickson's 25 and the only goal came just moments into the third period when Brown became the third player to claim a hat trick.

The Wasps were able to play out the remaining time without ever looking as though the points were going anywhere other than staying in the Cathedral City.

Durham remained in second place in the league on 17 points, a point behind leaders Murrayfield Racers with Flyers in mid table a further 3 points behind. For the record, the Flyers played at the Riverside 30 times from 1982 to 1996 and they returned home with a win on just four occasions!

Durham's Riverside Rink – if you were ever there you won't forget – often a painful place for Flyers and their fans

Saturday December 16th 1978

Crowtree Chiefs 8 Fife Flyers 10

Fife Flyers returned from a double header in the North East of England with another two good wins to their credit, the first of which was success in the Icy Smith Cup knock-out game at Sunderland against the local Crowtree Chiefs.

A win the following night in Durham stretched their winning streak on the season to eight matches. With Gordon Latto and Lawrie Lovell again among the goals and starting to show something like their best form, Flyers looked more like the squad which had dominated the British hockey scene in the past few seasons.

Without Canadian defencemen Doug Westwater — a back injury picked up off ice at his work — and Dave Medd, unable to make the trip, the Flyers, who had already beaten the Chiefs 9-3 at Kirkcaldy earlier in the season, had more of a struggle than expected in their first ever visit to the recently opened Crowtree Leisure Centre.

Westwater, who had joined the team a few weeks before, was a 21-year old from Bradford Ontario and had played Junior 'B' for Bradford Airgun Penguins. He also had trial for the Junior 'A' Peterborough Petes and while his father was playing football for St Johnstone the youngster had impressed player-coach Law Lovell in a try out for the Flyers.

The home team made a dream start with the opening goal a minute after puck drop. Flyers then proceeded to play some excellent hockey, scoring five times during the opening twenty minutes, which included a natural hat-trick by Chic Cottrell, with only one goal from the Chiefs in reply.

The visitors seemed well in command during the middle period but with the Wichenko brothers Brent and Mike and Hep Tindale forming a highly dangerous line, the Chiefs pulled back from a 7-3 deficit to tie the scores at 8-8 going into the final twenty minutes.

Crowtree goals came from Keith Havery, Peter Lund, Tindale and Rod Binns with the Canadian Wichenko brothers netting the other four.

For Fife, Chic Cottrell had added another to take his tally to four, Law Lovell had a brace with strikes also from John Taylor and Charlie Kinmond.

Flyers tightened up considerably and dominated throughout the closing period. With Gordon Latto getting the all-important ninth goal, it was left for Ally Brennan to put the issue beyond doubt and put the holders into the semi-final, where they would meet Glasgow Dynamos, who had triumphed over the Aviemore Blackhawks. The following week the Flyers recorded a more comfortable win against the Chiefs when they ran up a 21-8 win at home.

The former Crowtree Leisure Centre and its landmark bridge across Crowtree Road. Opened in 1978 it was pulled down in 2013.

Saturday December 17th 2005

Aberdeen Lynx 1 Fife Flyers 30

No, the score line is not a mis-print. Fife Flyers did indeed put *thirty* goals past a sad Aberdeen side, and this despite leaving four of their top players at home and icing a number of teenagers.

Although a historical event as it created a new club record, it did show, not for the first time that season, that Fife Flyers and the Scottish National League did not belong together.

Even before face-off the gulf in ability between the two teams was no secret. That did not stop the result from causing a great deal of shock and possibly even more damage in the sport. Pitting the oldest and most successful club in Scottish ice hockey history against a team taking its first steps into the sport was perhaps inviting an uncomfortable outcome.

The merit of bringing Aberdeen into the Scottish National League in the first instance and, if this was their level, keeping them there, surely now had to be questioned. To make up the numbers was simply not a strong enough argument.

Flyers were supposed to be using this season to develop their young players and help raise their game. How this could be achieved in an environment where they had to try to avoid scoring because the opposition were still learning to skate, let alone play, was the farcical situation for a club with such history and tradition to find itself in.

What made it all the more ludicrous was that this was only the first leg of a Scottish Cup tie. The two teams still had to go through the total formality of a second leg at Fife Ice Arena on January 14.

Fife averaged a goal every two minutes and pounded the Aberdeen net with 96 shots during this 60-minutes of humiliation. Not even a respected ex-BNL goalie in the shape of Chris Rugg and former Kirkcaldy netminder Matthew Savage could prevent the annihilation.

Fife moved defencemen up front, and vice versa, but still the goals rained in, some from outside the blue line, and at least three were clearly in the own-goal category.

Flyers chose not to ice Derek King, Steven King, Liam Greig and Scott Plews, while John Haig did not feature at all during periods two and three. Stephen Gunn fell a point short of equalling a single game points record for a Flyers British player, held jointly by Gordon Latto Snr, Les Lovell and John Taylor with 11 points.

In truth the Flyers couldn't have been accused of "running up the score" as it was the kids who were let loose on the home side with Fife Flames duo Steven McAlpine and Willie Nicolson and rarely used defenceman Paul Shevlin scoring almost half of the goals between them.

At least Aberdeen managed to get the puck into Fife's zone long enough to score one goal in the third period. Flyers had won the match but in truth nobody was a winner from this débacle ...... least of all the sport itself.

The stats on this "historic" albeit uncomfortable night were:

Steven McAlpine (5+3), Stephen Gunn (4+6), Gavin Fleming (4+4), Willie Nicolson (4+3), Paul Shevlin (4+2), Chris Linton (2+3), Tommy Muir (2+3), Chris Wands (2+3), John Haig (1+3), Gavin Holmes (1+2), Gordon Latto (1+3)

Blair Daly faced 14 shots.

Rugg in the Aberdeen goal is beaten by John Haig in an earlier game at Kirkcaldy where he faced 68 shots.

Saturday December 18th 1965

Fife Flyers 3 Polish National Team 5

The Flyers played one of their toughest games since the resumption of hockey at the Gallatown rink, three years before, when they met the Polish touring side.

It was certainly no disgrace to them to end up on the losing side and they didn't go down without putting up a fine struggle. It was the first visit to Kirkcaldy by a continental team since Swedish side Gota had visited back in December 1948.

While Flyers lost, it must be acknowledged that in the World Championships the previous year Poland were winners of pool 'B'. Such was the high esteem of the game in Poland at this time that the previous weekend saw three separate Polish club teams visit Germany, Russia and Sweden.

There was a mix-up pre-match and some language difficulties which resulted in a one-hour delay in the start of the match. The visitors' equipment had not arrived on time. When play did commence it proved to be one of the most exciting games of the season, with the teams fairly evenly matched for most of the 60 minutes.

Flyers were without netminder Roy Reid, who was in hospital after an operation, but in his place was the British keeper, Willie Clark of Murrayfield Royals who delighted the home fans with some fine saves for the Kirkcaldy side. Bryce Penny of Ayr Rangers and Johnny Carlyle of Murrayfield Royals also joined the home ranks as guests.

Carlyle, having already played with the Edinburgh team earlier in the day, was sent off for a ten-minute misconduct, which was a handicap the Flyers could well have done without. Ian Forbes would also fall foul of the referee for the same crime.

The game was at times pretty rough but started on friendly terms when both captains exchanged coloured team pennants and the Polish team were introduced to the crowd.

Flyers went straight into the attack after the face off and Jerry Hudson, Bert Smith and Tommy Paton made frantic attempts to push the puck in but were unsuccessful in their efforts. The first penalty came after only seven minutes when Polish defenceman Sitko was given two minutes in the cooler for tripping. Four minutes later Forbes who played an excellent attacking game scored the first goal with a long shot from the blueline.

At this point Flyers were well on top. There was great optimism amongst the Kirkcaldy faithful that with such a display of attacking moves the Flyers would once more rack up a home win.

Once the visitors however had settled into the game the crowd was not so sure. Two days journey with hardly a wink of sleep made no difference to the speed and accuracy of the visitors play and the Flyers were suddenly hard pushed to keep up with them at times. The visitors equalised in the fifteenth minute with a long shot from Cofala who neatly collected the puck from Skorski – one of the visitors' best players.

The second period began badly with both Williams and Skorski being sent off for two minutes. Shortly afterwards the visitors went ahead with a shot from the midst of a goal mouth melée.

Clark had one good save after another but with so many players around the net he missed the shot by Kowalski from a pass by Skulski. A minute later Czachowski put his side even further ahead with a magnificent shot from the blue line, which even the most ardent of Flyers fans applauded.

Johnny Carlyle found himself being given 10 minutes for misconduct but Tommy Paton helped reduce the margin in the 17th minute with a fine shot following a neat manoeuvre by Hudson and Andy Williams.

It was short lived, however, for only two minutes later Kowalski collected a pass from Wieczersak to make the score 4-2 and seconds later Wieczersak himself scored with a pass from Skulski.

The start of the third period saw more penalties with culprits Graeme Farrell and Skorski each being given two minutes for roughing. Flyers thought they had scored but there was great disappointment when the referee announced that an infringement had occurred before the goal. Seconds later however Farrell, from a pass by Penny, shot home for what was nothing more than a consolation goal.

Somewhat blurry account but Tommy Paton leads an attack against the Polish tourists with Jerry Hudson far right in support.

Saturday December 19th 1970

Fife Flyers 5 Dundee Rockets 6

No Breaks For Flyers

The visiting Dundee Rockets were still in with an outside chance of catching the Autumn Cup leaders, Murrayfield Racers. For the Flyers it had so far been a disappointing campaign with just a couple of wins, a position that did not change at the conclusion of the competition.

The visitors stole the game late on, however, with two goals within the space of 13 seconds in the final period giving them a hugely valuable two points.

This was one of the better matches of recent times at the rink and the general consensus was that had Flyers got their fair share of the breaks in the final period they would most likely have had at least had a point for their efforts.

Penalties proved costly for the home side. None so obvious as in the final stages when Rockets grabbed those two quick goals while Joe Baird and George Taylor were in the bin. Power plays bookended the match with the first penalty of the match also proving costly for the Flyers when Rab Petrie was penalised for hooking Mike Mazur and ex Flyer Sammy McDonald made his old club pay the price.

Les Lovell equalised after eight minutes and with only one second remain in the opening period Jimmy Hunter gave the home side the lead. Dundee levelled the score. This time it was Gus Cargill who was in the penalty box and Bertie Ross netted with the man advantage.

Flyers hit back and Lovell out-skated his shadow to give Baird an inch-perfect pass to score. Kenny Horne was also causing a lot of trouble and from one of his passes Petrie made it 4-2.

It looked as though the Flyers would go into the final period with just a slender one-goal lead when, in the final minute of the middle period, George Reid pulled a goal back for the Rockets. Joe McIntosh restored the two-goal cushion before the buzzer however with a fine shot from the blue line.

McDonald, with his second of the game, reduced the leeway at the start of the third period. As the pace of the game quickened tempers became ever more frayed. Joe Baird and Tam Stewart were dismissed for roughing and Baird went to the bin again this time for hooking. He was soon joined by George Taylor, and Rockets seized the opportunity when they had a two-man advantage. Mazur netted the equaliser and seconds later McDonald, with his hat trick goal, scored what proved to be the winner.

While the Flyers went on to have a less than enthralling rest of the season, things were much more severe for the Rockets. At the Northern Associations meeting on January 8th the Dundee representatives indicated that Ice Hockey Scotland Ltd were not prepared to pay the gate levy in full.

The Rockets were therefore expelled from the league and their Northern League results expunged from the record books. They would return to the fold for the start of the 1971/72 season.

1970-71 Fife Flyers team with the Skol Cup
Back, left to right: Chic Cottrell, Jimmy Hunter, Dave Medd, George Taylor, Allan Crooks, Angus Cargill, Kenny Horne, Stuart Muir, Joe McIntosh, Harold 'Pep' Young
Front, left to right: Jimmy Simpson, Rab Petrie, Norrie Boreham, Roy Reid, Les Lovell, Alistair Crombie

Sunday December 20th 1964

Fife Flyers 9 Murrayfield Royals 2

After winning the Television Trophy by a narrow one-goal margin over Murrayfield Royals the previous night, Flyers left nothing to chance when they met the Edinburgh side for a second time at Kirkcaldy.

Flyers opened their scoring in the third minute, were three up inside five minutes and virtually had the outcome decided when they completed the first session with a four-goal lead.

Royals were without star defenceman and coach Johnny Carlyle and they lacked the same levels of confidence they had shown the previous day. It was another sterling performance by netminder Willie Clark but even he could not prevent them from taking one of their heaviest beatings of the season.

Despite the fact that Clark was beaten nine times, Royals had him to thank for keeping the score down. Flyers iced former Ayr Rangers player Gordie Hughes and that made them even stronger than they were on Saturday. Hughes, who also played for Glasgow, had been released from Ayr and Flyers manager Sandy Nicol had made the signing in midweek.

Jimmy Spence found the target after only three minutes to get the Flyers off and running. They were much the sharper team and a mere twenty seconds later Graeme Farrell added a second goal. A second goal from Spence put Flyers three up with just 5 minutes on the clock. Mike Mazur hit home a great goal to open the Murrayfield account in the sixth minute but two more from Lawrie Lovell gave Flyers a 5-1 lead.

Johnny Flynn added a sixth goal for the home side four minutes after the start of the second session but Marshall Key snatched one back for the visitors before the end of the period.

Despite their healthy lead the Flyers stepped up the pressure even further in the final twenty minutes and Spence bagged his hat-trick with a great goal from the right wing three minutes after the start.

Two minutes later Lovell also collected his treble, when he once again beat an overworked Clark for the eighth time. The scoring was completed with another Spence goal with a couple of minutes of the game remaining. Sammy McDonald, along with Spence, Lovell and Farrell were the mainstay of the home attack while in defence Bill Sneddon and

Joe McIntosh were the stars. Roy Reid pulled off some fine saves to keep the visitors goal total in check and he could hardly have been blamed for the two shots which had him beaten. Mazur, Key and Gordon Ross were the outstanding Royals forward. Clark did a lot of hard work in goal while Glen Reilly was tops in their defence line.

There was a bizarre prelude to the game with the Royals. A situation arose that presented the Flyers with the choice of two opponents on the Sunday evening.

Shortly after Murrayfield had arrived at the rink another bus pulled into the car park carrying the Durham Bees and a number of their supporters. According to the Durham team's fixture list they thought they were due to meet the Flyers and were unaware of the Flyers-Royals match.

After consultation with ice rink manager Mr Tommy Horne, Flyers team manager Sandy Nicol decided to stick to the advertised programme and meet the Royals. However, coach Ian Forbes wasn't worried about who Flyers were to meet. "We'll play Durham between the periods" he quipped in the dressing room. And he might have had some justification for his optimism considering the way in which the Flyers coasted home in their win over Murrayfield.

Flyers captain Bert Smith receiving the Scottish Television Trophy won the previous evening.

Thursday December 21st 1939

Fife Flyers 5 Falkirk Lions 3

Flyers win over Falkirk broke a long series of deficits for the lads in blue-white-and-gold; rather unflatteringly the comment in the *Fife Free Press* was that the win "might well have inspired cartoonist Ripley of 'Believe or not' fame". It had been so long since they had chalked up a victory that it "was almost a job for the oldest inhabitant to try and remember when they had last finished on the right side of the scoreboard".

How horrible had their run of failure been? – five games! But clearly it had been a relief to see a win and even more pleasing had been the fact that the win was on merit and well deserved. It was true to say that during their win-less streak the Flyers had played some pretty average hockey with little dash in the forward line and their defence more than a trifle suspect on occasion.

Against the Lions the whole team seemed to be rejuvenated. Flyers started the game as if they meant business and in the second minute they took the lead. Glen Morrison paved the with strong skating and when he rounded and shot, net minder Maurice Gerth padded the puck out and the ever-ready Paul Rheault was on the spot to net.

Art Grant had looked lively to stave off a series of Falkirk raids, then George Horn set up Rheault whose effort struck the iron. Falkirk responded with Art Schumann prominent, but the Flyers defencemen were in sound form. In the fourteenth minute Glen Morrison passed to Tommy McInroy who slapped the puck past Gerth as if he meant it to finish up in the restaurant.

Into the second period and Arnie Pratt tested Gerth on a number of occasions but he stood firm. After a quiet period in the game the Flyers thought they had stretched their lead. Gerth padded out shots from Rheault and Pratt in succession but failed to even see Rheault's second attempt. Unfortunately, the referee failed to notice it had clearly gone into and out of the net and play was waved on.

Falkirk scored shortly afterwards through Gerry Davey from the rebound of a Schumann effort and the breaks seemed once again to be going against the home side. Rheault however restored the two-goal lead from a Morrison assist with a goal which this time Referee Foley seemed to like. A fine piece of work by Schumann saw Tommy Forgie reduce the leeway again but before the end of the session Glen Morrison helped Rheault to his hat trick goal.

The final period was played at a great pace with no further scoring until after the turnaround – teams would play 10 minutes of the third period and then swap ends. Rheault netted again from a Morrison play but once again the referee said "No!" while the Flyers faithful, in a variety of ways asked "Why? 'Red' Thomson then slipped up when he lost control of the puck in front of his own net and Davey took full advantage.

This was followed by a spot of bother between Arnie Pratt and Art Schumann, who came to blows, and with two minutes to go both were told by the referee that their services were no longer required in the game.

Schumann, of the Perth Panthers, was guesting for the Lions and as usual some of the Kirkcaldy fans liked to give Art a hot time. The fact, however, was that no matter how much they shouted themselves hoarse, tied their tonsils in knots and worked themselves up to the verge of apoplexy, Schumann was one of the cleverest skaters and most formidable attackers in the game of that era. In the final minute Paul Rheault set off on a solo dash and, by the grace of referee Foley, scored his fourth goal.

Flyers — Art Grant, George Horn, Red Thomson, Johnny Schofield, Paul Rheault, Glen Morrison, Arnie Pratt, Tommy McInroy

Lions — Maurice Gerth, Alec Purdie, Clem Beaton, Jock Taylor, Art Schumann (Perth), Gerry Davey, Larry Marsh (Dunfermline), Tommy Forgie

Referee—J. Foley

Blairgowrie born
Tommy McInroy in his days
with the Perth Panthers

Saturday December 22nd 1984

HEINEKEN PREMIER LEAGUE

Fife Flyers 22 Southampton Vikings 5

STOYANOVICH CLAIMS NEW SCORING RECORD

Welcome, readers, to the Dave Stoyanovich show!

Flyers Canadian shooting star re-wrote the Heineken Premier League record books with an astonishing 13-goal performance against the luckless or hapless, depending upon your perspective, Southampton Vikings.

Stoyanovich smashed the Flyers previous best individual scoring record by five goals (held by Jimmy Spence) and was just one short of equalling the British all-time record of 14 set by Roy Halpin of the Dundee Rockets in 1982.

His match total of 15 points was also at that time a Heineken record. Danny Brown collected a then club record of 10 assists to join Stoyanovich as the first two players that season to reach 100 points in competitive Heineken matches.

Flyers tally of 22 goals set yet another Heineken record of that time and in truth the magnitude of victory could have been so much higher. It was only in the final period that Flyers realised that the records were there to be broken and they scored an incredible nine goals in the final eight minutes.

They even withdrew netminder Scott O'Connor with 60 seconds remaining to give Stoyanovich a chance of the British record. The big Canadian would assuredly have done so had he had set his mind to it in the first two periods but settled for a hat-trick in each.

Flyers overwhelming victory was achieved while they also took the opportunity to ice three 15-year-olds for part of the match. Making their senior Flyers debut were Scott O'Connor in goal and forwards Bobby Haig and Dean Edmiston, who were both unlucky not to get among the goals.

Stoyanovich was the man who set the tone for the evening with a quick-fire hat-trick in the first period — all the goals scored with Flyers short-handed. Danny Brown and Neil Abel made the period score 5-0, and the only surprise was that Vikings did not concede many more goals.

Flyers tended to over-elaborate in front of net but Stoyanovich scored two more short-handed goals within the space of 30 seconds to open their account in the second period. Doug Merkosky pulled one back for Southampton in the 34th minute even though the puck appeared to have struck the post.

Stoyanovich again and two quick goals by Ron Plumb made it 10-1 at the end of the second period. Stoyanovich with two and Neil Abel increased Flyers lead early in the third period with Robert Waddell pulling one back. The home side really went to town after O'Connor replaced Craig Dickson in goal in the 42nd minute.

The goals came thick and fast with Stoyanovich netting four. Danny Brown, Andy Linton and Chic Cottrell, making his comeback after injury, all hit the net and Vikings countered through two from Merkosky who completed his hat trick and another from Waddell.

Flyers then iced six skaters in the final minute and Stoyanovich netted his 13th goal 30 seconds from time. It still wasn't over though and Danny Brown completed the scoring with 15 seconds remaining. As a match it was not much of a spectacle with Flyers out-shooting the visitors 90-16, but Stoyanovich gave the home fans a one-man show in the art of goalscoring, striking from all distances and angles and the Southampton netminder Charlie Colon must have been sick of the sight of him by the end of the evening.

It may come as little surprise to know that the scoring feat by Stoyanovich still stands at the time of publication as a Flyers club record for goals in a single game.

Unlucky for some, Stoyanovich bags his 13th against the hapless Vikings and helpless Colon.

Sunday December 23rd 1990

Murrayfield Racers 19 Fife Flyers 8

The exodus began after 37 minutes of play and continued throughout the rest of the contest as Flyers were routed in Edinburgh.

As a Flyers fan I couldn't have been alone in feeling a sense of trepidation each time I visited the 'cosy confines' of the Murrayfield Rink during the Heineken League era. Pretty much always on Sunday nights, it usually put me in a foul mood for the week ahead.

If the wounds were healing for those Fife fans who had witnessed, a little more than 12 months before, their side capitulate by losing 16 on a visit over the Forth then this was salt and some more to rub into a now gaping gash.

The first fans decided they had seen enough the moment Scott Neil completed his hat-trick to give Racers a 12-5 lead and the trickle towards the exits quickly became a flood. It was a night when even the most loyal supporter could take no more. I admit though, I stayed to the bitter end; well, it would only have meant longer to wait for my train at Haymarket!

It was a humiliating end to a vital weekend in which Flyers were run ragged by their old rivals, they were minus the calming influence of injured skipper Gordon Latto, who stripped but did not set foot off the bench, and first line defenceman Neil Abel. Mike Fedorko threw teenager Scott Plews into the deep end; while he may have just about stayed afloat the rest of his team-mates sank without trace.

The visitors, the epitome of Christmas Spirit, presented the Racers with three gift-wrapped goals in the opening seven minutes. Once again their physical limitations were exposed by a strong, dare it be said robust, Edinburgh side.

The lightweight, nimble and often artistic Fife side inflicted minimal damage on Moray Hanson's charge and all but disappeared in a harrowing second period. The rout started when Jim Mollard hammered a lethal shot past Craig Dickson at 2:21 and by 7:51 two Paul Pentland blue liners took that tally to three.

Sheer determination brought the visitors back into contention with Darcy Cahill and Lindsay Lovell making it 3-2 at 14:03. Flyers played their best hockey in the closing minutes of the first period when Steve

Gatzos cancelled out Mollard's power play with a fine short-handed strike and then struck with a power play at 19:48 to tie the scores at 4-4.

The two sides traded early second period goals, Mollard for Racers and Gatzos completing a straight hat-trick, but that marked the beginning of the end for the Kirkcaldy side. They conceded seven straight goals, and spent most of the period chasing white shirts. Tony Hand and Scott Neil shared the first three strikes between 25:15 and 30:06 as Flyers backed off every time Racers drifted deep into their zone.

The horror show continued into double figures courtesy of Brian Collinson and Neil. By the time the hooter sounded Flyers trailed 12-5 and they must have been tempted to pack up early and go home. It was a night of utter misery for all concerned. Darcy Cahill temporarily stemmed the flood at 43:29 but Tony Hand quickly restored the seven goal lead with a solo jaunt down the ice followed by a text-book finish.

The closing 17 minutes felt like the longest of the entire evening as Pentland and Collinson completed their hat tricks, and Jock Hay and Mollard also found the net. Single goals from Gordon Whyte and a hard-working Iain Robertson at least denied Murrayfield beating the November 1989's (16-3) record differential for a win over their arch rivals. You see, every cloud does have a silver lining.

MURRAYFIELD RACERS

M E R R Y

C H R I S T M A S

What the best dressed Racers wear when first-footing
as modelled by Brian Collinson!

Murrayfield Racers
v
Fife Flyers

Sunday 23rd December 1990
Face-off 6.30pm
Murrayfield Ice Rink

The programme from yet another braw night out in the Capital.

Thursday December 24th 1953

Fife Flyers 1 Murrayfield Royals 7

Flyers fans rolled up on Christmas Eve hoping for a Christmas Miracle and with the news that their player-coach and dependable blue liner, Floyd Snider, would be being moved up into attack.

Fife had yet to register their first National League win that season and they made sweeping changes for the visit of the league-leading Murrayfield Royals.

Snider, who was equally at home in attack or defence, was moved up to centre ice with Fred Kentner and Murray Banks, who had recently signed from Paisley, as his wingers.

Bert Smith was to lead the second line, flanked by the two Scotty's, Dowle and Reid. Although the move risked weakening the defence, the Flyers player-coach reckoned that the team would set out to score more than they would lose.

Always a sound coaching strategy, I think we'd all agree.

Wray Fallowfield, Jimmy Mitchell and Jim Smith would form the rear line with the inclusion of the ex-Dundee Tiger, Larry Ford, who had played recent games as a trialist.

Flyers had been putting in a power of practice recently and a win would be just reward for Snider's untiring efforts to ice a winning combine.

Even although they iced a full line-up the Flyers put up a poor, poor show and the opening 12 minutes of the game were disastrous for them. They lost four rather soft and avoidable goals and never looked like recovering.

Ironically the men whose mistakes were largely responsible for these goals, netminder Ron Collins and coach Snider, were also the two who did most to keep the game alive in the latter stages. Collins had many good saves and Snider's fighting spirit was as good to see but the Flyers were never in Royals class.

Flyers did most of the early attacking and went close but it was Royals who went ahead after three minutes. Ex-Flyers coach Bobby Burns made a typical solo burst up the ice and slapped the puck past Collins from the edge of the crease.

They fell further behind on a short-handed goal when Tick Beattie set up George Townsend to leave Collins helpless. A Jimmy Mitchell slapshot from the blue-line was Flyers best try for goal to this stage. Although Flyers continued to do most of the attacking the Royals got a third in 12 minutes when Snider was caught out of position and Cece Cowie netted easily. A minute later it was four when Beattie scored with a long shot.

Flyers had great difficulty in even getting play out of their own zone at the start of the second period. The Royals had much the better of the exchanges and Collins was keeping the hosts in it. However, about twenty seconds from the end of the period, Lennie Baker fastened on to a pass from the left and scored with a tight angled shot.

Flyers efforts became weaker and weaker as the game went on and it was no surprise when they fell further behind early in the third session. First Henri Leomine was left to drift in on goal unattended and then junior Dorry Boyle got a seventh.

Flyers attacking efforts were poor indeed and they were lucky not to fall further behind in the next few minutes. Eventually they managed to put a cohesive move together and broke the Royals shut out. Kenter out skated Burns along the boards and set up Banks to net.

Flyers were a livelier lot after that although the closest to another goal came from the Royals but Collins outguessed Beattie on a break-away and managed to block Cowie's shot from the rebound.

Flyers, Ron Collins, Wray Fallowfield, Larry Ford, Jim Smith, Jimmy Mitchell, Floyd Snider, Fred Kentner, Murray Banks, Bert Smith, Scotty Reid, Scotty Dowle, Harry Pearson

Royals, Hap Finch, Bobby Burns, Verne Greger, Henri Leomine, Lennie Baker, Jim Dunlop, Cece Cowie, Ron Phillips, George Townsend, Tick Beattie, Dorry Boyle, Stan Dunn

Referee — Nels McQuaig.

To further strengthen the team, Frank Facto, who played centre ice for the Kirkcaldy club three seasons ago had again put pen to paper and was expected to join the line up in the New Year.

Murray Banks continued his fine scoring form for the Flyers since joining earlier in the month from Paisley Pirates

Monday December 25th 1950

Dundee Tigers 3 Fife Flyers 4

In the National League the Flyers were going for their third championship in a row. It was a stuttering start from them with a win-one-lose-one sequence over the opening seven games. At this stage they had also lost Harold 'Pep' Young for the season to a leg cut sustained during Canada Cup action. Former players Scotty Reid and Hick Moreland had been drafted in to provide cover. Their lack of consistency was best summed up in this match. They stormed to a commanding lead but had to fight hard to hold on to their four-goal advantage.

Flyers began the game displaying a brand of fast, wide-open hockey which Tigers could not match. The visitors were first to score and indeed had limited the Tigers offence to sporadic raids on their net. When a double from Marshall Bentley and strikes from Al Campone and Sherman Blair had given them a four goal lead there looked no way back for the Tigers.

The home team however suddenly woke up and staged a fight-back which had Fife hanging on for the final bell. A Maurice La Forge hat trick saw Flyers defence reeling and it was just as well that Pete Belanger was on top of his game as without several crucial saves the points would have stayed on Tayside. The win brought the Flyers their fifth success against the Tigers in six outings so far that season and left the league table reading like this:

	P	W	D	L	F	A	Pts
Perth Panthers	8	6	0	2	43	29	12
Paisley Pirates	9	6	0	3	45	39	12
Fife Flyers	9	5	1	3	36	30	11
Dunfermline Vikings	9	4	2	3	47	42	10
Ayr Raiders	8	3	1	4	32	40	7
Falkirk Lions	8	1	2	5	24	39	4
Dundee Tigers	9	1	2	6	25	42	4

Both teams would later struggle and occupied the bottom two spots in the league at the end of the season with Tigers 10 points adrift of the Flyers.

Hockey matches played on Christmas Day are of course a very unusual occurrence in more recent years. At the time of publishing, you have to go back to 1965 for the last time the Flyers played a fixture on that date.

They lost 5-4 to the Paisley Mohawks at Kirkcaldy and their only other game on this date was in 1954 when they went up to Perth and were beaten 7-3 by the Panthers.

Patrons to Dundee Ice Rink that evening in 1950, though, could enjoy from 6pm a Christmas Dinner in the restaurant or a Special Supper after the match. Stovies or chips 'n cheese not on the menu it appears.

Nothing says Christmas more than some fake snow and a Santa costume as the Flyers Christmas card of 1996 shows Russ Parent, Mark Morrison and Frank Morris getting into the spirit of the season.

Saturday December 26th 1998

Fife Flyers 7 Paisley Pirates 3

On a night when the blast of winter was felt across Scotland the only storm at Fife Ice Arena was the one battering the old rink from the outside.

Flyers did what was necessary to pick up the two points to maintain their interest in the Vic Christmas Cup but were never extended against a Paisley side who looked more disinterested the longer the game went on.

There was little excitement or tension on the ice to reward the fans. Nearly 2000 had bravely come out on a bitterly cold and gale-lashed evening, but they gave their usual vocal support and witnessed a vastly improved display by Flyers, who responded well to the absence of coach and top scorer Mark Morrison.

It was a comfortable, if not spectacular, performance and in fact the only danger to the home side came from the weather as on several occasions the lights flickered and dimmed and some even went out at one point.

It was later revealed that if the conditions had become any worse referee Moray Hanson was quite prepared to call the game off — a decision that would not have gone down too well with the club officials or the fans!

Flyers didn't have the expected new face in their ranks, as the signing of Steve Brown, who would eventually debut in January, had not been completed in time for the weekend.

With only four imports to Paisley's eight it was the home-based players who caught the eye. The second line of John Haig, David Smith and Andy Samuel were in great form, the former enjoying his best game for some time, while 'Sammy' covered every inch of the ice in a really committed display and showed that he was back to approaching full fitness after his shoulder injury.

Frank Morris, who took on the responsibility of orchestrating things on the ice, contributed one of the goals of the season when he skated in behind the defence before cutting in front of the goalie and scooping the puck into the net on the backhand from what looked an impossible position.

There were no real failures but Flyers didn't have to play that well to secure the win. A disappointing Pirates side put up only token resistance and seemed to have given up the ghost long before the end.

Only the free skating Nicklas Jonsson, George Swan, Pierre Lindahl and the ever-committed Paul Hand could be pleased with their efforts and even the normally reliable Craig Lindsay had a poor night between the pipes by his standards.

An early unsportsmanlike conduct penalty on Lindahl saw the Flyers power play work as Smith knocked in a rebound from a Bill Moody shot at 4.22. 10 minutes later Pirates were level, Tobias Hall beating Ricky Grubb from a tight angle.

At 15.28, the third line notched its usual contribution with Gary Wishart finishing off a fine move and Flyers took the lead into the second period, adding to it at 22.38 with a clever finish from Jeff Sobb.

Pirates hit back again at 26.06 when Neil Donovan found the corner but two minutes later Smith showed great skill to beat Lindsay and restore the two-goal advantage. This was extended to three at 31.27 with Morris's solo special. Steven Lynch kept the visitors in touch with the final goal of the period at 34.25.

The third period belonged to Flyers, and in particular Lee Cowmeadow, the defenceman capping another fine display with a rare brace of goals. The first came on the power play at 41.54 and the second at 44.44 when he accepted Haig's pass from behind the net and beat Lindsay all ends up.

There was no further scoring and little in the way of any action as Flyers saw out time and coasted to victory and the points. The teams met 24 hours later at the Lagoon in Paisley, with the Pirates exacting revenge.

Mark Morrison attempts to evade capture by the Pirates Iain Robertson in an earlier encounter that season

Monday December 27th 2004

Belfast Giants 5 Fife Flyers 2

It was a brave effort from a threadbare Fife Flyers but it was not enough to avoid defeat in Belfast against the Elite League Giants.

With coach Mark Morrison in Canada and his assistant Karry Biette out after suffering a horror eye injury in Edinburgh the previous night it was left to long-serving import Todd Dutiaume to pick up the reins.

Steven King and Frank Morris were also missing due to work commitments leaving Dutiaume and Co with an uphill task against a team vying for top spot in the Elite League. But the stand-in coach was full of praise for the way his side competed in the face of adversity.

"To be honest, and I even told the players, I was surprised at how well we did. We were missing a number of key guys and a lot of people were predicting a different score line. We went with the two lines and although we were outplayed and out-skated there was no lack of effort."

Flyers lined up with a second line of captain John Haig alongside teenager Lee Mitchell and rookie Liam Greig. Up against three experienced Belfast lines it would have been classed as the result of the season, had the visitors taken anything from the game. Backed by a large travelling support, who would come to enjoy many trips over the Irish Sea in years to come, Flyers took the game by the scruff of the neck and grabbed a shock lead on 8.33 courtesy of 16-year-old Mitchell.

Flyers were only in front for four minutes when Diarmuid Kelly played a perfect pass for George Awada to level. The sharp shooting of Belfast coach Tony Hand and superb teamwork between Kelly and Marc Levers created the second goal in the final minute of the first spell.

Flyers amazing resilience showed at the start of the second period and for 10 minutes they kept Belfast on the back foot. The pressure paid off with an equaliser just after the midway point when Dutiaume found the net from Adrian Saul's set up.

But the home side ended the middle session with a one-goal advantage when Curtis Huppe and Hand stormed the net for defenceman Todd Kelman to crash the puck home from close range.

Curtis Bowen then netted on the power play in the opening two minutes of the final period to make it 4-2 and Fife's lion-hearted effort started to fade. A wonder goal from Levers made it 5-2 with 10 minutes to go but Fife took all the credit for a spirited display.

Giants scoring: Hand, Levers, Kelman (1+1) C Bowen, Awada (1+0) Kelly (0+3) Jamieson, Nasvall, Walton, Huppe (0+1).

Flyers scoring: Dutiaume (1+1) Mitchell (1+0) Saul (0+2) Kuznik (0+1).

SOGs: Belfast (Klempa) 15, Fife (Hay) 48.

PIMs: 8-6

Referee: Moray Hanson   Attendance: 3983

Over the weekend however most Flyers fans attentions had turned to the injury to Karry Biette. His career was considered to be hanging in the balance as he awaited news on his damaged eye. Biette had been struck in the face by the puck during the controversial Boxing Day clash against Edinburgh Capitals at Murrayfield. He was immediately rushed to the city's Western General Hospital before being transferred to Edinburgh Royal Infirmary. However, the amount of swelling on the injury stopped doctors from properly assessing the extent of the damage. Initial tests appeared to confirm that the 31-year-old had suffered a torn iris which could lead to further complications but until a full diagnosis was made it was difficult to speculate on Biette's ice hockey future. Karry would not play for the rest of the season and he would not return the following season as the Flyers dropped into the Scottish National League.

Flyers netminder Scott Hay

Tuesday December 28th 1999

Fife Flyers 4 Peterborough Pirates 5

The final game before the new Millennium.

An equal, it could be argued, for sheer drama and passion had never been witnessed before at the Auld Barn.

Had this been a film script then the onlookers would simply have dismissed it as being an unbelievable piece of sporting theatre.

Ahead of the Christmas break the Flyers returned from the first leg on the Pirates home ice having secured a very handy two goal cushion after a 4-2 win. A 2000-plus crowd still in festive mood turned up in the hope of seeing some further Christmas stuffing with the promise of some inventive off ice surprises in store.

Flyers were short benched with Kyle Horne and Stephen Murphy in Japan on GB International duty and coach Mark Morrison back home in Vancouver for the holidays with his family.

Flyers went with three defencemen and Ricky Grubb with the start in nets. It was the Flyers who resembled turkeys, however, as their two-goal lead lasted just 98 seconds as Pirates rattled in a quick-fire double.

Anyone remember Japanese-born Junji Sakata? Well, he netted the first, and the almost unforgettable Claude Dumas the second as Grubb was left horribly exposed.

Worse, indeed much worse was to follow. The Pirates mustered a total of 9 shots in the opening period but they lit the lamp on 5 occasions. Highly strung coach, Randy Smith, added a third after 13 minutes and Doug McEwan added a fourth with 90 seconds of the period remaining.

There was still time for classy defenceman Jimmy Anderson to make it a nap hand five seconds before the buzzer. The inquests in the stands were only limited by the sheer bemusement of what had been witnessed.

Grubb, more so than any other Flyer, was in the spotlight and great credit to the youngster with how he handled the next 40 minutes.

The Flyers had clearly regrouped after the break and started chipping away at what looked like an unassailable Pirates lead. They managed to get the puck behind Lindsay once in the middle period when John Haig broke the shutout on 35 minutes.

The full drama and indeed the somewhat pantomime-like scenes however were reserved for the final period. Rookie stripey Andy Allsopp, handling his first senior game, had called all indiscretions to that point meticulously, no fear or favour shown.

Pirates' naturally robust game led by the aforementioned Smith, the epitome of level-headedness, finally saw them hit the self-destruct button in what became a parade to the box.

They gave up two 5 on 3 power plays and were short-handed 5 times in the last 9 minutes of a game and that was enough to tip the scales as they relinquished the defence of their trophy. Russell Monteith brought Fife back within a goal on 43 minutes and three minute later the roof was almost lifted off when he struck again to tie the game on aggregate.

Ted Russell, formerly of the Pirates parish, struck the tie-winning goal in 53 minutes on a two-man advantage — oh sweet irony for Ted, who was unsurprisingly singled out for 'special' attention in most games against his old side.

To accompany the Flyers goals, the club had rigged up some indoor fireworks behind the net at the Curlers bar. The problem with three goals in 10 minutes was that by the time Russell hit the winner there was already a blanket of smog at that end of the arena.

The Pirates still had time to take another couple of daft penalties before Smith ushered his team off at the end ignoring the handshake and marching them almost full kit onto the bus.

The Flyers fans flocked rink-side and the best part of 1000 linked hands around the boards in a mass rendition of Auld Lang Syne. Amidst the celebrations, assistant coach Chic Cottrell seized the puck and nailed it to the wall inside the dressing room. A ritual that was to be repeated after key victories for the remainder of the season.

Russell Monteith and the King brothers put pressure on Pirates netminder Craig Lindsay

Sunday December 29th 1991

Fife Flyers 28 Blackburn Hawks 3

Poor Blackburn Blackhawks.

They headed north with a tiny squad and skated straight into the eye of a goalscoring tornado. In one of the most spectacular mis-matches of the modern era, they were torn to ribbons by a razor-sharp Flyers outfit which plundered goals and assists almost at will while rewriting the record books.

Hawks were beaten from all angles and distances, outshot on a harrowing scale (67-27), and probably scarred for life by a 17-2 third period humiliation.

A whole-scale demolition was always on the cards as the visitors started with a paltry *eight* skaters and finished with *six*, just sufficient to ice one line.

Perhaps it was a blessing in disguise that Flyers bench was limited to 13 bodies, which restricted coach Brian Kanewischer to just two lines.

The game was over as a contest within ten minutes, but Flyers simply refused to take their foot off the pedal and rammed home their superiority at every opportunity. In doing so, they finally delivered the victory which Kanewischer promised for some time.

They stole the puck from Hawks on countless occasions. Playing some spellbinding hockey around the opposition net, they could quite easily have crashed through the 30-goal barrier, but for the admirable endeavours of netminders John Dunford and Trevor Foster.

Never have two players more deserved a post-match refreshment in the Curlers bar than those two. They pegged Flyers to a mere three goals in a dull second period.

No fewer than ten players appeared on the scoresheet, while eight actually found the net.

Young netminder Colin Hamilton also shone during his 45 minutes between the pipes. He replaced the absent Colin Downie, who was on GB duty in Rome.

A third period blitz was always on the cards but few could have envisaged 17 excellent strikes. Hawks ran out of energy long before the final buzzer but earned widespread praise for not resorting to a negative and tiresome dumping game. They persevered in the knowledge that they were on a hiding to nothing and Gatien Dumalin's two goals were warmly applauded by the home fans.

For the record, Flyers scorers were: Frank Morris (9+5), Richard Laplante (6+11), Cal Brown (3+5), Kel Land (3+0), Iain Robertson (2+4), Gordon Whyte (2+2), Craig Wilson (2+0), Paul Berrington (1+2), John Haig (0+6), Bobby Haig (0+1).

Just for good measure, they kept a clean sheet in the disciplinary stakes.

Some Heineken First Division records were rewritten:
- Most goals in a game
- Most goals in one period (17) – also stands to date as a club record
- Most assists in one period—Richard Laplante (8)

Some of the numbers were just downright eyewatering!
- Goals 15 and 16 came in 50 seconds.
- Goals 17 to 20 inclusive were rattled off in 72 seconds.
- Goals 23 to 25 plus Blackburn's third were condensed into a 24-second spell — a goal every six seconds.
- Goals 26 to 28 were crammed into 23 seconds.

Frank Morris must also have come close to some sort of record by scoring a double hat-trick in the third period in just 7:39 minutes.

Richard Laplante adds one of his 17 points against Blackburn on his way to setting a Flyers club record best points total in a season of 264

Thursday December 30th 1954

British National League

Fife Flyers 3 Dundee Tigers 5

Tigers played spoiling hockey and simply waited for the breaks as they upset a desperate, but seldom consistent, Flyers side to steal two valuable points from this National League encounter.

Flyers easily had 75% of the play and were only penalised on four occasions to Tigers' eight but despite their territorial and numerical advantages they failed to exploit the situation. As a result they could not feel hard done by with their defeat.

Ron Hemmerling and Nebby Thrasher were once again the leaders for Flyers but unfortunately, with the exception of Johnny Andrews, the rest of the forwards failed to lend their whole-hearted support.

Goalie Walter Malahoff, along with blue liner Neil Matheson, were the only ones to garner any credit in Flyers defensive efforts. Their struggles were compounded by not yet having found a replacement for John Petry. A move would have to be made soon if there was to be any outside chance of competing for the top spots in the league.

A pep talk to the players just prior to the start of the game appeared to have the desired result. The home side started in whirlwind fashion and shots absolutely rained down on Don Grant's charge.

Hemmerling twice broke clean through to see his shots parried by Grant but then Bert Smith flashed the red light from a delightful Thrasher assist, only to see the goal disallowed owing to a previous infringement.

However, after three minutes Flyers took the lead; a great angular shot from Andrews was guided past Grant by Roger Landry. Flyers continued to pin Tigers in their own zone for lengthy periods, but it was Dundee who were able to add to the scoring when they collected a couple of snap goals through Art Sullivan and Jim McGeorge within a matter of three minutes.

Flyers looked temporarily stunned following these reverses but gradually they regained the initiative and just before the interval Henry Hayes slammed home the equaliser from a Thrasher flick.

Sullivan was the danger man and playmaker-in-chief of the Dundee attack and at this stage it was fairly obvious that if he could be subdued then Flyers task would be made much easier.

With Andrews still under penalty at the start of the second session Tigers were the aggressors but Flyers weathered the storm, thanks to many brilliant saves by Malahoff. Shortly after they returned to full strength, the net minder had to admit defeat when Johnny Quales netted from close in following a melée in front of the cage.

Grant was starting to frustrate the Flyers attack which appeared to have a depressing effect on their play with their finishing becoming more than a trifle erratic.

A Hayes penalty immediately followed by a Smith penalty did not improve their morale although somewhat ironically one minute later the Flyers scored a short-handed tally. Hemmerling gathered a loose puck to skate through on his own and at the crucial moment passed to Wayne Sutherland who bulged the net with a grand shot.

A procession of penalties ended with Bert Oig and Nebby Thrasher having a bout of fisticuffs which resulted in a seven minute spell for each in the cooler. Flyers continued to have the better of the exchanges until the second interval and it was simply the brilliance of Grant which prevented them from forging ahead.

After a spell of listless play Tigers regained the lead with a poorly conceded goal in the third minute of the final period when from an impossible angle, Johnny Kent shot and the puck slipped into the net between Malahoff's legs.

It was a pity for the net minder who had effected so many brilliant clearances early in the game. Tigers suffered two quick penalties to Dick Maday and Verne Greger but Flyers could not cash in on their numerical strength. They got a further chance a couple of minutes later when Quales was penalised but again they failed to exploit their advantage.

Four minutes from time Tigers made the points secure when Sullivan netted with the Kirkcaldy defence hopelessly out of position. As they had done for most of the game Flyers took over the initiative again but now there was little cohesion in their play, it was more inclined to be desperation. Just on the final bell Grant produced a magnificent save from Hemmerling.

TONIGHT'S LINE-UP

THURSDAY, 30th DECEMBER, 1954

FIFE FLYERS

DUNDEE TIGERS

The centre pages of the Flyers programme for the visit of Dundee Tigers

Friday December 31st 1948

Fife Flyers 6 Dundee Tigers 3

The headline following this game wasn't the score but a serious incident that occurred before the match.

The Flyers looked to continue their run of form in the first half of the season which had seen them win the Autumn Cup, and finish runners up to the Falkirk Lions in the Canada Cup. They were now embarking on the start of their march on the National League title.

In 27 competitive matches so far that season, only four losses had been recorded and the Tigers had lost on their earlier two visits to Fife. However, before all that there was this headline:

TIGERS IN ROAD CRASH

The Dundee Tigers ice hockey team were involved in a road crash at Glendoick, 12 miles from Dundee, when on their way to meet Fife Flyers at Kirkcaldy Ice Rink.

The team bus skidded and collided with an oncoming heavy lorry. Billy Frick, left wing forward, was the most seriously injured, having been thrown out of the bus door on to the roadway. Frick, after getting to his feet, collapsed at the roadside and had to be taken to a nearby house for treatment.

Trainer Gordon McIntosh, although suffering from injuries helped Frick to the house before he in turn collapsed. Facial injuries were sustained by Tigers skipper Bob Burns and a Dundee newspaper reporter, travelling on the bus, suffered a leg injury.

The remaining fourteen occupants of the bus apart from suffering from shock were thankfully uninjured. The bus was badly damaged and another bus had to come from Dundee to take the team to Kirkcaldy, where they arrived an hour late. Despite their mishap, the Tigers gamely played the game. Incredible to consider but here's how events unfolded on the ice.

Considering the ordeal that the Dundee Tigers had endured before the game they did remarkably well to hold Flyers to such a close game.

It was only in the final period that Flyers lived up to their reputation, but otherwise the game was scrappy. Tigers had a nippy front line in Johnny Rozzini, Johnny Evans and Archie Williams, but were shaky in defence, although George Kovac in nets was safe. Flyers were listless for most of the game but they got good service from Hick Moreland and Bert Smith in attack. Verne Greger was the most accomplished defenceman on the ice while 'Pete' Belanger made no mistakes in Flyers net.

Dundee impressed at the start with their open hockey and it came as no surprise when they opened the scoring after four minutes. Pat Donahue accepted a pass from Rozzini to skate in from the boards to net. Frick, who miraculously played, was penalised for hooking but while the Flyers power play provided plenty of goalmouth thrills it did not materialise into an equalising goal.

Bob Finlayson increased Tigers lead and the term 'bus legs' looked a contrary term to that applied in more modern time. Flyers got one back through Moreland following a two-way play by Bert Smith and Chic Mann. After a scrappy start to the second session Tigers took advantage of a defensive slip to increase their lead through Finlayson.

For a brief spell the spectators were treated to a first-class exhibition of ice hockey with star play-maker Mann excelling himself. During this time Bud Scrutton, from a Mann-Snider assist, and Moreland, from a Scrutton play, tied the score.

Scotty Reid provided a touch of slap-stick comedy; after breaking his stick he continued to manipulate the puck with the blade until the play was stopped for his obvious infringement.

Straight from the third period face-off the Flyers took the lead for the first time when Mann neatly connected from a Scrutton assist. Belanger distinguished himself with a daring clearance when he beat Evans in a race for the puck; although he broke his stick in the process he was on the spot to deal with a sizzler from Williams.

In the ninth minute Moreland scored his hat trick when he beat Kovac from just inside the blue-line with a raking shot and in the final minute Greger put the issue beyond doubt when he netted a Snider assist.

*Harold 'Hick'
Moreland with
a hat trick against
the Tigers*

Flyers Team Manager Jack Latto with the array of silverware won by the all conquering 1976-77 season Flyers team. Quite the bill for Brasso!

January

Josh Boni, who was with the Flyers for the first few months of the 1994/95 season before departing for the Durham Wasps

Thursday January 1st 1953

Fife Flyers 2 Ayr Raiders 2

Four games into their National League campaign and the Flyers were starting to show signs of recovery from their torrid run of one win in eleven matches. They were now unbeaten in their last two outings. Two goals in arrears at the start of the final frame, the home side staged a spectacular revival to gain a valuable point on New Years' night.

Still short of Canadian manpower, Flyers took a long time to settle. However, once they opened their account through a Marlowe McDonald goal in the fifth minute of the final session they set to with renewed vigour and in the end were more than a trifle unlucky not to gain both points.

In addition to their normal complement of Canadians, Flyers iced ex-Vikings winger Bert Simpson. The newcomer had been released by the Dunfermline line-up after only playing in a few games. He was seen as a short term fix until reinforcements arrived.

Hero of the match was once again veteran netminder Harry McQueston. Although having to admit defeat on two occasions, McQueston was in brilliant form and three of his clearances in particular had the international label firmly attached. He would have been the first to admit though that without the support of defencemen Bob Burns, Jim Mitchell and Moe Zubatiuk his efforts would have been useless. Those three blueliners were in inspired form and they dished out body-checks with accuracy and precision.

The attack unfortunately was not consistent. After racing around in circles for the first two sessions they eventually did settle and in a hectic final frame they made amends for some of their previous blunders. Bud Stock was the most enterprising and consistent performer although both Marlowe McDonald and Scotty Dowle stole much of the limelight with their clever and energetic final session displays.

Bert Simpson, who displaced Harry Pearson, was very subdued as were Jock Harley and Pep Young. Len Smigel was improving with every game and was becoming a real asset to the team.

Raiders were a smart moving and quick breaking outfit. Andre Girard and Ernie Domenico were the keymen in attack while Al Holliday, Herb Kewley and Ray Dinardo were outstanding in defence. The opening exchanges were very scrappy and the game did not warm up until Raiders opened the scoring after 11 minutes. Dave McRae gained possession in front of McQueston's net and following a melée he had little difficulty in beating the unsighted goalie.

Flyers were still wandering about aimlessly when Raiders struck again with Johnny Kent the marksman this time. Flyers tried hard to get organised but seldom was Holliday seriously tested. In the closing minutes Zubatiuk and Stock were penalised but Raiders failed to take advantage of their numerical strength.

McQueston was the outstanding personality on view in the second period. For the greater part of the session shots were fired at him from all angles but he was equal to every occasion. His highlight saves were when Domenico (twice) and André Girard broke clean through only for him to stonewall them. Towards the end of the period Flyers showed signs of staging a revival but despite some hectic pressure they failed to score.

However, only five minutes had elapsed in the final session when the home team got their reward. A nice inter-passing movement between Smigel and Burns ended in McDonald beating Al Holliday all ends up. This counter infused new life into the Flyers bench and Holliday was forced to perform acrobatics to prevent any further scoring.

Just when it appeared as if all Flyers pressure was going to go unrewarded Harley swept through on his own and his clever back flick was gathered by Dowle who neatly rounded Holliday before netting. Flyers put in a terrific finish but the winner eluded them.

Flyers 1952/53
Back row left to right: Harry McQueston, Nick Dubick, Gordie Blackman, Marlowe McDonald, Ron Biggar. Front row left to right: Moe Zubatiuk, Bud Stock, Bob Burns, Scotty Dowle

Monday January 2nd 1995

Fife Flyers 9 McGill Redmen 2

Flyers confidently disposed of Canadian university team McGill Redmen and turned on the style against a side who had already claimed the scalps of Humberside Hawks and Peterborough Pirates on their tour of Britain.

Fife played three-line hockey all night against a squad of over 20 dressed players from the Montreal-based team. Experience was the deciding factor in the match; the average age of the McGill team was just 20 with the eldest a wrinkly 24.

The young Canucks were definitely a decent outfit and they played ice hockey as it should be played, fast and physical. But they were shown up as promising youngsters, particularly when up against the Fife imports.

Flyers lined up with dual-passport holder Lee Saunders in defence, with the English-born Lee Valley Lions import on a one-game trial as a possible stand-in for broken jaw victim Ryan Kummu. He looked fairly impressive and collected a goal and an assist but didn't really come up against any top-class opposition to test his defensive capabilities.

The first period provided some cracking entertainment and Flyers were glad to be 2-0 up at the buzzer after young netminder Ricky Grubb had pulled off a couple of outstanding saves. Steven Lynch scored Fife's first at 13:03 after Doug Marsden had set him up and the youngster showed good pace and a cool head to beat netminder Richard Boscher.

The visitors were full of ideas in attack with Guy Boucher, Lou Forner, Pierre Genciron and David Vecchio the stand-outs in a hard-working squad. But they couldn't find the touch needed in front of goal and missed the target or fired straight at Grubb when it looked as if their pressure might pay off. Fife went 2-0 up in the final minute of the period when Tony Szabo's slap shot went through Boscher's pads.

Fife started the second period really on form with Mark Morrison netting his first of the night at 22:42. Grubb then made an amazing diving save from Martin Pouther as McGill tried to get themselves on the scoreboard but Steven King put Flyers 4-0 ahead at 25:26 with another shot through the goalie's pads.

The home team went nap two minutes later with a sweeping end-to-end move started and finished by Saunders, which did his contract prospects no harm. Boscher, who played his first game between the pipes on this tour after recovering from illness, was replaced by Robert Bobreau after the goal.

Redmen finally opened their account bang on the half-hour mark when a lightning break down the right was finished off by Boucher when he tipped a shot home from close range. It was no more than the visitors deserved.

Morrison made the score 6-1 at 31:35 but McGill scored again a minute later, Vecchio conjuring up a glorious snap shot over Grubb's left shoulder from a tight position. Fife's top scorer Morrison netted Flyers seventh at 34:44 after a cool piece of stickhandling by Saunders. There was controversy seconds later when Fred Brais blasted a shot past Grubb. Although the puck definitely went in the net and out again the goal judge didn't signal and referee George Nicholson waved play on.

The third period was a bit slower with Fife obviously concerned not to pick up any injuries, but Doug Marsden scored a double to end the game at 9-2 for Flyers. The former Paisley Pirate's second was the result of some great passing play with Morrison and was enough to earn him the Man of the Match award.

Flyers: Szabo 1+4, Morrison 3+1, Marsden 2+2, Lynch 1+2, Saunders 1+1, Steven King 1+0, Figala 0+1, Robertson 0+1.

Redmen: Boucher 1+0, Vecchio 1+0, Latulippe 0+1, Marcellus 0+1, Pouther 0+1, Shewfelt 0+1. Referee: George Nicholson. Crowd: 800.

Iain Robertson and Guy Boucher exchange mementos prior to puck drop. Boucher went on to coach in the NHL with the Tampa Bay Lightning and Ottawa Senators

Sunday January 3rd 1982

Streatham Redskins 5 Fife Flyers 0

FLYERS LONDON NIGHT OUT

Streatham Redskins proved that their standards were comparable with those North of the border with a 5-0 win over the Flyers.

Redskins, who were flying high in the English National League, were also still unbeaten in the Southern Cup with a 100% record. Streatham had maintained an unbeaten home record for over three years and boasted a full quota of Canadians in their squad.

Gary Stefan had a keen eye for the net while ex Flyer Robin Andrew was a steadying influence on the blueline. Young English-born forward Tony Goldstone had had a trial with Quebec Nordiques after spending the summer at a Canadian training camp, so there was no shortage of talent in the side.

The Mecca-owned Streatham Rink would normally see crowds of around 1000 but 1350 packed in to see this Grand Challenge Match featuring the first Scottish team to guest there in recent years. The rink had undergone a complete overhaul two years previously, and could boast some of the most modern equipment available, including plexi-glass and a clock-scoreboard which cost around £10,000 to install — significantly different facilities to those enjoyed by visitors to the then Kirkcaldy Ice Rink.

Coaching the London outfit was old-timer Red Imrie. The Scot was an ex-Brighton Tiger and a name familiar to many of the older generation of Fife followers of the game.

The Flyers were missing a number of regulars owing to injury problems and business commitments — goalies John Pullar and Willie Cottrell, defender Dougie Latto and forwards Rab Petrie, Dennis Clair and Chic Cottrell — and so consisted largely of the club's younger contingent. To provide cover in goal they called upon the services of young Canadian goalkeeper Paul Flamont who was currently living in London.

Flyers manager Sandy Nicol was very impressed with the young Canadians performance and he later said of the opponents "I'd heard teams from the South of England were sub-standard but I've changed my views somewhat. I must admit we had a weakened team but everything about Streatham impressed me."

At the other end they faced 17-year-old Gary Brine and the youngster fully merited his shut out. Richard Bacon and Tony Goldstone had opened up a two-goal lead for Redskins by the first buzzer. Although Flyers came more into the game in the second period they were unable to penetrate Streatham's well-polished defence.

The London side repeated their first period onslaught with three further goals in the final spell. Robin Andrew scored against his former team-mates. Bacon hit his second goal in 54 minutes and Canadian Gary Stefan completed the scoring three minutes from time. It was hoped that Flyers would not have to wait too long for revenge as it was suggested that Redskins made a return visit to Kirkcaldy in the near future. That meeting would be the following season but not in a Challenge match.

The Redskins were admitted into the British League for season 1982/83 and would further enhance their reputation with the Flyers management and fans when they won home and away in their initial two meetings.

Chic Cottrell (left) and Allan 'Bean' Anderson in action against Dundee Rockets, season 1981/82

Sunday January 4th 1987

HEINEKEN PREMIER LEAGUE

Solihull Barons 8 Fife Flyers 11

Following the earlier disastrous run that season of seven consecutive defeats, which culminated in the axing of import Mike Jeffrey, and Steve Moria joining the team, the Flyers had now gone on a run with only two defeats in their last eleven competitive outings.

The first game of the season between the two sides had seen the Flyers struggle in the home opener but had narrowly taken the points. This must have been at the back of their minds as they visited the Hobs Moat Road rink for their first ever competitive match.

The opening period did little to suggest that the Flyers would have to claw and scratch for the points this time as they carved out a two-goal lead midway through the first. The Barons however fought back with four unanswered including three in 91 seconds to lead 4-2 three minutes into the middle period.

The home side from that point onwards however destroyed themselves with penalties, when they conceded an astonishing *eight* straight power play goals between the 26th and 49th minutes. During this time Al Sims helped himself to a hat trick and as Barons Brian Puhalski sat out a 5-minute major he watched the visitors score five.

Steve Moria had made his debut at Kirkcaldy against the Durham Wasps the previous night when he picked up five points with two goals and three assists. Picking up from where he left off, he helped himself to six assists during the scoring spree and ended the game with seven helpers without finding the back of the net.

9-5 behind going into the final period, the Barons were in truth never really out of the game but they had left themselves with far too much to do. Although they won the period 3-2 the Flyers were happy to see the game out playing typical road hockey.

Dave Stoyanovich top scored with 4 goals and 4 assists while Sims also had 4 helpers to add to his trick. Jimmy Pennycook grabbed a double and there were singles form Gordon Latto and Charlie Kinmond. Dave Graham faced 56 shots to Andy Donald's 40. The Barons goals came from Jamie Crapper, Glen Skidmore and Brad Schnurr with two each and a strike each from Rod Turner and Peter Smith.

The Flyers season was most definitely re-ignited as they played catch up on their nearest rivals from across the Forth and Tay as the Racers and Rockets lead the way in the standings. Despite a further two wins against the West Midlands club the stuttering start to the league campaign however would ultimately prove crucial and too much to recover from.

Al Sims with a 7 point game against the Barons

Sunday January 5th 1975

Glasgow Dynamos 5 Fife Flyers 5

In what was a protracted competition that season, with the first puck dropped in September, the Autumn Cup was finally wrapped up in the depths of winter with the Flyers completing their schedule at Crossmyloof Ice Rink.

They shared the points with the Dynamos in a match spoiled by a rash of penalties. It must be noted however that the Flyers were the main culprits and clocked up 21 minutes. In relative terms to games played in the modern era, back then this was way above the average.

Flyers were minus skipper Les Lovell, who had the flu, but they opened the scoring after just five minutes through brother Lawrie. It was a milestone goal for Law — his 400th in Northern Ice Hockey Association matches.

The visitors had the bit between their teeth and were clearly intent upon extending their recent good form in which they had won their last two games. By the end of the first period Flyers had increased their lead to 3-0 with goals from Kenny Horne and Lovell again.

With nothing but pride to play for by both sides the Dynamos came back at the start of the second period when their coach and ex-Flyer, Joe Baird, scored twice in a four-minute spell. Flyers steadied the ship and Alex Churchill extended the visitors lead before Martin Shields netted for Glasgow to make it 4-3 for Flyers going into the final period.

Dynamos were quick to level proceedings when they drew level in the second minute but Jimmy Jack put Flyers back into the lead for the third time in the match.

The play this period was particularly feisty and one particular set-to between Gus Cargill and Shields saw them both off to the cooler for a lengthy stay. Fife couldn't hold their advantage and for the final time Dynamos drew level once again when Barrie Stevenson netted. As the table shows the Flyers finished in third spot with their most notable result being a 10-5 win at Murrayfield.

	P	W	L	D	F	A	Pts
Warriors	14	10	2	2	112	51	22
Racers	12	9	2	1	68	49	19
Flyers	13	7	4	2	85	62	16
Rockets	11	6	3	2	57	41	14
Dynamos	12	4	7	1	55	73	9
Mohawks	12	3	6	3	57	58	9
Wasps	12	3	5	2	52	69	7
+Bruins	12	0	12	0	14	64	0

+Bruins played all games away for double points

Next up for the Flyers was a tough match at home against Whitley Warriors as they commenced their Northern League programme. The Flyers were hoping to go one better than in their last encounter with the North East side when Warriors snatched the equaliser with only two seconds of the game remaining.

It didn't end well for Flyers as the Warriors trounced the home side 11-2 to set them on their way to repeating their Autumn Cup success with the top four placings in the Northern League also being replicated from the Autumn Cup.

From left to right, Law Lovell who scored his 400th N.I.H.A. goal in the match against Glasgow, Kenny Horne, Johnny Pullar, Angus Cargill and Les Lovell

Saturday January 6th 2001

Fife Flyers v Coventry Blaze

The stage was set for a classic game of hockey as the biggest crowd of the season poured into the arena, a good 2,000-plus with a healthy and as always noisy contingent from the Midlands sat behind the away bench.

Everything was set for this being the match of the day. Warm-ups were taken and as fans settled in to their seats with their stovies and the ice resurfacing almost at an end the Zamboni affectionately known as "Mabel" gave a cough, a splutter and then nothing.

Despite the best efforts of referee Graham Horner, linesmen Gordon Smith and Norrie Grieve and the rink staff to repair the damage caused by the hot water and oil from the stricken machine which had left four major holes in the ice the situation was too severe to fix.

A Flyers spokesman later said

> "Everyone is hugely disappointed by Saturday's last-minute cancellation and we want the fans to see the game they originally paid for, which is why we made tickets available for the return together with the added incentives of an exclusive prize draw for all who come to see the rearranged game. The fans also deserve praise for the excellent way they reacted to the news of the cancellation".

Flyers director John Waring also thanked the fans for their patience and their compliance with the announcements and the orderly manner in which they vacated the building.

Some other notable occurrences of hockey cancellations or alterations to opponents at the Auld Barn include January 1965 when Brighton Tigers failed to turn up owing to a strike at London Airports leaving the Flyers to hastily arrange a match against a Scottish Select.

In February 1968 the Durham Wasps were unable to travel from the North East because of severe weather and the crowd were entertained by a Flyers A v Flyers B match. More recently the 'Beast from the East' raged and caused the cancellation of a game with Edinburgh Capitals in February 2018.

The Coventry débacle was the first and thankfully only time to date that a home game was called off due to ice issues. Not the case on the road with the game on 15th December 1974 against Paisley Mohawks cancelled at Crossmyloof when the ice machine broke down.

This was a regular event in Glasgow; there are accounts of junior games taking place with the stricken machine parked up in the corner, such was the vastness of the ice surface at Crossmyloof, without it interfering with play.

On the 20th September 1985 up at the old Kingsway rink in Dundee with the Rockets leading 4-3 the match was abandoned as the ice surface slowly turned into a swimming pool.

FOOT NOTE

The rearranged game against Coventry took place on Tuesday 20th February and the league-leading Blaze failed to score for the first time that season in a gruelling match against a Flyers side that looked set to give them a tough challenge in the play-offs.

Coventry arrived at Fife Ice Arena late because the coach driver had taken a wrong turn and the travel-weary Blaze players appeared to be jinxed on their visits to the Kingdom.

The 2-0 defeat was the eighth game for Blaze in 12 days and saw both goals being scored on power plays in the second period. Steven King scored first in the 23rd minute as Claude Dumas sat out a holding minor and there were just 28 seconds of period left when Frank Morris netted as Kurt Irvine prepared to return to the ice after a slashing penalty.

The defeat meant that the Blaze would have to rely on other teams beating Fife if they were to stay above them in the BNL table. As it transpired both teams failed to keep momentum going with winners Guildford Flames and runners up Basingstoke Bison ahead of them in the final standings.

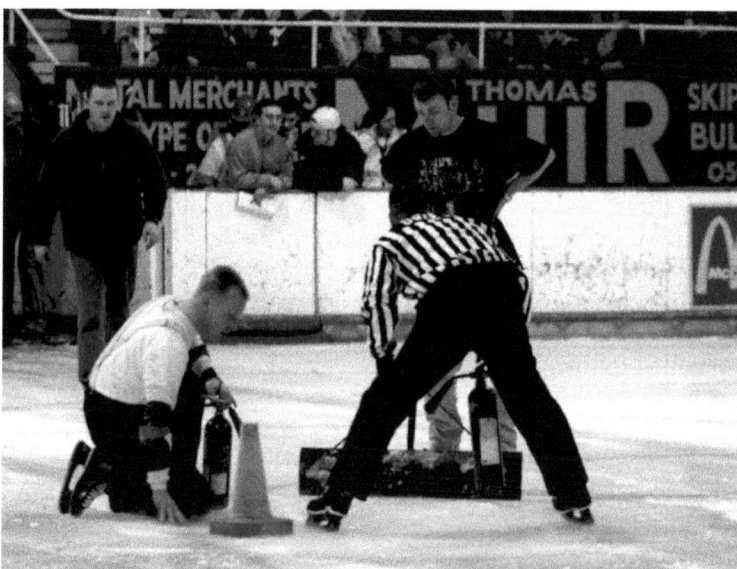

It reminds you of the old joke, a hole has been discovered on the ice – officials are looking into it!

Saturday January 7th 1967

Fife Flyers 3 Wembley Lions 2

The Flyers defied the odds in the Final of the BBC TV Grandstand Trophy and defeated the favourite Wembley Lions 3-2 in what was one of the most exciting matches seen at Kirkcaldy that season.

The Wembley team were possibly the more practised side but they lacked the individual brilliance of a few of the Flyers. The visitors and the eighty supporters who travelled with them were obviously surprised at the high standard of hockey played by the home team as were the majority of the home fans as the Flyers emerged suddenly from the doldrums to play to something like their old form.

There had been no games over the Christmas period and hockey came out of cold storage with the visit of the Lions. Willie Clark, Johnny Carlyle, Eric Grieve, Freddie Wood, Gordon Inglis and Pep Young all made guest appearances in a changed team that looked more like a Flyers/Racers select.

The pace was fast right from the start of the game with both teams trying hard to gain a quick advantage. The first crack at goal was from Lions Scot, Red Imrie, when he forced Willie Clark to his knees to make a good save. For the Flyers Johnny Carlyle retaliated with a well-taken shot at the Wembley goal and he was unlucky not to score.

This set the pace for the game and the first penalty was handed to Flyers Derek Reilly for tripping. Bill Sneddon in particular was key to killing the man advantage but Lions talisman George Beach generally made life difficult for the Flyers defenders. With just five minutes of the first period gone Les Lovell put Flyers ahead and rewarded them for their sustained pressure on the Wembley goal. Derek Reilly just failed to make it two. Flyers extended their lead when Lovell, assisted by Norrie Boreham, scored his second goal for Flyers to put them firmly in command of the match and possibly one hand on the Trophy.

Wembley retaliated by playing harder than ever and Flyers defenders had to work extra hard to keep them out. Freddie Wood and the visitor's Red Imrie were each sent off for two minutes for slashing and tripping but the score remained the same. Just before the end of the first period Tommy Whitehead scored for the Lions as he was assisted by Art Hodgins before he skated past three defenders.

Flyers did not slacken their pace at the start of the second period and Bert Smith put them another goal ahead in just two and a half minutes. After a short pass from Pep Young he had a beautiful solo run through the Wembley defence and gave goal-tender Glynne Thomas no chance to save.

This was Bert Smith's best period of the game. He had several good shots at goal and made use of every advantage that came his way. Despite constant pressure which completely disrupted the Wembley defence Flyers failed to add to their score and all credit was due to goal-tender Thomas for some fine saves.

Into the third and it looked as if this might be the final score as both sides were playing well and giving few chances away to their opponents. Then in the 7th minute Rupe Fresher with an unassisted goal made the score 3-2 when his cleverly taken goal gave Clark little chance of saving.

If anything, the pace of the game from this point increased and although there were no more goals Les Lovell with a clear break on goal missed the chance to clinch it for Flyers. In the last few minutes the Lions lost two players, George Beach and Rupe Fresher, for roughing calls and this allowed Flyers to ease through to the final buzzer and capture the trophy for the second time having also beaten the Lions in their first success.

Flyers — Willie Clark, Bill Sneddon, Joe McIntosh, Johnny Carlyle, Eric Grieve, Freddie Wood, Lawrie Lovell, Derek Reilly, Les Lovell, Norrie Boreham, Bert Smith, Pep Young and Gordon Inglis

Les Lovell giving Lions goaltender Thomas no chance from close range

Saturday January 8th 1983

Fife Flyers 8 Cleveland Bombers 4

Fife Flyers extended their unbeaten run to four games, their best sequence in competitive games that season, when they defeated Cleveland Bombers in a lack-lustre match at Kirkcaldy Ice Rink.

The Flyers had a familiar face back in their line up when Jimmy Jack returned to his former team following an amicable release from the Murrayfield Racers.

American Charlie Brown was on the Fife bench after two successful trial matches. Brown was working at that time in Aviemore and made several Second League appearances for the local Blackhawks before he was invited south for a try-out by Flyers manager John Haig and coach Kenny Horne. Making his first appearance after injury was Rab Petrie, who was obviously short of match practice. This showed, as he missed several early chances.

Canadian Jim Earle gave Bombers the lead after only three minutes, but Gordon MacDougall squared matters for Flyers soon after. In the first 13 minutes of the game there were 29 minutes of penalties handed out by the ref Ake Alm who had, as recently as last October, been the Flyers coach.

Brian Peat put Flyers ahead in 16 minutes and that was how it stayed until the end of the first period but the score line could have been very different if both teams had concentrated on playing hockey and refrained from the physical aspects of the game.

Charlie Brown made his debut for Flyers in the second period on the second line alongside Jim Lynch. Gordon MacDougall put the home side 3-1 ahead within 20 seconds of the restart when he pushed home a loose puck just a matter of inches from the Cleveland line. Flyers missed a succession of chances, including a penalty shot by Jim Lynch, who had been brought down by four Bombers during a solo run. Just before the buzzer Neil Abel picked up the puck from a face-off in the visitors area and slammed a shot past netminder Terry Ward.

The final period, at last, brought the action the fans had hoped to see with Flyers sweeping into an 8-1 lead. Neil Abel opened the third period scoring but Flyers fifth goal proved to be the best seen at Kirkcaldy this season and one of the all-time greats. Picking up the puck behind his own goal Jim Lynch beat every opponent on the ice before netting a superb goal which brought the crowd to their feet to acclaim his stick handling and skating ability.

Just 25 seconds later the fans were on their feet again as newcomer Brown scored a debut goal from a fine Petrie pass. Flyers final goal came from Gordon Latto, who netted the rebound from a Neil Abel shot. Jim Earle brought respectability to the score line for Bombers with three goals in the last eight minutes.

For this, the inaugural season of the British League the teams were split into three sections with the Bombers playing in what was generally the Northern of the two English groups. They were strong contenders to the winners, Durham Wasps, while the Flyers, along with the Murrayfield Racers, chased the Dundee Rockets forlornly for the top spot in the Scottish section.

The Rockets defeated the Wasps in a one-off game at Streatham to become British Champions in what was the forerunner to the Wembley weekends.

Jim Lynch (12) finishes off his solo move with a goal that was reckoned to be one of the finest scored at Kirkcaldy in many years

Saturday January 9th 1988

Fife Flyers 18 Dundee Tigers 4

The toothless Tigers of Dundee lay down like pussy cats as they were given a real mauling by Fife Flyers.

The Taysiders however had already suffered a similar fate against Fife twice before in the previous five weeks losing 24 goals and scoring just 6 in reply with both games having taken place on their home ice.

It was changed days in the Flyers/Rockets derby matches as the Rockets had ceased to be after the conclusion of the Autumn Cup matches earlier in the season, both won by Fife who scored double figures in each, and the renamed club the Tigers became an ever more dispirited bunch as the season progressed.

The beleaguered Dundee side, languishing third bottom of the Heineken Premier League, were powerless to contain a Flyers outfit firing on all cylinders. Coach Jack Dryburgh's policy of utilising his full squad took its toll on an admittedly understrength Tigers team left in total disarray by the final period.

Fred Perlini continued his recent scoring streak with a personal haul of five goals and five assists but the remainder of the goals were shared around the team with nine other players hitting the net. The busiest man on the ice was Dundee netminder Gerry Anderson who faced a barrage of 65 shots and picked the puck out of the net eight times in the final period as Tigers resistance crumbled.

Although the home fans revelled in the goal rush, it had to be admitted as is often the case with lopsided encounters that this match as a spectacle was a major disappointment. No criticism was directed at Flyers though who maintained a high level of performance throughout.

It was all so different from Tigers previous visit to Kirkcaldy in November when they recorded a victory which ultimately led to the resignation of Chic Cottrell as coach.

Flyers served early notice of their intentions to avenge that defeat when they raced to a 4-0 lead in little over seven minutes with goals from Fred Perlini, Jim Lynch, Steve Moria and Neil Abel. Two goals from Tigers 'temporary' import Brian Ludy and a power play score by ex-Flyer Charlie Kinmond pegged the score to 6-3 at the end of the first period with further Flyers goals from Perlini again and Jimmy Pennycook.

Flyers stretched their advantage to 10-5 in the second period through a Ronnie Wood double, Iain Robertson and then Perlini who collected his hat trick while Ludy and Gary Smith replied for Tigers.

Defenceman Al Sims, who iced for only a few shifts because of a broken bone in his hand, managed to get his name on the scoresheet while his teenage replacement Derek King earned a standing ovation with the last goal of the night which was his first in Flyers colours.

The other Fife goals came from Perlini and Moria, with two more apiece, Jim Lynch and Gordon Latto who was the sponsors' choice as Flyers Man of the Match.

Fred Perlini gets the goal procession underway with the opener against the Dundee Tigers

Tuesday January 10th 1939

Kelvingrove-Mohawks Select 0 Fife Flyers 7

The meeting of the Kelvingrove-Mohawks select team, representing Glasgow, and Fife Flyers, representing Fife, in the Simpson Trophy at the Crossmyloof Ice Rink in Glasgow provided a really hectic game which ended with what was considered at that time to be the greatest all-in scrap in Scottish ice hockey history.

Almost all the players were involved in the final period rammy with players who had set out to intervene with peaceful motives soon being stung to retaliation.

The referee, Mr Frank Chase, had a great job to restore order out of this bedlam. When he did manage to put a stop to hostilities he sent Flyers Len McCartney and Mohawks Glen 'Shorty' Morrison to the cooler for five minutes each, which meant that the two did not reappear on the ice as the game ended before their 'rest' was completed.

From the opening face-off it was obvious that the game was going to be played in a hard physical manner. Referee Chase handed out a string of penalties throughout in a vain endeavour to quieten down the exchanges. He had an unenviable job and he for one must have been glad when it all ended.

The 'Kirkcaldy' victory was well deserved as they were the faster and more combined lot. And yet Glasgow had 23 direct shots against 16 for Kirkcaldy which showed that the Flyers had placed their shots better and that was coupled with goalie Chic Kerr being on top of his game to record the Flyers first ever shut out in their history.

George Horn, Les Lovell and Len McCartney were the other Flyers who shone, while Mickey Shires and George Cummine starred for Glasgow in defence and Cadieu was their only attacker of note.

Flyers took an early lead in the first session when Tommy McInroy netted following a movement initiated by Tommy Durling. Willie Turnbull had blocked the puck but McInroy nipped in to net before the tender could recover. Then Les Lovell broke away and passed to Durling who netted a second. McInroy added a third following a shot by Jimmy Chappell and although there were vigorous protests about McInroy being offside the goal was allowed to stand.

KIRKCALDY ICE RINK

PROGRAMME
THURSDAY, April 27 to WEDNESDAY, May 3.

425

PRICE
TWO
PENCE

The Flyers programme for the 1938-39 season consisted of a weekly guide of events at the rink including skating, curling and hockey matches

The second period was more noted for the number of penalties than for good ice hockey. McQuade, Don Eaton, McCartney and Cummine were all visitors to the cooler. The third period was even more hectic and Morrison, Shires, McCartney, Chappell, Morrison, McCartney and Alec Fullerton visited the 'pen' in that order.

The visitors' goals in the last session were scored by Chappell assisted by Durling and then Chappell again with a solo effort, while Cummine was through on his own before being denied, as was Norman McQuade on a solo dash before he later added the final goal.

And so Chic Kerr recorded the Flyers their first ever shutout. He would go on to blank the opposition in two of his next four games for three shutouts on the season.

After the game it was announced that Flyers Tommy McInroy and Billy Fullerton along with Joe Collins of Kelvingrove would come into the reckoning in the selection for the British team to go to Switzerland for the World Championship next month.

The British Ice Hockey Association had decided to hold another trial at Harringay on Sunday in preparation to selecting the team of 13. Both of the Flyers players made the cut.

For Great Britain, composed mainly of home-developed players, it was to prove a disappointing tournament. It started well enough in the preliminary phase with a 3-1 victory against Belgium. The three British goals were all scored by Scots, two of whom were Flyers, Tommy McInroy and Billy Fullerton. Jimmy Kelly of the Wembley Monarchs scored the other tally. McInroy scored again in a 1-0 win against Hungary which allowed Great Britain to progress to the semi-final stage of the competition.

Many observers had criticised the BIHA for selecting what was considered to be an inferior side and they felt vindicated when Great Britain lost all three of their section matches without scoring a single goal.

Over 4,000 spectators witnessed Canada defeat Great Britain in Zurich, all of the Canadian goals scored in the final period. The British team then lost 1-0 to Germany thanks to another third period goal and finished the tournament with a 2-0 defeat to Czechoslovakia.

Great Britain finished the competition in eighth position, their worst performance in the World Championships since 1934.

Sunday January 11th 1998

Murrayfield Royals 3 Fife Flyers 9

Five-goal hero Frank Morris blasted a depleted Flyers squad to a comfortable win in Edinburgh. This completed their eighth straight win over the Royals so far in the season, with five matches having been played on 'enemy' ice.

Even without the services of five regulars, including player-coach Mark Morrison, the Flyers were still far too strong and quick for a lethargic Murrayfield side and once the visitors opened up a lead there was never really any doubt about the outcome.

After the disappointing 8-5 defeat in Hull against Kingston Hawks the previous night, it was imperative to their hopes of retaining the Northern Premier League crown that Flyers picked up the points and they did so in a professional manner.

They were led by the expert finishing of Frank Morris and John Haig and backed up by some fine netminding from Bernie McCrone and strong performances from the likes of Bill Moody, Gordon Latto, David Smith and the excellent Derek King.

As performances go though this was a real team effort and the commitment of the players was never better summed up than by Daryl Venters. The youngster stepped up to the first line and fitted in well, resulting in a thoroughly deserved goal early in the second period.

Royals started brightly enough and took the lead at 6.29 when Scott Neil took advantage of a mistake at the Fife blue-line and fired past McCrone. Flyers were level just 28 seconds later when John Haig was sent clear by Derek King's long pass to beat John Finnie through his legs. The Canadian netminder didn't have the best of nights and at 8.23 he was beaten again by a fierce shot from David Smith but this time it was Royals turn to hit back immediately and Neil Smith found the net 23 seconds later to tie it up again! To complete a scoring burst of five goals in four minutes Morris knocked home his first on the power play at 10.22 and with 28 seconds of the period left he added another with a back-hand finish after being left on his own in front of goal.

Flyers got the perfect start to the second period when Morris and Venters broke on a 2-on-1 and the latter beat Finnie just 14 seconds after the restart. The game became a bit scrappy after that with Flyers guilty of not taking their chances and they were made to pay when George Swan deflected a Paul Pentland shot into the net at 35.57 to leave the game finely poised.

But the third period belonged totally to the visitors and two goals from Morris in 22 seconds (42.24 PP, 42.46) made the game safe. John Haig knocked in another power play effort at 54.40 after good work from Smith and Morris and Frank made it a personal nap hand with a shorthanded effort at 57.49 as Andy Samuel sat out a hooking minor.

Royals scoring: Scott Neil 1+2, Neil Smith 1+0, George Swan 1-0, Paul Pentland 0+1.

Flyers scoring: Frank Morris 5+2, John Haig 2-3, David Smith 1--1, Daryl Venters 1+0, Lee Cowmeadow 0+3, Derek King 0+2, Steven King 0+2, Gordon Latto 0+2.

Shots on goal: Royals (Finnie) 33; Flyers (McCrone) 28.

Penalty minutes: Royals 10, Flyers 6.

Referee: Drew Fraser. Att: 608.

The two teams would meet twice more in the season with Flyers completing a clean sweep of the 10 matches. It meant that over the last two seasons the Flyers had won all 18 encounters with the Royals who would rebrand as the Edinburgh Capitals from the start of next season and they eventually won a game!

Wayne Maxwell lurks around the Royals net in an encounter later in the season at Kirkcaldy

Saturday January 12th 2008

Paisley Pirates 1 Fife Flyers 8

Flyers remained unbeaten so far that season, unless the opposition were the Dundee Stars — who had managed to hand two competitive defeats to their near neighbours.

The visitors wasted no time at Braehead Arena, putting another team to the sword as they sought their fourth win of the season against the Pirates while maintaining their 100% record in the Northern League.

Fife were anticipating an improved home team under the coaching of ex-Flyer Bobby Haig but were quickly out of the traps and surged into a three-goal lead inside the opening 10 minutes. The scorers were Andy Samuel, Stephen Gunn and Steven Lynch in what was a comfortable opening period.

The second period was a tighter affair but Flyers drew first blood again when at 22.42 Iain Bell made it 4-0. Pirates broke Blair Daly's shutout just two minutes later as ex-Fife defenceman Scott Plews found the net but the home side were punished on the power play at 37:23 as Flyers went 5-1 up through Todd Dutiaume.

Into the third period and seconds after the restart Pirates Chris Conaboy and Fife defenceman Dan McIntyre went toe-to-toe which resulted in 2+2+10 penalties handed out to both players. In a hectic opening minute the Flyers scored their second power play goal of the game with Plews once again in the bin when Chris Wands found the back of the net. Further goals from Lewis Glasgow and Dutiaume rounded off the comfortable win.

While a number of Flyers games that season had been high scoring and lopsided in their favour as was often the case this match saw 13 different Flyers on the scoresheet with goalie Blair Daly picking up two assists to bring his season's points total to four.

A victory the following night at home to the Pirates put the Flyers on the brink of winning their first trophy of the season. It set up the meeting the following week against Dundee Stars. Although a win would not mathematically clinch it even a loss to the Stars would still require Fife to lose all of their remaining games for the Tayside club to catch them.

Todd Dutiaume was full of 'coach speak' following the weekends victories saying

"If we beat Dundee we'll need one more point to secure it but I would certainly hope we could grab a point from the four remaining games. We're taking one game at a time but we know two points on Saturday will give us a chance to clinch it in Whitley next month. It's been a see-saw battle with them this year. They're an improved team but we've improved over the last month or so."

Referencing the two defeats against the Stars in December, as well as a reverse against the touring Concordia Stingers, which he said had opened their eyes and enabled them to recapture their full potential since then.

Derek King in action against Braehead Paisley Pirates

Saturday January 13th 1968

Durham Wasps 7 Fife Flyers 0

It was a result that sent shock waves around the Northern League. While the Flyers were far from a power house team, merely one of the pack chasing the Paisley Mohawks that season for honours, they were however still expected to bring the points home from the North East against a Durham side that was rooted at the foot of the table.

The Flyers had already enjoyed 15-6 and 7-2 wins in the earlier Autumn Cup matches. Incredibly the match was actually still on level terms after two periods with both goals intact.

The third period collapse left the Flyers to make a somewhat bewildered trip back up the A1. You had to go all the way back to October 1954 for the last time the Flyers were held goal-less when they were blanked 11-0 in an Autumn Cup match at Paisley.

Despite Durham being a difficult place for Fife to pick up points across various eras this remained the only time that they failed to score against Wasps on their home ice. Derek Metcalfe's shut out was the only one recorded in the Northern League that term; he was named as the All Star 'A' Team goalie at the end of the season along with Flyers Joe McIntosh on defence. The 'B' Team featured Wasps top scorers Hep Tindale and Fife duo of Les Lovell and Sammy McDonald.

The Northern Ice Hockey League would look back on its second season of operation with a fair amount of satisfaction. Although far from complacent, considerable progress had been made towards the ultimate aim of re-establishing ice hockey as a major British sport but a tremendous amount of work lay ahead.

Billy Brennan's well-drilled Paisley side continued to prove themselves a grade or two ahead of the other teams in the league but there were definite signs towards the end of the season that the gap was beginning to close.

Attendances at most rinks were marginally higher than in the previous year. There were clouds on the horizon, however, and by far the most serious of these was the problem of referees. A disagreement between the League and the established Scottish referees had led to the withdrawal of labour during the season from the latter. While the younger and less experienced men who stepped in had done a good job it was obvious that they had not had full control and gained the proper respect from the players.

The issues boiled down to both how referees were being deployed and how many had become "home" refs, where there was a question mark over neutrality. It's a problem which still persists to a lesser degree in the modern game.

Another cause for concern was the amount of bickering between clubs. It is natural to want one's own club to win but with the future of the sport at a critical stage it was felt that some sacrifices for the greater good was required.

Many of the problems which faced the British game at that time could it was felt be overcome by a greater degree of co-operation amongst club officials. Fast forward 50 years and it could be argued that these same issues are still fundamental in the growth of the sport in this country.

Referee Moray Hanson and Martin Mckay a picture of concentration from the goalies union.

Monday January 14th 1952

Dunfermline Vikings 4 Fife Flyers 4

VIKINGS BID JUST FAILED

If the Flyers were having a tough season then the Vikings were enduring a thoroughly miserable time of things — having already finished bottom of the Autumn Cup, they then swapped around positions with the Paisley Pirates to finish second bottom in the Canada Cup standings.

That said, the Dunfermline side were now starting to show some greater resolve in the National League but their 'achilles heel' that season had clearly been their county rivals.

They had met the Flyers six times already and had yet to record a win. Following such a disappointing 1950/51 season it was not a great surprise that the Flyers roster had undergone something of an overhaul in the off season.

Last years' captain Floyd Snider returned, the only ever-present in local post-war hockey and he was joined by Verne Greger, the sole Flyers representative in All-Star honours last season when he made the 'B' team.

Archie Williams, a dashing right winger, who had joined the Flyers midway through last season would also return. High scoring winger Sherman Blair had decided a good paying job at home this winter was his best option. Last season's centre Marsh Bentley, who the returning coach Al Rogers had hoped would be a certain starter, didn't return; he and his brother tended the crops on their farm back in Saskatchewan before he went on to play for Spokane.

Ice rink manager McGregor then pulled off what was considered one of the most sensational captures of the close season when he secured the services of netminder Jack "Stubby" Mason.

On the eve of the season the early assessment of the new look Flyers team was that they were a workmanlike bunch.

"... of all the Canadian ice hockey players who have crossed the Atlantic since the end of the war, the new Fife Flyers look the most workmanlike yet to come to Kirkcaldy. All of them have an efficiency and certainly don't lack bulk. The players will make up one of the oldest and most experienced line-ups seen locally, and should bring back some of the glamour and thrills missing in recent years."

As one wise-cracker put it, "at least they can all skate!"

The newcomers to the team were Fern Phillion, a rather short but well-built defenceman who was a swimming instructor in the summer and recruited from the Toronto Mercantile league.

Al Brown had played in the US the previous season and was joined by his team mate Frank Facto. Joe Millisin was the 'baby' of the team at 20 and had been with the Toronto Maple Leafs farm team while Johnny Pyryhora from Winnipeg had plenty of experience in England with the Wembley Lions and Nottingham Panthers.

Mickey Linnell was a 29 year old who had played with Swift Current Indians and finally a man who needed little introduction, Johnny Vanier, who returned to the club, two seasons ago having also played here with the Paisley Pirates.

The referee circuit was to be enhanced with the arrival of Gordon Gerrard who officiated in the Toronto Major League last season and who would take charge of most of the games.

Also in the pool were Bert Gemmell, Dave Cross and a couple of well-known faces in ex-Flyers coach Nels McCuaig and Harold 'Pep' Young, who had been lost to the Flyers last season when a skate blade cut through a tendon in his ankle forcing his playing retirement.

Returning to the game, the Vikings narrowly failed to lay their Flyers bogey but they didn't make the best start when with just five minutes on the clock the visitors took the lead through Johnny Vanier. Vikings were quick to respond and within two minutes were back on level terms through center Jerry Hudson.

The home side took the lead when Hudson again beat Mason but not to be outdone Vanier also got his second to put the scores level. Joe Millisin put the Flyers into the lead once again but they failed again to hold their advantage and within 50 seconds future Flyers coach Hudson equalised and completed his hat-trick.

Vikings were forced to defend a Flyers power play when Tiny Syme collected a penalty but they held out and on his return former Flyer Cliff Ryan put them ahead. With eight minutes of the game remaining the Flyers struck the equaliser through Frank Facto before they lost Vanier who went off injured.

Saturday January 15th 1994

Fife Flyers 6 Basingstoke Beavers 9

There have been some epic collapses by Fife teams over the years and one such has already been recounted just a few pages ago.

This game was another cracker. The Flyers were 6-2 ahead going into the final period. They completely crumbled in the face of determined opposition to lose seven unanswered goals in little over 12 minutes of play.

Yet, for the understrength Flyers, it had all started so well. They made their intentions clear within a minute when Doug Smail slipped a pass to top scorer Mark Morrison in the slot and he hit a cracking slap shot past Neil Peters in the Basingstoke goal on the 56 second mark.

Things looked even better for Fife when Ryan Kummu scored a short-handed goal five minutes later. At 7:03 the home fans began preparing for a massacre as Steven King collected the puck behind the Beavers goal and found Morrison in front for his second of the game. Basingstoke weren't completely out of the game and on a number of occasions only the reflexes of Fife netminder John McCrone kept them out.

The southern side did get some reward at 11:14 when an attack by the Fife second line broke down and Tony Redmond pounced on the mistake to hit a slap shot between McCrone's pads. Morrison netted his hat-trick goal to put Fife 4-1 up with less than a minute of the period left.

Fife continued where they had left off at the start of the second period when Smail nicked a Steven King shot high into the net past Peters. At the other end McCrone was still called upon to make several important stops but with the Flyers killing a too-many-men penalty Redmond set Nicky Landoli to tap the puck past the scrambling McCrone.

Two minutes later Fife re-asserted their command. Neil Smith deflected a Morrison snap shot into the goal. This saw the end of Peters night as Richard Baxendale replaced him between the pipes. Somehow this appeared to make Fife ease up on their opponents.

Something they were about to pay dearly for in the final period. There was no real danger when import Kevin Conway reduced the deficit to three goals with an enterprising goal at 44:07. But alarm bells should have started ringing some 30 seconds later when Anthony Page beat McCrone with a low shot, bringing the score to 6-4.

The visitors began believing in their chances now and at 45:35 sloppy defence allowed Russ Parent to find Belanger in the clear for a perfect finish. Flyers tried to rally and Smail, Morrison and Kummu all came close before youngster Craig Wilson missed a golden chance to steal the momentum back.

The equaliser arrived a 48:02 when Grant Slater hit a slap shot from the blue line which bounced through a crowd of players and past McCrone.

Not even the travelling supporters could believe that a team lying fourth from bottom in the league were running riot over the championship hopefuls.

But they certainly celebrated when Beavers did the unthinkable at 54:44. Kummu gave away the puck at centre ice. Conway passed to Belanger, who stayed super-cool to round McCrone and slide the puck home. At 56:19 Landoli gave his team some breathing room after Fife defenceman Alistair Reid slipped behind his own goal. Belanger tried a shot which sailed over but Landoli knocked the rebound past McCrone from a tight angle.

Amazingly, the visitors made the game safe just six seconds later. Total disarray in the Fife defence allowed Conway to skate clean through and prod a weak shot past the netminder. Beavers held on in the remaining minutes to send their surprised fans into overdrive celebration mode.

McCrone only faced nine shots on goal in the final period as his form deserted him but he was by no means the only culprit being booed off the ice by a shell-shocked home crowd.

Bobby Haig denied by Basingstoke netminder Neil Peters before it all went horribly wrong for Fife

Sunday January 16th 1977

Paisley Mohawks 3 Fife Flyers 28

It was a night where Northern Ice Hockey Association records were sent tumbling and the Flyers hit new heights at Crossmyloof Ice Rink when they annihilated Paisley.

The Mohawks, who shared the Glasgow rink with the local Dynamos, did not have their troubles to seek as they entered the New Year. Their captain, John McLachlan, and veteran defenceman John Connor were forced out of the rest of the season by injury. Goalie Pete Callaghan, perhaps as a result of a premonition, and winger Shawn Niskanen walked out on the club. Could things get any worse?

Well, this was a match that ripped the record books to shreds as the poor old Mohawks took the drubbing of all drubbings. Before this match the record for goals scored in one match was held jointly by Flyers and Whitley Warriors with 26.

Durham held the record for most goals scored away from home with 17. The highest aggregate was 30 (26-4) accumulated during a Flyers v Mohawks Skol Cup tie. Flyers held the record for the most goals in one weekend when they notched up 29 earlier in the season but having rattled 12 past Dundee Rockets at Kirkcaldy the night before that figure now stood at 40.

This game produced the highest score recorded by an away team, the highest aggregate of goals (31) and the most goals in a period when Flyers banged in 13 in the final period. It was nearing the stage now where the only side in the record books went by the name of the Fife Flyers.

If you were to script such a shellacking then you'd want there to be a surprise. So there was! Mohawks took the lead after 10 minutes of what had been a closely contested match. It was the briefest of moments to be savoured by the home fans though as the visitors were back on level terms straight from the resulting face off.

Mohawks managed to keep the score down to a 4-1 deficit at the first interval but what followed was nothing less than shooting practice for the Flyers. Yet even at the midway point of the game there was little to suggest the utter capitulation by the Mohawks who were only a modest 6-1 in arrears.

The final 30 minutes produced 24 goals as the teams practiced face offs at very regular intervals. John Taylor was Flyers main marksman with 6 goals and 5 assists to his credit which still stands today as a Flyers record, which is shared with Gordon Latto, for points in a game by a British player, Jimmy Jack and Lawrie Lovell both netted twice and also racked up six assists each.

Other scores were Gordon Latto and Chic Cottrell with four goals each and there were hat tricks for Les Lovell, Dougie Latto and Ally Brennan with Kenny Horne grabbing the other goal.

With the ink barely dry on the Flyers annotations to the record books a mere seven days later the Paisley lads had to endure this scoreline – Whitley Warriors 31 Paisley Mohawks 0 – so Whitley now held the mark for the NIHA. highest score.

Flyers had notched 65 goals against the Mohawks for the loss of 7 in their four meetings this season. Paisley went through the entire season without a point from their 28 games and with an eye watering 411 goals conceded and 50 scored. In contrast the Flyers went on to complete the Grand Slam and lost only one game. It was perhaps the perfect storm on a Sunday night in the south side of Glasgow.

Latto double act, Gordon, closest to keeper, scores in a game against Glasgow Dynamos earlier in the 1976/77 season

Saturday January 17th 1987

Fife Flyers 8 Murrayfield Racers 9

Fife Flyers and Murrayfield Racers combined to produce what ranks as one of the greatest matches seen at Kirkcaldy Ice Rink in recent years, if not ever.

It was hard to believe that the two old rivals could top their earlier season 11-10 epic at Murrayfield which the visitors won but that's how this one played out.

On a night of incredible drama, Flyers clawed their way back from what looked a hopeless position at 8-2 down to bring the scores level with just 90 seconds remaining.

Incredibly there was a bitter sweet final twist in this one as Racers still had time to snatch the winner, through Mike Jeffrey, who had been axed by the Kirkcaldy side just two weeks previously. A scriptwriters masterpiece — but sometimes fact is stranger than fiction.

Although Jeffrey scored a hat-trick for his new team, his replacement — Steve Moria — was instrumental in Flyers fightback and finished with three goals and four assists.

It was a remarkable climax to a pulsating match watched by a capacity crowd of more than 3000. As was common place at that time hundreds more were turned away creating a tremendous atmosphere inside the arena.

Flyers actually out-shot the league leaders 65-37 but netminder Moray Hanson gave an inspired performance in the Murrayfield goal to keep them at bay. Chic Cottrell's side, who were without skipper Gordon Latto, did not know what had hit them as Murrayfield raced to a 5-0 lead after just 13 minutes. The visitors displayed lethal finishing with Tony Hand grabbing two short-handed goals after intercepting slack passes to add to a double by Jeffrey and another by brother Paul Hand.

If Flyers were finding it easy to surrender goals then in stark contrast the Racers goal led a charmed existence. Flyers did everything but score. They missed numerous opportunities.

It was the opening minute of the second period before Al Sims finally found the net. However, Hanson's heroics continued when he denied Dave Stoyanovich and Moria when both were clean through and in a classic sucker punch with both teams a man short Rick Fera stretched Murrayfield's lead after 32 minutes. The same player struck again with Racers third short-handed goal after dispossessing Jimmy Pennycook five minutes later. Although Sims pulled one back on a power play Tony Hand completed his hat-trick with two minutes of the period remaining to leave Flyers with a mountain to climb.

Moria caught Murrayfield cold just 12 seconds after the restart but even when brilliant play by the Canadian set up a power play goal for Pennycook eight minutes later the task still looked beyond Flyers. However Stoyanovich, who still looked less than 100 per cent fit, scored his only goal of the night after 52 minutes before Moria reduced the deficit to 8-6 two minutes later.

Urged on by a cacophony of noise from their fans Flyers struck again through Moria with less than two minutes remaining and there was delirium as Pennycook fired home the equaliser with just 90 seconds on the clock.

In a twist of supreme irony however Jeffrey powered a slapshot past Andy Donald to give Murrayfield a dramatic victory just 40 seconds from the end and Flyers marvellous fightback counted for nothing.

Two "older heids" Flyers Charlie Kinmond and Racers Jock Hay battle for the puck

Sunday January 18th 2015

ELITE ICE HOCKEY LEAGUE

Hull Stingrays 2 Fife Flyers 3

Road performances continued to be Flyers saving grace as they claimed back the two points surrendered on home ice the previous night with a narrow victory in Hull.

In their last nine games on the road they had returned with six wins compared with their last nine at home, where the visitors had plundered the points in all but two of the games.

The previous night the Flyers had succumbed on home ice 6-3 to the Stingrays in a performance that head coach Todd Dutiaume described as "unacceptable".

Despite the recent good run of form on the road, a trip to face the Stingrays was an unlikely place to pick up further points. The Flyers only had one success on Humberside in their previous dozen visits stretching back to their first season in the EIHL.

Flyers were heavily outshot 44-20 with netminder Kevin Regan proving to be the match-winner with an outstanding display. For 50 minutes, Stingrays could not find a way past the Fife goalie as the visitors clung on for a gutsy victory.

Flyers spent large chunks of the match under pressure, mainly thanks to spending 22 minutes short-handed. With Regan on top of his game and some dogged penalty killing, Hull were restricted to a solitary power play goal from their 11 attempts with the man advantage. Matt Reber put Flyers ahead at 11.58 before Chris Wands sent a powerful slapshot into the roof of the net on 15.59 for 2-0. It was the defenceman's second goal in as many weeks and something of a purple patch as he notched all three for the season in the month of January.

The second period was one-way traffic towards the Flyers net, but Regan kept the home side out. It took a peach of a strike from Carl Lauzon at 49.58 during Hull's 10th power play to finally break Regan's resistance but Ned Lukacevic restored Flyers two-goal lead with his own rocket shot on the power play at 55.23. Hull pulled netminder David Brown with two minutes remaining and the extra skater finally paid off when Eric Galbraith tapped home at the back post for 2-3 at 58.55.

It set up a grandstand finish but Flyers were able to hold on to secure two crucial points which extended their lead to three points over the

Stingrays. At this stage of last season the Flyers sat ninth in the table; this year they were in sixth spot and seven points ahead of ninth placed Coventry and a spot in the play-offs.

Speaking after the weekend Matt Reber spoke of the team's inconsistencies

"We seem to be in a routine here where we'll come out and have a decent performance, then next game we'll lay an egg. We can't rely this season, like last season, on a purple patch. A lot of people continue to harp back to last season's run and that's great because we have a lot of the same guys and we remember that feeling. But it's hard to have lightning strike twice on the same spot so we can't just rely on that"

On the performances at home he was bemused

"We have some of the best fans in the league so it's not due to lack of support, I don't know what it is?"

Kevin Regan in action the previous night against the Stingrays – his performance in Hull put him top of the Mirror of Merit standings where he would remain for the rest of the season.

Goal hero Billy Fullerton played under the weather to secure the Flyers first ever silverware which is being presented to Les Lovell.

Thursday January 19th 1939

JOHN ANDERSON TROPHY FINAL

Fife Flyers 1 Perth Panthers 0

After Flyers two recent lapses, the home fans were delighted to see their favourites return to something akin to their old flashing form at the rink and win their own John Anderson Trophy, beating Perth Panthers by the only goal of a hectic game.

Flyers really played with some vim and vigour and with Panthers also skating hard there was fast play in a game full of interest. It was a keenly fought contest played in a great spirit. Referee Macdonald, who was also secretary of the Scottish Ice Hockey Association, handed out only two penalties, which came in the last period; one of these was for Perth having too many men on the ice.

A number of voices in the home crowd suggested that several more penalties ought to have been dished out, but a complaint all season long had been that referees were too quick to hand out tickets to the cooler. On many occasions this had only aggravated the players and made matters worse.

It had been refreshing see two whole periods without any excursions to the 'pen' and referee Macdonald had enjoyed a good night's work without ever letting the game get out of hand. Flyers were tightened up in defence and greatly improved in attack from their recent outings.

Les Lovell's body-checking was a revelation. Chic Kerr had a happy night in his cage registering his second shutout, in spite of a number of melées and narrow escapes around his net. In attack Tommy Durling and Jimmy Chappell skated well without much luck, but they gave the Panthers defence plenty to think about.

Norman McQuade was in one of his 'generalising' moods and that meant trouble and plenty of it for Panthers. Len McCartney stickhandled in his inimitable fashion. If Billy Fullerton did not find everything coming off for him, he had the satisfaction of scoring the all-important goal in the last period.

Panthers had a great personality and a grand player in Schumann. This giant defender nowadays operated on the left wing and played a hard, clean game coming close on a few occasions to scoring. Scottie Milne was in good form in goal and Bob Purdie and 'Breezy' Thompson were

359

others who impressed. A fast pace was set from the start and although long-range efforts were the order for a while, several of them came near enough to make both tenders uncomfortable.

Kerr, however, was by far the busier keeper and he had to sprawl to stop a Breezy Thompson special and later kicked out a Purdie drive. Art Schumann was grounded by Horn and a minute later Horn and Lovell closed in on Breezy Thompson as the physical play increased. Thompson almost opened the scoring with a shot that Kerr stopped brilliantly and three drives in succession from Schumann were saved by Kerr.

Flyers had their share of attacking but Milne was seldom troubled. It was a different tale in the second period with Milne taking his turn to shine. Flyers attacked with purpose. Billy Fullerton gave Milne some anxiety with a fast drive from the wing. Horn, on a burst up the ice, landed in a group of Perth defenders and his stick was held by an arm just long enough to prevent him reaching the puck to tap it into the net.

Chappell, Durling and McQuade all tested Milne. Billy Fullerton, on a McCartney pass, whizzed in a shot that Milne never saw but luckily deflected clear. A great run and shot by Chappell followed and then McQuade had a grand effort smothered.

In the last period both tenders were tested in fast end-to-end play. Flyers had an escape when Breezy Thompson shot and collected his own rebound from Kerr but missed the net by inches. With less than ten minutes remaining the breakthrough was finally made. Billy Fullerton passed the puck to Horn who shot. Milne made the save, only for the rebound to fall to Fullerton to skate swiftly in to net before Milne could recover.

Panthers fought hard to the end but Flyers held on to their lead with grim tenacity. It was Flyers first-ever piece of silverware. After the game Billy Fullerton, still feeling the effects of flu, withdrew from the British amateur half-mile speed skating championship to be held at Richmond the following day. Fullerton was a great exponent of the sport and had won the British one-mile speed title in 1936.

Saturday January 20th 1968

Fife Flyers 4 RCAF Lahr Arrows 8

The Canadians came to Scotland with the reputation of being one of the finest sides in Europe; after seeing Flyers performance many thought that the standard of Scottish hockey couldn't be all that far behind.

Admittedly the Kirkcaldy side did have four guests from Murrayfield Racers in their line up but the general display of every player must have made a very good impression on the Canadians.

The Arrows from Lahr in Germany played in the Canadian Air Division European League as well as also playing against other Continental outfits. Regular practice meant they were a very fit and energetic team and when they skated out on to the Gallatown rink few supporters expected Flyers to be in with a chance.

Roy Reid performed miracles in the home cage and he had the large crowd cheering time and again with some great saves. He was beaten several times in the final period but he could not be blamed after his earlier show.

In defence Joe McIntosh and Ken Horne were steady throughout and at no time was the latter out of his class. The youngster had improved almost out of all recognition throughout the year. Flyers went into the lead in the ninth minute with a great team goal. Joe McIntosh passed to Les Lovell who then laid on a fine pass to Ian Forbes who raced in and his shot seemed to burst the net. After some consultation the referees gave the goal. A minute later however the visitors were back on level terms when Breadner had a long shot at goal. It was well wide, but luckily for the visitors it bounced back from the netting around the boards and Kerry Stevens was on the spot to find the back of the net.

The Canadians then went into the lead in the sixth minute of the second period as Gordon Inglis slipped up in defence with a bad pass which let D'Armour through to score. A shock was in store, however, in the 13th minute. Mike Mazur took the puck down the left and passed to Norrie Boreham who then left Gordon Inglis with an easy chance to score to make up for his earlier booboo. Derek Reilly raced away from the Arrows defence. Although his shot was stopped by Baudoin, Lawrie Lovell followed up and he shoved the puck into the net and Flyers into the lead.

In the last twenty minutes the Airmen really flew through the home defence and scored five times before Flyers could do anything about it. In fifteen seconds Jerry Norum got the first goal of his hat trick with a shot that rebounded from the boards and landed at his feet. The same player then put them ahead with a fine shot that ended up right in the corner of the net. With still less than 10 minutes gone Don Martin made it 5-3. Goal number six again came from Norum and in the 13th minute Lampron scored when his own team had a man in the sin bin.

Flyers were now looking weary and ready to give up but Derek Reilly gathered the puck on the left wing and as a defenceman came in to check him his shot streaked into the top corner of the net. Even if the netminder had been able to see the puck it is doubtful if he could have saved it. With a minute to go George Buffet made it 8-4 from a Steele pass.

Flyers – Roy Reid, Bill Brown, Joe McIntosh, Gordon Inglis (Murrayfield), Kenny Horne, Ian Forbes, Sammy McDonald, Mike Mazur, Norrie Boreham, Les Lovell, Joe Baird, Lawrie Lovell, Danny Brown, John Taylor, Graeme Farrell, Glen Reilly (Murrayfield), Derek Reilly (Murrayfield).

Hat trick hero Jerry Norum scores the Arrows third goal

Ric Jackman marked his return to the team with the game winning goal against Storm

Saturday January 21st 2017

Fife Flyers 4 Manchester Storm 3 (after overtime)

Flyers victory over Manchester Storm in the Elite League was overshadowed by an altercation between a player and spectator.

In the 31st minute of the match, which attracted an attendance of almost 2000, Storm forward Eric Neilson was seen reaching into the crowd and throwing punches at a Fife fan sat immediately behind the away bench. The player was ejected from the game on a match penalty and the spectator removed from the rink by security.

The ugly incident sparked a huge reaction both rinkside and across social media. Storm coach Omar Pacha criticised the security arrangements at the Kirkcaldy rink, claiming that his player, who recently had eye surgery, was reacting to having "beer thrown in his face".

The shameful scenes overshadowed what had been a tense end-to-end hockey match, where two big points were at stake. Both sides looked to close the gap on Gardiner Conference leaders Braehead Clan.

With Ric Jackman returning from injury, Flyers finally got to experience the luxury of running with a full complement of imports although their most influential player and top scorer, Ryan Dingle, missed out through injury for the third match running.

Storm were backed by an impressive travelling support and saw their team dominate the opening minutes. Flyers weathered the early pressure and after a missed power play opportunity the hosts took the lead while short-handed, thanks to the tenacity and skill of Brendan Brooks.

As Storm tried to set up at the point Brooks intercepted a loose pass from Trevor Johnson and raced to the other end to pick his spot high past Mike Clemente with 6.30 on the clock.

If Brooks' goal was the highlight of the first period then the talking point was a diving penalty called against Fife defenceman Kyle Haines just two seconds into a five-on-three power play. It was one of nine minor penalties called by referee Pavel Halas in the opening period alone and it sparked a furious reaction from the Fife bench who clearly felt Haines had been tripped.

Flyers started the second period on the front foot and doubled their lead on the power play on 28.08. Bryan Cameron screened the netminder from a Justin Fox slapshot then as the rebound dropped onto his stick he cleverly shifted the puck wide to Chase Schaber who had the better angle to shoot home for 2-0.

Storm hit back just over a minute later. Flyers seemed to switch-off from a face-off in their zone to leave Trevor Johnson unmarked in the slot. Shane Owen couldn't hold onto his shot and Jack Prince snaffled the rebound.

The altercation between Neilson and the spectator followed, sparking a hostile atmosphere. The match was stopped for a lengthy period before Neilson was sent back to the away dressing room on a match penalty, as well as a five-minute major.

The incident seemed to affect the concentration of the players and officials alike. With the teams even-handed at four skaters each Cody Cartier fired an equaliser past Owen despite the Storm player appearing to go offside in the build-up.

With no margin for error in the Conference title race Flyers had to refocus for the third period and they made the perfect start as they regained their lead just 15 seconds after the restart. Cameron's shot hit the backboards and fell kindly in front of the net for Sebastien Thinel who rattled it past Clemente for 3-2.

Man of the Match Brooks hit the crossbar as Flyers pushed for a fourth, but Storm hit back again with just over seven minutes left of the regulation 60 as Darian Dziurzynski lashed a powerful shot into the Fife net on a delayed penalty.

There was growing tension on the ice as the clock ticked down with Fife coming closest to grabbing a winner when Matt Sisca was denied at the back post by a stunning save from Clemente.

The crucial extra point would be decided in overtime, but Storm proved to be their own worst enemies, taking back-to-back penalties. This gave Flyers almost a full two minutes of five-on-three power play, resulting in Jackman's slapshot which decided the contest in Fife's favour at 61.38. A great win for Flyers, but a bad night for the sport.

Monday January 22nd 1940

Dunfermline Vikings 3 Fife Flyers 8

The Flyers were looking to avoid losing their first two Scottish National League games on the road as they travelled to the West Fife rink.

They had already visited three times in the Scottish Points League and a Scottish Cup tie and the Vikings held the upper hand with two wins over their County neighbours.

As expected in derby matches there was a healthy rivalry building between these two teams in their first and second seasons respectively.

Helping undoubtedly to fuel the fire was the 'defection' of several of the Flyers squad from last season to the Vikings ranks.

Goalie Chic Kerr, who did not play in this game, which left the Vikings needing to borrow Scottie Milne from Perth Panthers as injury cover. Tommy Durling was also appointed Vikings player-coach and with him followed Jimmy Chappell and Norman McQuade.

All of these signings were primarily as a result of Kirkcaldy ice rink Manager Mr Rolland taking up the same position with the fledgling Fife club. The *Fife Free Press* reported events as follows:

FLYERS LOST 3 GOALS THEN SCORED 8

After being three goals in arrears against Dunfermline Vikings on Monday evening at the Dunfermline rink, Fife Flyers staged a remarkable recovery and scored eight goals in a string without any reply from Vikings. At the end of the first session, Vikings had sailed into Flyers to the tune of three goals, McQuade netting one and Durling two. Terrific power plays by Flyers in the second session saw Dunfermline's lead wiped out, Arnie Pratt netting two and Glen Morrison one. In the final session Paul Rheault notched four and Red Thomson smacked home one to put paid to the Dunfermline account. An injury to Norman McQuade early in the second period handicapped Vikings but this does not detract from Flyers victory. The way they played after they settled down would have rattled any team. Scottie Milne and Johnny Scott, both of Perth Panthers, who assisted Vikings for the night must have thought that Flyers make a speciality of notching goals against them. Playing for his own team at Kirkcaldy last Thursday Scottie Milne had nine goals scored against him by Flyers with the other two being scored against deputy-tender Ray Cheyne when Scottie was in the cooler. So in two games against the Kirkcaldy lot he had lost 17 goals. Not bad going if you don't happen to looking at it from Scottie Milne's point of view!

Vikings — Scottie Milne (Perth), Johnny Scott (Perth), Ernie Batson, Larry Marsh, Tommy Durling, Jimmy Chappell, Norman McQuade, Jimmy Shannon.

Flyers — Art Grant, Red Thomson, George Horn, Glen Morrison, Paul Rheault, Arnie Pratt, Frank Ney, Johnny Schofield.

Referee — J. Newton

Paul Rheault led the Flyers scoring that season and was second in the league to George McNeil of the Dundee Tigers. The Vikings Tommy Durling was a couple of points behind Rheault in third spot.

In the "Men of the Pen" standings the Flyers had two players in the top three in penalty minutes with Glen Morrison and George Horn behind Dundee's Merrick Cranstoun.

Dunfermline Ice Rink construction. A number of previous/current Flyers in the workforce — left to right Norman McQuade, John Fullerton (Falkirk), George Horn, Tommy Durling, F Woods (Harringay), Chic Kerr, Buster Amantea (Falkirk)

Saturday January 23rd 1988

HEINEKEN PREMIER LEAGUE

Fife Flyers 9 Ayr Bruins 7

In what was a make or break match for the Flyers the outcome also confirmed that indeed ice hockey was not a sport for the faint-hearted.

Controversy coloured Flyers first confrontation of the weekend with Ayr Bruins and it spawned an explosive edge to a heated match. In a major and bloody first period fight seven players were penalised.

Two Flyers had their wings clipped for the rest of the game in a brawl which had been quite unprecedented at the Kirkcaldy Ice Rink that season. It served to escalate the tension of a close contest which the home side just had to win to remain within a slapshot distance of the league pacesetting Whitley Warriors and Murrayfield Racers.

Those ingredients were emptied into the cooking pot. After an initial stirring about, what was dished up in the last 20 minutes was for the ice hockey connoisseur. It was vintage hockey played at a cheetah's pace which engendered a pulse-stopping spirit among the capacity crowd.

Indeed, the highly-charged game was equally balanced until the final five minutes when Steve Moria and Jim Lynch wrecked the Bruins stubborn challenge. Flyers, who were missing Al Sims and Gordon Goodsir, had the perfect start as Dean Edmiston slammed in a Moria assist from close range within the first minute. Three minutes later and Lynch edged the home side further ahead with his first strike of the night. Halfway through the opening period a ferocious bodycheck by Jimmy Pennycook on Bruins' netminder John McCrone sparked off the battle scene. Everyone knows that no one touches the goalie in hockey.

The result of the chaos was an early shower for Messrs Gary Fyffe and Jimmy Pennycook, much to the fury of the passionate home fans. Bruins players Frank Morris, McCrone and John Kidd were penalised as were Flyers Edmiston who also needed attention for a cut on his forehead and Neil Abel.

When play resumed Fife quickly added another brace through Moria and a brilliant unassisted effort from skipper Gordon Latto. Bruins hit back with a strike from import Claude Gagnon in 11 minutes but Lynch got his second just seconds later to restore Flyers four-goal cushion.

Power play goals from Scott Howe and Gagnon closed the gap as Flyers poorer penalty record took its toll before Gagnon slotted Bruins' fourth to complete his hat-trick. Just 15 seconds before the break Fred Perlini eased the frantic Bruins pressure to record Fife's sixth goal.

Compared to the first period the second was something of an anti-climax but goals from Alistair Reid and Gagnon for Bruins were separated by a fine shot by Lindsay Lovell to give the Kirkcaldy teamsters a single goal lead going into the last session.

With so little between the two sides the final 20 minutes adopted a cracking pace and when Bruins star man Gagnon levelled the score in the 47th minute the contest tottered on the sharpest of sharp edges.

But with four minutes left Moria snatched the lead and gave Flyers the sight of victory and Lynch then secured his hat-trick with 15 seconds left on the clock against an unguarded net.

Claude Gagnon went on to finish the Bruins top scorer that season by a mere 99 points over the second placed Frank Morris. He notched three fewer points that Flyers top scorer Fred Perlini who had 176 with Steve Moria bagging 151.

This is what happens when you 'bump' the goalie as Flyers Neil Abel is restrained by the linesman when tempers flared against the Bruins

Sunday January 24th 1993

Humberside Seahawks 4 Fife Flyers 2

After enjoying a promising start to the season on their return to the Premier League, during which time they had two early victories against Seahawks, the Fife side now found themselves mired in inconsistency. They had been fighting through a number of losses to injury and suspension, the most significant being the career-ending injury to their influential blueliner Cal Brown.

Looking to repeat their win in Peterborough the previous weekend the Flyers failed to alter their frustrating pattern of poor away results in Hull which meant they now had just one win away from Kirkcaldy in their last eleven attempts.

In a tight match the home side Seahawks ran out two-goal winners on the back of a convincing first-period display. Hawks ran up a three-goal margin by the 14th minute and Flyers netminder John McCrone was called upon time and time again to keep his side in touch as the Kirkcaldy side were outshot 36-24 over the 60 minutes.

With Bob Giffin back home in Canada on compassionate leave a slashing penalty on Darin Banister left the Flyers blueline pretty thin to kill the penalty and the home side opened the scoring at 4:47 through Dan Dorian. Less than two minutes later Hawks had manoeuvred into a two-goal lead when Dorian hit home Stephen Johnson's assist for his second of the match. The third came through Kevin MacNaught at 13:36 and it wasn't until the final minute of the period that Flyers managed to offer some resistance. A Frank Morris effort from the red line beat Humberside netminder Brian Cox all ends up.

The remaining two periods of hockey pretty much saw each side cancel the other out as chances were created but not taken and each side won a period each through single strikes. Anthony Johnson scored past McCrone at 36:22 and Dean Edmiston fired an unassisted effort at 42:55 to complete the scoring. The result preserved Flyers third spot in the Heineken Premier League but their near rivals Bracknell Bees, Whitley Warriors and Humberside were closing in and crucially all had games in hand.

Coach Jim Lynch reckoned that his side needed five more victories with only nine games remaining to secure a favourable play-off berth.

Several Flyers players were picked to represent Scotland in their game against the 'Auld Enemy' in Sheffield the following weekend. Jim Lynch, Iain Robertson, Bernie McCrone, Dean Edmiston, Ally Reid, Steven King and Moray Hanson were all scheduled to travel south.

In the end the Flyers snuck into the post season on goal difference with a win in their penultimate game against the Nottingham Panthers before being swept in their six qualification games for Wembley.

Match programme for Flyers game against the Humberside Seahawks

Tuesday January 25th 2000

CHRISTMAS CUP FINAL 2ND LEG

Basingstoke Bison 2 Fife Flyers 3

Remember that epic win against Peterborough Pirates a few pages ago? Once the smoke had cleared it paved the way to the Flyers reaching the Christmas Cup Final.

The first leg in Kirkcaldy the previous week had ended all square at 3-3 thanks to a last-minute equaliser by Mark Morrison. The Flyers had already visited the Playground rink in Hampshire twice that season and were unbeaten with a win and a draw with both games being tight affairs and this one would turn out no differently.

The Flyers travelled with Frank Morris being unable to ice due to a suspension and Todd Dutiaume wore the 'C' for the game. It was another great advert for the sport as the game swung from end to end with no team having the upper hand for any length of time.

Stephen Murphy and Joe Watkins each faced 31 shots but in keeping with the tight nature of the game it was defencemen Ted Russell and Dywane 'Dog' Newman that were awarded the beers after the match.

The first period appeared to be heading for a goal less stalemate but with 21 seconds remaining the Flyers made the break through. Andy Samuel collected the puck at the blue line and fired it towards Watkins. In front of the netminder, the puck took a couple of bobbles, which eventually threw him, and the all-important opening goal and lead went with Fife into the changing room.

The Flyers got the first power play of the game early in the second. On an excellent set up play John Haig saw a shot ring off the inside of the post. Watkins had another incredible escape moments later when a shot from Mark Morrison squeezed between his pads but sat on the goal line before he scrambled it clear.

Small margins, as the Bison then broke down the ice and Jeff Daniels beat an unsighted Stephen Murphy to tie the game and the score on aggregate. The post again denied the Flyers when Dutiaume returning from serving a minor penalty jumped onto the ice and broke in on Watkins only to ping the crossbar.

He stayed with the play however and collected the puck and fed it cross crease where Morrison effectively had an empty net to restore the Flyers lead. The see-saw nature of the game continued and within a minute the

Bison were back on terms when Mike Ellis fired a shot at Murphy who again looked as though he had been screened this time by Russell.

The next goal in the final period was likely always going to be decisive in such a closely fought game. It looked as though Bison had made the breakthrough when they scored with Derek King sitting out a penalty only for referee Cloutman to wash it out for a man in the crease.

The tension built and when Bison took a penalty with less than five minutes remaining Fife sensed this was to be their chance. Ted Russell, as he had done in the earlier game, scored the decisive goal when his blue line slapshot through traffic beat Watkins.

Or did he? Later he reported that while all of the news outlets had reported the goal as his, as it had been recorded that way on the gamesheet, he had spotted Morrison at the side of the Bison net on the power play and he had fired the puck to Mo who got a nick on it before it entered the net. Morrison was the unheralded match winner.

Bison pulled the goalie for the final 45 seconds and threw everything at the visitors, who stood firm to secure their first trophy of the new century — not their last however!

Captain Frank Morris with the N.T.L. Christmas Cup

In a season of many triumphs Steven King leads the celebrations of the 2007/08 Northern League Trophy

Saturday January 26th 2008

SCOTTISH PREMIER ICE HOCKEY LEAGUE
Fife Flyers 2 Solway Sharks 2

On paper this might have been a surprise result but anyone at the game could see it coming. What could not have been predicted was that the outcome of the game was not the one showing on the scoreboard at the end of the evening.

The result of the game was decided in a penalty shootout a week later as the two teams once again met at Fife Ice Arena. The rules of the Scottish Premier Ice Hockey League competition decreed that matches should be played to a result. No one had realised this until both teams were showered and Solway were on the bus headed back to the borders.

The 'solution' was to play for the extra point the following week when the point that the Flyers secured in the shootout amended the result in the record books to

Fife Flyers 3 Solway Sharks 2 (after a shootout)

Fife Flyers had played in a comfort zone which was normally enough to see them through games but there was a late sting in the tail in this one. Solway Sharks could flatter to deceive that season with a great win one week and a heavy defeat the next, but in Dumfries they were building their hockey history and their team had to be taken seriously.

A Flyers side playing at full pelt would have, nine times out of ten, been too strong for them as indeed they were pretty much too strong for anyone that season.

However, the Flyers bench had clearly instead opted for an easy night and it nearly cost them a point in a league where the EIHL Edinburgh Capitals reserve team were at least giving them a run for their money.

For the second week running Flyers let a 2-0 lead slip at home but this time Todd Dutiaume's side had nobody to blame but themselves. A defensive mistake for Sharks first was followed by a netminder howler for the second and Fife had left themselves no time to go for the win.

The first period proved that Solway were an improved side from their last visit to Kirkcaldy in December when they lost 7-1 but their tactics were cautious with defencemen venturing no further forward than the neutral zone. It made for a stuffy opening period and Flyers without the services of key players Steven Lynch, Andy Samuel and Derek King struggled to carve out clear chances. Sharks first misdemeanour was punished as Fife made their first power play count at 7:40. Steven McAlpine put the puck past Scott McMeeken while Tim McKay sat out for interference. The second goal followed shortly after at 13:49 as Lewis Glasgow flicked home Steven King's composed pass after Craig Mitchell's shot had been blocked by the netminder.

Without being brilliant Fife had managed to open a two-goal lead and that perhaps contributed to the lethargic mindset for the remainder of the game.

The first sign of trouble arrived at 36:43 as Solway hit back. Tom Muir dallied on the puck and gave up possession to Sharks veteran import Kevin Conway. He fed Mark Gallagher who passed to Bari McKenzie from behind Daly's net and the former Belfast Giants forward lashed the puck beyond the reach of the goalie's left hand glove.

By this point Flyers were well and truly stuck in a low gear. Although McMeeken had to make two or three decent stops the visiting defence wasn't being stretched nearly enough. As for their power plays the less said the better, but Fife were now down three top forwards; Stephen Gunn failed to re-appear for the third period after suffering a cut leg in the second.

That lack of spark was to cost Fife the win and with 1:30 to go in the match Solway earned a face-off in the Fife zone and called a time-out. It proved a masterstroke as Flyers re-appeared still in time-out mode and lost the face-off and a slapshot from the blue line ended up in the back of their net. McKenzie's effort was straight at Daly and should have been saved but the Fife goalie was slow to get his pads down and the puck wriggled through to the basket.

The roars did not come from a visiting support, as there wasn't any, but from all the Solway players who knew they were little more than a minute away from their result of the season. Flyers upped the pace considerably for that last 60 seconds, but by then it was too late.

Sunday January 27th 2013

Fife Flyers 5 Hull Stingrays 1

The Flyers needed a jump-start to get their engines going in this encounter but once they did they were too strong for bottom of the table Hull Stingrays.

It was a comfortable win in the end but it was only after the loss of the opening goal that Flyers stopped pussyfooting around and started showing some grunt.

Missing the injured trio of Casey Haines, Chris Wands and Steven McAlpine, a tentative looking Flyers came out the blocks with their guard up which was unusual for a team with such a strong home record.

Perhaps the defeat in Hull the previous night on top of being down on bodies led Flyers to doubt themselves as they sat back and invited punches before eventually one got through. Bryan Pitton's heroics were all that kept Flyers in the game until 12.42 when Dominic Osman whacked a shot into the top corner to light up the scoreboard.

That gave Flyers the jolt they needed. From then on they started imposing themselves on the game and it did not take long for the visitors' defence to crack. On one of the first occasions that Flyers managed to set up play in the Hull zone, Derek Keller hit a shot that deflected into the path of Todd Dutiaume. While he may have been approaching 40 the player-coach showed he still had good reactions with a sharp first-time finish that gave netminder Ben Bowns no time to re-adjust his position. Having been out-shot 19-8 over that first stanza Flyers could consider themselves somewhat fortunate to reach the first interval on level terms.

However, they turned the tables in the second period, firing 22 shots to Hull's 6 to take a 3-1 lead and set themselves up for an essential victory. Talk about night and day! Constant pressure on the Hull goal was finally rewarded at 34.44 with a goal made in Kirkcaldy and finished in Canada. Local lads Jamie Wilson and Josh Scoon both saw efforts saved in quick succession but defenceman Derek Keller followed up to make it third-time lucky with a rebound strike.

A power play goal from Jason Pitton when he tipped home Keller's blast from the blue line put daylight between the teams at 37.32 and gave Flyers some breathing space for the third period.

Hull applied some pressure at the start of the third but Bryan Pitton was having a solid night between the pipes with one stunning save in particular giving home fans a reason to chant the netminder's name. The next goal would be crucial to the outcome and Bobby Chaumont, as he so often did, found himself in the right place at the right time to skate onto a Pitton rebound to fire Flyers 4-1 up and effectively seal the win.

The match was meandering to a close when with three minutes left Kurtis Dulle took exception to a clean hit from Dutiaume against the glass and smacked him in the nose with an elbow. It led to a bout of fisticuffs between the two and resulted in Kurtis Dulle being assessed a 5 plus Game penalty for checking to the head. Dutiaume, with a nose turning more purple by the second sat out two minutes for roughing.

It left Flyers to play out time on the power play and they applied the icing to the cake in the final second of play as Hogg just beat the clock to sweep home the fifth goal on 59.59. This was a crucial home win that repaired the damage of the defeat in Hull the night before. However, until Flyers dreadful away record was addressed the home form would have to continue to simply bail them out of trouble.

In team sports, one man's injury is often another man's opportunity. That was certainly the case for Fife Flyers youngster Josh Scoon when he stepped into the space vacated by broken collarbone victim Steven McAlpine to pick up his first Elite League point of the season. Speaking afterwards he said that he was looking to make the most of his chance in the line-up. "You don't want to see guys getting hurt but one guy's loss is another guy's gain," he said.

Kris Hogg beats Ben Bowns in the Stingrays goal

Sunday January 28th 1979

Fife Flyers 7 Durham Wasps 2

The Flyers were looking to make it three wins from three in the Autumn Cup which, unusually, was not played as the season opening tournament this year so took on more of a winter feel.

With a snow storm raging outside, it was decided to reduce the length of the match to give the Durham Wasps more time for their long journey south. The first period was played without stopping the clock and the intervals were also reduced but Flyers still had enough time to run up a convincing 7-2 victory.

As if that was not bad enough for Wasps, they eventually had to spend the night at Kirkcaldy Ice Rink before making a start to their return journey at 5.30 a.m. on Monday morning. Even then the 30-strong party did not find the going easy. They got stuck at Berwick and didn't arrive home until Monday afternoon after nearly eight hours on the road.

Brian Peat turned in an excellent game in defence and was always in the right place at the right time allowing him to pick up three assists. Jimmy Jack opened the scoring after eight minutes, and with Wasps still reeling Chic Cottrell rammed home a second goal. Flyers moved into top gear in the second period with Charlie Kinmond quickly making it 3-0 and Jack scoring again after a pile-driver from Peat rebounded from a post.

Wasps continued to be under heavy pressure and on a power play, captain Kenny Horne made scoring look easy with a well taken goal. Flyers brought veteran Joe McIntosh on for his first shift just after the midway point and with his first touch of the puck he added to the total.

Joe, who was also GB head coach that season, then gave Flyers a 7-0 lead going into the last period when he back handed a shot into the roof of the net. Flyers eased off during the last period and Wasps collected two consolation goals through Ronnie Stark and John Nelson.

Overall this was a better all-round performance than of late by Flyers with a greater work rate from the players and it was good to see Murray McLellan stepping up from the Kestrels and fitting in well.

The Flyers topped their section with Durham Wasps, Ayr Bruins and Sunderland Chiefs and met Whitley Warriors in the semi-final which they won 14-9 over the two legs.

The Murrayfield Racers were in no mood to relinquish their grip on the trophy and in what were essentially the final two games of the season they were also only two wins away from a Grand Slam. The Racers won the first leg in Edinburgh 4-3 and without any ice at Kirkcaldy the Flyers "Home" leg was played in Aviemore where the Racers were stunned by a rampant Fife side who won 12-4 to lift the trophy and crush the slam.

Dougie Latto appears to be surrounded but still finds the back of the net in a match against Glasgow 1978/79

Thursday January 29th 1953

Fife Flyers 7 Dundee Tigers 4

Fife Flyers not only recorded their first National League win of the year; they also gained their first victory over Dundee Tigers for almost two seasons and at the same time achieved their highest score in a competitive game that season.

Quite a list of achievements for one night! It was a merited win with plenty of fight in both lines and the re-shuffle which took Marlowe McDonald to centre with Bud Stock and Scotty Dowle on the wings brought goals.

This line, along with coach Bobby Burns and junior Jim Smith, scored five of Flyers goals with a hat trick for Stock and a double for Burns. While Flyers showed plenty of spirit they were opposed by a surprisingly lack-lustre Dundee line-up.

The Tigers had not been blessed with the best of luck in recent weeks and looked as if they were quite prepared to accept their fate. They put remarkably little fight into the exchanges, except perhaps in the physical sense and their covering was slack and ineffective. It was a hard-fought game with a climax arriving in the second period when both teams were left playing 3 on 3 with 6 players sitting out penalties.

This situation caused some confusion. It appeared the officials were less than familiar with the delayed penalty process which was evolved to prevent teams having any fewer than three players and a goalkeeper on the ice through penalty.

It was particularly obvious in this game that confusion existed and the consequence was that Flyers played first 33 seconds and then 30 seconds longer under penalty than was required by the rules. Such mistakes could have been fatal to any team's chances and lose them the game.

Seven minutes into the game, after several good chances had been missed by both teams the Flyers took the lead. Dowle gave McDonald a nice pass in the corner. The centre's pass out in front of goal was promptly despatched to the back of the net by Stock.

Four minutes later Len Smigel increased Flyers lead with assists for Don Claydon and Jock Harley. Flyers always looked like going further ahead but they were frequently troubled by the Jake Favel, Art Sullivan combination at the other end. It was no great surprise when Sullivan reduced the leeway with a snap shot after Favel and Johnny Rolland had made the opening. Harry Pearson and McDonald contrived to give Burns a good chance following a face-off in Tigers' end and the defenceman promptly increased the Flyers lead.

This goal was nullified only two minutes later, however, when McDonald failed to get the puck out of his own end and Holland's shot was deflected past Harry McQueston by Pearson. Ed Williams restored Flyers two-goal lead again. When the teams were reduced to three men each Burns got his second to make the score 5-2 in Flyers favour after Stock and Dowle had made the play to leave him open.

Flyers had a further goal disallowed just on the bell marking the halfway mark when referee Gemmell ruled that McDonald was inside the goal crease the time. It made little difference. Dowle soon made an opening for Stock to shoot home number six and a few minutes from time the same player completed his hat-trick after Dowle had failed to beat the keeper on solo break.

Leading 7-2 Flyers slackened off in the last minute and lost two goals when Ferens and Lorne Goddard beat McQueston from scheming plays by Favel. Over the piece Flyers best were McQueston, Burns, Stock, Smigel and Williams, with Don Grant, Fred Ferens and Favel outstanding for Tigers.

Fife Flyers match programme for the visit of the Dundee Tigers

Sunday January 30th 1966

Fife Flyers 12 Murrayfield Royals 2

Fife Flyers were still smarting from their loss to the Paisley Mohawks in the final of the BBC Grandstand Trophy at Kirkcaldy the previous night when they met a determined Murrayfield side.

It looked initially as though the Royals were going to hold off the Fifers as after the first twenty minutes the home side had been held to a goalless draw.

Flyers seemed to get into their stride however and from then on it was one-way traffic to Royals net as goal after goal went thumping home. Murrayfield keeper Willie Clark, who suffered an injury some weeks ago, wasn't quite back to his usual top form.

Royals had a mainly young team and had improved immeasurably under the able coaching of Johnny Carlyle who had coached the top team Brighton Tigers for several seasons before moving back to Scotland.

Under the circumstances and with several juniors included in their line-up they did exceptionally well. The final score of the match flattered the Flyers somewhat as they seemed to lack confidence until they took the lead and at that point Murrayfield lost some of theirs.

All credit to the home team however as once they had the edge on the visitors they certainly showed their goal-getting ability. Jerry Hudson almost completed his hat trick but had to be content with two goals. Team mates Lawrie Lovell, Sam McDonald and Graeme 'Pinky' Farrell also had two goals to their credit. Only forwards Andy Williams and Andy Napier were unfortunate enough not to contribute to Flyers grand total.

Both teams had their defences working full-time in the first period but, although both pressed for the advantage, the score line remained blank at the first buzzer. Flyers efforts were rewarded in the second period, however, when Farrell collected the puck from Hudson and shot it home. Minutes later Joe McIntosh put Flyers two up from a Lovell pass. Murrayfield reduced arrears when ex-Flyer 'Pep' Young beat John Pullar after picking up the puck from a neat piece of play by Reilly and Shaw.

Shaw was sent to the penalty box for two minutes after tripping McDonald as he skated in for a solo attempt and Flyers put the pressure on. Andy Williams however wasn't long in joining Shaw in the box with a two-minute penalty for tripping and both teams were a man short. Jerry Hudson then took his chance with a beautifully taken shot assisted by Farrell. Shortly afterwards Williams made the trip to the sin bin again, taking with him Dunbar of Murrayfield, each with two minutes for roughing. Williams was only seconds back on the ice when he gave McDonald a neat pass to put Flyers three up. Ian Forbes was next to find the net giving the Flyers a 5-1 lead at the end of the second period.

The Kirkcaldy side were quick to press home their advantage and seven more goals were collected in the final minutes of the game. First came Jerry Hudson followed by Bill Sneddon with an unassisted goal. Then in quick succession came goals from Lawrie Lovell from Hudson and Sam McDonald with a well deserved goal from a yet another perfect Hudson pass.

McDonald got a his second followed by Verne Greger getting in on the scoring act from the blue line. Murrayfield replied when Les Lovell gave Gordie Ross a chance to beat keeper Pullar but in the closing seconds brother Lawrie Lovell got an unassisted goal to end the scoring.

Flyers — John Pullar, Bill Sneddon, Joe McIntosh, Verne Greger, Andy Williams, Jerry Hudson, Bert Smith, Lawrie Lovell, Sam McDonald, Ian Forbes, Andy Napier, Graeme Farrell

The result proved to be the last game played by the Edinburgh side who disbanded for the remainder of the season.

Action from a Flyers visit to Murrayfield as the players appear to be searching for the puck in the rafters

Sunday January 31st 2016

Elite Ice Hockey League

Fife Flyers 4 Braehead Clan 2

Playing a three-game weekend, the Flyers bounced back from Friday night's narrow defeat in Braehead with back-to-back thrilling home victories over Belfast Giants on Saturday and twenty for hours later the Braehead Clan.

Flyers clearly had Clan's number on home ice at that time as this win saw them chalk up their fourth win over the title-chasing Renfrewshire side — a thoroughly deserved victory. It was a different story, though, when Flyers travelled West as they had failed to win in their last eight visits to 'the shops'.

The win took Flyers back to the top of the Gardiner Conference. With the season swinging into the home straight, it opened the door to making up some ground from seventh in the EIHL — a must for their post-season aspirations.

If they could maintain the form they had shown over the weekend and in particular against the Clan then it would definitely be game on. There was a solidity about their performance that had been lacking on many nights in the first half of the season. Defensively they were strong and the bond between the blueliners and netminder David Brown had clearly grown and tightened. The smile on the goalie's face as the fans chanted his name after the buzzer pretty much summed it up. He was the clear Man of the Match candidate.

At the other end of the ice pad was emerging a rather tasty partnership between TJ Caig and Nico Sacchetti. Shayne Stockton was enjoying great form and Ryan Dingle as always was a driving force. They were all key players in the win over Clan in which Fife led from start to finish. Dingle fired them ahead at 9:58 and he had the last word with a long-range empty net shot just 16 seconds from the buzzer.

Flyers cracked the game open after 15 minutes with a big goal. A shot off netminder Travis Fullerton's pads saw the puck fly to the left where the unmarked Justin Fox spun round and netted with lightning speed.

They held the lead until the first break. Clan's response was instant at the start of the second, when they needed less than 90 seconds for Ben Davies to net the rebound off his own shot. Braehead applied some heavy pressure in a period which referee Neil Wilson happily allowed to flow. Quite why the whistler then started making back-to-back calls late on left players on both sides frustrated.

Flyers were given two power plays and they netted on the first with Paddy Cullen's left wing shot flashing past Travis Fullerton for 3-1 at 27:53. The third period saw more chances coming Fife's way as Caig and Sacchetti tormented the Clan defence, but the game wasn't a done deal.

With 52 minutes played the referee binned Danny Stewart for hooking and then left Fife facing a five on three for 1:36 as Phil Paquet went for roughing. The tap-in from Matt Keith for 3-2 set the stage for a fascinating last few minutes.

It got more intriguing as Fife lost Paquet to a ten-minute misconduct as he made two bids to confront a Clan player after a late check. It was a big loss, considering Kyle Haines had also taken a knock but the team stood firm and with 55 seconds to go, Clan pulled Fullerton in a last throw of the dice. But despite swarming round Brown's net the puck found its way to the stick of Dingle and he hit the empty goal from deep within his own zone to seal the victory.

Flyers goalie David Brown celebrates with the fans after another home win over the Clan

Shane Owen who broke the record (held jointly by the man on the previous page) during season 2021-22 for most shut outs all-time in the Elite Ice Hockey League for a Flyers goalie.

February

Kirkcaldy Ice Rink at the start of the 2021-22 season

Thursday February 1st 1940

Fife Flyers 10 Dundee Tigers 3

The Consolation Cup was a two-legged tie, involving the two teams that were eliminated in the first round of the Scottish Cup. The Flyers had returned from Tayside 24 hours earlier on the wrong end of an 8-4 deficit — but what a transformation they were on home ice.

Center Paul Rheault lived up to his nickname of "Thunderbolt" when he scored his first double hat-trick of the season, while also adding three assists, being involved in all but one of the Fife goals.

Flyers had their opponents hog-tied in the first session and Lane in Tigers net was machine-gunned with shots. Flyers simply outskated them. It was no surprise when Rheault took an Arnie Pratt pass to open the home account in four minutes. Two minutes later he doubled the lead from a Glen Morrison assist. Inside ten minutes, 21 year old Eddie McMillan scored his first goal at Kirkcaldy for the Flyers.

Dundee came more into the game and their cause was helped when Rheault took a penalty. They could make nothing of the advantage however and in the 19th minute Rheault bagged his treble on a solo play.

In comparison to the first session the second was pretty tame for a time. Williams, Tigers new Canadian, netted two minutes in and that was all that happened for a while. When Cranstoun and Roberts were sent off in quick succession, it looked like the home side would increase their lead, but Flyers advantage was offset when McMillan was also sent to the bin. In the closing minutes, Cranstoun and McNeil missed two good openings for Dundee.

The third period saw all of the real fireworks and with the Tayside team still ahead 9-8 on aggregate the Flyers needed to up their game even further. Inside three minutes that man Rheault tied the scores but before the midway point Roberts restored Tigers advantage.

This lasted only a minute as Rheault levelled the combined scores again on a Pratt assist. A minute later Glen Morrison scored an opportunist goal when Pratt was upended on a break-away. The puck went loose and Glen scored with a shot that went through a forest of legs and flickered the red light. The Flyers were ahead for the first time in the tie.

In the fifteenth minute Rheault scored from yet another Pratt assist. A couple of minutes later the tie looked completely dead when McMillan netted a Rheault assist. There was a glimmer of hope for Tigers when McNeil got one back but the man of the evening "Thunderbolt" scored his sixth in the dying seconds for what in the end was a comfortable looking Flyers win.

Flyers, Art Grant, Frank Ney, Johnny Schofield, Glen Morrison, Paul Rheault, Arnie Pratt, Red Thomson, George Horn, Eddie McMillan

Tigers, Bill Lane, George McNeil, Bunt Roberts, Laurie Marchant, Al Rogers, Merrick Cranstoun, H Williams, Scotty Cameron, Glen Braid.

Paul Rheault scored a couple of nap hands later in the season but didn't repeat his haul from this game on his way to unsurprisingly leading the Flyers in scoring with 104 goals in 50 games.

It's a goal scoring rate for a season only bettered by three players in Flyers history. Richard Laplante with 124 in season 1991/92, Dave Stoyanovich with 108 in season 1984/85 and Bud Scrutton who scored 107 in season 1948/49.

Unfortunately, the war interrupted his playing days with the Flyers although he appeared in a number of armed forces representative teams across Scottish rinks during the hostilities after which he returned to Canada in the autumn of 1946 hoping to play some more with his old club the Winnipeg Monarchs.

Paul Rheault who is fourth all-time in goals scored in a single season for the Flyers

Sunday February 2nd 2003

Dundee Stars 5 Fife Flyers 4 (after overtime)

There was a growing resilience and determination about the Flyers in recent times that suggested their aim of participation in the play-offs was going to be more than just a token gesture.

That made this overtime loss all the more difficult to take as Flyers came within 73 seconds of a notable victory against a Stars side who were trying to hang on to the coat tails of the league leading Coventry Blaze.

Flyers had received the news a couple of days before that the eye injury sustained by Frank Morris against the Newcastle Vipers would end his career. So, with two imports less than the Stars, and a number of the team less than fully fit, Flyers again showed that they were at their best when faced with adversity.

The task became even harder when Derek King was thrown out of the game for a match penalty for checking from behind just after the midway point. It was after this that the visitors hit back from trailing 3-1 to level the game by the break; when they took the lead soon after the restart the Flyers travelling support had high hopes of a confidence-boosting win.

They came mighty close but in the end the legs began to go and once Stars equalised there was only ever likely to be one winner in the extra period.

Remarkably, Flyers outshot their hosts, including an 18-8 middle period, but Dundee had the clearer chances only for Steve Briere to again make some outstanding saves.

Fife started the game well and stunned the home side at 3.17. An excellent goal came from the third line with David Smith and Andy Finlay teeing up Daryl Venters who rifled a shot high past Stephen Murphy. Flyers killed a roughing minor on Frank Evans but Dundee were level at 10.55 when Dan Ratushny's screened shot crept past the unsighted Briere. It was an unfortunate goal to concede and worse was to follow at 16.16 when Briere and Evans left a puck behind the net to each other and Martin Wiita fed Ratushny for his second from close range.

Both sides saw off a penalty at the start of the second but at 31.50 Finlay failed to clear a puck round the boards and Ken Priestlay passed inside for Teeder Wynne to beat Briere. The uphill struggle Flyers faced appeared even worse at 36.08 when Derek King checked Paul Sample into the boards and then did likewise to Laurie Dunbar who had his head down and went face first into the boards. The blood on the ice swayed referee Mike Rowe to hand the Flyer a 5+Match for checking from behind but the shorthanded situation was eased somewhat by Ratushny's minor for high sticks.

At 39.02, with the sides at 4-on-4 Karry Biette knocked in Mark Morrison's pass and incredibly 26 seconds later Evans got the final touch to poke the puck behind Murphy and suddenly Flyers were level.

The Dundee netminder was penalised for delaying the game soon after the restart. With the momentum with them Flyers capitalised at 42.10 when Biette banged in Jonathan Weaver's pass at the back post to stun the home fans in the 1707 crowd.

Flyers killed penalties on Weaver and Evans then Briere denied Tony Hand on a one-on-one breakaway and when Johan Boman and Jason Dailey were sent to the bin on roughing minors Dundee's efforts became more and more frantic.

Unfortunately, the extra space allowed Stars to move the puck about and at 58.47 Jan Mikel stole in to beat Briere with the netminder off balance to deal with the shot.

Flyers held on to secure a point as the game went into overtime but were out on their feet and failed to register a shot. Stars pounded their net and eventually grabbed the win at 62.27 with a scrambled effort from Wynne.

*Jason Dailey who played
one season with Flyers
after a year each at
Slough and Guildford*

Thursday February 3rd 1955

Fife Flyers 5 Nottingham Panthers 4

The Flyers earned their first ever competitive victory at home against the Panthers at the third attempt that season.

The Kirkcaldy management were at the end of their tether. With a run of six games, where they had secured but a single point, they had put the entire team on two weeks notice.

It certainly appeared to help with motivation of the players, although Flyers best performances that season appeared to have been reserved for their engagements with the leading English clubs. It was yet another giant-killing act but thoroughly deserved against the colourful Nottingham Panthers.

Both teams took a while to settle. Although it was Nottingham that played all the clever hockey it was Flyers who took the lead 30 seconds from the first interval with a clever goal through Nebby Thrasher from a two-way play by Roger Landry and Walter Davison.

The tempo increased in the second frame after Bill Ringer, from a Chick Zamick assist, had put the teams on level terms after five minutes. However, Flyers hustling type of hockey unsettled Panthers. It came as no surprise when Johnny Andrews regained the lead for the home side, with a grand shot assisted by Neil Matheson and Wayne Sutherland.

For the second time Panthers tied the score when Les Strongman netted from a Ringer pass. Three minutes later Flyers struck a purple patch to net two counters in 10 seconds. The first one came through Henri Labrosse after good set up work by Davison and Don Cox. Straight from the face-off Cox netted the fourth, with Davison and Labrosse being awarded the assists.

Nottingham really turned on the heat in the final frame but it was Flyers who got the all-important next goal when Cox scored but it was the clever inter-passing movement between Thrasher and Davison that was the highlight.

Panthers reduced the lead after the changeover when Zamick netted a picture goal and after many goalmouth thrills Kenny Westman notched a fourth 35 seconds from time.

For the remainder of the game as the Panthers stormed the Flyers net most of the Flyers fans focussed their eyes on the clock rather than the game. Net-minder Mike Luke performed miracles to keep the raging visitors at bay. Eventually the final whistle brought relief to a hard-pressed home defence who whooped and jumped with joy at their success.

Top honours in this exciting encounter were shared by centre-ice Nebby Thrasher and net minder Mike Luke. The former, who was forced to absorb a lot of punishment against a clean but hard-hitting Nottingham defence, was at his elusive best.

This was not a game which was confined to the odd personality, however, and it was through their combined efforts that victory was attained. Each goal was well worked and resulted from a three-way play and only one marksman counted twice.

Another important factor which simplified the road to victory was that Flyers were not penalised once in the match. Nottingham were an entertaining team to watch and they may well consider that they were a trifle unlucky not to have gained a share of the spoils.

They had a steady net minder in Jack Siemon, a safe bunch of blue-line blockers and two crafty forwards in George Chin and Chick Zamick.

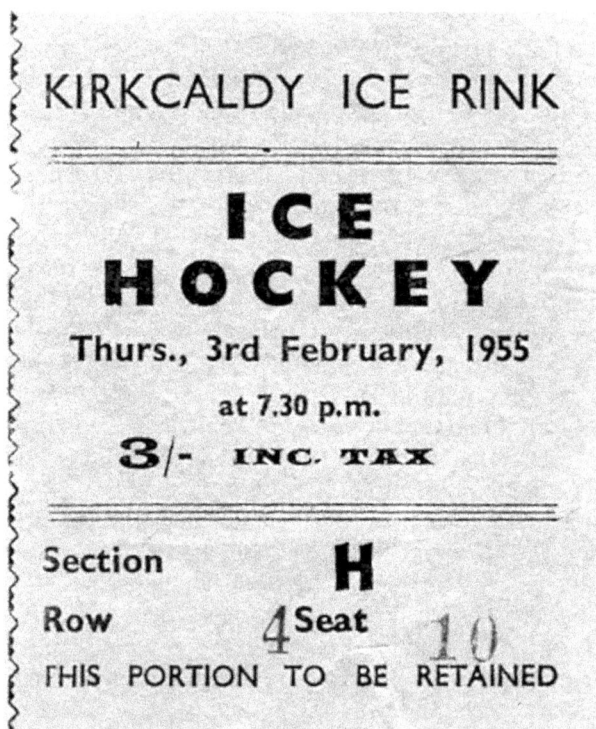

KIRKCALDY ICE RINK

ICE
HOCKEY

Thurs., 3rd February, 1955

at 7.30 p.m.

3/- INC. TAX

Section **H**

Row 4 Seat 10

THIS PORTION TO BE RETAINED

Was this still the hottest ticket in town? Fans in attendance this night certainly got value for money.

Saturday February 4th 2006

Elgin Tornadoes 2 Fife Flyers 13

Flyers through the years have always had a following on the road, with the exiles south of the border, not to mention the veritable masses who have descended on the rinks of their nearest rivals.

This night in Morayshire there appeared to be just a single Fife strip in a crowd of little more than 50. "'Welcome tonight's visitors, Fife Flyers," said the DJ as the team stepped on to the ice in total silence. In the cafe next door there was a children's birthday party which drew to a close with more noise and excitement.

This was almost certainly the smallest ice pad the Flyers had played on since the days of Ayr's Limekilns Road rink. Fife started the game playing hard and fast. They really didn't need to, but once again did their job as efficiently as ever.

Credit however the Tornadoes, who barely managed two lines and a handful of decent shots. The home players certainly did their very best and scored a fine goal to tie the game early on, only to wilt badly.

As the calendar had flipped over to February, attentions were starting to focus on next season and where exactly Fife would play. The British National League and its predecessors seemed a long way away and there was only so much enthusiasm even the die-hard fans could muster for non-competitive, one-sided hockey and a match night atmosphere that was flagging.

Indeed, there was only so much even the most committed opposition skater could learn from double-digit hammerings and only so much experimentation Fife could do to turn games into training drills.

For the game in Elgin, Todd Dutiaume made more changes to systems but the result was closer to target practice than a true game, as Fife got to grips with the restrictive ice pad.

He and the players needed competitive action. This was game 35 on the season and only Dundee had put a single dent in their loss column and the Edinburgh Capitals had also squeaked a draw.

The jolt of a wee defeat now and again keeps a team honest but that was never going to happen in a leisure centre in Elgin. At times the neutral zone resembled rush hour. The game was over after a 6-1 opening period in which the sides traded goals and then Fife got down to business.

With John Haig and Steven King both putting in shifts on the blueline Flyers subjected Tornadoes netminder to a barrage of rubber. They fired the puck in from the blue line and pounced on every rebound and struck metalwork twice.

It could easily have finished with the margin being doubled. Stephen Gunn took the scoring accolades as he netted five. Gordon Latto Junior also chipped in with a hat trick.

The second period saw Tornadoes handed a power play and it made no difference when Jamie Wilson accepted Steven King's perfect pass for a short-handed counter to make it 8-1. No disrespect to Tornadoes but Fife could probably have iced four skaters and still have won with goals to spare.

The gulf not just in skill but fitness was evident for all to see and by the time the third period came round Tornadoes were chasing shadows. Chris Linton, Steven McAlpine, Willie Nicolson and Liam Greig were the other scorers with no fewer than 13 players appearing on the scorers sheet.

Tornadoes did however have the last say with their second but it was another match completed. One step closer to the finishing line and the continued search for competitive hockey.

John Haig in action against the Tornadoes in a match at Kirkcaldy

Sunday February 5th 1989

Tayside Tigers 3 Fife Flyers 11

Flyers completed yet another comprehensive win over the Tigers that season as they recorded a hat-trick of Heineken League victories with this latest win on Tayside.

Once again they reached double figures at the expense of the ailing Tigers who were now fighting for their Premier League lives. Earlier season clashes were much closer affairs and the Tigers split the Norwich Union Cup series as they advanced to the National Final to be defeated by the Durham Wasps.

While they lost both of the lesser important Scottish League games they had bigger concerns as they battled with the to-ing and fro-ing of players which at one stage left Rick Fera as their only import. Flyers were simply too strong and too quick for the Dundee side and cruised to a comfortable win.

Fired by the return of Czech forward Vincet Lukac — and fellow countryman Milan Figala in defence back on the ice after taking a puck in the face the previous night — they eased through the first and third periods, hitting nine goals past the helpless netminders Mike Ward and Colin Downie.

Lukac in particular tormented the home side with his blistering speed and vision and claimed a hat-trick plus six assists to round off a thoroughly emphatic display.

Bobby Haig also contributed significantly to sending his old club on the road to defeat with four goals while Jindrich Kokrment had to settle for a mere two plus three after firing hat-tricks in the last three games.

It was Jim Lynch who got the proceedings underway with a fourth minute power play goal. Rick Fera levelled but a double from Kokrment put Fife on easy street at 18.01. Less than 20 seconds later Haig made it 4-1 before the buzzer.

Flyers were outshot 11-10 in the second period and 42-31 overall in the game but Martin McKay kept a clean sheet during the middle stanza as Tayside's finishing was less than impressive. Lukac fired a fifth goal at 31.47 and a strike from Haig four minutes later all but sealed the points.

The third stanza was simply one-way traffic towards Tayside's net and although ex-Flyer Jimmy Pennycook reduced the deficit at 40.40 the hosts were overrun in the closing stages. Kokrment and Lukac set up number six for Haig, and Lynch made it 7-1 with an unassisted effort in 45.38. Lukac hammered home two inside 60 seconds.

Ronnie Wood notched another consolation but the Flyers demolition job was completed by Haig when he hit the target twice in the dying minutes to round off an excellent team performance.

For the Tigers they were to welcome a saviour on board in the shape of Glenrothes based Lawrie Lovell who stepped in behind the bench to revitalise the team and vanquish the spectre of Division One Hockey.

It was to be a stay of execution as the Tigers could not compete when the 1989/90 season rolled around in September.

Bobby Haig (left) celebrated his call up alongside Derek King and Richard Phillips to the GB U21 side with four goals against the Tigers

Sunday February 6th 2005

Cardiff Devils 11 Fife Flyers 2

With the prospects of a fully integrated league looking increasingly likely, this season's crossover fixtures between the British National League and Elite Ice Hockey League sides were taking on more significance as the powers that be looked ahead.

This result however highlighted the current gulf, a veritable chasm on the night, that existed between the two leagues as a full strength Devils outfit with 16 skaters and 11 imports over-ran a brave Fife side with only 11 skaters and 7 imports.

It was the first and only time however that season that Fife had conceded double figures in these match ups. The early moments saw the home side pour forward pinning the visitors in their own end but a lightning break by Todd Dutiaume in the second minute nearly ended in an opener.

The Kent Davyduke, Judd Medak, Dutiaume line continued to pose problems for the home defence with some impressive counter attacks but Devils maintained territorial superiority, firing an astonishing 26 shots on Steve Briere. Devils eventually took the lead in the 15th minute when Dave Matsos found the far corner and they doubled their advantage only a minute later after an odd man break ended with the puck deflecting past Briere off Greg Kuznik.

Having acquitted themselves well in the first period and been unlucky to trail by two at the buzzer the Flyers simply fell apart in the opening minutes of the middle stanza. Devils fast paced three-line hockey carved open chance after chance as the visitors were pulled out of position time and again with the home side scoring four goals in as many minutes.

Adrian Saul then opened Flyers account at 30.07 with a clinical strike although when Jon Cullen hit the Devils seventh a minute later a cricket score looked on the cards. Flyers refused to lie down and they fought their way through to the second buzzer conceding only one more goal to Rob Davison.

The final period was purely academic. Nathan Rempell and Todd Dutiaume traded goals early on before the home side wrapped up the scoring through Jonathan Phillips and John Craighead.

Devils scoring: Matsos (2+2) Rempell (1+3) Cullen, Davison, Romaniuk, Sacratini (1+2) Tait (1+1) Craighead, Phillips, Manny (1+0) Burgoyne (0+2) Becker, DeWaele, Hill (0+1).

Flyers scoring: Dutiaume, Saul (1+0) Haig, Medak (0+1).

SOGs: Cardiff (Cugnet) 10. (Brabon) 17; Fife (Briere) 57. PIMs: 6-4

Referee Andy Carson

Attendance: 1500

In their next game, the following weekend, with the addition of Paul Spadafora and the return of Steven King giving Flyers three lines it was expected there would be no repeat of this one-sided encounter and Devils were given a much tougher game winning 6-4.

What these matches were telling everyone though was that Flyers management would need to look long and hard at the size and strength of the squad required to play at this level on a regular basis.

Adrian Saul was Flyers second top scorer in season 2004/05 behind Todd Dutiaume

Saturday February 7th 2015

Elite Ice Hockey League

Edinburgh Capitals 5 Fife Flyers 2

On a weekend where the Flyers faced the bottom two clubs, Edinburgh Capitals and Dundee Stars, and with the momentum behind them from recent good performances and results, their three-game winning streak came to a disappointing end with a 5-2 defeat at Murrayfield Ice Rink.

Edinburgh Capitals were a much-improved side from the one that last met Flyers, who handed them a 9-3 thrashing in Kirkcaldy on January 11th, but the Flyers, who had won all but one of their eight previous meetings with the Edinburgh side so far that season, played a significant part in their own downfall by failing to live up to the standards set in recent weeks.

Flyers were out of sorts, particularly in defence, where costly mistakes were made and the forwards had no answer to on-form Caps netminder Tomas Hiadlovksy. While he bemoaned the fact that his side came up against a hot goalie, Flyers head coach Todd Dutiaume also admitted that there were problems with the performance, most notably in defence where he blamed `mental errors' and said his defencemen 'weren't solid'.

Caps took the lead after 7.50 when Flyers played themselves into trouble in their own zone when Matt Nickerson passed the puck straight to Jade Portwood behind the net, who set-up Denis Rix in splendid isolation in front of the net to slot home.

Flyers put some pressure on the Caps net but with Hiadlovsky making several sprawling saves it took the visitors until the 31st minute to draw level. Bobby Chaumont was the beneficiary of some statuesque Caps defending as he skated in from the wing with purpose. Caps stood and watched he drew Hiadlovsky before sweeping the puck into the net for a sweet solo goal.

At this stage Flyers were having slightly more of the play but five minutes later Caps regained the lead as a breakdown in the Flyers defence saw Rene Jarolin left unattended at the back post and he rounded Kevin Regan to slide home.

Caps put daylight between the sides four minutes into period three as they hit Flyers on the counter attack with Jarolin bamboozling the diving Nico Suoraniemi with a dummy before firing in for 3-1. It was 4-1 and effectively game over on 50:50 as Jarolin pounced on his own rebound to beat an exasperated Regan, who rightly expected his defence to help out after he had stonewalled the first attempt.

Ned Lukacevic gave Flyers false hope on 57:58, tipping home a Kyle Haines rising slapshot and Regan was withdrawn for the extra skater as the Fifers went for broke. After failing to set up an attacking play with the extra man, Flyers lost the puck and left Jarolin to skate down the pad unopposed to grab an empty net fifth and seal his hat trick.

Ned Lukacevic pulled the Flyers back into the match but it was a false dawn

Saturday February 8th 2020

Fife Flyers 4 Dundee Stars 1

The losing sequence stood at 14 games on the bounce, equalling the modern-day record (at the time of publication) as the worst run of results for the Flyers in the EIHL. A defeat to the Dundee Stars, looking to claim their fourth straight victory at the Fife Ice Arena, would arguably have painted this team into the annals of Flyers history for all the wrong reasons.

The Stars were down a couple of players as import Alex Schoenborn and Kris Inglis remained unavailable because of injury while the Flyers were missing defenceman Sam Jones due to suspension.

With the Stars going for a clean sweep of wins in Fife it was the Flyers who took the early initiative as the first chance of the match fell for the home side. Just 40 seconds in Chase Schaber was in behind the Dundee defence but he could not hit the target.

The Stars created the next best chance in the third minute as they broke down the ice three-on-two after Jordan Buesa's shot was blocked but Fife goalkeeper Adam Morrison denied Dundee twice. Schaber incurred the first penalty of the evening on a tripping call but Omar Pacha's men could not open the scoring on the power play.

Instead it was the Flyers who almost opened when Danick Gauthier was denied by Dundee netminder Alex Leclerc and following up was Paul Crowder but he failed to hit an open goal in the 13th minute.

Fife deservedly took the lead however when Kyle Just netted from close range on 15 minutes. It was a short-lived lead as Egils Kalns skated onto a loose puck and quickly dispatched it past Morrison less than two minutes later to tie the score.

Into the second period and the action continued to go back and forth until a short period of pressure from Dundee midway through culminated with Kevin Dufour missing the target on a big chance for the visitors.

The Stars went on the penalty kill on 32 minutes as Reilly O'Connor was punished for a trip and it took just 21 seconds on the power play for Schaber to put the home team back in front.

Fife pressed well to keep the puck in the offensive zone and when the pass came out to him from James Livingston, Schaber drilled his shot into the top right corner. Dundee responded through Jagger Dirk and the defender saw his first shot from the left flank saved; after collecting his own rebound he attempted to wrap a shot around the far post only for Morrison to close the door at the last second.

Despite a few chances for both sides there were no more goals in the period. Stars started the third period with the man advantage as Gauthier boarded Dirk with 10 seconds left on the clock. The Flyers killed the power play and almost stretched their lead but Kalns made a great play with his stick to take away a chance from Tim Crowder in front of the Dundee goal.

A few moments later Mike Cazzola then misplaced his pass to Carlo Finucci as another chance to increase their advantage was wasted. Fife went on the power play again and Kyle Just played in Paul Crowder but he could not slip the puck past Leclerc.

Dundee were next to threaten with a shorthanded chance for Matt Marquardt but Morrison came up with a huge stop. Just was the next player in the sin bin for delay of game in the 54th minute and the Stars were rocked when they gave up a short-handed goal.

A stretch pass down the ice from Paul Crowder found Schaber and he beat Leclerc for the vital insurance goal. Dundee put up a strong fight in the final minutes but the puck bounces were falling on Flyers sticks. When Leclerc was pulled for an extra skater with a couple of minutes to go, Paul Crowder eventually hit the empty net with 12 seconds left to play.

Danick Gauthier and Tim Crowder around Leclerc in the Stars goal

Sunday February 9th 1964

Fife Flyers 11 Paisley Mohawks 7

The Flyers remained unbeaten in their Scottish League campaign.

The Mohawks, who were without home ice and played all of their games away from home, put up their best performance of the season against the 'champions elect' but as with all six encounters against Fife ended up on the losing side.

With the Flyers line up hosting the countries top three scorers in Jimmy Spence, Ian Forbes and Sammy McDonald attentions in this match had turned to someone in the line-up who had been finding it difficult recently to put the puck in the net.

As it was Bert Smith broke his 15-game goal jinx against the Mohawks. Could this have been because he changed jerseys? Before the game Bert told manager Sandy Nicol: "I'll try the number five jersey tonight. Maybe that'll change my luck". It certainly appeared as though it did as he scored from McDonald and Forbes in the second period. Incidentally, junior Ian Shields who took over Bert's number nine jersey didn't score!

This game coming as it did only 24 hours after their thrilling encounter with the Brighton Tigers at Kirkcaldy was something of an anti-climax, one of the few thrills being the goal from Bert Smith to break his unwanted drought.

It was noticeable how the pace of the Mohawks game was much slower in comparison to that of the previous night. It was top marks however to the Paisley side who showed great fortitude. Down 9-2 in the second period they not only hung on grimly but fought through to finish only four goals behind when it seemed certain that they would be on the wrong end of a very lopsided score.

It took Flyers only three minutes to find the net and they were able to add to their tally at regular intervals in the first two periods after which they were ahead 10-3. That said, their overall standard of play was sloppy. Had they turned in a similar performance against Brighton the previous night the English side would have walked away with an easy win.

In the third period the home side allowed the visitors much too much of the play with the puck and the Mohawks never-say-die attitude was rewarded as they stated a mini comeback to win the period 4-1.

A newcomer to the Paisley ranks was Norwegian Per Brandtzaeg, who turned in a fine performance and provided some punch in the West of Scotland side's attack. He was rewarded for his efforts with three of his sides goals while Bob Stevenson and Billy Brennan picked up doubles.

For the Flyers it was once again the top line that featured heavily with Forbes and Spence collecting four each. Smith, Lawrie Lovell and Joe McIntosh netted the remaining three.

Flyers lined up — Roy Reid, Bill Sneddon, Joe McIntosh, Verne Greger, Ian Shields, Ian Forbes, Jimmy Spence, Sammy McDonald, Bert Smith, Law Lovell, Graeme Farrell, 'Pep' Young, Jimmy Watson

Ryan Kummu who spent two seasons with the Flyers from 1993 to 1995 – uncompromising but hugely unfortunate as he twice suffered a broken jaw in his second season

Wednesday 10th February 1954

NATIONAL LEAGUE

Dundee Tigers 14 Fife Flyers 3

The saying is that pictures paint a thousand words. So, this picture of Flyers goalie Ron Collins being called into action yet again, this time by Dundee Tigers John Scrimgeour, was pretty much the story of a bad night on Tayside.

The way the season had gone for the Flyers there weren't many more words left to describe how dire the situation was. They found themselves in the middle of an 11 game win-less run and were handed a walloping from a Dundee side who finished the season a distant second bottom of the table but still with almost double the points secured by bottom club Fife.

Dundee Tigers kept up their "yo-yo" form in the National League game at the Kingsway when they recorded their highest score of the season against the hapless Flyers.

The visitors could do little about it and their defence simply wasn't good enough for a smart Tigers forward line that included juniors John Scrimgeour and Ian Flight and both local lads did well.

The home side opened the scoring in seven minutes and were three up before 10 minutes had elapsed on the clock. Flyers got on the board before the first period break but that was as close as it got all night.

The Tigers hit five without reply in the second period including four in a six-minute spell. It took them the grand total of eight third period minutes to really rub it in by adding another six. It could have been much worse with the Tigers passing up some clear-cut chances including Bert Oig and Vern Smith failing to find the net when clean through in the closing minutes.

It was now only three wins in 19 National League games with Flyers last win coming against the Tigers when they demolished them 12-4 in Kirkcaldy.

The Tigers goals came from Art Sullivan who along with Red Kurz and Bert Oig all had hat tricks. Marshall Key, John Scrimgeour and Dick Wolstenholme got the others. The Flyers consolations came from a double by Murray Banks and another from Scotty Dowle.

DUNDEE ICE RINK

KINGSWAY WEST
Telephone 85222

ICE HOCKEY   NATIONAL LEAGUE

Tigers v. Flyers

Wednesday, 10th February, 1954

AT 7.30 P.M.

PROGRAMME   ·   PRICE FOURPENCE

The programme for Flyers night of misery in Dundee

Sunday February 11th 1996

Fife Flyers 8 Humberside Seahawks 1

Flyers completed a perfect four-point weekend with victory over Humberside on Sunday night, but it has to be noted that it was with a little help from the referee and some crazy indiscipline by the visitors.

Even the most blinkered Fife fans had to admit that the ref spoiled this contest with what looked at times like a one-man crusade against the visitors.

Hawks came North ready to play their usual physical game where intimidation and cheap shots were never overly subtle. Flyers were prepared and their combination of higher skill levels and new-found determination looked like clipping the Hawks wings.

They didn't really need the referee's help. In any case Keith Simpson threw two Humberside players out of the game. First, he handed Ian Pound a second 10-minute misconduct penalty, presumably for verbal abuse; then he handed Bruce Bell a five-plus-game penalty for what looked a fairly soft spearing call which could easily have been penalised as a minor for tripping or slashing.

The Canadian simply jabbed Andy Samuel in the calf as the pair tussled in front of the net and that was his last action of the evening. Penalties like that — along with an even more curious incident when the stripey binned two Hawks on the same hooking call — simply provided the spark that caused Humberside to 'mix it up' and blow their tops.

Despite all of Fife's efforts to continue playing their classy brand of hockey from the previous night, the game never really reached the same heights, mainly because Flyers spent most of the night with a five-on-three power play.

Chris Palmer was the odd man out among the home imports, which was a surprise after his performance the previous night, but he made way for the return of Canadian defenceman Frank Evans.

Kevin St Jacques carried on where he'd left off against Slough with the only goal of the first period at 8:55 although Iain Robertson had a strike washed out three minutes later for infringing on the goal crease.

Player-coach Mark Morrison led by example in the second period creating his own chance and scoring at 24:31 and just over a minute later

Frank Morris showed that the Flyers were just as dangerous when killing penalties as they are on the power play.

With Craig Wilson binned on an accidental high-sticks penalty Morris robbed Pound on the Hawks blue line and deked the goalie out of his socks before he slid the puck home.

Further power play goals from St Jacques, Robertson and Evans gave Flyers a 6-0 lead but Hawks, with just enough players for two full lines following the Pound and Bell dismissals, wrecked Bernie McCrone's shut-out hopes with a Norman Pinnington goal just before the second buzzer.

The final period was dull, dull, dull. Hawks had seen enough and were just playing out time while Fife took their foot off the gas just a touch. Evans scored with a super low slap shot. St Jacques completed his hat-trick with a lovely goal at 57:27 when Flyers pinned the visitors in their own zone, kept possession and dodged the flying checks before the winger pulled the trigger.

The Flyers skated a lap of honour after the game with Man of the Match Evans bringing up the rear as the fans showed their appreciation for a job well done in difficult circumstances.

Shots on Flyers — McCrone: 20 Hawks -Wolfe: 54.

Scoring — Flyers: St Jacques 3+1, Evans 2+1, Morris 1+2, King 0+3, Marsden 0+3, Morrison 1+1, Robertson 1+0, Samuel 0+1.

Hawks: Pinnington 1+0.

Crowd: 1500

A caged Steven King battles with Hawks Cam Plante

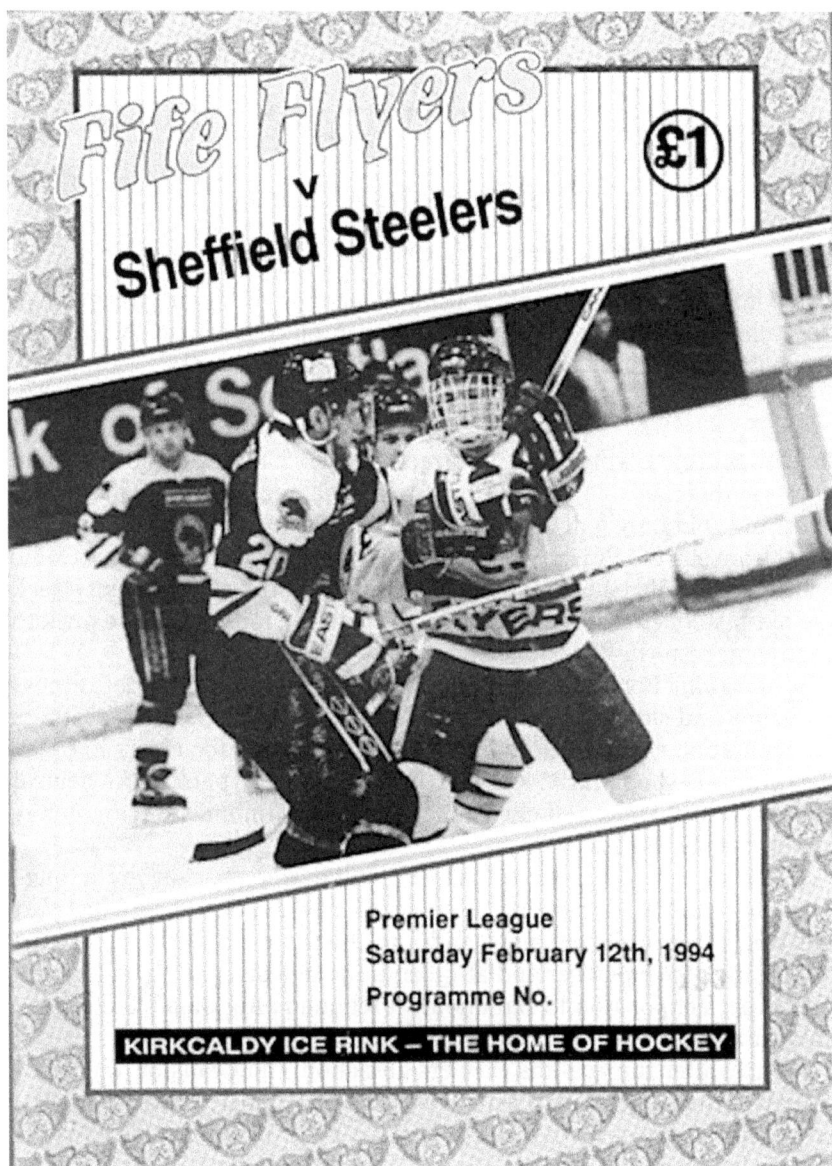

Craig 'Mookie' Wilson on the cover of the match night programme for the visit of the Steelers

Saturday February 12th 1994

HEINEKEN PREMIER LEAGUE

Fife Flyers 5 Sheffield Steelers 4

Ice hockey is undoubtedly a team game, but there are times where the influence, be that positive or negative, on a game can be directly attributed to one individual.

This game was one such case in point. Doug Smail returned from his extended business trip and led Flyers to victory over Sheffield in a real thriller. Since the winger's departure, the Flyers had failed to pick up any points in their last five games. His winning goal was a fantastic individual effort but told only half of the story as the former NHL all-star ran the show from start to finish.

The whole Fife bench responded to this and broke their losing streak the old-fashioned way by digging in and fighting for every loose puck to over-come a spirited Steelers team.

New signing Bobby Brown made his home debut. Despite some fitness problems and sloppy stick-handling he showed the physical robustness his reputation carried before him. It took until 8:38 for Flyers to break the deadlock when Mark Morrison picked up a loose puck in the neutral zone to outskate the Sheffield defence and beat netminder Martin McKay low on the stick side.

It didn't take long for the visitors, who were backed by a huge travelling support, to respond. Ron Schudra fired a perfect shot just past McCrone's out-stretched glove and into the top corner. Fife upped the tempo after the equaliser and at 15:41, burly defenceman Ryan Kummu was in perfect position to slam home a rebound after Smail had missed an opening.

Shortly after the goal the Steelers all-action Tim Cranston was lucky to stay in the game, after a ridiculous show of temper, when he slashed on the arm a steward who had picked the puck off the boards after the whistle had gone.

Flyers went further ahead with two minutes of the opening period remaining and it was all down to the skill and persistence of Smail. He forced his way to the net and despite being tripped he got up to bury the puck past McKay. McCrone almost paid for a real blunder when he came out to clear a puck dumped into the Fife zone and only succeeding in passing it straight to Sheffield's Les Millie but the netminder back-pedalled and got into position to block the shot.

Fife had played things pretty tight at the back but the home fans must have expected the worst when Steelers netted three times in just over a minute. During that short time the supporters must have imagined another collapse of Basingstoke proportions when they had led 6-2 with twenty minutes to go only to lose to seven unanswered goals! (Apologies, I've already mentioned that!)

Tommy Plommer started the rout at 27:40 after brilliant skating down the left by Schudra. Les Millie took advantage of a loose puck in front of goal to level the scores and then at 28:56, import Steve Nemeth out-skated Fife captain Iain Robertson to beat McCrone.

Now trailing for the first time in the game Fife pulled out all the stops. Teenage forward Steven King, icing on the second line to make space for Brown, showed some great skill to tie the Steelers defence in knots before hitting a back-hand shot which McKay saved well.

The equaliser arrived with under three minutes of the period left as Kummu bagged his second of the night in great style. Picking up the puck in the left corner behind goal he drew the defence out of position and made space for a shot which screamed past the goalie on his glove side.

Flyers came out in top gear for the final period and Smail scored what proved to be the winner less than 90 seconds after the face-off. In a quite brilliant individual effort he put the puck to one side of Sheffield's Man of the Match Schudra and rounded him on the other side before hitting a perfect shot which McKay hardly glimpsed.

In the final minutes Steelers GB coach Alex Dampier pulled McKay for an extra skater in an attempt to get the equaliser and although Robertson looked to have scored an empty net goal for Fife it was chalked off for a two-line pass before he shot. With 15 seconds left McCrone saved an effort from Nemeth to secure the points.

Tuesday February 13th 2001

N.T.L. CHRISTMAS CUP FINAL 2ND LEG

Fife Flyers 2 Guildford Flames 3

Christmas by now was but a distant memory and the glitter and tinsel of that time of year was sadly missing as the Flyers lost their grip on the N.T.L. Christmas Cup.

It was always going to be a tough task to claw back a three-goal deficit against a Guildford side who had won their previous 22 games; it was obvious from very early on that it was going to be beyond Flyers.

The team, which swept all before them last season, were certainly not firing on all cylinders at the moment. Goals were hard to come by against bigger, stronger teams, such as the Flames, who gave little away.

The vast majority of the Fife crowd seemed to have accepted that defeat was more than likely before the face off and the atmosphere created by the 2011 in attendance seemed hardly fitting for the final of a major competition.

More of a consequence perhaps was the midweek date for a competition where the Final surely deserved a weekend slot where the games could have been played in front of large excited crowds.

Instead, by the time it got to the third period it was after 10 pm and the Flames were well on their way to victory with the only noise coming from the bus-load of happy Guildford fans as the home support sat in resigned silence.

The whole occasion was something of an anti-climax, which might have been different if Flyers had scored early on, but that never really looked likely. It was more a relief than anything else when they finally managed to break Mark McArthur's shut-out.

Flyers were a little unfortunate with the goal that gave Flames victory but no one could begrudge the visitors their success. It was certainly deserved and the visitors had the look of a team who were hitting form at the right time for the play-offs.

Flames had spent big to try and achieve success and it finally came good for coach Stan Marple in Fife and he even iced himself just to savour the occasion more! It was also somewhat galling that Flames were missing three imports from their line-up and still had seven in the team! Flyers had defeated such odds before of course but never looked like doing so as Flames were able to play conservatively to protect their 4-1 first leg advantage.

It was an even first period that produced no goals but the destination of the cup was decided in the opening stages of the middle stanza as Flames took advantage of weak penalties called against the home side.

With Derek King off, Derek DeCosty redirected Wayne Crawford's pass beyond Stephen Murphy to break the deadlock at 21.03. Soon after, with Iain Robertson sitting out, former Flyer John Haig found space to beat the netminder from close range at 24.07.

Flyers needed to find five goals just to take the tie into overtime but they struggled to even manage one against an inspired and sometimes lucky McArthur. With under 10 minutes of the game left and the black and red ribbons already adorning the trophy the objective for Fife simply became to avoid being shut-out at home.

Eventually, they got a break as Frank Morris blasted a shot from the point that seemed to hit John Downes and deflect into the net at 51.45. The celebrations were muted, both on and off the ice, but spirits were lifted further at 54.03 when Morris rifled home his second to tie the game as Campbell sat out a slashing minor.

Fife went for the victory but Flames were not to be denied their win as Karry Biette's pass across the front of the net took several nasty bounces before hitting off a Flyer and past Murphy at 58.18. Guildford took the plaudits at the end as Crawford collected the trophy. The Fife players were left to reflect as they picked up something they had not been accustomed to receiving — runners-up medals.

The Cup didn't stay in Fife but a couple of Fifers helped take it back South – Flames John Haig and David Smith

Saturday February 14th 1976

Fife Flyers 21 Glasgow Dynamos 2

The old cliche about the St Valentine's Day massacre was certainly relevant to this battle at Kirkcaldy Ice Rink on Saturday night.

It wasn't much of a surprise as the Glasgow side had shipped 17 on their earlier season visit in the Autumn Cup and lost double figures at home in the other three meetings with the Flyers that season.

Although Lawrie Lovell had a field day in finding the net he didn't grab all of the headlines. He was outshone by Ally Brennan who set a new Northern Ice Hockey Association record with nine assists.

The previous best of seven assists was held jointly by Mike Mazur (Dundee Rockets), and Gordon Inglis (Murrayfield Racers). His feat also stands at the time of publication as a Flyers club record for a home-grown player and is jointly held with Gordon Latto.

Dynamos, who lined up minus their second top point scorer John Hester, were soon in trouble. Les Lovell scored with only 20 seconds on the clock. A further two goals inside the opening four minutes ended Dynamos chances of an upset. Another brace at the midway mark of the period from Ally Brennan and Lawrie Lovell signalled that the floodgates were open. John Taylor poured in two in a row to get a first period hat trick. As Dynamos watched the clock in anticipation of the buzzer Lawrie Lovell and Joe McIntosh brought the tally to nine.

Surprisingly it was Dynamos who opened the scoring in the second period when John Reid opened their account. However, although they got a second goal during this period Pete McGarvie in the visitors goal saw the puck pass him a further five times before Donnie McLaughlin put one past John Pullar.

Law Lovell had netted another three goals in between and one from brother Les and Dougie Latto kept the score board operator busy. A Brian Peat slapshot and a goal from Brennan made the score 16-2 at the buzzer.

Dynamos changed their netminder for the final 20 minutes but the one-way traffic continued with Dougie Latto once again finding the net on the opening play.

Lawrie Lovell and McIntosh added a further two to bring the score to 19 before Lawrie Lovell hit his seventh of the night to set yet another

NIHA record. His seven goals were the most scored by one player since the present format started in 1966. One more and he would have tied the Flyers club record for goals in a single game by a British player that was set by Jimmy Spence a decade before. The seven goals and three assists left Law only three points adrift of his own NIHA record for points scored in a game. Flyers defenceman Kenny Horne completed the scoring in the closing minutes.

Chic Cottrell contributes to the Flyers 21 goals against the hapless Dynamos.

Tuesday February 15th 2005

Fife Flyers 3 London Racers 4

Despite coming back from three down to level, the Flyers ultimately lost out to a heart-breaking late goal. London Racers denied them what would have been a deserved share of the spoils.

The Elite League side had a clear game plan in mind and played some of the most aggressive ice hockey seen from a visiting team in Kirkcaldy for some time.

The first period in particular saw Racers employ a tactic commonly referred to as 'goon hockey' as Flyers players were targeted for some heavy-handed treatment. It appeared to pay off as London bullied their way into a three-goal lead within the opening 23 minutes.

The visitors first was scored by player-coach Dennis Maxwell, whose shot found the net after Steve Briere originally appeared to have saved his effort.

Ian McIntyre turned Jason Robinson's long-range shot in at the crease at the start of the second period. Almost immediately afterwards Mark Gouett latched onto a set up by former Fife idol Steve Moria and hit a sweet strike that found Briere's net via the right-hand post.

The technique in the shot had to be admired as the puck was spinning viciously as he lined it up. Flyers looked a beaten side at this point but a great solo effort from Todd Dutiaume lifted spirits to spark a three-goal comeback in the 10 minutes that remained in the second period.

He out-paced the defence and cut in from the wing to score followed by Mark Morrison, who won the puck to shoot through netminder Joe Watkins and reduced the deficit to just one goal.

London went back on the offence but great defensive work sparked a counter attack that ended with Paul Spadafora lifting the puck past Watkins from Steven King's perfect pass for the leveller at 39.37.

Frustratingly for Fife a problem with Briere's net proved to be their downfall. There was a lengthy delay while rink staff re-attached the goal to its moorings and London took advantage of the confusion that followed to score within seconds of the face-off.

Jim Vickers had all the time in the world to skate towards Briere and although the keeper did well to save the initial effort Vickers was on hand to score from his own rebound. It was a tough break on Flyers who deserved more from their stirring comeback.

Given London's combative style it was perhaps inevitable that there would be at least one fight on the night and Flyers rookie Liam Greig took a brave but ultimately foolhardy decision to react to a slash from London giant Jeremy Cornish.

There was only ever going to be one winner as the pair went toe-to-toe. Cornish, a man mountain at 6ft 4in, held off the challenge of his much smaller opponent but full marks to Greig for standing up to the intimidation.

Flyers scoring: Spadafora, Morrison, Dutiaume (1+0) Horne, S King, Davyduke (0+1).

Racers scoring: McIntyre, Vickers (1+1) Maxwell, Gouett (1+0) Nichol (0+2) Robinson, Moria, Ciccarello (0+1).

SOGs: Fife (Briere) 34, London (Watkins) 27.

PiMs: 16-34

Referee: Neil Wilson   Attendance: 1193

The Racers had a reputation for tough hockey so Liam Greig thought it would be rude not to dance with Jeremy Cornish

Friday February 16th 1973

The Hague 11 Fife Flyers 0

Despite this hefty defeat at the hands of a Dutch All-Star Select the Flyers players and officials voted their one-game trip to Holland as a tremendous success.

It was hoped that the experience of playing abroad for the first time, and some of the tips picked up by the players, would help the team in the future.

Prior to visiting Holland, Flyers had only lost one match that season on their way to already winning two national trophies. Perhaps it was this factor that had clearly set their reputation at the highest level with their hosts.

Flyers were expecting to play a team called Veronica 538 who were a mainly amateur side in the Hague. Upon hearing that there were four GB International players and three Canadians in Flyers party the Dutch team called in some "outside assistance."

In the end Flyers took the ice against a select side that included seven Canadian professionals and a netminder who had previously played in the American leagues. The match was played at a new £2 million ice rink used solely for hockey and right from the start it was obvious that the Dutch combine were going to be a little too strong for the visitors.

Little wonder perhaps! Consider that in the Dutch League each team played over 50 matches with the players practicing four nights a week and playing matches on the other three nights.

Commenting, on his return to Kirkcaldy, Flyers coach 'Pep' Young said:

> "The Dutch team were not better skaters or anything like that but the teamwork was far above ours. They were able to move the puck around well knowing by instinct where a team-mate would be. If Flyers were able to take the ice every night of the week we would be just as good. As it was, we were well beaten but not disgraced. They were full of praise for our ability and we could have done better with a full-strength team as we were without Les Lovell and Bruce Libbos, and Lawrie Lovell was suffering from toothache and was not at his best. Some of the travelling party had been sea-sick on the boat crossing and were tired after the journey."

The Dutch side scored three times in both of the first two periods and Flyers tired towards the end allowing the hosts to get into double figures.

But apart from the score-line it was quite a trip for the Kirkcaldy party. Veronica officials were waiting at the quayside in Rotterdam to meet the tourists and they took Flyers to their hotel at Scheveningen, a coastal holiday resort on the outskirts of the Hague. On Saturday before leaving for home Flyers were taken on a tour of Amsterdam which included a visit to a clog-making factory.

This one game, it was hoped, would lead to future trips abroad as they left with an invitation to return to Holland next season and coach Young was keen to accept the offer.

He added: "It would be good for the team if we returned, but if we did I would prefer to fly and play two or three matches in a short tour."

Flyers also approached their hosts concerning a possible visit to Fife in March but the suggested date clashed with an important league match for Veronica. They were available to travel over in April as the hockey season in Holland was finished then, but that would have meant they would have had to engage their top players for a longer period which meant paying them extra money.

It was hoped that something could be arranged to allow the Flyers to host them next season as all concerned agreed that they would be a great attraction at Kirkcaldy. Negotiations however went cold and Flyers never did make a return trip, although in January 1975 they did host a team from Utrecht, a town a 60 minute drive east of where they had played.

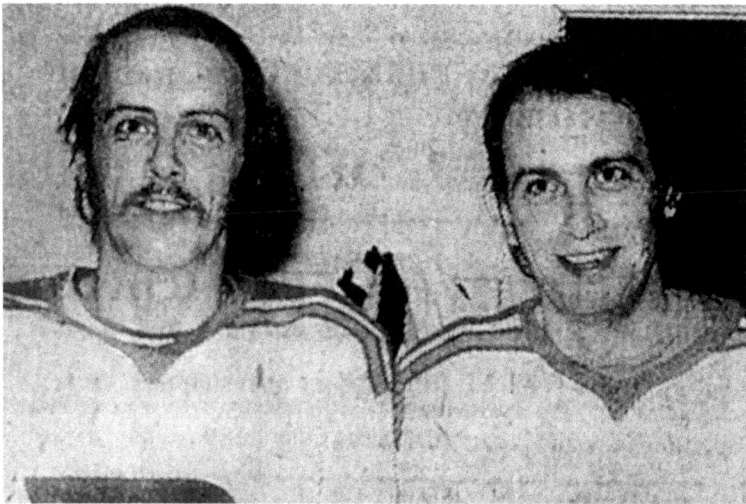

The Lovell brothers, Les on the left and Lawrie

Sunday February 17th 1963

Fife Flyers 4 Durham Bees 5

The history of hockey in the North East is complicated during the late 1950s and early 1960s with the rivalry between the rinks at Durham and Whitley Bay.

This resulted in, amongst other things, Whitley teams playing out of the Durham rink and vice versa and the switching around of the Durham team name between the Wasps and the Bees.

For season 1962/63 there was the added complication that the Durham Bees also found themselves virtually homeless as they competed in the newly formed Scottish League as well as English clubs 'Home Tournaments'.

The Bees had already visited Kirkcaldy in November and had been soundly beaten. The sparkling play from both sides gave the large crowd plenty to shout about; unfortunately it was a theme for fans at Kirkcaldy that the best games from a viewing perspective would most likely end in narrow defeats for the home side.

In this case the Flyers made a determined effort in the closing six minutes to equalise after Jimmy Spence had scored to bring them within one goal. Keeper Johnny Pullar was in the process of being withdrawn with two minutes to go but when the puck skittered back up ice towards his net he instinctively leapt back on to the ice to avert a goal.

However, this meant Flyers had too many men on the ice and the resultant team penalty left them with little chance of equalising. Yet with only seconds to go Forbes just missed scoring from a Spence pass which was not the first time this pair had been unlucky during the evening.

Bees really merited their win; despite their hard game at Ayr the previous evening they played with a zest and could build up attacks from their own goal area which Flyers could not match.

They also had to endure their share of bad luck; they lost Johnny Weston in the second period with a face injury which required five stitches and Mike Jordan missed the last few minutes due to a broken skate.

However, the outstanding player on the ice was Flyers defender Joe McIntosh who played his heart out checking raids and building up plays at every opportunity. Also starring in the home side were Ian Forbes and Jimmy Spence who, despite their lean evening as scorers, fought tirelessly throughout.

It would have been unfair to single out one of the Bees for extra praise for they all swung into action from the first whistle and their combined play always looked more dangerous than Flyers individual thrusts. Hep Tindal opened the scoring for the Bees when he slipped home a pass from Ron Stark but Flyers drew level when with Wasps Derek Adamson sitting out Dave Johnston smacked home a Cook assist.

With Bees captain Bill Booth benched for using a broken stick, Andy Napier put Flyers into the lead also from a Cook pass. However, in the second period a glorious weaving run up the right wing by Mike Jordan led to Tindale scoring his second to equalise and then Dave Lammin put the visitors ahead with a surprisingly easy solo counter.

Some great skating by Spence let Forbes unleash a terrific slapshot which just failed to hit the target and so, with Flyers having a blank second period, Bees entered the final session with a one goal advantage.

This was soon increased when Stark found the net from the blue-line but at long last Forbes and Spence got some reward for their diligence when the former's shot left Carlyle helpless from five yards.

Bees went through a sticky spell when Walter Bell took two minutes for roughing but they survived for Bell to return and slap home a Stark pass from the right wing. With only six minutes to go Spence set the game afire again when he scored from a Greger pass, but with Bees tiring rapidly, Flyers failed to notch the equaliser.

Flyers: Johnny Pullar, Verne Greger, Joe McIntosh, Pete Robertson, Bob Chalmers, Pete Grieve, Jimmy Spence, Ian Forbes, Andy Napier, Pep Young, Dave Cook, Dave Johnston, Jimmy Watson

Bees — Jimmy Carlyle, Bill Booth, Mike Jordan, Hep Tindale, Derek Adamson, Ron Stark, Peter Johnson, Ian Dobson, Walter Bell, Dave Lammin, Johnny Weston.

Verne 'Bones' Greger who took over coaching duties in season 1962/63 after 'Pep' Young stood down owing to business commitments

The Flyers team, management and travelling support celebrate capturing the Gardiner Conference title in Dundee

Sunday February 18th 2018

Elite Ice Hockey League

Dundee Stars 6 Fife Flyers 7 (after overtime)

A packed out Dundee Ice Arena witnessed a stunning third period comeback from Stars but despite taking the lead they could not postpone the Flyers Gardiner Conference winning party.

Flyers were given the best possible start to the game as they picked up a power play after just sixty-six seconds when Emerson Hrynyk was called for boarding. With 91 seconds on the clock Peter LeBlanc was found by Liam Heelis alone in the slot, where he dragged the puck around the pads of the Stars goalie Travis Fullerton to score.

Dundee slowly turned the game around and a fight between Stars' Adam Harding and Fife's Tommy Muir was enough to give the home side some momentum.

Muir also received a two-minute minor penalty for illegal use of his equipment and that gave Dundee their first man advantage. They seized the opportunity. Following a good move between Marc-Olivier Mimar and Lukas Lundvald the puck went to Gabriel Lévesque who found the roof of the net at 5:52.

A few moments later, Lévesque and Heelis both picked up unsportsmanlike conduct penalties after exchanging some words behind the play.

There was a great chance for Jimmy Jensen during the 4-on-4 period but he was denied by Andy Iles in the Fife net. Brian Hart's shot was also saved. Lévesque rattled a wrist shot off the goal post as Dundee came close to taking the lead. Chase Schaber picked up a slashing penalty but Dundee could not capitalise on their second power play of the night.

Chris Lawrence fired a backhanded shot but Iles gloved it. A good chance for Stars turned into a breakaway for Fife's Carlo Finucci, but Fullerton made the save with just two minutes remaining in the opening period.

Fife went ahead early in the second period following a bad giveaway by Omar Pacha to Shayne Stockton, who was denied initially by Fullerton, but he followed up to poke home the rebound. Finucci hit the post as Flyers were denied another, then a great play by Hart was thwarted by Iles.

The Flyers eventually extended their lead to 3-1 midway through the game when Stockton scored his second of the evening, converting yet another rebound on the wraparound. Less than 60 seconds later Liam Heelis set up Danick Gauthier who bulged the net. 4-1 ahead Fife looked like they had done enough to secure their first EIHL trophy.

Dundee were given a life line, however, as Mimar netted with barely a second left in the middle period. Flyers lost defenceman Ian Young early in the third after the puck struck him in the face. With Stars controlling the play it forced coach Dutiaume to call a time out.

Stars however got the next goal, when Pacha's shot off the glass unfortunately rebounded off Iles into the net. The travelling fans' nerves were calmed when Gauthier held off Hrynyk to restore the two-goal lead.

Dundee were not done yet; with Ricards Brizins in the box a Cody Carlson blast was saved, but Jensen was in the right place to shoot home. Stars were back on level terms with under two minutes of the game to go again with Birzins in the box and the rebound from a slapshot from Lundvald was buried by Lawrence.

Fife needed just the point to secure the title but with 90 seconds remaining Young was called on an unsportsmanlike penalty and Lundvald pounced at the back post to edge the Stars ahead.

Flyers pulled Iles after the restart. With just 16 seconds left on the clock the away side of the rink erupted. Charlie Mosey, who was all alone in front of goal, put the puck past Fullerton to secure the Gardiner Conference title amid wild scenes.

The extra point in overtime didn't matter as such. When Young was denied by Fullerton, the rebound fell straight to Dan Correale. The Flyers late season signing planted the puck into the back of the net, to complete an incredible night of drama and tension for both sets of fans.

Saturday February 19th 1972

Fife Flyers 0 Whitley Warriors 3

Flyers were sitting top of the Northern League in an epic battle against the auld enemy Murrayfield Racers.

However, they did not have their troubles to seek for the visit of a Whitley side that had already beaten Fife home and away in the earlier Autumn Cup campaign. Norrie Boreham (broken hand) and Billy Dunbar (leg injury) were missing from Flyers line-up. The Warriors were at full strength.

The first period produced numerous thrills and plenty of good hockey but no goals, although the visitors should have gone ahead when Terry Matthews was presented with an open net only to incredibly shoot wide.

It was eight minutes into the second period before the opening goal arrived. On one of his many forays up the ice, Matthews took the puck into the right corner and crossed for Alfie Miller, perfectly positioned at far post, to drive home.

Bob Gilbert was looking very solid in the Warriors net. He earned applause for two fine saves when first Stuart Muir and then Alistair Crombie broke clean through. In the thirty-sixth minute the Warriors struck again. Once more Miller was the man who did the damage with a goal very similar to his previous one.

Coach Young shuffled his lines but the visiting defence comfortably coped with everything that the home side could throw at them. Flyers worked hard throughout the final period to find a break through. The home fans, by now, had the feeling that if they could get that elusive first goal then more would follow.

Crombie broke through on his own but Gilbert once more saved the day with almost uncanny anticipation. At the other end Flyers defence was coping well with the Warriors forays but with five minutes to go Jim Pearson got his first real sight of goal on the night and gave Jim Taylor no chance. It was desperation stuff from the home side now as they tried to break the shutout and find a way past Gilbert. Les Lovell who had been closely watched throughout the match, sent Muir away but once again Gilbert pulled off a fantastic save and the final whistle handed the Flyers a crucial defeat. Or did it ?

There had already been a situation earlier that season when the Flyers match with Dundee Rockets was declared void owing to both sides fielding an ineligible player.

The result of that game had also been a home defeat but when replayed the Rockets were once again victors. The Flyers made a successful protest to the NIHA to have this defeat to the Warriors replayed and in the rescheduled match at the end of March they won 8-5.

By that time however they had fallen badly out of the race for the title which was comfortably won by Murrayfield with Dundee Rockets, Whitley and Fife trailing in that order.

Carlo Finucci celebrates; in his time between 2016-2020 he became the club's all time point scorer in the EIHL era

Monday February 20th 1950

Falkirk Lions 4 Fife Flyers 3

The Flyers were league leaders but for the second week in succession Lions got the better of them in a hard-fought game played at the Falkirk Ice Rink.

The previous Monday the Flyers had travelled in Scottish Cup action and were knocked out of the competition by a 7-3 reversal. More alarming than that — either side of that defeat they had lost National League games. They had now not won on their last five trips outside of the Kingdom.

The win for the Lions narrowed down Flyers lead over the Falkirk side to just three points. Penalties would prove to be very influential in this game with all but one of the seven goals scored when the teams were playing with a man advantage.

It took a grand shot from Phil Casey midway through the final session to bring out the winner but Lions fans would have suggested that the game should have been well won by that time. Flyers played well in defence but enjoyed more than their fair share of good fortune and 'Pete' Belanger was kept on the hop for most of the game.

Lions Tommy La Pointe had a most unfortunate night when on his first appearance on the ice he went down heavily after a check and was assisted from the ice and did not return.

Lions set out to stop Flyers play at the source and they did this with constant fore-checking and hard back-checking. Phil Casey and Bill Sneddon formed a clever defence line and their timely rushes had the Fife defence in trouble.

The rarely appreciated Willy Roe put in a power of work, in the forward line demonstrating that goal scoring is not always the principal feature of hockey. Once again Pat Casey was the play maker on the first line and Kenny Nicholson kept the second line moving.

Doing most of the pressing Lions took the lead after ten minutes when Phil Casey passed out to Roe for the winger to net. The home lot kept up the attack but just before the end of the period Floyd Snider equalised from a Chic Mann assist.

Starting the middle session where they left off previously Pat Casey put Lions ahead after clever play by Roe and Johnny Carlyle and then the same player made it three with a snap shot. This was when Lions should have added to their total but two simple goals from Chic Mann soon wiped out their lead.

Continuous pressure in the final period brought a goal from Phil Casey just on the change over. Flyers, in a desperate attempt to salvage the game, withdrew Belanger for the last two minutes to try and force the equaliser. The nearest thing to a goal however came at the other end when Snider deflected a shot from Pat Casey that slid past the empty net.

With his two goals Flyers Captain Chic Mann became the second player that season to go through the 100 points target. He brought his total to 102 (44 goals and 58 assists) eight behind George Sinfield of Dundee Tigers. Sinfield's clubmate, Bob Finlayson, and Nebby Thrasher, of Dunfermline Vikings were running neck and neck for third place. Thrasher, perhaps unsurprisingly due to his feisty style of play, looked like being the first man to have 100 points and 100 minutes in the cooler.

Match programme for Flyers match at Falkirk Monday February 20th

Thursday February 21st 1952

Fife Flyers 1 Paisley Pirates 3

Far from being the fast, thrill-a-minute game that Pirates and Flyers had served up the previous week at Paisley, this National League encounter packed little punch.

Keener in anticipation and harder checkers than the Flyers, Paisley were the superior team. However, Flyers gave them a fight for the points and impressed frequently with some scorching power plays.

With Flyers management warning of changes, the home line-up knew they were fighting for their place in the team and each one pulled his weight. As a team, however, they lacked cohesion.

Roy Hammond, playing his third successive game at centre for Pirates, laid on the first score for Joe Brown in eight minutes. A power play by Flyers Hal Kewley, Joe Millisin and Johnny Vanier line resulted in the equaliser off Kewley's stick.

A quiet middle frame resulted in only one goal. It came for the Pirates from a long shot off Hammond's stick. It was a goal that Flyers tried desperately to cancel with another but no dice. The duo of Hal Empie and Bernie Hill, small but rugged, were supreme on the visitors' blue-line. They were proving to be the Paisley clubs' biggest assets in their fight for a play-off berth.

There was an ugly little incident toward the end of the period which went unnoticed by referee Gordon Gerrard and which riled the fans. It gave yet another very sound reason for the call of the return to two officials handling games. After a slight contact with Joe Millisin, Joe Brown, Paisley's tough-as-nails defenceman, lifted his stick and slashed the winger in the face. This was the sort of thing that was fast creeping into games North of the border and many thought it was high time the Scottish Ice Hockey Association opened their eyes to the fact.

The third period resulted in a parade of players to the penalty box. Flyers enjoyed some further power plays but crucially the only further goal in the game came at the other end with the Pirates third counter.

Kewley and Vanier throughout looked the most likely men to break the Paisley iron curtain but the defensive set-up seemed to have an answer for every move. Bob Tripp in nets was cool and calm and courageous and, as the score-line suggests, was on well-nigh unbeatable form. 14 seconds from the final whistle with the Flyers pushing valiantly for the equaliser Empie broke way on a solo run to score with a low drive on Stubby Mason.

What was equally concerning was the empathy towards the team from the Flyers faithful. The low attendances at the Kirkcaldy rink appeared to directly affect play.

The finest team available would still look poor in front of the handful of spectators that turn out most Thursday nights to watch. The yawning gaps in the rink seats must, it was thought, be having a decided psychological effect on the players, which then dragged the standard of play down.

Flyers last game at Paisley perhaps illustrated the point clearly when with hardly a seat empty in the arena, every smart move, penalty, fine or weak piece of team-play was greeted with roof-raising reaction from the vast crowd.

The enthusiasm set spectators and players alike on their mettle, sharpened up their thinking and set a tempo of thrills and excitement for the whole game. With the arrival of new import Don Mann imminent it was expected that either Bob Bergeron or Verne Greger were the likely candidates to make way for him.

Flyers, in view of the proximity of the final stretch in the National League, were in need of new talent and maybe the change would be the spark to hoist them up the table.

Their position at the moment looked anything but healthy as they lay in fifth place behind the Raiders, Tigers, Lions and Vikings and were 11 points behind the leaders and four points behind Vikings.

With one game in hand over Vikings, a win at Dunfermline in her next outing would close the gap on their county rivals and within snapping distance of Lion's heels. Flyers had however only four wins and three draws out of 17 games to their credit.

Even the most optimistic amongst the dwindling Fife support thought their chances of making the grade to be slim. Flyers would in fact finish bottom of the pile.

Flyers later season line up 1951-52
Back Row, left to right: Ray Dinardo, Floyd Snider, Billy Fisher, Don Mann, Frank Facto, Mickey Linnell
Front Row, left to right: Bert Smith, Hal Keuley, Stubby Mason, Jimmy Mitchell, Bob Bergeron, Johnny Vanier

Saturday February 22nd 1975

Fife Flyers 15 Paisley Mohawks 6

It was fast approaching six years since Paisley last chalked up a win at Kirkcaldy Ice Rink; judging by their performance on this night at the Gallatown it would be quite some time yet before they improved on that miserable record.

In recent seasons Flyers had been hammering in goals against Mohawks with monotonous regularity. After what was their tenth successive home win against the West of Scotland men, the two points kept them within touching distance of the Murrayfield Racers and Whitley Warriors at the top of the standings.

It didn't take Flyers long to open the scoring. The first time the Paisley netminder touched the puck was when he had to pick it out of the net after Lawrie Lovell netted.

Flyers increased their lead to three goals with only five minutes gone with Les Lovell and Norrie Boreham scoring. The home fans were given a jolt, however. Two goals from the ever alert Billy Miller for Mohawks reduced the deficit.

The rapid scoring pace continued and before 10 minutes of the game had elapsed the score had jumped to 5-3 for Flyers. Jimmy Hunter and Les Lovell netted for the home side and Miller completed a quick hat-trick for Paisley. Tempers became a bit frayed. After a goalmouth flare-up three players found themselves spectating for a spell from the penalty box. Miller closed the gap to 5-4 before Boreham netted Flyers sixth near the end of the period.

The first period had certainly produced plenty of goals. As often happens, the scoreboard operators found themselves less heavily involved in the second session, although the Mohawks were hemmed in their own defence zone for long periods. Miller continued to be the sole threat to Flyers supremacy. Les Lovell completed his hat-trick with Flyers seventh goal and Chic Cottrell made it eight before Miller scored his fifth for Mohawks two minutes from the end of the period.

Two power play goals by Flyers at the start of the final session brought up double figures, with Alex Churchill and Cottrell on target. Two further spectacular goals from the stick of Cottrell brought his tally to four and

Flyers up to the round dozen. It was a performance that saw Chic awarded the Mirror of Merit award for the match and continue a rich vein of form with 10 goals in the last five matches.

Gordon Latto rubbed more salt into Mohawks wounds with another goal. At the other end netminder Johnny Pullar must, at this stage of the game, have been blue with the cold. In a rare moment of action around his goal he was however beaten by Shawn Niskansen. Moments later he pulled off a tremendous save from that man Miller which earned him a rousing ovation from the home fans.

Flyers completed their night's work with a further two goals in the closing minutes of the match from the Lovell brothers, first Lawrie with his second, then Les who matched Cottrell's tally of four as the Flyers notched up their highest score of the season.

Captain Les Lovell scores Flyers seventh against Paisley to complete his hat trick

Saturday February 23rd 1963

Fife Flyers 5 Murrayfield Royals 4

The big freeze continued to hit Scottish football.

At the request from Scottish Television that the match be played on the Saturday afternoon — so they could film it and air it later that evening on Scotsport — this was the Flyers debut on TV, something they would grow accustomed to as the decade wore on.

Altrincham Aces Sammy McDonald was a guest in the Flyers line up and 'The Perth Line' of McDonald, Forbes, Spence was born. Murrayfield also guested Dorry Boyle from Paisley. Producing their best team work of the season the home side deservedly beat Royals in a fast exciting encounter.

All Flyers points came from their magnificent first line of Greger and McIntosh, Forbes, Spence and McDonald. The second string, too, played their part admirably, forechecking and backchecking with a consistency which had not been apparent in the past.

Royals were by no means a poor side as the score line indicated but had netminder Willie Clark not been in such fine form Flyers victory margin might well have been much greater. Clark was well backed up by Bill Sneddon, who always played well at Kirkcaldy, and Dorry Boyle. It was Sneddon who twisted his way through Flyers defence from his own goal area to shoot his side into an early lead.

This came after five minutes of the fastest hockey seen at Kirkcaldy that year; although this frantic pace was not kept up the speed of the game was always well above average. After ten minutes Jimmy Spence broke clear on the right wing and drew the Royals defence before slipping a deadly accurate pass to his ace accomplice, Ian Forbes, who slapped home the equaliser.

Royals unfortunately lost Gordie Ross just after this with a facial injury. A Lawrie Lovell backhand flick found Joe Baird unattended and he put the visitors into a rather fortunate lead which they held until the end of the period.

Royals struck hard and fast in the second session when Dave Watt finished off the good work of Lovell and Baird while Flyers Danny McGeever was cooling his heels for interference. Flyers were desperately unlucky to find themselves two goals behind at this stage especially as the smoother more attractive brand of play had come from them.

Joe McIntosh seemed to skip over the ice to dispel danger. Along with Verne Greger, he lent valuable support to the fast interchanging first line forwards, who were lacking only in finishing power. Yet it was a solo effort from Jimmy Spence which narrowed the gap and this led to a period of all-out assault on Royals goal in which Clark had many fines saves.

The pressure finally told however two minutes from the end of the period when Forbes was left in the clear, after the visitors defence had been split open by Spence and Greger. Flyers coach was certainly in sparkling form after one or two indifferent performances. He combined well with Sammy McDonald to give Spence a clear run in on Willie Clark and he made no mistake. Only a minute later it was Greger's turn to score the best goal of the evening when a pass from McDonald allowed him to swoop down on a lonely Clark and put his side two goals in front.

Flyers really turned on the pressure but a solid defence and some first-class anticipation and catching by Clark kept them out. Indeed, in one of their infrequent visits to Flyers end, Norrie Boreham smacked home a Dave Watt assist to set the home hearts fluttering with anxiety once again. However, it was all Flyers in the dying minutes and they skated off as narrow but worthy winners.

Flyers: Johnny Pullar, Verne Greger, Joe McIntosh, Danny McGeever, Bob Chalmers, Sam McDonald, Jimmy Spence, Ian Forbes, Andy Napier, Pep Young, Dave Johnston, Jimmy Watson

Royals — Willie Clark, Bill Sneddon, Dorry Boyle, Eric Grieve, George Henderson, Gordie Ross, Joe Baird, Norrie Boreham, Lawrie Lovell, Bill Archibald, Dave Watt, George Buchan, Freddie Wood

Sammy McDonald who guested from the Altrincham Aces and formed part of the Flyers "Perth Line"

Thursday February 24th 1949

Fife Flyers 9 Dundee Tigers 5

A badly needed boost to Flyers goal-average came as a result of their sparkling attacking play against the Tigers.

Dundee picked up some strange goals, to keep them just behind all evening, but when the Flyers let loose in the last period they had no response.

George Kovac, Tigers net minder, was still trying to figure out how to handle Bud Scrutton when the game finished, with the Fife captain having bagged four goals. The Flyers opened the scoring when Bobby Burns was penalised on the 3rd minute. An end-to-end break by Floyd Snider was capped with a brilliant finish which left Kovac in a daze.

A minute later and a snap-shot by Verne Greger from the blue line was well held by Kovac. Clever passing between Whitey Frick and Archie Williams found an unmarked Johnny Evans but his shot was blocked by Pete Belanger. Seconds later Williams had a go from the right only to see his shot strike iron.

Despite numerous chances for both sides, in which Burns and Jim Yeaman in particular had glaring misses for the visitors, and Scrutton, Chic Mann and Reid all passing up glorious opportunities for the home side, it wasn't until the last minute of the period before the net bulged again. Scrutton and Mann combined and the former skated into the goal mouth to beat Kovac.

Tigers netted seconds after the restart of the second when Bob Finlayson out-skated the home defence. A minute later following a set up between Greger and Mann the red light flashed but no goal was awarded because the puck entered the net via Mann's skate. Two minutes after the start Bob Reid reduced Flyers ranks when he took a tripping penalty. Flyers managed to increase their lead while short-handed when Scrutton netted after some fine passing between Mann and Greger.

With the sides at even strength again, play developed into a fast paced end-to-end game but with few shots on either goal. A dash up the right by Scotty Reid looked good but his pass was off the mark and eventually cleared.

A bonny piece of skating in the next raid by Hick Moreland saw Kovac sprawl to save a certain goal after the Flyer had gone through the whole Dundee side. In the 15th minute a Tigers rally reduced the leeway when Evans shot through a mass of players. Scrutton then out-skated the Angus defence to net his hat-trick and only a fine save by Kovac prevented the winger netting again in Flyers next attack. The goalie had no chance, however, with a shot by Scotty Reid from Moreland's rebound as the period ended.

Finlayson missed an open goal at the start of the third, but managed a second attempt and scraped the puck over the line to bring Dundee back into the game. At the other end Kovac saved twice in succession and a few minutes later another Dundee breakaway was followed by a scrimmage round Belanger with Williams sending the puck home.

Evans skated down the left to unleash an accurate shot but Belanger cleared. With Dundee piling on the pressure Snider deflected another shot from Evans. Scrutton made his total four with a shot from the left which beat Kovac all the way.

A move between Scotty Reid and Ken Joy brought no reward. Following this the Dundee cage was knocked off its moorings and the game was held up while the damage was repaired. Moreland made Flyers total seven just before the midway point, after Joy had taken the puck up to the boards before sending it into the goal-mouth for the Kirkcaldy player to net.

A cross from Mann on the right came to the in-skating Snider who extended the lead with a strong shot. Tigers retaliated and only a huddle of players round Belanger prevented a goal. Snider was prominent in the next two Kirkcaldy attacks before Evans reduced the leeway in another scrimmage round Belanger.

Mann restored the balance after dummying a defender and slipping the puck round the side of the cage before Kovac could react. A breakaway by Yeaman saw Belanger save well but Flyers were well on top in the closing minutes with Kovac saving twice from Snider in succession.

Four goals against the Tigers for Bud Scrutton

Tuesday February 25th 2003

Fife Flyers 5 Dundee Stars 3

The Caledonian Cup this season was played as a four team round robin group to determine the semi-final match ups with the Newcastle Vipers the "guest" side.

Stars won the group and had knocked out bottom team Edinburgh Capitals in their semi-final while the third placed Flyers overcame the Vipers in the other. With eight games that season already in the books and the Stars with a stranglehold of six wins and two draws, the bookies odds on a Fife win were generous.

However, the Flyers would take the advantage into the following night's second leg against the holders at the Dundee Ice Arena. Flyers shocked their arch-rivals and were at one stage in the match ahead 5-1. Two Stars goals later on in proceedings put a better gloss on the scoreline for the Taysiders.

Tony Hand, Stars player-coach said post-match,

> "We'll have our work cut out at Dundee as this is not decided on aggregate. We have to win the game to collect two points and then win on penalties if we want to retain the trophy."

It was hoped that this result would be the massive boost the home side required ahead of the play-offs with this success built on a great desire and tenacity that perhaps surprised the visitors. Flyers were backed by another inspirational performance by netminder Steve Briere, who turned away 40 of the 43 shots fired at him. In comparison Flyers could only manage 18 shots on target but they took their chances when they had them; it had to be recognised that Stephen Murphy didn't have one of his better nights. Flyers player-coach Mark Morrison said, "This was a big win for us and we're quietly confident going to Dundee."

Karry Biette opened the scoring at 7.23 while the teams were 4-on-4 when he broke clear and finished well. When John Haig beat Murphy from an impossible angle at 15.46 and Biette claimed his second with another quality strike at 18.38 the home fans probably couldn't believe what they were seeing.

This was a Fife side without Jonathan Weaver and David Smith but Andy Finlay extended the lead to four at 23.35 when he tipped in Mark Morrison's mis-hit shot. It took a power play strike from Johan Boman at 32.44 to finally put Stars on the board.

Crucially, though, just over two minutes later Morrison knocked in Steven King's pass for 5-1 only for Tony Hand to beat Briere at 35.46 and set up a tense final period.

Flyers defended well, despite clearly tiring. Though Martin Wiita pulled one goal back at 49.15, Briere stood tall. Fife, despite having defenceman Frank Evans thrown out of the game for a check from behind, with seven minutes left held on to claim a notable victory.

Flyers: Biette 2+0, Morrison 1+2, Haig 1+1, Finlay 1+0, Dutiaume, S. King 0+2, Evans 0+1.

Stars: Hand 1+2, Boman, Wiita 1+0, Ratushny 0+2, Mikel 0+1.

Shots: Flyers (Briere) 43, Stars (Murphy) 18.

Pens: Flyers 20, Stars 6.

Referee: Andy Allsopp.

The next night in Dundee, Flyers completed the job when they held the Stars to a 4-4 tie to take the trophy.

Stars Martin Wiita trying to get to grips with Flyers Todd Dutiaume

Monday February 26th 2007

This was one of the more sombre moments in Fife Flyers history as fans came to terms with a major incident at Fife Ice Arena.

Newspaper reports carried headlines that "investigators were looking into the cause of a large fire at one of Fife's main sporting venues" in the early hours.

The blaze broke out at the Fife Ice Arena in Kirkcaldy shortly after midnight with a number of crews from around the region called out to tackle the incident.

It was understood the fire started in the south-facing roof space of the Rosslyn Street building. Police said later that the cause was thought to have been an electrical fault. A spokeswoman for Fife Fire and Rescue Service said there was nothing to suggest the fire was caused maliciously.

Two crews from Kirkcaldy plus one height appliance together with two engines from Glenrothes, one from Methil and one from Burntisland battled the blaze using three main water jets, four breathing apparatus sets and one aerial monitor.

Most of the crews were pulled back at 3am after the fire was extinguished, although one firefighting team from Kirkcaldy remained to dampen down the exterior of the smouldering building for most of the morning.

Thankfully, no one was injured. There was thought to be no risk of the building collapsing although the normal structural assessments still had to be carried out. Most of the damage was confined to the roof and the south corner of the building above the Curlers bar with a sizeable portion of the grandstand in that corner charred through.

Firefighters said the blaze in that area would have been intense and suggested that temperatures had reached between 500°C and 600°C at the height of the fire. The 3200-capacity Fife Ice Arena had been built in 1938. As well as hosting ice sports, it had been thrust into the lime-light in recent years for playing host to major boxing events, with high-profile title fights being broadcast from the arena on satellite TV.

Earlier that month Methil boxer Kevin Anderson lost his Commonwealth welter-weight title in front of almost 2000 fans in the "Auld Barn"; negotiations were still under way about Anderson defending his British title against Eamonn Magee at the venue later that year.

Those plans were of course to be put on hold until the full extent of the damage could be ascertained. Fife Flyers chairman Tom Muir said officials would try to get the building operational as soon as possible. However, the visit of Dundee Tigers who were to face Fife Flyers in a challenge match that Saturday evening would almost certainly be cancelled, club officials added.

Within the next few days it became apparent just how much damage the fire had caused. Of the Flyers three remaining home games, two were played at Edinburgh and the other at Dundee and it would be September before they would once again hit the ice in familiar surroundings.

The aftermath of the devastating fire at the Curlers Bar end of the arena

Sunday February 27th 1994

Teeside Bombers 9 Fife Flyers 14

Three teams battled for second top spot in the league. The Flyers, Murrayfield Racers and Sheffield Steelers were all locked on 48 points after the weekend action.

The chase for the top spot was officially ended, as the Cardiff Devils wrapped up two wins to take the title. Flyers continued their winning ways in Teesside with a high-scoring victory over Bombers.

The bottom placed club had already been put to the sword three times by Fife in their meetings that season, all by fairly comfortable margins.

Flyers however had to survive something of a mini third-period fightback from the never-say-die Bombers. Young netminder Ricky Grubb lost six goals from 13 shots but with an 11-3 advantage at that stage it was always on the cards that the Flyers could ease off a bit.

It was a match littered with minor penalties, 56 minutes in total, and the home side proved to be stuffy opposition in the tight opening period. A Ryan Kummu double on power play goals saw Fife just edge in front after Scott Young scored for the home team.

In the second period Flyers hit the goal trail in grand style with Mark Morrison and Doug Smail each grabbing hat-tricks and they both included a short-handed strike each. Also on the score sheet were Bobby Brown, who netted only his second goal for Fife, Craig Wilson and Neil Smith. Tim Delay and ex-Fife import Todd Bidner countered for a ragged Teeside team.

Grubb took over from John McCrone between the pipes in the third period and got off to the worst possible start losing three goals in just over a minute. Paul Davison struck first at 41:41, Bidner netted at 42:40 and Delay rammed one in 16 seconds later. Smail lifted Fife spirits with another short-handed goal at 47:02 taking him to just one short of the club's all-time record. Neil Smith followed his lead with a similar strike with 10 minutes of the game left. Bombers continued to fight on and goals from Delay, Young and former Flyers favourite Jimmy Pennycook narrowed the gap to four goals. But Kummu had the last word with the hard-hitting defenceman completing his second hat-trick of the weekend with 20 seconds of the game remaining.

Bombers: Delay 3-0, Young 2-1, Pompeo 0+3, Bidner 2-0, Davison 1+1, Pearey 1+1.

Flyers: Morrison 3-4, Smail 4+2, Kummu 3+1, Smith 2+1, Robertson 0+3, Brown 1+0, Wilson 1+0, Derek King 0+1.

Referee: Alex McWilliam. Crowd: 600.

Coach Jim Lynch said after the game

"Ricky will be disappointed with the shots he let in but he just needs some more match practice. He's more than capable of stopping these shots. We're going to get him some more ice time, either with us or the Kestrels. Because if anything happens to Bernie McCrone we need Ricky to be ready"

The coach added that he had intended to use more fringe players but both games over the weekend ended up being too tight to take any risks.

Doug Smail would go on to set a new club record for short-handed goals in a season for the club, which still stands today, with 13 tallies.

Messrs Smail, Haig and Robertson against Teeside in an earlier encounter that season at Kirkcaldy

Saturday February 28th 1970

Fife Flyers 7 Ayr Bruins 3

1969/70 wasn't exactly a season that was brimming with highlights for the Flyers. There were very few opportunities to include events. In fact this is the only occurrence within these pages.

The decade was to finish with a 10-team Northern League with Edinburgh icing two teams, the Racers and Royals, as did Whitley with the Warriors and Bandits, who joined the Flyers, Dundee Rockets, Paisley Mohawks, Glasgow Dynamos, Ayr Bruins and Durham Wasps.

The team comprised of a much more youthful bunch: Jimmy Taylor, Kenny Horne, Dave Medd, Jimmy Simpson, Bill Brown (captain), George Pearson, Jimmy Hunter, Ian Shields, John Taylor, Rab Petrie, Angus Cargill, Jimmy Jack, Andy Dryburgh, Allan Crooks, Douglas Wilson, Hugh Taylor

The League campaign saw them finish bottom of the pile with the following record:

GP	W	D	L	GF	GA	Pts
18	2	3	13	63	118	7

There was the now customary exit from the Icy Smith Cup at the first time of asking when Dundee Rockets knocked them out, winning 4-2. Once again there was no Mirror of Merit award but it was hoped that better times were just around the corner into the new decade.

The other competition played for that season was the Flyers home based tournament, the Skol Cup.

FLYERS WIN, AT LAST

was the headline and after a run of narrow defeats and draws, the Flyers finally gave their fans something to shout about with a fine 7-3 win over Ayr Bruins.

It was a run that had last seen them last taste victory in early December, almost 3 months ago! Ayr came to Kirkcaldy with the distinction of being the only team in the league to beat top-of-the-table Murrayfield Racers that season. However, Flyers got on top from the start and didn't look like losing. Player-coach Joe McIntosh spearheaded most of the attacks but still found time to hold a tight grip on the defence. He was ably assisted by netminder Jim Taylor who had an inspired game.

Jimmy Hunter and John Taylor were the brightest in attack for the home side and shared four of the Flyers goals but generally the team as a whole played very well.

There were goals also for Rab Petrie, Jimmy Jack and Allan Crooks. Ex-Flyer Joe Baird managed to break through to score twice for the visitors with John Hogg netting the other consolation goal for the visitors.

Dundee were the team who had the best score against the Flyers in the Skol Cup when they won 5-2 and so they were invited back to contest the final in which they rudely repeated the feat.

Fife Flyers 1969/70 Back, left to right: Tommy Horne, Ian Danton, Dave Medd, George Taylor, John Taylor, Kenny Horne, Allan Crooks, Jimmy Hunter, Bill Brown, Doug Wilson
Front, left to right: Jimmy Jack, Andy Napier, Ian Shields, Iain Ritchie, Jim Taylor, Rab Petrie, Jimmy Simpson, Alistair Crombie, Joe McIntosh
Mascots are Gordon and Dougie Latto

Sunday February 29th 2004

Edinburgh Capitals 7 Fife Flyers 5

Flyers had secured the League crown on the road the night before in dramatic fashion after overtime in Hull and "on the road home" stopped off 24 hours later in Edinburgh.

Murrayfield had never seen anything like it. The loss of a derby game was simply shrugged off and the 'auld enemy' had to watch as Fife paraded the league trophy on their ice pad.

Well, they paraded *a* trophy as the actual shield wouldn't arrive until the following weekend.

In what looked like a hastily cobbled together presentation, Mark Morrison turned photographer to capture a defining moment in the careers of his squad, after they brought their own cameras on to the ice at the end of the game.

It was obvious how much this Championship meant to the team and to Morrison. The changes made in summer were all for the better and what emerged after a sticky start was a team in the true sense of the word.

One that was as tight-knit as the Grand Slam squad from four seasons ago and a team that got big seasons out of numerous individuals as well as working for each other game in, game out. It was surely a formality that All-Star honours would be in the post heading for Fife.

Was there a better sniper than Dan Goneau or a more influential player than Karry Biette, indeed, a defenceman more imposing and focussed than Greg Kuznik? Also, had anyone skated through games with as much enthusiasm as Morrison himself? Ten years on and a bit greyer round the temple he remained welded to the team and the town.

While a win over Caps would have been nice the result mattered little to anyone North of the Forth. The summit had already been reached and there were more than a few fuzzy heads to be found under hockey helmets as Fife skated until their legs gave out.

Only when the adrenalin started to diminish did Caps get into this game. Fife found themselves 3-0 up inside six minutes without actually doing anything. They logged five shots on goal, scored with three, rattled the metalwork and saw netminder Ladislav Kudrna make one save.

Daryl Venters picked up the scraps from a Caps' attack deep in the Fife zone to send John Haig clear for a thumping finish for 1-0 at 2:36 and

Todd Dutiaume polished off a slick Morrison move for 2-0 at 4:21. The third line struck again at 6:35, this time Haig setting up Venters as Caps looked to be in disarray. Adrian Saul at 11:00 steadied their ship but Fife went into the first break 4-2 ahead thanks to a Dutiaume strike at 16:33.

A power play gave Dutiaume his hat-trick at 27:23 and it looked as though they might round off the league campaign with a derby win. They were however outshot 18-4 in the middle period and the increasing number of times Caps broke out of defence and the growing number of tempting rebounds coughed up suggested Fife were running out of gas.

Goals from Steven Kaye and Tony Hand made it a 5-4 hockey game at the halfway stage, and Martin Cingel's strike at 36:06 gave the hosts the momentum to go for the win and secure third place which was a superb achievement for a club that played to the smallest crowds in the league.

The game winner came as early as the 44th minute as Miroslav Droppa let rip with a cracking shot but Cingel made sure with a late strike.

The third period produced a spot of stick fencing between Paul Spadafora and Kaye and some wide open play in which Tony Hand looked as predatory as ever. As the clock wound down, few on the Fife side of the rink spent much time fretting about the scoreboard.

Caps won the game but the plaudits and the encores belonged to Fife

Capitals scoring: Kaye (2+2). Cingel (2+1), Sa 11+2). Hand.Droppa (both 1+1), Krajicek (0+3), Dunbar. N.Hay (0+1).

Fife scoring: Dutiaume (3+0), Haig, Venters (both 1+1), Forsyth, Fletcher, S.King, Morrison, Finlay, Biette, Spadafora (all 0+1).

PiMs: 6-4 SOGs: Caps (Kudrna) 32, Fife (Briere) 47

Attendance: 1682 Referee: Wilson.

*John Haig in action
against old rivals
Edinburgh Capitals*

Flyers John Coyle who moved mid season from the Telford Tigers is up against his old team mate Adrian Lomonaco later in the 1998/99 season

March

Andy Samuel in season 1996/97

Friday March 1st 2019

Fife Flyers 5 Milton Keynes Lightning 2

The Flyers were looking to achieve a top half finish for the first time in the EIHL but firstly they were out to strengthen their position within the play-off places, with an essential victory at home to bottom club Milton Keynes Lightning.

On a rare home Friday night game, with no other teams in action, the two points lifted the Flyers up to sixth in the table above Sheffield Steelers, and more importantly opened up a six point cushion to the danger zone.

Scott Aarssen, Evan Stoflet and Paul Crowder were still missing from the line up through injury, so Fife once again started with 12 imports against a Lightning side who were also running short-benched.

Flyers took a 1-0 lead into the first break courtesy of Brett Bulmer's opener which took a fortunate bounce to deceive netminder Patrick Killeen. The other talking point from the first period was a Danick Gauthier hit on Martin Mazanec that left the Lightning defenceman motionless on the ice for a period of time before he eventually recovered.

Flyers were the team with most of the concerted pressure but Lightning certainly had their sporadic chances. The visitors eventually made one count in the second period with a power play equaliser at 21.16 from Robbie Baillargeon. That provoked Fife into an immediate response, as Mike Cazzola restored the lead little more than a minute later, when he tipped home Ricards Birzins pass.

Referee Blake Copeland took centre stage with a verbal spat with Fife head coach Todd Dutiaume. This was shortly followed by a soft slashing call against Cazzola, coupled with a bench penalty for unsportsmanlike conduct, as the Flyers had a two minute five-on-three to defend.

The penalty killers excelled and Fife took a 2-1 lead into the final period. Flyers struggled to put the game to bed but a gifted goal from the visiting defence looked to have given them the cushion they needed to see it out. A misplaced pass left Gauthier with an empty net tap-in for 3-1.

However Milton Keynes hit back with another power play strike as Carlo Finucci was robbed of the puck and Baillargeon fired home his second of the night at 49.20. Once again the home side responded to losing a goal and Flyers upped the intensity to grab a couple of late goals to ensure there would be no nervy finish.

Cazzola, the architect of goal number four, won the puck in the neutral zone before motoring over the blue line to set up Brett Bulmer who stepped past his marker and backhanded past Killeen. Evan Bloodoff was fortunate to avoid injury as he was clattered into the boards by defenceman James Griffin, who was served a 2+10 for checking from behind. From the power play the game was killed as Joe Basaraba pounced on a loose puck at the net to complete the scoring.

Six points from the last eight was a good return for a team nursing several injuries and had put the season back on an even-keel after a recent tumble down the standings. The victory, while deserved, was far from comfortable. Todd Dutiaume admitted his team struggled at times with Lightning's style of play but he was happy enough with the performance.

"It was always going to be a dangerous game but we played well again at times. It's tough when teams want to run and gun for guys to stay engaged and do the right things. We saw along the walls a little bit of sloppy puck management and not being committed with a bit of swinging going on. When your opponents are doing that it's easy to fall into that trap. But we did enough to win the game, and stuck with the programme for the most part."

For the second match running Brett Bulmer was voted Man of the Match with the ex-NHL er bagging two goals to take his season's tally to 22. That his consistent run of form had mirrored Flyers upturn in fortunes was no coincidence according to his coach.

"When Brett is skating like that we're a completely different team," said Dutiaume.

Mike Cazzola celebrates as the puck nestles behind Milton Keynes netminder Patrick Killeen

Saturday March 2nd 1991

HEINEKEN PREMIER LEAGUE

Fife Flyers 5 Durham Wasps 11

Chic Cottrell must have been sorely tempted to sneak into Durham's dressing room and un-cork their champagne to drown his own sorrows. The heavy defeat at the hands of the newly crowned Champions brought the reality of relegation to the dressing-room door and left the Flyers coach with numerous problems.

Cottrell's bench was decimated by injuries and a dismissal during the match. He simply could not match Durham's sheer strength, power or experience. In a nutshell Flyers came off second best to a side which did not even need to move out of second gear. The game was over within ten minutes.

By then Wasps were 3-0 ahead and Flyers defence was in complete disarray, resulting in Craig Dickson being replaced in net by Colin Downie, but Cottrell's problems were only just beginning. Paul Cain traded places with Les Millie and the Canadian actually looked more comfortable in the second line after a series of utterly anonymous performances. Unfortunately a back injury forced him out after the opening period. Defenceman Gordon Whyte also bowed out of the action at the same time.

The biggest blow however came when Rick Fera was turfed out of the game after a moment of sheer madness. The Canadian centre tangled with Ian Cooper and tried once too often to re-engage in hostilities. He skated through a cluster of players and officials to have a second go at Cooper before being ushered away to cool down by a linesman. The real mayhem, however, came inside the penalty box as Fera looked for round three. In doing so he sent the time-keepers scurrying as he attempted to throw a chair at Cooper, who by this time was frantically looking for an escape exit. Both players collected double minors for roughing but it was no surprise when Fera received game and gross misconducts penalties for his abuse of the officials.

The player's actions stunned as many people as they amazed and his subsequent suspension all but hammered the final nail in Flyers Premier League coffin. Fera's fight also sparked off a series of niggly incidents which culminated in a ten-minute misconduct penalty to Stephen

Cooper little more than 90 seconds from the final buzzer. In total eight players collected roughing penalties. Wasps, as always, hit hard and fast and Flyers had nobody with the brawn to respond in kind. The defence struggled to dump the puck beyond the blue line and Downie experienced one of Dickson's season-long frustrations by coming up with the big saves only to be beaten by uncleared rebounds.

There was no indication of the necessary leadership from the sole remaining import, Justin Butorac, who turned in an awful performance before walking off the ice prior to the post-game handshakes. He also un-sportingly snubbed the formalities on Sunday after another inept outing. Butorac was Flyers last card and billed as a high-scoring uncompromising defenceman he had contributed an average of just one point per game while adding nothing to the most fragile defence in Britain. Against Wasps he was very suspect under pressure and too many passes either drifted aimlessly down the ice or ended up on the stick of a Durham player.

Flyers had gone through eight imports that season and had failed to improve in any way since the collapse of the 'Czech experiment'. They had yet to find a more composed defenceman than Lubos Oslizlo and they had been unable to sign a winger to complement Fera.

Flyers hardly troubled Wasps and had slumped to 4-0 at 9:20 before finding some form. The Fifers best play came in the closing minutes of the first period but even then they still gave up a short-handed goal. Mike O'Connor and Ian Cooper scored within 20 seconds to give Wasps a two-goal cushion at 3:39 and they saw off keeper Craig Dickson just six minutes later.

The Flyers netminder had already dealt with close on 1,300 shots this season and in a mercy pull, there was little sense in exposing him to more rubber. Stephan Cooper destroyed Butorac with a delightful body-swerve to set up number three for the unmarked Brebant and Paul Dixon caught Downie cold with number four at 9:20. Goals from David Smith and Les Millie dragged Fife back into contention but only briefly. Wasps took the first period 5-2 and the second 3-0 to allow their supporters to unfurl banners which proclaimed them as the 1991 League Champions.

The third period was a niggly affair with Millie, Blair Page, Michael Tasker and even Gordon Latto picking up minor roughing penalties. Flyers pulled back from 8-2 to 8-4 with goals from Butorac and Fera but Durham replied with a swift double courtesy of Stephen Cooper and O'Connor when both sides were down to four skaters. Paul Hand found the net for Flyers fifth but Brebant, who else, took his tally to four and three assists with the final goal of the evening at 57:40. By then Flyers fans had stopped counting.

Rick Fera in more typical pose – his frustrations on the season were clear for all to see against Durham Wasps

Derek King along with the rest of the Flyers defence had a torrid night at the Skydome

Sunday March 3rd 2002

Coventry Blaze 7 Fife Flyers 0

Following a positive start to their play-off campaign the night before when they had overcome the Hull Thunder at Kirkcaldy, the Flyers were comprehensively outplayed by a full-strength Blaze who never allowed the visitors to settle. They hammered seven goals past Shawn Silver.

It was the first time the Fifers had been shut out that season and their first whitewash in the league or play-offs since going down 4-0 in Slough back in February 1999. To cap a bad night the Edinburgh Capitals had also won, to create the very real prospect of a three-horse race for the two playoff final qualification slots.

The Flyers went into the weekend with something of an injury crisis. Derek King, Gary Wishart and Frank Morris were all struggling to be fit but would all make the line-up. Not the case however for goal machine Russell Monteith who was lost, not just for the opening weekend but the entire remainder of the season. It was a stunning blow and player-coach Mark Morrison was visibly distraught in his press conference ahead of the action saying

> "I thought we were the strongest we have been all season and looked a dominating force and suddenly it all changes. Nick Poole has come in and added speed and great skating while Bob Quinnell has settled well and gets better each week and it's so sickening because it took us a long time to put together what we thought was a Championship winning team".

The patched-up squad suffered further injury problems as player-coach Mark Morrison and Kyle Horne both required time out of the game for attention to head knocks. Flyers fell behind to a Steve Roberts goal at 4:56 with the Coventry player making the hit to create the chance and then bagging the rebound off a Mike Shewan shot.

Horne left the game for treatment following a big hit from Steve Carpenter with Flyers pushing Gary Wishart into the first line. A tripping penalty against Stephen Cooper put Flyers on the power play and Iain Robertson shot narrowly past, but Blaze killed the penalty before extending their lead through the unmarked Roberts at 13:53. The home side then added a killer third at 18:58 through Tom Watkins to leave Fife with a mountain to climb.

Indeed the Flyers had lost four of five encounters against the Blaze that season with all those defeats coming in the league. Their one success was the highlight of the season, as they downed the Blaze 6-3 in the Findus Cup final. That defeat was now being avenged with interest.

Morrison and Horne were back for the second period but with several players clearly carrying injuries they struggled to get their game going and couldn't capitalise on a 2+10 checking from behind call against Hilton Ruggles at 34:54.

Two quick goals early in the third period killed their hopes of a comeback. Shaun Johnson converted on a three on one break at 41:27 and then just 19 seconds later it was five as Fife hesitated over a bouncing puck and Claude Dumas knocked it into the net.

While there were good chances at both ends as the game moved into the closing stages, home goalie Ian Burt stayed on top of his game to savour a rare play-off shut-out. Blaze underlined their dominance with further goals from Tom Watkins and Rob Eley.

Thursday March 4th 1954

NATIONAL LEAGUE

Fife Flyers 5 Dundee Tigers 3

In a game of many penalties, most of them for trifling offences, the Flyers eventually snapped their six-week losing run in the National League at the expense of the Dundee Tigers.

The visitors took the lead in the first period when Art Sullivan slashed home a Bert Oig pass from the edge of the crease. It was the only goal of the session but there should have been several others. Both Murray Banks and Jim McGeorge missed the net when right through and there were other shooting failures almost as bad.

The second period put a different complexion on matters however. Banks netted the equaliser with a blind back-hand swipe and Floyd Snider put Flyers ahead from close range. The sides were often reduced to three-on-three in this session. Midway through Red Kurz missed a penalty shot for Tigers. The big defenceman simply skated straight at Ron Collins then shot wide of the post.

Flyers dominated the last period. Despite Scotty Reid stretching their lead, their finishing was weak, and they had always to keep a wary eye on Tigers marksmen. Oig reduced the arrears for Tigers but goals from Fred Kentner and Bert Smith in a two-minute spell made the last goal of the game by Tigers Sullivan a mere consolation.

It was not a game to be remembered for its hockey, but rather the penalties, the fights and the many near misses, when both teams were under strength. There was a whole lot of good goalkeeping as both Collins and Ron Gross were in tip-top form. The respective defences were wide open for long spells, but the forwards did not make the most of their chances.

No fewer than 57 minutes in penalties were handed out. Many of the 'offences' which were penalised were pernickety and made the whole thing slightly ridiculous. For example, Tigers left-winger Jim McGeorge had to sit out two minutes for a perfectly legitimate slap-shot which was executed when there was absolutely no danger anyone being hit by his stick on either the back-swing or the follow-through. Contrast that to an incident in the second period, when Kurtz and Kentner were intent on swopping blows with their sticks. Everyone else was keen to join in, making the scene more like a wrestling contest than a hockey match. But the total penalties imposed totalled only four minutes, which hardly stood comparison with the previous incident involving McGeorge. The penalties and varied lively scenes did not add to the value of the game from the point of view of good hockey but they certainly added to the excitement. It had been a long time since such a small crowd made so much noise in the Kirkcaldy rink.

Flyers deserved to win, of that there could be no doubt. All of them skated hard. Although their luck round the net never improved the pressure told in the long run. There were long spells when they had Collins to thank for keeping them in the game, but over the piece the home side had the better of the exchanges. They were all triers, and that counted for a great deal. Buddy Stock showed greatly improved form, but still couldn't get into the play often enough, simply because Snider and Kentner rushed the puck on almost every occasion without passing. Kurz, Sullivan and Oig were the best Tigers, but it was goalkeeper Gross who kept them in the game.

Flyers, Ron Collins, Floyd Snider, Jimmy Mitchell, Wray Fallowfield, Jim Smith, Bud Stock, Murray Banks, Bert Smith, Scotty Reid, Harry Pearson.
Tigers, Ron Gross, Red Kurz, Alf Krober, Dick Wolstenholme, Bert Oig, Art Sullivan, Jim McGeorge, Marshall Key, Jake Grant, Johnny Rolland, Larry Ford.
Referee — R. Gemmell

The win proved to be Flyers only one in a 21 game spell stretching from 21st January to the end of the season on the 8th of April!

From an earlier 1953/54 encounter with the Tigers – Ron Gross watches as Flyers Hayes shot flashes past the post

Sunday March 5th 1967

Fife Flyers 21 Paisley Vikings 1

Flyers came of age in a goal-scoring spree in which they cracked twenty-one goals past a woefully weak and inept Paisley Vikings side.

Although Flyers won, by scoring an average of one goal every three minutes, the question being asked was — is this the sort of entertainment to bring the crowds back to ice hockey?

Clearly the answer was an emphatic "no" as the attendance was down again; one reason might have been that before the game even started there was never any doubt that Flyers would not only win but do so by a large margin. The match as a spectacle wasn't helped by the fact that the Paisley side —which had a record of played twenty lost twenty, goals for 4, goals against 144 — turned up short of two players, one of whom was their netminder.

There was a certain amount of context to this mismatch. Many were left wondering that if Flyers could score 21 goals against the West of Scotland side then how many would some of the top teams score? This, however, didn't detract from the merit and the stature of the Fife side's win, which was achieved without one of their most experienced campaigners in Bert Smith.

Vikings turning up short benched bizarrely offered up an opportunity for a couple of Fife's younger players. Jim Taylor took his place between the Paisley pipes and was joined by fellow Flyers Junior team mate Drew Motion. Even with those two additions the Vikings still only had a bench that numbered 10 skaters which was just enough to field two complete lines.

The standout performance in a Flyers side that obviously looked good against such opposition was yet another youngster, Danny Brown, who helped himself to five goals and an assist. However, with so many goals flashing past Jim Taylor, it was a real feast for the forwards. Les Lovell netted four times and had a hand in five others. "Pep" Young, who was wearing Bert Smith's jersey, took over the veteran's position by continually setting up Flyers moves towards goal. He finished with five assists and a hat-trick of goals.

The only defender to net was Joe McIntosh, who scored Flyers final goal, but Bill Brown also proved his worth again with three assists and was up helping his attack on numerous occasions. As for the rest of the defence, Roy Reid in nets would have been better at home watching the Sunday film while Ken Horne and Dave Medd were continually getting mired up in their efforts to block the rare Vikings pressure.

The first period started with the Flyers strangely looking as if they couldn't care less. At least that was the impression given by the first line, who were outshone in the opening stages. All of Flyers three goals in the opening twenty minutes were scored by the second line with John Taylor, Pep Young and Danny Brown each getting their name on the score sheet.

Les Lovell and D Brown again netted inside four minutes of the start of the second period before Vikings scored their only goal. It was a good one, too, as Kane received a through pass from Grant, rounded Reid and slipped the puck into the net.

After that the first line really showed what they could do with Norrie Boreham grabbing a double and Lovell and Ian Shields each scoring. With five minutes to go until the end of the period Jimmy Watson flicked the puck into the net after a Young shot had rebounded off the post to make it 10-1. There was still time for Lovell and Brown to complete their hat tricks.

Nine more goals in the last period gave Flyers goal column a very welcome boost. Les Lovell netted again in the fourth minute, followed by goals from John Taylor and Boreham with his third. Then came another from Jimmy Watson, which was quite a handy performance considering he was on the ice for the shortest period of time. Brown scored the next two goals and within a minute Young had performed the same trick. Three minutes from time Joe McIntosh completed the rout.

Teams—Flyers — Roy Reid, Bill Brown, Joe McIntosh, Dave Medd, Kenny Horne, Pep Young, Les Lovell, Ian Shields, Jimmy Watson, Norrie Boreham, John Taylor, Danny Brown

Paisley Vikings — Taylor, Black, Hamilton, McLachlan, Miller, Tate, Grant, Lawson. Kane, Devlin. Motion

Referee — T. Watt.

BRITISH ICE HOCKEY LEAGUE
SPONSORED BY THE SCOTTISH BOTTLERS OF

COCA-COLA
(Trade mark registered)

ICE RINK, PAISLEY
SUNDAY, 20th NOV., at 7·30 p.m.

PAISLEY MOHAWKS

FIFE FLIERS

Things go better with
COKE

Get Your Tickets NOW!   **Adults, 5/-; Juveniles, 3/-**

TICKET AGENCIES:
Paisley Ice Rink; Lumley's, Sauchiehall St., Glasgow; Sportsmen's Emporium, St. Vincent St., Glasgow; P. Keenan, 97 Maxwell Drive, Glasgow, S.1—Telephone IBRox 1622.

A bill poster from the same season for the Flyers match with the senior Paisley team the Mohawks.
The Vikings were run that season as the Mohawks "Second team"
(Note the spelling mistake, this was a common occurrence around that time)

466

Friday March 6th 2020

Elite Ice Hockey League

Belfast Giants 3 Fife Flyers 1

The Flyers made their first ferry trip of the season in the League having already completed their home series with the Giants. They were due back two weeks later, for a St Patrick's weekend double header, but this game became their final one in the coronavirus-curtailed season.

Liam Morgan came up with the game-winner 5:45 from time as the Belfast Giants rode a 34-save display from netminder Shane Owen for a 3-1 win. Mere seconds after Fife netminder Adam Morrison, with 39 saves had made a sensational sprawling stop to deny Matt Pelech on a two-on-one breakaway, the Giants got the crucial strike when Elgin Pearce fed the onrushing Morgan to finish smartly for his 14th goal of the season.

Winger David Goodwin took his personal tally to 15 for the season. He extended his scoring streak to five consecutive games with a two-goal night. After netting the opener on the power play, he wrapped things up 1:20 from time with an empty-netter.

The Giants also got a two-point night from captain Matt Pelech, At the other end, Owen was exceptional in turning away 34 of the 35 shots on his net. The Giants improved to 28-16-4 on the campaign and clawed back some ground in the Elite League title race.

Also key to Belfast's success was an impressive 3-for-4 penalty kill which, although it gave up the Flyers only goal of the night to Carlo Finucci in the first period, came up big in the final frame to keep the visitors at bay when it was still a one-goal game.

The first period had been a tale of two power play goals as the sides, having traded successful special team spells, went in level at the first intermission. The Giants had been ahead when James Isaacs was binned for holding the stick. Goodwin extended his scoring streak at 13:58 when he fired in the angled rebound off Curtis Hamilton's initial shot for his 14th goal of the season. The Flyers pulled level when Kevin Raine was sent to the box on an interference call. When Owen couldn't handle Paul Crowder's shot, it was Carlo who was quickest to react to the loose puck to make it 1-1 with 1:02 until the intermission.

If the first period was fairly uneventful then the second was even more so, with the action limited at both ends to two Giants penalty kills while playing out a Raine high sticking minor and Ryan Lowney's cross-checking call.

Flyers nearly lost netminder Morrison to an innocuous looking injury when he needed treatment after stopping a shot from the blue-line. Then they did lose Jordan Buesa for the rest of the period after the young forward was checked off the puck to no penalty. The two sides headed in level at the second intermission after a scoreless middle frame. Bobby Farnham, perhaps, should have done better after he seized on a Morrison misplay behind the net, but couldn't force it into the empty net as the Flyers scrambled around the play.

Patrick Mullen thought he might have scored the go-ahead goal early in the third, when he walked in from the left circle and cranked one off the bar. The video review confirmed that the shot hadn't snuck in and out off the back bar instead. At the other end Finucci thought he might have his second of the game and a winner for the visitors. He went on a clean breakaway, only to be denied by a massive stop from Owen, who thrust out a pad to deflect the puck to safety.

That prefaced Morgan's winner, with the winger set up beautifully by Pearce for the finish. When Goodwin slid in the empty-netter with 1:20 remaining for the shorthanded tally, after the Giants' penalty kill came up huge that was game over. Without knowing it at the time, it also brought the curtain down on Flyers season.

Adam Morrison makes another save against the Giants on an earlier visit that season to Kirkcaldy

Sunday March 7th 2010

Fife Flyers 4 Dundee Stars 3 (after overtime)

Although Flyers and Stars had played each other too often that season for the rivalry between them to sustain any real meaning, come the play-offs they both jettisoned the jadedness of the regular season and served up a cracking and at times raw and error-strewn final.

For the best part of the opening 30 minutes the Stars were the better side and worthy of their first period lead. Then the momentum turned. Their big-game players melted into the shadows. After shaking off their own defensive jitters Fife started to skate with purpose. By the time we got to the third period the one goal hockey game could have gone either way.

Stephen Gunn's 52nd minute goal should have sealed the trophy but Stars rallied. They forced sudden death overtime with a dubious call from the very referee they were later to berate with undisguised fury. Just 10 minutes later, Stars were twice reduced to three skaters because, despite what tradition decrees, referees don't always leave their whistle in their pocket for everything more minor than decapitation.

Marius Nawrokch called what he saw and heard — all of it against Dundee. This resulted in some old-time hockey mayhem at the final buzzer as Andy Samuel sealed victory in the 68th minute. Stars coach Bobby Haig hurled his water bottle on to the ice. This was followed by six more before the whole bottle carrier and then a stick was smashed across the barrier.

Not all the visiting players went up to collect their medals or shake the hand of the referee as the old barn fair shook with verbal indignation. All credit to Bobby Haig, though for stepping on to the ice and picking up the bottles, after the lively end to a wide open final between two well matched teams.

After two dull semi-finals the tournament needed to deliver a showcase finale to justify the price hike at the door and the fans certainly got their money's worth. Stars started strongly and were settled by a trademark rocket from David Smith at 4:39. It took a disjointed Fife 22 minutes to draw level and even then they needed a wicked bounce off the back boards to allow Iain Beattie to net. John Dolan twice skated through on solo rushes but Daly came up with huge saves; they proved to be two of the game's pivotal moments. Flyers mucked up a three-on-one break with one pass too many in the 33rd minute which beggared belief.

The home side did go ahead through Steven Lynch at 45:59, and Stephen Gunn's strike at 52:01 should have sealed victory. Stars grabbed a lifeline with a peach of a blue line shot from Dolan at 55:26. Going into the final two minutes Fife kept Stars pinned in their zone denying them the chance to pull netminder McGill. They couldn't endure however and the goalie raced to the bench with 54 seconds remaining. Then a moment of huge controversy at 59:45 as Gary Wishart's left-wing shot was blocked by Daly. The whistled sounded only to have the puck roll under his pads and over the line a second later. The ref awarded the goal.

If the fans thought that was controversial then what followed in overtime had them on their feet. With Stars down to four skaters Jeff Marshall was binned for delaying the game. It was a huge call but Stars survived short-handed but when they repeated the feat later it was one step too far. Harper took his second minor in sudden death and words from the bench saw a second penalty called. It saw the momentum turn one last time and this time Fife struck with the tireless Andy Samuel fittingly getting the winner from close range.

Contrasting emotions as Mark McGill is beaten by Andy Samuel for the sudden death winner to lift the Celtic Cup Play Off title

Saturday March 8th 1997

Fife Flyers 15 Dumfries Vikings 5

For two periods of this game the Dumfries Vikings threatened a major upset as they matched Flyers in every department and only trailed 6-4 after 40 minutes.

Eventually the strain of playing with only nine outfield skaters took its inevitable toll. The home side crushed the visitors in the final period to ensure qualification to the second round of the play-offs.

With Martin McKay at home with his new-born daughter, and Colin Hamilton injured, Flyers had to turn again to their junior netminding duo of Sean Goodsir and Andy Moffat. The pair performed admirably with the latter picking up the Man of the Match award.

The antics of the young goalies rather over-shadowed the feat of Steven King who returned figures of 5+5. The quality of the opposition may not have been the greatest but it was a fine performance in any circumstances by the International forward who looked to be back to his best at just the right time.

Vikings, who emerged with great credit, were kept in the game by a virtuoso show by veteran netminder John McCrone, who produced one of the best displays of keeping seen at the arena that year.

In the end 'Bernie' was withdrawn after 46 minutes, having faced 47 shots and looking completely shattered, but his efforts were warmly applauded by the Fife crowd.

After King fired Flyers ahead at 2.58 the fans awaited a goal feast but it didn't materialise. When Goodsir was beaten by a quick shot from Michael Tasker at 7.40 and a John Churchill effort which deflected off Richard Danskin less than two minutes later it was clear things weren't going to plan.

Vikings held the lead until the first break and drew first blood in the second period through Tasker again before Flyers eventually stepped up a gear. It took a tripping penalty on Richard Dingwall to get them going and when Frank Morris netted shorthanded at 23.31 it signalled a burst of scoring with four goals in four minutes through King, Lee Mercer, Morris and Wayne Maxwell who finished off a great play by the kid line.

The visitors refused to buckle, however. When Martin Grubb forced the puck home past Moffat, who had replaced Goodsir at 25.29, there were only two goals in it entering the final period. As expected the Flyers strength in depth told. They added nine further goals with King taking his tally to five. Morris completed his hat-trick with Tasker doing likewise with a consolation power play for the gallant losers.

In a game with few incidents Russ Parent talked himself into a ten minute misconduct after picking up a tripping penalty at 49.49 and sat out the rest of the match.

Flyers scoring: Steven King 5+5, Frank Morris 3+1, Mark Morrison 2+4, Wayne Maxwell 2+1, Lee Mercer 2+1, Craig Wilson 1+0, Mark Slater 0+3, John Haig 0+2, Russ Parent 0+2, John Reid 0+2, Gordon Latto 0+1.

Vikings scoring: Michael Tasker 3+1, John Churchill 1+1, Martin Grubb 1+1, Andrew Holmes 0+2, Richard Tasker 0+1.

Shots on goal: Flyers 24 (Goodsir 10, Moffat 14); Vikings 65 (McCrone 47, Langford 18).

Penalty minutes: Flyers 14, Vikings 2. Referee: Drew Fraser. Crowd: 1600.

The Flyers completed a clean sweep of ten victories against the Vikings that season for a combined 97-30 goals total and it would be eight years before the clubs would meet again by which time the Vikings were known as the Solway Sharks.

Steven King on his 10 point performance in action around the Vikings net.

Saturday 9th March 1985

Fife Flyers 9 Toronto Eagles 3

TOURISTS TROUNCED

This challenge match gave Flyers the chance to relax from the pressures of the Heineken Premier League.

The Toronto Eagles were playing the fourth match of their Scottish tour and looking for their first win. Despite giving a good account of themselves the Flyers proved too strong for them. The Kirkcaldy side were without Stuart Drummond, who was still completing his period of suspension, and so player-coach Ron Plumb took the opportunity to ice young defencemen Blair Page and Gary Fyffe.

The first period was closely contested with Flyers going ahead through Dave Stoyanovich. This was short lived as Jeff Newby equalised for the visitors with a well-taken goal. However, Stoyanovich restored Flyers lead within a minute to give his side a 2-1 advantage at the first buzzer.

As had been the case so often in recent times it was a middle period burst that put Flyers firmly in the driving seat. In the dying seconds of a power play Danny Brown brought the crowd to its feet with one of the goals (and there had been many) of the season. Picking the puck up in his own end the big number 19 weaved his way the length of the ice, leaving the tourists trailing in his wake, before calmly beating netminder Trithart.

Another power play goal by Brown followed four minutes later. Soon after that Stoyanovich completed his hat-trick from a Brown assist. Stoyanovich then snapped up the rebound from a Neil Abel pile-driver, which was blocked by the netminder, to give Flyers a 6-1 lead at the break.

Just a minute into the final period and Abel himself got on the scoresheet when he crashed an unstoppable shot into the top corner from the blue line. Two minutes later it was Brown's turn to complete an excellent hat-trick when he capitalised on good work by Murray McLellan to scoop an angled back-hander into the roof of the net.

Eagles persistent efforts were rewarded by a second goal from Newby. Within 25 seconds Stoyanovich brought up his nap hand, after McLellan had again done the spade work. With Flyers threatening to run riot, the visitors to their credit raised their game sufficiently to prevent any further goals against. Indeed, it was the Canadians who had the final word when Clark scored just two minutes from time. After the game the Man of the Match awards were presented to Danny Brown of Flyers and Newby of Eagles and the crowd gave the visitors a rousing send-off after an entertaining and clean-fought encounter.

Prior to the Toronto Eagles match Dave Stoyanovich received the mounted puck from his record breaking 129th goal of the season from Bob Fernie, Chairman of Kirkcaldy Ice Hockey Club. The previous record of 128 was set by Dundee Rockets Roy Halpin

Thursday March 10th 1949

NATIONAL LEAGUE

Fife Flyers 7 Perth Panthers 1

FIFE FLYERS CORONATION TROPHY WINNERS

"It was a long road, but it was worth it. It is great honour to be known as National League winners and naturally I am very happy." These comments were made by Fife Flyers captain Bud Scrutton when interviewed after the game.

After reporters duly extended congratulations to the victors they returned to Bud who remarked "lt would be just right if Raith Rovers completed the 'double' by beating [Glasgow] Rangers in the League Cup final." Bud added "To-night the Raith players were rooting for us, well on Saturday, we will be rooting for them." [Author note – two days later and the Rovers went down 2-0 in the final – a result it has to be said that does not disappoint this Fife football fan].

Flyers, who had everything to gain and lose on the night, showed no signs of nerves and straight from the face-off they opened in a business-like manner. Their first raid had the spectators on their feet and their opening blitz was so demoralising that it took Panthers about eight minutes to register their first shot on Belanger's net.

The strength of Don Irons in the visitors net, however, was as tough as his name implied; it was not until the 16th minute that Chic Mann succeeded in finding a loophole to open Flyers account. For the remaining four minutes of the opening period the Flyers went goal-crazy and by the time the gong sounded they had added three more to their account.

Following these early reverses the Panthers, who had no interest in the National play-off, but were purely playing with the honour of their club at stake, set out to do all in their power to prevent Belanger from collecting a "shut-out" and after 50 minutes they succeeded in their quest.

For the fourth successive game, the solitary counter to beat Belanger was of the scrappy variety, although no blame could be attached to "Pete", who with a little luck in the last four games could now have claimed his seventh clean sheet of the season but had to be content with a well-earned three.

Panthers, although clever individually, lacked striking power and as a result the game as a spectacle suffered accordingly. Flyers, on the other hand, were a swift moving scientific combine that ripped an indifferent

Panthers defence to shreds. Mann was the play-maker superb and his cheeky stick-handling and long sweeping passes combined with deadly finishing made him the scintillating star of the match. By collecting a well deserved hat-trick and two assists he was now tied with "Bud" Scrutton as joint leader of the snipers list, each having scored a total of 145 points.

Belanger may justly claim that he was out of luck on the night but lady luck also dealt more than one unkind blow to "Bud" Scrutton. Three times he flashed the red light. With one exception, the scores were chalked off for previous infringements. On another occasion, he sizzled through but his shot rebounded off the steel work with Irons helpless.

The Flyers captain, although dogged by bad luck, gave one of his most impressive displays and, while he did not get his usual quota of goals, he was instrumental in originating many of the attacks which resulted in scores. Bert Smith completed a smooth and efficient first line; he helped himself to a goal and assist which kept him amongst the top scoring juniors.

The second line were more polished than usual. The Ken Joy, Harold 'Hick' Moreland and Scotty Reid combine had the beating of the visitors' defence for the better part of the game. Floyd Snider and Mann took most of the defensive honours, although for good solid defending Jimmy Mitchell and Rab Reid took a lot of beating. Panthers were best served by Irons, Joe McGuire, Lorne Goddard and Tom La Pointe. The goals in the game that secured the Flyers their first post war National League title were:

1st period – Flyers: Mann (Mitchell), Joy, Snider (Mann), Mann. 2nd period – Flyers: Mann (Scrutton) 3rd Period – Flyers: Smith (Mann), Scrutton (Smith), Panthers: Forbes (Chard)

Chic Mann in typical action around the net.

Thursday March 11th 1948

Fife Flyers 6 Czechoslovakia 1

The Czechoslovakian touring side gave a disappointing display against a Flyers side that was bolstered by the addition of guest players Pete Belanger (Glasgow Bruins), Norm Gustavsen (Dundee Tigers) and Art Hodgins (Paisley Pirates). With a re-enforced defence the Flyers restricted the visitors attacking flair. Contrasting that with other teams, such as Paris Racing Club, the Continentals' raids were all the same unimaginative pattern. Hodgins and Floyd Snider in particular were never really stretched. Belanger in net made the shots coming his way, particularly in the last period, look easy to stop.

Flyers started off with a bang but poor passing inside the Czech blue line spoiled their moves. It was the touring team who opened the scoring. Prchal slipped one past Belanger after Hanzl had brought the puck up ice. Cliff Ryan roamed down into the visitors area and was unlucky not to connect when the puck rebounded off his skate, but he made certain with his next shot when he sent home a lovely cross from Roy Hawkins. Soon after Hawkins saw his first shot saved, Les O'Rourke fed him the puck once more and he made no mistake with his second try.

Jarkovsky, in the tourists net, was having a busy time and had now settled down after those two snap Flyers goals. He had to look lively to deny Scrutton and then Snider. Flyers then had to kill a tripping penalty on Ryan. Shortly after, Kenny Potts collected the puck at the red line and wove his way through the defence but was well off the mark with his parting shot. Flyers increased their lead in the 16th minute when Ted Fowler skated in to the corner and slipped the puck to Bob Londry. The defenceman's shot whistled passed Jarkovsky.

In the second period Belanger was put under a little more pressure. That included killing a penalty after Scrutton had pulled the puck under his body when he slipped and was called for delaying the game. The keeper was playing a strong game, however. At the other end, his counterpart Jarkovsky came right out of his net, and with Fowler dithering over taking the shot, shoved the Flyer off the puck.

Although the visitors were creating more chances now, it was the home side who should have scored next when Hawkins was pulled down and Flyers were awarded a penalty shot. Scrutton nominated Hawkins to take the award. As he skated slowly in on Jarkovsky, his attempt to deke the keeper ended in his shot slithering past the post. Jarkovsky was playing with much more confidence. He was out of his net time and again to unsettle the Flyers before they could shoot. Despite repeated attacks, the home defence held out. In the 17th minute Hawkins put his side further in the lead after a set up by Ryan and O'Rourke. The visitors then had a goal chalked off as the puck was deemed to have been kicked in.

The third period started with the Flyers again doing most of the pressing. The Czechs seemed to feel the loss of Plocek who had suffered a broken nose towards the end of the second period. There was a bout of roughing between Kobranov and Scrutton. In the 12th minute Flyers scored again when Ryan notched another with a left-handed flick.

With two minutes to go the Czechs bombarded Belanger with five shots in quick succession, which brought their period total to 20, compared to Flyers 4. Londry was sent off for playing with a broken stick only, for the short-handed hosts to break away in the final few seconds for Scrutton to complete the scoring.

Roy Hawkins who had two goals against the Czechs

Sunday March 12th 1989

HEINEKEN PREMIER LEAGUE

Whitley Warriors 17 Fife Flyers 2

The back drop to this match was the end of the Flyers title contention the previous weekend leaving them to wrap up their league campaign with their sights firmly trained on second place.

The previous Saturday's defeat at the hands of an increasingly impressive Nottingham Panthers shattered the Kirkcaldy side's hopes of snatching the Heineken League crown at the very last hurdle. But they could still finish a roller-coaster season as runners-up and head into the play-offs brimming with confidence.

The fact that Flyers were even quoted in the closing stages underlined just how much work had been put in at the Rosslyn Street rink in recent months. Since the arrival of coach Rab Petrie, the side had regained its early season confidence and adapted to his own game plans, to produce a string of superb performances to zoom from a depressing fifth place into contention for the league title.

Ten victories from eleven outings transformed a predictable two-horse race between Murrayfield Racers and Durham Wasps into an unexpected three-way contest. Many thought it ought to have seen Petrie awarded with the Heineken 'coach of the month' award for February which had gone to Ayr's Rocky Saganuik. If he could get a fully-fit squad at his disposal Petrie was confident of finishing the season as runners-up to Champions-elect Durham.

Flyers had missed the experience of Jim Lynch last weekend and a doubt still hung over his fitness. Defenceman Richard Phillips was also struggling to shake off a viral infection as the team prepared for a home tussle with a Solihull Barons team who had nothing left to play for except their pride. Flyers on the other hand had everything going for them. Victory over Barons, plus two points from Sunday's journey to Whitley Bay, would put them within touching distance of second place which would augur well for the play-offs.

That season for the very first time the Champions and runners-up would be seeded to head Groups 'A' and 'B' respectively with all other qualifiers going into a hat. The move was designed to bring to an end the traditional sight of clubs jockeying for position in a bid to land the 'easier' play-off opponents. Seven busloads of Flyers supporters were already Wembley-bound. Saturday night's match against Solihull went as most had hoped and even without Jim Lynch the Flyers easily disposed of the visiting Barons 13-8.

The following night was not in the script, however, as the Flyers rounded off their league season with a record they didn't want – their all-time equal worst ever defeat on the road and their worst in the Heineken Premier League. Minus Gordon Latto, Milan Figala and the influential Jim Lynch, Flyers were no match for the hard-skating and full-strength Warriors.

Coach Rab Petrie gave his young protégés considerable ice time and threw them into power play situations simply for the experience. Warriors, however, showed no mercy as they cruised to a 6-1 lead in the first period, then hit Flyers for seven without reply in the second and wrapped things up with a 4-1 margin in the final stanza.

John Iredale began the rout at 4.04 and Garry Fyffe levelled 60 seconds later but that turned out to be Fife's last goal for over 40 minutes. Mike Rowe headed the scoring charts with four plus two, Hilton Ruggles chipped in with three plus two and Scott Morrison earned his corn with a three plus five. Neil Abel scored the visitors other consolation goal as they gave up a season high 60 shots against.

When the newly formatted draw took place, there was controversy as the BIHA split the teams finishing 3rd to 6th into two hats rather than all four teams going into one hat. With Fife and Nottingham in one bag and Whitley and Ayr in the other the Flyers reward for finishing in 3rd spot was to be grouped with the Champion Durham Wasps and face the prospect of a return to the Hillheads Rink to face Whitley Warriors – a tough ask.

Scorer of one of Flyers consolation goals, Neil Abel, the previous weekend chalked up his 200th Heineken Premier League appearance.

Thursday March 13th 1947

Fife Flyers 9 Dunfermline Vikings 4

In their final game in the competition the Flyers jumped into top spot in the Airlie Trophy race when for the first time that season they beat their Fife rivals. The teams had met nine times previously with Vikings winning every game.

Playing for the third time that week both teams looked rather leg-weary but Flyers were faster on the move and fully deserved their win. Vikings were without star centre-man Johnny Myke and played local junior Johnny Rolland in his place. Rolland made the first line at left wing with Joe Aitken playing centre and Jim Davis the right. Rolland held his place in the first line for 30 minutes of the game before defenceman Stan Stewart stepped forward.

Although Flyers were by no means world-beaters they were the superior team on the night's showing. Bud Scrutton hadn't yet managed to hit top form but lady luck was obviously not on his side. Going several games without scoring on Ivan Walmsley it was refreshing to see Earl McCrone hit the limelight with four goals. Harry O'Connor was a worker on the left, but he had lost a lot of his early season sparkle, which was perhaps due to him not getting as many passes as before.

Nobody on the ice worked harder than Pat Ratchford, who never gave in, and was epitomised by his goal, when he chased what looked like a lost cause to recover the puck after a face off. Bob Lantz wasn't brilliant on the right wing on Flyers second line. While John Drummond was a sound trier he made little progress. Frankie King and Floyd Snider in defence had apparently learned much from the Flyers loss to the Vikings in the National League Playoff Final second leg as they were rarely both found out of position. Bob Londry and Jim McKenzie also looked as if they had found out that games are not won from the cooler.

The absence of Myke upset Vikings play. Little was seen of Jimmy Davis. Vikings match winner two nights ago Joe Aitken tried hard, but his play lacked its usual verve and snap. Joe Kromptich bulged the mesh behind Don Dougall twice, but looked as if he was capable of doing it oftener. Dougall slipped up on Kromptich's second goal when he failed to track a knee-high shot from the right. Herb Kewley was Vikings best defenceman with Walmsley backing him up well.

Scoring Summary

First Period Goals – Vikings: Stewart (Allan) 4th min; Flyers: McCrone (Snider) 10th min

Penalties – Flyers: O'Connor (14th min – hacking)

Second Period Goals – Flyers: Snider 21st min, Ratchford 22nd min, McCrone (O'Connor & King) 32nd min, Lantz (Ratchford & Drummond) 32nd min, Scrutton (O'Connor & Snider) 34th min, Connor (Scrutton) 30 mins; Vikings: Kromptich (Allan) 37 mins

Penalties – Vikings: Lay (31st min – charging)

Third Period Goals – Vikings: Kromptich (K. Kewley) 43rd min, Stewart (Aitken) 53rd min; Flyers: McCrone (King & Scrutton) 55th min, McCrone (Snider & Scrutton) 59th min,

Penalties – Vikings: lrwin (49th min – tripping)

Flyers, Don Dougall, Floyd Snider, Frankie King, Earl McCrone, Bud Scrutton, Jim McKenzie, Bob Londry, Pat Ratchford, Bob Lantz, John Drummond

Vikings, Ivan Walmsley, Herb Kewley, Joe Lay, Arnold Irwin, Joe Aitken, Jim Davis, Stan Stewart, Joe Kromptich, Jimmy Allan, Keith Kewley, Johnny Rolland

Referees — G. McNeil, L. Marchant

There was disappointment for the Flyers a few days later when as a result of Dundee Tigers defeating the Vikings 5-2 at Dunfermline the Tigers gained custody of the Airlie Trophy with Fife Flyers as runners-up one point behind.

Programme for Vikings and Flyers match earlier in season

Saturday March 14th 1998

Fife Flyers 10 Cardiff Rage 2

With just ten seconds left in the final competitive game of the season at Fife Ice Arena, along came a moment that all those who witnessed it would cherish for a long time to come.

With Flyers coasting to victory after doing no more than necessary to see off the Cardiff Rage, Frank Morris won a face-off in the visitors zone and slid the puck across the face of the goal where number 16 was waiting to knock it into the net.

The crowd went wild as young and old alike rose as one to acclaim the fitting end to the astonishing career of Gordon Latto. The legend explained afterwards with tongue firmly in cheek.

> "It was a text book finish. Actually the plan was that when we were far enough in front I would move forward and try and score a goal but I didn't mean to leave it quite as tight as that! It was obviously special to score in my last home game and the reception of the fans at the end to all the players was great to hear."

The script could not have been written better to round off the season in Kirkcaldy.While the game itself was little more than a training session for Flyers, against a brave but vastly outclassed Rage team, the fans made sure things finished with a bang, especially in the final period when they virtually ignored events on the ice and celebrated in style.

Victory chants and rousing renditions of "Geordie Munro" and the bizarre spectacle of the now famous giant Flyers flag being transported right round every section in the rink by the fans and even through the Fife Lounge!

Victory was never in doubt. Those expecting a goal avalanche were disappointed as Mark Morrison quite rightly took things easy and iced his big guns sparingly once the game was safe. The final period saw Flyers attempt to set up young Gary Wishart for his first goal for the club prove successful. Once he had a taste for it he added a second just over a minute later.

Somehow, amid the rather dull fare in the opening two periods, Wayne Maxwell was handed a rather harsh 5+game for slashing by American referee Dave McGowan. We also had the rare spectacle of the Rage coach

Peter Smith being sent to the stand on a game misconduct with the score at 9-1. Both Fife netminders were given valuable ice time. Bernie McCrone must have had difficulty staying awake during his stint, as the crowd was treated to some excellent goals at the other end, most notably from Morrison and a fine effort by Andy Finlay. The players were cheered off the ice individually at the end, as the fans lifted the roof to send them on their way to the play-off finals at Hull with the belief that further glory was possible. And as Gordon Latto himself admitted what a way to finish that would be.

Flyers scoring: John Haig 2+2, Frank Morris 2+2, Gary Wishart 2+1, Mark Morrison 1+2, Andy Samuel 1+2, Andy Finlay 1+0, Gordon Latto 1+0, Derek King 0+3, David Smith 0+2, Lee Cowmeadow 0+1, Steven King 0+1.

Rage scoring: Wesley Spencer 2+0, Richard Townsend 0+2, Scott Carter 0+1.

Shots on goal: Flyers (McCrone 15, Hamilton 22) 37; Rage (Van Der Velden 24, Douglas 24) 48. Penalty minutes: Flyers 37 Rage 32

Referee: Dave McGowan. Att. 1690.

The match programme for the first and last visit of Cardiff Rage to Kirkcaldy

Sunday March 15th 2009

FFDR Cup

Fife Flyers 8 Paisley Pirates 0

Flyers young players like Josh Scoon and Callum Adamson would have grown up dreaming about scoring their first ever goal in the gold white and blue. In that dream it would not have involved a near-empty arena and a game that could best be described as a complete waste of time.

A 26-6 drubbing at Solway the previous week had given Fife fans an inkling of what to expect from a Pirates side wheezing its way over the finishing line. Sure enough they turned up for their final fixture with just seven skaters and no goalie. Such a situation was reminiscent of how the game was back in the 1960s, when there was at least an excuse that the sport was rediscovering itself in an amateur form after the professional game in the mid-1950s had gone boom.

Flyers provided the visitors with four juniors to at least try make it a spectacle worthy of the entry fee. In doing so the Pirates broke competition rules which did not allow the borrowing of players and so the FFDR Cup points were awarded to Fife before a puck had even been dropped. The pretence of the game was changed to that of a challenge match but where that challenge was going to come from was hard to find.

With the visitors in such obvious disarray the last thing that the fans expected was a goalless first period but by that stage everyone knew what was coming and the inevitable had merely been delayed. Flyers scored four in each of the last two periods with the up and coming talent taking centre stage for the night. However it was hard to imagine what they would have learned from this that they wouldn't have in any training scrimmage on any night that season.

The highlights were the first ever Flyers goals for Adamson and Scoon and a shut-out for teen netminder Craig Holland. The rest of the night was best forgotten although for Flyers, the Pirates were the only team they took points from in a competition dominated by the Elite League Edinburgh Capitals 'reserve' team.

Flyers scoring: Steven McAlpine (2+0), Iain Bell (1+), Callum Adamson, Josh Scoon, Lewis Glasgow, Stephen Gunn, Daniel McIntyre (1+1), Steven Lynch, Andy Samuel, Willie Nicolson (0+2), Aaron Greger, Steven King (0+1).

It was their 10th win from 10 matches against the struggling Paisley side in all matches that season. In the S N L era 2005-2010 the Pirates visited Kirkcaldy 19 times and lost all 19 although they were awarded a 9-3 defeat in March 2006 as a 3-0 win after the Flyers had iced John Haig when he should still have been under suspension.

The 2008-09 Flyers with the Scottish Cup – their third trophy of the season

Sunday March 16th 2003

BRITISH NATIONAL LEAGUE PLAY OFF

Guildford Flames 5 Fife Flyers 2

The Flyers 2002-03 competitive season came to a close in familiar fashion. Yet another defeat on the road, albeit sustained with a side weakened by injuries.

In a game that meant nothing for either side with the Flames and Dundee Stars already assured of progressing to the play off finals, the Flyers iced without Jonathan Weaver, David Smith and Andy Finlay.

They soon found themselves a goal behind, when the unmarked Nicky Chinn hit the far corner on a Derek DeCosty pass from behind the net after only 70 seconds. Despite the early set back the visitors looked to ice their whole bench with Chad Reekie, Tommy Muir and Adam Walker all gaining useful senior hockey experience.

Flames continued to dominate play and the hosts out-shot Flyers 38-11 up to the second buzzer although they could only add a David Clarke power play counter at 29.13 while Karry Biette sat out a soft hooking call.

The home side also scored on their only other power play of the evening when Derek DeCosty finished off a move involving Corey Lyons and Jason Lafreniere at 47.03 to increase their lead to three. Todd Dutiaume, Jason Dailey and Steven King all went close on a Flyers power play before Tony Redmond stretched the Flames lead further with a wrist shot into the top corner at 51.23.

Flyers deservedly got on the board at 54.17 when Dailey rifled a slap shot past Mike Torchia after good lead up work from Steven King. Mark Morrison then cut the deficit to two goals when he scored on the break-away after a pass by Dutiaume. Tempers flared three minutes from time when Steve Briere and Chinn tangled on the edge of the Flyers crease. The ensuing altercation resulted in both receiving double minors for roughing. With Briere sustaining a cut in the fracas, the Flyers took the opportunity to give Craig Arthur the last few minutes in goal. He saw plenty of action, before being beaten by a Ricky Plant slapshot in the closing seconds. This wrapped up the scoring and a disappointing season for the Flyers who had only the Caledonian Cup Final victory over the Stars to show for their efforts. In 30 road games that season they returned to Kirkcaldy on just five occasions with the two points.

Flames scoring: DeCosty (1+2), Plant (1+1), Clarke, Redmond, Chinn (1+0), Lyons (0+2), Lafreniere, Bowen, Galazzi (0+1)
Flyers scoring: Dailey, Morrison (1+0), Haig, Dutiaume, S King (0+1)
SOGs: Flames (Torchia) 21, Flyers (Briere 53, Arthur 4) 57
PIMs: Flames 8, Flyers 8.
Ref: Matt Thompson. Attendance: 1620

Net front action from an earlier Flames and Flyers game

Sunday March 17th 2013

ELITE ICE HOCKEY LEAGUE

Edinburgh Capitals 2 Fife Flyers 4

Flyers eventually banished their road blues after they had failed to win any of their previous 12 games. At the same time they put themselves into pole position to qualify for the play-offs with this huge win at Murrayfield.

The match was not only Flyers last away fixture of the league season it was also their last chance to prove they could win outside of Kirkcaldy ahead of the play-offs. It was one of their most committed and physical performances of the season and they were backed by a superb travelling support. The grit and determination shown by the team's imports was proof if anyone needed any that they were not quite ready to fly home for their summer vacations just yet.

With local players such as Stephen Gunn, Jamie Wilson and Tommy Muir also stepping up their game there was not a notable difference in productivity between imports and Brits. The three lines clicked perfectly and rolled like a dream all night. Even when Flyers lost a player late in the game they had depth on the bench to see them through.

Flyers forced the play from opening face-off with a physical forechecking game that saw them regularly steal puck possession from the Caps in their own half of the pad. Flyers took the lead at 5.05. Derek Keller's shot from the blue line bounced off Tomas Hiadlovsky's chest to the lurking Kris Hogg, who pounced on the rebound. Caps were no pushovers at home, however, and they came storming back to equalise following a neat move that eventually saw Richard Hartmann bundle the puck over the line.

Though Flyers second period must have ranked alongside one of their best periods of road hockey that season, they only managed one goal for their pressure. Josh 'Podge' Turnbull pounced during a stramash in front of Hiadlovksy's net. Having been the hero for his explosive fight with Patry the previous night, Jason Pitton then risked becoming Sunday's villain by stupidly getting himself thrown out of the game in the 43rd minute. He aggressively chased after referee Neil Wilson when he thought he had been unfairly dumped on his rear, and earned himself a Game Misconduct for abuse. When Capitals equalised just three minutes later through a Jade Portwood power play goal there was a real sense of foreboding of another self-inflicted road defeat.

Caps were beginning to build up a head of steam for the final 10 minutes when Flyers did to them what other teams had been doing to Flyers and they hit them with a sucker punch. Tommy Muir played a crucial part. After a spell of intense Caps pressure he could have easily iced the puck but he fought his way down the boards to the red line before sending the puck spinning round the boards. Casey Haines picked it up and spotted Bobby Chaumont in space at the back post where he played the perfect pass for the Flyers top marksman to shoot home.

There had been few more important goals this season and it gave Flyers their mojo back. When Turnbull cracked home a stunning wrist shot from just inside the point they had a crucial insurance goal going into the last seven minutes. After throwing away points at Dundee and Braehead the previous week there was no way they were going to let this one slip away.

Defenceman Jeff Caister reckoned the team answered its critics with the weekend win over the Caps, as the team had been subject to some heckles from sections of the support following their fourth defeat on the spin in Braehead. However the back-to-back wins had pushed Flyers back into position to qualify for the play-offs and provided a perfect response to any doubters in the stands. Caister said

"We don't mind the critics. Our fans are so passionate that when things go wrong they are going to let us hear it. We understand that there's pressure and responsibility with this team. We have the best fans in the league and we owe it to them to be the best we can."

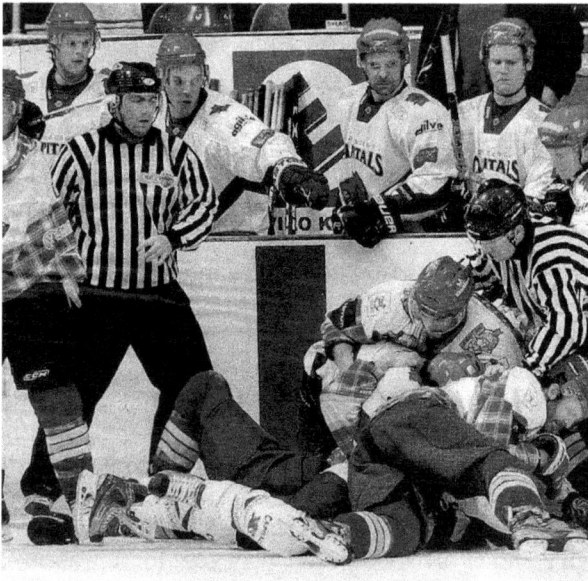

A good old fashioned rammy in the derby match with Capitals

Saturday March 18th 1972

Fife Flyers 3 Murrayfield Racers 9

Fife were competing in their first ever Icy Smith Cup final and were up against four-time winners Murrayfield Racers, who had enjoyed the better of things over their rivals in their last three meetings since the Flyers had beaten them back in November in the season's first encounter.

Flyers got off to a great start when Les Lovell beat Willie Clark with a low wrist shot in the first minute. Seconds later John Taylor had a great chance in front of the empty net but didn't quite get his shot away. Racers came more into the game and it was no surprise when Lawrie Lovell tied the scores just before the end of the first period.

For the opening six minutes of the middle frame the Flyers stayed in contention. Pat Hare put Racers in front; they responded when Norrie Boreham equalised 13 seconds later. Derek Reilly put Racers ahead once again, only for the Flyers to retort with another equaliser; this time Les Lovell netted within 40 seconds. That was to be the end of Flyers challenge, however, as defensive errors let in Derek Reilly for two more goals. Willie Kerr made it 6-3 by the second bell.

The final period was virtually one-way traffic towards Jim Taylor in the Flyers net. Again the Fife defence was suspect. Lawrie Lovell was left unmarked for an easy score. Derek Reilly underlined Racers superiority with two late goals to complete his nap hand.

Flyers hopes of winning the "Icy Smith" Cup for the first time had now virtually vanished, with the second leg on April 9 at Murrayfield, where Flyers had only won once in their last 10 visits. Though much of the blame for this defeat lay with the Flyers defence, one man completely exempt from criticism was the recently returned Joe McIntosh. The former coach worked ceaselessly to rally his mates, and thoroughly deserved his award for that week's Mirror of Merit award.

Ahead of the game Flyers were presented with a cheque for £217 which was a donation from Lees Limited, the well-known confectionery firm. The money would be used to pay for two new sets of jerseys which Flyers had ordered from Canada. The cheque was handed over by Mrs Lynn Sim, wife of Lees managing director Mr Drew Sim, and daughter of the company chairman Mr John T Lees.

As for the origins and name behind the Icy Smith Cup it was a knockout tournament originally contested from 1966 to 1982. The competition began in 1966, contested mostly by Northern League teams. In 1976 the Icy Smith Cup became the national British Championship award and saw teams from all leagues participate. Retroactively, the tournaments played between 1966 and 1975 were recognized as serving as the British Championship during that time period and the cup was last awarded to the British Championship winner in 1981.

John Frederick James Smith (1889-1965), known simply as "Icy", was a Durham businessman who would go on to become one of the forefathers of British ice hockey. Smith made his fortune running an ice business out of Bishop's Mill, selling blocks of ice to the public, most of whom didn't have a fridge. By the late 1930s, fridges had became more common. Icy's business was rendered far less profitable than it had once been.

He decided to move away from ice production but stuck with what he knew, devoting his time and money to the construction of an ice-rink on the bank of the River Wear. Full construction of the Riverside Rink was hampered by the lack of manpower during World War II, and so Icy made do with a massive marquee which, legend has it, was one of the largest in the world at the time. The new rink was hugely popular among locals and Canadian pilots alike.

After the War, Icy was finally able to construct a more permanent rink, famously using wood from coffins to construct the stands. In 1946 the Durham Wasps emerged, formed by an ex-Canadian airman, Michael Davey, and a handful of his countrymen who had made their home in Durham. The rest as they say was history.

Flyers being presented with a cheque from the confectionery company Lees Limited which helped them purchase two new sets of jerseys.

Thursday March 19th 1953

Fife Flyers 9 Dundee Tigers 1

At long last Flyers had done it. For the first time in the National League series they had broken away from the bottom of the league table, albeit only on goal average. Against the equally lowly Dundee Tigers, with whom they swapped places with in their final game of the season, they were in rampant form and the score might easily have been doubled.

There was little to enthuse over for the fans, as the visitors — without player-coach Red Kurz — were a weakened bunch, and never challenged the home sides lead. Apart from a bright spell in the first period, Dundee were on the receiving end throughout. The one-way traffic grew monotonous as the minutes ticked past.

In the end it became a Flyers race for double figures but the clock beat them to it. Once again, coach Bobby Burns was the inspiration in the Fife line-up. His two long-range counters were real opportunist efforts. Jimmy Smith, who had improved with every game, along with Ed Williams, formed a strong defence. Moe Zubatiuk was once again too impetuous, however, and against a better team his needless penalties would have proved costly.

Young Harry Pearson was only iced in the last ten minutes and had little chance to show his paces. Many thought coach Burns had erred. This surely was the perfect chance for the local lad to gain some invaluable experience in the senior team. With the outlook next season for three juniors in the line-up he was considered a certainty. Scotland's leading scorer Art Sullivan only had two real shots at goal, and those were easily dealt with by Harry McQueston in Fife's net.

Flyers started off well and Grant was a busy man in the opening minutes. Len Smigel opened the scoring from close range and Burns made it two with a slap shot from the right. The Fife captain again found the net seconds later with a similar shot from near the blue line.

Tigers did not take this reverse lying down and in their first real raid Len Hilton rounded off a good movement with a well-taken goal. For a spell after that the Tigers swarmed round McQueston but Burns and company soon turned the tide. Twice the post came to Tigers rescue before Bert Smith restored Flyers three-goal lead just before the end of the period.

After the resumption, following a long spell of pressure, Don Claydon increased Flyers lead. Bud Stock and then Smigel once more added to the score. When Tigers were penalised, Flyers went out for more goals but Claydon hooked the puck past when left in front of an empty cage. Dundee never, at any time in the second period, look like penetrating the Kirkcaldy defence.

With Flyers going all out for double figures it was a case of "shooting in" during the last session. But despite repeated attacks they failed and had to be content with nine: firstly, a second from Smith and near the end Smigel broke clean through to complete his hat-trick.

Flyers, Harry McQueston, Bobby Burns, Moe Zubatiuk, Jim Smith, Ed Williams, Bud Stock, Scotty Dowle, Don Claydon, Bert Smith, Marlowe McDonald, Len Smigel, Harry Pearson

Tigers, Don Grant, Bill Melville, Fred Ferens, Alf Krober, Jake Favel, Art Sullivan, Len Hilton, Lorne Goddard, Hal Moreland, Johnny Rolland

Key Referee – Nels McQuaig Linesman — S. Cameron

The 1952/53 season had been a struggle but there was some silverware — Airlie Trophy winners and Bob Burns and Harry McQueston sharing the Mirror of Merit award being presented by Les Lovell Snr. Burns had been awarded the accolade at the final home game when a recording device measured the volume of the crowd who cheered for either him or McQueston and so Burns with the highest recording tied the seasons votes.

Saturday March 20th 1982

Fife Flyers 22 Billingham Bombers 1

Both Flyers and their fans were disappointed to see that Billingham Bombers had arrived several men short for this Flyers home tournament match, with a number of young reserves filling in for first team regulars.

Matches against the Bombers that season had been reasonably close, especially in the two Northern League encounters Despite Flyers coming out with two wins they were restricted to scoring single figures and won each by a 3 and 4 goal margin.

The Flyers had also triumphed in the Bombers home tournament, the Cleveland Cup, the previous month when they won 11-5.

Jim Lynch opened the floodgates in the 37th second. From then on it was virtually a one-horse race. In total eleven different Fife players hit the target, with amazing regularity.

Lynch notched up his second in four minutes followed closely by Allan Anderson, Dougie Latto, Murray McLellan with a double and Richard Black. Black was making his first appearance with the senior squad after moving up from the Kirkcaldy Kestrels. He joined youngsters Gary Fyffe, who had made his debut two weeks ago against Ayr Bruins, and Gordon Goodsir, who had broken into the team earlier in the season.

Leading 7-0 at the end of the first period Flyers knocked in another eight goals to finish 15-0 up at the second interval.

Into the third period, and the second score-sheet; by now the Bombers had obviously become resigned to their fate. In the 42nd minute they decided that a token effort was better than none. Tony Burdon, assisted by Ian Noble, scored a consolation goal and toppled Andrew Donald in his shutout bid.

Flyers continued their relentless attack on the Billingham net. They managed to score an average of one goal every 171 seconds before they eventually called it a night at 22. It was the highest goals total for the Flyers at home since January 1977 when they had popped in 28 against the Paisley Mohawks. The spread of goals scored was; Jim Lynch (5), Allan Anderson (4), Chic Cottrell (3), Murray McLellan (2), Ake Alm (2) and Richard Black, Brian Peat, Gordon Goodsir, Dougie Latto, Kenny Cruden, Steven Kirk with one each.

With the formal competitions such as the Northern League, Autumn Cup and Scottish National League all completed the Flyers had spent the last few weeks playing challenge games and home tournaments to keep things ticking over before they were due to meet Murrayfield Racers in the semi finals of the Spring Cup a couple of weekends from now.

Flyers player-coach Ake Alm adds to the rout against the Bombers

Sunday March 21st 1965

Fife Flyers 4 Paisley Mohawks 6

For the second time in three seasons a West of Scotland team had won the Scottish Ice Hockey Championship.

Paisley Mohawks, who were winners in Section 'B' of the tournament, clinched the title that year when they beat the Flyers, who had been the top team in Section 'A', in a one off game at Kirkcaldy.

This end-to-end thriller was climaxed with four penalties being handed out in the last five minutes. One of those penalties banished Flyers top-scorer Jimmy Spence for the rest of the game and the other took out the ever-influential Bert Smith for two minutes.

Even in the closing minute-and-a-half, when both teams were playing a man short, the Flyers took the desperate step of withdrawing net minder Roy Reid and adding another forward, without success.

As far as Paisley were concerned their victory over Flyers meant more than simply taking the Scottish Championship Cup back to the West of Scotland, as it was the first time they had recorded a win over Flyers since January 1963. There was a measure of revenge in their victory also. Paisley had lost the title last year when they were beaten 6-3 by the Flyers at Kirkcaldy.

Jim McDougall in the Paisley net held the home forwards at bay during the first session, when they looked most dangerous. It was primarily due to his performance in the early stages that the Flyers were two goals down at the first interval.

Although Flyers had the edge during the opening exchanges it was Paisley who opened the scoring. Billy Miller snapped up a chance after Bill Crawford had pulled Reid out of position in the 12th minute. Two minutes later Jimmy Spence slipped neatly round John Milne to pick his spot high in the Paisley net. The visitors recovered with a great counter from Billy Brennan 30 seconds later. Tom Lemon, an ex-Paisley Pirate in the old professional days, made a come-back in this game and proved a constant danger to the home defence. Lemon was on the spot to assist in the Mohawks third goal from Miller.

Flyers exploded into action with two goals in 30 seconds at the start of the second period, but that was the final show of fire power from the

Kirkcaldy side until the closing stages of the game. Spence accepted an Ian Forbes pass and caught the Paisley defence napping in the third minute. Graeme Farrell put the Kirkcaldy side back on level terms from a Johnny Flynn assist.

Billy Miller, with his hat trick, restored the Paisley lead four minutes after the start of the final period before Crawford added a fifth goal in the sixth minute. 60 seconds later Milne scooped the puck away from Reid and picked his spot in the empty net as the Mohawks put clear daylight between themselves and the hosts.

Six minutes from the end Sammy McDonald soloed through to cut the leeway. Paisley claimed the goal should have been disallowed for a high stick. Spence and Roy Collins were banished for the rest of the game when a scuffle started between them a minute later and they were followed to the bench within 20 seconds by Bert Smith and Alastair Brennan.

The loss of these two top players effectively stopped any chance of a late Flyers recovery and they were left with the desperate move in vain of pulling Roy Reid out just before the final whistle.

The 'Goat' Danick Gauthier who spent three seasons with the club in the EIHL from 2017 to 2020

Saturday March 22nd 1986

Fife Flyers 11 Peterborough Pirates 3

Peterborough Pirates, in their second ever visit to Kirkcaldy, never looked capable of breaking their Premier League duck; the under-strength Flyers carried too much fire-power for the struggling English side. The Flyers were still without Bobby Haig and Dean Edmiston, who were both representing GB in the World Junior 'C" Pool Championships in France.

Todd Bidner and Danny Brown both grabbed four goals. Gordon Goodsir claimed a rare hat-trick. It was a case of one in and one out for the Flyers who were missing Neil Able again, with a twisted back. It was Bidner — back in action after completing a three-match suspension — who opened the scoring with a short-handed goal after eight minutes.

Although Pirates levelled within 60 seconds through Canadian John Lawless, Danny Brown then rattled home three goals inside four minutes to give Flyers a comfortable 4-1 lead. Alan Walker pulled one back for Peterborough after 17 minutes but Brown scored his own fourth and Flyers fifth just 30 seconds later. Gordon Goodsir then finished the period scoring with a fine solo goal to make it 6-2.

The second period threatened to turn into a non-event with Flyers always in command but unable to increase their lead until Bidner struck in the 26th and 32nd minutes to complete his hat-trick.

It seemed that the final period would be as non-productive as the second until Goodsir netted a power play goal after 50 minutes. Bidner put Flyers into double figures two minutes later before collecting a 10-minute penalty for spearing, after letting his temper get the better of him. Five minutes from the end Sean Sherman grabbed a third goal for the visitors. The last word of the evening went to Flyers with Goodsir completing his hat trick with an angled shot from the right wing.

The win meant that the Flyers were now finding their form at just the right stage of the season, with only one defeat in their last ten league outings. With a win the following night at Ayr they had given themselves every chance to claim fourth spot in the league heading into the play offs.

Looking to the longer term future though, the news wasn't quite as optimistic for the Flyers faithful, as the club revealed that Danny Brown would not be returning to the club for a third season. The popular Canadian had decided to retire from the sport to enter into a business career in his native Toronto.

Speaking after the weekend games he said "I have always planned to go back to Canada to start up a business. However, I would love to leave after another Wembley success and I think we can do it".

Inevitably it also sparked speculation about Flyers other two imports with Todd Bidner indicating that he would like to return to the club for a second term and unsurprisingly player-coach Ron Plumb commented "I am not discussing anything as far as what my future plans are until the season is over".

Dean Edmiston (left) and Gordon Goodsir who notched a hat trick against the Pirates

Saturday March 23rd 1974

Fife Flyers 10 Whitley Warriors 6

This match saw the completion of the preliminary rounds of the Skol Cup. The home side's win meant that the Flyers would meet the Murrayfield Racers at the Gallatown rink to contest the final in two weeks' time.

The Skol Cup or Skol Trophy, as the title seemed interchangeable, was the Flyers home rink tournament. Over the years it was played for under a variety of formats. The most usual was on the basis of playing a round of preliminary games against all opponents and the team that scored the best result against the Flyers would be invited to return to play in a Final match for the silverware.

In this case the Racers had been the only team to defeat the Flyers when they met the previous November and the final was expected to be a close and exciting tie with the Flyers in excellent recent form.

Indeed, the defeat for Warriors was only their third of the season and the first time they had lost double figures. To be fair, they had to travel to Kirkcaldy without five of their regulars, including the Matthews brothers.

Nevertheless, Flyers had won well; more importantly the result would give them a psychological edge for the following weekend's Spring Cup semi-final second-leg tie in England between the clubs.

The home side quickly got into their stride. After only 30 seconds had elapsed the Flyers found themselves a goal up when Chic Cottrell converted a pass by Jimmy Hunter. The only other goal of a disappointing first period came just before the bell when Lawrie Lovell scored to make it 2-0 for Flyers.

The visitors hit a real purple match in the middle period when they scored three times in 50 seconds with their goals coming from Alfie Miller, with a double, and Dave Taylor. Les Lovell soon grabbed the equaliser and Flyers play gradually improved. Ally Brennan steadied the team with some fine constructive passes out of defence and from one of them Lawrie Lovell skated in on goal and slipped the puck past Bob Gilbert to restore Flyers lead.

When goals from the Lovell brothers early in the third period increased the team's lead to 6-3, it looked as if the game was sealed but Warriors showed why they were Northern League Champions and never gave up the fight.

Miller completed his hat-trick and Taylor scored his second to bring the visitors to within one. As the match looked finely balanced the crucial next goal came from the Flyers, when Dave Medd kept them ahead by two at 7-5.

The final five minutes saw a spate of goals. A couple from the home side by Lawrie Lovell and Dougie Latto apparently easing any pressure that there might have been with just a two-goal lead.

The scoring wasn't over in this frame when the final 60 seconds brought two more goals to remind everyone that ice hockey wasn't labelled the fastest game in the world for nothing!

First Lawrie Lovell collected his fifth and his team's tenth goal. With just three seconds left Jim Pearson dispatched the puck into the corner of the net for Warriors sixth tally, nothing more than a consolation.

Although Lawrie Lovell notched five goals to prove he had completely recovered from a recent injury, the Mirror of Merit Award went to Ally Brennan, who was back at his best after a disappointing spell. As well as collecting four assists, he had steadied the team at a time when Warriors could have asserted themselves in the game.

Action against Paisley Mohawks from the 1973/74 season as Chic Cottrell scores

Saturday March 24th 1984

Fife Flyers 5 St Albert Thunderbirds 9

St Albert Thunderbirds, a Canadian team, taught Fife Flyers a few lessons as they opened their week-long British tour with a comfortable victory at Kirkcaldy Ice Rink.

The visitors, who had won their own league for the past three seasons, seemed to play well within themselves and were content to do enough to ensure they got off to a winning start.

Flyers opened the scoring after only 40 seconds when Chic Cottrell caught the Canadians cold, but the Thunderbirds quickly got into their stride and fired home three goals by the first buzzer.

Both teams could only manage a goal apiece in the second period but Thunderbirds stepped up a gear in the final spell and hit three goals in as many minutes to stretch their lead to 7-2.

The tourists then seemed to ease off which allowed the Flyers to find the net three times themselves to cut the deficit to just the two goals but St Albert made the victory safe with another pair to complete the scoring.

Scorers: Flyers — Gordon MacDougall (2), Chic Cottrell, John Maskiewich and Gordon Latto one each Thunderbirds — Schafers (3), Hunter, Labrie, Ferguson, McLaren, Paplawski and Wilkinson one each.

Although just a Challenge game the defeat to the Thunderbirds was now the Flyers sixth consecutive game without success. The following weekend it was to be make or break time for them, as they entertained the British Champions, Dundee Rockets, in a match they simply had to win if they were to retain any hope of making the end of season play-offs.

Hardly ideal timing; the Flyers would be without netminder Andy Donald and Gordon Goodsir who were both in Italy with the Great Britain squad at the World Under-20 Championships.

Donald, somewhat bizarrely, travelled with the squad as a non-playing member, having originally been picked for the squad only to be told that he was 10 days too old to be eligible for the tournament. The British team in Italy which was managed by Flyers team manager John Haig had lost both of their opening games going down 12-4 to Italy 'A' and 7-4 to Spain.

Despite it being a long shot, the Flyers did upset the odds by beating the Rockets, but their efforts ultimately fell short as they finished seventh and a place outside of the play off places.

The 1983–84 season, the second of the British Hockey League, saw the introduction of the Premier League and First Division format that would continue until the disbandment of the British Hockey League in 1996. Nine of the fifteen teams which had taken part the previous season joined the Premier League. That season also saw the reintroduction of the Autumn Cup and the first season of sponsorship by Heineken. Flyers had disappointed in the opening competition of the season as they finished bottom of their all-Scottish section of the Autumn Cup.

TONIGHTS MATCH

LUCKY No. 64

FIFE FLYERS
V
ST ALBERTS THUNDERBIRDS

ON SATURDAY 24TH MARCH 1984

SPONSORED BY:
I.C.C.S. (Nothern) Limited Incorporating
Bar-Tech Services Limited
457 Clepington Road, Dundee
Telephone (0382) 815660

ICCS

Match programme for the visit of the touring Thunderbirds, who were from St Albert in Alberta

Tuesday March 25th 1947

Fife Flyers 5 USA 4

The Flyers entertained the USA Amateur Hockey Association team who were touring the UK, following their participation in the Ice Hockey World Championships in Prague the month before. Those players who were unavoidably left behind on the continent had now caught up with the team. The visitors were noted as being at full strength for their match in Kirkcaldy.

Ten players would take the ice. Unfortunately, owing to lack of substitutes, the Americans had never had a fair chance to show their prowess so far in their games. It would be considered a feather in Flyers cap if they recorded a win against the full touring team which, when down South, defeated an English representative team and also created quite an impression while participating in Czechoslovakia.

Perhaps the newspaper headline of the game report tells it all, **MEDIOCRE FLYERS PIPPED TIRED YANKS**, There wasn't really an awful lot of credit in this narrow victory as the USA squad had clearly played far too much hockey in too short a time.

"Galloping Gus Galipeau" had received a great welcome from English sports-writers when the tourists landed down South and he was described as one of the "best defencemen ever seen here" by one writer. Against the Flyers he was slow in his rushes and indifferent in his passing. How could anyone blame him, however. Since he left his native shores about three months ago, he had played over forty games; this applied to the whole team.

Some of the Americans reckoned they had played a game every other night, and travelled 10,000 miles, since leaving the US. In spite of this, the Americans impressed many with their neat teamwork, fast skating and accurate shooting.

H.J. Rousseau was a speedy winger, who only used his speed in bursts, generally when it was most needed. "Red" Linton was a hard-to-hit centre. The biggest surprise of all was Kenny Darling, of Perth Panthers, who helped the tourists out with their manpower difficulties. So far this season Darling hadn't hit it off too well at Perth but he played a grand game in defence with "Galloping Gus". The two outstanding performers in the game, however, were John Meoli, the five foot two U.S.A. netminder, and Don Dougall the Flyers "in and out" netminder. Meoli had better protection than Dougall, but caught the eye with his nonchalant manner when stopping shots from all angles. He was cool and confident and was ever on the alert while Dougall touched top form again and was extremely steady under pressure.

Had it not been for him, the Flyers could possibly have been the first team in Scotland to fall to the tourists. Bud Scrutton was his usual self, being slippery as an eel and tricky as ever. His goal in the first period was a beauty when he dragged the puck past Meoli and flipped it into the corner of the net.

Earl McCrone, who was still suffering from a shoulder injury, played steadily enough while Floyd Snider and Frankie King caught the eye with individual rushes and Pat Ratchford tried hard both on the first line and when pivot to John Drummond and Bob Lantz. Flyers stars were Dougall, Snider, Scrutton, Ratchford and King, while the tourists got best service from Meoli, Darling, Galipeau, Rosseau, and Linton.

Goals: — First Period: Flyers — Snider (O'Connor) 4th min, Scrutton (Snider & McCrone) 16th min, U.S.A.- Darling 18th min, Second Period: Flyers — Snider (Scrutton) 24th min, U.S.A.- Darling (Heavern & Rosseau) 26th min, Third Period: Flyers — Drummond (Lantz) 45th min, King (Scrutton) 52nd min,

U.S.A — Heavern (Rosseau) 44th min, Savard (Darling) 55th min

Penalties — Londry and Kilmartin 29th min high sticks, Scrutton 38th min high sticks

Flyers, Don Dougall, Bob Londry, Floyd Snider, Jim McKenzie, Earl McCrone, Bud Scrutton, Harry O'Connor, Pat Ratchford, Bob Lantz, John Drummond.

USA, Johnny Meoli, Linton, Gus Galipeau, Robert Bingham, Hector Rosseau, Savard, Chris Ray, Gerald Kilmartin, Bob Heavern, Kenny Darling

Referees—D. Cumming and G. Horn

The first ever visiting team from the USA – Flyers had hosted two Canadian teams in their inaugural season.

Sunday March 26th 1995

Whitley Warriors 7 Fife Flyers 8

Fife finished their season with a 50% winning record in the League courtesy of this narrow victory in Whitley Bay. The visitors looked comfortable with a three goal lead going into the final minute but two goals from the home side threatened to rock the Flyers bandwagon. They held out grimly for the win.

The result cemented sixth spot in the final standings and meant they had now only suffered one defeat in their last nine outings. A six-goal middle-period performance by the visitors held the key in this traditionally tough fixture. This ultimately allowed Jim Lynch's men to lose their concentration, thankfully without losing the match late on.

Playing with passion from the first face-off, both teams did their best to make the supporters forget that there was nothing really at stake to play for, with the home side out of play-off qualification contention. Despite a number of early scares at both ends, Flyers netminder Bernie McCrone and Whitley shot-stopper Peter Graham, a 'favourite' of the Flyers support did their best to keep the score line blank.

When McCrone was eventually beaten at 14:08 it took something a bit controversial. When Steve Brown drove hard to the net he took the goalie completely out of action in the collision and left Dean Richards with a simple finish into the empty net. Despite Fife's protests referee George Nicholson allowed the goal to stand. Flyers hit back in the perfect manner with Mark Morrison tying the match up 18 seconds later with a dazzling display of stickhandling and a cracking finish.

Goals, which were in scarce supply during the opening 20 minutes, were provided aplenty in the second period. Warriors seized the initiative just over a minute in when Brown stabbed the puck home from close range. Fife fought back to level the scores when Man of the Match Steven Lynch tipped Laurie Boschman's pass through the netminder's pads at 22:11. Just 19 seconds later Flyers went 3-2 ahead when Doug Marsden's pass sent Craig Wilson in one-on-one against Graham and the young forward executed a smart dummy before knocking the puck in.

Whitley certainly weren't finished yet. They battled back into the game through an excellent individual goal from David Longstaff at 24:52. Last season's young British player-of-the-year mesmerized the static visiting defence with his stickhandling in the left corner and emerged untouched to ram his shot past McCrone.

The young players appeared to be taking over the game at this stage and it was one of Fife's most promising starlets, Lynch, who created another go-ahead goal for the visitors. He intercepted a pass outside the blue line then took on his marker with great confidence and laid the puck off in front of goal for NHL veteran Laurie Boschman to get the final touch at 27:02. Flyers hardly looked back for the rest of the period with Morrison accepting a gift of a loose pass out of defence to beat Graham at 29:32 before Steven King showed great strength to hold off his marker and convert Ally Reid's pass at 34:38.

Netminder Graham was getting wound up by the visiting crowd but looked to have silenced them with a classy glove save from Wilson's slap shot. Unfortunately his attempt to clear the puck hit off a defender's skate and skittered past the goalie and into the net for Wilson's easiest goal of the season at 36:30.

It took until just over seven minutes into the final period for Warriors to mount their comeback. Longstaff found the net at 47:05 and the game's only penalty was called two minutes later with a minor against Morrison for slashing which gave Whitley the chance to reduce the leeway further.

A tactics discussion during a time-out clearly worked with Longstaff netting his third to make the score 7-5 to Fife. The game appeared to be over when King and Smail broke out on a two-on-one following a period of sustained Whitley pressure with King getting the final touch at 58:53. But a smart finish from Brown at 59:08 and a lightning strike by Dean Richards with 15 seconds remaining added a bit of spice to the proceedings although Warriors had left it all too late.

Mark Morrison about to pull the trigger against the Warriors in an earlier match in October at Kirkcaldy

Sunday March 27th 1988

Murrayfield Racers 9 Fife Flyers 6

After a season of tremendous promise with Flyers chasing their first ever Heineken Premier League title the last eight days had been a bitter disappointment.

The previous weekend Fife crucially lost their two encounters against title rivals; Whitley Warriors at Kirkcaldy, then on the Sunday they went down to the Racers in Edinburgh. The league was gone, as was the chance to play in the European Cup the following season. It was a devastating weekend for the club and the fans.

The title was wrapped up 48 hours before this match. The Racers travelled to Dundee on the Friday night and recorded a win to finish two points better off than the second placed Warriors, and clinch the crown. It was a travel weary Flyers side that were eclipsed by their arch-rivals, who won their second piece of silverware in two nights when they lifted that season's Scottish Cup.

Flyers had secured third spot in the league with a win against the Solihull Barons in the Midlands the night before. That game had been delayed by an hour. The match officials were unable to get to the rink on time, as they were delayed by a car accident.

The squad headed North following the game, having managed less than three hours sleep at a Darlington hotel, before continuing their journey to Edinburgh, as the clocks were put forward one hour that Saturday night for British Summertime. Murrayfield realised that the Fife side would be tired and hit the visitors hard early on.

The Edinburgh side, not surprisingly, looked the sharper outfit from the start, despite losing a superb goal to Fife playmaker Steve Moria after three minutes. Racers took just two minutes to equalise with a power play goal from Tony Hand as the home side went 4-2 ahead by the first buzzer.

Racers continued to stay on top during the second period which they also won 4-2 before Flyers finally rallied in the third period. Al Sims scored a power play goal in the 49th minute and Moria scored Flyers sixth three minutes later to reduce the arrears to two goals but Mike Snell settled the tie with four minutes remaining.

Moria scored three goals during the televised match and was voted Flyers Man of the Match and there were other strikes from Fred Perlini and Ronnie Wood.

Mike Snell, with five goals for Racers, was the obvious vote for Murrayfield's Man of the Match. Stand-in coach Jim Lynch — who was in charge as Jackie Dryburgh was laid low with a virus — said his side were always up against it, with the match in Solihull the night before particularly when it started late.

Murrayfield, he added, had been able to switch their match with Dundee to the Friday night and that had been to their advantage. For Lynch, who was due to retire at the end of the season, his aim was to taste Wembley success with two different teams, having won there before with the Racers, and to do so they would have to qualify from their group with this weekend's two opponents. The games that season with Racers had been shared with four wins each, while against the Barons the Flyers had taken nine of 12 points.

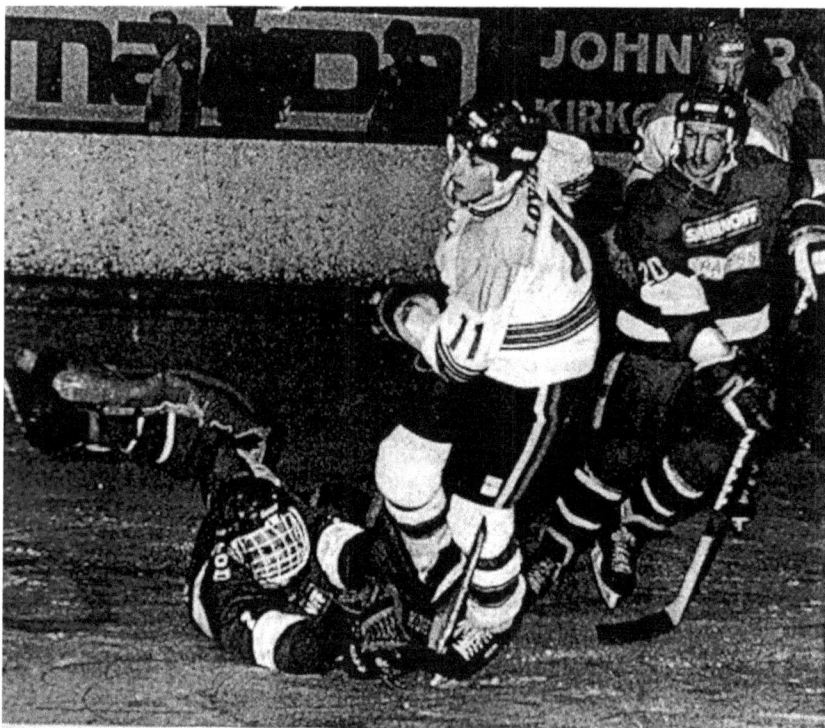

Lindsay Lovell denied by Racers keeper Andy McLeod

Saturday March 28th 1987

Cleveland Bombers 4 Fife Flyers 17

Despite a run of only four defeats in 20 league matches since the turn of the year — where crucially two of those were at the hands of arch rivals the Murrayfield Racers, who were on their way to the league title — the Flyers had to be content with getting themselves ready for another assault on the Wembley weekend.

This was their penultimate league match of the season. Their final road trip was against a Bombers team who were firmly rooted at the foot of the table, with just three wins to their name all season.

Fife's last visit to the Forum Ice rink back in January had yielded two points for the visitors, but only by a margin of two goals in an 8-6 win. It wasn't ever going to be as close in this encounter. The Bombers never recovered from an early Dave Stoyanovich hat trick which helped the Flyers to a 4-1 head inside the opening 10 minutes.

With the usually dependable Chris Newton having a nightmare match in the home net, the heart quickly went out of the Bombers during the second period. They trailed 6-2 at the end of the first then 11-4 by the second buzzer.

The match is remembered however for a piece of Flyers history. Playmaker extraordinaire Steve Moria excelled himself by being involved in all but four of the Flyers goals. 13 assists in the game (no goals incidentally) still stands (at the time of publication) as a Flyers record for most assists in a single match.

The Flyers added a further half dozen in the final period with Bobby Haig netting a hat trick. Stoyanovich was involved in all but two of the Flyers goals as he registered 15 points with 8 goals and 7 assists. This was only good enough to equal his own club points record in a single game (13+2 v Southampton Vikings in December 1984) with that performance. That number would later be surpassed by Mike Jeffrey who scored 20 points in a game in December that year. Again (at the time of going to press) that feat against Glasgow remains a record for points scored in a single game

Al Sims also had a hat trick, with singles from Neil Abel, Charlie Kinmond and Andy Linton. Linton had returned from the horrific injury he sustained at home against Murrayfield Racers in the Norwich Union Cup win, when he was hit in the face by an Al Sims slapshot as he stood at the top of the crease – the puck going into the net. All the more remarkable as he had lost the sight in his left eye as a result of the incident.

Moria had recorded 91 helpers in only 21 games and with 53 goals it was a points-to-games ratio that would have placed him second in the league to only Rick Fera. As it was Fera and Tony Hand stood atop the scoring charts with Dave Stoyanovich third ahead of Panthers Fred Perlini, Moria lay 7th with Al Sims in 9th spot. The Flyers finished third in the standings and their road to the Wembley final was through the group qualification with the second-placed and sixth-placed Dundee Rockets and Ayr Bruins respectively.

The record breaking Steve Moria – the original 'Mo'

Thursday March 29th 2007

Dundee Stars 2 Fife Flyers 6

Player-coach Todd Dutiaume led by example as the Flyers shot down the Stars to win their third ice hockey trophy that season and keep their back-to-back Grand Slam hopes alive.

The razor-sharp Canadian fired a double in the second-leg win after the previous Sunday's 5-5 draw.

Flyers — forced to play both legs at Dundee Ice Arena because of the recent fire at the Fife Ice Arena — coasted to victory thanks to a five-goal burst in a penalty-filled game with both teams recording 40 minutes each.

The visitors went into the pressure clash minus experienced duo Derek and Steven King, owing to work commitments. The Flyers who had gone through a 90-minute training session at Murrayfield on Tuesday night admitted through assistant coach Martin Grubb that "the pressure was on".

Dundee, who outshot the visitors 43-40, were first to score when John Dolan fired the home side ahead on the power play after 94 seconds; the Flyers were back on level terms just over two minutes later when Dutiaume netted.

The Flyers then fired five straight goals between the 15th and 33rd minutes. Dutiaume doubled his tally with a short-handed strike to put Flyers ahead and Chris Wands put the Kirkcaldy club 3-1 in front with a power play strike 41 seconds into the middle period.

Worse was to come for the home side. Jamie Wilson scored in the 22nd minute. Skipper John Haig then netted number five with 30 minutes on the clock. Wands scored his second on the power play after 33 minutes. The scoring was competed when Dolan netted his second for what was only a consolation for the Stars in the 50th minute.

The pair were scheduled to clash head-on again in the semi-final of the Northern League play-offs the following week and Stars coach Roger Hunt said,

> "We'll have to lift the guys but I'm proud of what they did in the first game when we held them 5-5. They are a class outfit and their quality players rose to the top tonight. We were right in the game at

the end of the first period with the score line at 2-1 but that second period when they scored four goals in 15 shots killed us and we'll have to re-group and be ready for them."

Flyers had already won the Scottish National League and the Northern League titles and it was their 8th game against the Stars that season without defeat. That all ended the following week when Stars savoured their first win over the Flyers in almost 18 months and took the semi-final tie 7-4 in what was one of only two defeats suffered in 55 games played — enough to deny them their back to back Grand Slam aspirations.

Flyers match programme as they add the Autumn Cup to the trophy cabinet as they went for back to back Grand Slams

Monday March 30th 1998

Fife Flyers 10 Latto's Legends 10

They came in their droves to salute a sporting legend — regular Flyers fans, ice hockey enthusiasts from other clubs and many who had been tempted back into the old rink after several years simply because they could not miss the chance to pay tribute to everyone's favourite player — Gordon Latto.

The ice arena was packed to the seams for the celebration of Gordon's staggering 25-year career in senior hockey. The turnout only emphasised the high regard he was held in by all of those who followed the sport.

A star-studded collection — of former team mates and opponents, NHL stars and top Superleague talent — gathered to form the "Latto's Legends" including the reappearance in Kirkcaldy of great names from Flyers past like Doug Smail, Laurie Boschman and Cal Brown.

The match against the current Flyers team kept the huge crowd thoroughly entertained and the final result of 10-10 was irrelevant; what mattered was that the curtain was brought down on Gordon's career in glittering style.

The fans were able once again to admire the skills of Smail, Boschman, Tony Hand and John Lawless alongside the likes of Hilton Ruggles and Jim Lynch. There were former Flyers Iain Robertson, Bobby Haig and Jimmy Pennycook and even a veteran line of Dougie Latto, Charlie Kinmond and Allan 'Bean' Anderson.

Gordon hit a hat-trick in the game. Smail astonished everyone with his incredible accuracy in the 'Slapshot Challenge'. Veteran Flyers were introduced to great applause. At the end each player was presented with a special certificate from the star of the night to mark their appearance at a poignant but memorable moment in the club's history.

There was an air of nostalgia, but also one of fun and delight, as Gordon himself smiled his way through the entire night's proceedings and the crowd smiled with him.

Even when it came time for him to hang his famous number 16 strip on a coat-hanger, dangling from a wire, and watch it slowly make its way up into the rafters, he did so with a style and grace that was symbolic of the way he had conducted himself both on and off the ice for all those years.

It was a night of high emotion. The feeling that what we were all witnessing was the end of an era only added to the poignancy of the occasion. Everyone there was part of something that may never be repeated. John Waring, Flyers director and member of the organising committee, described the night's events and the reaction from the crowd as "over-whelming" and few could disagree.

Mementoes were presented to Gordon from the BIHA and SIHA, and he became only the third person to receive an Ahearne Medal – named after the former president of the association and awarded to those who had made an outstanding contribution to the sport in this country.

Long after the presentations were over his famous number 16 still hangs in the rafters as a permanent reminder of his achievements.

For anyone who was keeping count then the night's statistics were as follows:

Period scores: 2-2, 1-4, 7-4.

Legends scorers: Gordon Latto 3+1, Doug Smail 2+2, John Iredale 2+0, Laurie Boschman 1+2, Dean Edmiston 1+0, Bobby Brown 1+0, Tony Hand 0+3, John Lawless 0+2, Iain Robertson 0+1, Bobby Haig 0+1, Neil Abel 0+1, Hilton Ruggles 0+1, Jim Lynch 0+1, Scott Neil 0+1, Paul Pentland 0+1.

Flyers scorers: Frank Morris 2+1, Mark Morrison 1+3, Daryl Venters 1+2, Wayne Maxwell 1+2, Andy Finlay 1+1, Bill Moody 1+1, Andy Samuel 1+0, John Haig 1+0, Lee Cowmeadow 1+0, Steven King 0+3, David Smith 0+1.

Shots on goal: Legends (O'Connor 28, Grubb 22) 50; Flyers (McCrone 25, Hamilton 27) 52.

Penalty minutes: Legends 0, Flyers 0.

Referees: Alex McWilliam, Keith Simpson, Moray Hanson.

Attendance : Full House.

Gordon and Doug Smail during the after-match presentations

Tuesday March 31st 1981

Fife Flyers 5 Don Mills Comets 11

Kirkcaldy ice hockey fans saw the good and the bad sides to the sport, when Canadian touring team Don Mills Comets were the guests of Fife Flyers.

On the positive side spectators witnessed the speed skill and superb stick work of the Comets, which Flyers simply could not match. Without a hat trick by guest player Alex Dampier of Murrayfield Racers, Flyers would have been on the wrong end of a much heavier defeat.

But surely to the detriment of the sport particularly as this was a challenge match were the outbreaks of violence. The Comets certainly were no angels and showed that they were well versed in the cruder aspects of the game. The Flyers in turn showed no great hospitality to their guests and involved Brian Peat in two incidents which might have seen him locked up if they had taken place in the street.

Ice hockey, as we know, is a contact sport, but there was no excuse for a second period flash point when Peat and Sims of Comets got to grips with each other on the ice for fully 30 seconds before the referees could separate them.

The pugilistic instincts were obviously aroused in the fans. One of them quipped "they could nae separate them; that was terrific". Both players picked up five-minute penalties for the episode, but Peat was again guilty in the final period when he landed a left hook squarely on Jim Prosser, who would have retaliated but for the intervention of a match official.

Peat's punishment was a paltry two minutes in the cooler. He was a lucky man. Comets Dave Wilson and Chris Kelland, who was Flyers other Murrayfield guest, were later given match penalties for another session of close combat on the ice.

These events overshadowed what had been a reasonably entertaining evening with Comets displaying their skills. Flyers, who seemed to be in awe of their opponents in the first period, were two goals down in less than 50 seconds when Garland and King inflicted the damage.

The home side pulled one back a minute later through Jim Lynch before Green made it 3-1. Flyers scored again through Jimmy Jack following a defensive mistake but Dave Wilson took the period score to

4-2. Comets seemed to let up in the second period but increased their lead through Bruce Sims. Guest star Alex Dampier struck twice for Flyers but in between Sims had countered for the visitors and King took the score to 7-4 at the end of the middle period.

The Canadians displayed their full repertoire of skills in the final period, scoring through Kosswan, Mitchell, Collier and Howard in the first seven minutes with Dampier completing his hat trick for Flyers five minutes from time. The match saw the final appearance of Flyers Canadian Steve Crummey before he returned home and he was given a rousing send off by the fans.

Nº 5546

KIRKCALDY ICE RINK

presents

FIFE FLYERS

VERSUS

DON MILLS
COMETS
●
TUESDAY
31st MARCH, 1981

Face-off 8.00 p.m.　　Programme 15p

Flyers match night programme for their "challenge" match against their Canadian visitors

Joe Watkins is under pressure from Slough Jets Joe Stefan in the 1999 BNL Play Off Final

April

Action from season 2021-22 as the Flyers celebrate a goal against the Manchester Storm

Sunday April 1st 2018

Manchester Storm 1 Fife Flyers 5 (after overtime)

In a season often defined by the team's never-say-die spirit, this match saw the Flyers produce undoubtedly the bravest comeback of them all.

This was no 'April Fool' but more of an Easter miracle in Altrincham. Fife Flyers came back from the dead to book their place in the Elite League Play-Offs the following weekend at Nottingham.

Less than 24 hours earlier it had all gone wrong for the Flyers, as they succumbed at the Fife Ice Arena. Not just another defeat, their fourth in five games against the Storm this season, but a seemingly terminal 4-1 reversal.

The odds were heavily stacked against them as they and an army of hundreds of fans travelled south. However, in a heroic performance, Flyers fought back with a 4-1 victory of their own to take the tie into overtime, where Carlo Finucci struck an unforgettable winner greeted by a wall of noise from the ecstatic travelling support.

In stark contrast to how the match finished the previous night, with Storm players swaggering as they left the ice, the ice was littered with stunned Storm players, many lying flat out in abject despair of what had just happened.

It was hugely important that the Flyers got a positive start to plant seeds of doubt, to take the home crowd out of it, and to give themselves a platform to build on. With the help of the travelling masses that's exactly what they got, as Danick Gauthier opened their account in the fourth minute, a lead they held until the first break.

Head coach Todd Dutiaume had picked his team up off the floor the previous night and set them a target of winning each period in the second leg. Part one was accomplished, and part two followed in period two as Carlo Finucci reduced the deficit further just 74 seconds after the restart, before a Jim Jorgensen power play strike in the 31st minute brought the score to 0-3, and the teams were level on aggregate.

In what could have been an almighty momentum changer Storm pulled one back and reclaimed a one-goal advantage on aggregate through the EIHL's top scorer Mike Hammond. There was clearly a strong belief amongst the road team as they set about completing mission improbable in period three. With another man advantage, Liam Heelis put the visitors 4-1 ahead in the 46th minute, dragging them level on aggregate once again.

Despite referees Neil Wilson and Stefan Hogarth becoming heavily involved in the closing stages, with Flyers forced to defend back-to-back minor penalties, the visitors held firm to force overtime. Simply getting to that stage was an achievement. Glory, or heartbreak, were the only options now.

The atmosphere in the Storm Shelter was immense, nerve ends were every bit as raw as the voices in the stands who willed their respective clubs to grab the next goal. In hindsight it's easy to say, but genuinely at the time amongst the maelstrom of emotion there was a calm and somewhat inevitable outcome expected.

It arrived just 47 seconds into sudden death with a goal that will live long in the memories of all those who were there that night. Scored at the end of the rink where the travelling support were located, the stand erupted as Carlo Finucci's solo dash and back hand ended up nestling in the back of the net. The Flyers were on their way back to "Scottingham" for the third time in five years.

The Flyers bench clears as they rush to mob overtime hero Carlo Finucci

Sunday April 2nd 1967

Fife Flyers 1 Paisley Mohawks 5

Three goals in the last ten minutes by Paisley Mohawks gave them a rather flattering victory over Fife in a match where the home side, for most of the game, had held the table-topping Mohawks to a single goal lead.

It was the final home match for Flyers. There was no mistaking, over the course of the evening, who were the better team. The Paisley side finally made the points safe on their way to an eventual title win. Flyers fought hard through-out, sometimes they just fought, and the players put in a grand effort as the team finished in sixth spot.

The 1966-67 Northern Ice Hockey Association season was the first season of the Northern League, the top level ice hockey league in northern England and Scotland. Nine teams participated in the league. The league was officially known as the Scottish League for this one season and saw its schedule left uncompleted.

The man mainly responsible for keeping the margin of defeat down was net-minder Roy Reid. He brought off some daring saves time and again when under constant pressure and could not be faulted for any of the goals.

Player-coach Joe McIntosh also played a big part in Flyers rear guard, working hard to relieve the strain and get the attack going. The main stars in what was a relatively poor front line were Norrie Boreham and Les Lovell. Les was able to work his way through Mohawks defence with ease and came close on a number of occasions.

Flyers other attack formation had a quiet time with only Ian Shields making any impression at all. Fast earning himself a reputation of a player who would stand no nonsense was Kenny Horne, who was penalised twice for getting involved in fights.

Flyers started the game well and were clearly looking to improve on their recent dismal record against the West of Scotland side. They had lost all three previous league games and their only victory was in the Television Trophy when they came out winners by the odd goal in three before going on to win the competition.

They opened the scoring in nine minutes when Pep Young picked up a pass out of defence from Joe McIntosh and slipped it to Norrie Boreham who, flying down the left wing, picked up the puck and netted brilliantly. The visitors however regained their composure and after some continuous pressure Dave Ferguson equalised.

Unfortunately for Flyers with three minutes to go in the first period Ally Brennan put the visitors into the lead with the Flyers defence bunched in front of goal trying to protect Reid.

Following an evenly contested, but goalless, middle period it was Brennan again who netted the next goal. He caught Flyers defence covering play at one post, picked up a pass at the back post and edged it into the almost empty goal as the defenders couldn't react in time.

Mohawks fourth goal was hotly disputed by Flyers when Billy Miller netted from close in. Home protests that he had used his hand to score instead of his stick faell on deaf ears. With only seconds left Dave Ferguson made it five.

Flyers – Roy Reid, Bill Brown, Joe McIntosh, Dave Medd, Kenny Horne, Pep Young, Les Lovell, Bert Smith, Jimmy Watson, Norrie Boreham, John Taylor, Ian Shields, Danny Brown

Mohawks – Billy Laird, John Milne, Tom Reid, Ally Brennan, Billy Dempsey, Alistair McCrae, Billy Miller, Dave Ferguson, Joe Conway, Jackson McBride, Bill Crawford, Billy Brennan, Roy Collins

Ref – Mr T Watt.

Before the match the annual Fife Free Press award to their player of the year, the Mirror of Merit, was presented. The recipient was Bert Smith who received the trophy from the sports editor Sandy Beveridge.

Tuesday April 3rd 2001

Fife Flyers 7 Mighty Mo's 7

It was a night for fun and frolics at the rink as many of the biggest names in British ice hockey united to pay tribute to Fife Flyers long-serving player coach Mark Morrison.

As Testimonial matches go this one, surprisingly, had some outstanding hockey played with quality goals. Of course, there was a rink full of pranks and tomfoolery, and a whole load of family entertainment. Almost every seat in Fife Ice Arena was filled, which was a measure of the esteem of the man and his incalculable contribution to the Flyers during his eight years at the club.

The Mighty Mo's team read like a Who's Who of ice hockey, including the much-loved Gordon Latto, "Mr Fife Flyers" and the not so much-loved, in this parish at least, Tony Hand who re-wrote the record books and is still regarded as the best hockey player Britain has ever produced.

It could have been expected that the Flyers would be given a bit of a "showing up". This was not the case as they put up a good fight and dominated the early stages of the game. The fun element of the night was highlighted when Flyers captain, Frank Morris, received a two-minute penalty for wearing a silly helmet, and an impressive goal scored by Todd Dutiaume was disallowed because he skated too fast.

Todd and his younger brother Mark, who iced for the Mighty Mo's, were each sent off for two minutes for swapping jerseys amid an amusing scuffle which delighted the crowd.

In the final few minutes of the game, by which time the score line was totally irrelevant, all the players from both teams took to the ice and chaos took over to the tune of a Scottish reel. The final score probably should have read 7-6 to the Mighty Mo's, but there was the puck that was sneaked into the net by Flyers when around 40 people were on the ice.

The outcome was of course totally irrelevant but for those who were counting the game stats were:

Flyers: Iain Robertson 2+0, Russell Monteith 2+0, Dean Edmiston 1+1, Gary Wishart 1+0, Todd Dutiaume 1+0, Steven King 0+2, Craig Nelson 0+1, Andy Samuel 0+1.

Mighty Mo's: Paul Morrison 2+0, Mark Dutiaume 1+2, John Haig 1+2, Doug Marsden 1+1, Tony Hand 1+0, Paul Hand 1+0, Steven Lynch 0+2, Bill Moody 0+1, Ally Reid 0+1, Mark Slater 0+1, David Smith 1 assist.

The Officials were McWilliam, Craig and Smith.

On what had been an emotional night a rather bleary-eyed Mark said post-match

> "I thought it was outstanding and I would like to say a huge thank you to the committee who organised the event and all the others in the background who did a tremendous job. The turnout was brilliant, but there again I didn't expect anything different from the people who have always supported me. After being here for eight years it's obvious I wasn't here just for the hockey and I have made many good friends. The game itself was a lot of fun and everyone in the Mo's enjoyed themselves. A lot of these guys took a night out of important schedules to be here and some travelled a long way which I was very grateful for."

Mark would continue his hockey career with the Flyers for another four seasons before leaving them after the 2004-05 season. His career totals stand at 562 games played, scoring 516 goals and 593 assists for 1109 total points. As well as presiding over a number of trophy wins, including a Grand Slam season, he was also voted Coach of the Year on three occasions, to match the feat achieved by Al Rogers in the post-war years.

The Mighty Mo's post-game photo call

Monday April 4th 1949

Falkirk Lions 4 Fife Flyers 2

The Flyers travelled to Falkirk still looking for their first win in that season's Scottish Cup competition.

In what was a hard-fought game in which the Lions allowed Flyers to get a lead of two goals in a dull opening period it looked as though the men from Fife would crack that particular nut.

The Lions were accused in recent games of being slow to come out of the gate and that was the case once more. Although they had most of the pressure in the opening session, the Flyers played a canny road game and were content to lay back and wait for any breaks which came their way.

A significant factor in the home team's resurgence in the match however were the penalties given away by the visitors which took a heavy toll of their energy. In the end the Lions were worthy winners as they battled for top spot in the standings.

When Pat Casey got going in the second period, he had the Flyers defence completely outwitted with his superb stickhandling. It was said at the time that people would be hard pushed to name a more accomplished stickhandler on the circuit than that Casey brother.

In the opening period however it was all about the opportunist play from Fife. After defending for most of the period Flyers scored in the 12th minute. Bert Smith poked the puck home after a Chic Mann shot had hit the post. Five minutes later and wee Bert struck again with Mann picking up the assist.

It looked as if the Lions were going to be "robbed" of the points because the Kirkcaldy line-up had defended for 90 per cent of the time and scored two goals in the other 10 per cent.

At the start of the second period the home side set about reducing arrears. But for the brilliance of Pete Belanger in the Fife net, Lions would have overwhelmed Flyers during the middle session.

Lions went into all-out attack but stubborn defending initially kept them out. When Verne Greger was penalised however, Lions got through for two goals within a minute to square matters, Phil Casey and Ken Nicholson were the scorers.

Lions kept at it in the final frame and in six minutes Phil Casey put them into the lead. Flyers tried hard for the equaliser but three minutes from time Pat Casey scored to give Lions what was a comfortable win.

For Flyers, with Scrutton and Mann marked men and penalties weakening an unsteady line-up they had a hard time holding on to their opening period lead. Despite the fact that the Falkirk fans undoubtedly 'helped' Flyers find their way regularly to the penalty box the Kirkcaldy team were most definitely second placed to the Lions play making. Perhaps if the Flyers had not tried to make sure of increasing their advantage they might have taken something from the match by continuing to frustrate the home team. Playing open and attacking hockey Fife met nothing but penalties and power plays, which tied the score at the end of the second session. In the third the Flyers were still taking the heavy end of the whistle as the game "toughened" up. Best in the Fife line-up were Smith in attack, 'Pete' Belanger in goal and Greger in defence.

In more favourable news, reported in the *Kirkcaldy Times*, just 24 hours after the Falkirk game coach Al Rogers was confirmed as putting pen to paper as he committed himself to the Flyers for a fourth successive season. There had been great competition for the services of the distinguished coach who for the last three seasons had been unanimously voted as Coach of the Year in Scotland

Glen Robertson presents Kyle Horne with the Flyers award for 1996/97 Rookie of the Year

Saturday April 5th 2014

Elite Ice Hockey League Play Off Semi Final

Nottingham National Ice Centre

Fife Flyers 0 Belfast Giants 1

This was the Flyers first visit to the EIHL Play Off Final weekend at Nottingham.

In what was the opening game of the weekend it was intense, physically and mentally draining, and utterly absorbing. One goal was the cruel, heart-breaking difference between success and defeat. Flyers did nothing wrong, apart from not score, for 60 minutes. They stuck rigidly to the game plan where focus and discipline were qualities that took the League Champions, Belfast Giants, to the absolute wire.

A scoreless opening period was perfect for Fife. At the end of period two it was still 0-0 – the Flyers were on track to spring the surprise of the weekend.

At 47:12 Kevin Saurette fired from the right point and the puck flew through traffic and found the net. One shot. One goal. One huge result.

Flyers made the best possible start when Fulton drove the net inside 10 seconds as Fife moved quickly into their game plan. Giants made sure dangermen Ned Lukacevic and Jordan Fulton were closely patrolled and Kevin Regan was playing as he needed to between the pipes.

The game flowed back and forth with few stoppages and at 10:20 Colin Shields found himself at the back door, but his one-time shot was poor. At 13:46 David Phillips caught Bobby Chaumont with a high hit which left the Flyer slightly dazed and the Giant took 2+10 for checking to the head. Flyers couldn't cash in and the period ended in a 0-0 stalemate.

Flyers started the second period as they did the first with some early attacks – Fulton shooting narrowly past, Matt Reber tried his luck with a wrist shot and Stephen Gunn saw his effort turned high into the back nets. The Flyers then had a power play chance but Regan had to bale his side out as Dustin Whitecotton and Jeff Szwez charged down on his goal.

Into the third and net minder Stephen Murphy kept out Roehl before Belfast finally cracked the deadlock. Back came Flyers as the tireless Danny Stewart buzzed round the Giants zone, Darryl Lloyd got the gate for an uncontrolled elbow mid-ice at 51:49 and Fulton's great set up for Reber was matched only by the save by Murphy, Flyers fans had seen those game winning saves before. Fife continued to drive on in pursuit of the equaliser, the chances that were fashioned landed just inches the wrong side of the posts. With 1:44 to play Cody Brookwell took a penalty and Fife, after calling a timeout, pulled Regan when they gained control of the puck.

It was heart-stopping stuff. Giants saw one puck fired down the ice slide inches wide of the empty net, but Fife re-grouped and bodies flew across the goal in the hope of a tip or touch to get the goal that would force overtime.

The final seconds were incredible to watch as Flyers laid siege to Belfast's goal. Amid the intensity, Murphy remained calm, tracking the puck round his net and crease. The clock finally wound down on the game and a stunning two-month run of amazing and inspirational victories that propelled Fife into the finals.

As much as there was pain in defeat there was also immense pride in the performance levels across the team. Flyers main threats were in the main shackled by Giants but still they created chances, which on another night might just have delivered. The record books show a 1-0 defeat, a rare score in ice hockey, and an indication of just how close the Flyers pushed the runaway champs — who themselves were beaten in sudden death overtime 24 hours later by the Sheffield Steelers in the final.

The coolest head on the ice, Stephen Murphy, denies Bobby Chaumont on the way to his shut out.

Sunday April 6th 1980

Fife Flyers 3 Tarnby (Denmark) 3

As the season was drawing to a conclusion, the Flyers, who had finished in a mid-table position in the Northern League, had not had a competitive match now for over a month.

Other than the challenge match against the Old Timers side, the UK Grousebeaters, their last competitive game had been when they had defeated Whitley Bay in the Icy Smith cup to advance to the semi-final meeting with the Autumn Cup and runaway league winning Murrayfield Racers.

Having been completely inactive during the past two weekends the Flyers were in need of some game time with the tie against Racers still two weeks away. They returned to the fray with a draw and a victory against overseas touring opposition. The previous night they faced the Vancouver Eagles and clinched a 9-6 victory in a high scoring match.

It was a pleasing result for Flyers who had been out of action at home because of a lack of available ice time with an Old Timers tournament taking place. There were hat tricks for both Chic Cottrell and Rab Petrie against the side from British Columbia with a double from Gordon Latto and also one from Jimmy Jack.

The following day they met Tarnby Ice Hockey Club from Denmark who had played the previous night against the Glasgow Dynamos at Crossmyloof and had been walloped 11-3. Taking their name from the town in which they were based, Tarnby had played one season in the Danish top league a decade before.

Since then they had been a fixture in Division Two. It proved to be a much closer fought match with Flyers goals coming from Chic Cottrell, Jimmy Jack and Gordon Latto. Four years later, Tarnby would be no more, as they merged with Tre Falke to form Tarnfalkene. The team lasted one season in the top league before dropping out and ceasing to exist.

Another notable event across the weekend was the inaugural Eddie Haggerty Memorial Cup competition. It saw Kirkcaldy Kestrels hit top form to become the first winners of the Trophy. Six teams took part in the tournament in memory of Eddie Haggerty, an up and coming hockey player who tragically died in a car accident the previous year.

Eddie had been a regular Kestrels player. He had made a scoring debut for the Flyers against Durham in December last year, a week before he was involved in the terrible accident. Fittingly it was the home team who clinched the trophy.

Kestrels faced Glasgow Redwings and Aviemore in section one of the tournament. They narrowly defeated Redwings 3-2 but had a more comfortable 5-2 victory over Aviemore to go through to the final where they met the winners of section two, Ayr Rangers, and went on to win 5-2. The full results were as follows:

Section 1 — Glasgow Redwings 6 Aviemore 2: Glasgow Redwings 2 Kirkcaldy Kestrels 3: Aviemore 2 Kirkcaldy Kestrels 5

Section 2 — Ayr Rangers 4 Irvine 1; Ayr Rangers 1 Murrayfield Raiders 1: Irvine 2 Murrayfield Raiders 2

Final — Kirkcaldy Kestrels 5 Ayr Rangers 2

Captain Derek King parades the Scottish League trophy in 1997 with Andy Samuel and Richard Danskin

Friday April 7th 2000

Fife Flyers 2 Basingstoke Bison 1

The Flyers had forged ahead by two games to nil in the best-of-five British National League Play Off series against the Bison, having won home and away the previous weekend.

Two of the final three games would be played at Kirkcaldy. The Flyers wanted to avoid another energy-sapping road trip south by winning this one and sweeping the series. 2500 packed the rink with the face off delayed by the late arrival of referee Graham Horner.

The delay perhaps impacted the visitors more as it was the Flyers who came out and seized the initiative with the opening goal with a little over three minutes on the clock. With Danny Meyers sitting a holding penalty, Russell Monteith did what 'Monty' does: putting the puck behind Watkins, his final man advantage tally as he set a new club record of 38 power play goals in a season. The visitors had most of the first period pressure and Stephen Murphy, as he had done the previous Sunday on the road, faced a barrage of shots from the Bison. He looked unfazed by the occasion and performed heroics, making one incredible double save to deny Tony Redmond and Wayne "Reggie" Crawford. The early goal was all that separated the sides at the first interval.

The second period was very much like the first. Bison had plenty of the puck and shots through at Murphy. Fife were content to play a fast counter attacking game, almost as though they were playing the way of a road team. Midway through the period Todd Dutiaume stripped Jeff Daniels of the puck and charged down the ice on a breakaway before clearly being pulled down by Rick Strachan. A certain penalty shot? Horner ordered Strachan to the box for a two minute minor, much to the chagrin of the home fans.

The Monteith goal still separated the teams. The third was barely two minutes old when some tape was discovered to be protruding through the ice. Horner, as he had done on a previous visit, spent 25 minutes trying to fix the issue with the teams returning to the dressing room. The Zamboni and fire extinguishers were deployed to try to repair the defect and the crowd grew ever restless. The solution was that Mark Morrison swapped ends so the Flyers were defending the 'bad ice' end just to get the game back underway.

It's a moot point to speculate what might have happened had he not intervened with this offer. Bison were back on level terms just four minutes after the restart. Jeff Daniels shot home from an angle and the emotion from the stands was palpable. In a roller-coaster last 14 minutes both teams traded attacks and the stoppages were kept to a minimum. Dru Burgess was binned for holding in the 48th minute and Fife sensed this was to be their chance.

The power play unit set itself up and delivered a textbook Fife power play goal with an angled pass from Ted Russell finding Dutiaume at the back post who shot it past Joe Watkins. Bison were forced to throw caution to the wind and were vulnerable to Fife's high man breakouts. Watkins was pulled in the last minute and Monteith missed the empty cage but it mattered not a jot as the final seconds counted down.

The team poured off the bench and swamped Man of the Match Stephen Murphy to signal the start of the party as hundreds flocked rink side along the boards.

The Championship baseball caps were handed out and skipper Frank Morris stepped forward to lift the trophy for the second consecutive season and the completion of the Grand Slam for the season.

As the champagne was uncorked and sprayed each player took the cup on a lap of honour to the delight of the home fans. Basingstoke's players sportingly remained on the ice for the presentations, a classy move.

Grand Slam winner and Goalie of the Year Stephen Murphy

Saturday April 8th 1978

Fife Flyers 13 Southampton Vikings 0

VIKINGS CRUSHED IN ICY SMITH FINAL

SECOND LEG A FORMALITY

That was the headline after Fife Flyers had all but assured themselves of retaining the British Championships with a crushing win over Southampton.

The long journey to the south coast to play the return leg on April 22 was surely confirmed as a mere formality following an utterly ruthless display. Such was the margin of victory that many followers of the game pondered the suggestion that the present format where the Northern Section winners played the winners of the Southern Section would probably have to be changed. The gulf between the two was undeniably vast.

The two teams had met 12 months ago and, without spoiling things for readers turning the page, the aggregate score line had not been close. In a season where the Flyers had run up some pretty hefty scores this first leg victory was considered the biggest mismatch of the season and the visitors were overrun from the minute they skated on to the ice.

Fish Robertson, their veteran goaltender, managed to keep the home side at bay for a while but it was obvious the floodgates were to be opened. In the sixth minute Gordon Latto waltzed through the Vikings defence and lifted the puck into the corner of the net.

That was the beginning of the end for the Englishmen, perhaps still trying to shake the long trip north from their legs. The same player chose the other corner of the net for Flyers second. There was a brief moment of hope for the Vikings. Jim Taylor had to pull off a fine double save as the visitors made their first assault on the home goal. Back came the Flyers and Jimmy Jack and Les Lovell added to their tally to bring up a comfortable 4-0 interval score.

After the restart, goals from Les Lovell, who beat the advancing keeper, and a close-in score by Charlie Kinmond were added to when Chic Cottrell rifled the puck home. Having a much easier time of it, Jim Taylor dealt capably with Vikings infrequent sojourns up the ice during the middle period.

Flyers captain Les Lovell brought up his hat-trick at the start of the final period and the Vikings team — a more mature lot with an average age of 34 — ran out of steam and resorted to some foul play.

Three goals in less than a minute shot the home side into double figures. Ally Brennan hit the first with a slapshot which looked as though it was going right through the net and the Lovell brothers collected another one apiece.

The Latto brothers got the final counters inside the last five minutes with Dougie then Gordon collecting his hat-trick.

The Mirror of Merit award on the night went to goaltender Jim Taylor. He had enjoyed a relatively quiet game but had recorded Flyers first shut-out of the season by making some good saves from the Vikings breakaways.

Flyers were now faced with the formality of travelling down to Southampton to make sure the Icy Smith trophy remained in the Kirkcaldy rink's showcase. It did so after a 10-5 win.

Charlie Kinmond scores in the rout over the Vikings – note goalie Robertson without any face mask

Saturday April 9th 1977

Fife Flyers 9 Southampton Vikings 5

The first leg of the British Championship Final (Icy Smith Cup) was spoiled by two incompetent referees who many considered should not have been allowed to take charge of such an important game.

It says much for an official's performance when those comments come from the team who had won the game, more easily than even the score line suggests. Flyers should really have taken the English side apart, but there was an utterly bizarre decision in the middle of the second period. On reflection it broke the momentum of the game and allowed the visitors to come back from the dead.

With Flyers leading 5-2 Vikings captain Alan Hindmarch scored, following a delayed penalty call which had been imposed against a Vikings player.

The rule states that play may continue as long as the opposition, in this case the Flyers, have possession of the puck. However, Hindmarch of Southampton won the puck and skated to the other end to hit the Flyers net. The referee's decision on the play was that the goal stood and Hindmarch went to the sin bin for his original penalty. It clearly unsettled the Flyers but ultimately had little impact on the overall outcome.

Flyers lined up minus captain Les Lovell through injury and Kenny Horne was also out through suspension. Vikings had their player-coach Pete Murray back in the side following a two-match suspension.

The first period started with heavy pressure on the Vikings net but Flyers failed to turn their advantage into goals. Surprisingly, Don Reycroft opened the scoring on Vikings first venture into the Fife end in 11 minutes. Two minutes later Gordon Latto equalised from a penalty shot, neatly side stepping the enormous Vikings goalie Pete Lane. Lawrie Lovell gave Flyers the lead but Murray put the visitors back on level terms minutes later. The Fife Flyers captain for the night, Ally Brennan, gave his side a period lead with a solo goal a few seconds from the interval buzzer.

Vikings came close to squaring matters at the start of the second period, but it was Flyers who found the net next. Lawrie Lovell deflected a Chic Cottrell shot past Lane, followed by Dougie Latto who netted after John Taylor had set up the chance. The controversial goal followed these two counters but Chic Cottrell was next to score after good support work from Law Lovell and Brennan.

Only the great work of Lane kept the Vikings in contention in the first two periods. Their accurate shooting on their few chances gave them the lifeline during their third period fight back.

A good solo effort by Steve Parrish was followed by a goal from Walt Dirks to bring the score to 6-5 but a quick one-two knockout blow put the Flyers in the driving seat. Gordon Latto, who was assisted by Lovell, scored in the 46th minute and a minute later Chic Cottrell scored a fine solo goal.

The final ten minutes of the match was ruined by penalties which amounted to a game total of 66 minutes with Vikings collecting 46 of them. John Taylor increased Flyers lead to four and left home supporters worried that this might not be an adequate enough advantage for the return leg on Southampton's postage stamp rink. They needn't have worried as Flyers won 18-6!

Gordon Latto with the Flyers opening and equalising goal finishes his penalty shot

Saturday April 10th 1971

Fife Flyers 8 Ayr Bruins 3

Fife Flyers, in their final outing for the season, put in one of their best performances of the season to bring the Skol Cup back to Kirkcaldy for the first time since 1968.

The previous week the Bruins had visited Kirkcaldy in a qualifying game and had beaten the Flyers 6-4. They were the only club to record a victory against the Flyers and so here they were back a week later at the Flyers rink to compete for the trophy.

The winners over the previous two seasons had been the Paisley Mohawks and Dundee Rockets. Flyers were keen to ensure that they managed to place the Skol Cup silverware back in the Kirkcaldy trophy cabinet at the third time of asking.

The home team got off to a dream start when Rab Petrie opened the scoring within 15 seconds of the start and the Flyers never looked back. Ayr Bruins had no answer to the Flyers attacking play. Les Lovell had another outstanding match and he helped himself to a hat-trick while at the other end of the rink netminder Roy Reid had a very good game and even managed to save a penalty shot. Flyers finished the first period three up with Dave Medd and Norrie Boreham adding to the lightning quick strike from Petrie.

Bruins strangely had enjoyed the best of the forward play but couldn't find a way past Reid. Their endeavour however eventually paid off and early in the second period Jackson McBride opened their account. Any thoughts of a comeback were shattered by two quick goals by Les Lovell. John Taylor, who had endured a season of misfortune through injuries, once again saw the hockey gods conspire against him and he was forced to retire with a leg injury. However, Flyers were looking slick and increased their lead through Allan Crooks and Jimmy Hunter.

The visitors started the final frame with a bang. McBride and Alistair McCrae flashed the red light in quick succession. Ian McCord was then brought down in full flight for goal but Reid brilliantly saved Ally Brennan's penalty shot. From that point on, Flyers never looked like letting victory slip away. With one minute to go Les Lovell, who in addition to Bruins Jackson McBride was named to the First All-Star team, completed his hat-trick.

Flyers 16-year-old right winger, Chic Cottrell, picked up the Mountford Trophy when he was voted by the NIHA as their best young prospect – Rookie of the Year. A few silver linings on what had been a fairly difficult season for the Flyers, who had managed a mere six wins from their 22 competitive fixtures in the Autumn Cup and Northern League.

Les Lovell was presented with the National Ice Hockey Association's "Player of the Year" Shield and also the Fife Free Press Mirror of Merit Trophy before the game with the Bruins. The photograph shows Mr Bernard Stocks, editor of the Ice Hockey Herald, making the presentation.

Tuesday April 11th 1950

Paisley Pirates 6 Fife Flyers 4

The Flyers season so far had been a huge success. After narrowly losing out on the Autumn Cup by a single point to the Dundee Tigers, the Kirkcaldy men had captured the Canada Cup and retained the Coronation Cup as winners of the Scottish National League for the second year in succession. They were in the final of both the Scottish Cup and the National League Playoff. The final group competition, the Association Cup, was proving to be somewhat of a chore.

Despite the opening to the match report reading, "Once again Paisley Ice Rink proved to be Flyers bogey, when they were well licked by six goals to four by a strong fast skating Pirates line-up" the Flyers didn't have an awful record at the East Lane Rink; it was their sixth visit of the season and the series would end with three wins a piece. Perhaps with only four wins from their previous 14 post war appearances this somehow gave the scribe a feeling of déjà vu.

Flyers team play had the Pirates in a daze for long spells but it all came to an end when they were in front of the net. On the other hand, Paisley were not brilliant stick-handlers but they never wasted an opportunity to have a go. 'Pete' Belanger played well in the Flyers cage, but faded badly towards the end of the match. Floyd Snider worked hard in defence and his was a valiant effort to force the pace. In the forward line, Marsh Bentley and Chic Mann were the pick of the bunch. The Pirates had one particular line of Ken Head, Stu Robertson and Doug Ringrose that simply skated Flyers off their feet.

Pirates junior Johnny Quales, another speed merchant, also caused the visitors some anxiety. This result meant that the visitors would now have little interest in the Association Cup. Flyers had opened the scoring. It was ding-dong stuff throughout the first period with the score ending three each, with Mann and a double from Scotty Reid scoring the Flyers goals. Paisley really went to work in the middle session and added two goals without reply. The third period saw Mann reduce the leeway but another Paisley goal in the final minute restored their two-goal advantage. Pirates goals were scored by Robertson 2, Head, Elwood Shell, Quales and Sid Arnold.

A little bit of background on the Paisley Ice Rink of that era. During the dark days of the 1940 "phoney war", when rationing, gas masks and baffle walls were the order of the day, a new exciting winter sports stadium for Paisley first opened its doors to large crowds of people.

East Lane had never seen such crowds since the days when Abercorn Football Club played on the same piece of ground. The ice rink brought a fresh breath of air to the East End of Paisley. It was the most up to date arena in Great Britain and boasted an ice space of 20,000 square feet, seating for 5,000 spectators, a first-class restaurant, cafe, milk bar and a well-appointed shop.

The streamlined, shell like building was large. The car park could provide 800 spaces, enough to accommodate all of the privately-owned cars in Paisley at the time.

On 20th August 1965, a wee bit of history was made when Cassius Clay, the then 23-year-old Muhammad Ali, the heavyweight boxing champion of the world, gave an exhibition bout to excited Scottish boxing fans. Paisley had never seen the likes since Benny Lynch fought a world title at Love Street in 1933!

Like many ice rinks in Scotland, however, East Lane was eventually consigned to the history books. It was closed to ice sports in 1970 and a few years later it was demolished for what is now the location of a supermarket.

The original Paisley Ice Rink at East Lane

Saturday April 12th 1986

HEINEKEN PREMIER LEAGUE PLAY OFF GAME 1

Fife Flyers 8 Durham Wasps 5

As defending British Champions, the Flyers took the first vital step on the road to returning to the Wembley Finals with a Saturday afternoon match in front of the BBC Grandstand cameras.

The Flyers had a full squad available to them, having had a scare earlier in the week about the fitness of Danny Brown. The impetus for their victory came from a devastating three-goal burst inside 60 seconds late in the second period which knocked the fight out of the Wasps.

In a tension-laden and often bad-tempered match, a significant factor was Durham's penalty count, which enabled Ron Plumb's men to gain the upper hand, with Flyers first four goals all coming from power plays. The English side looked the more impressive outfit when they had a full complement of players on the ice, but faced with an 8-3 deficit at the start of the final period, there was no way back.

It was the visitors who drew first blood after eight minutes with goal by Paul Tilley, but a five-minute major penalty for high sticks against Paul Smith proved costly. Flyers scored three times in his absence. Wasps were in fact down to three skaters before Neil Abel set the home fans alight with a shot, partially stopped by netminder Frankie Killen but with just enough momentum to cross the line.

Two minutes later Danny Brown cut in from the right to fire Flyers into the lead and they went further ahead when, with Durham again skating two men short, Todd Bidner neatly rounded Killen before flicking the puck home. However, with Durham back at full strength, the home defence looked suspect on a number of occasions before Paul Tilley scored two minutes from the buzzer.

Flyers were denied what appeared to everyone but the officials a blatant penalty shot early in the second period when Brown was tripped in front of the net. Bidner made the resultant power play count with a blistering wrist shot low into the corner. As Durham began to take control of the match, Anthony Johnson pulled the score back to 4-3, and it was against the run of play when Brown broke away to score. That sparked off a real purple patch for Flyers, who buried Durham with three goals in less than a minute. Chic Cottrell gained just reward for his endeavours when he made no mistake after a Brian Peat effort had not been properly cleared. Dean Edmiston then got into the act with a brilliantly taken goal following a Jimmy Pennycook pass. When Danny Brown completed his hat-trick from a Bidner cut-back just seconds later, the match was effectively over as a contest.

Flyers dominated for long spells in a low-key third period, but a combination of careless finishing and excellent net-minding prevented them from increasing their lead. Indeed, it was Durham who found the net twice in the closing minutes through Ivor Bennett and Tilley to complete the scoring.

Danny Brown, who covered every inch of the ice as well as his three goals, was Heineken's choice as Flyers Man of the Match. Stephen Cooper picked up the award for Durham. Ron Plumb said later: "It was a very physical game, but Durham's heads went down when we hit them with those four quick goals."

The bookies had Flyers fourth favourites to win the Championship with Murrayfield as favourites. Disposing of the Premier League Champion Wasps however had the Kirkcaldy faithful once again believing.

Andy Linton celebrates scoring against the Wasps in an earlier season encounter with Todd Bidner in the background

Friday April 13th 1951

Ayr Raiders 1 Fife Flyers 5

In a somewhat strange set of circumstances, these two teams met in a game which would decide the winners of the Bairns Trophy.

Strange because both sides were in direct competition to land the more prestigious Autumn Cup that season, the fixtures having taken almost the entirety of the season to conclude. The two teams had tied on points after the group games had been completed in mid-October. Rather than award the title on goal difference which would have made Flyers winners it was decided there should be a two-legged play off.

Those games took place in December and February. The teams were still tied on aggregate, so a further two games were scheduled. A week before this tie, the Flyers had visited the West Coast in the first leg and were soundly beaten 7-3. It was a clearly rejuvenated Flyers side, however which gave one of their more assured performances since the New Year that thrashed Raiders to the tune of 5-1.

"Pete" Belanger, magnificent in the Fife nets, was decidedly unlucky not to record a shut-out. The only shot to beat him came from Bill McIntosh with just four minutes remaining on the game. Ray Dinardo was once again the outstanding Flyers defenceman, while Marshall Bentley and Archie Williams were the most impressive play-makers for the visitors.

It was a Flyers performance, nevertheless, that still lacked consistency, a problem that had beset the team in recent months. Indeed, while this was their third win in a row, what preceded that was a run of 15 consecutive defeats, a club record (at the time of publishing) for games without picking up a point.

Most nights there had simply been too many passengers. Tonight was no different, despite the result. Al Campone, after a couple of indifferent games "gate-crashed" back into the limelight with couple of picture goals. His first counter gave the Flyers a slender lend at the end of the first session. Williams and Bentley brought the total to three in a keenly contested second session, and in the final stanza Scotty Reid and Campone added two more. Raiders opened their account with a McIntosh counter in the closing minutes of play.

The Bairns Trophy was traditionally the "home" tournament trophy for the Falkirk Lions. This season however the silverware was put up for competition for the bottom three teams in the National League who did not qualify to participate in the play-off series for the Anderson Trophy.

As the season came to a close Falkirk grabbed the final spot by two points from the Ayr Raiders to avoid competing for their own trophy. The table below shows that the Flyers win, in what was just one game home and away for the three, resulted in them winning the trophy for the first time since it was competed for in 1939. Unfortunately, they would retain the trophy under similar circumstances the following season.

	GP	W	D	L	GF	GA	Pts
Fife Flyers	2	2	0	0	13	4	4
Ayr Raiders	2	0	1	1	6	10	1
Dundee Tigers	2	0	1	1	8	13	1

What about the Autumn Cup you ask? A week later the Raiders came to Kirkcaldy for the second leg, and were beaten 11-5. So, with only one week left in the season the competition that opened the season in September was finally settled with the Flyers victorious 14-12 on aggregate. Something to brighten up what had turned out to be a fairly miserable season for the fans.

Raiders netminder Dutch Erion denies Sherman Blair in an early match from the season

Sunday April 14th 1985

Ayr Bruins 3 Fife Flyers 5

The Flyers travelled west to the tiny Limekilns Road rink to meet a Bruins side still smarting from losing just over 24 hours earlier, live on TV in an epic odd-goal-in-17 thriller at Kirkcaldy. It was an all Scottish home-and-home to open the play off quest for Wembley for both teams. After the first weekend Flyers were in a commanding position. Bruins had only come out on top in one of their previous six Autumn Cup and Premier League encounters with the Flyers and the Kirkcaldy side continued their dominance, albeit in a pair of games that were much closer than any others before.

The atmosphere in the Ayr rink was electric with the doors closed 15 minutes before face-off. At the best of times there was never much space for fans to stand around the ice pad — but there had to be some in attendance that night who left to go home with the criss-cross pattern of the netting across their faces, such was the way people were packed in to the 'bijou surroundings'.

Flyers, without Stuart Drummond and Gordon Latto, went ahead when Dave Stoyanovich scored in the eighth minute. Minutes later Flyers had a couple of golden opportunities to extend their lead but were denied by the brilliance of John 'Bernie' McCrone.

Bruins stunned the big Fife support with two quick goals at the start of the second period. Paul Bedard equalised on the power play. Two minutes later Steve Slaughter put Ayr ahead with a fierce slapshot from just inside the blue line. The home side looked capable of extending their lead but some dogged defensive work and sound net-minding by Andy Donald kept Bruins at bay. Midway through the period Andy Linton scored a fine unassisted break-away goal to tie the scores going into the final spell.

With both teams looking for the vital opening goal of the third period it was Flyers who went ahead when Gary McEwan calmly slid the puck under McCrone following a Jimmy Pennycook pass. The Kirkcaldy side kept up the pressure and increased their lead four minutes later when Ron Plumb found the corner of the net with a slap shot from the blue line. Bruins pushed forward and laid siege to the Fife goal and their efforts were finally rewarded 55 seconds from time with a power play goal by

Slaughter. Ayr withdrew McCrone for the extra forward in a desperate bid to grab the equaliser but their hopes were dashed 10 seconds from the buzzer when Jimmy Pennycook flicked home a Stoyanovich pass.

The result meant that the Flyers would secure qualification to the Wembley Finals if they took just a single point from their final two remaining games against the Cleveland Bombers.

The Bombers were the weakest team in the group, against whom the Flyers had won all four of the meetings in convincing style that season. There were already seven fully booked coaches in the expectation by Flyers fans that Fife would make it. Readers can find out what happened a little later on in the book.

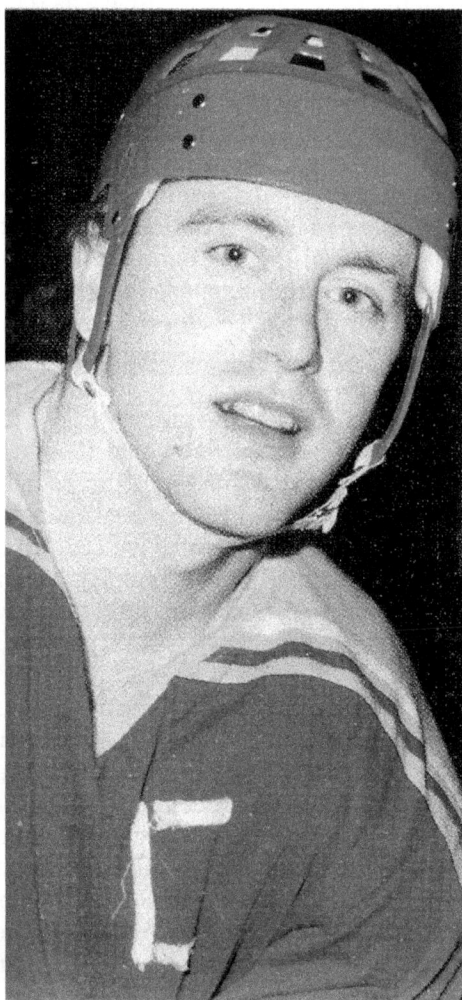

'Gogs' Latto was missing from the Flyers line up with a troublesome stomach injury but Flyers put one foot in the Wembley final without him at Ayr.

Sunday April 15th 1990

Durham Wasps 10 Fife Flyers 2

With nothing at stake, the Flyers having qualified from the group along with Murrayfield, the events at Durham's Riverside rink veered from the ridiculous to the farcical as the play-off campaign staggered to a disgraceful, chaotic finish.

Much of the mess was due to the man in the middle, Nico Toeman, who must shoulder the burden of responsibility. He handed out three match penalties, dismissed Flyers coach Rab Petrie from the bench, and then left the ice altogether as the Fife side contemplated quitting in disgust.

Confusion reigned as some players headed for the dressing room, a few sat in the penalty box and Durham's dreadfully undisciplined younger players started a victory dance. It would be very easy to blame the referee for everything that happened in front of a noisy, and increasingly tetchy crowd, but the players — primarily from the home ranks —displayed a couldn't care less attitude and far too many challenges were maliciously late or high.

Toeman allowed the game to flow and it was his biggest mistake. Hindsight suggested he should have clamped down on the nonsense which transformed this game into an ugly mess. Time after time players followed through with late checks long after the puck had been played and as a result petty scrums were blown up out of all proportion.

The first period was shambolic, 28 minutes in penalties and a mere 18 shots on goal. Rick Fera fired a superb 69-second opener, and John Ollson replied with two power plays to make it 2-1 with six minutes played.

By then Neil Abel had come and gone. Flyers assistant captain had a brief shoving match with Adrian Smith prior to a face-off and round two came along the boards seconds later. Abel collected a match penalty for fighting and a gross misconduct for allegedly striking the official trying to separate them. Smith walked into the bin on a two plus two.

The period ended on a ridiculous note as Anthony Payne indulged in a piece of juvenile brinksmanship as he denied Fera his customary want of being the last player to leave the ice. Payne simply skated to his own team bench and kicked his heels until Toeman ordered the Canadian centre off the ice. Similar scenes occurred at the end of the second with Payne being joined by Damian Smith and their gloating dance earned them both ten-minute misconducts.

All three second period goals came on power plays, with Ollson and Ivor Bennett netting for Wasps and Fera keeping Flyers within striking distance. In that period Flyers were short-handed for the best part of 12 minutes and Petrie was given his marching orders.

Any hopes that some sanity might be restored finally evaporated in the 47th minute with Wasps leading 5-2. Mike Rowe collected an elbows penalty and Gordon Latto, sitting in the bin, threw his gloves into the air in an expression of disbelief and frustration. Toeman gave him a match penalty and that proved to be the final straw.

Flyers bench directed their players off the ice and the referee took his officials out of the arena. Confusion reigned and when some semblance of order was restored Toeman gave Flyers another bench minor and re-started the action.

Wasps hit five goals to notch up a meaningless result. Brebant fired a straight hat-trick but Craig Dickson pulled off a string of superb saves to prevent a cricket score. Iain Robertson, Colin Wilson and Gary Fyffe all had fine games on what was a night to forget. Both Abel and Petrie were set to be banned for the Flyers Wembley showdown with the Cardiff Devils although on the eve of the game the BIHA allowed Abel to play and "downgraded" Petrie's punishment to a £500 fine.

Craig Dickson who, despite this pose, literally stood on his head against the Wasps

Sunday April 16th 2006

Edinburgh Capitals 6 Fife Flyers 6

Flyers moved a step closer to their fifth trophy of the season. After finishing the second leg of their Scottish National League Play-Off all square they progressed through to meet the Dundee Stars in the final on a 12-9 aggregate score line.

The previous night in Kirkcaldy Flyers had recorded their fourth win in five matches that season against the side from the Capital. However, they had to work hard to secure their place in the showpiece event after Edinburgh raced into a two-goal lead to reduce the deficit to just one overall.

Matthew Rich pounced on a loose puck in the middle of the ice and fired a low shot into Blair Daly's right-hand corner. As Flyers struggled to find their rhythm Edinburgh again caught them out on the counter attack at 7.19 when Craig Wilson broke forward and squared to Ian Simpson who finished with aplomb.

In reality it was just what the tie needed and the atmosphere began to hot up in the stands as some heavy checks were put in on the ice. Flyers began to come more into the game as Jamie Wilson missed a good chance and Capitals netminder Alisdair Flockhart saved well from Derek King.

Flyers persistence eventually paid off when a Chris Wands cutback was slammed home by John Haig. The visitors were level on the night only 39 seconds later. Haig did well to make room for a shot only to see his effort come back off the inside of the post but Caps made a hash of clearing and Haig converted at the second attempt.

Edinburgh looked stunned at this point after their strong start and Flyers took advantage and rattled in another two goals with Stephen Gunn and Steven King both getting on the scoresheet.

Edinburgh started the second period as they had done the first with most of the possession and the better chances. Their dominance was rewarded when Ian Simpson netted his second goal of the night. Flyers then contrived to miss a host of chances before Edinburgh pulled level on 29 minutes when Ross Hay scooped high past Daly.

A flurry of goals late in the period meant the teams were level at 5-5 going into the final stanza. A clever reverse pass from Jamie Wilson allowed Liam Greig to put Flyers ahead at 37.43 but Capitals equalised less than a minute-later through Steven Lynch.

Into the third period and Flyers went ahead again with only ten minutes remaining. Haig forced Flockhart into the save but Chris Wands was on hand to net the rebound. Edinburgh realised they weren't going to make the final but they fought hard for a draw on the night and Lynch scored his second of the match to give them some credit.

Steven King in action against the Edinburgh Capitals

Thursday April 17th 1952

Fife Flyers 3 Paisley Pirates 3

Flyers got off to a fine start in this nothing-to-lose-or-win final game of the season in the Victory Cup.

The meeting of the League's basement sides — Flyers had finished last — resulted in a low-key affair throughout. That was reflected by the penalty count of only a single penalty, Bob Bergeron of Flyers and Joe Brown of Pirates, to each team.

The Flyers had lost their first two games in the competition but had beaten local rivals Dunfermline Vikings in their last outing three days before.

They had also annexed the Bairns Trophy in recent weeks, the "runners up" competition for those teams that didn't qualify for the Anderson Trophy play-off matches. Their record against the Pirates across the season was good and they, together with the Vikings, were a team against whom Fife fans knew Flyers were in with a shout of getting a great result.

The home crowd didn't have long to wait before they were out of their seats with a goal, after only five minutes, netted by Bert Smith. This stung the visitors into action. They replied just five minutes later when one of their local lads, junior Bob Bremner, equalised.

The Pirates were well on top now and stunned the home side by going ahead with a strike a minute later by Roy Hammond. Flyers got back on level terms before the first period buzzer when Hal Kewley set up Billy Fisher, who had joined the previous month from the Brighton Tigers, to score.

The only goal of the second period was netted by Hal Brown for Paisley to regain the lead but midway through the final frame the Flyers secured a point when another late season addition to the squad, ex-Wembley Lion Don Mann, netted off a Mickey Linnell assist for the tie.

Flyers – 'Stubby' Mason, Floyd Snider, Bob Bergeron, Ray Dinardo, Jimmy Mitchell, Billy Fisher, Mickey Linnell, Johnny Vanier, Hal Kewley, Frank Facto, Bert Smith, Don Mann

Pirates – Bob Tripp, Bob Reid, Bernie Hill, Roy Hammond, Joe Brown, Moe Fife, Hal Brown, Bob Kelly, Dave Hebenton, Rheal Savard, Maurice LaForge, Bob Bremner

Referee: Gordon Gerrard

The competition was scrapped after just one season.

It had been a rather casual slap-happy affair and for that reason the *Ice Hockey World* newspaper stated that it would not be rated as a major tournament for statistical purposes.

The winners were Falkirk Lions, with the Dunfermline Vikings as runners-up. The Mirror of Merit was awarded in its inaugural season to 'Stubby' Mason – he had endured a tough term with the Flyers, the lowest scoring team in Scotland, with only the Pirates having shipped more at the other end.

Despite this he finished second in save percentage bettered only by the Rookie of the Year Al Holliday of the Scottish National League and Autumn Cup winning Ayr Raiders.

A youthful looking Dougie Latto, who served the Flyers for 13 seasons.

Thursday April 18th 1940

Fife Flyers 4 Perth Panthers 4

The Flyers had pipped the Panthers by just a single point to win the Scottish National League regular season. The Panthers bested the Flyers in the earlier Scottish Points competition. The two were to meet over a series of five games to determine the overall Scottish Ice Hockey Champions. In the end the title was competed for over three games, details of which come later in the book.

After a series of brisk opening exchanges, it was Flyers who went ahead in five minutes. Red Thomson fired in a shot from distance which Scottie Milne saved with his stick but the ever-alert Glen Morrison fastened on to the rebound and netted. Art Grant then saved an Art Schumann drive and then Frank Ney broke away and slipped the puck to Arnie Pratt who hurried his shot wide of the net.

Another break-up ice saw Ney just fail to pick up a Pratt pass in a melée in front of Milne. After this promising start Ney was penalised for bringing down "Breezy" Thompson. The Panthers, after many good chances, eventually beat Grant when "Breezy" managed to level the scores.

Morrison was upended in a Flyers attack, but Red Thomson fastened on and missed narrowly. The Flyers regained the lead in the 16th minute when Morrison batted the puck over to Paul Rheault who, standing just outside the crease, left Milne wondering where the draught had come from. Panthers levelled however before the interval. George Horn had been penalised after a collision with Les Lovell and Schumann set up Thomson to score again.

The second period began with a bang with two goals inside the opening two minutes. Horn battled his way up ice and he fed the puck to Rheault who put Flyers ahead again. The lead was extended 30 seconds later when Pratt, on a solo dash, skated right through and netted Flyers fourth.

Into the third period and Flyers looked as though they were in full control. Big Art Schumman, a fan favourite at Kirkcaldy for derisory calls from the Flyers faithful, had other ideas. In the opening minute, George Horn made his first real slip of the game when he completely missed the puck and Schumann simply skated in and left Grant helpless.

A couple of minutes later with Johnny Schofield alongside Frank Ney, Flyers had their youngest defensive pairing on the ice, they could do little to prevent Schumann, who was in sparkling form, from scoring with another solo goal. A somewhat ironic situation, given the local reporter having advocated giving the youngsters a break.

Clearly, though, one at time in partnership with either George Horn or Red Thomson would give the stabilising influence of the old and experienced hand. After these lapses Flyers made great efforts to get the winner and the closest they came was a Red Thomson shot that Milne did well to block with his pads.

Although there was a hectic finish to the game neither side could break the deadlock with a winner. Panthers Schumann was the Man of the Match.

Flyers — Art Grant, George Horn, Red Thomson, Frank Ney, Johnny Schofield, Glen Morrison, Arnie Pratt, Paul Rheault, Eddie McMillan

Perth Panthers — Scottie Milne, Les Vickery, Ray Cheyne, "Breezy" Thompson, Art Schumann, Les Tapp, Jimmy Allan, Les Lovell, Verne Reilly

Referee: J. Foley

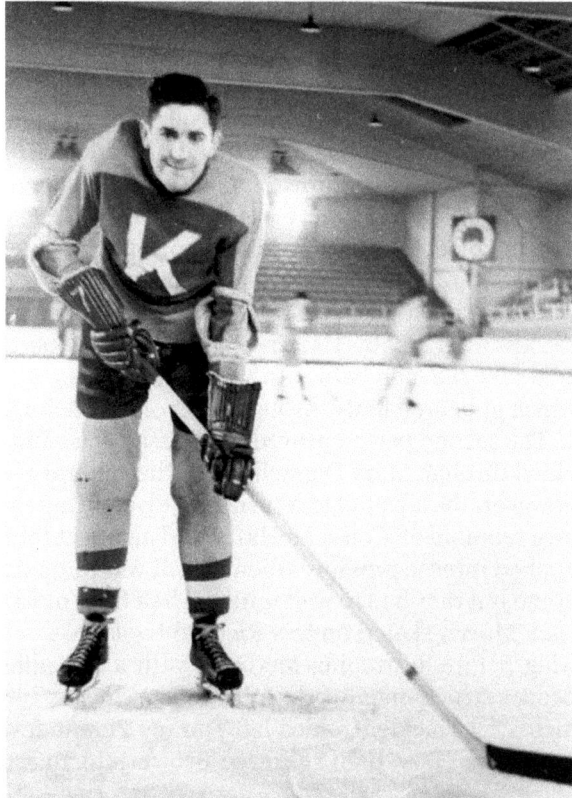

Glen Morrison who also appeared in a George Formby film from 1938 called "I See Ice"

Sunday April 19th 1992

Ayr Raiders 8 Fife Flyers 6

Flyers clinched promotion at the Summit Centre in Glasgow, but only after an incredible fright.

The First Division Champions were coasting to victory and a return to the Premier League when Ayr staged the fightback to end nearly all fightbacks. The West coast men needed to win this game by three clear goals to top the play-off group. They trailed 6-4 with less than seven minutes to play but an incredible four-goal blitz produced a grandstand finish which very nearly caused the sensation of the season.

The game was balanced on a knife edge for two and a half nerve-wracking minutes as Flyers clung by their fingertips to promotion. The tension was unbearable, the pressure immense and the atmosphere simply unbelievable.

Raiders blitzed Flyers goal throughout an opening period which was played at a whirlwind pace. They outshot their visitors 15-6 with the action ragged and frantic. A goal was inevitable and it came when Colin Downie failed to freeze the puck. Warren Rost nipped in ahead of Cal Brown to set up Russ Parent, who made no mistake with a fine shot. Raiders then had a power play chance, but they couldn't capitalise and were caught with a sucker punch. Frank Morris netted the equaliser one second after Bobby Haig returned. Flyers took the lead with a second goal just seconds before the buzzer, courtesy of a Gordon Latto strike which appeared to fly through McCrone's catching glove.

The second period proved to be just as fast and furious. Ayr drew first blood through Mark Dennehy to tie the game at 2-2. Within two minutes, however, the advantage returned to Flyers. Paul Berrington picked up his own rebound off Collin McHaffie and netted at the second attempt. Flyers applied intense pressure when Parent was binned on a holding penalty at 26:26 but they had to wait until the half hour mark before extending their lead. Morris skated on to a Richard Laplante pass and hurtled down the wing before destroying McCrone with a magnificent long-range strike. Brown struck metalwork. Iain Robertson was binned for an accidental high-sticks incident which left Tommy Plommer with a broken nose and a cut face. Rost then suckered Brown into an interference penalty and

AYR Raiders
BARR CONSTRUCTION

v
TELFORD TIGERS

Promotion/Relegation
Play-Off

Saturday 18th April

v
FIFE FLYERS

Promotion/Relegation
Play-Off

Sunday 19th April

Face-Offs 6.00 p.m.

Programme
£1.00

The programme from the momentous game in Glasgow

the niggly but highly effective winger netted on the power play to make it 4-3 at the end of the second.

The game was all-square again at 41:55 courtesy of Tony Redmond's counter against Fife's second line but the odds were still stacked against an Ayr revival as the clock ticked away. They needed to score three times without reply to avoid relegation. Their hearts must have sunk when Laplante robbed Parent on the blue line, fired the puck off McCrone's pads and chipped home the rebound to make it 5-4. Ten minutes later it looked all over for the home side. Gordon Latto picked up the puck behind his own net, skated the length of the rink, and drilled a fabulous shot between McCrone and the near post.

Raiders now needed to score five without reply, and they had six minutes 32 seconds in which to perform the greatest of escapes. Dennehy narrowed the deficit with a long-range drive at 54:54. Terry MacLean came up with the all-important equaliser at 56:05. Raiders still needed to score three more. They netted twice through Dennehy and Parent before Fife called a time-out to take the heat out of an increasingly tense situation.

Ayr's Premier League status and the entire future of the club hinged upon one more shot flying past netminder Colin Downie. Flyers entire season rested on winning the last face-off, dumping the puck down the ice and willing the clock to reach zero before Raiders could strike again.

Flyers managed to retain possession from the very last face-off and Raiders had no time to pull McCrone for a six on five advantage for one last shot on goal.

Phew!

Saturday April 20th 1968

Wembley Lions 11 Fife Flyers 4

After hovering on the brink for several matches, George Beach, Wembley Lions popular captain, became the second player to be credited with 1,000 goals in British ice hockey; Nottingham Panthers Chick Zamick had been the first.

This was the Flyers final match of the season and was their third meeting with the Lions that season. The previous two had been in the British Cup, where they had lost 5-2 in the "big smoke" and 4-2 at Kirkcaldy. The Flyers were always well received by the Wembley fans although clearly most of the crowd – there were 5500 in attendance, which was slightly above the average — had come to see if Beach could reach the milestone.

The Lions were looking to record their tenth successive victory and were unbeaten on home ice so far that season in what was to be their penultimate game. There were a number of players who guested for the Flyers. Kirkcaldy son Jackie Dryburgh had of course been a prolific goal-scorer with the Brighton Tigers and on his last visit to Wembley Arena had bagged four goals in a 9-7 Tigers win.

Roger Turner was in the Flyers net. Roger had been the back-up goalie for the Brighton Tigers in their final season, 1964/65. The Flyers had lost the services of Roy Reid a few weeks earlier, when he emigrated to Canada. This had left Ian Nelson, Johnny Bayne and junior Jim Taylor to cover the net-minding duties. Roy Yates was the last of the guest players; he was Brighton born and had started and ended his career with the Tigers while also appearing for the Southampton Vikings.

The event that all were anticipating, Beach's goal, came during a rather drab and uninteresting clash. After six minutes of desultory play, Lions player coach Johnny Murray slipped the puck to Beach. Beach headed towards the Fife goal but defenders converged on him from all directions. He seemed to give up all hope of making a direct scoring attempt by skating past the side of the goal and round the back of it. But if Beach had gone this way the puck had not gone with him; before many spectators realised that it had already left his stick, the inside netting on the far side of the goal jerked as the puck slammed into it.

Once the red light came on for a goal pandemonium broke loose. Players from both teams swarmed round Beach congratulating him. Sections of the crowd rose to their feet cheering and shouting while "Good old George" suddenly appeared on the giant telewriter screens at each end of the arena.

As it was, it was very fitting that the chance should come from Johnny Murray who would retire after the game the following week, after 30 years of service to the club and five years as player coach.

The Lions held a 4-0 first period lead with further goals from Tony Whitehead and a Red Imrie double. Les Lovell and Graeme Farrell were on target for the Flyers in the second but by the buzzer the Lions were 9-2 ahead. Imrie added another two and Roy Whitehead and Les Strongman ended with doubles while Rupe Fresher, Murray and Roy Shepherd each had one by the end. Norrie Boreham and Jackie Dryburgh had but mere consolations in the final period.

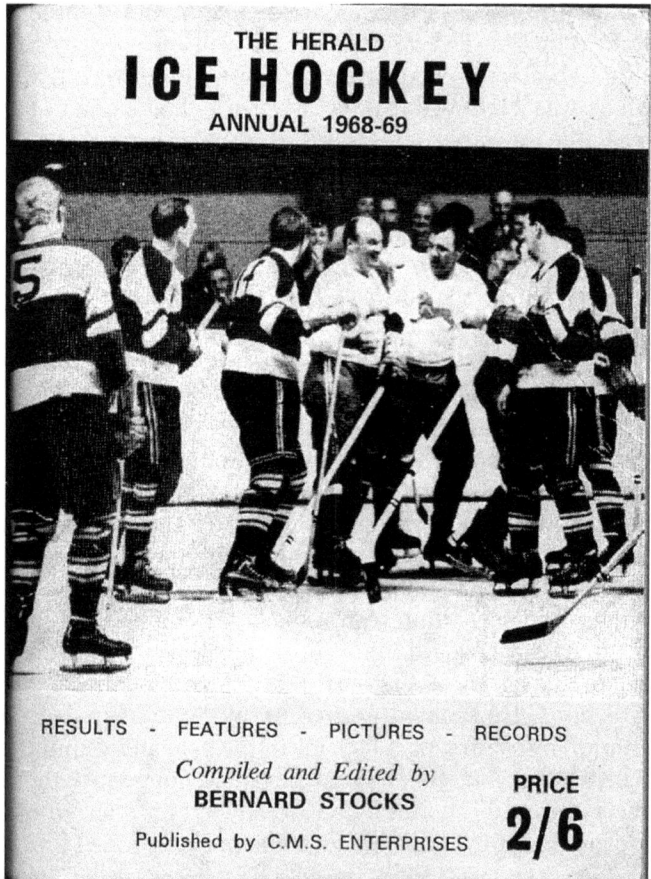

The historic moment of Beach's 1000th goal, captured on the front cover of The Herald Ice Hockey Annual

THE HERALD

ICE HOCKEY

ANNUAL 1968-69

RESULTS - FEATURES - PICTURES - RECORDS

Compiled and Edited by
BERNARD STOCKS

Published by C.M.S. ENTERPRISES

PRICE

2/6

Sunday April 21st 1974

Fife Flyers 4 Dundee Rockets 7

Fife Flyers bid to land the Spring Cup, considered to be the Northern Ice Hockey Associations premier trophy at that time, was foiled at Edinburgh's Murrayfield Rink.

The biggest crowd of the season saw Flyers play the better hockey at times, but it was not to be their night and Rockets, who had been beaten finalists in the past two seasons, took the trophy back to Tayside.

The Flyers and Rockets had chased the Whitley Warriors for the Northern League title. Although they had shared the points in their league meetings, the Flyers had also won the two local cup encounters between the sides. Fife had reached the Final by virtue of a 14-11 aggregate win over the League Champions, Warriors.

The Flyers were first to threaten in the game but after these early attacks it was ex-Flyer Sammy McDonald who opened the Rockets account after only three minutes. Flyers were soon back on level terms when the Lovell brothers combined with Lawrie getting the final touch.

However, Dundee were to take decisive control of the match when Mike Mazur made it 2-1. Before the end of the first period Flyers lost two more goals. Firstly, a shot from the blue line by Willie Murray entered the net with Jim Taylor unsighted, then Charlie Kinmond scored to put the Rockets well on top.

It was to be a different story in the middle period, however, as it was Flyers turn to shine. Goals by Lawrie Lovell and Norrie Boreham reduced the deficit to 4-3 and midway through the period Dougie Latto looked to have scored a perfectly good equaliser, only to have it chalked off by the referee. The ruling by the referee was that a team mate had been standing in the goal crease at the time.

Try as they might Flyers just couldn't get the equaliser. One shot from Chic Cottrell had Dundee netminder Mike Ward more interested in getting out of the way than stopping the puck but unfortunately the shot passed just over the bar.

Rockets increased their lead at the start of the final session when a long shot by Pete Reilly slipped through between Taylor's pads. Les Lovell pulled it back to 5-4, scoring from a pass by brother Lawrie. That's the way it stayed until Dundee scored twice to clinch the win. McDonald cashed in on a poor defensive clearance to make it 6-4. Twenty seconds from the final bell Kinmond scored from a penalty shot.

It was maybe a little harsh on the Flyers, who came close to equalising on a number of occasions, when they were down 4-3 in the middle period and again at 5-4 in the third. However, Flyer fans' views were that they contributed to their own downfall through their frequent change of line-ups, never the best signs in a vital cup final they mused. The Lovell brothers, Flyers most dangerous forwards, should have been iced together more often.

Flyers still had three more finals to play before the season ended, at Dundee, Durham and Whitley Bay for the silverware in the local tournaments. After a promising start to the season it was now a distinct possibility that the Kirkcaldy boardroom, which at one stage of the season looked as though it might be crowded with silverware, might end up empty.

Flyers 1973-74
Back, left to right: Dougie Latto, Gus Cargill, Reggie Smith, Ian Ferguson, George Taylor, Ken McAuley, Stuart Muir, Norre Boreham, Harry Cottrell, Pep Young
Front, left to right: Ally Brennan, Chic Cottrell, Rab Petrie, John Pullar, Law Lovell, Jimmy Hunter, Les Lovell, Dave Medd

Saturday April 22nd 1950

NATIONAL LEAGUE PLAY OFF FINAL 2ND LEG

Falkirk Lions 6 Fife Flyers 1

It was a grim struggle for the Flyers but a match in which there was plenty of excitement for the spectators in the packed rink.

With the home side trailing 4-1 after the first game the Lions prospects for a comeback were not considered to be particularly bright but the final result only went to prove how unpredictable ice hockey form can be.

Flyers were League winners but the Lions were eager to put one over on their bitter rivals to retain the most sought-after prize of the season, the Anderson Trophy.

Playing in top gear from the opening whistle the Lions hammered at the Flyers defence and never let off until the final five minutes when they were content to let the visitors bring the play to them. By that time however both teams were feeling the effects of the cracking pace which had been set.

Every player in the home side was a hero with this grand win but several were worthy of a special mention. Ken Nicholson, apart from his three goals, was the coolest man on the ice and one of the cleverest thinkers in the game. His combination with Pat Casey, who was in one of his better moods, had the Flyers defence in trouble for most of the game.

Warner Carlson, Lloyd Penner and Tom La Pointe were in a "Thou shall not pass" mood, even more remarkable considering that Carlson shouldn't have taken the ice. His ankle was heavily strapped, following an injury on the previous Thursday.

When Lions opened the scoring they had their tails up but Flyers showed them they had no intention of playing second fiddle. Lions started off with a rush and after a scramble in front of Pete Belanger, Chic Mann went close at the other end. In the fifth minute Nicholson opened Lions account after Penner and Leo Carrey had carved open the visitors' defence. There was a shock however for the home fans when two minutes later, with Hap Finch at full stretch, Earl McCrone had the simple task of getting the Flyers back on level terms. Thrills at both ends followed with Lions having the bulk of the pressure and just when it looked like level pegging at the first interval, Lions scored with ten seconds left for play. A breakaway attack saw Pat Casey pass to Penner who banged a fine shot past Belanger.

Four minutes into the middle session Nicholson netted from Casey's pass and Lions pressure increased. Line changes were frequent as the pace of the game was maintained and in the final moments of the period Pat Casey flashed the red light to level the aggregate score.

Excitement was intense in the final period and Flyers came close to scoring but after seven minutes Nicholson's coolness was rewarded when he beat Belanger cleverly at the post.

Both teams were handicapped by penalties now and with only three men out to Flyers four, Wilson Roe harassed the Flyers defenders and a loose puck was deflected into his own net by Floyd Snider.

This finished the visitors' chances, although they tried manfully to the end. It was elation for the Lions and despair for the Flyers who after winning their opening two games of the season at the Falkirk Rink had now capitulated in each of their last five visits.

After a period of adjustment Bill Moody became a highly accomplished defenceman in his three seasons with Flyers in the 1990s

Saturday April 23rd 1994

Cardiff Devils 9 Fife Flyers 5

In what was to be the Flyers last ever appearance at the annual Wembley hockey jamboree — the Championships would end two years later with the advent of the Superleague — they were bedevilled by misfortune in London in the opening semi-final of the Championship weekend.

Devils supremo John Lawless said afterwards "That was a game of mistakes". Indeed, it was a highly unusual affair and the opening period alone contained more goals than most final matches.

Throw in two short-handed counters and an own goal and neither coach was set to be very happy with what had transpired. Flyers reached the weekend by producing tight defensive hockey, even in the most intense games. It all went wrong as early as ten seconds. There was no immediate danger from the face off to the right of 'Bernie' McCrone's goal but the keeper could do little to anticipate the unexpected flip back from Ryan Kummu. The puck found the net. Even the BBC commentators were momentarily speechless.

The early jitters settled slightly when Mark Morrison slammed home a fine equaliser at 2:36 but at 4:40 Ian Cooper couldn't fail to miss the gaping hole in McCrone's net and Cardiff were ahead courtesy of a short-handed goal. They moved smartly and efficiently to a 4-1 lead as Flyers struggled to find their fluency on a rather slushy ice pad. Bobby Brown made it 4-2 at 12:26 before the Fifers moved on the power play. The chance of a breakthrough power play goal became a short-handed nightmare as Hilton Ruggles rang the red light.

Just to underline that it wasn't going to be Flyers day, Gordon Latto took two minutes for slashing. Along with the rest of the arena, he could only watch in disbelief as Doug Small's certain breakaway short-handed goal was wrecked when he just had Jason Wood to beat. As he went for the wrist shot it bobbled and the ex-NHL man was left with an air shot. Ian Cooper made it 6-2 on the same power play although Flyers had the last word of the opening period, courtesy of Iain Robertson's slapshot.

The damage had been done for Flyers in particular, but neither side emerged with any defensive credit during the opening 20 minutes. A tighter middle period ended all square at 1-1 and Flyers certainly picked up the tempo but they were always playing catch-up hockey against a side which rarely coughed up a lead. Their spells of pressure couldn't produce the goals necessary to put the skids under Devils' own defence. The end was in sight when Hilton Ruggles slammed home number eight just six seconds into the third period. It was a disappointing trip south for the 1000-plus Fife army. Not so much the result but the manner in which they saw their side beaten. Even in the midst of the chaotic, freakish opening period, Flyers could see Devils were well within their sights. The Welsh defence had its own moments of uncertainty but they covered up their errors by carefully policing Smail and Morrison.

The Stats for the match were as follows:

Devils: Hilton Ruggles 3+2, Stephen Cooper 2+1, Ian Cooper 2+1, Rick Brebant 1+5, Doug McEwan 1+0, Shannon Hope 0+2, Nicky Chinn 0+1, Jason Stone 0+1

Flyers: Mark Morrison 2+0, Bobby Brown 2+0, Iain Robertson 1+1, Doug Smail 0+1, Ryan Kummu 0+1.

Attendance: 7909

In the Final the following day, after the Steelers had blanked the Panthers 8-0 in the second semi- final, the Devils romped home in one of the most one-sided Wembley Finals ever when they retained their Championship crown with a 12-1 shellacking.

Mark Morrison scores the Flyers opening goal at Wembley

Sunday April 24th 1988

Durham Wasps 8 Fife Flyers 5

For the fourth successive year the Flyers were on the glory trail at the Wembley Finals weekend. After easily disposing of the Whitley Warriors in their semi-final on Saturday they were up against the Durham Wasps in an attempt to emulate their last Final success in 1985. Demand as usual from Fife fans for the end of season event was high. With an initial allocation of 860 briefs selling out weeks ago, a further 200 tickets were then snapped up from returns from other clubs.

It was a horrible start to the game, however, that cost Fife the game. Three goals were conceded in the first eight minutes; the Flyers never quite recovered from that early setback as they succumbed to what was a powerful Durham Wasps side.

It was a match which offered little excitement for Fife fans in the arena and those watching at home on television. The Flyers supporters had approached the final with confidence after their impressive semi-final display and excellent play-off performances so it was a major disappointment.

Durham, looking as sound in defence as any British side in recent years, were always going to be difficult to catch once they were in front. Wasps went ahead after just 35 seconds with a power play goal after Dean Edmiston had been penalised just 12 seconds earlier. Edmiston, given the role of unsettling Rick Brebant, was penalised for an interference offence involving the tall Canadian.

Brebant, who had been in devastating form in Durham's semi-final with Murrayfield, had a much quieter game in terms of points in the final. Conversely netminder Chris Salem, who had looked vulnerable in the Murrayfield match, turned in an inspired performance which helped turn the game.

It was captain Paul Smith who took the Durham Man of the Match award with three goals and two assists but there were no weaknesses in the Wasps side. The English side did in fact lead 7-2 with just 33 minutes gone as they dominated the early play.

Inspirational goals by Steve Moria and Jim Lynch helped reduce the deficit to 7-5 four minutes into the third period as Flyers staged a brave rally. Mike O'Connor then scored Durham's eighth goal and there was no way back for the Flyers. Al Sims turned in a heroic final performance and he scored the Flyers opening goal.

Fred Perlini was voted Fife Man of the Match; he got the second counter to bring the score to 4-2 at the end of the first period and the third goal which made it 7-3 in Durham's favour. Sims said afterwards that the three early goals had made all the difference.

Had Flyers scored first Durham would have been forced to play a more open game, resulting in less stringent marking on Perlini and Moria. Flyers who preferred to carry the puck across the opponents' blue line had been forced to dump and chase far too often he said.

Mike O'Connor commented that each member of his side managed to keep their discipline very well. To compound a hugely disappointing weekend the Flyers then made some national tabloid newspaper headlines 24 hours later; the club's flight back into Edinburgh was forced to abandon its landing as a couple of Flyers players, goalies Craig Dickson and Andrew Donald, did not obey the landing instructions of the cabin crew.

Almost immediately the club slapped a £500 fine on each and a lifetime playing ban. A significant move against two of the most talented netminders in the entire league. For Donald it would be his final involvement with the club although Craig Dickson would be reinstated the following season and went on to play a further four years with the Flyers.

The seconds tick away on another Wembley dream

Saturday April 25th 1987

Durham Wasps 7 Fife Flyers 5

By now readers will have spotted the similarity of events around this time of year; once again the Flyers faithful were re-acquainted with the strains of Brass Bonanza and over-priced beer.

It did however have an inevitable feeling. The Flyers were perhaps always destined to be the "Bridesmaids" this season as they crashed out of the Wembley showpiece at the semi-final stage against Durham's "Big Blue Machine".

Having lost to the Panthers in the Norwich Union Cup Final, the Flyers were also denied silverware when the Dundee Rockets annexed them on home ice from the Scottish Cup at the semi-final stage. The Wasps finished the regular season just a point behind the third-placed Flyers and matches between the two were very keenly contested with both sides winning their respective home games.

The games played in Durham, however, were close affairs. Confidence in the Fife camp was naturally high as the teams took to the ice in the first semi-final of the weekend. Flyers had somewhat upset the form book by winning their qualifying section. This relegated the regular season runners up, Dundee Rockets, into the second semi-final where they would meet the League Champions, Murrayfield Racers.

It was a tightly contested opening period which was dominated by each teams' prowess on the power play. Firstly, Jimmy Pennycook scored with the man advantage with assists from Steve Moria and Al Sims. That lead lasted barely 90 seconds when Kevin Conway struck for the Wasps as Neil Abel and Gordon Goodsir, along with Wasps Ian Cooper, watched from the box.

The Flyers upped their momentum however in the middle period and took what looked like a formidable lead given the circumstances of the game, into the final period. Durham, however, were first to strike after the interval when the Johnson brothers combined with Ian Cooper for Stephen to score. The Flyers took advantage of a couple of power plays to regain the lead. Steve Moria from Neil Abel levelled and on 28 minutes Al Sims fired the Flyers ahead with an assist from Moria. It was another short-lived lead however as 90 seconds later Stephen Johnson struck his second.

There was drama as Wasps Frankie Killen was taken out of the game after he was hit by a shot from Sims and his back up Neil Campbell played 32 seconds to allow him to recover. Midway through the game and it was all tied up but Fife then struck out for a lead before the second intermission. Their third power play goal of the period, this one from Dave Stoyanovich assisted by Sims was added to by the Sims grabbing his second, again from a Moria assist but this time at even strength. A two-goal lead looked significant.

In a penalty-free third period however, the Wasps did a number on the Flyers. Three goals in the space of 54 seconds was a devastating burst and swung the momentum of the game their way. Anthony Johnson got the first followed 48 seconds later by Mario Belanger to tie the game up. Incredibly just 6 seconds later and Belanger had edged the Wasps ahead. Fife pushed for the equaliser but with time running out Belanger helped himself to a natural hat trick and iced it for the Wasps to leave the Flyers looking a bewildered lot.

Wasps Anthony Johnson bears down on Andy Donald as Al Sims watches on in the Wembley semi final.

Thursday April 26th 1951

Fife Flyers 13 Dunfermline Vikings 1

In what had ultimately turned out to be a disappointing season, compared to the last few, the Flyers all but secured another piece of silverware with a thumping win over their Fife neighbours.

Shortly after Verne Greger had taken a penalty for tripping, the Vikings opened the scoring. A shot from George Sinfield went into the net and came out at the back. It was only after the referees discovered a hole in the net that they awarded the goal. That would be all there was to shout about, if you were a Vikings fan.

Sherman Blair equalised not long afterwards. It was a grand effort. Marsh Bentley swung a hard shot across the goalmouth. Although the puck was two feet off the ice, the left winger first-timed it home. Penalties spoiled further play and Flyers pounded the Dunfermline cage. Don Anderson was defying their efforts to gain a lead but a pass round the goal by Bentley was tapped home by Scotty Reid.

Twenty-eight seconds after the restart Bert Smith flipped in a Blair rebound and Flyers were set for their big win. The Flyers forwards were scrambling round the visitors' net when Floyd Snider popped in another. Fifteen seconds later Blair hit home an Archie Williams rebound. Then the right winger got one for himself when Bentley's pass left him with a clear shot. A tangle between Snider and Ross Atkins resulted in a minor penalty to each but the Dunfermline player was displeased and managed to talk his way into getting ten minutes added.

Vikings indiscipline didn't help their cause, as they always appeared to have a player in the 'cooler'; as a result they never looked like catching up. The final session was a stormer. A Greger play resulted in Snider adding to the Flyers lead. Following that came the best goal of the evening. Pete Belanger, in the home cage, passed the puck to Williams who body-swerved clean through the opposition to net and give his tender an assist-point on the score sheet.

Then Bentley went hat-trick hunting. He had quite a bit to make up on his team mates but he netted two goals within a minute and from a Williams' pass got his third. Within 47 seconds three different Kirkcaldy players had chalked up goals to complete their hat tricks. Williams followed Bentley to get his first 'triple' this season; hot on his tail was Sherman Blair scoring his ninth set of three for the season.

Penalties were handed out to Atkins and Con Switzer just before the whistle. Both players decided not to sit out the penalties as the game was almost over and went for an early shower. The rules however didn't allow for that and we then had the spectacle of referee Cross attempting to retrieve them both from the dressing room.

Twice he tried and each time he returned alone and held up his hands to signify that each had been given a misconduct. On the restart Flyers had decided they had done enough and gave the Vikings plenty of scope but they had already packed up their tent and were beyond caring about the match.

The teams met two nights later for the second leg in Dunfermline, where the home side at least recovered some pride in front of their own fans, when they won the match 10-6.

№ 29113

Kirkcaldy
Ice
Rink

PROGRAMME
4ᴰ

Readers will enjoy this programme, for the Flyers Jubilee Trophy win against the Dunfermline Vikings, reproduced over the next few pages.

TO-NIGHT we play Vikings in the first leg of the Jubilee Cup, and on Saturday our boys travel to Dunfermline to play the Final leg.

The match here to-night is the last of our home games this season, and our match on Saturday at Dunfermline completes this season's programme. These two games will be very keenly fought and are sure to be full of thrills from beginning to end.

A local "derby" is a very fitting ending to our hockey fixtures.

To-night, at the first interval, Mr Ian Stevenson, Director of Dunfermline Ice Rink, has very kindly promised to present the Autumn Cup and Bairns Trophy.

With regard to our Summer Programme, to-morrow will conclude our Old-Time Dancing for the season, but there will be Modern Dancing every Saturday, and we shall be putting on "Name Bands" from time to time, the first being Hedley Ward and his Radio Band on Thursday, 10th May.

The Club premises will be open on certain evenings during the week, and these will be notified.

As this is our last programme, the Management would like to take this opportunity of thanking all Patrons, Officials, Players and Staff, and the Red Cross for their services during the year.

FLYERS' FIXTURES

DATE			COMP.	VENUE	OPPONENTS	RESULT
1951						
Sat.	Feb.	10	Nati'nal	Away	PERTH PANTHERS	4—2
Mon.	,,	12	League	Away	DUNDEE TIGERS	4—3
Thurs.	,,	15	,,	Home	DUNFERMLINE VIKINGS	5—3
Wed.	,,	21	,,	Away	PAISLEY PIRATES	7—12
Thurs.	,,	22	,,	Home	FALKIRK LIONS	3—5
Mon.	,,	26	,,	Away	FALKIRK LIONS	2—3
Thurs.	Mar.	1	,,	Home	DUNDEE TIGERS	4—5
Mon.	,,	5	,,	Away	DUNFERMLINE VIKINGS	2—8
Thurs.	,,	8	,,	Home	PERTH PANTHERS	6—7
Wed.	,,	14	,,	Away	AYR RAIDERS	3—8
Thurs.	,,	15	,,	Home	PAISLEY PIRATES	6—9
Mon.	,,	19	,,	Away	DUNDEE TIGERS	3—5
Thurs.	,,	22	,,	Home	DUNFERMLINE VIKINGS	3—7
Thurs.	,,	29	,,	Home	AYR RAIDERS	5—6
Sat.	,,	31	,,	Away	PERTH PANTHERS	4—7
Wed.	April	4	Canada	Away	PAISLEY PIRATES	5—7
Thurs.	,,	5	Cup	Home	FALKIRK LIONS	3—2
*Thurs.	,,	19	,,	Home	AYR RAIDERS	11—4
Sat.	,,	21	,,	Away	PERTH PANTHERS	4—7

* Final Autumn Cup.

HOCKEY PLAYER AND SKATER WED

By courtesy of the "Kirkcaldy Times."

"Pep" Young, Flyers' right winger, pictured with his bride, Miss Sheena Balfour, Scottish Amateur Figure-Skating Champion, following their wedding at St. Peter's Church, Kirkcaldy.

CANADA CUP.

FINAL STANDING.

	P.	W.	L.	D.	For	Against	Pts.
VIKINGS	12	7	2	3	58	47	17
LIONS	12	7	5	0	51	40	14
PANTHERS	12	6	4	2	52	46	14
PIRATES	12	6	6	0	53	50	12
FLYERS	12	5	8	1	53	48	11
TIGERS	12	4	6	2	40	48	10
RAIDERS	12	3	9	0	53	72	6

582

583

584

Rink Announcements

TO-NIGHT

SENIOR HOCKEY.   JUBILEE CUP (First Leg).

FLYERS v. VIKINGS

FINAL at Dunfermline—SATURDAY, 28th April.
AUTUMN CUP AND BAIRNS TROPHY BEING
PRESENTED TO-NIGHT.

FRIDAY, 27th April.   Old-Time Dancing.

To JOHN SMITH and his Old-Time Quartet.

(This Season's concluding Old-Time Dance).

8-11 p.m.   Admission 1/6.

EVERY SATURDAY.   Modern Dancing.

To BILL DUFF and his Orchestra.

8-11 p.m.   Admission 2/-.

Coming on **THURSDAY, 10th May.**

HEDLEY WARD & HIS RADIO BAND

OFFICIALS:
Announcer—Victor Beattie.
Timekeeper—J. C. B. Carr.
Scorer—J. Oates.
Penalty Timekeeper—J. Kilpatrick.

GOALS	ASSISTS	PENALTIES

TO-NIGHT'S

THURSDAY, 26th AP

FIFE FLYERS

Colours: BLUE AND GOLD.

1. ADRIAN BELANGER   GOAL
2. VERNE GREGER   DEFENCE
3. FLOYD SNIDER (Capt.)
5. RAY DINARDO
12. J. MITCHELL   FORWARD
6.
7. M. BENTLEY
8. "SCOTTY" REID
4. AL CAMPONE
11. BERT SMITH
10. A. WILLIAMS
9. S. BLAIR

Coach: Al Rogers.
Trainer: Tom Elder.

Referees:
D. CROSS and N. McCU

......13....GOALS

IT'S LINE-UP

AY, 26th APRIL, 1951

VIKINGS
Colours: RED, WHITE & BLACK.

			GOALS	ASSISTS	PENALTIES	
GOAL	DON ANDERSON	1.				
DEFENCE	VINNY KEYES	2.			X X X	
	~~TUCK SYME~~	3.				
	TINY SYME	4.			X X	
FORWARD	D. HEBENTON	5.				
	ROSS ATKINS	6.			X X	
	GERRY HUDSON	7.			X	
	CON SWITZER	8.	X		X	
	~~WILF THRASHER~~	9.				
	JUNIOR	10.			X X	
	~~KEITH CRIGHTON~~	11.			X	
	JOHN ROLLAND	12.				

Referees:
SS and N. McCUAIG.

Coach: Joe Aitken.
Trainer: J. Johnstone.

...........GOALS

SUPPORTERS' CORNER

TO-NIGHT'S Derby with Vikings is the first leg of the Jubilee Cup and should create a keen game. Vikings are winners of the Canada Cup, while Flyers have won the Fife Championship, the Autumn Cup and the Bairns Trophy. Both clubs have had some rare tussles this season and they break about even on results. This will be the last ice hockey game of season 1950-51. Presentation of both the Autumn Cup and the Bairns Trophy will be made at the first interval. Mr Ian Stevenson of Dunfermline has kindly consented to hand over the trophies to Flyers' popular captain, Floyd Snider. 2-4-6-8, Etc.

The final of this Jubilee Cup will be played at Dunfermline on Saturday, 28th April. The supporters are keen to see the last game, and buses will be run from the Rink, leaving here approximately one hour before advertised face-off time. You can book for this game immediately after to-night's game in the Skate Hire Room.

Supporters' Whist Drive held in Drummond's Cafe was a very enjoyable one. Prize-winners:—Ladies—1 Mrs Mitchell, 2 Miss Lima; gents.— 1 Ray Dinardo, 2 Miss Hamilton. Consolations—Miss Jean Spence and Mr Tom Knox. Winner of raffle—Mrs Niven, St. Andrews. Cardmaster, Mr Watson. M.C., Mr Mitchell. Prizes presented by Mrs Adamson. The Social Committee wish to thank those who donated prizes, and all who helped to make it a success. They hope to hold a Hostess Whist Drive in the near future and will give notification in the local Press.

Flyers Supporters' Annual Drive, Sunday, 29th April, 1951. Buses leave Rink at 9 a.m., picking up members en route via Junction Road, Dunnikier Road, Bennochy Bridge, Fidelity Garage and Burntisland. Lunch in Cross Keys Hotel, Peebles. Destination St. Mary's Loch, via Traquair. Tea in Kings Hotel, Galashiels. Here's hoping for a good day, boys!

This being our last Supporters' Corner, we take this opportunity of thanking the Directors of Kirkcaldy Ice Rink for their courtesy in granting us this space in the programme. We also wish all our members and all Flyers' fans a nice summer and a good holiday. Hoping to see you all in September to shout that 2-4-6-8, Etc., and follow Flyers everywhere in Season 1951-52! Cheerio, Fans!

FLYERS LAST HOME GAME

Vikings Provide the Opposition

FOR their last game of the season at Kirkcaldy to-night, Flyers oppose County rivals, Dunfermline Vikings, in a two-legged play-off for custody of the Jubilee Trophy.

Both teams have enjoyed their share of the limelight in the various tournaments throughout the season. Flyers, winners of the Autumn Cup and Bairns Trophy, will want to add the Jubilee Trophy to their list of successes, while Vikings, winners of the Canada Cup, will be keen to gain a second award to be upsides with the Kirkcaldy boys.

Quite a number of the players will be making their last appearance in Scottish ice hockey, and although neither of the clubs have announced their retained lists, rumour has it that at least four or five players will be released from the respective clubs at the end of the season. The players who are returning home for the close season will depart from this country on the 1st or 3rd of May.

We take this opportunity of wishing the team, the coach and trainer, a pleasant vacation, and to those that are going home, a safe journey. To those who will not be returning—Good-bye and the best of luck.

ICE HOCKEY RULES

THE ICE SURFACE between the two goals is divided into three zones by two Blue Lines, DEFENDING ZONE, NEUTRAL ZONE and ATTACKING ZONE.

THE RED LINE is drawn completely across the rink on centre-ice parallel with the goal lines. It is known as the Centre Line and divides the rink into DEFENDING and ATTACKING HALVES.

OFF-SIDE. Any attacking player entering the attacking zone before the puck is off-side.

BODY CHECKING is permitted only against the puck carrier and only after he has crossed the red line.

CROSS-CHECKING. A minor penalty shall be imposed on any player who cross-checks. (Note: a cross-check is a check delivered with both hands on the stick and no part of the stick on the ice.)

THE PUCK may be stopped with the hand, body or skate at any time and in any Zone.

KICKING THE PUCK is permitted in all Zones, but a goal may not be scored by the kick of an attacking player unless the puck is deflected into the net by a defending player other than the goalminder.

PENALTIES. Penalised players are sent off the ice for varying periods according to the nature of the offence. No substitute player is allowed on the ice, except in the case of Misconduct Penalties, while the offender is in the Penalty Box. Penalised players must skate behind their Blue Lines before re-entering play after the expiration of the penalty.

SUBSTITUTES. Players may be changed at any time from the players' bench provided that the player or players leaving the ice shall be at the players' bench and out of the play before any change is made. Only six players from each side may be allowed on the ice at any time during the match.

THE FACE-OFF. The Puck is "faced" by the Referee dropping the puck on the ice between the sticks of the players taking the "face-off." At the beginning of each period and after each goal the face-off takes place at the centre face-off spot. The other face-offs take place at the appropriate face-off spot marked on the ice surface on either side of the goals and on spots adjacent to the blue line, or in some cases where the actual stoppage of play occurred.

ASSIST. A player who passes the puck to the goal-scorer is credited with one point in the scoring list. A double assist arises where a goal results from more than one pass and provided the passes are made within the attacking half of the rink.

DURATION OF MATCH is three 20-minute periods of actual play with time out for stoppages and for intervals between periods.

TALKING TO THE REFEREES. Only the team Captain or his Deputy shall have the privilege of discussing with the referees any question relating to the interpretation of the Rules.

ICING THE PUCK occurs when any player shoots the puck from his own half of the ice behind the goal line of the opposing team. Play is stopped and the puck is faced-off at the rink end spot of the opposing team. This rule does not apply if a goal is scored, if it results from a face-off, if an opposing player other than the goalminder could have played the puck, if the puck should touch any part of a player of the opposing team, or if in the opinion of the Referee a proper pass has been attempted by the player shooting the puck.

BROKEN STICK. A player whose stick is broken may participate in the game provided he drops the broken portion.

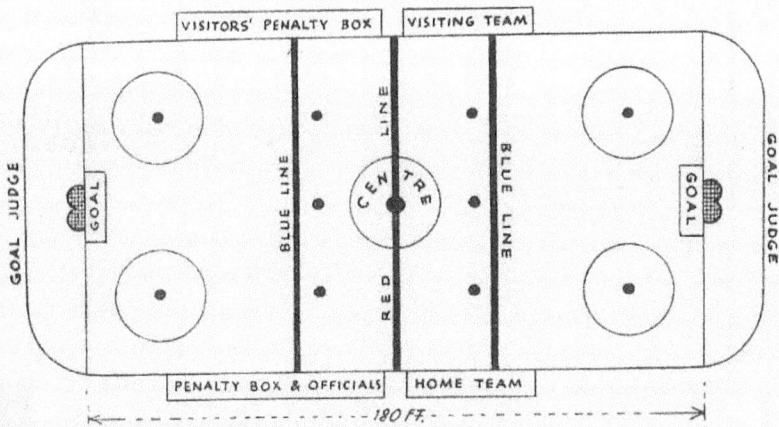

Refresh yourself!

DRINK
Coca-Cola

TRADE MARK REG.

Tuesday April 27th 1948

Paisley Pirates 8 Fife Flyers 4

With only one win in their last five matches, the Flyers were playing their penultimate Canada Cup game on their way to finishing bottom of the table in the competition.

Flyers were more enthusiastic than of late at Paisley, but a deficit of four goals at the end of the first period reduced their chances of winning to a minimum. The defence would want to forget the disastrous first session when an enterprising Paisley attack took full advantage of their defensive gaps.

The hockey in the second period was a great improvement but Flyers lacked that extra bit of combination and enterprise which marked the home side. Once again Bud Scrutton was the best Flyer, playing a dour never-say-die game, and Ted Fowler showed greatly improved form. Kenny Potts was still absent through tonsilitis but he had an able deputy in junior Bert Smith, who played a hard game.

The second line had an off-night with Roy Hawkins being best. Bob Londry was the best defenceman but Floyd Snider was ever ready to turn defence into attack. Sholtz had a hectic night in net, but as was the case most nights could can take a lot of credit for his effort.

Pirates took an early lead through future Flyer Johnny Vanier in the second minute after Paul Therriault and Leo Carrey had made the play. The cheering had barely died away when Doug Leadbetter managed to outmanoeuvre a puzzled Flyers defence to beat Sholtz from close quarters. A bright spell from the Flyers saw Fowler reduce the leeway from a pass by Smith behind Danny Kewley's net.

The balance was soon restored however when Vanier picked up a Carrey pass to net Pirates third in the seventh minute. Leadbetter came near to scoring but a full-length clearance by Sholtz saved the day. The puck came right back into the goalmouth but Pat Good was on the line to save. A few minutes later Pirates went further ahead when Therriault stickhandled his way into the goalmouth before netting. Flyers hit hack and a cunning Fowler-Snider move resulted in the latter scoring.

In the final minute of the period Pirates ran amok, scoring through Tommy Lauder and Leadbeater with both goals being assisted by Ted Watson. In the second period Pirates kept up the pressure and after

Leadbeater and Jack Thaler had worked their way through the Fife defence Sholtz brought off two praiseworthy clearances. Play switched to the other end with Kewley clearing in a goalmouth scrimmage from Fowler and Smith. Scrutton puzzled the home defence more than once but the puck was always cleared. Another Paisley goal looked imminent after Watson had drawn the defence but Sholtz saved magnificently from Leadbeater. A breakaway by Cliff Ryan came to nothing when the puck skimmed over the top of the cage. Back came the relentless Pirates and Sholtz saved two powerful shots. He was unable to stop a shot from Vanier in the 17th minute to put Pirates five goals ahead.

Sholtz had a hectic opening three minutes to start the final period in which Carrey and Leadbeater were prominent. A minute later Scrutton netted from close range following some fine combined play by Fowler and Ryan. Things looked a bit brighter for Flyers when Fowler netted two minutes later following a great combination with Scrutton which left the home defence completely helpless. Thaler came near to scoring but a last minute save by Sholtz kept the score at 7-4.

It looked as though the Flyers would get their fifth when Les O'Rourke gave Roy Hawkins a perfect pass in the goalmouth but he sent it past the post. Vanier and Therriault tested Sholtz and Flyers goal had a break when Carrey shot wide after Sholtz had been enticed from his charge. In the closing minutes Bernie Hill brought the Pirates total to eight with an individual goal.

Murrel 'Babe' Sholtz
who had a busy night in Paisley

Thursday April 28th 1955

East Canada 8 West Canada 5

With only one away game remaining to play for the Flyers to complete the one and only season of the British National League, this challenge match would prove to be the final senior hockey game played at the rink for over seven long years.

Both sets of players went about the game with great enthusiasm in front of a larger-than-usual crowd. If it was to be the end of professional hockey played by the Canadians imported by the Scottish Ice Hockey Association members then it was at least a glorious finish. Here for all to see was a perfect example of experience versus youthful enthusiasm, with the older Easterners proving themselves just a bit too good for the youngsters from Canada's Western provinces.

When the teams for this challenge match were announced it was obvious that the East side had a monopoly on the finer points of the game. Against this the Western line-up looked capable of skating and perhaps getting right on top in the latter stages of the game.

In the first two periods, the older Eastern team was much too good for the West. Perth Panthers deadly combination of Tommy Forgie and Bruce Hamilton with Flyers coach Henry Hayes on the right wing repeatedly ripped huge gaps in the West defence with great ease and the other line of Thrasher, Sullivan and Domenico repeatedly hemmed in their opponents.

The West however missed big chances in the early stages. Twice they broke away and should have scored and that was before the East opened their account. Then the East began to make their pressure pay dividends. Domenico popped in two in 20 seconds, Hayes completed a Forgie play two minutes later to put the East 3-0 ahead.

Goals by Andrews and Beattie for the West made it a bit more respectable at the start of the second period. It was just then that the Hayes, Hamilton line began to reap the reward of their polished passing movements. Hamilton was as ever the sharp-shooter and netted three in ten minutes with a beautiful goal by Burns in between making it 7-2 for the East with twenty minutes left.

The leeway was much too big for the West. Even though they were the much stronger team in the last 20 minutes they lacked the skill to utilise their power to its full extent. Led by the elusive Jake Favel, they did stage a revival, but they rarely looked like closing the gap and only bad finishing prevented the East piling up an even bigger lead.

Johannson reduced arrears only for the East to counter through Sullivan. Davison and Beattie brought the scoring to an end. The game as a whole was a treat for those hockey enthusiasts who delight in accurate passing moves and the crowd, incidentally the largest since New Year, was not slow to show its appreciation. Particularly noteworthy was the combination of Forgie and Hayes who, despite both being well over forty years old,and easily outskated by their opponents, were so shrewd in their positioning and passing that their physical disadvantage hardly seemed to matter.

These two and Hamilton were the real dangermen of the East team but special mention must also be made of goalkeeper Mike Luke, who survived the loss of one or two bad goals and went on to a grand game. For the West it was Johannson and Kurz who had the right ideas but they had poor support from the forwards. Individually they were strong and fast but they rarely combined and were often easily disposed by the East defence.

East Canada – Mike Luke (Flyers), Bobby Burns (Royals), Henri Labrosse (Flyers), Verne Greger (Tigers), Nebby Thrasher (Flyers), Art Sullivan (Tigers), Ernie Domenico (Flyers), Tommy Forgie (Panthers), Henry Hayes (Flyers), Bruce Hamilton (Panthers)

West Canada – Walter Malahoff (Panthers), Red Kurz (Tigers), Ken Johannson (Flyers), Neil Matheson (Flyers), Jake Favel (Royals), Johnny Andrews (Flyers), Tick Beattie (Royals), Don Cox (Flyers), Walt Davison (Flyers), Wayne Sutherland (Flyers)

Referees – M Beaton, B Tierney

Flyers hard-hitting center ice 'Nebby' Thrasher being presented with the Mirror of Merit Award for season 1954/55 by director of Kirkcaldy Ice Rink, Victor Beattie

Saturday April 29th 1997

Fife Flyers 0 Swindon Ice Lords 5

It was always going to be a hard task. Ultimately Flyers could not match the sheer power and strength of the Swindon Ice Lords in the British Premier League Final at the Nynex Arena in Manchester. The difference between the import-laden Southern League and the Northern League's policy of giving British players a chance was never so obvious. A brave Flyers effort found the handicap of playing with three import players to Ice Lords' *ten* — and a further two were injured — too much to overcome.

With Canadian netminder Mark Cavalin in top form, Flyers also suffered the indignity of being shut-out, although they did create a few chances which on another day they might have taken. In the end, the shots on goal total of 51-21 told its own story. The over-worked Martin McKay was a real hero in the Fife net in what was his last game before joining the police. The reception he received from the huge contingent of Sheffield fans and the magnificent Fife support — which looked much larger than the 1000 estimate — was a fitting tribute to end his hockey career.

It would have been nice for him to go out with a winner's medal as well, but the brute strength of the Swindon defence was just too much for the Flyers. They formed a virtually impenetrable barrier across their blue line. On the few occasions that Fife did manage to break through, Cavalin was there to deny them — one save in the second period with the score at 3-0 was particularly amazing. If that had gone in who knows what might have happened?

Certainly, it would have been interesting if the game had been played to Northern League rules with Swindon only allowed to pick their best three imports and packing their team with British players — something they would end up having to do the following season with their main financial backer walking away at the realisation of his "dream" of championship success.

The benefits of developing your own talent was ably demonstrated on the Fife bench where youngsters like Lee Mercer, John Reid and 16-year-old Kyle Horne all gained valuable experience and let no-one down with their efforts. In fact, none of the team could really be faulted for their commitment but the step up to a higher level of intensity after a season of playing in the Northern League was never going to be an easy one to make. Russ Parent found himself under constant pressure in defence, the main forward line usually had nowhere to go and the second line were unable to break free of the tight checking.

For all that, Flyers actually started the brighter as both teams took a while to size each other up. Mark Morrison failed to convert a difficult chance in the first minute and if the early pressure had brought a goal the complexion of the game could have changed. As it was, a lucky bounce off the boards at 9.42 saw Robin Davison fire Swindon ahead and a crucial second at 16.31 from Chris Eimers — again with more than a hint of luck about it — gave the English team a cushion at the break. With the Ice Lords content to defend in depth and try to catch Flyers on the break, the Fife fans were still confident that their team could get back into the game but unable to capitalise on a few power play opportunities, there seemed no way past the impressive Cavalin. Eimers grabbed his second at 33.28 with a shot that seemed to deceive McKay in flight and then two goals in the final two minutes of the period from Barclay Pearce and Lee Braithwaite — the latter with just one second to go -wrapped up the game for Swindon.

The final period was a low-key affair, only brightened briefly by a flare-up involving Pearce and Mercer, as Ice Lords protected Cavalin's shut-out. Flyers did have a couple of good chances to score but it wasn't to be and Swindon took the title.

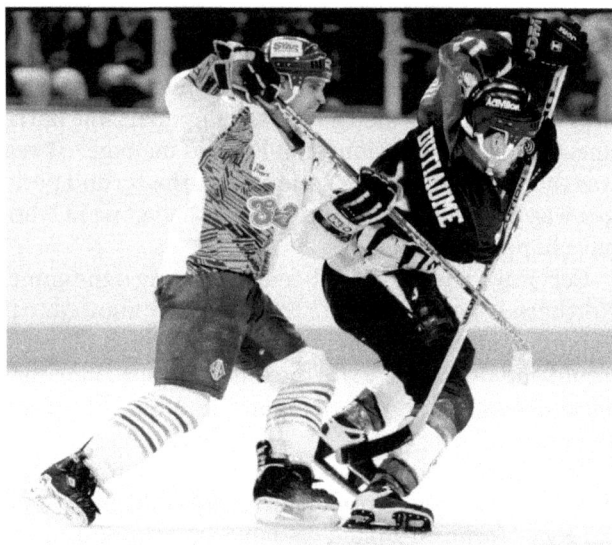

Russ Parent attempts to slow down the Ice Lords Todd Dutiaume during the Final at the Nynex Arena

Thursday April 30th 1947

Fife Flyers 8 Falkirk Lions 3

Was there ever a team like Fife Flyers?

It was a rhetorical question after the Flyers had run themselves into a 6-4 deficit at Falkirk the night before, in the opening game of the Simpson Trophy, before they walloped Lions the following night in the return game at Kirkcaldy.

Inconsistency had been an issue for much of the season, but games were usually very interesting and intriguing! If you were late to your seat for this one then you had already missed the first significant piece of the action. In exactly thirteen seconds Bud Scrutton flashed an Earl McCrone assist past Clair O'Connell. Then after only 55 seconds McCrone did ditto on a Scrutton assist. Visions of a cricket score rose in the imaginations of the local fans. However, as might have been expected this was too good to last.

No team can go on scoring goals at the rate of two a minute — well, not strictly true in his game, if you discount the lengthy intervals between them. Lions recovered from the early shocks and fought back. By midway through the period Flyers had lost their lead. In seven minutes Johnny Savicky took advantage of a defensive lapse, whizzed a shot from the right wing — this had been a weakness on a number of occasions for Flyers netminder Don Dougall — and suddenly the deficit was one.

Then just to show that this two goals in a minute business was quite easy Savicky scored another in the eighth minute. This perhaps gave the home side the jolt they needed. Just before the interval gong Earl McCrone on a Scrutton-Snider assist, gave them the lead once again.

The second period also opened surprisingly, this time a two-minute penalty award against McCrone for tripping. Play in the middle period raged from end to end at a terrific pace and there were times when it looked as if hostilities would start at any time. Bud Scrutton was the chief "victim", the worst example being when Keith Tolton literally "took the feet" from him without penalty.

Bob Lantz scored on a John Drummond assist in nine minutes. Shortly after, Scrutton hit the post with a terrific shot. John Drummond then scored on a Lantz assist after 12 minutes. Lion's defence — with the exception of goaltender O'Connell — were rattled and only a spectacular clearance by the netminder kept a McCrone drive out. A score was only delayed, McCrone netting from a Harry O'Connor assist in 18 minutes. A minute later Frankie King took a Scrutton pass to score yet another quick-fire double.

With a 7-2 lead Flyers were guilty of giving Lions too much rope in the final session. Tolton was penalised for what was described as "knees-up." while a little later Lantz was sent to the box on a tripping call. Scrutton was given a gift from the gods when he received the puck and had a clear skate in on O'Connell but the netminder cleared.

Lions showed their appreciation of this let-off by racing to the other end. Paul Pelow assisted by Norman Watts placed the puck in the rigging. Flyers made more of the turn-round, and O'Connell's goal had a series of narrow escapes. In 17 minutes McCrone crowned a good night's work by scoring his own fourth goal on a Scrutton assist.

For Flyers Dougall, Londry, King, Scrutton and McCrone were the pick, while Lions were best served by O'Connell, Clair "the mighty midget" Parker and Savicky. It was a good fast game. Although beaten the Lions' team, as ever, showed many clever touches.

There were only a further two Simpson Trophy games for the Flyers before the end of the competitive action for the season. They finished the competition with 2 wins and 2 defeats.

Action between the Flyers and Dundee Stars from the 2019/20 season

May

Law Lovell and Gordon Latto (16) combine for a goal against the Racers earlier in the 1976/77 season

Sunday May 1st 1977

Murrayfield Racers 4 Fife Flyers 5

Flyers secured their place in the Spring Cup Final for the fourth year running with this narrow win over rivals Murrayfield in the second leg of the semi-final.

Flyers took a two-goal first-leg lead into this match. After only five minutes they added to that when Gordon Latto netted the only goal of the first period. Flyers had Les Lovell and Jimmy Jack back in the side while Willie Cottrell took John Pullar's place in goal. It was a first-class performance from Cottrell, which kept the Racers off the scoresheet as they fought hard to establish a breakthrough.

Flyers really took control of the match and the tie in the second period and opened up a 4-1 lead on the night. Although Racers had equalised early in the second period it was once again Gordon Latto who restored the lead. Towards the close of the period a brilliant move between Les Lovell and Dougie Latto produced one of the best goals of the season for a 3-1 lead. The two best players worked their way forward and Latto took an inch perfect pass from his captain to give Main no chance in the Murrayfield net. Jimmy Jack notched another quick goal before the buzzer.

The final stanza was full of action as Racers came storming back to try to salvage the tie. Freddie Wood got a first minute goal for the home team before Derek Reilly slammed one home on a power play. Wood with his second goal tied the scores on the night with six minutes to play but Cottrell was proving a heartbreaker to Racers with several class saves. As the minutes ticked away it was the Flyers who took the game and the tie. With only 16 seconds left, Angus Cargill let a shot fly from the blue line and rang the red light. Flyers had now brought their tally to an incredible twelve straight wins over the auld enemy and the following week they extended this to unlucky thirteen when they annexed the Racers home tournament, the Evening News Trophy. Flyers who had already won the Northern League, Autumn Cup and Icy Smith Cup had now only one hurdle to leap to emulate what only the Paisley Mohawks in 1967/68 and the Murrayfield Racers in 1970/71 had achieved in Northern Ice Hockey Association history, the Grand Slam, when they would meet Whitley Warriors in the Final over two legs.

Saturday May 2nd 1964

Fife Flyers 5 Wembley Lions 4

Two shock goals in a hectic final 30 seconds saw Flyers beat Wembley Lions 5-4 to become the first ever winners of the B.B.C. Grandstand Trophy in a match played at the Sports Stadium Brighton. It was the Fife side's tenacity and — it has to be acknowledged — a liberal sprinkling of luck that enabled them to pull back Wembley's slim one-goal lead in the dying seconds and go on to turn almost certain defeat into victory.

Flyers had hammered the London side 9-2 at Kirkcaldy a month ago but there was never going to be a repeat of that, as on this occasion the Lions were at full strength. Top scorer Chick Zamick and defencemen Art Hodgins and Vic Fildes, who all missed the previous game, played a major role in this thrill-a-minute affair. Ahead of Flyers hitting the ice for the Final, they received a number of telegrams and good wishes from ice hockey fans in Kirkcaldy.

If the game ended in dramatic fashion then the start was equally exciting. Lions Canadian George Beach soloed through to put Wembley into the lead with five minutes played on the clock. Flyers coach Ian Forbes netted in the 14th minute to equalise. Winger Sammy McDonald added another five minutes later to give the Flyers the edge at the end of the opening session. Wembley turned in the more attractive type of hockey over-all, and fought back hard in the second period with Vic Fildes, Zamick and Beach the danger men.

Six minutes into the middle session and the Lions were back on level terms when Fildes cut through to finish off a Beach move. Flyers held out under mounting pressure, then failed to cash in on a chance to go ahead when Lions Reg Board collected a two-minute penalty. The Flyers power play could make little inroads on the Lions net. It was Wembley who almost went ahead just as Board returned to the ice when Beach tried a solo move but was stopped just inside the blue-line. Minutes later Beach had a golden opportunity when he left Roy Reid sprawled in front of Flyers net but luck was with the Fife side, however, as the puck hit the net minder and bounced over the cage. Lions had another chance when Flyers defenceman Andy Williams was sent to the penalty box for two minutes after a high stick. Only some brilliant play from Roy Reid kept the eager Lions out.

Flyers picked up another goal early in the third session when Forbes netted his second. Just after the change around in the final period the Lions broke through and equalised then forged ahead into the lead with two brilliant goals. Firstly, Beach put Stan Bremner in possession and the Wembley forward rocketed from his own defensive zone round Flyers defenceman Joe McIntosh and whipped the puck into the net to tie the game. Five minutes later Chick Zamick soloed through a thunderstruck Fife defence to hammer home what looked like the winning goal. But a shock was in store for the jubilant Wembley supporters. Lions coach Johnny Murray collected two minutes in the sin bin for tripping Jimmy Spence. Flyers staged attack after attack but Glynn Thomas in the Wembley net seemed unbeatable.

In a last-ditch effort Flyers withdrew net minder Reid and added another forward and this heralded a blunder on Thomas's part. He dropped the puck for a second and Flyers coach Ian Forbes was on the spot to slam home his hat trick goal and the equaliser. Then with only two seconds left Flyers broke the hearts of the Lions when defenceman Bill Sneddon carried the puck from his own end and dumped it in front of the Wembley net. Before Thomas had time to gather the loose puck McDonald had passed to Sneddon again, who came up to drive the puck home and secure the silverware in the most dramatic fashion. The following week, at the end of season awards ceremony in which Flyers celebrated a "Grand Slam" season, coach Ian Forbes paid tribute to the team by saying, "We had to beat the best team in Britain to win the BBC trophy and I consider this to be virtually the British Championship"

Flyers captain Bert Smith receiving the BBC Grandstand trophy from actress of stage, film and television Dora Bryan

Saturday May 3rd 1986

Dundee Rockets 7 Fife Flyers 3

The Regal sponsored Scottish Cup had its critics in its first season. Many felt the qualifying series had too many meaningless games to play. The sole objective was to remove one of the five teams, for four to progress into the Finals weekend. The fixtures were all played at either Fife, Dundee or Edinburgh with many televised by either Grampian TV or the BBC. Perhaps this was a little hard on the Ayr Bruins and Glasgow Dynamos. Not all planned fixtures were played. The ones that were completed eventually eliminated the Dynamos.

The Flyers had a record of five wins and two losses from their seven matches in the competition. In the wake of the previous weekend's disappointment at Wembley, when they relinquished their British Championship crown after a semi-final defeat at the hands of the Murrayfield Racers, they played out their final game of the season. It was Flyers third journey to Tayside in the competition. As expected, the absence of three key players proved too great a handicap for them to overcome in Saturday's second semi-final against the hosts, Dundee Rockets.

Danny Brown was already back in Canada, and Jimmy Pennycook had returned offshore to the oil rigs. The Flyers were also without injured skipper Gordon Latto, who had broken a bone in his foot at Wembley. The understrength Kirkcaldy side saw their last chance of a trophy that season slip away in the first period as they conceded four goals without reply. In what was his 500th appearance for the club, it was a disappointing way for Chic Cottrell to end his Flyers playing career.

Three of Dundee's first period goals resulted from power plays. Garry Unger put them ahead after five minutes with Brian Peat sitting out his two minutes; three minutes later Graeme "Peem" Lafferty made it 2-0 with an unassisted effort. Flyers had both Ron Plumb and Charlie Kinmond under penalty when Ronnie Wood scored after twelve minutes. The roof threatened to fall in on the visitors less than sixty seconds later when the same player added a fourth goal.

The Flyers were presented with a golden opportunity to get back into the match when Rockets were left skating two men short at the start of the second period. They took full advantage when Andy Linton netted assisted by Plumb and Dean Edmiston. Just eleven seconds later and Todd Bidner also scored on the power play to make it 4-2. However, Flyers comeback was cut short by Roch Bois in the 25th minute. With Ronnie Wood restoring Dundee's four-goal advantage three minutes from the buzzer it looked like mission impossible for the Fifers.

That was confirmed when Wood scored his own fourth goal of the night a mere 22 seconds into the final period. With Rockets coasting to victory Dean Edmiston at least had the last word, three minutes from time, for Flyers with a goal assisted by Linton and Peat. Flyers were outshot 47-22 and were served with ten minutes in penalties compared with eight minutes for Dundee.

Todd Bidner evades Rockets Garry Unger and Roch Bois

Saturday May 4th 1974

Whitley Warriors 7 Fife Flyers 3

Flyers ended the season without a trophy — a stark reality for a team that at one stage looked as if they could sweep the honours board. Not winning any silverware on the face of it doesn't seem that incredible — no team has a divine right to win of course — but for this Flyers team they had made the slogan "often a bridesmaid ... never a bride" their own. That season, they were defeated in no fewer than five Cup Finals.

For what was the Flyers last match of the season the Gallatown men travelled south for the game with only eleven players and had to call on Glasgow netminder Pete Callaghan as a stand in.

There had already been six meetings between the sides that season with the honours evenly split at two wins each. The Warriors had not lost on home ice all season, but the Flyers had twice come close to ending that record. They had returned north with a couple of draws and on this occasion they put up a brave show somewhat against the odds.

The visitors trailed 5-2 going into the final period. When they pulled another goal back they had Warriors rattled for a bit. However the Northern League Champions regained their composure and added two more goals to finish worthy winners. Flyers three goals came from the Lovell brothers, with Les getting two and Lawrie the other.

It seemed incredible that Flyers finished the season without a trophy but they appeared to have been a victim of their own relative success. They qualified for so many finals that they ended up facing a back-log of fixtures and a hectic end to the season.

With Kirkcaldy Ice Rink having closed for the summer several weeks ago the players had to contest Cup Finals when they had been short of practice. On occasions the team had been under strength, owing to injuries and other commitments. Flyers had finished third in the Northern League and, along with Dundee Rockets and Murrayfield Racers, the Scottish sides could never catch the runaway Warriors. They were defeated in the finals of their own Skol Cup, the Rockets Angus Challenge Cup, Spring Cup, Durham's Dunelm Trophy and the Warriors Northumbria Cup.

On a happier note, and in contrast, the Kirkcaldy Kestrels had won every competition in which they had competed. That same weekend they picked up their third trophy of the season. Kestrels were already the holders of the League Championship and Coca-Cola Trophy when they had also travelled to the North East of England for the final of the Billingham Trophy. They defeated the home side, Bombers, by six goals to two. Gordon Latto was Kestrels Man of the Match with four of the goals while brother Dougie got one and Chic Cottrell the other. The young talent in the Kestrels would come into its own for the club over the next few years and it would be season 1978/79 before the Flyers would next go without silverware.

Les Lovell and Ally Brennan both passed 200 goals scored in the N.I.H.A. during the 1973/74 season – here being welcomed to the "200 Club" by N.I.H.A. Vice- President, Bernard Stocks

Sunday May 5th 1985

HEINEKEN PREMIER LEAGUE PLAY OFF FINAL

WEMBLEY ARENA

Fife Flyers 9 Murrayfield Racers 4

The Wembley Wizards — Fife Flyers 1985 Heineken British Ice Hockey Champions! Ron Plumb's magnificent men were crowned the new kings of British ice hockey amid tremendous scenes at Wembley Arena as they swept to an emphatic 9-4 victory over Murrayfield Racers. Around 1000 delirious Fife supporters in the 7000 crowd raised the roof as skipper Gordon Latto lifted the Heineken Trophy aloft to begin a long night of celebrations.

In one short season they had been transformed from mediocrity to a team of champions. After experiencing the disappointment of losing in the Bluecol Cup final and finishing runners-up in the league, the Flyers peaked at exactly the right time with their 17th consecutive victory. Ron Plumb, without doubt, was the architect of their triumph, along with fellow Canadians Dave Stoyanovich and Danny Brown, who both grabbed the goal-scoring headlines. But their influence had rubbed off on all the local players with outstanding success and winning the Championship was testament to how they had risen to the challenge.

Flyers powered their way to their first title in seven years with a magnificent first period performance which left Murrayfield wondering what had hit them. Andy Linton hit the post after only 40 seconds and then Stoyanovich had a goal disallowed in the second minute. However the huge Fife contingent did not have long to acclaim the opening goal when Danny Brown raced down the right wing before squeezing the puck into the net from a narrow angle.

Flyers played out a two-minute penalty on Neil Abel before taking advantage of a power play situation, with Murrayfield's Gordon MacDougall off the ice. Brown was the scorer again when he snapped up the rebound off a Stoyanovich shot which hit the boards behind the goal to make it 2-0 after six minutes. Three minutes later Plumb increased Flyers lead with a typical rasping shot from the blue line on another power play. Murrayfield finally opened their account when Jock Hay forced the puck home in a goalmouth melée.

Flyers really emphasised their superiority however with four further goals before the buzzer. Chic Cottrell was credited with the fourth goal after his shot was deflected into the net off a Murrayfield player and then

Stoyanovich snapped up the rebound off a Plumb effort. Two brilliant pieces of skating by Danny Brown set up the next two. He tore Murrayfield apart down the left before presenting Andy Linton with a simple chance to round Hanson and score, then claimed his hat-trick in the final second of the period with a tremendous shot into the corner of the net for his 123rd goal of the season.

As expected, Racers came out for the second period firing on all cylinders and Flyers were kept pinned into their own end but with Andy Donald in sparkling form the score line remained the same going into the final period despite the Racers having outshot the Flyers 16-6.

All Flyers had to do in the final period was contain Racers but they lost a goal after three minutes when Jim Lynch netted with Ron Plumb in the penalty box. Within 20 seconds Stoyanovich made it 8-2 with his 162nd goal of the season before becoming involved in an ugly scene with Murrayfield's uncompromising defenceman Paul Heavey, which earned the Fife man a seven minute penalty and the Racer five minutes.

Racers reduced the deficit to five goals when a Paul Hand shot was inadvertently deflected into the net by MacDougall. When Hay rammed home Racers fourth goal with seven minutes left the Flyers fans anxiously began watching the scoreboard clock. Hay then missed a simple opportunity to make it 8-5 before Jimmy Pennycook eased the tension on the Fife bench. He capitalised on a dreadful error by Hand to slot home Flyers ninth goal. There was no way back for Racers – cue Brass Bonanza!

Wembley Wizards
Back Row, left to right, Chic Cottrell, Gary McEwan, Danny Brown, Colin Braid, Dave Stoyanovich, Andy Linton, Ron Plumb, Blair Page, Neil Abel, Brian Peat, Dougie Latto. Front Row, left to right, Gordon Goodir, Murray McLellan, Gordon Latto, Andy Donald, Jimmy Pennycook, Stuart Drummond, Steven Kirk, Craig Dickson

Thursday May 6th 1948

Flyers brought the curtain down on a hugely disappointing 1947/48 season. It saw them finish bottom of the Autumn and Canada Cup standings, with only the Perth Panthers below them in the National League final table. The final action of the season was in the Silver Jubilee Tournament which was played over two nights, the first of which was in Kirkcaldy. The games were played as one period with a stop clock.

The Flyers opened the proceedings in game 1 — FLYERS 1 AYR RAIDERS 0 — Raiders came quickly into the attack with 'Babe' Sholtz saving well from Bob Lantz and George Gibbison. A break-away by Bob Leckie was saved by a fine body-check by Bob Londry while a cunning piece of stick-handling by Bud Scrutton brought no result for the Flyers before a drive by Les O'Rourke was saved by Johnson.

Back at the other end Sholtz was in outstanding form and saved a number of certain counters. Floyd Snider too proved his worth in defence. A piece of clever inter-passing by Raiders was intercepted by Pat Good to be followed by some Flyers pressure in which they did everything but score. A narrow miss by Doug Free in an unmarked position gave Flyers a let-off before Ken Johnson did well to stop a point blank shot from Scrutton and also Snider's rebound.

In the closing minutes Raiders almost broke the deadlock and Sholtz again received applause for repeated saves. O'Rourke then flashed the puck across Johnson's net which allowed Free to break away but once again Sholtz did his job. With only twenty seconds go Kenny Potts got the winner for Flyers when he smacked the puck home from the blue line.

In Game 2 the Perth Panthers defeated the Raiders 2-0 and in the final game of the evening it was FLYERS 2 PANTHERS 2. Flyers were first to threaten with a dangerous move between Scrutton and Potts. After weaving his way through, Scrutton again had hard luck. It seemed as though Flyers, and in particular Ted Fowler, were destined not to score. He hit the wrong side of the post when well placed. After breaking through, he saw George Leonard save what looked a certain goal. Panthers retaliated and only a master save by Sholtz prevented a score.

It was Panthers who opened after a spell of sustained pressure when Nebby Thrasher poked the puck home when it came round from the back of the cage. Play was end-to-end and only a fine save by Leonard stopped a Scrutton score. The equaliser came through Fowler who lifted the puck over the prostrate Leonard into the cage after the tender had partially saved. Flyers kept Panthers defence busy but a break-away by Thrasher was only saved through a trip by Londry. While a man short, the home side took the lead through Snider from a Cliff Ryan pass then a beautiful piece of skating by Potts saw him shoot past, followed by Leonard blocking a point-blank shot from Snider.

A desperate clearance by Good saved the day for Flyers in a Perth breakaway but he later received a 5-minute major penalty and with just 30 seconds to go Johnny Sergnese equalised for Panthers with the man advantage.

The following night Panthers started the second leg of the Silver Jubilee Tournament at Ayr with a slim goal-average lead over Flyers. Both gained the same points in Thursday's triangular contest but Perth had a goal more in the "for" column. Raiders had no points and no goals. Flyers gained custody of their first trophy for two seasons when they defeated the Panthers in their first game of the evening after the host Raiders had held the Panthers to a goal-less draw in the opener. The Flyers goal heroes against Panthers were Scrutton, O'Rourke and Ryan. In the final, 'dead rubber', game of the tournament the Flyers went down 3-2 to the home side with a double from Potts.

Ted Fowler who seemed destined not to score

Sunday May 7th 2006

HOCKEY UK TOURNAMENT DAY 2

Fife Flyers rounded off what was arguably their most successful season in their history by making their debut in their annual Hockey UK tournament.

The traditional season closing competition for junior hockey teams across all age groups would see the all-conquering Kirkcaldy outfit take on Dundee Stars and Edinburgh Capitals during a weekend full of action at Fife Ice Arena. Todd Dutiaume's team had swept all before them, in his first season in management, winning all six competitions.

They had lost only once in their 54 competitive match schedule, if you discount having beaten the Paisley Pirates in the Scottish National League, then having the result awarded to the Pirates due to icing the suspended John Haig.

No other Flyers team in history had dominated so, not even the Grand Slam side of 1976/77, who lost only two of their 39 competitive matches. After the demise of the British National League the previous season, there was no disguising the fact that the level of hockey that Fife had played at in the last eight months was not where a club of this stature should have been competing.

Politics in UK hockey have often thrown curve balls and teams had come and gone. At least the hockey lights were still on in Kirkcaldy. Dutiaume was hoping for even further success in the six-team Hockey UK tournament and the strongest line up saw Slough Jets, Sheffield Scimitars, Edinburgh Capitals, Dundee Stars and Whitley Warriors all in action with matches played with a running clock over two 15 minute periods.

A plethora of former Flyers would also be competing in the shape of Kyle Horne, Euan Forsyth, Gary Wishart and Chad Reekie. The action was spread over two days with round-robin games taking place all day Saturday and Sunday morning. The knockout phase commenced on Sunday afternoon and concluded with the final in the evening.

The Flyers hopes of a complete sweep of all tournaments entered were however dashed as the seemingly all-conquering Kirkcaldy side fell short in the final competition of the season. Flyers cemented their place in Sunday's semi-final by finishing second in the group following Saturday's qualifiers but Dutiaume's men failed to reach the showpiece final after losing 1-0 in the semi-final to a Sheffield team they had defeated 8-1 just 24 hours earlier. A 2-1 win over Edinburgh in the third/fourth play-off did little to soften the blow of missing out on a clean sweep of silverware.

Scores: Saturday — Fife Flyers 3, Whitley Warriors 0; Flyers 2, Dundee Stars 1; Flyers 2, Slough Jets 2; Fife Flyers 3, Edinburgh Capitals 4; Fife Flyers 8, Sheffield Scimitars 1. Sunday — Fife Flyers 0, Sheffield Scimitars 1; Edinburgh Capitals 1, Fife Flyers 2.

Tournament awards:

Top netminder — Steven Wall; Defencemen — Paddy Ward, Kyle Horne (all Slough); Forwards — Robert Dowd (Sheffield), Steven Lynch (Edinburgh), John Haig (Fife).

Derek King, coach Todd Dutiaume and Tommy Muir with the Northern League Play Off Trophy, one of six pieces of silverware won in season 2005/06

Saturday May 8th 1954

FLYERS WILL PARTICIPATE IN BRITISH LEAGUE

was the headline in the local *Fife Free Press* as weeks of speculation about the future of hockey in the town following the far-from-enjoyable last few seasons was finally answered. The article read;

"It was announced yesterday that the directors of Kirkcaldy Ice Rink, after careful consideration of the whole question, have decided to take part in the British Ice Hockey League next season. This ends all the uncertainty about the future of Fife Flyers and ice hockey locally next season and steps are now being taken to secure the services of a non-playing coach who will in turn be given a free hand to select his own team. This being the case it is obvious that the selection of a coach is going to be vital to the success of the whole venture. A well-known personality with considerable experience of ice hockey in Britain is being angled after."

In an interview with the chairman of Kirkcaldy Ice Rink directorate, Mr Glen, he had made it perfectly clear that although there had been a great amount of national publicity given to the British Ice Hockey League that this project was not yet finalised. Flyers continuation in ice hockey depended entirely on the British League reaching fruition and while there were several difficulties still to be ironed out he fully expected the new British League would eventually go ahead as planned. In the very unlikely event of the British League project falling through then the Kirkcaldy Ice Rink directors would have to reconsider their position.

So far as the British League was concerned it was reported that Streatham were already considering withdrawing although there had been no official confirmation. Streatham with a rink capacity of only 2,500 (including 1,026 standing) were in an exceptional position. Perth, the smallest of the Scottish rinks, had seating for 2,300 and with the addition of standing room could accommodate up to the 3,000 mark. As the other London rinks were all in the vicinity of 10,000, it was prudent that Streatham were carefully considering their financial viability before embarking on the ambitious British League project. Should they withdraw it was anticipated that Earls Court Rangers, who dropped out of the regular English competitive hockey series last season but continued to play friendly games on Sundays to capacity attendances, would join the new set up. In the event that the Rangers decided otherwise then Portsmouth, Durham and Liverpool were said to be interested and one of them might make up the English representation to five clubs as originally planned. Now that Fife, who had been one of the doubtfuls, had indicated that they would join, it was expected that the full complement of seven Scottish clubs would eventually come forward. Dundee, another of the doubts, had retained coach Red Kurz which rather indicated that they would also line up.

It had been provisionally arranged to commence the new season on Monday, September 27 with the oversees players due to arrive on September 15th. The season would terminate on Saturday, April 16, 1955. There would be an Autumn Cup series and a National League series with each occupying eleven weeks. The seven Scottish clubs would play for the Scottish Cup over a six-week period and the five English clubs would play for the English Cup over a similar period. The winners of the Scottish and English Cups would meet at the close of the season to play for the British Championship. This would give a season of 39 weeks. So far as Flyers were concerned the retained list consisted of Floyd Snider, Wray Fallowfield, Fred Kentner and Murray Banks. However, nothing much would be finalised regarding the team until the new coach was appointed.

Auld Lang Syne – the Flyers join in after the final game of 2000 – left to right Bill Russell, John Downes, Kyle Horne, Iain Robertson, Steven King, Mark Morrison

Thursday May 9th 1940

SCOTTISH NATIONAL LEAGUE PLAY OFF GAME 3

Fife Flyers 5 Perth Panthers 4

FIFE FLYERS – SCOTTISH LEAGUE CHAMPIONS

The Flyers, by virtue of winning Game 3 of the play-off series, were crowned Champions. The Scottish Ice Hockey Association took the somewhat controversial decision to reduce this to a best-of-three series from best-of-five. Having drawn Game 1 and won Game 2 in Perth the previous weekend, this meant a draw was all that the Flyers needed to take the title.

Panthers surprised Flyers within thirty seconds when Art Schumann received the puck from Breezy Thompson and he caught the home defence napping to give Art Grant no chance in net. This shock opening ramped up the intensity for Flyers. When Thompson and Ray Cheyne were penalised the Flyers launched a power play that had the visiting defence groggy.

George Horn netted the equaliser with a lovely wing shot which sped into the corner of the net, with Scottie Milne vainly down on one knee. Schumann came into the picture with a burst up-ice which baffled the defence but not Grant who brought off a chest-high save from the Perth Goliath. Verne Reilly was the next Perth player to try his luck and his close-range effort caused Grant some trouble.

In the 10th minute Arnie Pratt treated the spectators to one of his speedy efforts in which he stickhandled his way past Les Vickery, rounded Cheyne and drew Milne from his net before slipping the puck home. Before Perth could regroup, the Flyers extended their lead. Eddie McMillan, in a goalmouth melée, slammed the puck past Milne for Flyers third. Grant brought off a couple of quick saves from Les Lovell and Thompson while at the other end Glen Morrison shook Milne to his foundations with a rocket shot from the boards. Horn was penalised but the Perth power play was of no avail.

In the early stages of the second session it was evident that Paul Rheault's ankle injury was causing him considerable trouble. Although handicapped by this he gave valuable passes to his team mates. In the fourth minute, however, Rheault scored a brilliant goal. Arnie Pratt carried the puck into the Perth zone, drew the defence and flicked the puck on the backhand over to the Flyers top scorer, who beat a further two players before netting. One minute later, however, Les Tapp managed to squeeze the puck home for Perth after Thompson had done the spadework. Red Thomson was brilliant in the Flyers defence when Horn had a spell in the cooler. Grant also played as if inspired at this stage but when Pratt followed to the sin bin Thompson and Tapp took advantage of the home side's handicap and levelled the scores. Play flashed from end to end at this stage. In one of the Flyers raids Rheault drew the Perth defence to the boards before sending a perfect cross-goal pass to McMillan who experienced little difficulty in scoring to put the Flyers ahead again. The closing incident of note in the second period came when Grant sprawled to clear a Thompson shot.

Rheault and Pratt were prominent in early Flyers attacks in the last session. Milne was exceedingly fortunate to keep his charge intact. Schumann was penalised tor tripping and Flyers organised a power play in which dame fortune once again pulled her weight in Milne's favour. In a breakaway Grant was forced to throw himself at Schumann's feet to clear. Panthers gave the Flyers keeper a hectic time. When Horn was penalised he managed to keep the red light from glowing with many acrobatic saves.

Horn marked his return to the ice with a characteristic wander in the direction of Milne and the Perth tender was forced to sprawl twice before the danger was cleared. In the last four minutes Perth went all out to get the equaliser but with the Flyers defending stoutly they seldom looked like turning the tables.

Fife Flyers, Art Grant, George Horn, Frank Ney, Glen Morrison, Paul Rheault, Arnie Pratt, Red Thomson, Johnny Schofield, Eddie McMillan

Perth Panthers, Scottie Milne, Les Vickery, Ray Cheyne, Breezy Thompson, Art Schumann, Les Tapp, Jimmy Allan, Les Lovell, Verne Reilly

Referee—J. Foley SIHA

Flyers 1939/40 Championship winning team. From left to right: Red Thomson, Arnie Pratt, Frank Ney, George Horn, Art Grant, Tommy McInroy, Paul Rheault, Glen Morrison and Coach Nelson McCuaig

Sunday May 11th 1975

Glasgow Dynamos 6 Fife Flyers 15

It was a bit of a stuttering end to the season. The Flyers had played only two matches during April. The second was the Spring Cup play-off semi-final at Whitley Warriors, a surprise win to become the only team to beat them on home ice that season.

Their opponents in the Final would be Murrayfield Racers. It was decided to hold that contest over until the start of the following season as the ice at Kirkcaldy by that stage had been melted for the summer.

The Flyers however still had one 'competitive' fixture remaining. They were invited to play the Racers in the Final of their home tournament Edinburgh Evening News Trophy. A few days ahead of that game, having not been on the ice for almost a month, the Flyers arranged a warm-up/training match against the Glasgow Dynamos at Crossmyloof Ice Rink.

Flyers trailed 3-1 early in the game but came storming back to win comprehensively with Gordon Latto top scoring with 4 goals. There were hat tricks for Lawrie Lovell and Alex Churchill with doubles from Jimmy Jack and Chic Cottrell and a single for Les Lovell.

The meeting with the Racers the following Thursday ended in bizarre circumstances. Flyers Cup Final bogey struck again, when they finished runners-up for the eighth time in two seasons. Despite having had the game against the Dynamos, the Flyers were badly out of sorts with so little time on the ice and the odds ahead of the game were heavily stacked on Racers side.

Although Flyers were well out-shot in the first period it took Racers until the final five minutes to open the scoring when Freddie Wood, who had twice been allowed to hover uncovered on the centre line, bagged a couple of quick-fire goals.

The second period held no better joy for Flyers support as Willie Clark in the Racers goal was ably controlling any shots on his goal. Similarly, at the other end John Pullar in Flyers goal was doing all he could to prevent the Racers from increasing their lead. It was a real blow to the Flyers trophy hopes when the only goal of the period came the way of the home side while they were playing short-handed. Wood was left clear again and he marked up his hat-trick.

Flyers started the final session with a bang and by the fourth minute incredibly found themselves on level terms. Lawrie Lovell poked one home after just 21 seconds, then brother Les controlled a Brian Peat pass in the third minute to score. A cracker of a shot from Chic Cottrell equalised a mere 17 seconds later. Chic Cottrell scored again but this was cancelled out by the home side. The Flyers almost snatched what could have been the winning goal when a shot from Lawrie Lovell came back off the post and there was no more scoring in normal time.

What followed in the overtime period was certainly no true reflection of the tie. Rather than play a sudden death overtime period the teams were made to play 10 minutes and early in the extra session the Flyers were forced to kill a major penalty followed by a misconduct. That was where the game ended as a contest. Racers ran up seven unanswered goals with the Fife players completely out on their skates.

Mrs Helen Horne, wife of Rink Manager Tommy Horne, presents Les Lovell, left, with the Mirror of Merit for season 1974/75. Also pictured is Gordon Latto who won the Kirkcaldy Kestrels merit award.

Thursday May 13th 1976

EVENING NEWS TROPHY FINAL

Murrayfield Racers 1 Fife Flyers 9

Flyers reversed last year's result of the Evening News Trophy final when they demolished Racers at the Edinburgh rink. This was the Flyers 11th meeting of the year against the Edinburgh side and their eighth success over their rivals, which had included victory in the Spring Cup held over from the previous season.

Flyers secured their place in the final the previous month when they defeated the Racers 6-4 to record the best result in the qualifications rounds. The result was heralded with the welcome return to the scoresheet for Gordon Latto who picked up his first goals for the Flyers since his return from Sweden. It was expected that with that pressure now off his shoulders that would be able to settle down in future matches.

Not to be outdone by his younger brother, Latto put the Flyers on their way to victory with the opening goal when he neatly flicked the puck past Willie Clark. Derek Reilly almost countered for Racers when he cracked a shot past John Pullar but Brian Peat was back on the line to block the puck from entering the net. The visitors took a firm grip on the Trophy before the first period was concluded, when Racers saw the puck hit the back of their net three times in as many minutes. Peat cracked one through Clark's legs. This was followed by Chic Cottrell and Jimmy Jack opening their accounts, before John McIlwraith pulled one back for Racers right on the buzzer.

Flyers found themselves being continually penalised in the second period but Racers still failed to make any impression. It felt that it was going to be the Flyers night when Dennis Clair even failed with a penalty shot, although credit should go to Johnny Pullar for a great save. To rub salt into the home side's wounds Les Lovell collected the only goal of the period when Flyers were playing short-handed. Racers were skated off the ice in the final stanza as Flyers moved into top gear and Les Lovell left Clark all-at-sea to increase their lead. Gordon Latto opened his account soon after and added his own second and the teams eighth minutes later. In a game that was played at a furious pace the Flyers were faster and more determined. A final strike by Kenny Horne underlined this, as they fully justified the transportation of the trophy to the Kirkcaldy boardroom.

Gordon Latto, far right back row, with the Vastra Frölunda U21 team that visited Fife in 1975/76 season.

Wednesday May 14th 1944

The *Leven Mail* reported the following —

REGAL CINEMA'S NEW MANAGER

"The former Fife Flyers ice hockey coach and captain, Les Lovell has been appointed manager of the Regal Cinema in Kirkcaldy in succession to the late Mr A. P. Casey. Les, who is a native of Montreal and thirty years of age, was educated at Montreal Public School and High School and afterwards worked in the office of a big electrical firm. He began his ice hockey career with one of the oldest amateur teams in Canada, the Montreal Victoria, and came to Britain some years ago when ice hockey was introduced to this country on an organised scale. He played for Brighton Tigers and later came north to Perth Panthers. In 1938-39 he was player-coach for the newly formed Fife Flyers at Kirkcaldy Ice Rink and the following season, which was his last owing to the war, he renewed his association with Perth Panthers. A defenceman with a flair for rapier-like attacks, Les was one of the outstanding players in the country and he took part in several International games for Scotland. He was always a favourite with local fans and he was extremely popular with the young lads whom he introduced to the intricacies of the new sport. Of a quiet and unassuming disposition he has many friends, all of whom will be delighted at his new appointment. Lately he has been acting as manager of the State Cinema in Leith. Although organised Ice hockey has fallen a temporary victim to the exigencies of wartime, Les has kept up his connection with the game by acting as referee on several occasions for Armed Forces representative matches at rinks around the country."

At that time in cinemas, Errol Flynn and Julie Bishop were starring in the World War II film set in Canada called Northern Pursuit. Later that week at the rink, patrons were able to enjoy British orchestra leader Billy Ternent, who was popular from the 1940s to the 1970s, and best known for backing Frank Sinatra and his work at the London Palladium.

Les Lovell (Senior) had his playing career cut short not just because of the war but through injury. He wasn't able to complete the season with Fife in their inaugural campaign. After taking a heavy dunt in a game at Kelvingrove in January where he injured his collarbone, he had appendicitis. He made a comeback with Perth again the following season, but eventually he was forced to quit playing when he lost the sight in his left eye. He did continue to be involved in the game during the war years as a referee. After his retirement from ice-hockey Les moved into cinema management and became a well-known and respected figure. He is fondly remembered as one of the old school of smartly-dressed, "front-of-house" managers, who liked to establish a rapport with his regular customers. It could be suggested that he was at that time most fondly remembered in Kirkcaldy for his cinema duties. Known as "Uncle Les" to the bairns in 1952 he made the move over the water to manage the ABC in Edinburgh's Lothian Road and the family followed. There he broke new ground by opening the cinema as a rock venue with top stars such as the Beatles and the Rolling Stones performing.

REGAL

High Street, Kirkcaldy. Phone 2143.

WEEK COMMENCING MONDAY, 15th MAY – AND ALL WEEK
Continuous Daily from 2.0 till 10 p.m.

ERROL FLYNN - JULIE BISHOP

IN

Norther

HELMUT DANTINE

GENE L

SHOWING APPROX., 2.0

ICE RINK
kirkcaldy
THE CENTRE OF ENTERTAINMENT

BILLY TERNENT
(Direct from the B.B.C.)

AND HIS DANCE BAND

WITH

RUTH HOWARD   LESLIE WALSH
DON LORRAINE   PAT FISHER

THURSDAY, 18th May—7 to 10.30

ADMISSION 3 6

Adverts for the wartime entertainment in the town at Les Lovell's Regal cinema, and for the sound of big bands rather than big hits at the rink.

Thursday May 15th 1947

Fife Flyers 4 London All Stars 6

An augmented Flyers team built up a three-nil lead at one stage in this game against a select team heralded as the London All-Stars, but they were very lucky to be in the lead at all on the balance of play. Once the more experienced visitors found the way to the net, they were not long in changing the complexion of the game. This changed Flyers team lacked the combination and understanding of their more familiar line-up and many considered had it been the "real" Flyers then they would have been able to put up a better showing. Also many commentators were disturbed that the team was referred to as a Scottish Select which inferred a best strength team from the Scottish League which it certainly was not.

The Flyers line up was missing regular netminder Don Dougall, Frankie King, Earl McCrone and Pat Ratchford. It was widely agreed that the best player on the ice was one of their guest players, Jim Davis of the Dunfermline Vikings. Until his injury George Hayes of Ayr Raiders along with Flyers captain Bud Scrutton were next to shine. In a clever London team Ricky Ricard especially caught the eye. This may have been a "goodwill" game but there was little peace on earth or ice about it. The speedy and impetuous play of the Flyers youngsters caused a lot of trouble to the visitors. It was only the superior defensive tactics of the All-Stars which turned the scales.

It was a hugely enjoyable game. No one could have complained at not receiving value for money, not just for the hockey alone! There were also the skating displays by Miss Britta Rahlen, the Swiss amateur champion, along with Miss Margaret Gibson from Kirkcaldy, the Scottish amateur champion, and Dennis and Winnie Silverthorne, the British pairs champions.

The contrast between the English and Scottish brands of hockey could hardly be summed up by one game as these two teams were so evenly matched, in terms of effort at least. Many reflected that the visitors were more hefty and more skilful and ultimately that was what brought about their deserved win.

Flyers led at the end of the first period by a Davis goal assisted by Jim McKenzie and John Drummond. Although this flattered the home side there were soon more shocks in store for the visitors when Scrutton netted in the first minute of the second period assisted by Al Gordon and George Hayes. Just four minutes later Harry O'Connor set up Gordon for a third goal. Perhaps the Flyers thought that this was already their night or perhaps a sense of pride amongst the visitors spurred them into greater efforts. However, after this the All-Stars buckled to and by the end of the period they led 4-3. Duke scored the first before Davey reduced arrears to a single goal. Glennie netted the equaliser before Davey scored his second to stun the Flyers. Hopes of a Flyers revival were dashed early in the final period with further goals from Trottier and Glennie with the Flyers only crumb of comfort provided by a Davis goal from a Drummond assist with the puck entering the net via an All-Star defender.

Flyers — Joe Cleary (Dundee Tigers), Bob Londry, Floyd Snider, Harry O'Connor, Jim McKenzie, Bob Burns (Dundee Tigers), Bud Scrutton, Al Gordon (Ayr Raiders), Bob Lantz, George Hayes (Ayr Raiders), Jim Davis (Dunfermline Vikings).

All-Stars— Kenny Duncan (Streatham), Gerry Davey (Streatham), Frank Kuly (Greyhounds) Verne Greger (Streatham), George Baillie (Streatham), Wyn Cook (Greyhounds), Bill Glennie (Greyhounds), Frank Trottier (Streatham), Ricky Ricard (Greyhounds), Johnny Eisenzoph (Greyhounds), Art Duke (Racers)

After the game Johnny Drummond who had done a lot of work in coaching the Kirkcaldy juvenile players was presented with a fountain pen by the youngsters as mark of their appreciation.

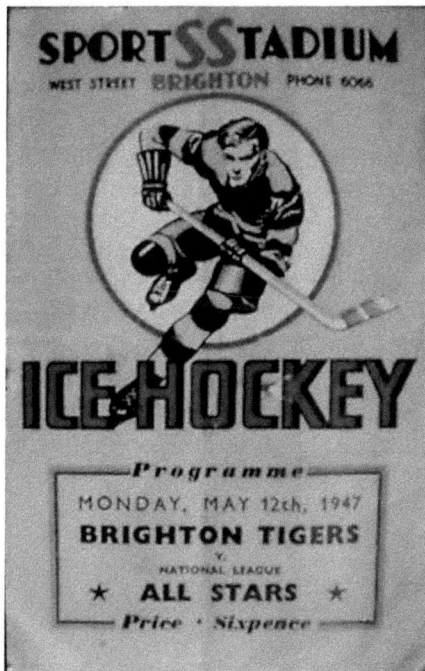

The programme for the previous outing of the All Stars team before they travelled to Fife

Thursday May 16th 1940

Fife Flyers 6 Dunfermline Vikings 5

Playing to be crowned Fife Champions, it was the Flyers who caused Dunfermline some trouble in the opening stages but they were denied by stand-in Perth Panthers goalie Scottie Milne who executed a lovely save from a breakaway by Eddie McMillan and Paul Rheault.

Ex Flyer Tommy Durling broke away next but the combined attentions of McMillan and Frank Ney prevented Art Grant from becoming unduly worried. The Flyers opened the scoring in the ninth minute when Paul Rheault had been pulled down on the point of shooting. The referee awarded a face-off in front of Milne and the centre-ice flashed the puck home with a beautiful back-flick. One minute later the Vikings, after an initial cruise around Grant, equalised when Durling lifted the puck into the roof of the net from just outside the goal crease. This added confidence to the Vikings play and in the 17th minute Pinky Downs broke away and outwitted Ney before netting with an angular effort.

Flyers retaliated. McMillan managed to evade the Dunfermline defence but at the crucial moment Milne materialised to deny him. Vikings were then warned for having four men in defence. Some of these earlier rules of the game are obscure to modern day hockey fans. In this instance only a maximum of three players including the goalkeeper could be in the defensive zone once the puck had exited – so you couldn't simply pack players into your own zone and defend.

After a delightful piece of combined play another loanee, this time from Dundee Tigers, Laurie Marchant slid the puck home for Vikings third after 15 minutes. The referee eventually had enough and Jimmy Shannon, also a Tiger loanee, was penalised for Vikings for playing four men in defence. Rheault then injured himself and had to retire from the game, so with the Flyers top scorer gone and trailing things looked ominous for the home lot.

After some reorganisation by the home side they eventually found a way past Milne who had begun to look unbeatable when Arnie Pratt drove the puck home from close in. Glen Morrison came close to equalising as did Pratt who hit the iron with a shot that had Milne completely beaten.

The third period began at a fast pace. It was the Flyers who were back on terms after just a minute, when a scorching shot by Red Thomson from just within the defence zone rebounded off the boards for Arnie Pratt to slam home. Pratt was also instrumental in obtaining the Flyers next goal when he neatly drew the puck round the defence and slipped the pass to McMillan whose lightning shot almost burst the net. Downs and Marsh broke away for the Vikings and only Grant's timely intervention prevented the latter from netting. After the change-over the Flyers added to their slender lead. Morrison, who had been handing out the headaches freely to the Halbeath defence all evening, forced his way through and smashed the puck past Milne.

At the other end Durling, who was hovering around the goal crease, brought Grant to his knees to clear with a quick flick. When Horn was penalised the feelings of the Flyers supporters were about as sweet as lemon juice to referee Foley. Anger and angst quickly turned to joy and delight in the stands, however. Pratt treated the spectators to one of his individual rushes, which had the Dunfermline defence groggy. After drawing Milne from his cage he flicked the disc home. With Flyers still handicapped by the absence of Horn the Vikings pepped up their attack and in one of their numerous raids Marchant netted from close range.

At this stage McMillan and Marsh came to blows and were sent to the cooler. Downs followed a short time later for a minor infringement. With each team having three skaters on the ice the excitement reached fever pitch with Durling bringing the visitors to within a goal. Although Vikings continued to press to gain the equaliser they hit the home trail minus the Championship of Fife silverware.

Flyers, Art Grant, Frank Ney, Johnny Schofield, Glen Morrison, Paul Rheault, Red Thomson, George Horn, Arnie Pratt, Eddie McMillan

Vikings, Scottie Milne, Pinky Downs, Ernie Batson, Larry Marsh, Tommy Durling, Jimmy Shannon, Laurie Marchant

Referee—J. Foley. SIHA

The advert for the Anderson Trophy match from the local Fife Free Press newspaper

Saturday May 21st 1966

Wembley Lions 7 Fife Flyers 6

This was the final match for the Flyers 1965/66 season. It had been a season of relative success. They had won 18 of their 22 matches to win the Scottish based Coca-Cola league. They had competed in the finals for another couple of trophies bearing the same sponsors name when they beat Paisley Mohawks in the League Trophy final and repeated the feat in the Challenge Trophy Final.

Incredibly the Flyers hadn't been on the ice in almost a month after meeting the Mohawks over two legs in mid-April in the Final of the Coca Cola League Trophy. Despite the obvious rust and the long journey South, it was the visitors who were out of the gates quickest. Jimmy Spence scored unassisted before the Flyers grabbed a second goal when Jerry Hudson put one behind goalkeeper Thomas from an assist from Les Lovell.

The home side were stunned into action and proceeded to dominate the game from that point and they fired six unanswered goals. Firstly, Tom "Red" Imrie and then Les Strongman each started on their way to collecting hat tricks before Rupe Fresher struck before the first buzzer to put the hosts in front.

In the second period it was Strongman and Imrie again to stretch the Lions lead, before Strongman completed his hat trick. At this stage it looked like the Flyers would be defeated heavily but they stemmed the tide and Les Lovell scored to bring them within three at the second period break.

This momentum was carried through into the final period. The Flyers looked set to make a remarkable comeback. Spence got the next goal followed by another from Sammy McDonald before, unbelievably, Jerry Hudson tied the game at 6-6. The fairytale comeback however was to be denied when the wee Scot 'Red' Imrie, who had signed a few weeks before from the Brighton Tigers as they went defunct, completed his hat trick to give Lions the win. It was revenge for the Lions over the Flyers who had been the only team to win at the Empire Pool Arena that season. Back in March in an equally thrilling match they had triumphed 6-5 although they had almost capitulated having been ahead 5-2 at the end of the second period.

The Flyers lined up with Willie Clark in goal that day who played despite needing an operation to fix a badly injured arm that he had sustained at work on a broken sheet of glass. Bill Sneddon, Joe McIntosh and Jim Mitchell were joined in defence by Bert Smith. The forward lines were Jerry Hudson, Jimmy Spence, Les Lovell and Harry Pearson, Lawrie Lovell, Sam McDonald.

Lions line up was Glyn Tomas in net with the defence being Roy Shepherd, Art Hodgins, "Red" Devereaux and John Cook with the forward lines of "Red" Imrie, Les Strongman, Johnny Murray, Tony Whitehead, George Beach, Mike O'Brien and Rupe Fresher.

Incredibly the Lions still had three games left in their schedule with the last one being June 11th.

WEMBLEY

EMPIRE POOL AND SPORTS ARENA

THE HOME OF THE LIONS!

OFFICIAL PROGRAMME—SIXPENCE
Saturday, May 21st, 1966

LIONS OUT FOR REVENGE!

Tonight we welcome back to Wembley that crack Scottish squad, Fife Flyers, who are the only team to have beaten the Lions here at the Empire Pool this season.

The Flyers, rated by Lions' player-coach, Johnny Murray, as one of the finest sides in Britain, brought off a thrilling 6-5 victory over Lions here in March. This followed a 7-4 home win against the Wembley squad at Kirkcaldy.

So the Lions, with three more home games to follow this season, really have something to go for this evening—especially as they came so close to pulling off at least a draw in that last match against Fife.

Then, the Scots had to fight as hard as they could to stave off a sustained attack from Lions in the Final Period, after leading 5-2 at the end of the second stanza.

Hero for Flyers in this match was their competent coach, Gerry Hudson, who notched a great hat-trick to enable his squad to run out narrow winners.

Lions' scorers were skipper, George Beach, Johnny Murray, Red Imrie,

Les Strongman and Mike O'Brien—all with a goal apiece.

TIGERS NEXT!

Next week's special Whit-Saturday match here at the Empire Pool will be against Brighton Tigers, and not Ayr Rangers as originally planned.

The Bengals sportingly agreed to "fill the breach" after news came that the Ayr squad had disbanded and consequently could not fulfil the fixture.

Lions v Tigers matches always create a fervour and excitement all of their own here at the Empire Pool, and next week's match will prove no exception.

This will be the Tigers' fourth visit to the Pool this season. The fact that they have lost by the narrow margins of 5-6, 2-4, and 3-4 in the previous three games typifies the keen rivalry that has always existed between the two teams.

The match night programme for Flyers visit to Wembley Arena which later became a spiritual home for many hockey fans

Sunday May 22nd 1977

Fife Flyers 7 Whitley Warriors 9

The Flyers final game of an incredible season and arguably the club's finest ever season in their history. Game 42 and almost eight months to the day from when the first puck dropped on their historic journey, during which there had only been two previous defeats. One of these had been a Challenge match. Fife Flyers were on the brink of achieving a Grand Slam and becoming only the third team to dominate in such a way in Northern Ice Hockey Association history.

A week ago the Flyers had travelled to the North East to meet the Warriors in the first leg and the game also doubled up as the Final of the Northumbria Cup. This had been the sixth meeting the sides so far that season and the Flyers continued their 100% record with a comfortable 13-7 win to give them a healthy cushion going into the second leg. The Warriors treated the home side with the respect they had commanded throughout the year by applauding them on to the ice — but that was as far as the niceties went.

Although Flyers took a 4-2 first period lead there was an uncharacteristic lack of urgency in their play which perhaps was as a result of their cushion from the first leg. Warriors capitalised on this during the second period and reversed the first period score as they gradually gained the upper hand. Bob Gilbert, in the visitors goal, greatly inspired his side during this period and brought off a fine penalty save from Gordon Latto.

Starting the final period with the score at six goals each the Warriors seemed to go from strength to strength and it was no surprise when they took the lead for the first time in the game. Flyers battled on gamely and managed to equalise, but Warriors justly won the battle — but not the war! — when they rifled another two goals past Pullar.

The Flyers scorers were Chic Cottrell with two, Les and Lawrie Lovell with a goal apiece with Gordon Latto, Kenny Horne and Ally Brennan who remarkably received 83 out of a possible 84 votes for the All-Star team also on target.

There were a host of other end-of-season All Star awards for Flyers players. Kenny Horne, Les Lovell and as coach Lawrie Lovell joined Brennan on the All-Star 'A' team, while the 'B' team had John Pullar and

632

1977/78 Fife Flyers team with their haul of silverware from the previous Grand Slam winning season
Back Row, left to right: John Grant (Trainer), John Taylor, Charlie Kinmond, Brian Peat, Chic Cottrell, Jimmy Jack, Gordon Latto, Kenny Horne, Dave Medd, Angus Cargill
Front Row, left to right: Willie Cottrell, Dougie Latto, Laurie Lovell, Tommy Horne (Manager), Les Lovell, Ally Brennan, Jim Taylor

Lawrie Lovell, who also received the Earl Carlson trophy as top points scorer, representing the club.

This was the third year in a row the Flyers had won the Spring Cup and their unsurpassed collection of silverware also included the Icy Smith Cup, Northern League trophy, Autumn Cup, Skol Cup, Edinburgh Evening News Trophy and the Northumbria Cup. In the four major competitions Fife hit the net 391 times shattering the old record of 307 set by Murrayfield Racers in 1971/72.

The night belonged to Fife Flyers who were presented with the Spring Cup and were also officially given the Northern League Trophy. To round off a perfect evening Gordon Latto was also presented with the Player of the Year Award from the NIHA after also having won the *Fife Free Press* Mirror of Merit.

Sunday May 23rd 1976

Ayr Bruins 5 Fife Flyers 7

The Flyers season came to an end as they retained their grip for a second time on the Spring Cup, the end of season play off competition involving the top four teams in the Northern League — their fourth piece of silverware, having already won the Autumn Cup, Skol Cup and Evening News Trophy

The night before, in the first leg, the Flyers adapted well to their 'home' surroundings as they sought to exact revenge on a Bruins team, who a few weeks earlier had inflicted a shock 8-1 defeat on them in the Final of the Icy Smith Cup.

That game was played at Murrayfield Ice Rink with the ice at Kirkcaldy having been melted for the summer season. Revenge was served. The Flyers demolished the Bruins 10-2, to set up what was almost a foregone conclusion 24 hours later in Ayr.

The second leg proved to be a history-making match for the Flyers coach Lawrie Lovell when his assist on the Flyers opening goal made him the first player in National Ice Hockey Association play to reach the 1,000 points plateau. Lawrie's points total comprised 494 goals and 508 assists at the end of the game.

The Ayr challenge was over when Flyers raced to a four goal lead in the opening 10 minutes of the game. Gordon Latto, Lawrie Lovell, Ally Brennan and Jimmy Jack all lit the red light to put the Cup beyond Ayr's reach.

A quick one-two by Bruins late in the second period gave them a boost, when Jackson McBride and Stewart Hendrie scored.

In the final period each side netted three goals. Flyers scorers were Brennan, Lawrie Lovell and Jack with a double from Jimmy Young and one from John Gibson making the aggregate score 17-7 for the 1976 Spring Cup Final. Flyers iced young goaltender Willie Cottrell in the final period. He had several good saves and looked a good prospect for the future.

With the 1975-76 Spring Cup final having been held over until the start of this campaign the Flyers had somewhat unusually won the same cup twice in the one season. The Flyers could possibly have run the table that year. They finished just a point behind Murrayfield in the race for the Northern League title. This was attributed to the rhythm of the team being interrupted by five players — Pullar, Brennan, Horne and both Lovells — being involved with the GB World Championships squad which had trained on the same night as the Flyers. Before leaving for Poland the Flyers had lost at home to the Whitley Warriors.

That said, their capitulation in the Icy Smith Cup was an anomaly of epic proportions. Lawrie Lovell once again topped the scoring to win the Earl Carlson Trophy and Jimmy Jack won the Mirror of Merit. The only disappointment for all the people involved in the game at Kirkcaldy was, however, their attendance figures. Ten years ago the Fife Flyers had been among the top teams in the country. Now they probably were the best side in Britain, but what had happened to the thousands who used to go to the games?

Action from an encounter with the Bruins earlier in season 1975/76 as Law Lovell scores

Saturday May 25th 1940

Perth Panthers 7 Fife Flyers 3

These two teams had battled all season for the major honours. Given the controversy surrounding the Flyers playoff series win, when the number of games were reduced from five to three, the pair somewhat strangely decided the finish their campaign with a couple of challenge matches. It seemed as if there was still some unfinished business and they were still trying to prove which outfit was indeed the best.

The final game of the season was described as "Wild Stuff At Perth" It was the second of the two challenge games. The Flyers, who had narrowly won 48 hours before in Kirkcaldy, were beaten by a substantial margin at the Perth Rink. It was a game that was more noted for its toughness than anything else.

The highlight in the way of incidents came in the last period when Glen Morrison was given his marching orders by referee, and former Panther, Johnny Scott. The two men did not see eye-to-eye on this outcome and after a brief argument they came to grips. Other players feeling in the mood joined in before order was restored and the game proceeded with the Perth side on top with two goals each from Ray Cheyne and Jimmy Allan with Art Schumann, 'Breezy' Thompson and Verne Reilly also on the mark. The Flyers consolations goals came from Eddie McMillan, Glen Morrison and 'Red' Thomson.

The closing notes on the Flyers Championship season were as follows:

"The Season Closes — The Kirkcaldy team has had a most successful season. The Scottish Championship the Fife Championship and the Consolation Cup have all come to the Lang Toun and incidentally the Anderson Trophy went with the Fife Championship.

Comedy and Capers — The final home game this week was quite a study in contrasts. The boys fought a spirited battle for the first two period but just to show that it was all good sport they had a comic face-off prior to the last period when netminders Scottie Milne and Art Grant gave a demonstration on how centre ices should play perhaps.

Strange but true — Referee Jim Foley SIHA who has refereed all Flyers games or at least practically all of them has never been a

Cover of the programme for the opening of Kirkcaldy Ice Rink on 1st October 1938

popular figure at Kirkcaldy. A new referee has been clamoured for frequently by those who thought the breaks were going too much against the home team. This being so one would have thought that Frank Chase who deputised for Jim Foley on Thursday would have been welcomed with open arms. But what actually happened was that some of the crowd were soon declaring that they wanted Referee Foley. This was undoubtedly tough on Frank but it just shows that no matter who is referee the fans will never be pleased. Indeed, when ice hockey enthusiasts are thoroughly satisfied with the whistling officials the game of ice hockey will be on the decline.

Two Absentees — It was a pity that there were two absentees from the teams for the last home game. Paul Rheault the leading goal-scorer in Scotland was unable to play because of an ankle injury while in the Panthers Les Lovell who had sustained a serious eye injury and a fracture to his skull in a recent game was lying seriously ill in Dundee Royal Infirmary. One of the finest fellows in the game Les was a great favourite with Kirkcaldy crowds even after he had swopped the Flyers colours for those of the Vikings and latterly the Panthers. All will join in hoping that he makes a good recovery.

A Closing Note — Someone should really send Lord Haw Haw a copy of the Kirkcaldy Ice Rink programme for the last game of the season. In this issue Manager Wake thanked the boys individually for their good work in the past season and gave Coach McCuaig a well-deserved pat on the back. But in the bit that would particularly interest the 'Hamboorsch' hombre is the last sentence. "Don't forget that the Flyers will be on the ice again next October, until then. 'Au Revoir.' And on behalf of all ice hockey fans, we may say that Haw Haw can put that in his pipe and smoke it!'

It was to be over six years before the Flyers would take to the ice in their next competitive action.

Perth Ice Rink or, as it was known originally, the Central Scotland Ice Rink. St Johnstone's Muirton Park is beyond it.

Saturday May 29th 1954

It seems only appropriate following the events described on August 12th in the book that we return to another coaching headline from the *Fife Free Press*;

FLYERS FIX A COACH — HENRY HAYES SIGNED

The article went on to read

"While down in London, Mr J. K. F. Glen chairman of the Kirkcaldy Ice Rink directorate, signed Henry Hayes the ex-Dunfermline Viking as coach for Fife Flyers next season. Hayes was player-coach for a short spell with Flyers last season and certainly impressed. Unfortunately, he was held to a contract with the Staag Club in Switzerland and had to leave Kirkcaldy about a month after his arrival. A strict disciplinarian as far as practices are concerned Hayes is just the type of man to get the best out of the team. While he will be a non-playing coach Hayes will be ready to step into the team if the need ever arises.

News of this latest development should please Flyers fans who will look forward with interest to further developments before the new season opens. In an exclusive interview with the new coach who paid a fleeting visit to the Kirkcaldy Ice Rink yesterday to check up on equipment and other essential items we were pleased to learn that he is quite happy with his new appointment and feels confident about next season's activities. He feels that the formation of a British League should improve support at the Gallatown Stadium but he is a trifle apprehensive about the number of matches which may have to be played on successive nights and particularly if the previous day has been spent in travel.

In respect of next season's team Henry said that he had an exceptionally good friend and ex-colleague whom for obvious reasons we cannot name whose help in the procuring of players would undoubtedly prove invaluable. This colleague of his is a well-known and highly-respected personality in hockey circles and with his cooperation the chances of Flyers icing a first-class team look exceptionally bright. Referring to Flyers retained players Henry plumped for Wray Fallowfield whom he felt had the main attributes of a good defenceman. He had the proper approach to the game was keen and ever ready to try and improve his play. However at this stage coach Hayes was wisely non-committal regarding the retained list as a whole particularly as he was not personally acquainted with the ability of Murray Banks and Floyd Snider.

How many of the retained players will be invited to re-sign for Flyers remains to be seen. Henry is due to return to London at the weekend to start his search for players and we have no doubt that long before the new league is due to start Flyers will have the nucleus of a team worthy to carry the blue white and gold colours of Fife Flyers. Flyers fans will wish him well."

Flyers would find it tough going in the new British National League with the team finishing in the bottom three of both the Autumn Cup and League competition. It was too much to hope that overnight Hayes could turn Flyers into world-beaters but with a bunch of kids he gave fans fast pleasing hockey and helped keep the interest in the sport at a decent level within the town. For an expectation of playing only when required Hayes appeared in 28 games that following season which was almost 50% of the total played and recorded six goals and six assists.

Henry Hayes eventually took up his coaching position with the Flyers.

Illustration Credits

Every effort has been made by the author to determine the source of the images contained within this book and approval for their use has been sought and given.

Where the source has been identified it has been noted opposite. A number of images are from private collections which include sources such as programmes, scrapbooks and photographs where the source cannot be identified. These are identified below mainly as the Author's collection.

Given the period of time this book spans it was not always possible to use original images and as such the resolution of some are less than desired but their inclusion will, it is hoped, add to the overall nostalgia contained within the pages.

Source	Page Numbers
Fife Free Press	xxii, 2, 9, 11, 13, 15, 17, 39, 44, 46, 51, 64, 72, 74, 76, 77, 85, 89, 93, 101, 106, 125, 133, 137, 141, 145, 150, 154, 156, 158, 173, 175, 177, 193, 201, 210, 214, 217, 227, 238, 242, 244, 246, 248, 252, 258, 260, 268, 289, 293, 297,306, 310, 317, 324, 326, 328, 330, 332, 334, 336, 338, 343, 347, 351, 353, 355, 362, 369, 373, 374, 380, 398, 400, 412, 417, 419, 423, 437, 441, 445, 447, 459, 470, 472, 474, 476, 480, 486, 490, 492, 494, 496, 500, 502, 508, 510, 512, 526, 529, 531, 535, 537, 539, 541, 547, 549, 553, 570, 572, 574, 594, 596, 602, 605, 607, 609, 613, 615, 617, 619, 625, 629, 636, 641
Mike Smith	42, 49, 53, 182, 240, 320, 408,452, 454, 520, 568, 598
Derek Young and Jillian McFarlane	18, 22, 26, 40, 61, 114, 184, 219, 388, 406, 430, 456, 468, 498, 600
Steve Gunn	29, 30, 32, 34, 37, 59, 68, 70, 79, 83, 95, 123, 135, 161, 179,190, 272, 279, 281, 357, 363, 378, 387, 404, 426, 522, 644
Gordon Latto Archive	6, 129, 139, 147, 163, 169, 195, 197, 199, 256, 264, 266, 270, 291, 318, 425, 439, 449, 466, 478, 517, 551, 557, 566, 611, 621, 623, 633
Author's Collection	ii, xxviii, 4, 24, 55, 67, 87, 91, 97, 99, 109, 111, 112, 116, 127, 131, 143, 152, 165, 171, 181, 186, 191, 207, 212, 220, 223, 229, 234, 250, 262, 274, 277, 283, 285, 295, 300, 302, 315, 322, 340, 358, 367, 371, 383, 385, 390, 392, 396, 409, 410, 413, 423, 435, 463, 482, 484, 504, 506, 514, 519, 524, 543, 545, 559, 561, 564, 627, 631, 638, 639
Fife Flyers	81, 104, 119, 121, 188, 203, 205, 231, 233, 287, 304, 308, 312, 345, 394, 402, 421, 443, 451, 488, 533, 555, 577-592

Fife Flyers in post-match handshakes from the 2021-22 season. Left to Right: Kristian Blumenschein, James Isaacs, Bari McKenzie, Andrew Little, Mike McNicholas, Carson Stadnyk, Jacob Benson, Jonas Emmerdahl.

Left to Right: James Anderson, Scott Jamieson, Greg Chase, Imants Lescovs, Craig Peacock, Richard Krogh, Erik Naslund, Matt Carter.

Fife Flyers Players Index

A

Aarssen, Scott: 20, 219, 455
Abel, Neil: 81, 119, 167, 169, 194, 210, 213, 217, 237, 238, 296, 297, 298, 335, 336, 337, 368, 369, 473, 480, 511, 516, 546, 552, 553, 573, 610, 611
Abel, Rob: 52, 54, 100, 102,
Adamson, Callum: 485
Alm, Ake: 86, 335, 495, 496
Anderson, Allan 'Bean': 119, 169, 210, 326, 495, 515
Anderson, James: 645
Andrew, Robin: 172, 209, 325, 326,
Andrews, Johnny: 16, 17, 211, 225, 313, 314, 395, 595, 596
Arthur, Craig: 487, 488
Auger, Chris: 35

B

Baird, Joe: 98, 126, 127, 255, 256, 263, 264, 266, 290, 291, 329, 362, 438, 439, 449
Balfour, Robbie: 75
Banks, Murray: 274, 301, 302, 410, 462, 463, 617, 641
Bannister, Darin: 159, 160
Basaraba, Joe: 20, 456
Bayne, Johnny: 174, 563
Beattie, Iain: 31, 245, 469
Beausoleil, Luc: 81
Bekkering, Justin: 56, 71, 72
Belanger, Adrien 'Pete': 3, 96, 97, 128, 129, 153, 154, 170, 171, 185, 186, 250, 267, 268, 303, 317, 431, 432, 440, 441, 475, 476, 477, 478, 530, 531, 544, 548, 567, 568, 575
Bell, Iain: 75, 76, 148, 150, 344, 485
Benson, Jacob: 644

Bentley, Marshall: 153, 154, 170, 171, 249, 250, 267, 268, 274, 275, 303, 348, 544, 548, 575, 576
Bergeron, Bob: 164, 166, 434, 435, 556
Berrington, Paul: 54, 312, 560
Bidner, Todd: 92, 93, 215, 282, 446, 447, 499, 500, 546, 547, 607
Biette, Karry: 43, 44, 73, 144, 145, 202, 203, 239, 240, 243, 307, 308, 394, 417, 442, 443, 450, 451, 487
Biggar, Ron: 108, 322
Birzins, Ricards: 271, 428, 455
Black, Richard: 92, 495
Blackman, Gordie: 108, 322
Blair, Andy: 119, 173,
Blair, Sherman: 64, 154, 170, 250, 303, 348, 549, 575, 576
Bloodoff, Evan: 60, 61, 62, 271, 456
Blumenschein, Kristian: 644
Boni, Josh: 47, 48, 176, 320
Boreham, Norrie: 98, 126, 139, 140, 206, 207, 228, 255, 256, 266, 291, 333, 334, 361, 362, 429, 436, 439, 465, 491, 525, 526, 542, 564, 565, 566
Boschman, Laurie: 507, 508, 515, 516
Bott, Bryan: 263
Bouchard, Ray: 268
Boulaine, Martin: 81
Bradbury, Bill: 129
Brencis, Aigars: 159, 160
Brennan, Alistair: 136, 137, 147, 175, 241, 242, 270, 285, 353, 418, 498, 501, 502, 526, 539, 540, 541, 543, 566, 609, 632, 633, 635, 636
Briere, Steve: 73, 74, 144, 145, 202, 203, 393, 394, 401, 402, 420, 421, 442, 443, 451, 487, 488
Brooks, Brendan: 28, 364, 365
Brown, Al: 349

D

DaCosta, Justin: 190
Dailey, Jason: 144, 394, 487, 488
Daly, Blair: 31, 94, 95, 148, 193, 233, 245, 246, 287, 344, 376, 470, 554
Danskin, Richard: 471, 535
Danton, Ian: 449
Davis, Jimmy: 481, 482, 626, 627
Davison, Walter: 16, 17, 211, 224, 225, 395, 596
Davyduke, Kent: 401, 421
Deacon, Don: 128, 129
Delahey, Matt: 279
Dickson, Craig: 80, 92, 102, 167, 169, 213, 214, 238, 283, 297, 298, 457, 458, 553, 572, 611
Dinardo, Ray: 267, 268, 321, 435, 548, 556
Dingle, Ryan: 29, 34, 364, 386, 387
Dingwall, Richard: 48, 89, 124, 125, 156, 471
Dobos, John: 7, 8, 64, 274
Doig, Bert: 64, 274
Dolan, John: 78, 469, 470, 513
Domenico, Ernie: 276, 321, 322, 595, 596
Donald, Andy: 86, 87, 92, 100, 118, 169, 172, 209, 210, 216, 217, 253, 254, 327, 355, 495, 503, 550, 572, 574, 611
Dorr, Michael: 34, 279
Dougall, Don: 180, 181, 481, 482, 505, 506, 599, 600, 626
Dowle, Scotty: 63, 64, 108, 274, 301, 302, 321, 322, 381, 382, 410, 494
Downes, John: 48, 417, 617
Downie, Colin: 38, 39, 84, 311, 457, 458, 560, 562
Drummond, John: 180, 181, 481, 482, 506, 599, 626, 627
Drummond, Stuart: 119, 169, 200, 473, 550, 611
Dryburgh, Andy: 448
Dryburgh, Jack: 50, 151, 152, 337, 510, 563, 564
Dubick, Nick: 108, 322
Duffield, Howard: 180
Dunbar, Billy: 98, 429

Durling, Tommy: 111, 115, 117, 339, 341, 359, 360, 366, 367, 628, 629
Dutiaume, Mark: 15, 43, 239, 244, 528
Dutiaume, Todd: 15, 19, 20, 21, 22, 27, 28, 29, 31, 32, 33, 36, 59, 65, 66, 70, 73, 74, 75, 76, 79, 82, 84, 85, 94, 120, 121, 145, 148, 149, 160, 178, 179, 187, 193, 203, 204, 205, 218, 232, 233, 245, 259, 281, 307, 308, 344, 345, 356, 372, 375, 377, 378, 397, 401, 402, 403, 420, 421, 428, 443, 451, 455, 456, 487, 488, 513, 523, 527, 528, 536, 537, 598, 614, 615

E

Edmiston, Dean: 54, 56, 84, 85, 100, 130, 131, 169, 217, 226, 227, 296, 368, 370, 371, 499, 500, 516, 528, 547, 571, 607
Emmerdahl, Jonas: 644
Evans, Frank: 393, 394, 411, 412, 443

F

Facto, Frank: 164, 166, 262, 302, 349, 435, 556
Fallowfield, Wray: 8, 64, 273, 274, 301, 302, 463, 617, 640
Farrell, Graeme 'Pinky': 126, 127, 140, 141, 151, 221, 222, 235, 236, 255, 256, 264, 266, 289, 292, 362, 384, 385, 408, 498, 564
Fera, Rick: 80, 93, 213, 214, 237, 355, 399, 457, 458, 459, 512, 552, 553
Ferguson, Ian: 566
Fiddler, Jim: 63, 262, 274
Figala, Milan: 11, 47, 50, 51, 130, 131, 194, 195, 324, 399, 480
Finlay, Andy: 71, 72, 393, 443, 451, 484, 487, 516
Finucci, Carlo: 28, 29, 219, 406, 427, 430, 455, 467, 468, 523, 524
Fisher, Billy: 435, 556
Fleming, Gavin: 84, 287
Fleming, Scott: 35, 134, 135
Fletcher, Ian: 73, 74, 451
Flynn, Johnny: 292, 498

287, 298, 327, 336, 338, 342, 343,
353, 354, 368, 398, 418, 437, 458,
472, 480, 483, 484, 503, 515, 516,
527, 534, 538, 539, 540, 541, 550,
551, 553, 560, 562, 569, 602, 603,
606, 609, 610, 611, 620, 621, 622,
623, 632, 633, 634, 635, 643
Latto, Gordon (Jnr): 84, 85, 193
Latto, Richard: 193
LeBlanc, Peter: 27, 271, 272, 427
Lee, Jeff: 34, 278
Lescovs, Imants 645
Libbos, Bruce: 157, 206, 207, 270, 422
Linnell, Mickey: 4, 164, 166, 261, 262,
349, 435, 556
Linton, Andy: 169, 297, 511, 547, 550,
606, 607, 610, 611
Linton, Chris: 31, 32, 84, 121, 193,
287, 398
Little, Andrew: 644
Livingston, James: 219, 405
Londry, Bob: 128, 129, 180, 181, 477,
478, 481, 482, 506, 593, 600, 612,
613, 627
Lovell, Lawrie: 136, 137, 138, 139, 146,
147, 151, 152, 157, 163, 196, 199, 201,
206, 207, 228, 241, 242, 264, 269,
270, 284, 292, 329, 330, 334, 353,
361, 362, 384, 385, 400, 408, 418,
422, 423, 436, 437, 438, 439, 491,
501, 502, 539, 540, 541, 565, 566,
602, 608, 620, 621, 631, 632, 633,
634, 635, 636
Lovell, Les: 78, 98, 99, 126, 132, 133,
136, 137, 138, 139, 140, 141, 146, 147,
151, 152, 157, 172, 197, 206, 207, 228,
242, 255, 256, 269, 287, 290, 291,
329, 330, 333, 334, 346, 353, 361,
362, 385, 418, 422, 423, 429, 436,
437, 464, 465, 491, 501, 525, 526,
538, 539, 540, 542, 543, 564, 565,
566, 603, 608, 609, 620, 621, 622,
630, 631, 632, 633, 636
Lovell, Les (Snr): 13, 111, 115, 117, 195,
339, 358, 359, 360, 494, 558, 559,
618, 619, 624, 625, 639
Lovell, Lindsay: 298, 369, 510
Lukac, Vincent: 50, 51, 130, 131, 194,
195, 399, 400
Lukacevic, Ned: 134, 135, 280, 356,
404, 532
Luke, Mike: 396, 596
Lynch, Jim: 48, 50, 52, 100, 118, 119,
130, 200, 213, 247, 335, 336, 337,
338, 368, 369, 370, 371, 399, 400,
447, 479, 480, 495, 507, 510, 515,
516, 518, 571, 611
Lynch, Steven: 31, 32, 75, 121, 149,
177, 204, 232, 233, 245, 306, 323,
324, 344, 375, 470, 485, 507, 508,
528, 555, 615

Mac, Mc

McAlpine, Steven: 31, 121, 148, 178,
287, 376, 377, 378, 398, 485
McAndrew, Marc: 84
McAndrew, Scott: 243
McAuley Ken: 566
McCartney, Len: 91, 111, 117, 339, 341,
359, 360
McCrone, Earl: 180, 181, 268, 481,
482, 506, 567, 599, 600, 626
McCrone, John 'Bernie': 45, 46, 48,
141, 194, 195, 257, 258, 342, 343,
350, 351, 368, 370, 371, 412, 414,
415, 446, 447, 471, 472, 484, 507,
516, 550, 551, 560, 562, 569
McCuaig, Nels: 349, 619, 639
McDonald, Marlowe: 108, 321, 322,
381, 382, 494
McDonald, Sammy: xxiii, 98, 141, 152,
163, 199, 221, 222, 235, 236, 255,
256, 263, 264, 290, 291, 292, 346,
362, 384, 385, 407, 408, 438, 439,
498, 565, 566, 604, 605, 630, 631
MacDougall, Gordon: 118, 119, 209,
335, 503, 610, 611
McEwan, Gary 550, 611
McGeever, Danny: 438, 439
McInroy, Tommy: 117, 294, 295, 339,
341, 619
McIntosh, Joe: 63, 64, 98, 132, 133,
138, 139, 141, 143, 147, 157, 163, 199,
221, 222, 236, 242, 256, 264, 266,
290, 291, 293, 334, 346, 361, 362,

Lightning Source UK Ltd.
Milton Keynes UK
UKHW020943130422
401497UK00009B/238

9 781849 212281